THE UPHOLSTERER'S BIBLE

THE UPHOLSTERER'S BIBLE

PERCY W. BLANDFORD

TAB BOOKS
Blue Ridge Summit, Pa. 17214

FIRST EDITION

FIRST PRINTING—APRIL 1978

Copyright © 1978 by TAB BOOKS

Printed in the United States
of America

Reproduction or publication of the content in any manner, without express permission of the publisher, is prohibited. No liability is assumed with respect to the use of the information herein.

Library of Congress Cataloging in Publication Data

Blandford, Percy, W.
   The upholsterer's Bible.

   Includes index.
   1. Upholstery. I. Title.
TT198.B53   684.1'2   77-18914
ISBN 0-8306-9986-4
ISBN 0-8306-1004-9 pbk.

Introduction

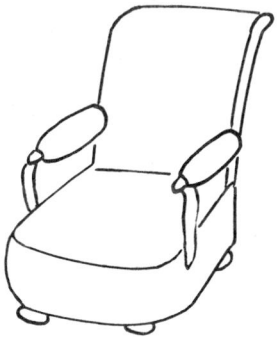

In these mechanized days there are not that many things about which a craftsman can stand back and say, "I made that." Most things we use are the products of factories where individuals only do part of a process. The finished item may be the result of the combined efforts of a very large number of workers. A worker may be skilled in his own job, but he does not have the satisfaction of seeing a piece of work through from the raw material to the finished product. He may not even see the finished product, if the output of his own factory goes somewhere else to join the products of other factories to be assembled at that time into the final whole.

Custom upholstering is different. A qualified upholsterer is able to make a chair or similar item in its entirety. He may still do nearly all of it by hand. Some mechanical aids have their uses, and electric power may be used to drive the sewing machine, but it is unlikely that an upholsterer, for whom every job is different, will have much other use for mechanization.

Upholstery is the art and craft of covering furniture with padding. This is done primarily to make the furniture comfortable. If it fails in that aspect, its aims have not been achieved. It also aims to make the furniture look more attractive. With the very large range of materials available it is possible to get an enormous range of effects. This is the art part of upholstery. The work done to make the furniture more comfortable is the craft. It is the combination of art and craft that go a long way towards making upholstery such an attractive activity.

Upholstery as a craft goes back into antiquity. Anyone practicing it today is carrying on an honorable tradition. At one time, like so many other crafts, upholstery had its trade secrets, and was only practiced by those who had served apprenticeships. Those days have gone. Obviously, there is much to be gained from experience and the beginner cannot expect to get the same results as a man who has spent a lifetime at the trade; but much of the work may be regarded as applied common sense, and the difference between the expert and the beginner is mainly a matter of time. If a beginner is willing to devote time and care to the work, he can complete many upholstery projects successfully the first time. It is important to be selective and work progressively from simple to more advanced types of upholstery.

Besides the *making* of upholstered furniture, there is much that can be done to *repair* and *recover* old furniture. Frames usually outlast their covering, sometimes many times over, so an old frame can be used as the base for more than one chair over a long period. An old chair that has been discarded and considered of no further use may yield a frame that gives an interested amateur or an enterprising professional something to work on that could end up as an apparently new chair.

The aim of this book is to cover all information and techniques that a modern upholsterer ought to know. It is not a guide to simplified methods for the amateur looking for an easy, but not necessarily good, way out. The techniques described are all those that a professional upholsterer should know. The keen amateur should want to follow the same methods. The majority of steps can be carefully followed to achieve satisfactory results without the need to resort to quick methods or shortcuts.

The book covers traditional methods as well as modern ones. Much furniture in use, and much being made today, is upholstered in ways that do not differ much from those used by earlier craftsmen. There is much to be said for these methods even if newer materials are being used. Synthetic materials, particularly padding which can be inserted as single blocks, have many applications. They can simplify construction and can often give a better results. With a knowledge of all methods of upholstery it is possible to assess a particular job and decide on the most satisfactory approach, instead of being confined to one method—which may not be the best.

Upholstery is not dirty work. It does not require elaborate equipment. There is no need for a special shop, although if much upholstery is to be done a separate workplace is worth having. Much of the work can be done in an ordinary room without making any more mess than when dressmaking. Stripping can be the dirtiest job, but it can be done outside.

Except for a sewing machine, which is necessary for all but the simpler projects, the hand tools needed can be kept in a quite small box. Their cost is not great, but the correct ones should be obtained. In particular, a good selection of proper needles should be obtained. An amateur buying all new upholstery tools will find they cost much less than the tools for most other hobbies.

Most upholsterers do not make their own frames, but buy them ready to assemble or get them from old chairs. Nevertheless, enough instructions are provided in this book for anyone keen on woodwork to make frames completely. In any case, an upholsterer needs to be able to make repairs and alterations to a frame. The book tells how.

Whether the aim of the reader is to do a small amount of upholstery repair and recovering to the household furniture or to deal with all that may come into a professional upholsterer's shop, it is the hope of the author that this book contains all the basic instruction needed. The reader should be able to face any problem in upholstery and deal with it. The instructions provided are based on methods found successful by the experts, yet most beginners should be able to do them, too. Of course, there are always new developments, and anyone interested needs to keep abreast of progress, but it is unlikely that anything new will make existing methods obsolete. Upholstery has survived for thousands of years and all the signs are that a skilled upholsterer will find he is needed for a long time to come.

Percy W. Blandford

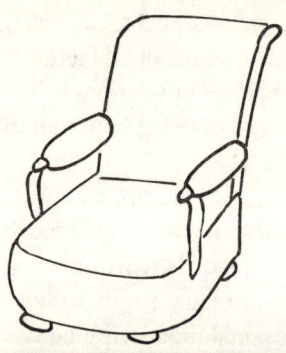

Contents

SECTION 1: BASIC UPHOLSTERY

1 History and Development 13
Roman Furniture—Egyptian Furniture—The Middle Ages—The Guilds—The Great Cabinetmakers—Materials and Techniques—Modern Upholstery.

2 Materials 24
Webbing—Tacks and Nails—Twine and Thread—Springs—Stuffing—Inner Coverings—Covering.

3 Tools 42
Cutting—Ripping—Needles—Web Strainers—Measuring and Holding—Woodworking Tools—Special Tools.

4 Springing 73
Webbing—Rubber Webbing—Tension Springs—Coil Springs.

5 Simple Seating 91
Loose Rigid Seats—Loose Soft Seats—Box and Tool Seats—Plywood Chair.

6 Other Seating 112
Piping—Piped Stool Seat—Buttoned Stool Seat—Round Seat—Office Chair.

7 Cushions 129
Filled Cushions—Molded Cushions—Covering Scatter Cushions—Wall-Edged Bunk Cushions—Small Wall-Edged Cushions—Chair Cushions.

8 Lounge Chairs 149
Covering—Fixing Cushions—Padded Arms—Side Panels.

9 Upholstered Arm and Wing Chairs 165
Padded Arms—Saddle Arms—Wings.

SECTION 2: ADVANCED UPHOLSTERY

10 Planning Materials Needs for Fully Upholstered Furniture — 181
Measuring—Curved Covers.

11 Fully Upholstered Chairs, Traditional and Modern — 189
Furniture Periods—Chair Designs.

12 Fully Upholstered Chairs: Seats — 213
Springs and Webbing—Springs and Burlap—Front Edging—Tension Springs—Stuffing and Covering.

13 Fully Upholstered Chairs: Arms — 234
Inside Arms—Covering Arms—Outside Arms—Front Arm Panels.

14 Fully Upholstered Chairs: Backs — 253
Light Springing—Coil Springing—First Padding of Back—Second Padding of Back—Outside Back—Underneath a Chair.

15 Fully Upholstered Chairs: Finishing — 270
Buttoning—Decorative Nails—Gimp, Ruchings, and Welt—Bottom Band—Flounce or Skirt—Curved Parts—Glides and Rockers.

16 Fully Upholstered Chairs: Special Styles and Effects — 293
Bowed Backs—Pillow Back Chairs—Channel or Fluted Backs—Tufting.

17 Beds, Divans, Ottomans, Head Panels, and Boxes — 306
Bunk Seats—Boxes and Ottomans—Beds and Divans—Head Panels.

18 Repairing Minor Damage — 329
Torn Fabric—Webbing—Renewing Burlap—Buttons—Loose Fastenings—Broken Springs—Repairing Foam—Dining Chair Back—Loose Covers.

19 Stripping and Recovering — 355
Removing Upholstery—Partial Recovering—Adapted Recovering—Full Recovering.

20 Rush and Cord Seats — 375
Materials—Tools—Rush Pattern—Checker Pattern—Other Patterns—Cane Seating.

SECTION 3: FRAMES

21 Frame Types — 401

22 Frame Construction Details — 410
Dowelled Joints—Clamps—Mortise and Tenon Joints—Dado and Lap Joints—Dovetail Joints—Screwed Joints.

23 Stools and Simple Frames — 429
Assembly Sequence—Ottomans—Seat Tops.

24 Open Frames — 440
Armless Chairs—Adjustments.

25 Enclosed Frames — 450
Curved Parts—Frame Design.

26 Wood Finishing — 464
Sanding—Wood Blemishes—Staining—Filling—Varnish and Shellac—Lacquering—Oil and Wax Polishing—Painting.

27 Repairing and Restyling Frames — 478
Looseness—Scarfing—Frame Finish—Restyling—Finishing.

28 Safety — 492

Glossary — 497

Index — 507

SECTION 1
BASIC UPHOLSTERY

History and Development

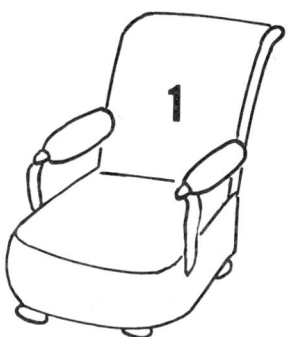

Primitive man sat on a rock and found it was hard and cold. He padded it with skins or grass—and upholstery was born. At least, that seems like the probable beginning. At what point in time man actually made seats and padded them, we do not know. Simple stools must have come very early in man's development. When he started making furniture an early need would have been for some sort of table to eat off or work on and the user would have wanted to sit alongside that table. If he had to sit for long, he would have wanted to do something to soften the hard wood, and it is likely that his loose padding of natural materials would have been fixed in some way, perhaps marking a further step in the early development of upholstery.

We know of earlier civilizations that have come and gone. While mankind in one part of the world was existing at a very primitive level, his fellow men in another part were living at a very high level of civilization, often with amenities comparable with ours today. The Egyptians and the Persians reached very high peaks in civilization while the Western world lived at little better than animal level.

ROMAN FURNITURE

When the Roman legions spread across Europe, they found Britons, as well as other residents of Europe, living at a comparably low standard. Even the leaders and the more wealthy members of the population lived in crude dwellings with furniture that was sparse. Little of it was more than temporary construction. The Romans took with them many of the comforts they had known at home. As they settled in the conquered lands they built substantial houses and equipped them with such amenities as central heating and furniture that would be acceptable today. Enough information exists from two thousand years ago for us to be fairly certain of details of domestic life and, for our purpose, details of how the Romans made life more comfortable with upholstery.

Surprisingly, when the Romans withdrew their occupation forces, there is little evidence that the local people made use of the new aids to comfort and a better standard of living that their masters had shown them. For another one thousand years or more western man was still dependent on agriculture and was often nomadic, so his furnishings had to be simple and portable.

EGYPTIAN FURNITURE

The best evidence of early furnishing and upholstery is provided by the Egyptian practice of burying their kings with all the equipment they were expected to need in their afterlife, and decorating the tombs with carved pictures of contemporary life. Although wood is a fairly durable material, it would not survive the many thousands of years from the days of burial. Some explorers have had fleeting glimpses of complete wooden articles that have held their form in the sealed tomb conditions, but have then disintegrated into dust with the change of air once the tomb was opened. The stone carvings were more durable. They provide proof of the way the Egyptians lived as much as 5000 years ago.

The Egyptian standard of living was quite high, even two or three thousand years before the birth of Christ. Drawings show chairs and other furniture that was obviously padded. There are even details of construction. The craftsmen of those days understood the making of joints, with dowels or pegs or something very like our mortise and tenon joints. Tools are shown, too. The early cabinetmaker had the means of sawing and shaping wood with tools that probably had bronze, rather than steel, blades. The making of holes did not seem to have been as successfully accomplished. Holes were kept small and worried out with inefficient tools. Needles may have been made of bronze or bone. The results were pieces of furniture obviously of good design, both functionally and in appearance. The Egyptians of that time had yet to learn of the wheel, so an early Egyptian chair could not have been fitted with casters.

Greek civilization was contemporary with that of the Romans, and there were other civilizations of the East and Middle East at that time, but in the Western world of Europe, as we've said, there is little evidence that the Roman influence had made much impact. Firm information on the development of civilization and of furniture, which is our interest, does not show real progress until the Middle Ages—those centuries from about 1000 AD until about 1600. This is the time when people of the countries that were to become Europe were advancing and eventually spreading their influence by exploring and colonizing. It is the period when most people, from the lowest to the highest, were to learn and appreciate the comforts of civilization. All of this was reflected by the production of furniture and other trappings of increasing civilization. People led a more settled existence. There were still wars, but they did not involve everyone in the way that earlier inter-tribal battles had.

Earlier, man had existed by hunting. This was followed by a type of subsistence farming, where there was little time for anything except eking out an existence. If a home was to be built, furniture made, clothing produced, or agricultural equipment made, there was no specialized craftsman to turn to and the family had to use what skill it had to meet its own needs. Anyone with a particular skill may have helped neighbors, but the blacksmith or carpenter only used those skills as a sideline to his main activity of farming. Any payment would have been by barter.

THE MIDDLE AGES

With the changing circumstances of the Middles Ages, particularly the growth of town life, specialization became more prevalent. There was work for craftsmen who could make a living by using their skill full time, in exchange via money or barter, for the needs of life and often for luxuries. Rising standards of living for a greater number of people meant more demand for things that added to comfort and were good to look at. The status symbol had arrived.

Upholstery as a craft or trade probably started as an incidental to another craft. Early woodworkers were men who tackled anything in wood, but their activities became divided by specialization and the cabinetmaker moved away from the carpenter doing rougher work, the joiner doing precision constructional work, and the carver and turner, who had their own speciality. Early cabinetmakers probably did whatever upholstery was necessary on the chairs they produced. There were workers in fabrics and skins who may have made chair covers. The tentmakers of the East probably also made cushions and other padding for seats. Amongst the nomadic tribes of the Middle East, tentmaking was an honored trade. St. Paul, of Biblical fame, was a tentmaker. Maybe he was also an early upholsterer.

The many crafts that developed in the Middle Ages were carefully regulated. Before anyone could practice a craft he had to serve an apprenticeship, which might last as long as seven years. During that time he was tied to his master and often lived with him, usually with little or no wages and maybe even a premium to pay for the privilege of the apprenticeship. At the end of this time he spent a year or so as an improver before becoming a *journeyman*. The term comes from the practice of traveling to work elsewhere to gain a wider experience, even if the man eventually returned to work for his original master, or set up a shop on his own.

THE GUILDS

All of the crafts had their guilds, which were associations of master craftsmen, either employers or those who had proved their skill and had been admitted to membership. They were not trades unions, but they controlled the standards of workmanship. Being able to say you belonged to a guild was a testament to your capabilities.

The guilds were based in London and many of them still survive, although they no longer serve their original function. In fact, they are now rather archaic, serving as exclusive clubs that maintain traditional pomp and ceremonies.

The guild for upholsterers was one of the earliest. This was called the 'Worshipful Company of Upholders,' and was in existence at the middle of the thirteenth century. The fact that the members were also concerned with tentmaking seems to be indicated by the fact that their coat of arms shows three tents.

The progress of weaving ran parallel with the progress of upholstery. Early upholstery would have been done mainly with leather, although the comparatively coarse fabrics of early days were also used. A few early weavers made some exceptionally good fabric, but this was not generally available and would certainly not have been available to the ordinary householder, nor to his lord. The church played a large part in education, including the practical activities as well as the academic, so much of the finer furniture-making and upholstery was found in churches. It is still possible to see evidence of this early development in some of the cathedrals and abbeys of Europe.

THE GREAT CABINETMAKERS

In Britain, weaving and upholstery benefited by the influx of Flemish weavers who fled from persecution in what is now part of Belgium and Holland. The finer fabrics that were woven brought with them an incentive to do better work to use them, and this resulted in a raising of the standards of cabinetmaking and its associated upholstery.

As the Middle Ages passed into the more gracious times of the eighteenth and later centuries, there came the period of the great cabinetmakers. Where utility was the prime aim in earlier furniture—and there was often beauty in fitness for purpose—the great cabinetmakers such as Chippendale, Sheraton, and many others, strove more for fineness of appearance. Much of their work was also very functional, but there is still in existence some of their ornate work that showed too much striving for an unusual appearance, with little regard for use.

This emphasis on decoration reached a peak with some of the furniture of Victorian days. Attitude seems to have been: if there are a few square inches of wood exposed, carve it. This carving was accompanied by upholstery that was altogether too fussy by modern standards. Victorian social prudery called for legs to be hidden, and this value extended even to furniture legs, which had their own bits of upholstery.

Examples of upholstered furniture of considerable antiquity can be found in palaces, castles, and old houses as well as ecclesiastic buildings. The covering and stuffing may not be original, but in most cases those who have done the work over the centuries have been careful to repeat the original methods. Even when some craftsman of other times has updated the upholstery, it is still possible to see how the original work was done.

Since the days of the European explorers from the fifteenth century, furniture and upholstery in North America has echoed European styles and methods. Distinctive Colonial styles developed, to be sure, but the methods were those of the parent countries. Early furniture was imported, either complete or as parts to assemble. Early upholstery materials must have been imported, but the use of local natural resources soon became apparent.

Sailing ships of those days had to be prepared to defend themselves. The captain lived in a fair degree of comfort aft, even if his crew lived in crude, wet discomfort forward, but the captain's cabin might have to be converted to a gun position for defense if the boat were chased by a privateer. To allow for this, much of the furniture, which looked like contemporary furniture of the period, could be dismantled for storage. Some of this may have found its way ashore. Examples of the type can be seen in Nelson's H.M.S *Victory*, at Portsmouth, England.

MATERIALS AND TECHNIQUES

Softening of seats, backs, and arms was done with materials available nearby. Grasses, rushes, and similar vegetation only had a short life as padding, so upholstery using such items needed to be opened for refilling frequently. There was also the problem of the grass moving. One way of reducing this was to weave the grass into a mattress form on a primitive loom (Fig. 1-1).

A better early upholstery stuffing—and one that has continued to the present day—was hair. Wool from sheep has a natural curl that made it fill well, with a springiness that gave comfort. Other hair, from horses, cattle, pigs, and similar animals may not have as much natural curl, but it was teased loose

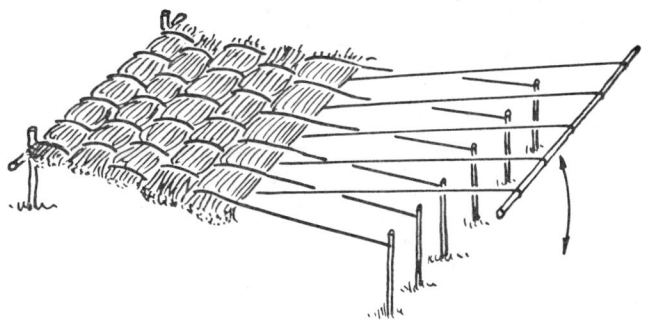

Fig. 1-1. Grass was woven into a mattress form on a primitive loom to avoid separation.

to open it up as much as possible. In fact, hair has been the most used filling for Western upholstery for as long as records are known.

With better communications offering understandings of wider possibilities, other stuffing materials were imported. Fibers from grasses and plants in other parts of the world were found to offer some permanent padding possibilities without deteriorating if properly treated. Sometimes these fibers were used as backing for hair stuffing. It is only in recent times that these materials have fallen from favor.

Early covering material was almost always leather. It may have been used in the form of a skin with its fur facing outwards for comfort, and little further treatment. But as a knowledge of tanning was gained, the skin was converted to leather more like we know it. This made a very durable covering and it would probably outlast the stuffing.

Woven fabric followed and became progressively better as weaving knowledge and skill improved. In Europe most fabric was woven from wool, with flax and other materials being used for coarser cloths. As communications improved, other materials came in. Silk passed through an upholstery phase and was sometimes used for unsuitable things. The development of cotton brought an alternative material for use in America and Europe.

Not all upholstery was padded. An appreciation of the comfort to be gotten from letting the support conform to the body seems to date from very early days. Some Roman seats had interleaved leather bands (Fig. 1-2). The hammock princi-

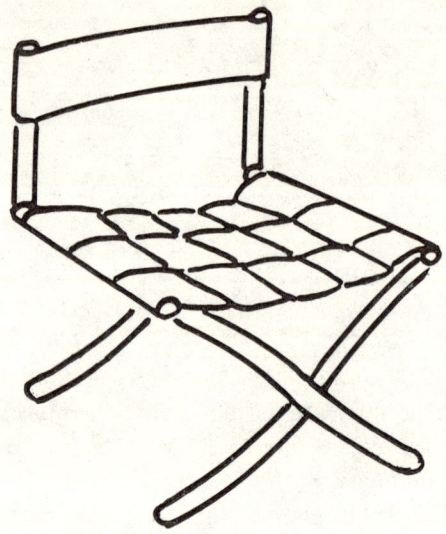

Fig. 1-2. Some Roman seats had interleaved leather bands..

ple of rope netting (Fig. 1-3) is still used under cushions in India and elsewhere. The limitation of this lies in that it is only suitable for single seats. However, a hammock is comfortable for reclining, and seaman slept comfortably in canvas hammocks until quite recent days. With spreaders at the ends (Fig. 1-4) the comfort of a hammock for relaxing is still welcomed.

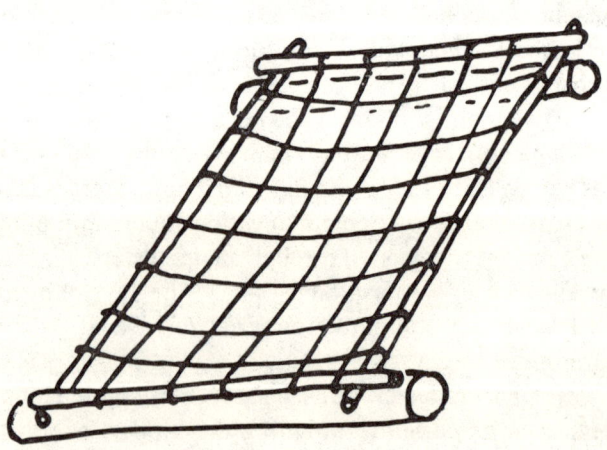

Fig. 1-3. The hammock principle of rope netting is still used under cushions in parts of the world.

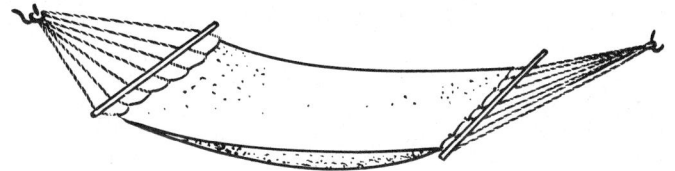

Fig. 1-4. Early attempts at softening seats used the still-common hammock idea.

Another alternative to padding was weaving a seat from rope, thongs, and natural materials like rushes. The rush pattern chair is still with us (Fig. 1-5), although the material used today may not always be the rushes from the riverside used by earlier workers. Interwoven cane used as a seating material came later; suitable cane was not local to workers in the Western world and it had to be imported.

Fig. 1-5. Rushes were worked into a seat top.

Like blacksmithing, upholstery has used the same techniques and similar tools for many centuries. It is a craft that does not need much mechanization. It is essentially handwork. Some crafts have changed completely with mechanization. The woodworker no longer has to laboriously hand saw pieces of wood to size from the tree. Besides power sawing, the wood is finished smooth by machine. Modern design is geared to power tools. Some crafts have gone. The wheelwright is no longer needed. The cooper has almost gone, with the diminished demand for wooden barrels. But the upholsterer endures. His materials may change, but his techniques are likely to continue and his skill will be required for some time to come.

Loose pillows and cushions have been used to supplement fixed upholstery and the hammock type of support could be further softened with a pillow. These loose pieces of padding have been used from earliest times. Besides stuffing with similar materials to fixed upholstery, a pillow was most comfortable with down, with other feathers coming next. With most people engaged in agriculture, and with poultry forming part of their subsistence property, feathers were readily available. Bedding probably had the first choice of feathers, but other feathers went into pillow for chairs. A snag experienced with down and feathers is their tendency to move and accumulate in one part. The idea of buttoning to prevent movement was not known, or was not found effective with feathers, so they were used for loose things that could be shaken to respread the contents.

MODERN UPHOLSTERY

Throughout history, for the thousands of years that upholstery is known to have been practiced, the materials used have been natural. They may have been manufactured or processed, but the base material has come from a natural source. It is only in recent times—mostly post-World War II—that synthetic materials have taken over a large part of modern upholstery. The word 'synthetic' might not have been understood by a pre-war upholsterer. Of course, everything in this world comes from a natural base, but a synthetic material starts from a stage where natural materials have been reduced to their constituent chemicals.

Some natural fabrics are still used. In fact, there is often a virtue claimed for furntiure covered in natural fabrics. Many synthetic fabrics are indistinguishable from natural ones, however; they are more durable and they have a better resistance to water and many fluids, although most will melt with heat. Few pieces of furniture are now covered with leather, but here again there are synthetic alternatives used instead.

The greatest changes are in stuffings. Plastic and rubber foam and pads have taken the place of hair and other traditional fillings, particularly in production upholstery. Besides simplifying upholstery, these materials are more hygienic and should keep their shape longer.

The widespread use of electricity as a source of power has not had much effect on the upholsterer. The frame maker is now able to benefit from power machinery in the same way as other wood workers, but the upholsterer still depends mainly on hand work. Electricity powers his sewing machine, were previously he turned it by hand or used a treadle. In earlier days all sewing was by hand. In production upholstery a power tool drives staples, which have taken the place of tacks, but there are places where tacks have to be used, and the custom upholsterer may not use staples. There are mechanical aids to pillow stuffing, button covering and other processes, but they are hand operated. In a world of mechanization, the modern upholsterer can still proudly claim to be a hand craftsman.

Possibly the nearest thing to a revolution in upholstery has been the development of molded chair shapes (Fig. 1-6), which may be made of several plastics and give the whole chair shape

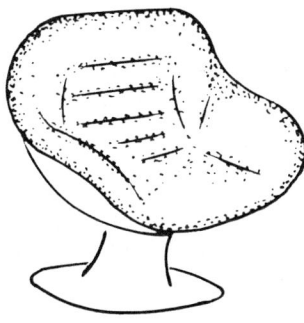

Fig. 1-6. Today whole chairs are molded in plastic.

in one piece, instead of being built up from a large number of parts, as in a traditional wooden frame. Their shape and the method of covering have produced what may be regarded as a twentieth century style of upholstered furniture, but many of the styles of earlier years, and even centuries, are still acceptable and in demand. Good design is always appreciated. Where it can be adapted to modern materials it is still good contemporary furniture.

It seems unlikely that there will be any significant change in furniture. Upholstery may be expected to continue with little fundamental change for a long time to come.

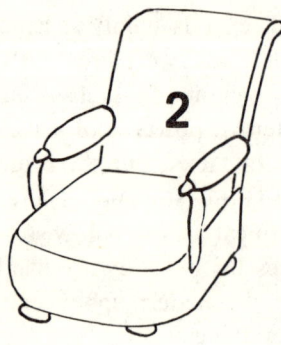

2

Materials

To achieve his aim of making furniture comfortable to sit on, the upholsterer uses many materials to pad seats, backs, and arms. He has to do much more than just provide simple cushioning. The section of any properly upholstered piece of furniture shows a combination of many techniques that will produce a shape designed to conform to the body and be comfortable to the user.

There have been changes in the materials used in recent years and some of these may allow simplification of construction, but there are still needs for traditional materials and techniques. An upholsterer who claims to have some mastery of his trade should be able to use all methods. He should be able to follow the techniques of centuries when repairing antique furniture or dealing with reproductions, yet he should appreciate the values of modern advances and be able to take advantage of them in suitable cases.

The simplest seating is made of padding held by covering over a flat board seat. This token softening may be found in simple dining chairs, but more comfortable conventional upholstery has a pattern of springs over webbing, which gives some resilience to the covered padding on top (Fig. 2-1). There are more recent variations, but this is still the basic way of achieving comfort in a seat.

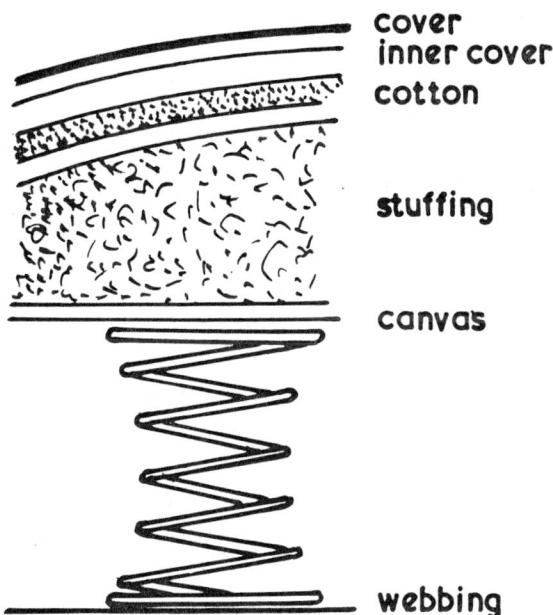

Fig. 2-1. Upholstery is made up of covered paddings supported by springs.

WEBBING

Webbing is made in many grades and qualities and from several materials. Most of it is two inches wide. This size is suitable for most purposes, but it can be had as narrow as 1 1/2 inches or in several sizes up to 3 inches in width. It is bought in rolls and cut to length as it is fixed. The best webbing has a twill weave. This is recognized by the pattern of diagonal lines on it (Fig. 2-2). Common webbing is made of jute, but the best is made of flax. Many varieties are woven from a mixture of jute, cotton, and hemp. Including linen threads near the edges (*sel-*

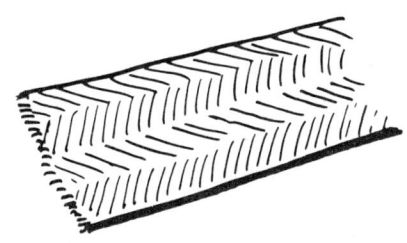

Fig. 2-2. Twill weave webbing has diagonal lines.

vedges) is supposed to contribute strength. Cheaper webbing has a plain weave.

Webbing is also made of synthetic materials. Natural materials may deteriorate with age and will suffer from rot in a damp situation. Synthetic materials should have a longer life. To achieve satisfactory results comparable with the use of webbing made from natural fibers, synthetic filaments have to be chosen with similar degrees of stretch and flexibility. Polypropylene is one synthetic material that is being used for webbing.

Rubber webbing is much used in modern upholstery, particularly below foam padding. A natural or synthetic latex rubber is used, with natural or synthetic fabric embedded so there is some stretch. Although elastic, this is quite powerful. A new length is fixed with about 5 percent or 10 percent stretch. Then, with the other pieces that make up the pattern to support the weight, the amount of sag permitted is not great. The standard width of rubber webbing for seats is 2 inches, but it can be had wider and narrower. Narrow webbing is useful for some types of back upholstery. Although rubber webbing can be fixed with tacks in a way similar to ordinary webbing, there are special clips and other means of attaching the ends to frames and these will be described later.

TACKS AND NAILS

Most webbing is fixed with tacks. A tack differs from a nail in being tapered for all (Fig. 2-3A) or most of its length (Fig. 2-3B) under a fairly large head. A nail is parallel for all of its length, except the point (Fig. 2-3C). Tacks are described by their length (mostly 3/8 inch to 7/8 inch) although they may be classed by their weight for a quantity. Common sizes classed in this way may be between 4 ounces and 16 ounces. Some makers describe their tacks by number—some examples being 3 for 3/8 inch, 6 for 5/8 inch and 12 for 7/8 inch. A tapered tack or nail may be described as 'cut', while the parallel type is 'wire'.

Gimp pins are very fine nails which may be cut or made of wire. They are used for fixing a decorative strip of fabric called gimp, but they have other applications where an inconspicuous nail is needed.

Nails with larger heads than those used only for woodwork are needed to provide a better grip over fabric and these are

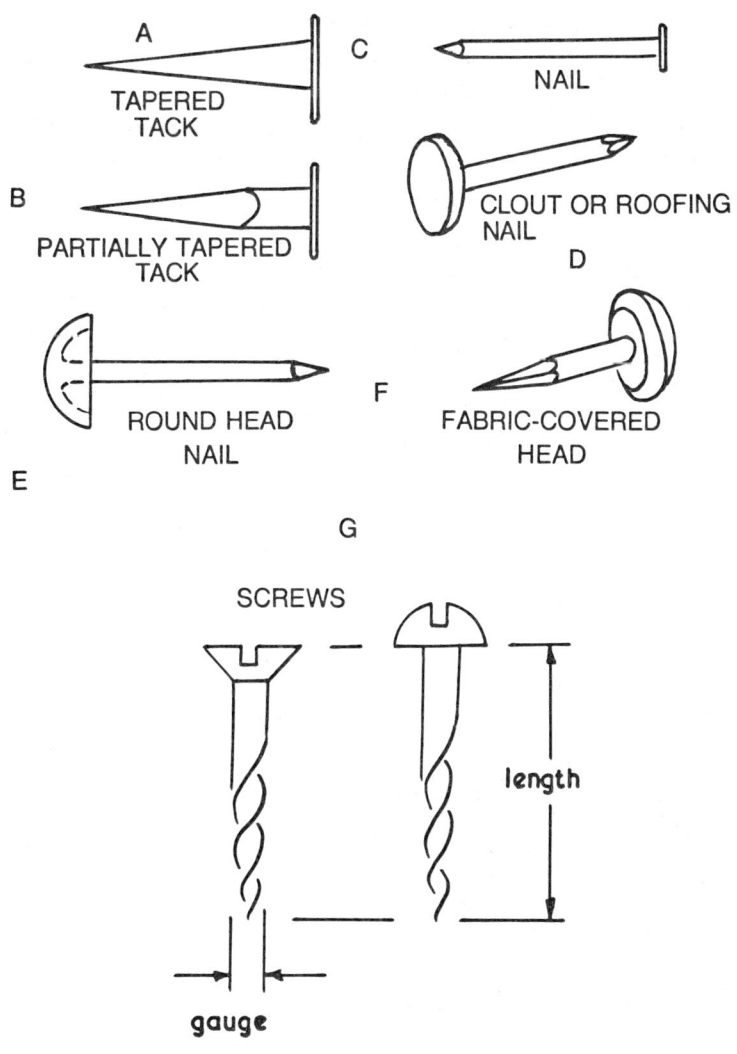

Fig. 2-3. Common tacks, nails, and screws.

clout or *roofing* nails (Fig. 2-3D), which may also be used for some types of springing. Common nails have some upholstery uses. *Casing* or *finishing* nails (panel pins) have narrow heads and are used where they may be punched below the surface and the hole filled with stopping.

Where a nail head will be visible on the surface it may be given a special decorative head. A *round head* (Fig. 2-3E) is an example, but there are several patterns with a plated or other finish used particularly on leather or imitation upholstery. It is also possible to get nails covered with fabric or leather (Fig. 2-3F). Special nails need care in driving so the head is not damaged, but this can be done with a matching punch or even a piece of wood hollowed on the end.

Few screws are needed with the actual upholstery, but they are found where framework comes apart, where there is a hinged back, or where other parts are arranged to move. Ordinary screws are graded by their length from the surface of the wood and by a gauge size for the diameter. General-purpose screws have flat heads (Fig. 2-3G). Round head screws have limited uses. There are other special shapes, too. Besides screws with slots for normal screwdrivers there are star-shaped sockets in Phillips head screws which require special drivers. Lengths may go in 1/8 inch steps for small screws, but above 3/4 inch, steps are more commonly by 1/4 inch intervals. Gauge sizes increase as the diameter increases. In small sizes they may be in single figure steps, but above gauge 6 only even number sizes are usual. Some commonly used screw sizes are 1/2 inch by 4 gauge, 3/4 inch by 6 gauge, 1 inch by 8 gauge, and 1 1/2 inches by 10 gauge.

Staples have taken the place of tacks in industry for many applications. It may be possible to use a hand-operated staple machine for some individual upholstery, but to drive the more substantial staples often requires a power-operated device. For much individual work it is better to use the traditional tacks and nails.

Adhesives now play a larger part in upholstery. With the development of plastics and synthetic materials there has been a parallel development using some of the same base ingredients to make adhesives of a quality that was unknown only a short time ago. These go much further than the traditional glues and other older adhesives, and can hold with a strength not previously possible. There are still some materials that cannot be satisfactorily bonded with adhesive, but there are now adhesives suitable for the majority of upholstery materials.

Unfortunately, there is no universal adhesive. It is important to select the adhesive to suit the material and to follow the instructions provided with it. There are adhesives that are used wet and pressed or hammered immediately to produce a tight bond between fabrics. Others have to be applied to both surfaces and left until almost dry before pressing together. Not all adhesives are flexible. Some that set hard are suitable for gluing fabric to wood. In this case the adhesive may take the place of tacks or staples or it may be used to reinforce them.

TWINE AND THREAD

Twine or string is used in spring assemblies for linking springs together at the correct distance and for sewing the springs to the webbing. Spring twines are sold by specialist suppliers, but in a repair it may be possible to find a twine from another source that matches the existing lines. Twine may be made of flax, hemp, or cotton, but there are synthetic twines which are stronger for their size. Synthetic twine is made from continuous filaments instead of short fibers that give a hairiness to the surface, so they are more slippery and may need special knots or standard knots with extra turns to make secure fastenings.

Lighter twines (stitching twines) are used for sewing with needles. These may be similar to the spring twines, or be thinner and better described as thread. For sewing on the surface there may have to be threads that match the covering materials being used. It is false economy to use cheap twines because these may break or fail in a position that is difficult to get at in the completely upholstered seat.

Sewn joints in coverings may include piping. This is fabric enclosing a cord (Fig. 2-4). Although piping may be bought

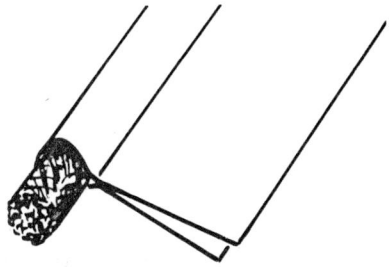

Fig. 2-4. Piping consists of fabric that encloses a cord.

already made, it can be made by sewing fabric around a length of cord. There are special piping cords, but any cord of suitable diameter may be used. A braided cord is better than one made from laid-up strands because its pattern is less likely to show through the covering. As the cord does not have to provide strength, but only shape, there is no need for an expensive line; there are compressed paper and plastic piping cords available that will give a firm shape.

SPRINGS

For many years springs were found in all upholstered furniture. Modern materials have modified this practice, particularly in quantity production using machine methods; but springs are still used extensively by the individual upholsterer. A properly sprung seat is very comfortable to sit on.

The traditional spring is known as *double coil* (Fig. 2-5A). This has top and bottom nearly of the same size (top may be slightly larger), but the center coils are smaller. There are many sizes made and these can have varying degrees of stiffness due to the thickness of wire used. Overall uncompressed lengths may be between 4 inches and 10 inches. These springs can be used individually. The upholsterer mounts them on webbing and links them with twine to retain their position. The ends of the wires may be joined into the end rings or this may only be done at the top, to prevent the wire from penetrating the covering.

It is also possible to get sets of springs mounted on a metal bar. These are *single coil*, with a large top reducing to a small coil attached to the bar, and may be arranged as a drop-in unit to fit over the frame (Fig. 2-5B) or on steel webbing (Fig. 2-5C) to fit the frame like fabric webbing. This idea may be extended to include a block of springs on a light metal frame, so the whole thing is a ready-made unit (Fig. 2-5D), possibly with a sprung mesh top to spread the load under the cushion. Nine or twelve springs are usual for a chair seat.

The pattern of springs on metal mounting may also be sprung by using tension coil springs attached to the frame (Fig. 2-5E). A further variation is to use tension coil springs instead of solid metal between the bottoms of the main coil springs.

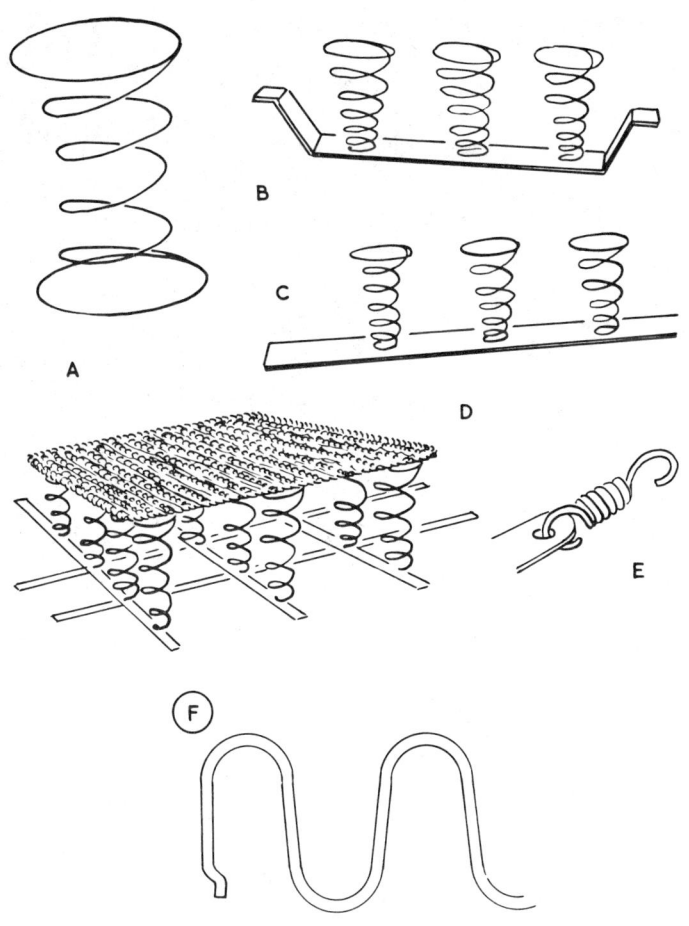

Fig. 2-5. Several types of coiled springs and flatter tension springs are used.

Another method of providing some horizontal springing to supplement the vertical springing of the main coil springs to use zig-zag, sinuous coil or serpentine springs instead of solid metal supports (Figs. 2-5 F and 2-6).

Double coil springs may be enclosed in a sleeve of muslin or other cloth, and a batch of these sleeves may be joined together to make a complete unit (Fig. 2-7A). The method is used for bed mattresses and for seat and back assemblies.

For lighter supports, as in a back with a removable cushion, there can be zig-zag springs fixed to the framework. They may

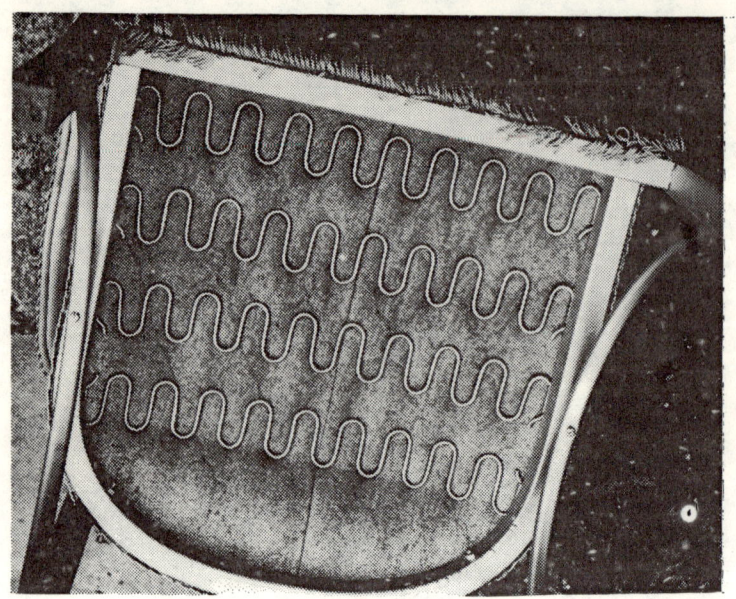

Fig. 2-6. The underside of a chair seat supported by zig-zag springs.

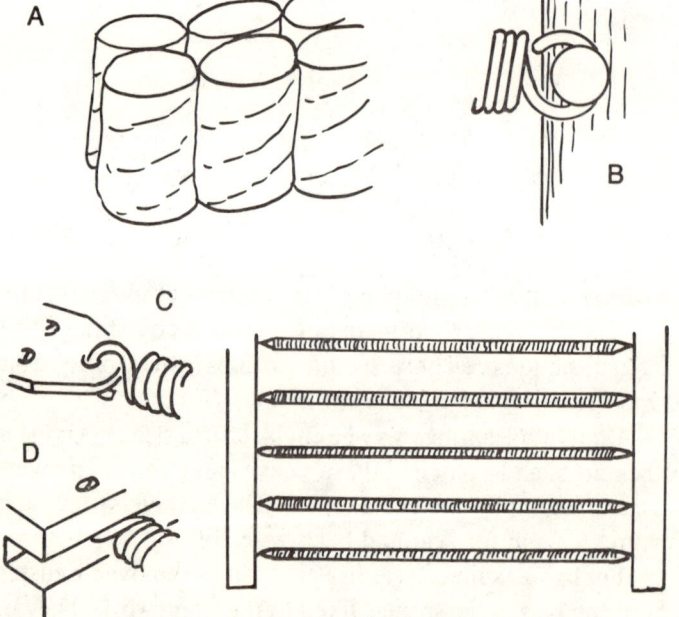

Fig. 2-7. Springs are used in even more variations.

be used without other springs under a seat, but it is more usual to use *tension springs* or a pattern of rubber webbing under a loose cushion. Tension springs are long, closely coiled springs with hooked ends. The end may engage with a stout nail (Fig. 2-7B), a steel plate (Fig. 2-7C), either continuous or individual in each position, or be screwed into a slot (Figs. 2-7D and 2-8). The number of tension springs used under a cushion depends on their strength and the area, but a spacing about every 4 inches is customary. Tension springs for seats may be about 1/2 inch diameter, while those for back cushions are slightly smaller.

STUFFING

An enormous number of materials has been used to provide padding in upholstery. Nearly all of these have been natural substances and a great many of them are still used, although some of the more primitive things, like grass, are obviously no longer found. However, many of these stuffing materials have been replaced by foam, which can be natural or synthetic latex rubber or a plastic. Whatever material used, its cushioning is created by the air bubbles in it. These can be regulated during

Fig. 2-8. Plastic-covered tension springs used to support the cushioned seat of a lounge chair.

manufacture to give soft, medium, or firm cushioning. Other qualities can be included in the material, such as special resistance to oil or burning.

The latex or plastic foam material may be plain with a smooth surface on both sides, but this is usual in thinner pieces up to about 1 inch thick (Fig. 2-9A). If the foam is intended for a seat it will be about 4 inches thick and will give a better cushioning performance if its top surface is smooth, but its underside is a mass of cavities (Fig. 2-9B). Of course, these cavities are additional to the air bubbles and merely supplement the effect of the bubbles in achieving comfort. Another way of making more cushioning is by using a pin-core sheet (Fig. 2-9C).

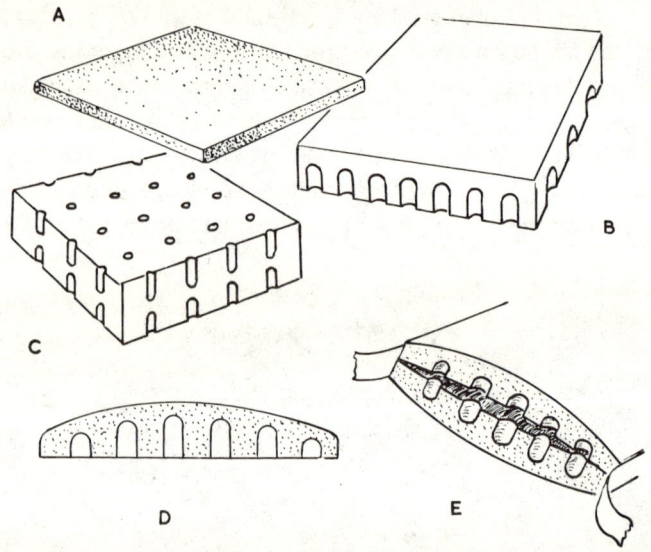

Fig. 2-9. Modern stuffing material may be made of plastic foam or latex rubber which has cavities in it to improve the cushioning effect.

Foam cushions can be molded into any shape during manufacture, so it is possible to get pads already made in a required size, with rounded edges and tapered or rounded sections if required (Fig. 2-9D). If latex foam has to be shaped, it can be cut with a knife or scissors for thin material. There are adhesives for joining pieces to make up special shapes, with tape to cover joints as well. Two cavity-type pads can be fixed together in this way to make a cushion (Fig. 2-9E).

Traditional stuffing materials that may still be used include fiber, hair, wool, kapok, and feathers. Whatever the stuffing material it is important that it remains twisted or curled so it does not pack tight, but encloses many air pockets. It is also important that the material return to its original shape after being compressed. Latex foam does, but some of the older materials lose this quality, to varying degrees, with age.

Fiber is not commonly used. However, vegetable fiber such as coconut fiber, which is the lining of the nut husk, or split leaves from an Algerian palm, can be curled to provide cushioning. Long fibers are more effective than short ones. As a natural material fiber may attract insects, although it can be treated to proof it against them. Some fibers get hard and turn to dust as they get older.

Hair may be described as *horse hair* or *hogs hair*, but that hair supplied for upholstery is more likely to be a mixture of hairs from cattle, and other animals as well. It is cleaned and sterilized and may be dyed black, then twisted into ropes. This gives it a curl when it is separated, which should be retained throughout the life of the hair. Long hairs make better padding than short hairs and they are easier to place. Hair stuffing makes good cushioning. It has a long life and is next in popularity to latex foam.

There are rubberized hair sheets, in which the hair is backed by rubber. This can be cut to shape and is used for such work as seat arms where loose hair would be difficult to place and retain evenly.

Wool in various forms has been used for stuffing. It may have been used at one time directly as cut from the animal with little preparation, but that form is not found today. Wool is more likely to be found in the form of flock. This is made from woollen rags that have been cleaned and carded into tiny particles. These may be made into felt, which consists of a sheet built up of flock particles bonded together. A similar item may be made from tiny pieces of cotton formed into linter's felt or cotton felt batting. This is related to the cotton batting, wadding, or cotton wool used for other purposes. For upholstery it may be supplied about 1 inch thick and held in shape by paper. It comes in rolls and can be cut as needed. Price is probably determined by weight and not size. Felts are used over hair and fiber fillings as part of the seal to prevent ends from coming through as well as to provide cushioning in itself.

There are other prepared supplies. Stuffing pads have hair or fiber on burlap. These are convenient for using in places like chair arms, where it would be difficult to get an even covering of loose stuffing. There are prepared fox and roll edges which simplify the arranging of seat edges. Piping can be bought all ready for sewing in seams. These items are described where instructions are given for their application.

Feathers are used more for stuffing cushions and pillows than fixed seats or backs. The highest quality feather is eiderdown, which is hand plucked from the breasts of eider ducks. This has the greatest capacity for regaining its original shape after severe compressing. Ordinary poultry feathers are more common. They have been cleaned by the suppliers. Feathers provide warmth, but their cushioning effect is not as good as many other stuffing materials.

Kapok is a vegetable padding something like feather stuffing. It was much used for upholstery at sea because a cushion made from it would float, at least for several hours. Although it has a good capacity for regaining its shape after compression, this quality diminishes with age, and the material may get hard and lumpy eventually. Kapok was also used in lifejackets, but this use has been abandoned because the material does not retain its buoyancy indefinitely, especially if it absorbs oil from the water.

The alternative for making buoyant cushions is to use closed-cell plastic foam. It is important that it is closed-cell foam because other foams, satisfactory for many shore uses, have connected air cells that act like a sponge if they come into contact with water.

INNER COVERINGS

The actual facing material that is exposed and sat on directly should do little more than provide an attractive covering. The stuffing, particularly if it is made up of loose material arranged as padding, should be enclosed by other fabric before the covering is fixed. Similarly, the underside of a piece of furniture should not have the springs and other structure exposed to view if it is turned over. As well as covering, there may be extra material needed between the springs and the cushioning matter. Materials used for these purposes are not exposed to normal view; they have to be adequate for their purpose, but no more costly than necessary.

Burlap is a coarse material made from jute. It is produced in many qualities and tightness of weave. The heavier grades are best, but lighter material may be quite satisfactory in some situations. The better quality may be nailed to the underside of a frame to give a good finish to the bottom of a chair. Burlap is normally supplied in wide rolls and cut as needed. It is a general-purpose material for hidden parts of upholstery.

Scrim is even more loosely woven than burlap. Scrim may be used as the first covering over hair or other loose stuffing, which is then sewn into place. Muslin is also used for holding stuffing in place. Material used for this purpose must be able to flex and stretch in both directions. Loosely woven nylon may be a synthetic that has possibilities for this purpose, but most synthetic fabrics are too tightly woven and inelastic. Black cambric is a commonly-used alternative to burlap for nailing below furniture to hide the springs and webbing.

COVERING

Chairs have been covered with a great many different types of flexible material, mostly woven cloths; but hides and leather of various sorts have also made tough, long-lasting covers, while plastics have brought a large variety of man-made materials to upholstery.

It is helpful if the covering material has a good resistance to creasing and will remain flexible at all times. Some plastics get hard and stiff when cold. The material should be comfortable to the touch. It is helpful, when fixing, if it has some elasticity and its weave allows it to be pulled to shape with the minimum risk of creasing. There is a limit to the amount of compound curve that any cloth will take, and pleats have to be allowed for. These may be regarded as decorative. Still, the material should take modest compound curving without trouble. Excessive stretch is not wanted and most upholstery made of plastic material has a woven fabric backing to keep stretch within the necessary limits.

Leather is broadly divided into *hides*, meaning cowhides, and *moroccos*, meaning skins of goats. A *roan* may mean a sheepskin, very similar to a morocco. Of course a cowhide produces a much larger piece of leather with greater possibilities for chair covering. However, leather covering is extremely expensive and chairs are more likely to be covered with a plastic imitation leather, which may be described as *leather cloth*.

A point to consider is the effect of condensation and perspiration on the material. Woven cloth made from natural materials will "breathe"—which means it allows the passage of moisture. This also applies to leather, which is porous. Some woven synthetic materials have a sufficiently open weave to allow them to breathe. Other plastic coatings, such as the imitation leathers, are completely waterproof and impervious to moisture.

All bodies exude moisture. This is inevitable. With normal clothing, the moisture evaporates to the atmosphere. An upholstered seat that is porous enables the process to continue, and is comfortable to sit on for any duration. If the surface does not allow moisture to pass, long use will cause a build-up of moisture under the body. It may not be much, but it can cause discomfort after a few hours. If such a surface is slept on for a night there will be a very pronounced layer of moisture remaining on the covering.

There are a number of other considerations in choosing cloth for covering. If there is any pattern, the covering has to be consistent and match at seams. If the pattern is large it may have to be arranged so the main motif is centered on a seat or back. In any case, the direction of pattern has to be kept the same. All of this means that the cloth has to be cut wastefully to get the desired results. As the covering material will almost certainly be the most expensive part of the upholstery, this waste has to be taken into account. Pieces of the required size and shape may be cut much more economically if the material is plain. It is possible to join most material, but this can only be done in hidden or inconspicuous places.

Besides the pattern, some materials look different when viewed from different directions. This applies to moquettes, velvets, and pile fabrics, and has to be allowed for in scheming the way the cloth is to be fitted. This, too, may result in waste.

Woven cloth is made on a loom with the lengthwise *warp* threads at right-angles to the *weft* threads. The weft threads go backwards and forwards across the cloth, turning back without a break at the *selvedges*. These selvedges, with no cut threads to bother about, cannot fray; but cuts anywhere else may need sewing or turning under and tacking. Normally, even with un-patterned material, it is usual to lay the cloth on the furniture so warp and weft are symmetrical in relation to the framework or the outline of the chair or other article. It is very rarely satisfactory to have the weave at an angle to the main lines.

Warp and weft threads are not always spaced the same, but for upholstery they should be, if possible. This may be seen if the fabric is held up to a light. The cloth with the greatest strength and the best prospect of long wearing is closely woven. This may be graded by the *pick* of the cloth. If there are 40 warp threads and 30 weft threads in a square inch the pick is 1200 (30 × 40).

In a plain weave the warp and weft thread cross each other "over and under one." This weave is both simple and durable and should produce a hard-wearing fabric. In a twill weave the effect is of diagonal lines on the surface. It has a good resistance to tearing, but stretches more than plain weave. A satin weave has the warp threads crossed by every fifth weft thread or so. This leaves threads rather prominent and liable to wear rapidly. There are also many combination weaves that produce special effects.

Some fabrics used for upholstery are listed below, but there are others and names may vary:

Brocade is a finely woven material which may be a natural material such as silk or cotton, or a synthetic. It is made in many designs.

Brocatelle is a heavy, stiff fabric with a raised design over a plain ground, made from cotton only or cotton mixed with other fibers.

Buckram is a canvas stiffened with glue.

Corduroy is an extremely durable ribbed fabric. It has a short pile and may be made of cotton or wool or one of these blended with other fibers.

Dacron is the trade name of polyester fabric which is strong, water resistant, and fire resistant.

Linen is a traditional plain or patterned flax-woven fabric.

Matelasse uses two sets of warps and wefts to form a design with a quilted effect and to produce a heavy fabric.

Moquette has a pile-like velvet, which may be cut or uncut or mixed. It can be cotton, wool, synthetic, or a combination.

Nylon is a synthetic that is woven into fabric which is water-resistant and difficult to burn. Several effects are possible.

Silk is not frequently used for modern upholstery, but it is interesting and is the product of the silk worm.

Tapestry is a stout fabric, closely woven, and it may have a pattern included. It is made of wool or cotton or a mixture.

Velvet is a cloth with a pile. Although traditionally made of silk it is now more likely to be synthetic.

Vinyl (polyvinyl chloride or PVC) is a soft plastic which may come on a woven cotton backing.

The choice of a covering material will be dictated by many requirements, such as the need to match other furniture or the decor of a room. For much-used furniture in a public place, the durability of the covering will be high on the list of requirements, with comfort and appearance rather lower in priority. Conversely, a chair planned to be used occasionally in a bedroom is unl kely to get rough use and the fabric may be chosen for its appearance and comfort, with less regard for how hard-wearing it is.

For early attempts at upholstery it is advisable to choose a fabric that is easy to work. A plain cloth avoids the problem of matching designs and allows the beginner to concentrate on fixing. The suitability of plain material for economical cutting is also an advantage to a beginner. If a mistake is made, it may be possible to alter or recut or join in a new piece, without having to cut wastefully to find a matching pattern.

Availability and price are important considerations. Although some materials not primarily intended for upholstery may have possibilities, some of these are best kept for small things like stool tops. For more ambitious upholstery it is advisable to get covering and other materials from a supplier of upholstery requirements. Some materials that are satisfactory for curtains, clothing, and other things may not have the qualities required for upholstery. Sometimes they may have to be used for the sake of matching other furnishings, but a beginner should obtain the advice of an expert before going ahead with them. One attraction of doing individual upholstery work is the ability to produce things that match in a way that no quantity-produced furniture can.

Most synthetic or plastic materials will melt if heated sufficiently. This can be a nuisance if a cigarette or something else hot is dropped on a seat. It will make a round hole with sealed edges. But the property of melting can also be used to advantage, as in sealing edges of material. Twine or rope made from synthetic fibers, for instance, may have the ends sealed, so they do not fray, by heating with the flame of a match or cigarette lighter. If finger and thumb are moistened, the ends can be rolled to a tapered point while they are still soft.

Some woven synthetic material will fray easily if it is cut. Using pinking shears instead of ordinary scissors will leave a sawtooth edge that resists fraying. Or, it is possible to both cut and seal the material with a hot tool. There are electrically heated knives for the purpose, but it is possible to use an electric soldering iron. Its end may be filed to a knife shape so it cuts as well as seals, or it can be used unaltered to draw along an already cut edge.

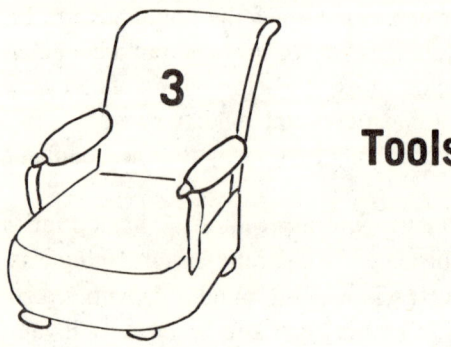

3

Tools

An upholsterer does not require a very large number of tools for his basic work, but he often has to repair and alter frameworks and he will require some general hand woodworking tools to do this. Much depends on how far he is prepared to go. If an old chair framework is to be adapted to a different purpose or shape, the woodworking skill and equipment needed may be fairly extensive; but if this sort of work is to be done by someone else and the upholsterer confines his activities to working with coverings and fillings, he can manage with a quite compact tool kit.

It is possible for a beginner to do a certain amount of upholstery with tools intended for other purposes, but tools to suit the needs of the upholstery craftsman have evolved over the years, so anyone planning to go far with upholstery will be advised to buy the right tools.

Any hammering required is usually light and it may be done in confined spaces. Because of this an upholsterer's hammer has a long narrow head. The general-purpose hammer (Fig. 3-1) has a face not much more than 1/2 inch across. The other side has a notch to give it a claw for withdrawing tacks. Because there would not be much strength if a wooden handle was merely wedged in a hole in such a small head, two cheeks from the head are usually carried along the handle.

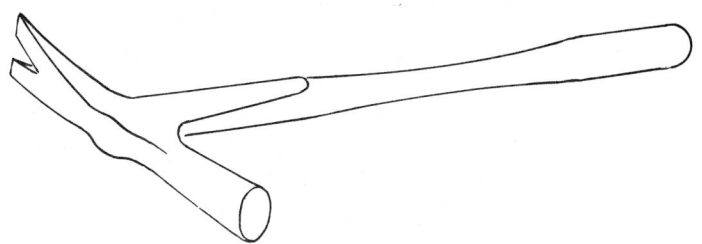

Fig. 3-1. A special-purpose hammer.

A *cabriole* hammer is a hammer with a narrower head. With a face only about 1/4 inch across (Fig. 3-2), it will get into very restricted places. It has to be more carefully aimed, however, so a hammer with a wider face is usual for general hammering.

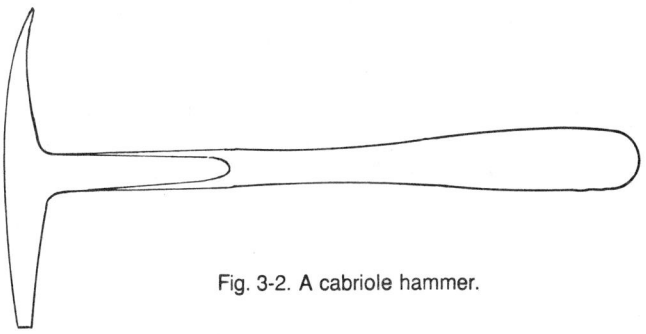

Fig. 3-2. A cabriole hammer.

Several handle shapes are used. One that is nearly parallel (see Fig. 3-1) encourages light blows by its feel, but it does not give a very good grip for the normal-sized hand. The handle may be ringed to improve the grip and prevent slipping (Fig. 3-3). A pear-shaped handle, as was shown in Fig. 3-2, offers more for the hand to hold and is probably the most favored.

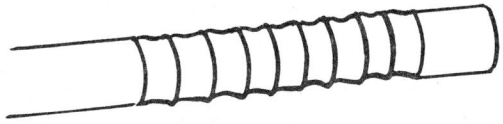

Fig. 3-3. A hammer handle may be ringed to prevent slipping.

Hammers have been magnetized. This property allows them to pick up tacks or to take them one at a time from the mouth, which was the practice of the traditional upholsterer.

Anyone tackling upholstery seriously must have one or more hammers. In commercial work, however, much of the work formerly done with tacks has been superseded by the use of staples and staple guns. The industrial staple gun is pneumatic or electric and the staple size needed for most purposes is too large for a hand-operated stapler. If antique furniture is being repaired, it would be wrong to use staples in any case because tacks would more appropriately follow the original methods.

CUTTING

Scissors are needed for most materials, but knives also have a use. Scissors should be fairly heavy, without being awkward to handle. Weight gives steadiness, which is valuable when following a line in thick material. There may be evenly matched blades centrally arranged, but there is an advantage in having the blades to one side, offset in relation to the handles (Fig. 3-4). Similar types are used for dressmaking and tailoring, but there is no need for the very large ones used for some tailoring operations. An overall length of 10 inches should suit most purposes.

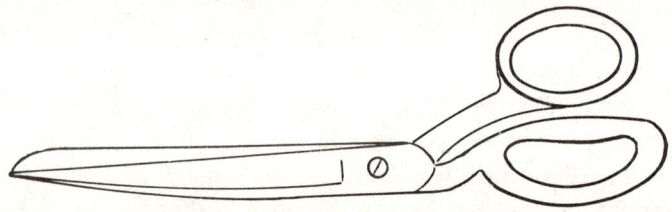

Fig. 3-4. Upholstery scissors come with blades offset to one side.

Much cutting can be done with a general-purpose knife, such as is used for leatherwork and other trades, but for end cutting a type with stout disposable blades is useful (Fig. 3-5). Sometimes a cut has to be made some way into a chair or other piece of furniture and a long-bladed knife is needed. This can be a kitchen carving knife (Fig. 3-6). Foam padding is best cut by hand with a thin-bladed knife. Special power saw/knives are

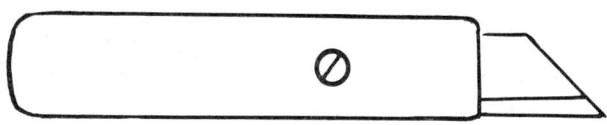

Fig. 3-5. Knives with stout, disposable blades are useful.

used for this purpose in industry. Some modern synthetic materials are surprisingly abrasive on cutting tools. It is advisable to get good quality cutting tools, which will keep their edge longer and cut more successfully than cheap tools.

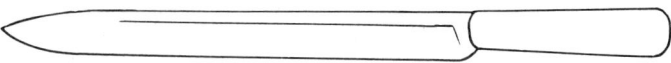

Fig. 3-6. Long-bladed knives are also useful.

An upholsterer needs to keep his cutting tools sharp, so an oilstone is essential. A combination stone, with coarse grit on one side and fine grit on the other is worth having. A size about 8 inches by 2 inches by 1 inch is better than a small stone, as it gives a good surface to work on. The stone should be kept clean, and a box or hollowed piece of solid wood makes a good base, which can be fitted with a cover (Fig. 3-7). Use a thin oil, or the

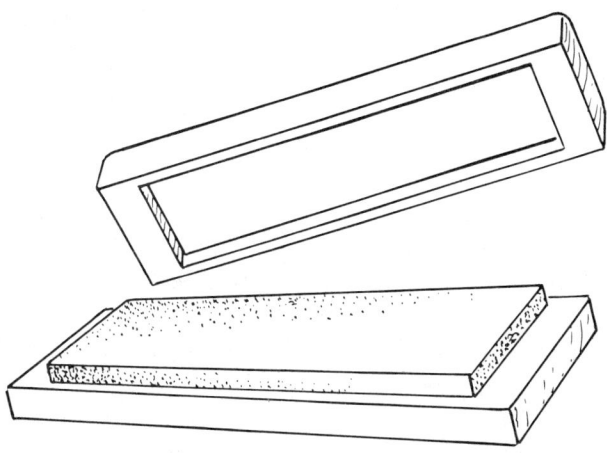

Fig. 3-7. Sharp tools are essential and knives should be sharpened on an oilstone kept in a box or on wood fitted with a cover.

type intended for sewing machines or bicycles rather than a car oil. Oil is necessary, but a thick oil keeps the steel away from the grit which does the cutting. The oilstone base may have nails driven in and the heads cut off and pointed (Fig. 3-8A) to prevent the oilstone case from moving on the bench. Strips of leather underneath will serve purpose (Fig. 3-8B).

Fig. 3-8. Nails driven into the oilstone base or strips of leather underneath it will keep the case from moving.

To sharpen a knife blade, hold the handle in one hand and control the angle with this hand, while the fingers of the other hand apply pressure (Fig. 3-9). Put the blade flat on the stone and tilt it until the edge touches. Keep it at this angle while rubbing it along the stone. If the edge is curved, move it about so all the edge is dealt with. Move the knife about the surface of the stone. As well as wearing the steel away, the surface of the stone will wear away. In order to keep this wear even, any tool being sharpened should be moved as evenly as possible over the surface.

When one side seems to have been rubbed enough, turn the knife over. Either change hands or face the knife the other way. Maintain a similar angle to that used for the first side. Wipe the oil from the blade with a cloth and examine the edge. The new bevelled surface will be seen on each side. These surfaces should meet at the edge for the whole length of the blade. They probably will not meet at the first sharpening and there will have to be more rubbing on the stone.

When you judge that the wiped edge is sharp, stroke a finger from the back towards the edge on the side that was uppermost at the last rubbing on the stone. If the newly-rubbed

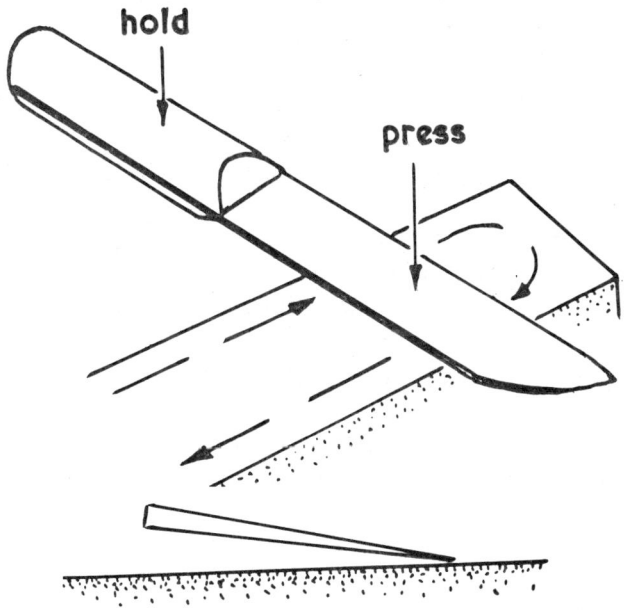

Fig. 3-9. Sharpening a knife blade..

surfaces are meeting there will be a tiny sliver of steel that has been rubbed away but is still clinging to the sharp edge. This "wire edge" will be felt curled upwards (Fig. 3-10). It can be removed by lightly slicing the blade across the edge of a piece of wood.

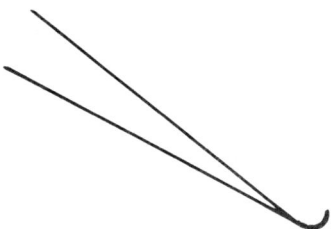

Fig. 3-10. A wire edge will remain after sharpening.

If the edge is touched up frequently during use, it need only be rubbed on the fine side of the stone. If a knife has been allowed to get very blunt or a notch has been made by cutting against a nail, sharpen it well on the coarse side of the stone. Remove the wire edge across a piece of wood, then sharpen again on the fine side of the stone. If a sharp edge is examined under a microscope it will be saw-like, with the size of the teeth and grooves matching the size of the grit in the stone. The teeth formed by coarse grit have to be rubbed away on the fine side of the stone and replaced with finer teeth. These are so fine that for practical purposes the edge may be assumed to be straight and sharp.

The edge produced on a fine oilstone should be adequate for all upholstery purposes, but if an even finer edge is needed, use of the fine oilstone can be followed by *stropping*. A leather strop is used for this purpose. It may be made of the flexible strip used for oldtime razors, or a piece of leather glued to a piece of wood. Its surface is dressed with a light oil containing very fine abrasive dust. The knife is drawn along this on alternate sides and the very fine abrasive will rub away the grooves and teeth made by the oilstone.

The existing bevels on a knife will give a clue to the angle at which it should be held on the oilstone. An acute angle is sharpest, but a razor-like edge may be so fine and weak that the first attempt to cut tough fabric may cause it to crumble. The best edge has to be a compromise, being as fine as possible for the sake of its cut, but with the minimum of obtuseness to provide strength and reduce the frequency of resharpening sessions.

RIPPING

An upholsterer uses a *ripping chisel*, which is more like a screwdriver than a carpenter's chisel. It is used for removing old coverings, levering out tacks and staples, and generally breaking away old materials. In new work it lifts tacks that have been wrongly placed, and it may be needed when there has to be experimenting to get the best fit or effect. A simple chisel is straight (Fig. 3-11A), with an edge not quite thin enough to cut. It may also be cranked (Fig. 3-11B) and either type may also have a notch to provide a claw for getting under tack heads (Fig. 3-11C). The corner of a thin, wide, straight tool can be eased under one end of a staple to loosen it, then the width can be used with a twist to lever it out. A broad screwdriver, taken to a fine edge by grinding, may be better for this than a conventional ripping chisel.

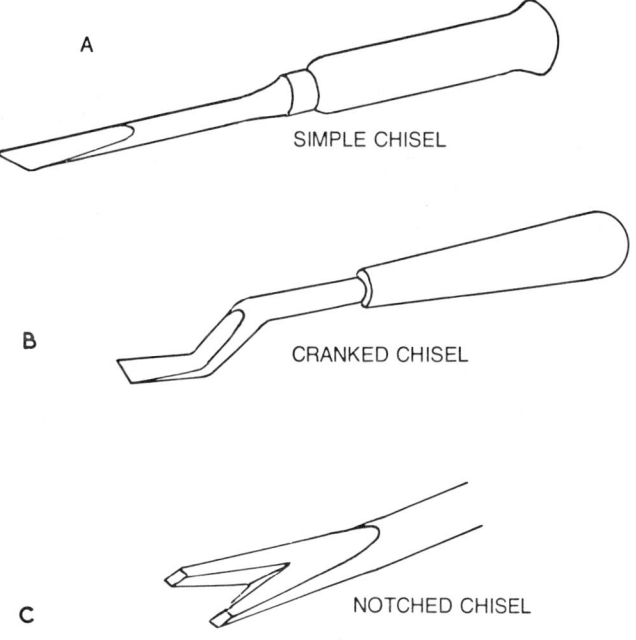

Fig. 3-11. Tools are needed to lift tacks.

The ripping chisel is used with a mallet. An upholsterer's hammer is too light and narrow for this work. The mallet may be a carpenter's type (Fig. 3-12A) or one with a round head. As the mallet may be used for other hammering, it should have a head least likely to do damage. A rawhide one (Fig. 3-12B) could be used, or one with plastic faces (Fig. 3-12C) is suitable.

NEEDLES

With changes in materials and methods, there is not as much use for needles today as there once was, but a craftsman still needs a selection of needles, even if he does not use them frequently. Curved needles are used where the needle has to go in and out when used from one side. This is often the case in upholstery, because padding and filling or the construction of the piece of furniture does not usually allow access to the other side. Such a needle may be described as half-circular, but it is not usually quite a full semicircle. It may have points at both ends (Fig. 3-13A) or at one end (Figs. 3-13B and 3-14). Upholstery needles have round points. Similar needles with trian-

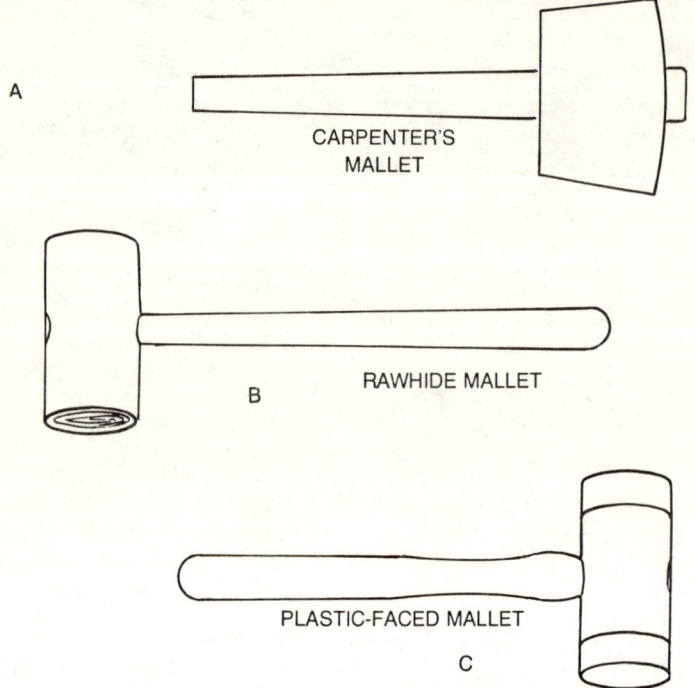

Fig. 3-12. A mallet with a wood, hide, or plastic head is preferable to a hammer for hitting wood and fabric.

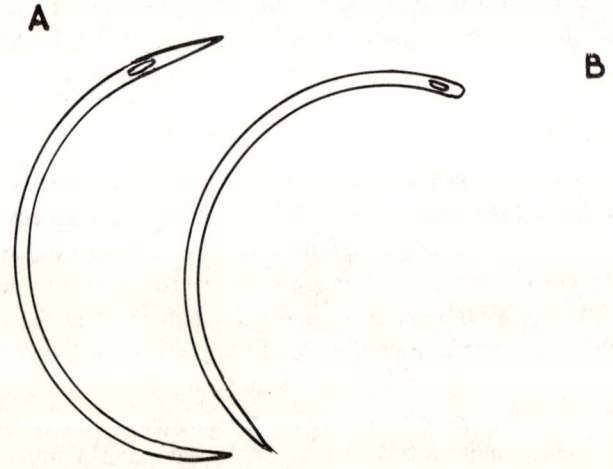

Fig. 3-13. Many types of needle are used in upholstery and the craftsman also needs spikes and special pliers for straining materials.

Fig. 3-14. Some examples of needles: at the top, a diamond-pointed bent needle, a large double-ended curved needle, a small curved needle, and a straight sailmaker's needle.

gular bayonet points are intended for leatherwork. Needles may be described by their length around the curve and by a gauge thickness. Sizes range from 1 1/2 inches to 6 inches or more. Table 3-1 shows usual sizes, with the approximate distances across the ends.

Table 3-1. Needle Dimensions

Curved Needles		
Length	Gauge	Across ends
1 1/2	19	1 1/8
2	17 or 18	1 1/2
2 1/2	17	1 3/4
3	16 or 17	2
3 1/2	16 or 17	2 3/8
4	15 or 16	2 3/4
4 1/2	15 or 16	3 1/8
5	15	3 3/8
6	14	4

Spring needles are also curved for most of their length, but the eye end is straight (Fig. 3-15A). They are thicker (10 ga.) and 4 inches to 6 inches long.

Mattress needles, long enough to go through a considerable thickness of seat, are also needed. Such needles can range between 4 inches and 16 inches long, with round points at both ends (Fig. 3-15B) or only one end (Fig. 3-15C). Triangular bayonet points may be used (Fig. 3-15D) in places where there is an advantage in forcing a wider hole. A needle may have a round point at the eye end and a bayonet point at the other end. Some usual sizes are shown in Table 3-2.

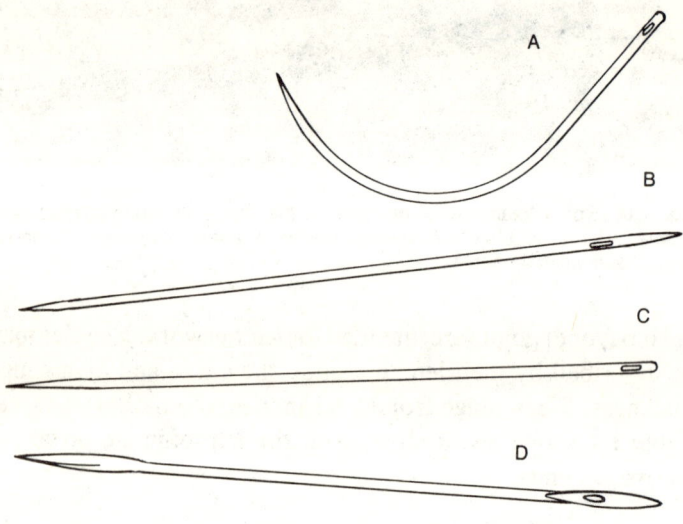

Fig. 3-15. Examples of spring and mattress needles.

A *regulator* (Fig. 3-16A) is made from a steel spike with a flattened end to form a handle, and is used to adjust some types of stuffing. It may be 6 inches to 12 inches long and 6 ga. thickness. An upholsterer uses *steel skewers* (Fig. 3-16B) as pins to temporarily hold materials together when arranging and adjusting them before fixing. They are 3 inches or 4 inches long and 16 ga. or 17 ga. thick.

There are occasions when general-purpose pliers or pincers are needed, but when cloth or webbing has to be strained, something with a wider grip is needed to get a better pull and

Table 3-2. Common Needle Sizes.

| Mattress needles ||
Length	Gauge
4	15
5	15
6	14
8	14
10	13
12	13
14	12
16	11

lessen any risk of tearing the material. The tool used is called upholsterer's or web *pincers* (Fig. 3-17). The corrugated jaws

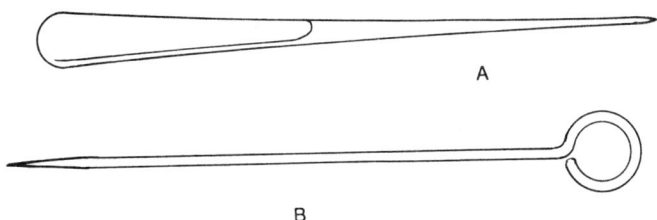

Fig. 3-16. Regulators and skewers.

provide a good wide grip and the projection below one jaw gives a fulcrum to lever on. This must be padded if it has to be used against an exposed polished surface.

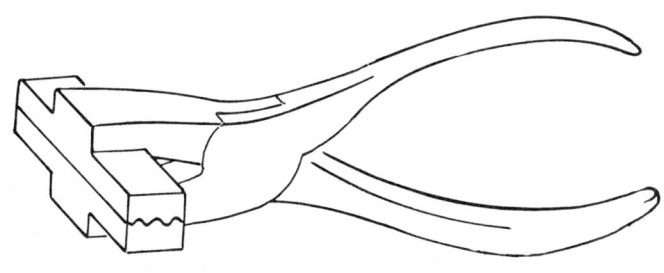

Fig. 3-17. Pincers.

WEB STRAINERS

Upholstered furniture does not rely quite as much now on stretched webbing as it once did, but this construction is still used and many types of stretcher have been devised to stretch and hold webbing while it is tacked. A plain strip of wood may be used as a lever against the frame side (Fig. 3-18A). It may have a piece of split rubber or plastic tube over the end to prevent damage to the frame and reduce the risk of slipping. Taking the webbing under the end also serves this purpose (Fig. 3-18B). The side may be hollowed for a comfortable grip and some of these strainers are given spikes (Fig. 3-18C), but there is a risk of the spikes damaging the webbing. Instead of a rounded

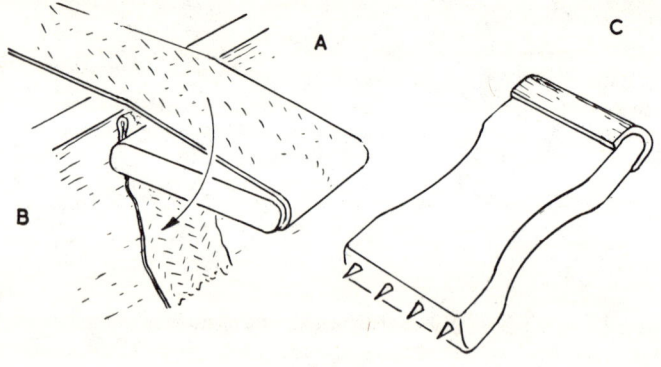

Fig. 3-18. Leverage has to be used to get a good tension on webbing and there are several types of strainers.

end against the frame, there may be a V notch (Fig. 3-19A) or a groove with legs of different length (Fig. 3-19B). In both cases, the end goes over the frame edge and levers from there (Fig. 3-19C).

Another type of strainer loops the webbing through a slot, where it is held by a peg (Fig. 3-20A). This device may have any of the ends to rest against the frame described for the plain strainer, although cutting to an angle (Fig. 3-20B) is another way of helping to apply leverage. This strainer can be made from close-grained hardwood. Some approximate sizes are shown (Fig. 3-21). The important dimension is the size of the slot,

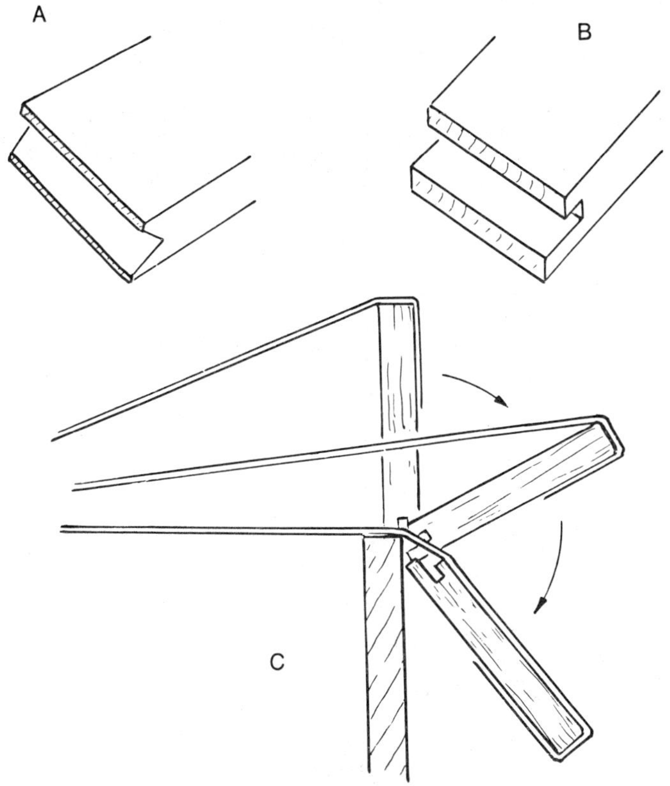

Fig. 3-19. Some strainers have V notches or grooves with uneven legs.

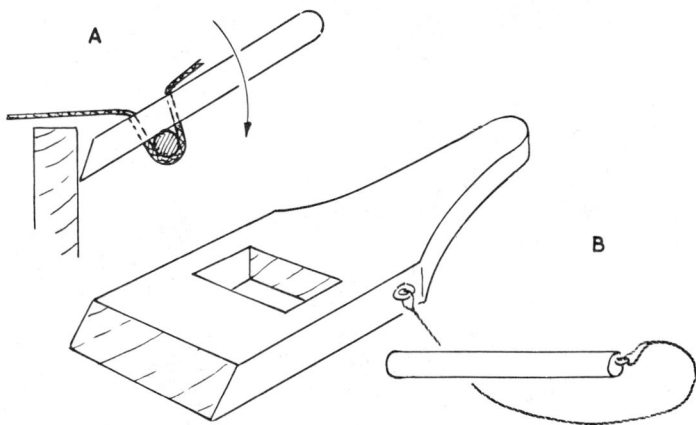

Fig. 3-20. One type of webbing strainer uses a peg under a slot. Another type gets a similar effect with a metal band over a rabbet.

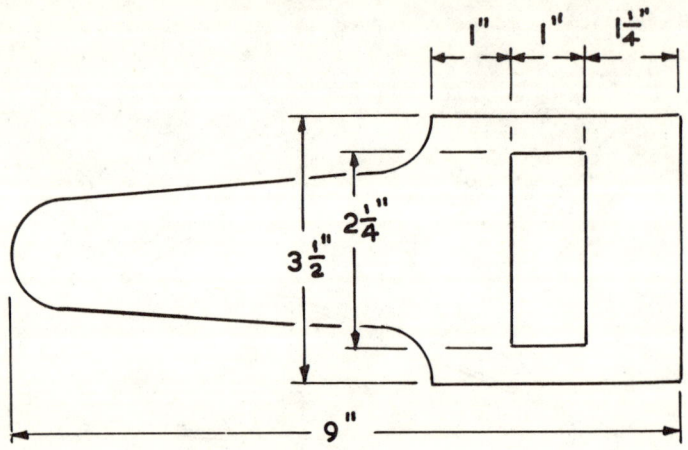

Fig. 3-21. Approximate sizes of strainers.

which should suit the webbing used and allow enough clearance for this to be passed around the peg. Because a loose peg might be lost, it is advisable to secure it with a cord.

There are metal strainers which use a similar principle (Fig. 3-22). But wood is kinder to fabrics and less likely to mark the

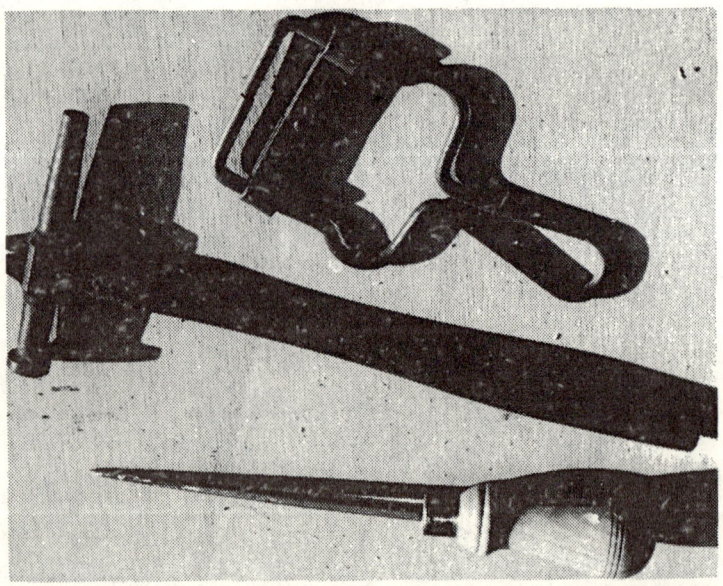

Fig. 3-22. A spike, a hammer with a tack lifter at the end, and a metal webbing strainer.

framework, so wood strainers—often made by the craftsman—are favored.

A variation on the lever strainer uses a piece of strip metal to grip the webbing in a recess (Fig. 3-23A). The webbing passes around the strip metal and over the end of the strainer, which is pressed down to stretch the webbing (Fig. 3-23B). The strip metal can be a section of steel about 3/8 inch by 1/8 inch, and

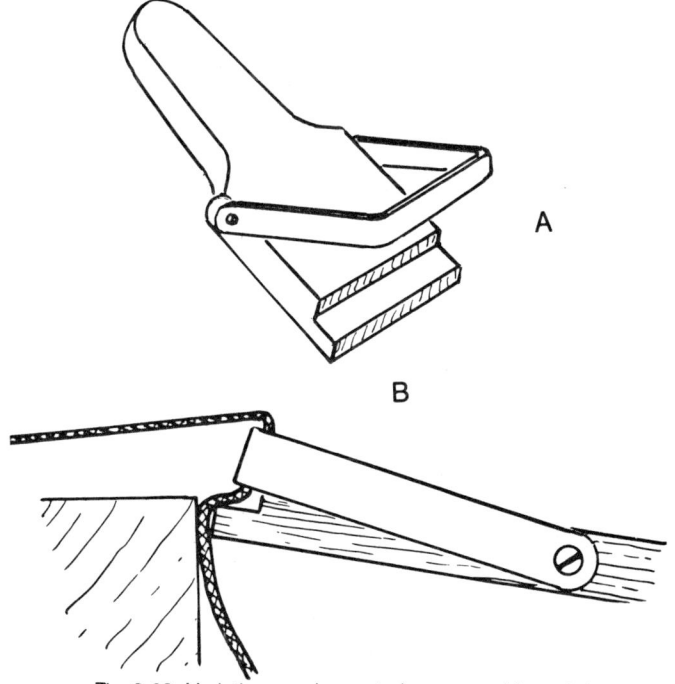

Fig. 3-23. Variations on lever strainers use strip metal.

may be bent cold in a vise. This pivots on two screws. The overall sizes suit average work (Fig. 3-24). Round the handle well for a comfortable grip.

With this last strainer the surplus webbing has to be passed through the strainer. This can be done by slipping the webbing through before passing it across the framework to fix at the other side, but if the webbing is already fixed and the remainder is on a long roll, it cannot be passed through the strainer without cutting off and wasting a short length. The other strainers are used on a loop of webbing so it does not matter how much more there is besides what is needed for the particular strip.

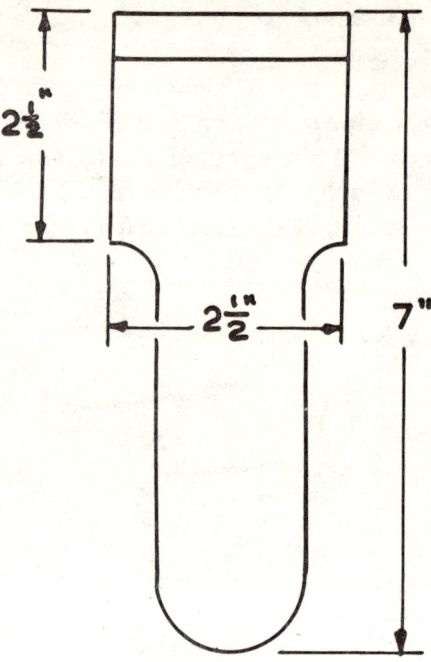

Fig. 3-24. Overall sizes suit average work.

MEASURING AND HOLDING

For measuring materials, an expanding steel rule or tape measure can be used for longer lengths, but a wooden or steel rule without a joint is convenient for shorter lengths and for drawing straight lines. The steel rule can act as a straightedge guiding a knife to cut straight lines. A piece of wood about 5 feet long with one edge planed straight is likely to be as long as needed for drawing lines on the usual widths of materials.

Marking can be done with a pencil, but chalk sharpened to a chisel edge may make a clearer mark on dark materials, and its line can be dusted away easily so nothing is left to spoil the appearance. For marking in places that will be out of sight, a felt pen or similar marker may make a line which is more easily seen. For inconspicuous edge markings you can make small nicks with a knife or scissors. With some materials a sharp crease may be all that is needed to indicate a position. If many identical parts are to be made, you can make paper patterns, or you can use cheap plywood as a template to cut around with a knife. For many items, an oversized piece of material can be formed to shape over a rigid frame, and surplus can be cut off later; but for loose cushions and similar items that don't have a rigid framework, more care is needed in marking out and cutting to size, especially if several matching items are needed.

Covering materials need to be kept clean. If exposed woodwork is already polished or varnished it has to be protected from scratches. This should always be remembered, particularly if upholstery is done in a shop that is also used for other crafts. Sawdust, metal filings, and other small debris may be just as damaging as the more obvious sharp edges of a vise or bench top.

If a chair or other piece of furniture has to be inverted to get at the underside, make sure the seat rests on clean padding and not on hard wood, even if that is clean. The necessary moving about would cause a hard surface to wear and mark cloth. If the woodwork is tilted and moved on a hard bench top, it may have its finish spoiled or even one of its edges splintered. Several thicknesses of blanket on a tabletop make a good working surface for inverted furniture.

For an occasional piece of upholstery it may be satisfactory to work with the furniture on the ground, but if this is done, the usual seat height of about 1 foot 6 inches requires much back bending. It is preferable to have the work at a height that does not require this bending. Standing a chair on a bench, however, puts it too high. There is a solution, though. Most furniture to be upholstered stands on four legs and it is helpful to have a pair of trestles of the same height and size to put under two legs each. The trestles should be higher than a carpenter's sawing trestle, but not as high as a bench—24 inches to 28 inches should be right—and a length of 3 feet should accommodate most furniture (Fig. 3-25A).

There should be border around the trestle top so the legs will not slide off (Fig. 3-25B). Fillets nailed on the top are more secure than lips nailed around the sides. Although the main use of these trestles is to support furniture by its legs, sometimes the trestles may be used to support furniture in other attitudes. If the upholstered surface has to rest on a trestle, the trestle should be padded. This can be taken care of with a padded insert (Fig. 3-25C) which can be dropped in when needed.

If fabric has to be cut off a roll, it is convenient to have a large flat area to work on. If a permanent cutting and marking table is not justified, you could use a sheet of plywood supported on the trestles.

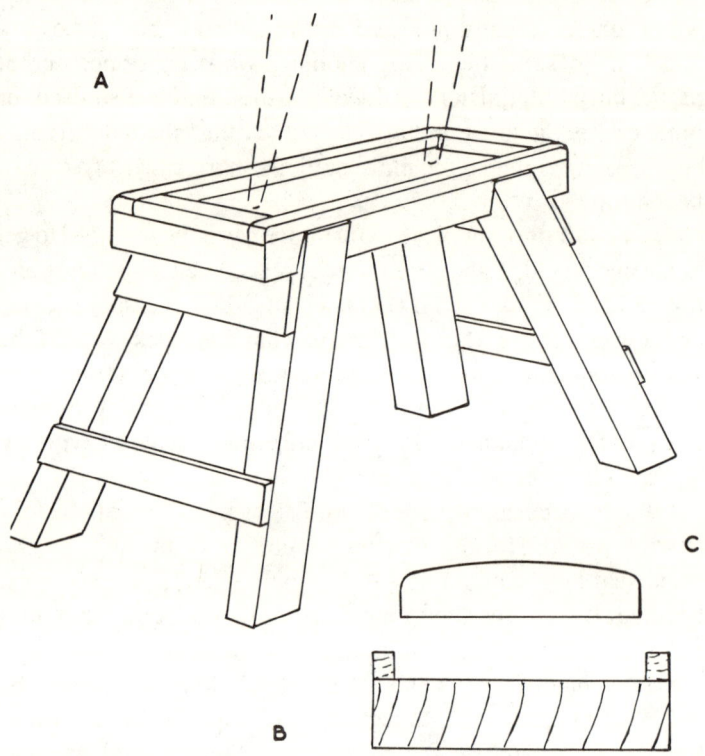

Fig. 3-25. To get a chair at a convenient height it is usual to use a pair of trestles. These may be fitted with strips to prevent legs from sliding off. There may also be a padded insert for use when the fabric part of the chair has to rest on the trestle.

The traditional method of protection for the worker is an apron with a large pocket in front. This is made of heavy white cloth and it wraps around far enough to cover the thighs, even when the legs are spread wide around the corner of a chair. The pocket may be in one width or divided down the center. It will hold all the odds and ends that accumulate during a working session. There may be a square of cloth sewn on the bib, into which needles can be pushed. These are high enough to be out of the way, with little risk of catching in the work or scratching the hands.

The traditional upholsterer kept his various sizes of tacks and other nails in cloth bags, either separate bags or one with several compartments. His tools were also carried in a bag. More recently, a plastic or metal toolbox with a tray for tacks and other things has been considered more convenient.

WOODWORKING TOOLS

Even if alterations and repairs are not being done to the framework by the upholsterer, he needs a few woodworking tools. How many depends on the extent of the woodworking he expects to do.

Wooden frameworks often need rounding. There should be no sharp angles against fabric. Rounding can be done with a coarse file or a rasp. A file has its teeth made by cutting grooves across it, usually crosscuts at different angles leaving standing points. A rasp is made by raising each tooth individually. A fine file clogs with wood dust quickly and becomes ineffective until it is cleaned by wire brushing across it. A metalworking file is unsatisfactory on wood. It is better to choose a fairly coarse woodworking file; a woodworking rasp may be even better. A 12 inch length should suit most work.

The alternative is the type of tool with rasp-type teeth cut through sheet steel and supported by a frame and handle. When the teeth blunt, the blade is replaced. Most shaping is done on straight surfaces, but a curved blade is needed for hollows. Rasps and files may be half-round (Fig. 3-26A), but for the disposable-blade type of tool separate blades are needed.

Further rounding of wood can be done with abrasive paper. Sandpaper is often used, but the abrasive may be glass, garnet, or a manufactured grit. For woodwork that is exposed in the completed furniture, it is necessary to finish with a fine grit, but for shaping internal woodwork fairly coarse paper will be quick-cutting and long-lasting. The usual size sheets for hand sanding may be torn into four and used in the hand for shaped work, or they can be wrapped around a block of wood, hard rubber, or cork (Fig. 3-26B) for flat or straight work.

If wood has to be cut, a fine-toothed backsaw (Fig. 3-26C) is usually preferable to the larger hand saw, which has coarser teeth and may not get into confined spaces. Most frames are made of hardwood and this material cuts better with a fine saw than with the big teeth which are more suitable for softwoods. A backsaw 10 inches or 12 inches long, with about 16 teeth per inch, is a good general-purpose tool that leaves an edge that may need little or no further work on it for inside a piece of upholstery.

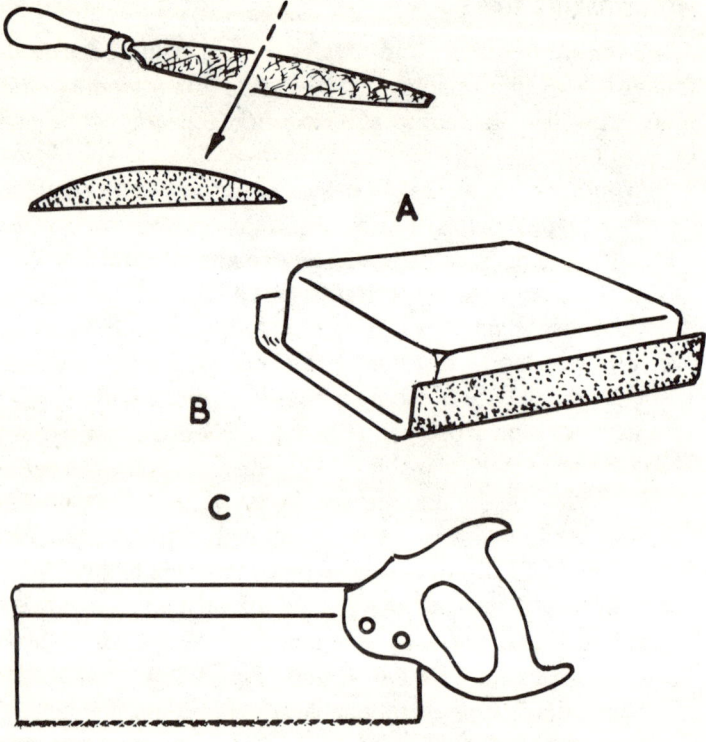

Fig. 3-26. An upholsterer often has to make modifications to the wood frame and needs files and a saw.

If wood has to be shaped more than can be done with a file or rasps it may be cut with a chisel. There are a large number of chisels graded according to their widths. They may be square-edged or bevel-edged (Fig. 3-27A). A bevel-edged chisel will do all that the square-edged one can and get into corners as well, so it is worthwhile getting bevel-edged chisels. Be careful to get the general-purpose type, sometimes called *firmer*, and not the slimmer, *paring* chisels or the very heavy *mortise* chisels, which were used for chopping out mortises before the coming of power tools and the more general use of dowels. A firmer chisel can be used in the hand or it can be hit with a mallet. Most modern plastic handles will stand up to hitting with a hammer, but a mallet delivers a better blow for chiselling.

If there is only one chisel, it should have a 1/2 inch width. This will get into most grooves and be suitable for general paring. A second chisel might be 1 inch or wider, as the broader cutting edge is more convenient for paring. A chisel has one side absolutely flat and all of the sharpening is done on the other side. There is usually a long bevel, which is made by grinding and a shorter bevel that is made by rubbing on an oilstone (Fig. 3-27B). There can be many sharpenings before the oilstone bevel gets so long that fresh grinding is needed. If a chisel is ground on a power wheel, follow the angle of the old bevel and be careful not to overheat it. Dip the point into water frequently. Overheating is apparent when rainbow colors come on the end. When this happens, the temper has been drawn and the tool is softened for the extent that has colored. Nothing practical can be done about this, except grinding past the affected part.

To sharpen a chisel on an oilstone, keep the surface coated with thin oil and hold the chisel with one hand on the handle, while the fingers of the other hand apply pressure (Fig. 3-27C). Maintain the angle for the length of the stone and move the chisel about on the surface to keep wear on the stone as even as possible. At first, there is a tendency to dip the hands at the far end of the stroke, and this should be resisted. The best edge is obtained by keeping a constant angle.

Continue sharpening until the result looks sufficient. Wipe off the oil and examine the edge. If the new bevel appears to have reached the edge, wipe a finger along the flat side towards the edge and a wire edge similar to that described for knife sharpening. If this is present, rub the flat side of the chisel absolutely flat on the stone (Fig. 3-27D) with a circular action. Do not be tempted to lift it to get more pressure on the edge. Slice the edge across a piece of scrap wood and the chisel should

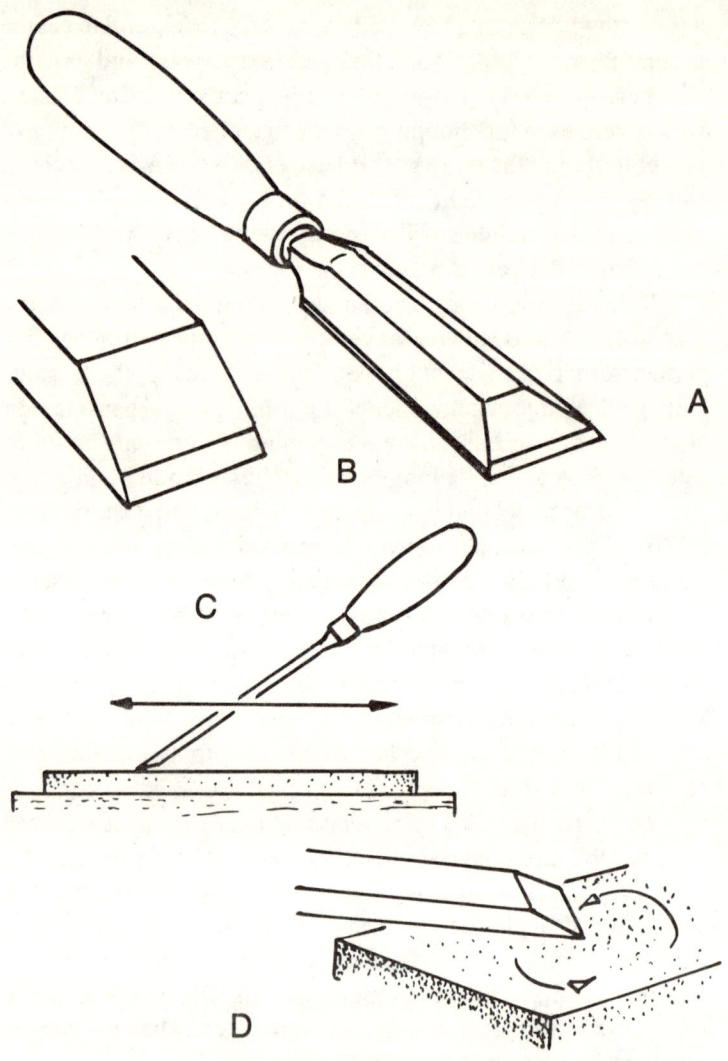

Fig. 3-27. Chisels are also necessary.

be ready for use. If much has to be taken off a blunt chisel, sharpen on the coarse side of the stone and repeat on the fine side.

For most chiselling the tool is held with the flat side against the wood. For hand work, one hand holds the handle and does the controlling, while the other hand is held across the top of the blade, applying some pressure. It is also ready to restrain if the tool tends to surge forward too quickly. For hand paring, it is best to take off many fine shavings and to use the tool with a slicing action, rather than push directly ahead (Fig. 3-28A).

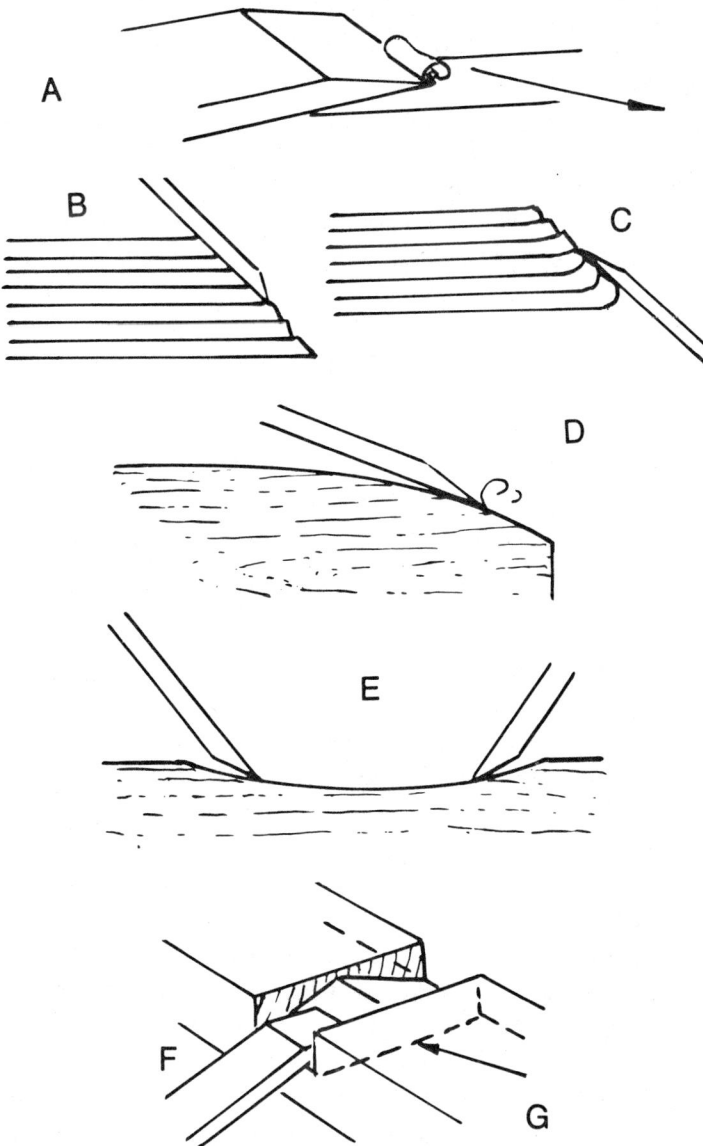

Fig. 3-28. Care is needed to use the chisel correctly in relation to the direction of grain. Technique is important.

Be aware of the direction of grain. Imagine the fibers as a bundle of loose straws and make cuts in the direction that would stroke them straight (Fig. 3-28B) and not the opposite way that would lift them (Fig. 3-28C). This may not be immediately obvious when working apparently parallel with the grain, but the first light cut will show if it might be better to change direction.

If a chisel is used with the flat side downwards it can cut a flat surface or follow an outside curve (Fig. 3-28D). If it is used with the bevel downwards it can scoop out a hollow (Fig. 3-28E). If a chisel is used across the grain, as it must be when levelling a narrow groove across a piece of wood, work from each side between saw cuts (Fig. 3-28F), but slope upwards to the center before finally levelling right across (Fig. 3-28G). If this is not done and heavy cuts are made right across, the far side is liable to break out and splinter.

Heavier cuts can be made by hitting with a mallet, but be aware of grain direction at all times, otherwise a split may develop. If there has to be heavy chopping with a chisel and mallet, have the far side of the wood supported, or it may crack or break. If much wood has to be removed, it is advisable to take away as much as possible by sawing, drilling, or other means so the amount of chiselling is not great.

There should be one or more planes available. If there is only one, it should be a Stanley No. 4 or its equivalent. This is large enough to use with two hands for levelling a surface, but it is light enough to use with one hand for work across end grain.

The actual cutting is done by a blade like a chisel with its bevel downwards. Over this and quite close to the edge is a cap iron (Fig. 3-29A), which stiffens the blade and breaks off shavings so the surface produced does not roughen or split in normal conditions. In many planes there is a screw adjustment to alter the width of the mouth through which the shavings come. This should be narrower for hardwoods than for softwoods, but the maker's setting will probably serve for most woods. The recommended plane has a screw adjustment to advance the blade and increase or decrease the cut, and a lever action to tilt the blade and set it to cut the full width of the blade or as required.

The plane iron (still called this, although it is made of steel) is sharpened like a chisel except that because it is thin, the one bevel goes right across (Fig. 3-29B). Ideally the cutting edge will be straight across with slightly rounded corners to prevent them from digging in the wood (Fig. 3-29C). In fact, the edge is more likely to develop a slight curve with rounded corners (Fig. 3-29D). This does not matter for the planing likely to be needed on a framework, but it would not be so satisfactory for something like a broad tabletop.

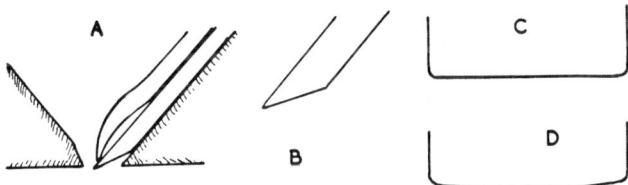

Fig. 3-29. A plane may be set and sharpened in several ways according to its purpose.

The need to watch the direction of the grain is the same with a plane as with a chisel. If the wood tears up on the first stroke, it will probably plane smoothly the other way. Normally a plane is pushed straight, but with difficult grain it helps to use it at an angle so the cut is more slicing. If a plane is being used to get an edge or surface straight, hold the whole length of the plane in contact with the wood to get the benefit of maximum length of flat surface. There are very long planes made that way particularly for ensuring straightness, but they are not needed by an upholsterer unless he plans to make frameworks.

For nearly all work of adapting a framework to suit his covering, a craftsman can do all he needs better with hand tools. If holes have to be made there is a use for a power drill, although similar work can be done with a wheel brace for small drills or a carpenter's brace for larger holes. With a power drill there is always the need to restrain it from going further than intended or marking or damaging other parts.

For screw holes and similar drilling, the usual small twist drills, originally intended for metal, can be used in sizes up to about 1/4 inch. For larger holes it is better to use proper woodworking bits that cut a cleaner outline to the hole. Of the several types, all have a central point that provides for accurate location. If it is possible to get at both sides of the wood, drill for one side only far enough for the point to come through (Fig. 3-30A), then use this hole to locate the point to drill back from the second side (Fig. 3-30B). If this cannot be done, clamp or otherwise hold a piece of scrap wood for the drill to go into (Fig. 3-30C). Otherwise the drill breaking through may splinter and split around the hole.

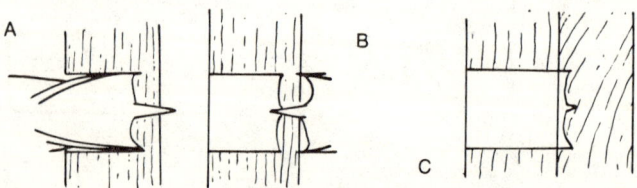

Fig. 3-30. Care is needed when drilling wood not to break out at the far side.

There are screws in many pieces of furniture. Fine screws may be used in some fittings, but most furniture screws are fairly large. There is a need for good leverage rather than quick action in the screwdrivers used. Because of this it is probably better to have several plain screwdrivers in a number of sizes than to use ratchet or pump-action types, although obviously any screwdriver already owned will have its uses. The simpler the screwdriver, the less the risk of its jumping off a screw and damaging the fabric.

Parts have to be pulled and held together. Several holding devices can be used. A few C clamps of different sizes are worth having. Bar clamps are also useful, but alternatives can be improvised. Parts can be pulled together with twisting rope in a *Spanish windlass* (Fig. 3-31A). Wedges can also apply considerable pressure at places where sprung parts have to be pressed and held together for refastening or gluing. Two blocks of wood can be fixed to a strip of wood and a wedge driven against one of them (Fig. 3-31B). A more even pressure is obtained by using a pair of *folding wedges* (Fig. 3-31C). This avoids the sideways leverage that comes with the use of a single wedge.

There are also uses for a number of punches. A center punch (Fig. 3-32A) is intended for marking metal before drilling, but it can be used on wood for the same purpose. A tool with a finer point can be used to make a deeper hole for starting nails

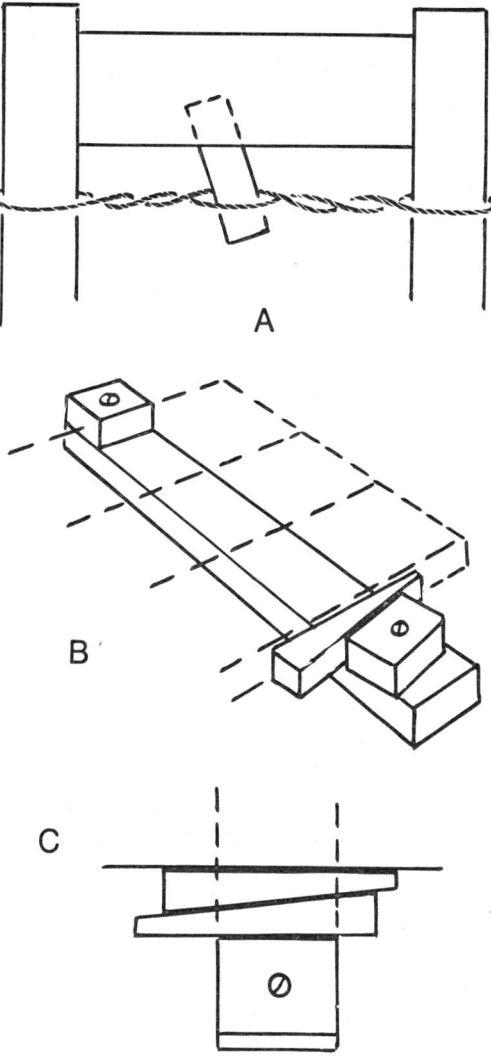

Fig. 3-31. Several improvized methods of tensioning can be used.

and tacks. A skewer might serve for this, but an ice pick is better to handle (Figs. 3-32B). Flat punches (Fig. 3-33C) in a few sizes will drive nails below the surface, knock bolts through holes, or drive tacks or nails closer without the risk to surrounding fabric or surfaces that there might be if the hammer was used directly. A carpenter's hammer is the best tool for hitting punches and it has many other uses when framework repairs and alterations are undertaken. If a hammer is used in wood, spread the shock by hitting over a piece of scrap wood. This makes the blow more effective and reduces the risk of splitting or denting due to a localized blow from hard steel on soft wood.

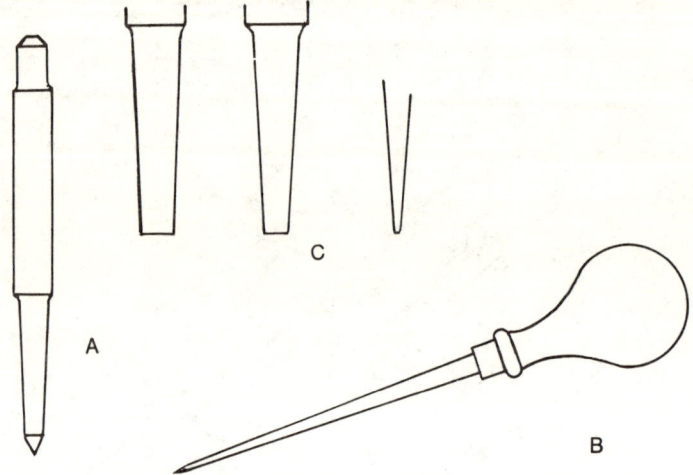

Fig. 3-32. Punches are needed to start nails and to make sure nails go below the surface.

Almost certainly an upholsterer will need to glue wood and he may have to finish it by staining and polishing. Equipment for these processes and tools for other special uses are dealt with in later chapters as the need arises.

SPECIAL TOOLS

There are appliances which may not be justified for an upholster doing a small amount of custom work, but which will help him if his activities get more extensive or if he does an increasing amount of repetition work. Button-covering and cushion-stuffing machines fall in this group. If much frame-making is undertaken, there will be an advantage in having power tools to lessen the labor of sawing and planing and to make possible the purchase of lumber in sizes and quantity that will allow conversion to the sections and shapes needed. Much of the wood in chair frames is not stock size and it is convenient to be able to prepare your own wood as you need it. However, to do everything that may be needed with the aid of power tools means equipping a special wood shop, and that is more than most workers—whose interest is in the fabric-working part of upholstery—would want to do.

There have been hand tools devised to use for sewing with a similar stitch to that of a sewing machine, but most of these are intended for lighter fabrics such as those used for clothing, and would not be suitable for the majority of upholstery fabrics.

One form of awl, intended originally for saddlery and other leatherwork, makes a lock stitch similar to that of a sewing machine and is stout enough to use on hide and heavy upholstery material. As supplied, the awl has waxed nylon thread inside the handle and there are curved, as well as straight, needle points (Fig. 3-33).

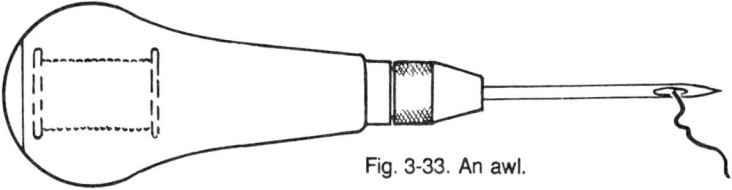

Fig. 3-33. An awl.

The awl point is pushed, at the end of the seam, through the thicknesses of material being joined. Then you pull out thread in sufficient length to go along the seam, with a little extra (Fig. 3-34A). Pull the awl back and push iththrough again at the

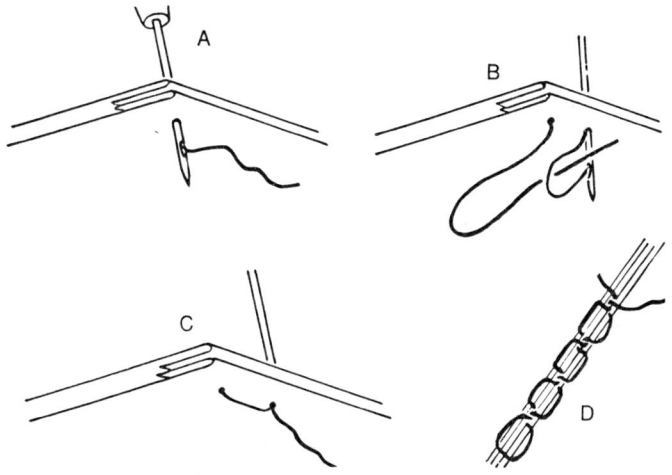

Fig. 3-34. Creating a lock stitch.

distance a stitch is intended to be—figure on using about five to an inch. This time, take the end of the thread through the loop that the awl brings through (Fig. 3-34B). Pull the awl back (Fig. 3-34C) and this will make a lock stitch. Do this all the way along the seam. If tension is regulated carefully, the upper and lower threads will loop together in the center of the thickness, like a machine lock stitch (Fig. 3-34D).

4

Springing

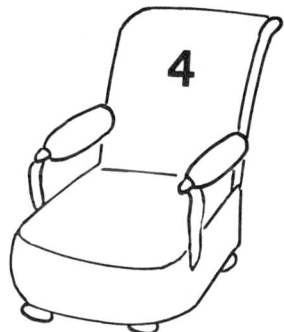

The base of nearly all upholstery is some form of springing. This backs up whatever cushioning is provided, giving some controlled resistance to sag and permitting the padded surface to conform to as large a part of the anatomy as is reasonably possible. Comfort results from the spread of the load over as large a surface of the body as possible, with a consequent reduction in the amount of weight to be taken by any particular part.

It is possible, with a sufficient thickness of latex or other foam, to provide an acceptable amount of cushioning even on a solid base. This means using something like 6 inches of foam over a wooden base (Fig. 4-1). There are problems in providing foam of this thickness, but for a bunk in a boat cabin or a similar application where the weight of the body will be spread out, it is possible to get acceptable comfort with a foam mattress 4 inches thick or more. For sitting it is likely that whatever thickness of foam there is, the presence of a solid base will become apparent to the user. Consequently, it is usual to have a seat with a sprung underpart, even if foam over a more solid support is used for the back or arms of the chair.

WEBBING

The arrangement of the pattern of webbing has to be planned to suit the intended number of springs. It is usual for the

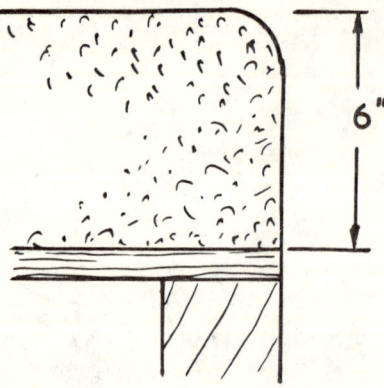

Fig. 4-1. Foam or latex padding can be used on a solid support.

pieces of webbing to cross under each spring, although this arrangement is not essential. If the webbing provides support for cushions directly, or if it is used in some other way that does not involve springs, the spacing will have to be arranged to provide what is estimated to be adequate strength. A reasonable pattern has gaps between the pieces of webbing slightly wider than the width of each piece, but this obviously has to be arranged to give even divisions in the available space. Also, any taper has to be allowed for (Fig. 4-2A). Although geometric precision is not important, aim to get a reasonable spacing by marking the frame. It is helpful to start with a center strip of webbing. If there are to be springs it may be helpful to sketch the arrangement on paper before fixing the webbing (Fig. 4-2B).

The wood used in chair framing should be a hardwood, for most hardwoods have good resistance to splitting. It is unusual to find softwoods used in chair framing, even for hidden parts, because there can be considerable strain on the attachments to framing. Wood's strength lies in lengthwise fibers. They are unlikely to break across, but they may pull apart. This is a split. To avoid this, tacks and other fastenings should be driven in as far as possible and so that not too many enter the same line of grain. As grain tends to wander and is not always parallel to the edge of the piece of wood, tacking can usually be arranged in different grain lines without much difficulty.

The end of a piece of webbing must be folded back so the load comes on the rolled part and not on a cut open end,

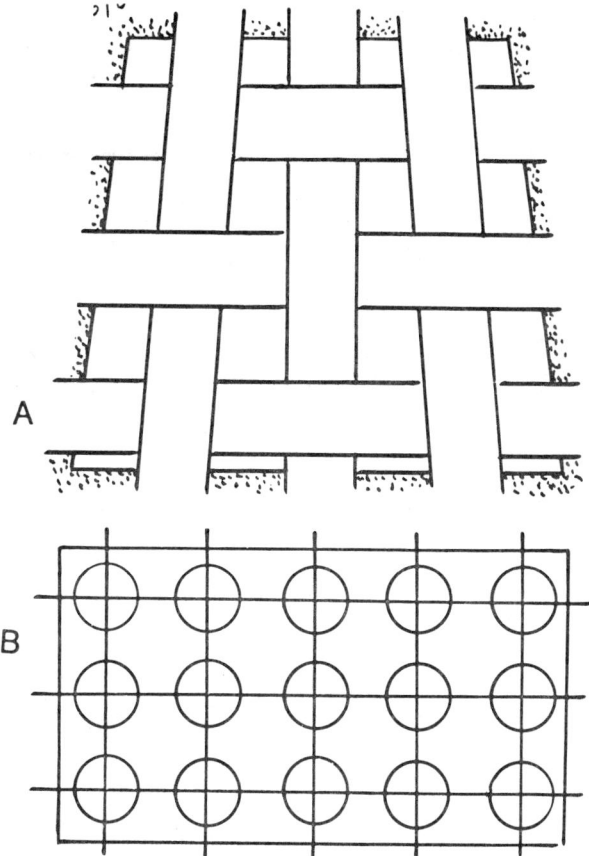

Fig. 4-2. More comfort is provided if springs are arranged over a pattern of webbing underneath the padding.

otherwise strands may pull and the end may break away. How the tacks are arranged through the double thickness is not important, as long as there are enough of them. Rows of three and two, or four and three, should do (Fig. 4-3A), staggering positions slightly to move into different lines of grain.

If the webbing can be taken over an edge and be tacked to the outside of the frame instead of its edge, the turn over the frame edge will contribute strength and relieve the tacks of some of the strain. In many parts the webbing outside would be visible or would interfere with other work, but it may be possible to arrange the webbing in this way at the back of a seat, even if it is tacked on the surface elsewhere.

At the other end one of the stretchers is used (refer back to Figs. 3-18 through 3-21). While the strain is kept on, one row of tacks is driven near the outside edge (Fig. 4-3B). These will hold

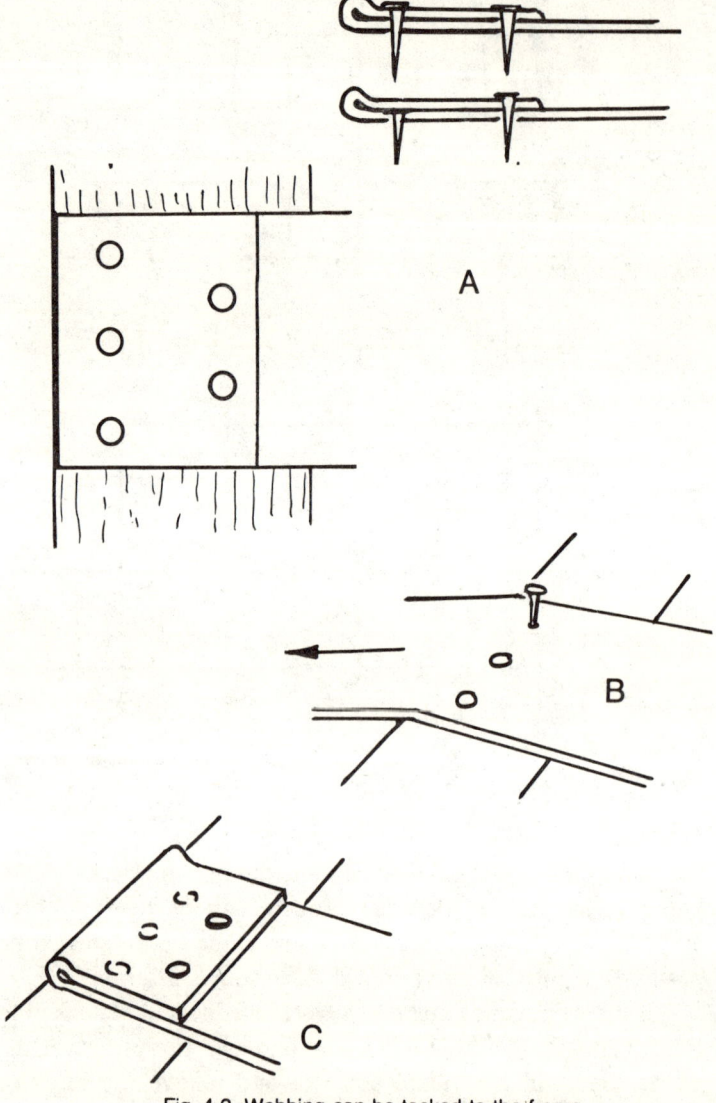

Fig. 4-3. Webbing can be tacked to the frame.

the load while the webbing is cut off long enough to turn back and take a second row of tacks (Fig. 4-3C). Arrange the webbing alternately over and under in each direction. Keep the turned-in ends of webbing within the bounds of the frame so they do not interfere with any covering going outside, and will not show if the wood is exposed in the finished chair. Some webbing is quite stiff and it is helpful to hammer down the crease before tacking to the frame.

RUBBER WEBBING

It is possible to tack rubber webbing to a frame in the same way. Although there is less risk of a tack pulling away the cut end, it is still advisable to turn back an end and tack through a double thickness. Although a stretcher has to be used, the fact that the material is elastic means there has to be some restraint on the amount of stretch permitted. It depends on the job, but 5 percent to 10 percent stretch is usual. This means that if the chair is 18 inches across, the amount of stretch given should be approximately between 1 inch and 2 inches. To get a similar stretch in each piece, mark the unstretched length on the webbing and note the amount this is to be stretched past the edge. Then drive the first row of tacks before cutting off and turning over for another row of tacks. The strength of tacked rubber webbing is increased if it can be taken over an edge and tacked outside—as was suggested for ordinary webbing—if this does not interfere with appearances.

There are special ends for rubber webbing. One is a metal clip that is squeezed on to the webbing with a vise. The points pass through the webbing and spread the load (Fig. 4-4A). The frame may be grooved on the inside so the clip can go into it and be held by a nail or screw down through the hole in the clip (Fig. 4-4B). The frame may have a groove cut at an angle in the top edge, so the clip will press in and the angle of the pull will prevent it from pulling out (Fig. 4-4C). A possibly stronger method has the groove outside and angled upwards, so the webbing goes over the edge (Fig. 4-4D). This is only suitable where the projecting webbing will not interfere with a covering or show on the outside. For attachment to metal frames there are clips that pass through holes in the turned-back ends of the rubber webbing (Fig. 4-4E).

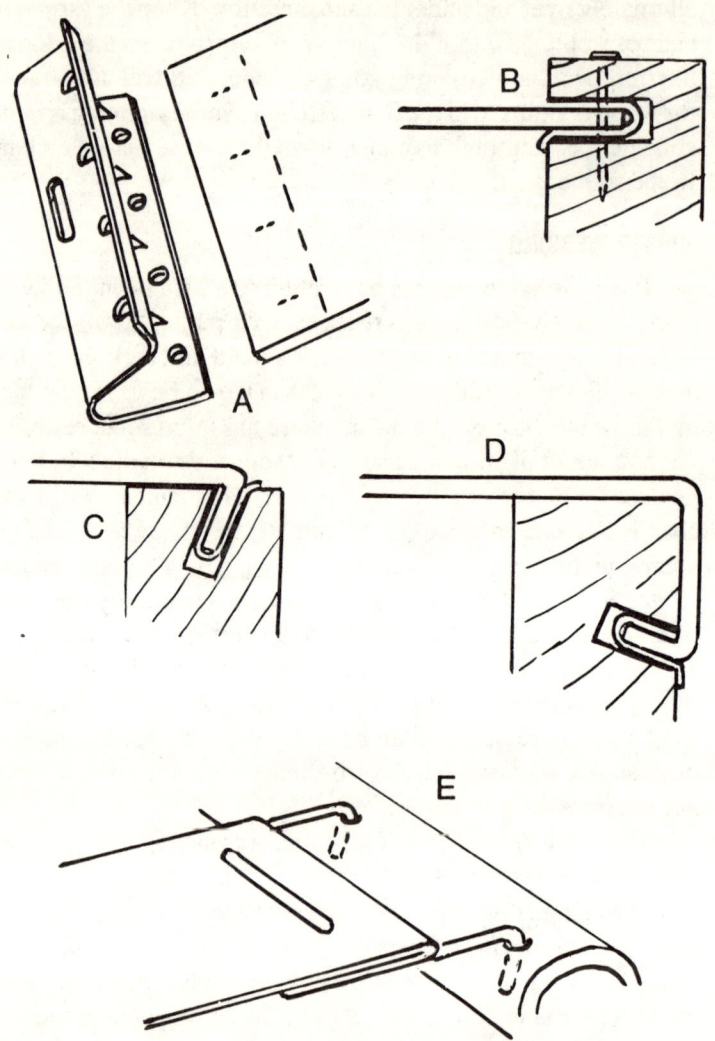

Fig. 4-4. There are metal fittings that allow rubber webbing to be attached to metal or wood frames.

TENSION SPRINGS

Tension springs are supplied with the ends already hooked. Although it is possible to cut a spring and bend a new hook, this practice is not advised because the steel is tempered and tends to be brittle. It will blunt a cutting tool and may snap in the attempt to form a new hook. The only safe way to cut and reshape an end is to heat the spot quickly so there is little time for the heat to spread. Make it just red hot and let it cool slowly. That part of the spring will then be soft enough to cut and reshape without breaking. Rehardening and tempering is not practicable in the home shop, so the shortened spring will have to be used as it is. It is obviously better to obtain springs of the right length.

A seat spring is usually satisfactory if stretched about 1 inch for every 1 foot of length, so this allowance should be made between attachment points, although there can be a little tolerance to accommodate a standard length of spring.

There are several ways of attaching these springs to the framing. If no provision has been made in the design of the woodwork and the springs will be out of sight, they may be held with nails or screws (Fig. 4-5A). A washer under a screw head makes a neat secure fastening. As it may be preferable to have the spring below the surface of the frame, the hook may go into a groove and be held by a screw (Figs. 4-5B and 2-7). In some

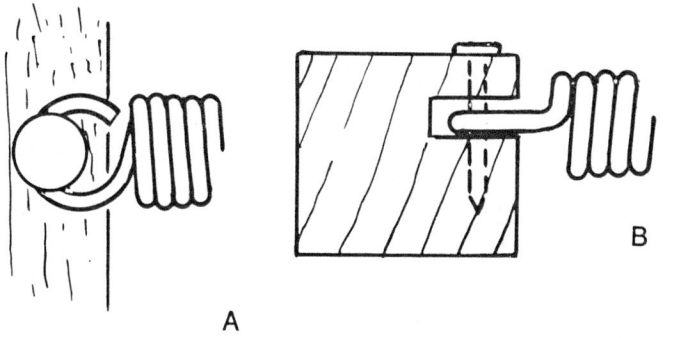

Fig. 4-5. Tension springs may be held by screws or nails.

constructions a metal plate is used. Lengths can be bought with holes already drilled sufficiently closely for any spacing of springs to be arranged. On some frames the metal strip is fixed at an angle (Fig. 4-6A) or it may be let into a rabbet (Fig. 4-6B). Individual plates may be used, but these require two screws at each spring end to provide sufficient strength.

For zig-zag springing there are clips for the ends (Fig. 4-7) which will pass over the wire and be fixed to the surface of the

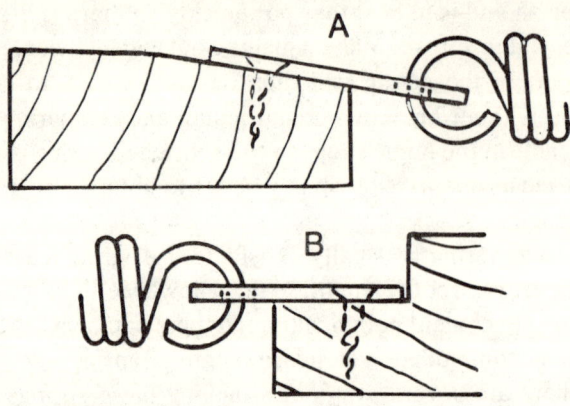

Fig. 4-6. In some cases it is more convenient to have metal plates attached to the frame.

frame with one or two screws in each position. As with tension springs the amount of tension for zig-zag springs has to be regulated. It is advisable to buy zig-zag springs of the right length, as cutting a longer piece to size is not satisfactory. Where this type of springing is used behind the cushions of a chair back, there is a curve across the spring. This curve has to be allowed for so the result is comfortable, with sufficient springs to give the right conformity to a reclining body.

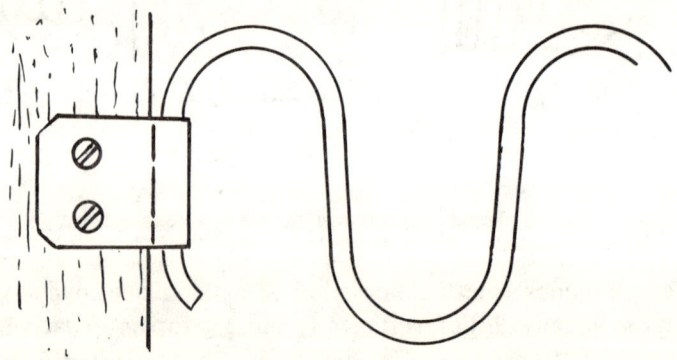

Fig. 4-7. For zig-zag springs there are clips for the ends.

Short stabilizer springs are used to keep zig-zag springs in the correct relation to each other. These are short tension springs that hook on and are used between spring and spring, and spring and frame.

Some seats and backs use other types of springs. There may be a metal mesh that provides the support, but this is held by shorter tension springs around the sides. These are fixed to the frame in the same way as tension springs. There are also units where all of the springing is fitted to a metal frame which only has to be screwed down to the wooden frame.

COIL SPRINGS

A drop-in spring unit (Fig. 2-5B) comes as a complete assembly, but it has to suit a particular frame because there is little opportunity of adjustment. There may be a small amount of tolerance due to bending the ends, but except for this it is necessary to match the unit to the frame. This factor limits its application. Where a series of these *can* be used, however, a satisfactory pattern of springs can be built up without the use of webbing.

This same principle applies to the steel webbing unit (Fig. 2-5C), but because the ends overlap the framing it is possible to adjust by a few inches if screw holes are located to suit the frame size. However, not much adjustment is possible if the springs are to retain a satisfactory pattern within the framework—not too close nor too far from the edges. For this sort of springing the thrust tends to push the steel webbing away from the wood, so it is advisable to fix with screws and not nails, to be able to better resist this load.

When single coil springs have to be fixed it is necessary to sew them to the webbing and use twine to link their tops so they keep in position. Sewing is done with a conveniently-sized needle, usually curved. Some workers favor the double-ended needle because it can be entered either way without the bother of turning round a single-ended one. Against that convenience is the need to remember that there is a sharp point upwards as well as downwards. If it is expected that much pressure will have to be put on the needle to get through tough material, it is probably wiser to use a single-ended needle.

Upholsterers use a special slip knot to start sewing. It may be used to start sewing springs to webbing, but it is also used to fasten the end of a length of twine to anything, such as a button or a piece of fabric. One idea for greater security is to include a small piece of cotton batting in the loop when the knot is used through coarse fabric, such as burlap. This helps prevent the knot from pulling through.

The complete knot is a variation on the figure-eight slip knot. In the basic figure-eight knot the end is taken around the long part and worked around itself (Fig. 4-8A). In the upholsterer's slip knot a part of the figure-eight knot goes around the long part as well (Fig. 4-8B). The knot can be made in stages by taking the end around the long part twice (Fig. 4-8C), then around itself and under the second twist (Fig. 4-8D).

There is another method of achieving a similar result. The long part is held in the left hand and the first finger extended behind the short part (Fig. 4-9A). Pull the short part behind the long part by bending your first finger (Fig. 4-9B). Without loosening your grip, turn your left hand over (Fig. 4-9C). Work the short end over and under the long part (Fig. 4-9D). If the left hand is removed and the long end pulled, the knot will be seen to have two sliding half hitches.

When this knot is pulled tight, it may be necessary to tension the short end as well as the long part; then any surplus short end can be cut off so as to leave a little projecting.

The front of a seat gets most use and needs support closer to the edge than at the back and sides. It is usual to position the front springs quite close to the front rail, but there can be gaps at the other edges (Fig. 4-10). The springs are sewn to the webbing at three or four points each, preferably with the knots arranged equally spaced around the circumference of the spring, although this is not always possible.

Although thick twine used singly might be satisfactory, it is more usual to have double twine in the needle. Do not try to put enough twine in the needle for the whole job. This would result in time wasted pulling it all through, and there would be frequent tangling around springs. A reasonable length is just long enough to reach up comfortably with the arm as each stitch is made. When a new piece of twine has to be introduced, start again with the special knot.

The knot through the webbing and around the spring is a simple overhand knot (Fig. 4-11A). If this does not appear to grip well, and if synthetic twine is used, put a second twist in the

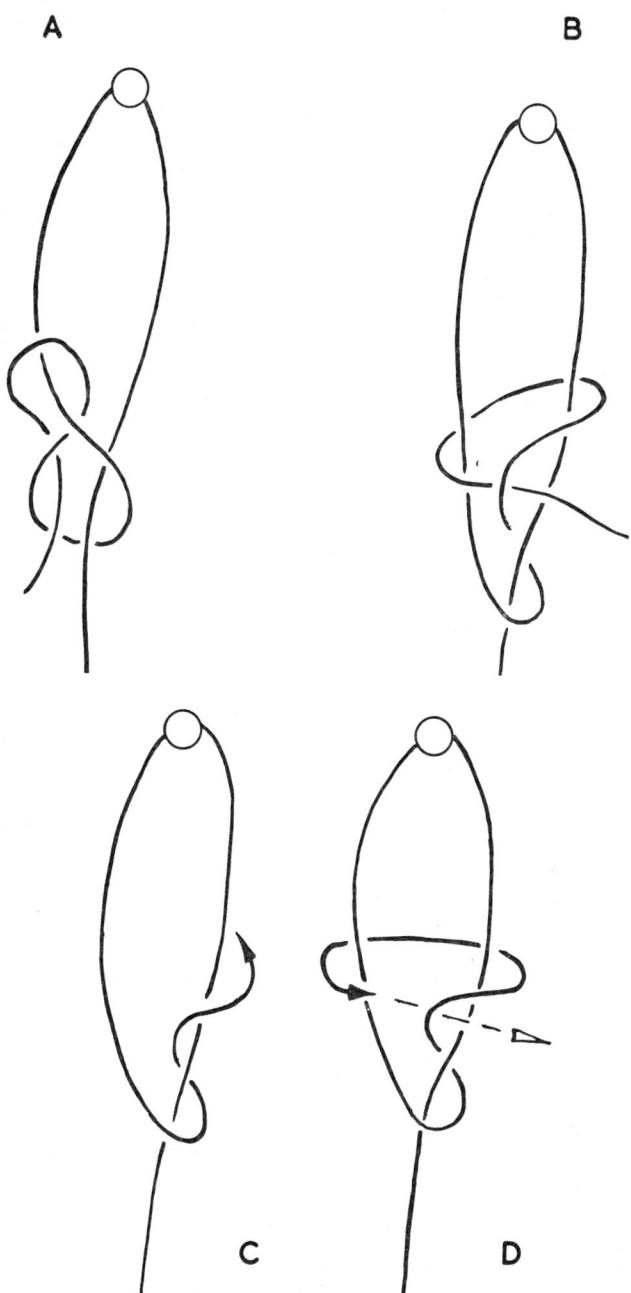

Fig. 4-8. A special slip knot is favored by upholsterers as it allows tension of twine to be adjusted and then locked.

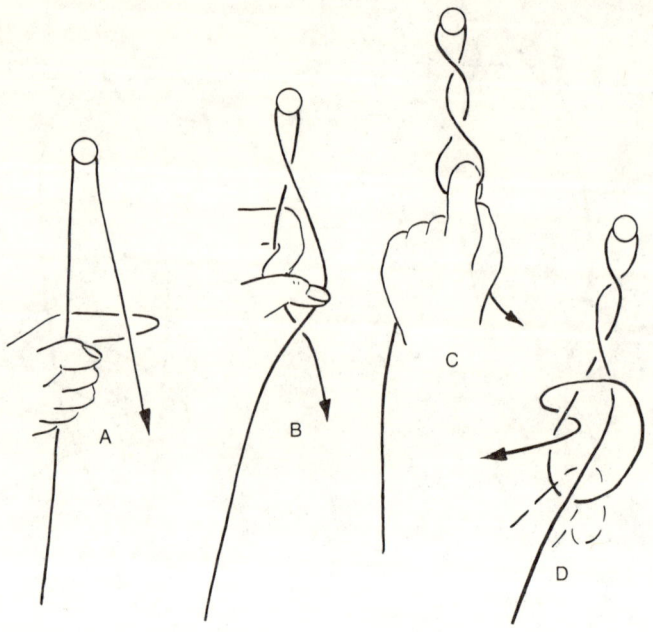

Fig. 4-9. An alternate method.

knot for extra security (Fig. 4-11B). When the end of the twine is reached, half-hitch back around the last part (Fig. 4-11C).

If each spring is to be sewn at three points the twine follows a zig-zag path across each circle and is knotted at each crossing

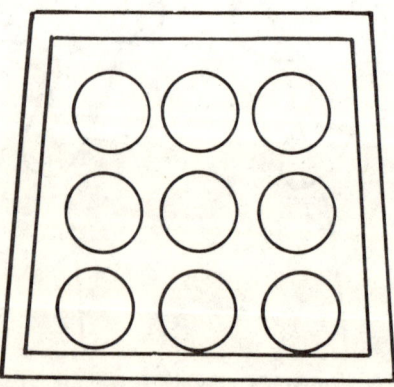

Fig. 4-10. Front springs are usually positioned close to the front rail of a chair.

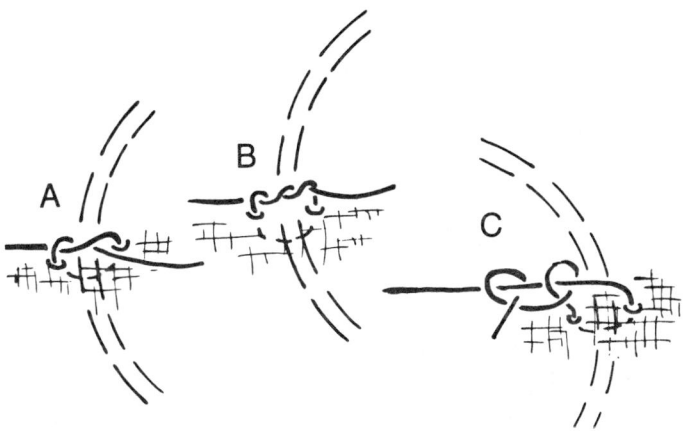

Fig. 4-11. Besides attaching springs to webbing the tops have to be kept in position by a system of crossing twines knotted to them in several ways.

(Fig. 4-12A). For four points it can go around the circle or be taken across between the second and third knots (Fig. 4-12B). It is not difficult to scheme out a way of going around the whole pattern in a single line, but if this does not work out, it does not matter so long as each spring gets its knots.

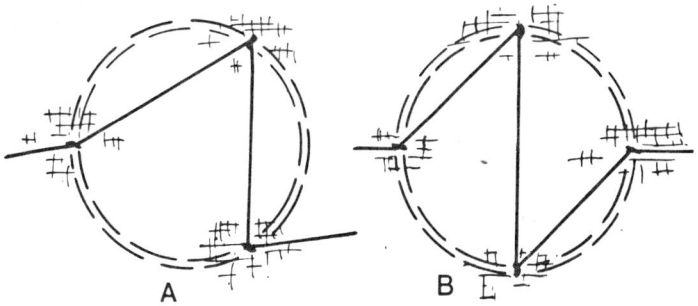

Fig. 4-12. Sometimes twine must follow zig-zag paths.

There are many ways of fastening the tops of springs with twine so they can still compress, but are kept in the right positions relative to each other. This is additional to any sewing to burlap or other covering that may come at a later stage over the springs and under the stuffing and further upholstery.

The twine used may be single or double. It is started at a tack on the frame. There may be the special slip knot for a single piece. There can be a double loop if the twine is to be used in two parts. A loop is allowed to fall back on itself (Fig. 4-13A) then the two eyes are put over the partly driven tack, which is then

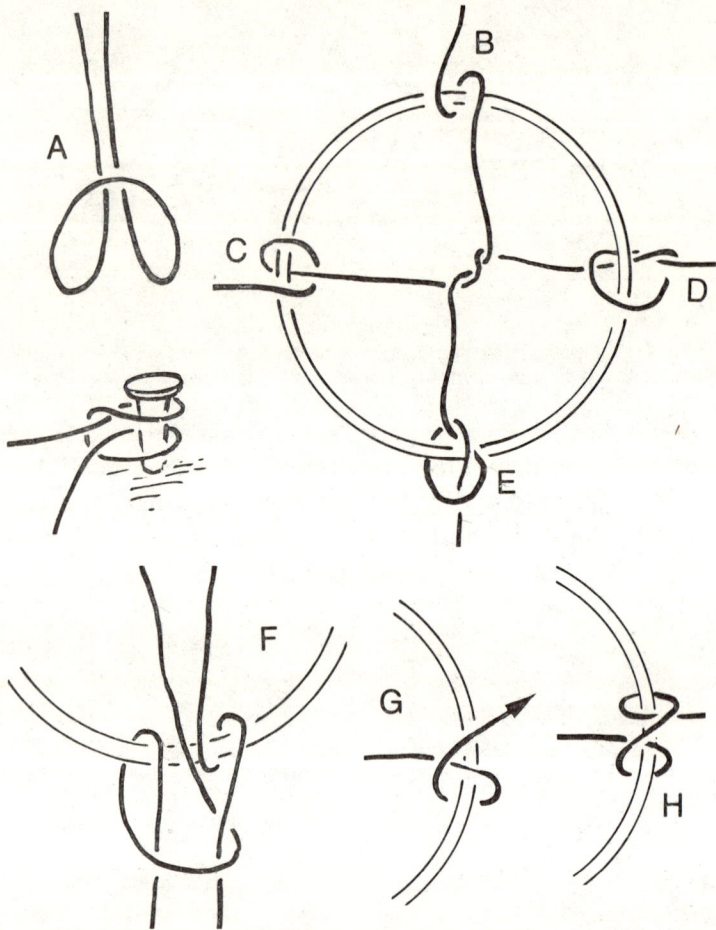

Fig. 4-13. There are several other variations for attaching twine to springs.

hammered tight. The simplest attachment to a spring is a loop taken completely around the wire (Fig. 4-13B). A better tie doubles this back (Fig. 4-13C). Both of these loops allow easy adjustment, but they have to be followed up with further ties with the second part of the twine.

Another way to attach a single twine is to use a simple overhand knot (Fig. 4-13D), the same as is used for sewing to webbing. In a slight variation the wire is included in a different part of the knot (Fig. 4-13E).

If the second part of the twine follows over after the springs have been adjusted using loops of the first part, locking is obtained by using a Y knot. This has the twine parallel to the first piece. It goes over the wire and around the far side of the first line before making a half hitch back around the wire (Fig. 4-13F). This is adjusted to match the first twine, then pulled tight. The line is then taken to the next spring and eventually down to a tack on the frame.

A clove hitch is a good knot for a single piece of twine. This is a jamming form of two half hitches. The twine is taken around the wire, over itself (Fig. 4-13G) and continued the same way around the wire and under itself (Fig. 4-13H). The second turn can be made some way from the first, if that is more convenient, then slid close to the first to tighten.

The method of lacing the tops of springs will vary according to the type of seat, but it is necessary to arrange ties square across in both directions as well as some taken diagonally in many cases (Fig. 4-14). This is not the complete sequence. The ties have to keep springs at even heights and arrange them to

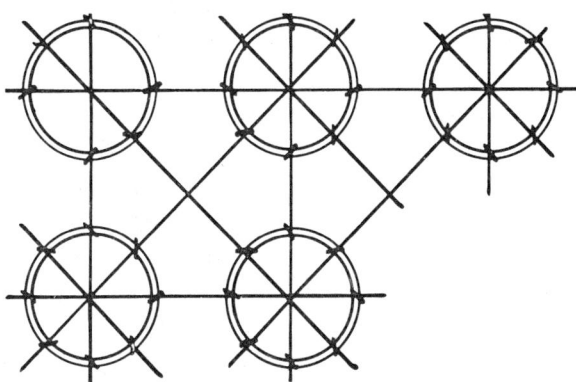

Fig. 4-14. The tops of springs may be adjusted to conform to the cushion shape by twine.

follow approximately the intended contour of the finished upholstery. While it may be satisfactory to tie the tops of the springs in the main body of the seat area, at the sides some springs have to be tilted. This is done by taking some ties through the springs to lower parts (Fig. 4-15A). In particular, springs along the front of a seat may be tilted to give a slightly diagonal thrust to the covering. There may be linking canes or

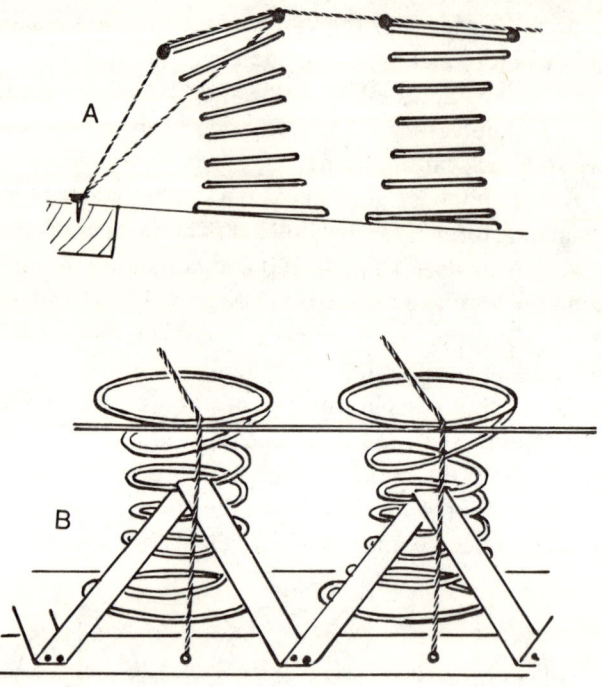

Fig. 4-15. Springs have to be tilted at the sides.

other material along this edge and the springs may be further encouraged to deflect in the way desired by narrow pieces of webbing around lower rings of the springs (Fig. 4-15B). The two parts may be knotted together on some springs with double twine, while one part goes to a lower turn on springs that are near edges.

Marshall units are normal springs, but they come in rows linked together with metal rings. A complete unit may be the right size for a chair seat or back, but if there have to be alterations, the metal ring links can be cut and the shape altered by re-arranging the enclosed springs. The outlines of the springs are apparent through their coverings and they are sewn to webbing in the same way as separate springs.

For many seats and some backs there is an edge wire around the tops of the springs. It may only come at the front edge, and cane or other material may sometimes be chosen instead of wire. This is a specially springy wire, but it is not as hard as the wire in the springs and it can be bent in the hands. The length should be sufficient to go all around, with a little to spare for the joint. There are different sizes to suit different types of seat and the gauge wire used in the springs.

It is useful to have a short piece of tube to slide over the wire. If the wire is held in one hand or a vise, the tube can be slid up to the point where there is enough exposed wire to make the intended curve. It can then be pulled around (Fig. 4-16). The wire can be tied to the springs or you can use special clips,

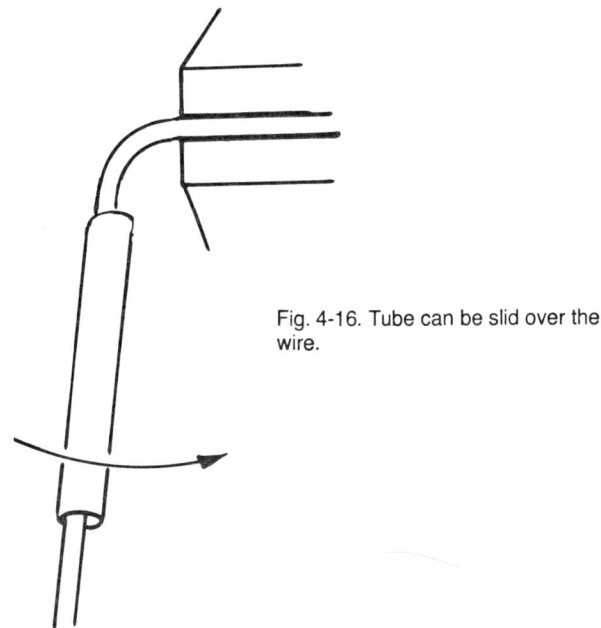

Fig. 4-16. Tube can be slid over the wire.

which need their own pair of pliers to tighten. The overlapping ends may be held with clips or be tied (Fig. 4-17), and this part should be out of the way at the back of a seat or the bottom of a chair back.

If all springs are to be at a uniform height the edge wire can be fixed around before the springs are tied with twine; but where

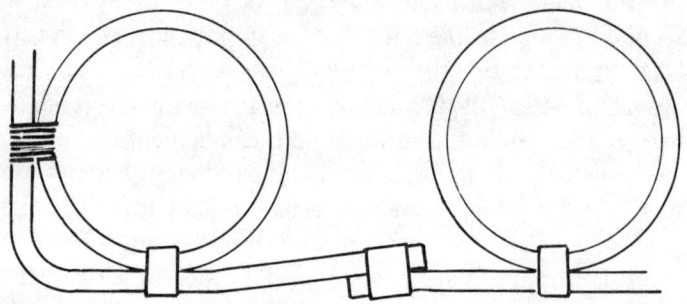

Fig. 4-17. In some cushions there is a metal wire edge put around a pattern of springs.

there is some shaping of the springs with twine it is better to complete this stage before adding the wire, and manipulate this to conform to the intended shape.

There are modifications and variations to the way webbing and springs are used, but these will be explained as examples occur in later chapters.

Simple Seating

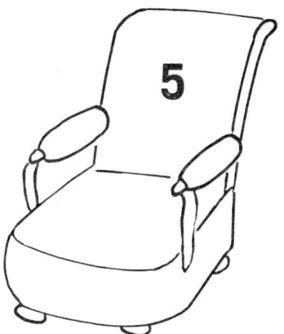

5

There are several chairs, stools, and other pieces of furniture that do not warrant full upholstery. These are items that are normally only used for brief periods and are not intended to be relaxed on. Dining chairs are examples. Their use is planned only for the time needed for a meal. An office chair may warrant better padding if it is to be sat on for most of the day. Like the dining chair, it is being used while the occupant is engaged in some activity, possibly only mental. In these circumstances, some people could argue against providing too much comfort on the basis that over-relaxed conditions might encourage laziness.

Things like boxes and chests, stools and window seats may be given a moderate amount of padding, but they may not need full upholstery, nor have uses that warrant any covering. Some chairs have wooden tops that offer a concession to comfort by being shaped. Examples are Windsor chairs, which are hollowed to very approximately match the contours of the body. Some plastic seats may have even more shaping. Plywood seats may be given a shaping back to front, with a rolled front edge, but as plywood can only curve one way and will not take a compound curve, lines across the width of the seat are straight.

If a seat has compound shaping in the solid material from which it has been made, it is usually unwise to attempt to add upholstery directly to it—although there may be a good case for cushions, which could be of fitted shape and held in with tapes, or merely loose ones of simple shape. There are shaped bases intended for upholstery, but these usually are designed to suit the arrangement of stuffing and stretching of cloth.

LOOSE RIGID SEATS

Many dining chairs have lift-out wooden seats. In the simplest form the base is a flat piece of plywood, which may be thick enough to have enough strength in itself, or it may be thinner plywood framed around (Fig. 5-1A). In some cases the front and back edges have slight curves, but the sides are straight. It may be worthwhile putting one or two 1/2-inch holes near the center of the seat. These allow air in and out as the seat compresses under load or expands when pressure is released.

This seat usually drops into rabbets (Fig. 5-2) in the frame and the amount of clearance should be noted as any covering has to be kept thin enough to fit into this space. If the covering material is thick, it may be necessary to plane the woodwork smaller. In any case, make sure there are no sharp edges anywhere that will come against the covering. Do not round excessively, particularly at the corners, where curving inside the angular corner of the rabbet might spoil appearances in the finished seat. A light cut with a plane along the edges, followed by hand sanding, should be sufficient. If the thickness of the wood without covering comes above the frame, bevel the edges (Fig. 5-1B).

Padding will come on the surface and only the covering material goes around the sides to be tacked underneath. The amount of padding is not usually great. It can be a piece of latex or plastic foam about 1 inch thick, cut to the same size as the base. It may be a manufactured latex cushion pad, if one can be found in the right size. Flat sheet will almost certainly pull down sufficiently at the edges when the covering is tightened, but if it is a stiff foam, this can be helped by bevelling the lower edges (Fig. 5-1C).

Although the seat could be covered with one of the loose stuffing materials, it is simpler to use felt or cotton batting. A domed effect can be obtained by packing in loose stuffing or

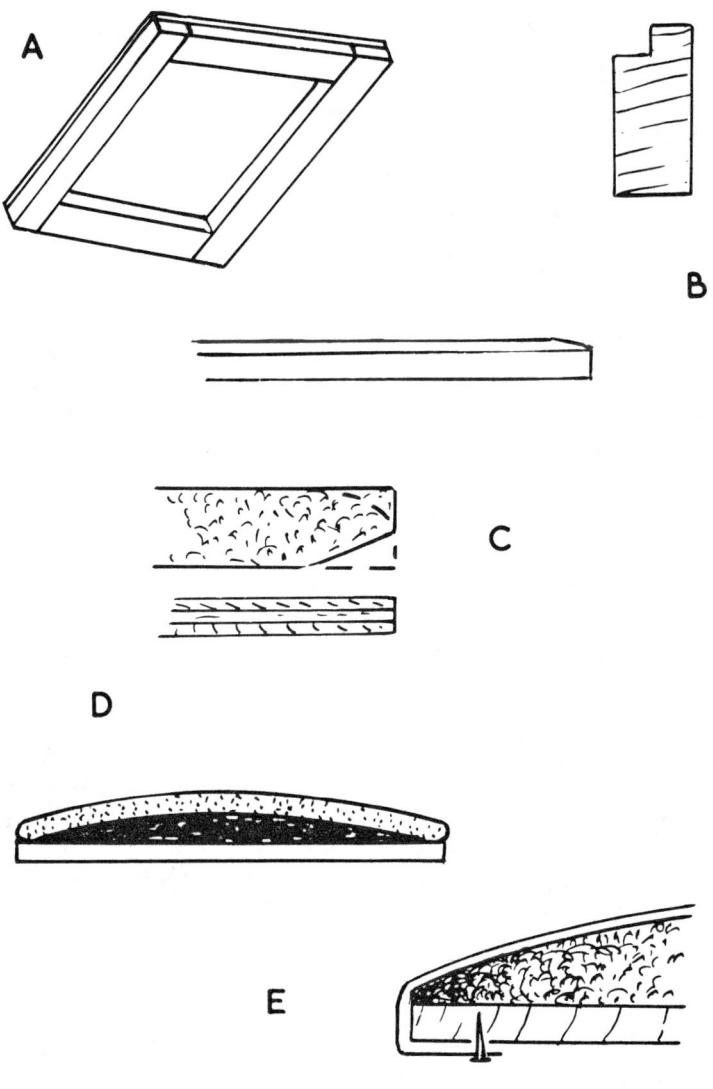

Fig. 5-1. In a simple drop-in seat top the padding is fixed over a solid base covered by material that wraps and is tacked underneath.

using pieces broken and teased out of the felt to build up under the fitted piece (Fig. 5-1D). Putting the smaller stuffing pieces under the large piece should give a smoother appearance to the finished surface.

The covering of a much-used dining chair is usually vinyl or other plastic material. This stands up well to the type of use expected, and is easily cleaned. As this is non-porous and there is no fear of stuffing material coming through, it can be applied directly to the stuffing. If the covering is a cloth or other material to match the rest of the furniture in the room, it may be advisable to use muslin or scrim over the stuffing first. If the stuffing is loose, a first covering in this way allows the padding to be adjusted to give a good shape before the outer covering is fixed.

The covering material should be cut big enough to wrap over and go far enough underneath to be tacked (Fig. 5-1E). Surplus can be trimmed off after tacking, but if the material is cut with nothing to spare, it may be difficult to grip and hold at an even tension while tacking.

Back and front are parallel, but the front is usually wider than the back. Fit the covering material in the parallel direction first. Stand the seat on one edge over the covering and stretch this over the other edge. Put in some temporary tacks (Fig. 5-3). Turn the seat over and check the appearance. See that the covering flows evenly over the stuffing and there are no bumps.

Fig. 5-2. Typical dining chair seat with a solid plywood base and the padding covered with vinyl.

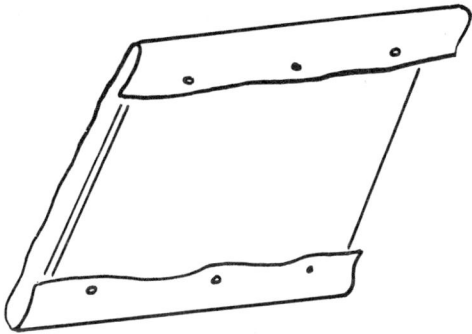

Fig. 5-3. Put in temporary tacks.

You can smooth out some flaws by rubbing the hand or a piece of wood over the surface, but if there is obvious unevenness due to misplaced stuffing, tacks may have to be lifted and the fault corrected. It may be possible to reach under the edges of the covering and poke the stuffing into place with a strip of wood.

Do the same the other way, with a few temporary tacks (Fig. 5-4A). Ignore the corners of the covering at this stage. Check the appearance of the top. Lift tacks and make adjustments if necessary. Do not drive any more tacks along the sides yet.

Deal with the corners next. Stretch the point of the material outwards first, then up and over the corner in a direction towards the center of the seat (Fig. 5-4B) and drive in a tack on the line of the pull. This may be enough, although some material may require two more tacks to hold the strain and shape. Keep them close to the first. Cut into the folds on each side of the tacks, but do not let the cut go further than the edge. Cut off waste material inside the tacks. Notch into the first cuts so two flaps are left standing (Fig. 5-4C).

Pull one flap over the corner, regulating the direction of pull to get the smoothest effect on the top surface. Some materials may crease a little on the edge, but this does not matter if it does not extend to the top. Tack this flap (Fig. 5-4D). Do the same the other way, with the second flap going over the first. Do the same at the other three corners. With vinyl or similar material the flap can be pulled over with the cut edge exposed, but with woven cloth turn under the cut edge before tacking (Fig. 5-5).

Tack all round the edges with about a 1 inch spacing and keep the line of tacks at an even distance from the edges. It may be necessary to regulate the tension to get an even appearance

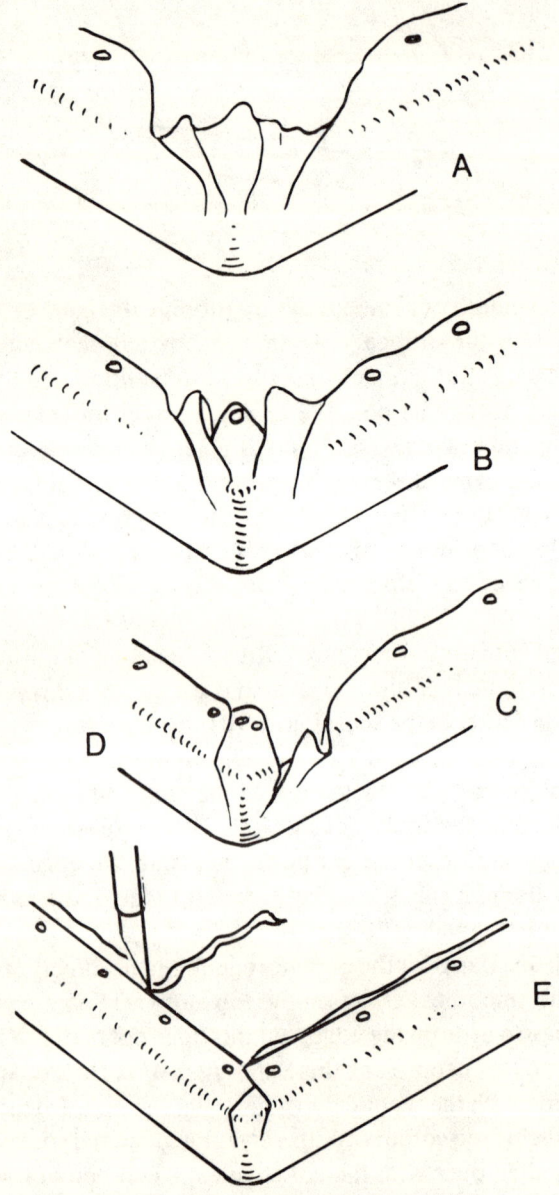

Fig. 5-4. Corners need special attention.

Fig. 5-5. The underside of the top of an office stool showing the method of folding around the curved corners.

on top, so examine the top frequently and drive tacks accordingly. If the first temporary tacks do not fit into the lines of final tacks, withdraw them as tacking progresses. Trim off surplus material inside the line of tacks (Fig. 5-4E). Use a steel rule to guide the knife if you do not trust freehand cutting.

The underside could be covered with cambric or other fabric, with its edges turned under on the tacked edges of the covering; but this is not usually done for this type of seat.

It is usual for the tops of legs to either be cut away to match the sides (Fig. 5-6A) or the construction be designed so the leg does not project into the rabbet line (Fig. 5-6B). If the top of the leg does project into the rabbet line and cannot be altered, this means cutting into the shape of the seat. The hollow created is difficult to cover because of the inside angle (Fig. 5-6C). A cut into this corner leaves a space in the covering. If the material has enough stretch, it may be pulled down so the gap is hidden, otherwise a piece of material can be put around the inner corner to disguise it (Fig. 5-6D). It is better to design or adapt the chair so the need for a hollow corner is avoided.

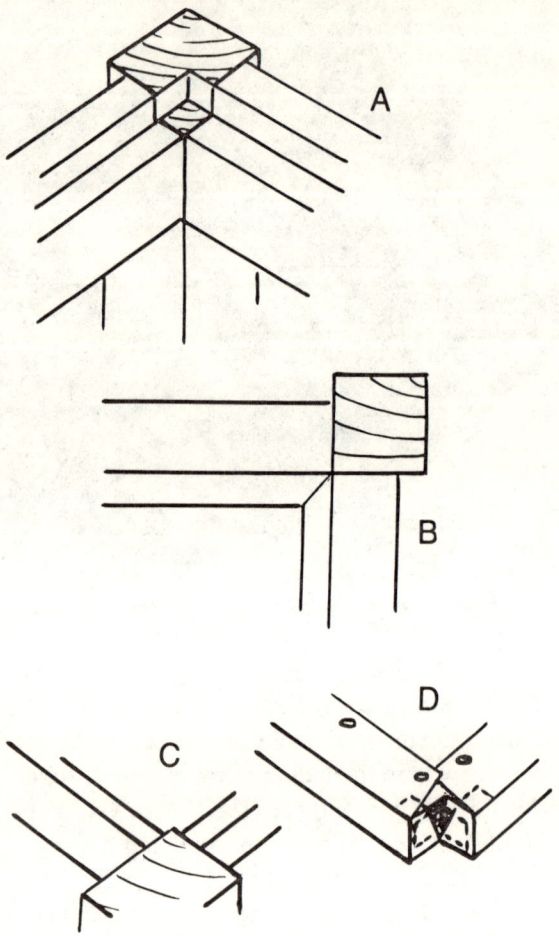

Fig. 5-6. Leg tops are treated in various ways.

LOOSE SOFT SEATS

A dining or similar chair can be given more comfort in the lift-out seat if that has a rigid frame around the outside and support at the center provided with webbing. The frame needs to be stout enough and will probably stand above the chair frame, so its edges should be bevelled (Fig. 5-7A). It should be checked for fit and roughness then sharpness taken off, as described for the simpler loose seat.

The amount of webbing to be used depends to a certain extent on the amount of stuffing that will go above it. If only a thin layer is contemplated there is a risk that after considerable use the filling will have compressed enough to have sunk into gaps between widely-spaced strips of webbing. The pattern of the webbing will show through the top. If a greater amount of padding is to be built up, there may not have to be as much webbing to support it. Of course, too much webbing stretched tightly will give a firmness to the support that might be little different from using a piece of plywood.

For the average dining chair measuring 14 inches to 16 inches across, it should be sufficient to arrange two strips of webbing each way (Fig. 5-7B), but this could be increased to

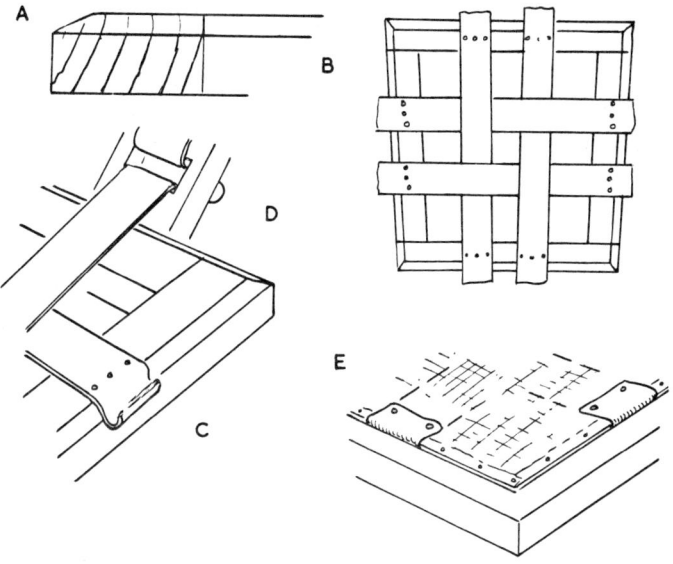

Fig. 5-7. A lift-out seat upholstered in the traditional way has a base of webbing.

three in one or both ways if it is felt that there would be insufficient support for the intended top. For a larger chair, increase the webbing accordingly. As a rough guide to spacing, it should be satisfactory if the spaces are slightly wider than the webbing.

Webbing goes on the top surface and is fitted, as already described in Chapter 2. It is important that the turned in and tacked edges are far enough in from the outsides of the frame not to show through the covering. If they are kept inside the bevelled edge that should be about right (Fig. 5-7C). Leave the second tacking until burlap is fitted. Strain in the usual way (Fig. 5-7D). Working on a light frame instead of a whole piece of furniture means that as the stretcher is levered, the far side of the frame will want to lift. Have an assistant hold the frame or fix it to the bench with a C clamp. Pull ordinary webbing quite tight—it will still have enough spring in it to give comfortable support.

Rubber webbing can be used if preferred, but this should be arranged closer than ordinary webbing, otherwise it may sag too much in normal use.

Cover the webbing with burlap. This should be big enough to fold in about 1/2 inch all round. Surplus can be removed after fixing. Fold and tack along the back—3/8 inch or 1/2 inch tacks will do. Pull to the front and tack at the center first, then position a temporary tack towards each corner, while more tacks are driven through the turned in edge. Do the same at the sides. Watch the weave of the burlap. The loose weave can easily distort with uneven stretching. This may not matter, but it is better craftsmanship to keep it square, with one line parallel with the back and front of the seat. Finally turn in the ends of webbing, tack them, and cut off (Fig. 5-7E). Trim off any spare edges of burlap.

The stuffing can be foam. A cushion of matching size with rounded edges will be best, and these are obtainable in many stock sizes to suit dining chairs and other chairs. This only needs positioning and covering, but it is also possible to use cut pieces of slab latex or other foam. Bevelling underneath allows the edges to pull down to a curved edge, as described for the simpler seat. It may be possible to adapt a larger prepared cushion by using its rounded edge at the front and bevelling other cut edges.

Many of these seats are stuffed with hair. This has to be held with loops of twine, otherwise the stuffing may move about when the chair is used. The surface may become irregular and the padding less comfortable. One way of doing this is to sew in loops of twine before adding the hair stuffing. Use a curved needle and arrange loops of twine through the burlap, allowing enough slackness for the twine to become embedded in the hair, but not so high as to actually be on the surface of the total amount of filling. The loops can be quite large. Knot them into the burlap so they do not slip. For an average seat it should be sufficient to have two loops near each edge and two more across the middle (Fig. 5-8A).

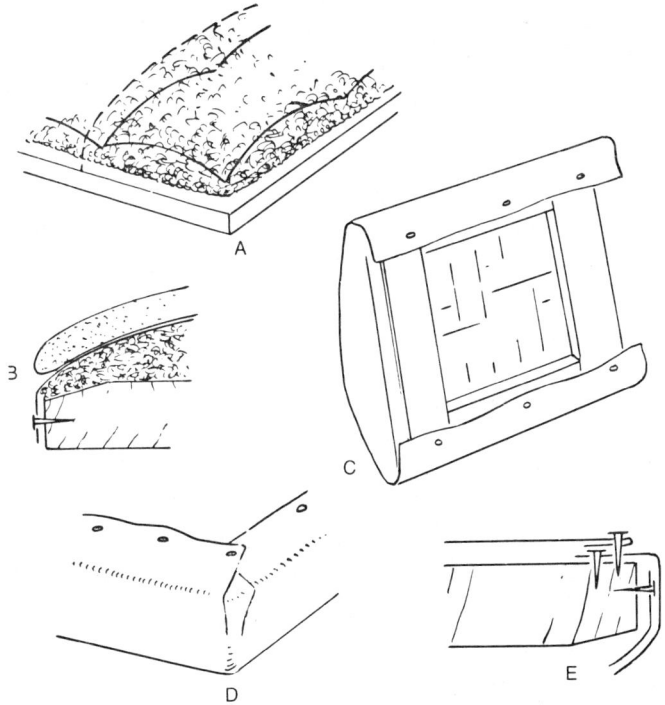

Fig. 5-8. A lift-out seat also has a stuffing of hair with the covering material taken over and tacked underneath. A piece of material is then tacked under that to make a neat finish.

Put quantities of hair or other loose stuffing on the seat. Push it under the back loops and work forward as more is added, progressing around the sides to the front without paying much attention to the center at this stage. See that the hair is gripped by the loops of twine towards the edges. Work more into the center, making sure the loops there grip it, but build up above the twine loops as well. Keep the hair interlocked with that under the loops and aim to get a domed shape with an even concentration of stuffing. This can be felt by handling the hairs and pressing on them. The amount to use depends on experience, but aim to get a firm stuffing because there will be a degree of loosening as the seat is put into use.

The first step in covering is to arrange an inner cover of calico or other light cloth that will hold the stuffing in place. Allow enough to tack under the frame or around its sides if the tack heads will not interfere with the fit of the frame in the chair. Probable sizes in each direction are best obtained by stretching a tape measure over the same way that the cloth will go.

Fix this inner covering with temporary tacks along the back, then pull to the front for more temporary tacks and do the same at the sides. Check the tension in all directions and the general appearance of the top, which should follow a domed shape. Stand back and view from several directions to see that the doming follows a consistent and satifsying outline.

Use sufficient tacks around the sides to hold the calico in place. There is no need to turn under the edges; the surplus edges can be trimmed below the line of tacks. Once the other covering is in place, most of the load will have gone from these tacks and there should be no risk of the calico shifting.

If a woven outer covering material is to be used, there is a risk that hair might find its way through the calico and through the outer cloth if nothing is done about it. If the outside is to be a stout, closely woven material there may be little risk of this happening, and if vinyl or other plastic material is used hair cannot come through. There would then be no need to put anything between the calico and the outer covering, but it may still be desirable to add to comfort and disguise any slight inequalities showing from the stuffing. A layer of cotton batting can be used for this purpose (Fig. 5-8B). This should be cut to size so it does not go over the edges, where it might cause too much thickness for the seat to fit the chair.

Cut the covering material to size with about 1 inch to spare all round. If it is patterned, arrange for the pattern to be centered on the seat. Even if the cloth is without a prominent pattern, arrange it so the weave is symmetrical on the chair and see that it is not distorted as it is stretched during fixing.

Locate the covering material on the seat with a few temporary tacks underneath the back and pull across to the front to drive some more tacks there. These tacks are unlikely to be right the first time, so leave their heads standing enough for them to be easily removed later. It is convenient at this stage to hold the seat on edge (Fig. 5-8C), so the top surface can be watched and the evenness and smoothness can be regulated as you stretch and tack on the underside. Put some temporary tacks under the edges. If the top surface is satisfactory, final tacks can be driven along each edge at about 1-inch intervals, with a constant check on the appearance of the top. Stroke the top and strain as necessary. Remove tacks and try again if you do not like the top appearance at any part. Get final tacks along each side to within about 2 inches of each corner.

Treat the corners in the same way as described for the covering of the simpler seat. Pull the point outwards and then over the frame corner towards the center of the seat and tack it. Then cut and arrange the flaps from each side to pull and tack over each other on top of the first part of the corner. Do not cut any further than is necessary. With many materials it is possible to make the stretch in the fabric take care of some of the shaping, so the cuts for the flaps do not have to come very high (Fig. 5-8D). First experiments after tacking the center piece at the corner can be made with the material folded. This will show how far cuts need to be made. With thin fabrics it may be possible to fold and tack without cuts, but with most coverings this would make a rather thick part at each corner.

Trim the surplus covering inside the lines of tacks. It will be satisfactory to leave the work at this stage for many purposes, but there can be a piece of burlap or other material turned in and tacked over the covering edge. This may be advisable if it is a woven fabric that tends to fray. To avoid too much build-up of thickness in a rabbet that is not very deep, it may be advisable to arrange the tack lines and the burlap so they come inside the frame (Fig. 5-8E) and only the thickness of covering material is in the rabbet (Fig. 5-9).

The fit of a loose seat affects appearance as well as convenience. It should be tight enough not to fall out when the chair is moved, yet not so tight that the covering is chafed against the wood and is difficult to remove. It looks best if the final covering slopes down to the wood level at the edges. If it is high, the

Fig. 5-9. The underside of a lift-out seat showing the covering material tacked below.

exposed edge is unsightly, while if it is low it also looks bad and the ledge catches dirt. These things have to be considered during the planning stage, and checked at intervals as upholstery progresses.

BOX AND STOOL SEATS

Latex foam is convenient for putting a soft top on a plain wooden stool or a box or chest that is also used as a seat. It can also be used to make a padded back along a wall where the chest is placed to act as a seat.

For a flat wooden stool with an overlapping edge, a piece of foam is cut to the same size as the top. It may be just a 1 inch piece of plain foam for a simple seat with minimum softening or a thicker piece of cavity latex foam for a more comfortable seat. However, if it is only a small stool, be careful of making it look top-heavy by building up too great a thickness of seat.

It is convenient to use a calico strip held to the latex with adhesive or self-adhesive strip to pull a curve into an otherwise square-cut edge. The strip should be wide enough to go over the top surface and hang over the side enough to pull under the woodwork. Use the appropriate adhesive to fix the strip to the top surface only (Fig. 5-10A). Do this all round, but at the corners cut away some of the foam on the underside (Fig. 5-10B). This will remove the tendency of the foam to pile up awkwardly there as the sides are pulled down.

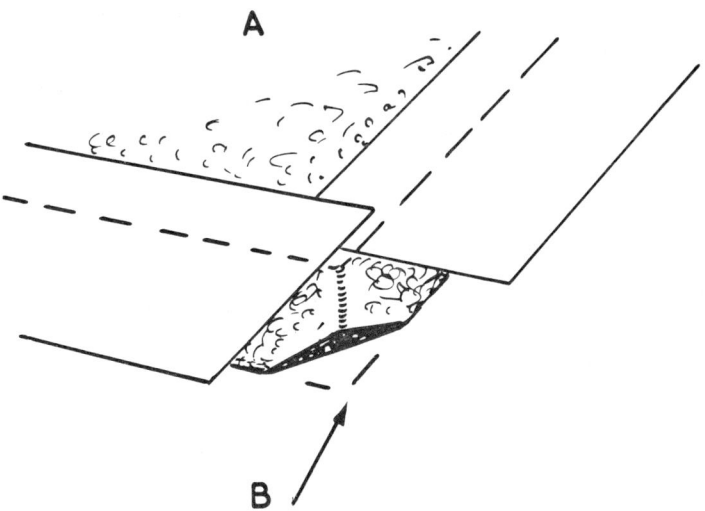

Fig. 5-10. Latex or plastic can be pulled to shape to give a rounded edge.

Position the foam on the stool. Adhesive can be used under it, but this is probably unnecessary. Pull the strips down on opposite sides to force the edges into curves (Fig. 5-11A). Adhesive can be used to hold the calico to the edges or undersides of the stool top, but there will have to be tacks as well (Fig. 5-11B).

Let the adhesive dry thoroughly before covering. Locate the covering so the pattern is symmetrical and the weave is parallel with the stool sides. Follow the same sequence as suggested for a chair top. Put some temporary tacks under the wood top along an edge. Stretch across and do the same at the other edge. Repeat in the other direction. If all is well, either drive the final rows of tacks (except at the corners), or deal with the corners as on the earlier tops and drive the edge tacks later. How neatly this can be done depends on the amount the top overlaps the rails below. Surplus covering will probably fold up the rails and can be trimmed with a knife in the angle between top and rail (Fig. 5-11C).

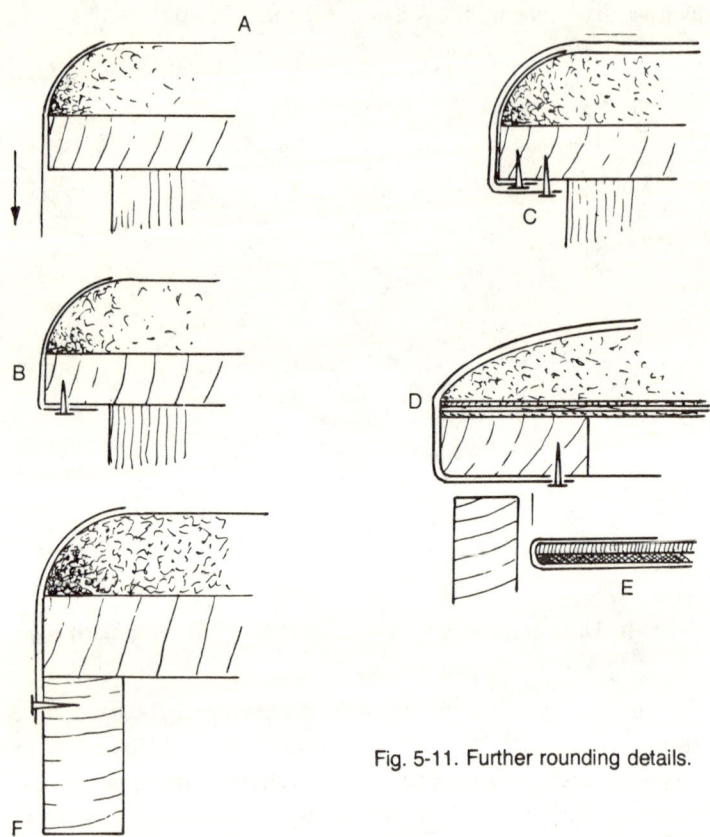

Fig. 5-11. Further rounding details.

A box top can be treated in a similar way if the lid will lift or hinge. The covering goes far enough inside the lid for tacks to miss the box sides (Fig. 5-11D). What is done inside depends on the intended use of the box. If it is for storing bedding or clothing, it may be lined, including the lid. A cloth lining can be tacked inside a wooden box. It may be better to have card or Masonite panels to fit, and cover them with cloth wrapped over their edges and glued. A further step is to have quite thin foam under the cloth. This is particularly luxurious under a lid, where the panel covers the tacks and edges of the covering material (Fig. 5-11E).

If a stool top or a box is unsuitable for the covering to wrap underneath, it has to be finished on the outside and this needs a special treatment to cover the ugly row of tacks.

The covering of such a top can be similar to that described for the other stool and box, up to the fixing stage. The top foam matches the wood top and calico strips are stuck on. These are pulled down all round to curve the edge. Tacks are kept reasonably high on the wooden edge (Fig. 5-11F). When you are satisfied that there is an even tension and the top is a good shape, hammer the tacks tightly so the heads do not project and cut the calico off below them.

It is advisable to lightly pencil how far down the covering material is to finish so the line of tacks through it will come just below the cut edges of the calico.

Position the covering material. A prominent pattern carefully centered usually looks good on a stool. In any case, see that the cloth is symmetrical and the weave is parallel with the sides. Tack temporarily, as with the earlier similar projects. The final tacks are to be covered with a comparatively narrow strip, so it is necessary to keep all tacking within close limits. This includes temporary tacks, as holes they leave may show if the tacks have to be withdrawn from an exposed part.

Much of the pleating at the corners will show in the finished work so keep it neat. The appearance is helped if the work on adjoining corners is paired. Let all ends overlap first, followed by the sides, or all the other way round. Drive tacks tightly so they do not project above the surface of the cloth.

The tack heads and the cut edges will be hidden by a strip taken around the stool and held on with pins. For leather or vinyl, it may be possible to cut a strip of the actual material, but for cloth it is better to use prepared *gimp*. This is a decorative form of fabric strapping, which can be obtained in many colors, widths, and patterns.

It may be possible to glue some gimp to suitable fabric, but it is probably better to use gimp pins, which need be no more than 3/4 inch long. They are usually colored black and are fine enough to be inconspicuous after driving, particularly in a patterned or embossed type of gimp.

Trim the edge of the covering below the tacks along a line that will ensure it being hidden by the gimp (Fig. 5-12). Start the gimp along one side and stretch it around the stool to finish with an overlap on the starting end. Use sufficient gimp pins to keep it in place, staggering them in a zig-zag pattern to hold the edges and avoid the tacks.

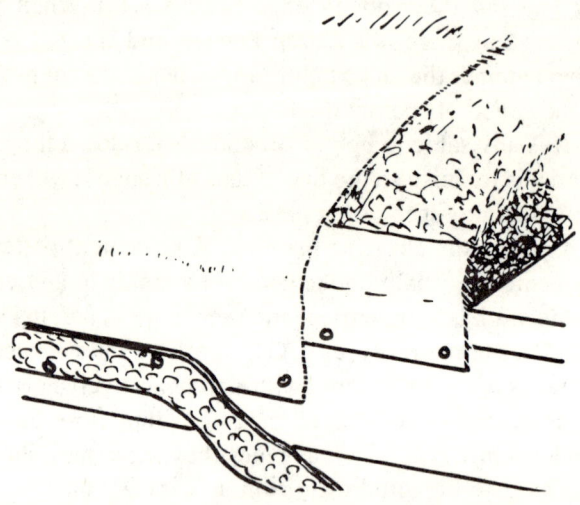

Fig. 5-12. Gimp strips are sometimes used.

PLYWOOD CHAIR

A plywood seat that is shaped back to front, but straight across from side to side, can be made much more comfortable with upholstery. This type of seat is usually mounted on a tubular steel frame by riveting (Fig. 5-13A). This makes it difficult to remove and replace the seat, so upholstery has to be done in position. Some of these chairs are arranged to stack. If that property is still required, care is needed to see that the upholstery does not project in a way to prevent stacking or be damaged when the chairs are stacked.

The usual plywood is not more than 1/4 inch thick and this is not really enough to give a secure grip to tacks. It may be satisfactory to substitute small, office-type staples which can be driven by an office stapler with the base turned back, or by a spring-action staple gun or trigger tacker.

An alternative is to thicken the edges. This is simple at the straight back and front. If there is not enough overlap on the tubular metal frame for thickening to come outside, strips can be placed inside (Fig. 5-13B). At the shaped edges the thickening need not be much, and a strip of 1/4 inch wood, 1/2 inch wide may be adequate. This is thin enough to pull into shape. It can be glued and held by nails or screws from the top, and held with C clamps while the glue sets (Fig. 5-13C).

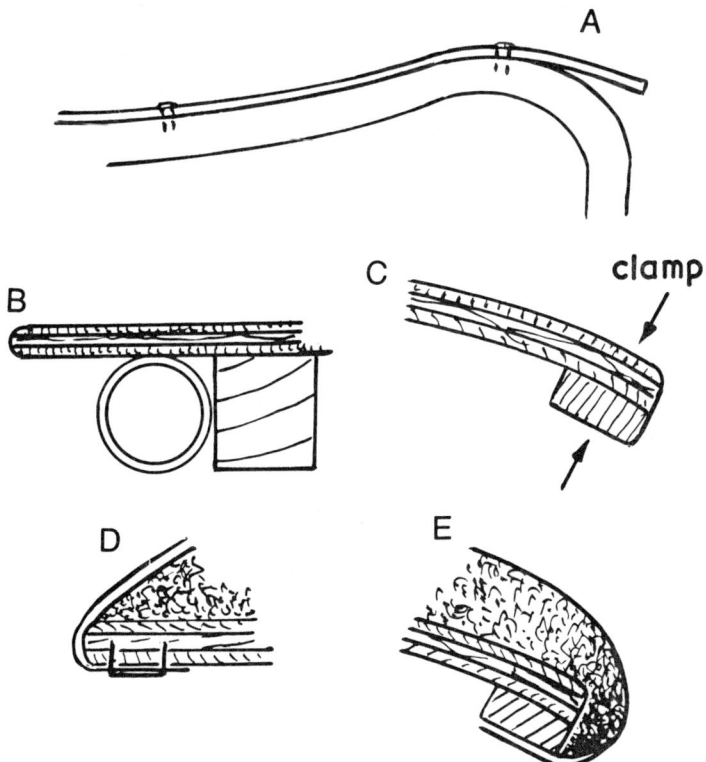

Fig. 5-13. A plain wooden seat can be given a foam upholstered top with strips stuck on and pulled underneath.

The top is covered first with plain latex or plastic foam about 1 inch thick. It is worthwhile using an adhesive to hold the foam to the plywood shape. If the chair seat has been painted or varnished, sand off the finish completely, or at least sufficiently to remove gloss and expose wood fibers. This will give the adhesive a good grip.

If possible, use self-adhesive strip around the sides to pull the foam close to the plywood and round the edges (Fig. 5-13D). In most cases it is best to cut the foam to the same size as the plywood, but it can be given a slight overhang at the front (Fig. 5-13E), if the curve of the plywood is not considered sufficient to give a comfortable edge otherwise. If the plywood has rounded front corners, trim the foam to match, but bevel the underside slightly so it will pull down and match the shaping of the adjoining edges.

When the covering material is fitted, tack or staple at the back and put just a moderate tension on with temporary tacks or staples under the front. Work forward from the back, stretching across and fixing underneath at about 1 inch intervals (Fig. 5-14). Watch the behavior of the weave if it is a fabric and see that tensions are kept even. Deal with the hollow in this way so the covering is brought tight over all the rear half of the seat.

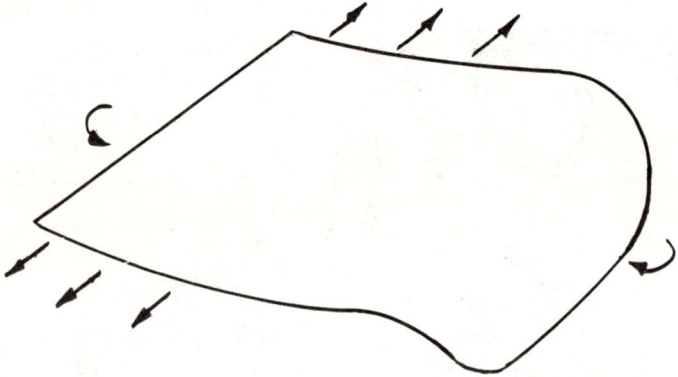

Fig. 5-14. Stretch and fix at 1-inch intervals, when fitted covering material is used.

The covering can now be pulled to its final tension over the convex part of the plywood, but not so hard that the hollow part is made to lift. If this part does lift, despite only moderate front tension, the crosswise pull is not enough and some of the side fastenings will have to be adjusted before the front is pulled and fixed underneath.

Complete tacking or stapling under the sides. This leaves the rounded front corners. As these are quite large curves

Fig. 5-15. Making pleats.

compared with the almost square corners of earlier projects it will not be possible to merely pull the center at the corner and overlap a pair of flaps underneath. If the curve is not great and the cloth is very flexible and elastic, this may just be possible, but in most cases the method has to be rather different. The surplus due to the curve has to be taken up in two or more pleats. The art in getting a neat effect is to divide the spare cloth into two or three bundles of equal size. It is very easy to get a large pleat alongside a small one.

Fold each pleat and crease the folds tightly. Pull the center of each pleat and fasten it underneath. Much of the crease over the edge will pull below, so there is a smooth edge and the pleats are underneath. Fold them all so the front goes towards the back (Fig. 5-15) and the effect will be quite neat.

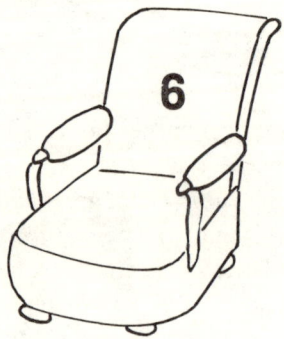

6
Other Seating

A lift-out chair seat provides softening near the center and this gets progressively harder towards the edge where, in a dining chair, it becomes just the hard wood rim. A stool or chair cover that has one piece of material stretched over a base that is either solid wood or webbed may have some softening taken to the edge, but the edge is much less comfortable than the center because the single piece of covering material strains and compresses the edge of the filling. This does not produce such a good cushioning effect. Even a piece of foam filling of original even depth becomes compressed at the edges.

Such seats have ample comfort for many purposes and may be all that is needed, but for greater comfort the upholstery has to be altered so there is more support and cushioning at the edges. The center may still be slightly domed, but the edge is kept thick and it may also be reinforced to give the maximum cushioning possible when anyone sits on the edge. This may happen when anyone sits forward in a reclining chair, and it is also possible with stools such as those used at a dressing table or piano.

To avoid compressing the edges by stretching a single covering piece over them, the cover has to be arranged boxed, with sewn seams. With some materials the effect is attractive with a plain seam, but piping is commonly used and this gives a pleasant line around the upholstery edge.

PIPING

To make a plain seam, the two parts of material are brought together with the right sides (outside) facing each other, and sewn by machine with a single line of stitching (Fig. 6-1A). The line to be followed should be pencilled on the wrong side (inside) of the top, and a slight rounding should be allowed at a corner.

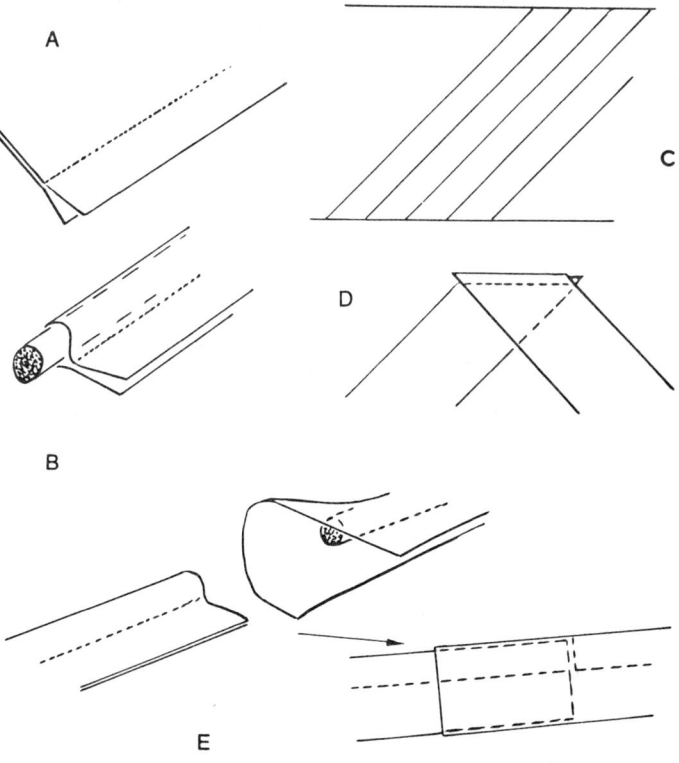

Fig. 6-1. Piping is used to make an attractive seam. It is cut from material on the bias and sewn around a cord or other round material to give it shape.

Piping can be made from the same material or it can be made in a contrasting color. Vinyl looks best with a contrasting color, usually white against a plain dark color. Some fabrics may give the best appearance with piping of the same material.

Other fabric may look better with a plain colored piping, either matching or sufficiently different to make a division between top and side.

Piping can be bought ready-made in many finishes and sizes. For stools and other small seats it should not be more than 1/8 inch in diameter. If piping is to be made from the covering or other material, a piece of cord has to be enclosed in a length of cloth and enough must be left for sewing into the seat (Fig. 6-1B). Ideally, the cloth should be cut on the *bias*, diagonal to the weave (Fig. 6-1C). The width of strips must go around the cord and leave about 1/2 inch for sewing. Bias cutting results in smoother fitting.

If cotton cord is used and it is expected that the cover will be washed, it is advisable to boil the cord before using it. If dry cleaning is anticipated, this step is not necessary.

The strips of cloth can be joined by machine sewing to make up a sufficient length. Use the ends as cut or make new cuts at a more acute angle. Put one piece over another with the right sides together and sew across (Fig. 6-1D).

The cord is sewn into the cloth with a line of stitching as close as possible. An upholsterer's sewing machine has a cording foot that allows close sewing. With any other machine, use the foot that allows the line of stitching to come reasonably close. Meeting ends should come at the back of a stool (if there is one). Use a strip of piping longer than necessary. When the piping has been sewn nearly all the way, cut the piping to overlap about 3/4 inch. Unpick the stitches for the length of the overlap on one end and cut off the cord, so the remainer will butt against the other end. Wrap the unpicked part over the other piece and complete the sewing (Fig. 6-1E).

When piping has to be taken around a corner, sew it up to the angle and make two V-shaped darts in it (Fig. 6-2). Of course, the cover is sewn inside-out, with the right sides of material towards each other and the piping with its cord inwards between them (Fig. 6-3).

PIPED STOOL SEAT

A suitable stool frame may have any sort of legs and underframing, but the important part for the upholsterer is a stout top

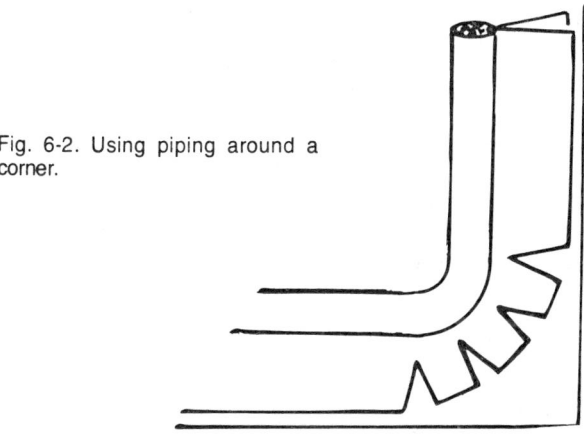

Fig. 6-2. Using piping around a corner.

frame 2 inches or more deep. The legs may be plain in a modern-style piece of furniture, or they may be turned or shaped with carved feet. They may be chosen to match other furniture in the room. It is usually best to finish the woodwork before upholstering the top. This includes sanding, staining, and either varnishing, spraying, or polishing, as will be described later. The final coat may be left until after upholstering, in case any damage occurs. There is less risk of marking the cloth with polish or other materials, if these steps are taken first, however, so it may be better to complete the polishing and then take care not to damage the surfaces during upholstery. The finish should

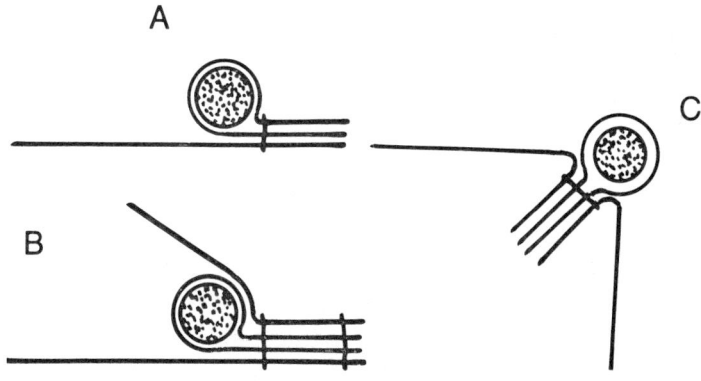

Fig. 6-3. The cover is sewn inside-out.

115

be carried high enough to be certain it will be covered with the top, but there is no need to treat the whole stool. Make sure, however, that sharp edges are sanded off and any roughness removed from the wood that will be in contact with cloth.

Start by fixing the webbing to the top. In most stools there will be two pieces lengthwise and three the other way, or four if it is a very long fireside stool (Fig. 6-4A). Cover the webbing with burlap. Turn in its edges and turn the ends of the webbing over it (Fig. 6-4B).

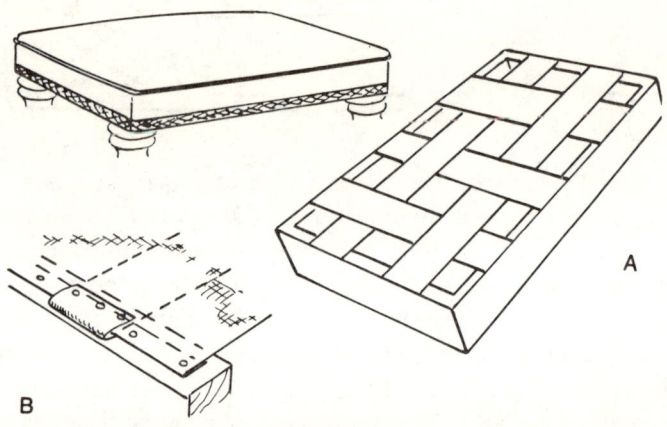

Fig. 6-4. A deep upholstered top starts with webbing.

A piece of cavity foam or pin-core latex foam could be used for the top. This should have its edges cut square and be slightly too big—1/4 inch more all round should suit an average stool. This allows it to be compressed to a close fit as it is covered (Fig. 6-5).

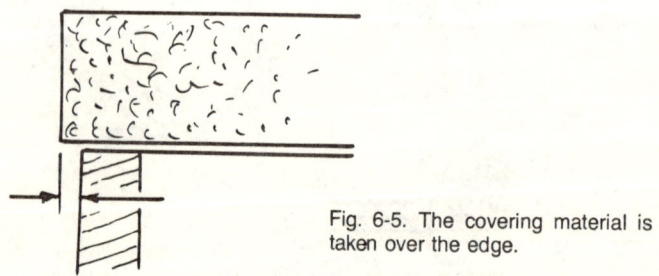

Fig. 6-5. The covering material is taken over the edge.

In making a comfortable and true shape for other types of stuffing it is a help to fix a *fox edging* (also called a *roll*). This edging also covers what would have been a sharp angle over the wood. It is used along the front edge of a chair, but on a stool it should go all round. Fox edging can be bought in many sizes or it can be made to suit each job as it is tackled. The commercially-produced fox edging is probably more even.

For the stool, fox edging no more than 3/4 inch diameter need be used. It is made of a strip of burlap containing hair or other filling the same as is used for the body of the stool. It could be made by sewing in the same way as piping is made, but with sufficient filling laid along as the seam is sewn (Fig. 6-6A). Fixing is done through the extending burlap. Bought fox edging has a band of burlap for sewing. For a stool with a sufficient width of wood for tacking, the roll or fox edging can be made in position.

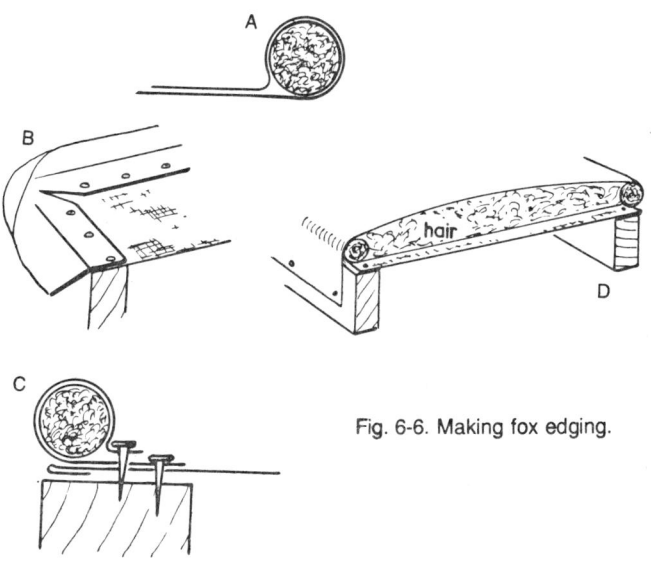

Fig. 6-6. Making fox edging.

Fix a strip of burlap all round the stool with tacks. A total width of about 3 inches should be ample. Nicks can be cut at the corners to avoid a build-up of surplus burlap on the flat of the stool top (Fig. 6-6B). Make up a long even roll of filling hair or other material and wrap the burlap over it, and fix down with fairly close tacking (Fig. 6-6C).

The central area is filled, using large loops of twine to locate the hair. Pick the filling evenly to fit close to the fox edging and give it a domed section. Over this put calico, muslin, or scrim. Take this over the sides and tack, but do not go down as far as the outer covering will come (Fig. 6-6D). At the corners fold the surplus from one side on to the other and tack, but adjust the tension to give a good shape to the combination of stuffing and fox edging.

With some covering materials there is no need for using anything else over the inner covering; but a layer of cotton batting or thin plastic foam adds to comfort and provides something resilient for the edges of cloth and piping along the seams to sink into inconspicuously.

Measure the size of the top allowing about 1/2 inch all round for the seams, but mark where the lines of stitching should come. This, of course, is only the top, and not the size extended down the sides. Cut four pieces for the borders. Allow 1/2 inch at the top for the seam and 1/2 inch at each corner for seams there. Having seams at the corners ensures a better fit than would a continuous length used all round the sides. The lower edges of the border will be covered with gimp or a strip of material. It may be sufficient to merely cut the bottom edge to what is expected to be the final line, or it may be better to allow for turning under a loosely woven material that might fray. In any case, final cutting to width should be left until actual fitting.

Sew the top to the borders, with piping between, if it is used, working inside out (Fig. 6-7A). Check the size on the stool and sew the borders to each other with plain seams. Some materials may benefit by ironing at this stage. Turn the top the right way and fit it over the stool. Lightly tack, while adjusting the cover to fit symmetrically. Let the cotton batting or foam extend down the sides.

On some stools the border may have to be tacked on the outside (Fig. 6-7B) or it may be possible to wrap it underneath, with a notch and the edge turned under at each leg (Fig. 6-7C). In either case the stool is given a finish by a border along the bottom edge of the rails. With soft covering this border may be gimp, held with adhesive and gimp pins. It may be a fairly plain pattern or it may have hanging tassles if that effect would be

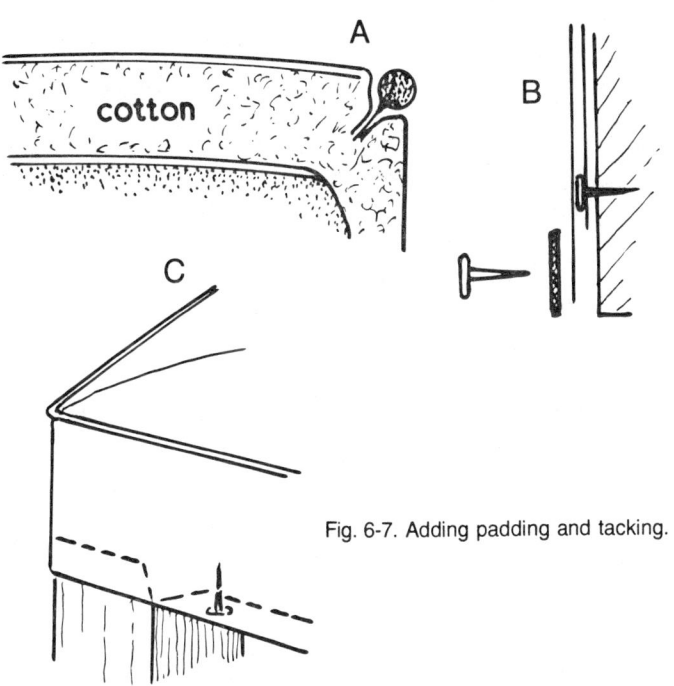

Fig. 6-7. Adding padding and tacking.

appropriate to the intended use. If the covering is made of hide or plastic, it may be more appropriate to use a strip of the same material held on with nails having decorative heads.

BUTTONED STOOL SEAT

The stool just decribed is satisfactory in all usual sizes, but for a larger top it is better, both for appearance and stability of the filling, to use buttons. Without them a large top may appear too domed, and this may flatten in use to become slack around the center. Buttons hold the original shape much longer and most people regard the appearance of buttons superior to a plain top (Fig. 6-8). Because of this, buttons may be considered for a stool of only modest size. However, for the sake of appearance, buttoning should not be arranged too closely. An arrangement in 5 inch squares in about right and anything less than 4 inch squares is unusual.

The stool with piped edges could have its top buttoned, with no other alterations. But if tradition is to be followed, the edge will be without a seam and the covering will be vinyl, either

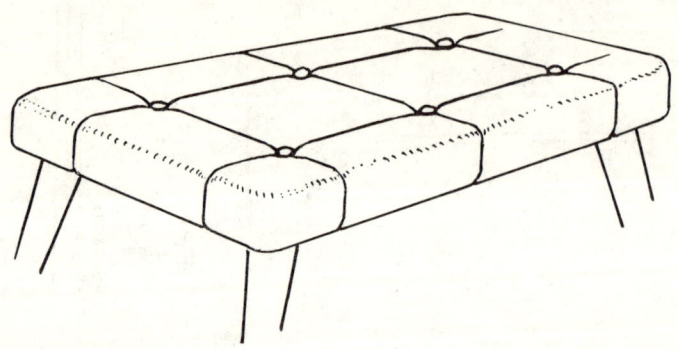

Fig. 6-8. A large stool top may be improved by a pattern of buttons on the top surface.

a plain color or simulated leather appearance. Of course, hide could be used, but plastic imitation leather is easier to work, much cheaper and just as effective, unless the furniture is intended to be a reproduciton antique.

The seat could be supported by webbing, but it is better for maintaining the tension of the twine from the buttons to have a solid base. This is made of plywood fixed on the frame Mark out the positions of the buttons on it and drill holes to pass doubled and knotted thread—1/4 inch should be large enough (Fig. 6-9A).

Besides having buttons, it improves the appearance of the top to sew pleats across the button positions, so that stitched lines show as a pattern on the top. Cut the top material with some to spare around the sides. Mark out the underside of the covering, the same as the plywood, but allowing about 1/4 inch to make each pleat (Fig. 6-9B). Sew these seams (Fig. 6-9C), so the final pattern matches the pattern on the plywood. Put the inverted stool on the top material and draw its outline on the underside as a guide to later shaping.

The filling is made of a piece of foam or latex padding about 2 inches thick. Its outline should be about 1/4 inch bigger all round to allow for compressing to match the wood. If cut exactly to size a hard edge might become visible through the covering. An adhesive can be used to locate and fix the filling to the base, but keep this to the central area so the edges are not prevented from compressing.

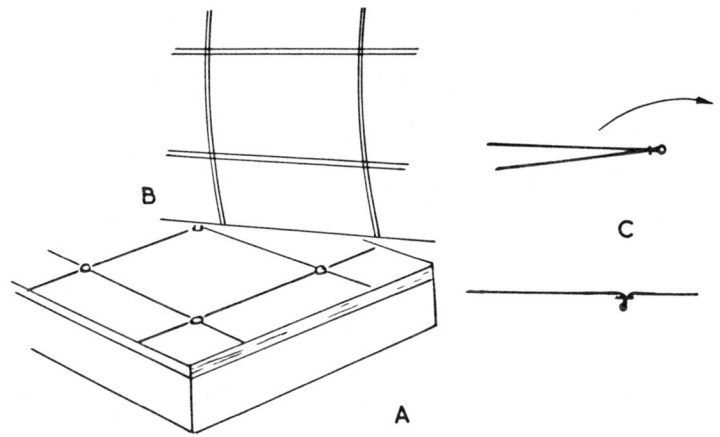

Fig. 6-9. A solid base and pleats are pleasing.

The cover can be marked out and cut with the borders in the same piece (Fig. 6-10A). A problem comes in making allowance for the corner seams, which have to taper in to nothing (Fig. 6-10B). The difficulty of stitching there can be relieved by folding in some of the uncut material above the corner (Fig. 6-10C). With fabric-backed vinyl this is satisfactory, but there is

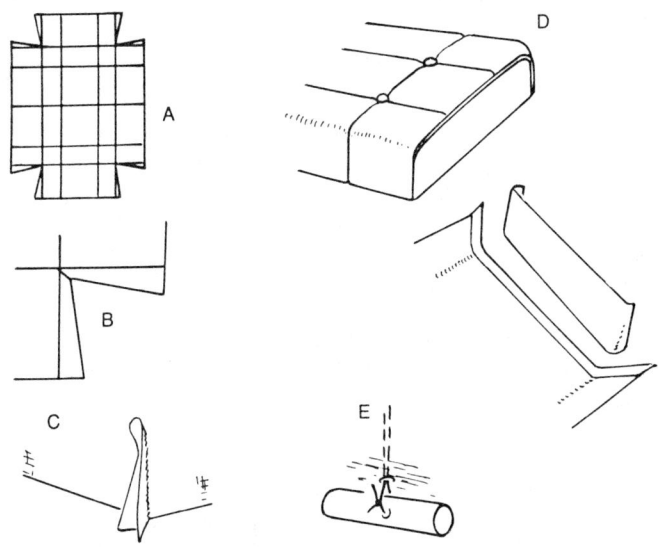

Fig. 6-10. Marking the border and making seams.

a risk of threads pulling in a loosely woven cloth and for this material a different method should be used. There may be a separate piece used for each end, with or without piping (Fig. 6-10D).

In either case, use the marked plywood outline as a guide. As the filling compresses and rounds at the edges, experiment with the top temporarily in position and arrive at a size and shape that will fit closely without unduly squeezing the filling. Sew the seams and try the cover in position. Secure with a few temporary tacks.

Use a long needle to poke through the filling to the matching hole in the base at each seam crossing on top. Put a button on the twine, with both parts of the twine going through the same hole in the cover. Below the plywood take in a plain button or use a small piece of wood, either around it or through a hole in it (Fig. 6-10E). At this stage, knot the twine temporarily. Fix all buttons in this way.

Check that the cover and filling match and that there will be a uniform appearance all round. Then pull down the borders and tack, either below the rails or outside them. If the material can be taken under the framing for tacking, this type of seat looks best without anything around the outside at the lower edge; but if tacking is outside, cover it. Use gimp if a woven material is used, or use a narrow strip of vinyl, if that is the covering, held with adhesive and some nails with decorated heads.

Adjust the tension on the buttons. They should pull in enough to come just below the general surface level. When the correct adjustment is obtained on the twine, compress the cushion enough to slacken the twine and lock the knot. If possible, regulate the twine so it can be pulled to get the knot out of sight above the hole in the plywood. The underside can be left at this stage, although the neatest finish is created by tacking burlap or other cloth under the frame, a short distance in from the outside edge, with surplus turned under.

ROUND SEAT

With a rectangular seat it is usually possible to cut cavity latex material so cavities are not exposed to the edge. The holes in pin-core material are not large enough to matter if holes are cut through and come against an edge. Plain foam does not have any of these problems and can be cut to any shape without bothering about the condition of an edge. Cavity material is probably most comfortable, so it may be desirable to use it, even if shaping will cut through cavities.

Plain latex foam is available in strips which can be used for walling around cut cavity latex. This need only be about 1/2 inch thick, but such a strip held with adhesive can make a good curved-edge cushion (Fig. 6-11A). It is helpful too to use a flat piece of this latex foam under the cavity foam (Fig. 6-11B).

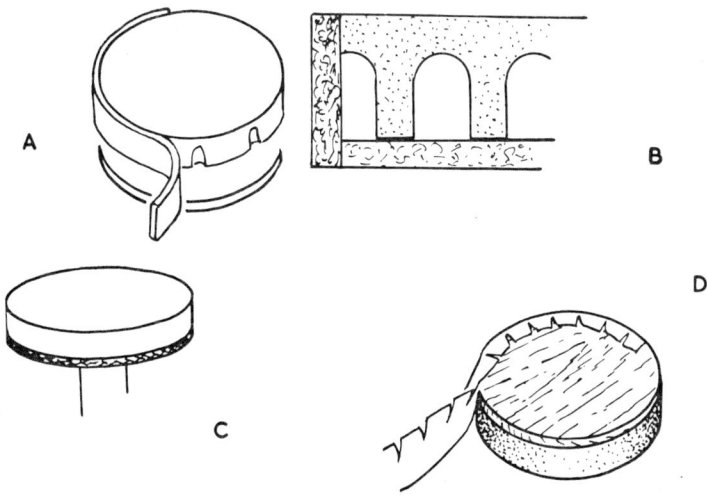

Fig. 6-11. Cavity latex padding can have strips sewn under and around the edge when it is cut. Adhesive strip may be used to secure it to a base.

For a round, or curved shape, the base will be made of stout plywood or blockboard. It should have a few holes through it to allow air in and out as the seat compresses under pressure and expands again when the load is released. Without these holes, the air has to find other ways out and something may break or strain.

Draw the shape of the foam, allowing for the thickness of the walling piece, which is wrapped around and held with adhesive. It is the top edge that is important. See that this follows around in a smooth line. The ends should meet as closely as possible. An alternative way is to stick the ends together before putting the piece around the cushion, allowing a little stretch so the ring of walling goes on tightly. Arrange the finished size so the cushion is a little bigger than the base—how much depends on the softness of the cushion. With an average type, 1/8 inch all around should be enough. If a flat piece of latex foam goes under the cavity foam, this may be inside or under the walling piece, depending on the width of walling strip available (Fig. 6-11C).

The cushion may be stuck down, but it helps in getting a close fit and a neat edge to use a strip of muslin or calico around the base. Use a strip about 3 inches wide. It need not be a single piece all around. Use adhesive to fix half the width around the cushion. The rest will fold under and be stuck to the plywood base. To avoid creases, cut darts into this edge (Fig. 6-11D). You'll have to experiment to find out how much to cut and how frequently to make the darts.

The covering is made up of a disc of material for the top. The seam line is slightly smaller than the size of the wooden base. This allows for the curving down of the foam, and about 1/2 inch outside this for the seam. For the sides the strip has a 1/2 inch allowance at the top and enough below to wrap under the base. There can be piping included in the seam if desired. The strip around should be a continuous piece; it may be made up from pieces sewn together if necessary. Sew the round seam (Fig. 6-12A). The edges may pucker when the cover is turned the right way, but this can be minimized by trimming to about 1/4 inch from the stitching.

Try the cover in place and tack it temporarily. Adjust the tension so the top is pulled evenly and a regular appearance is seen all round. How the final tacking is arranged depends on the material. A light material can be creased and arranged in an even pattern of folds underneath (Fig. 6-12B). With a stouter material it may be better to arrange darts towards the rim, but not up to it (Fig. 6-12C).

If the underside is to be left uncovered, use a notched block of wood to mark a line parallel with the rim and cut to this (Fig. 6-12D). For a neater finish use a piece of burlap or other material to within about 1/2 inch of the edge, turning in as it is tacked

(Fig. 6-12E). This should be open-weave cloth to minimize creasing as it is turned under.

This type of seat is often supported by a central pillar, or there may be independent legs. If there have to be bolts through or other special provision made for fixing removable supports, see that anything that will come inside is secure and properly fixed before doing the upholstery.

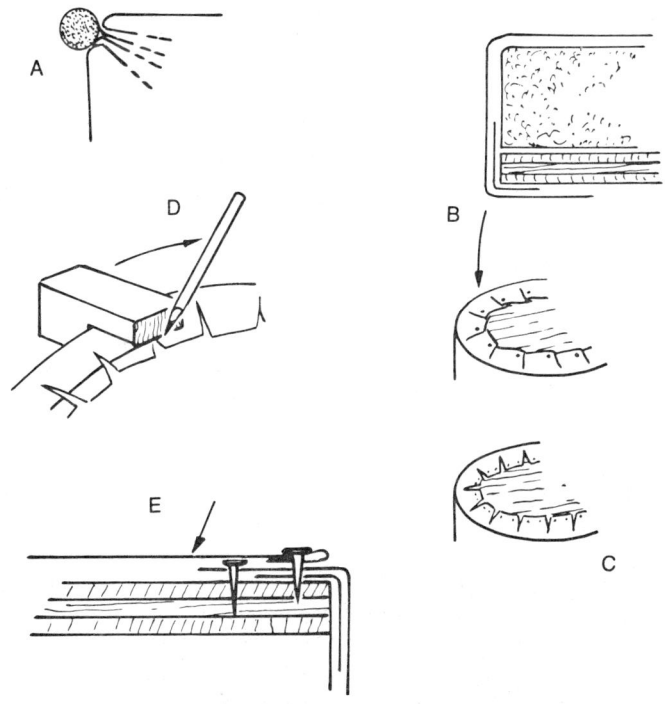

Fig. 6-12. Making round seams, and attaching them.

It is possible to button such a round top. The usual arrangement has one central button and four or more others arranged evenly around it about midway between the center and the rim.

OFFICE CHAIR

Office chairs and stools often have seats with a shaped outline on a plywood base, so the method of covering is very similar to that for the round stool. Many of the shapes suit standard cavity foam cushions so it may be possible to make or adapt a wooden seat shape to suit a cushion that is already profiled to the outline and shaped on the surface to provide a comfortable seat.

Covering may be done with cloth or with vinyl. For most seats there may be a continuous strip around the sides, with the joint at the back (Fig. 6-13). Cloth with a plain pattern may be best with a simple seam, but vinyl can have piping included (Fig. 6-14). If the filling has been cut to size and a walling strip stuck

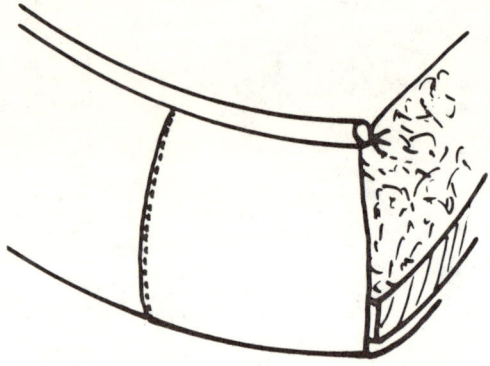

Fig. 6-13. For office chairs there may be a continuous strip of covering around the sides with a joint at the back.

Fig. 6-14. A vinyl office stool top with a piped seam in the same material.

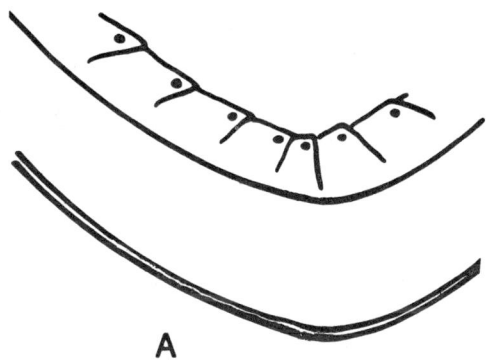

Fig. 6-15. Covering can be turned under and folded, or darted.

on, there can be calico or muslin used around the bottom; but if a prepared latex cushion is used it should be sufficient to put it on the plywood and position it with a small amount of adhesive.

The covering can be turned under and folded or there may be darts to reduce bulk. If the edge is likely to fray if exposed, it should be turned under when tacking. Burlap or other material may go over the bottom, but in much office furniture this is omitted (Fig. 6-15).

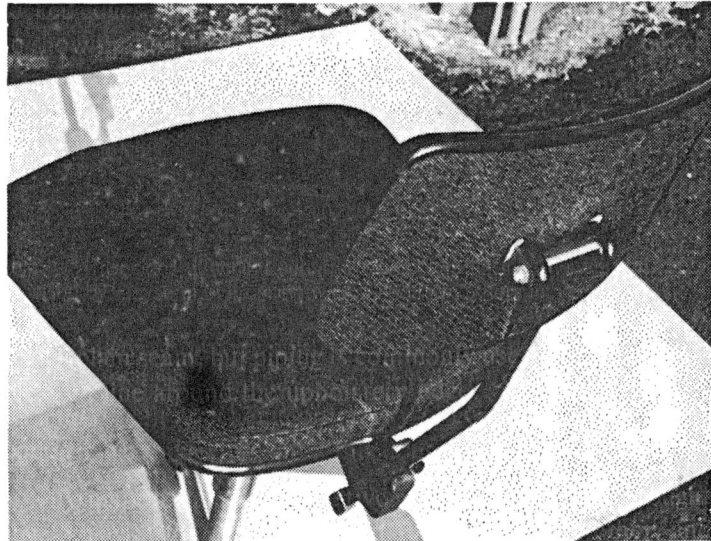

Fig. 6-16. A typical office chair with a simple padded back and the seat covering taken underneath.

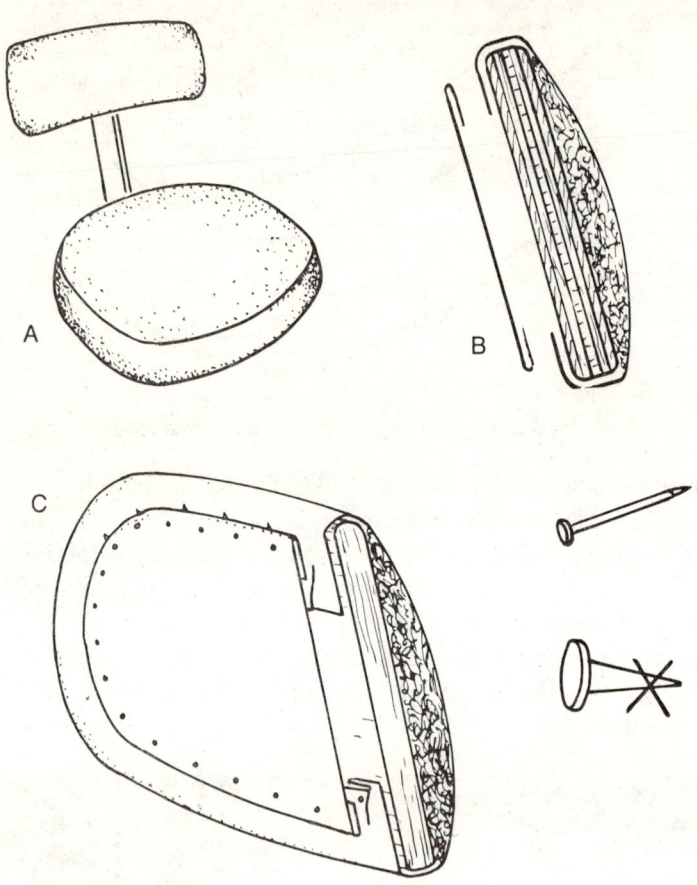

Fig. 6-17. An office chair with a padded back is made in a way similar to that of a lift-out dining chair seat.

If there is a shaped back to an office chair (Figs. 6-16 and 6-17A) it is usually made of plywood and the method of covering is simple and similar to that of a lift-out dining chair seat. Padding is provided by a shaped shallow cushion or by a piece of foam about 1 inch thick, which is held by a single piece of covering material stretched over and tacked to the other side of the plywood (Fig. 6-17B). This should be done neatly and evenly. Instead of burlap, a piece of the same material is used on the back. It is carefully turned in to come parallel with the outline of the back and is held with gimp pins or other thin nails, which are not as conspicuous as tack heads (Fig. 6-17C).

Cushions

7

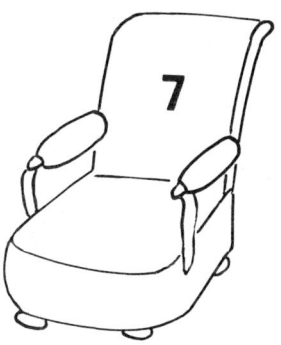

A cushion may be regarded as a loose piece of upholstery. There are two broad divisions. A cushion or pillow may be made without regard to where it will be used. Such a *scatter* or *throw* cushion can be of any convenient size and it can be carried about and used wherever temporary softening is required. The other type is a fitted cushion intended to be used with a particular piece of furniture. It is removable, but its size and shape match a chair or other item of furniture. It may rest on tension or zig-zag springs, or it may supplement a more fully upholstered seat, increasing the depth of softening and increasing comfort.

FILLED CUSHIONS

The simplest scatter cushion is a pillow intended for a bed. It may be a cloth bag filled with feathers or down. The covering material needs to be a down-proof type or the feathers may work through. This is usually sewn up completely, but it is given an outer cover of a washable material that slides over and is held by buttons, tapes, or other fasteners (Fig. 7-1A).

The same idea is used for loose cushions, which are square or round and covered with material to match the furniture they are to be used with. A cushion of this type may still be considered superior to one filled with one of the more recent foams for resting the head on against the back of a chair. Foam be-

129

comes more suitable and acceptable for larger cushions that may be used to soften a hard seat or provide softening on the ground.

Feathers or down need careful handling if you are to avoid losing some and spreading others around the working place. Get the down in a sealed plastic bag. Work in a draft-free room. Make the inner bag from down-proof material, either folded over or made of two pieces. Sew it inside-out, with two lines of stitches around the edge and partway across the edge that will be used for filling (Fig. 7-1B).

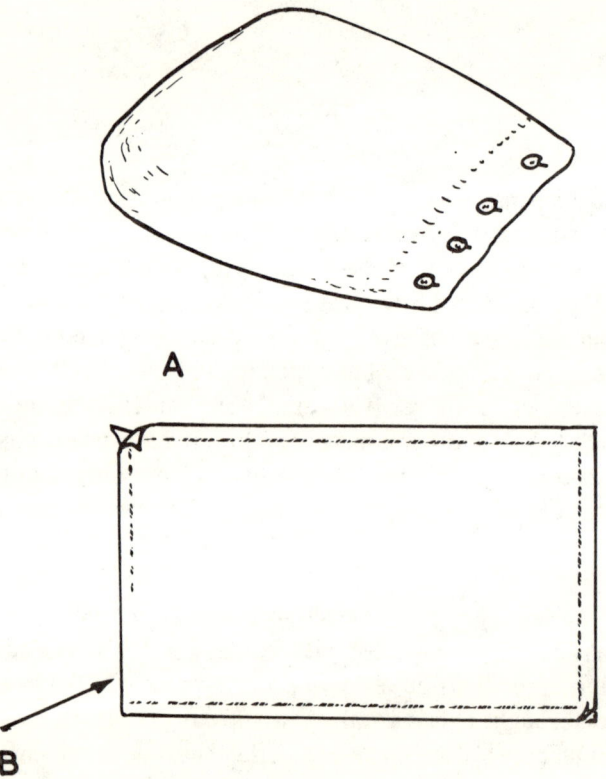

Fig. 7-1. A simple pillow or cushion cover comes or is made in the form of a bag.

Although the material may be down-proof there is a risk of feathers getting through the stitching. This risk can be minimized by rubbing the stiches on both sides with hard soap.

Then turn the bag the right way. The safest way to get all the down in is to cut a corner off the plastic bag that contains the down and insert this into the opening. Work the down from the bag into the cover by squeezing and easing it through. Coax most of the feathers to the far end and sew across the opening on the outside.

The same method can be used for a filling of particles or crumbs of latex or plastic foam. These should be built up to a fairly tight content, as a slack filling eventually becomes too loose for comfort. There are other plastic fillings supplied as loosely bonded compressed material between temporary cardboard covers. In this case, the whole assembly should be slid into the cover, then the cardboard withdrawn, so the plastic expands and fills the cover.

MOLDED CUSHIONS

There are molded latex cushion shapes, which are domed and rounded (Fig. 7-2A). A single one may be used on a seat, but to make a scatter cushion, a pair can be fitted together (Fig. 7-2B). Their meeting surfaces are joined with adhesive and the joint around the outside is covered with tape or thin cloth stuck on.

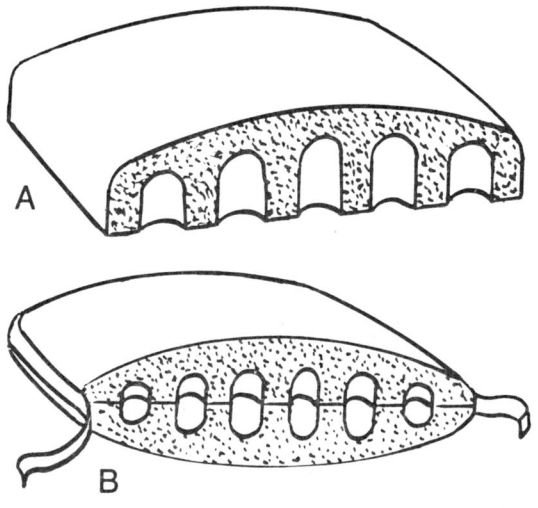

Fig. 7-2. There are also molded latex cushion shapes.

If a molded cushion of the right size is unobtainable and sheet material has to be cut, the undersides may be bevelled (Fig. 7-3A). These, as well as the flat surfaces, are stuck together. Follow the directions that come with the adhesive. Usually both surfaces are coated and then left to become tacky before pressing together. The adhesive should have sufficient strength to hold the edges to curves, but there should be tape around as well (Fig. 7-3B).

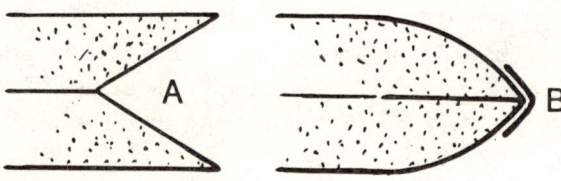

Fig. 7-3. Undersides may have to be beveled.

For many purposes two pieces of cavity latex material joined together will give a cushion of satisfactory bulk. If a greater thickness is wanted, pieces of plain sheet foam can be put in the center. One piece may be enough, or there can be several pieces cut to different sizes (Fig. 7-4A). If thin foam (about 1/2 inch) is used there is no need to cut tapers, but if one

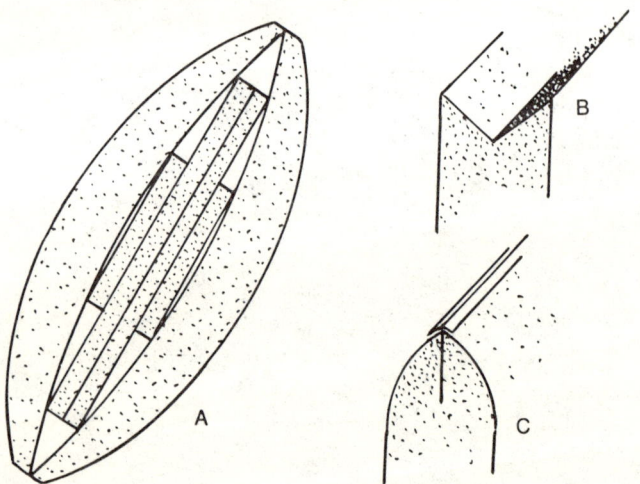

Fig. 7-4. The fillings can be made up from foam or latex joined together.

thick piece is used it may be advisable to taper the edges. Let these filling pieces be parallel with the edges of the cushion and if it is a shape with corners, round the corners of the inner pieces slightly to get the best form.

If the cushion is to be made from a thick piece of plain or pin-core foam that is of sufficient total thickness without joining pieces, another way of rounding the edges is to cut a V around the edge (Fig. 7-4B) and squeeze this together with adhesive and tape around (Fig. 7-4C).

COVERING SCATTER CUSHIONS

For any cushion with rounded edges, whether it has a loose filling in a bag or a molded pad, the cover is made from two pieces sewn together. There is no need for any walling or other strips. In some material there may be piping, but this is unusual. Mark the shape with 1/2 inch to spare all round. Sew the pieces together face to face completely on three sides. How far to go around the fourth side depends on how much the filling will compress to get it in. The cover has to be turned the right way and the filling pushed through the space. With some types of padding you may have to leave the full width of an end, but some fillings, such as feathers, will compress to go through only part of an end (Fig. 7-5). What is not machine sewn in this way will have to be hand sewn.

It is convenient to be able to remove the interior so the cover can be washed or cleaned. Buttons may suit a bed pillow, but for other cushions the edge may be slip (or blind) sewn, or fitted with a zipper.

Slip sewing makes the stitches inconspicuous and they can easily be cut and picked out when the cover has to be removed. Use a needle and thread appropriate to the material, but for most cases a general sewing needle will be better than a heavier upholstery needle. For heavy cloth use a small curved needle. Turn the edges in. If parts of the edges have already been machine-sewn, they will already be creased inwards. Rub down a fold that follows the edge line across. Take the needle along a fold. Knot the end. Bring the needle out and into the opposite fold exactly opposite (Fig. 7-6). Go a short distance along this fold and out again, to cross and into the first fold (Fig. 7-6B).

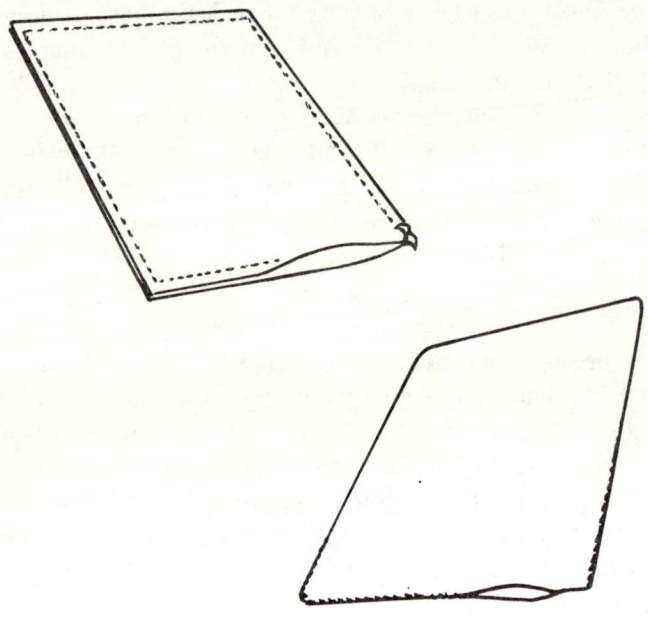

Fig. 7-5. For loose filling the cover can be sewn almost all the way and then closed by stitching externally.

How far to take the thread along inside each fold depends on the particular material, but 1/4 inch is a reasonable distance. Finish by knotting at the other end.

A zipper can be sewn across an opening instead of using slip sewing. It has a certain bulk, which cannot be avoided. This does not matter on a wall-edged cushion because it does not show along the center of a side. If the plain cushion cover is made of a fairly stout material and there is a full curve to the edge, a zipper may not be very conspicuous. If a zipper is used, the cloth opening should be a little more than that for slip stitching because the zipper reduces the space. If a zipper is to be used, it is sewn in as described in the next section.

WALL-EDGED BUNK CUSHIONS

Foam in any of its thick sheet forms is an appropriate material for plain mattresses or cushions, such as those used for bunks in yachts. The outline does not have to be rectangular. It

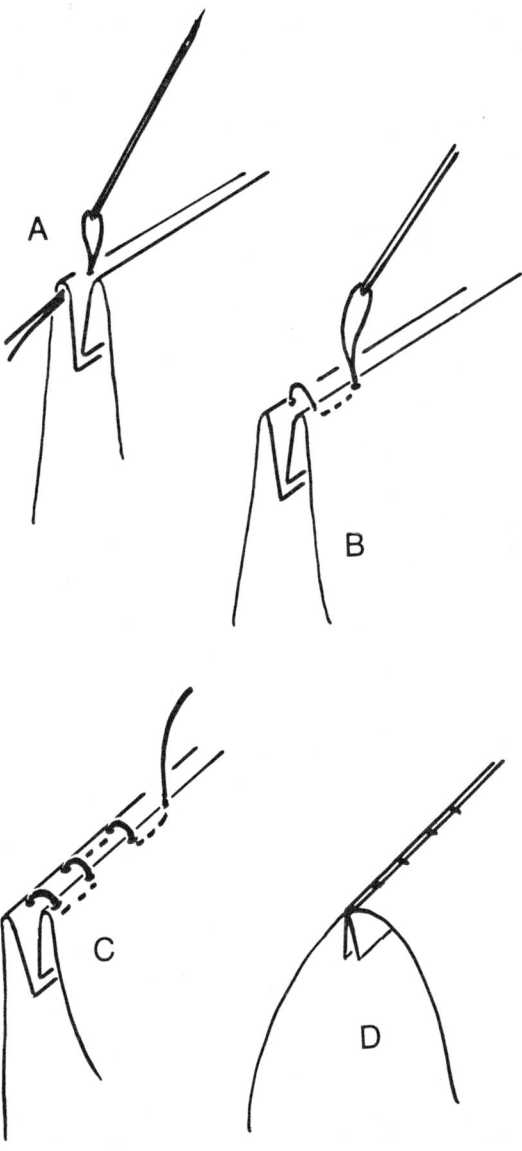

Fig. 7-6. Slip sewing makes stitches inconspicuous.

can conform to the shape of the ship and there can be notches to clear obstructions if necessary. If the cushion is to rest on a solid base it should be 4 inches or more thick for comfort when sitting or sleeping. Although quite a large cushion can be made in one piece, it may be more convenient to make it in sections, particularly for some boats where access may be restricted. For trailers, motor homes, and similar vehicles, access is not such a problem, but it may be necessary to make cushions in sections if they are arranged differently during the day for sitting and at night for sleeping.

The first step is to make a paper pattern showing all the details of the finished shape (Fig. 7-7A). Usually the edge is square, but if the maximum area is needed in a confined space it may be necessary to let a tapered part follow the flare of a boat's

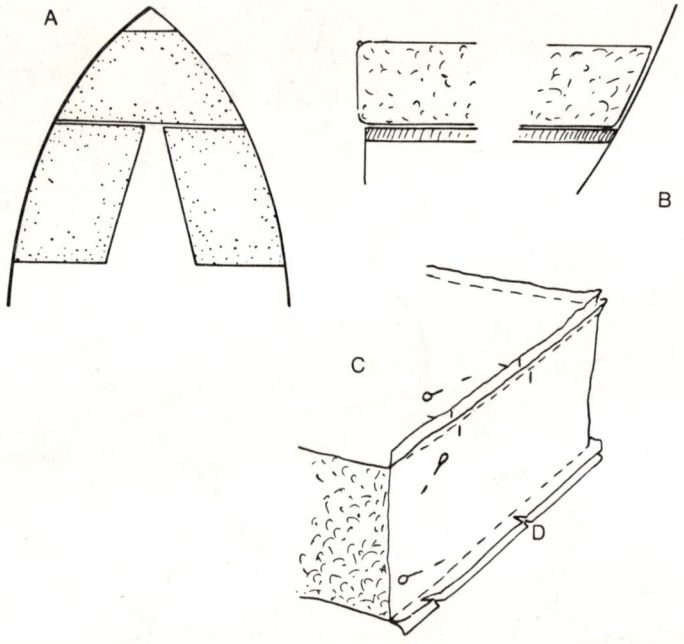

Fig. 7-7. Plastic foam can be cut to make shaped cushions and the covers made with piped edges.

side (Fig. 7-7B). If this is also curved when viewed from above there is a complication in the developed shape of the walling, which is not just a parallel strip wrapped round. This shaping is better avoided. Cutting that edge squarely like the others will have very little less area unless the side is extremely flared.

Use the paper pattern to mark the foam to shape and cut it to this outline. If there is to be a straight front edge, let this be the manufactured edge, so that any faults in hand cutting will appear at the back and be less obvious.

For a utilitarian finish on a cushion that is to get much use, vinyl is a good choice, but a woven cloth is more comfortable to sit on and certainly to sleep on. You will probably want to use a synthetic cloth or a mixture of synthetic and natural materials. These are acceptable, but a wholly natural material such as cotton or wool does not have as great a perspiration problem when slept on. The supporting plywood base should be provided with many holes for ventilation.

If the cushion is rectangular and may be turned over, it should have the same covering material all round. If it is a fitted outline such as a shaped bunk cushion, the hidden parts need not be of the same material as the rest of the cushion. There can be a saving in cost if a plain material is used for the bottom instead of a patterned material the same as the top. However, the two materials should be compatible. A light, plain material may have more stretch than the top material. The seam may work around the edge in use and the different material from below might become visible at the front.

Use the pattern to mark the shape of top and bottom with an allowance of about 1/2 inch all around for seams, but allow the sewn cover to compress the foam slightly. Before cutting to the outline try on the actual foam so any slight discrepancies can be noted and allowed for. Cut strips for the walling. There may be seams at the corners. Joints along a hidden back may not matter, but the front should be in one piece. For a simple rectangular cushion there may be no need to make register marks, but for an involved shape it is wise to pin the covering in place on the foam and to make marks opposite each other at intervals. The position lines for stitching should be marked, in any case. The register marks may be made by pencil or ball pen (Fig. 7-7C), but if the material will not take these, there can be cuts in the edges (Fig. 7-7D).

Piping the top edge improves the appearance of most square-edged cushions. Piping will have to run around the bottom edge as well if the cushion will turn over, otherwise a plain seam will do there. For plain colored vinyl, white or black manufactured piping is convenient and attractive. For a patterned cloth the piping can be a plain color, usually matching the predominant color of the pattern. Alternatively, piping can be made from the same material.

Sewing of the outer cover has to be planned keeping in mind the way to fit the slab of foam. In most cases the slab will fit via an end. If there is any shaping, it will have to be the broader end. Usually, the walling can be sewn all round to the top, and the bottom sewn on everywhere except across the end. The covering is turned the right way and the foam fitted in (Fig. 7-8). Then the bottom seam is slip stitched.

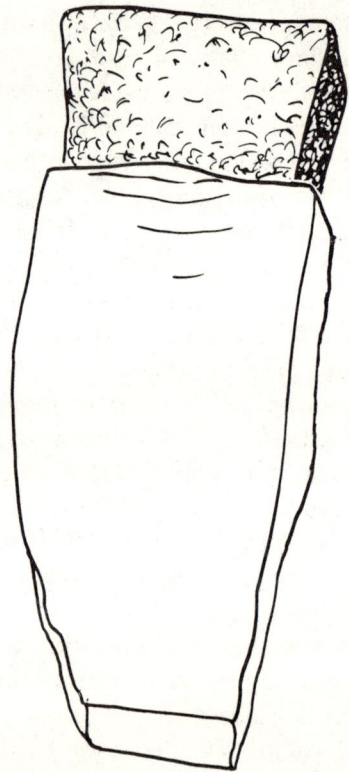

Fig. 7-8. The fit of the foam must be kept in mind when sewing the outer cover.

Another way is to use a zipper across the center of the end and preferably a short distance along the back (Fig. 7-9A). This allows the foam to be put in easily, and leaves enough room to get an arm in to adjust the foam's position. This is the main reason for the zipper although, obviously, it is more convenient than slip stitching if the foam has to be taken out later.

The cloth is cut and turned under at the point where the zipper is to be placed. The amount of cloth that can be turned under depends on the width of the cloth border of the zipper, but it is sufficient for a line of stitches (Fig. 7-9B). Have the zipper closed when it is sewn in and see that the two parts of the walling

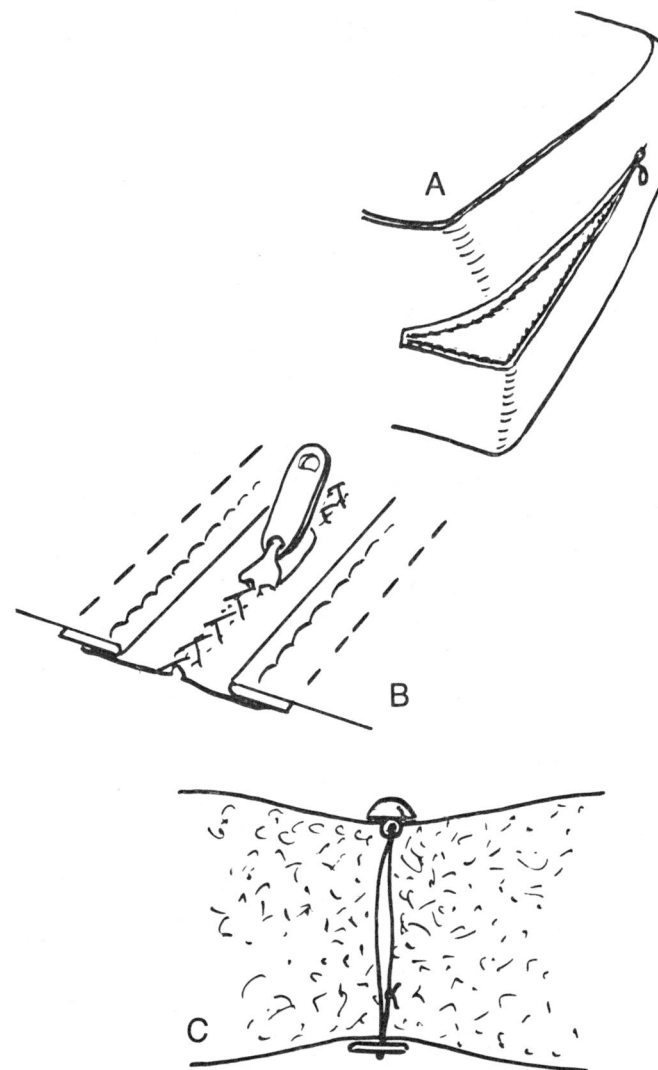

Fig. 7-9. A zipper and buttons can be used if desired.

material do not move in relation to each other. The zipper may be sewn into the walling strip before the cover is made up, then the whole cover can be sewn all around top and bottom. It is then pulled the right way by drawing everything through the opened zipper.

Latex and plastic foam slabs are fairly stable and there is usually little risk of the covers moving in relation to them, particularly if it is a one-purpose cushion, such as a bunk mattress. But if there is much lifting and altering of the use or situation of the cushion, the cover and contents may move in relation to each other. If there is a zipper it is possible to open and rearrange the slab, but if the cushion is closed, it is better to use buttons.

A large area of cushion top without any break in design does not look as good as one with a pattern of buttons, so besides using buttons to stabilize the interior, their use improves the appearance. A pattern with buttons at the corners of 6 inch squares should suit a bunk mattress.

The buttons should be in the same pattern on top and bottom. If the cushion does not turn over, the buttons underneath need only be plain, but they should be about the same diameter as those on top. Sew through with a long needle and take in top and bottom buttons, using the thread through single holes on each surfaces. At first temporarily slip knot the twine. When all of the buttons have been loosely attached, tighten their twines to get an even tension and lock the knots. Compress the cushion so the knots can be pulled inside (Figs. 7-9C, 7-10, and 7-11).

SMALL WALL-EDGED CUSHIONS

Smaller wall-edged or box-edged cushions can be made in the same way and they need not have blocks of foam inside. Loose filling material can be used, such as feathers, down, or small pieces of latex or plastic foam. A cushion without walling has its greatest thickness near the center, which may be all that is needed for resting a head, but if the cushion is used for seating, it is better if the thickness is maintained towards the edge. Walling allows for this.

Fig. 7-10. The appearance of a cushion can be improved by adding buttons, in this case covered with the same material as the cushion.

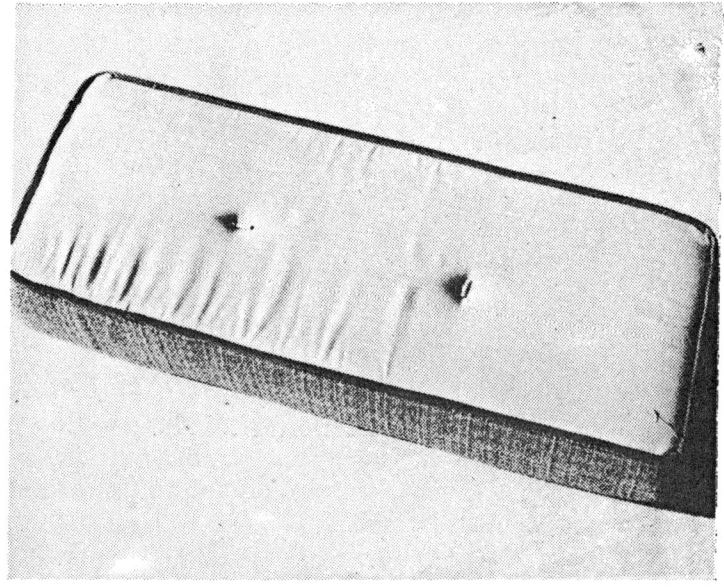

Fig. 7-11. The underside of a cushion showing the twine held by pegs.

A smaller cushion can be made with piped seams (Fig. 7-12A). Stitching is carried all round one seam and on three sides of the other seam, although it may be helpful to locate the piping with a line of stitches on one part (Fig. 7-12B) before turning the cover the right way. A slab of foam may need this full width to be inserted, but if a loose filling material is used only a narrow opening is needed. Machine stitching can be carried partly along the fourth edge. When the cushion has been filled, the opening can be closed by squeezing the filling away from the edge and running a line of stitches across close to the piping (Fig. 7-12C).

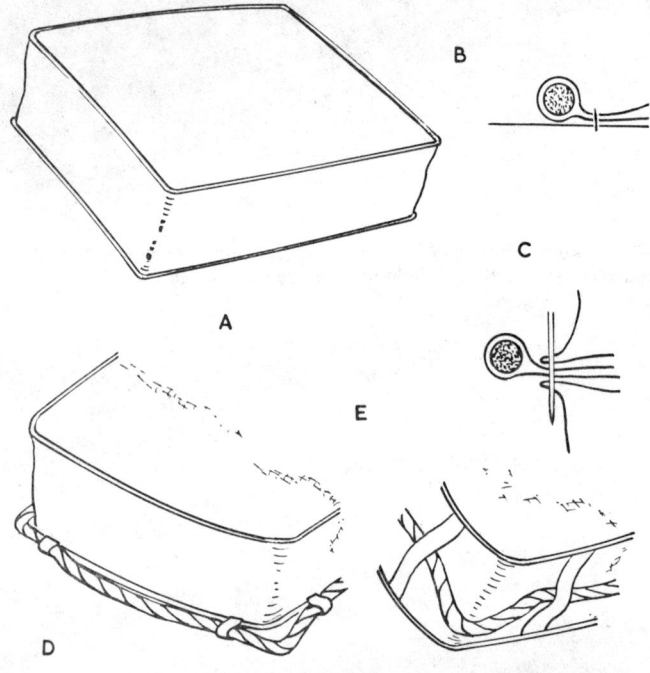

Fig. 7-12. A buoyant cushion with rope around the side.

This type of cushion may be used for emergency buoyancy on a yacht. Colored canvas is the appropriate covering material. The filling must be buoyant; it could be a piece of closed-cell plastic foam. A loose filling could be made of kapok. If the cushion is to be thrown to someone in the water, it must have something to hold onto. This attachment can be a piece of rope around the cushion. There could be loops of tape included in the seam stitching along one edge (Fig. 7-12D)—two each side on a cushion up to about 1 foot square and three for a larger one. Or, you could take the tape across to the other seam and let the rope be loose under these straps (Fig. 7-12E). The rope should be reasonably thick (not less than 3/8 inch diameter) to provide a safe grip, and it should be loose enough to hang in loops. Its ends can be simply knotted; they will look more nautical, though, if spliced (Fig. 7-13).

CHAIR CUSHIONS

In some chairs there are tension or zig-zag springs attached to the frame, but there is no fixed upholstery. Instead, the seat is made of a cushion resting on the springs and the back is either wooden or another loose cushion against springs. Other chairs may be fully upholstered on seat, arms, and back, but there is a fitted cushion additionally on the seat and there may be another at the back. These cushions are shaped to fit tightly, but they are not fixed in any way.

Such chair cushions are wall-sided and can be made in several ways, including those described for bunk cushions. In

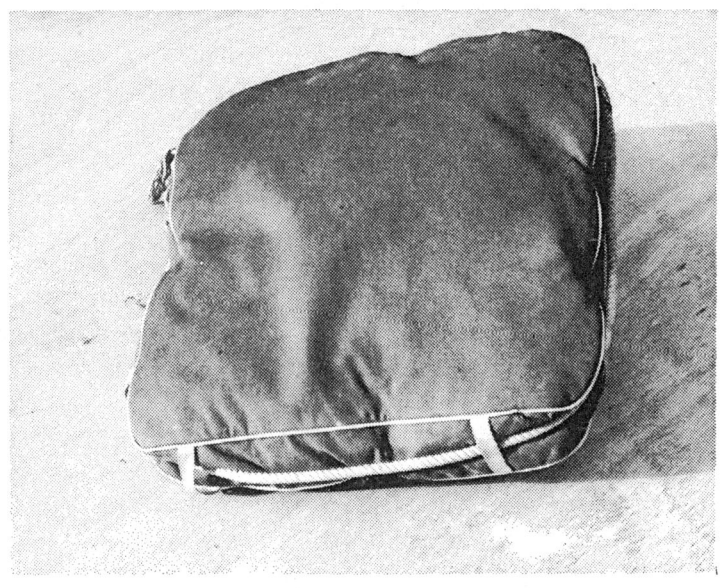

Fig. 7-13. A cushion made as shown in Fig. 7-12.

the simplest chairs, both seat and back cushions are plain rectangles and construction with a foam filling is quite straightforward. Although most bunk cushions are made with the covering directly over the foam, in better quality furniture a better finish and a more comfortable seat are obtained by encasing the foam in muslin or other light material before fitting it into the outer covering.

If there is any shaping needed, make a paper pattern. A seat cushion may be hollowed around the chair back (Fig. 7-14A). Allow for the cushion fitting closely at sides and back, with a full enough edge for comfort over the front. Too much overhang would be unstable, however.

The cushion may be made of a single piece of foam. If a variation in thickness is required, it could be made of two pieces with more foam sandwiched between (Fig. 7-14B). The front edge could be rounded by bevelling the underside of the top part and pulling it down to stick to the lower part (Fig. 7-14C). However, if the cushion is going on top of another upholstered part, the shape and behavior of this part must be allowed for. In most of these cases a wall-edged cushion of uniform thickness is best.

In a chair cushion that is not intended to be turned over, its lower surface can be a cheaper fabric and the part of the fixed upholstery that comes under the cushion need not be of the same quality as that used for the visible parts. The face material should be taken far enough back from the front edge, on the chair and under the cushion, for there to be no risk of any of the plainer material showing.

For ease of assembly and adjustment of this type of cushion it is worthwhile using a zipper across the back and forward about 6 inches at each side (Fig. 7-14D). This is out of sight normally, yet the cushion can be lifted out and the cover removed easily.

Traditional cushions are made with springs surrounded by padding. In commercial production, an adjustable machine or jig is used to maintain the cushion shape and arrange the stuffing evenly, but such a cushion can be made by hand.

The inner muslin or other cloth cover forms the case into which the various parts of the filling are put. It is made to the

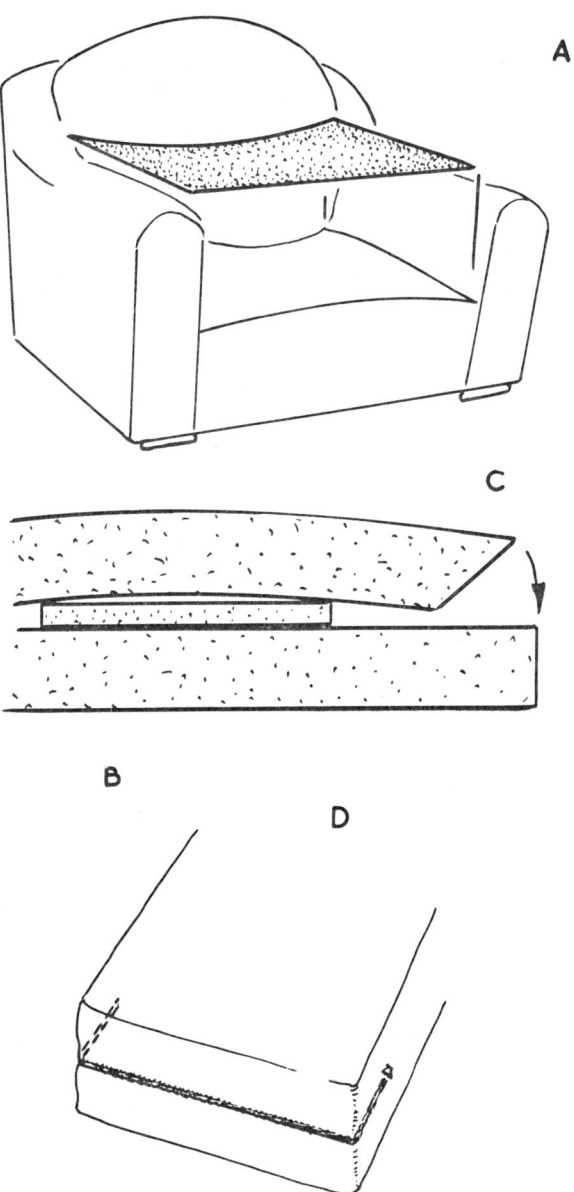

Fig. 7-14. A fitted cushion has to be made to a template.

template with enough all round to stand up to the full depth, except the part that comes at the front is long enough to fold completely over to the back (Fig. 7-15A). Edges are turned up and corners sewn. This cloth must rest on a flat surface and it is helpful to have temporary strips of wood to support the sides and front (Fig. 7-15B).

Have a piece of cotton batting that will fill the width and be long enough to wrap over the finished filling (Fig. 7-15C). The side facing downwards will eventually be the top of the cushion. Spread hair over the cotton. Do this evenly to a loose depth of about 2 inches. Above this goes a Marshall unit of small springs surrounded by rolled cotton. This gives some tolerance in size. The nearest Marshall unit size can be selected and the width adjusted by altering the amount of rolled cotton (Fig. 7-15D).

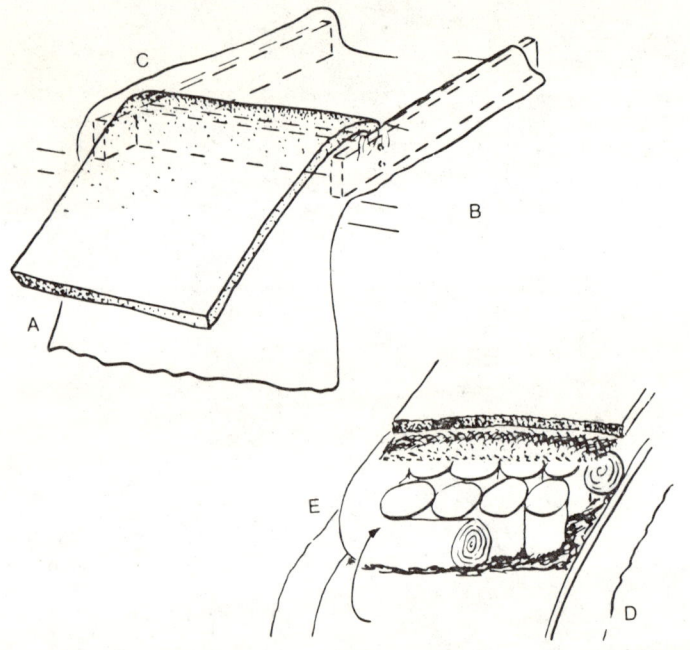

Fig. 7-15. The cushion can be filled with foam or built up with traditional stuffing and springs.

The rolls are made fairly tightly. They do not have to be continuous, but can make up the perimeter in sections. Keep them close, using adhesive tape if necessary to hold the rolling tight and to hold adjoining rolls close together.

The Marshall units should be close so the springs are not exposed and there are no gaps between parts. If there is any doubt, put burlap over the hair before placing the units, otherwise hair may become lost between the springs.

When the springs and rolls are located satisfactorily, put more hair over and wrap over the cotton (Fig. 7-15E). Pin this at the back. Compress the cushion as much as reasonably possible by hand, and draw over the muslin cover. This has to be sewn, but it is helpful to strain and pin the parts together, adjusting until an even tension has been obtained. Check final sizes in relation to where the cushion is to fit. See that the hair is evenly distributed. If the whole pinned assembly is satisfactory, sew the muslin casing by hand, taking out pins as you progress.

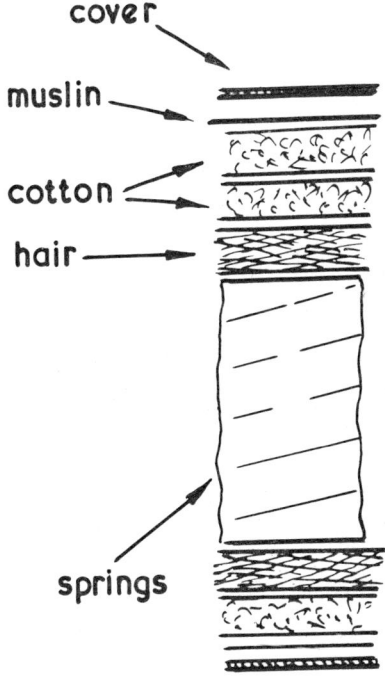

Fig. 7-16. The final cushion has a great many layers to provide comfort.

With this inner assembly encased in muslin, the final covering is similar to that described for using a foam interior, except it may be advisable to add a further layer of cotton batting on what will be the top side, or on both sides if the cushion may be turned over. This has to be carefully arranged between the outer cover and the sealed inner part. The cushion then has a great many parts building up to provide comfort for the human body (Fig. 7-16). Although this was once the usual way of making upholstered chair cushions, it will probably only be needed today in specialist work and in the making of reproduction furniture or the restoration of antiques. For most other furniture the various types of foam offer a much simpler method and usually as high a degree of comfort.

Lounge Chairs

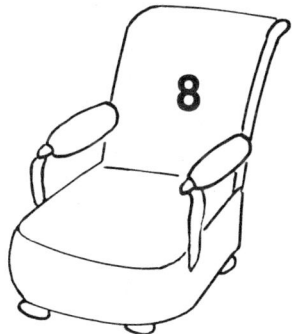

The simplest form of reclining chair, as distinct from one used for dining and similar purposes, has an open frame with uncovered plain arms and padding provided in a simple way at seat and back. The padding may be in the form of cushions that are entirely removable or the back upholstery may be fixed and the seat swab arranged to lift out. There are variations which take the upholstery further, but this type of chair is distinguished by being smaller and lighter than the majority of fully upholstered chairs. Frames are of the type described in Chapter 24.

If the only upholstery is cushions, they are made as described in Chapter 7. Seat supports are usually made of tension springs, but rubber webbing and other methods of springing can be used. If the cushion is thick enough to provide ample comfort without the aid of springs, there could be a piece of plywood as support, but it is more usual to provide some flexibility in the support. One problem with loose cushions is the risk of their slipping through the bottom. To prevent this and improve appearance when the cushion is removed there may be a piece of cloth fixed above the springs (Fig. 8-1A). This cloth should have some stretch. It may be a piece of open weave burlap. Turn in the edges and tack them to the frame. A double turn in over the spring ends may be carried far enough over them to reduce the risk of chafe on the cushion (Fig. 8-1B). There should be enough tacks, but if the springs ever need attention the tacks will have to be withdrawn, so allow for this when fixing.

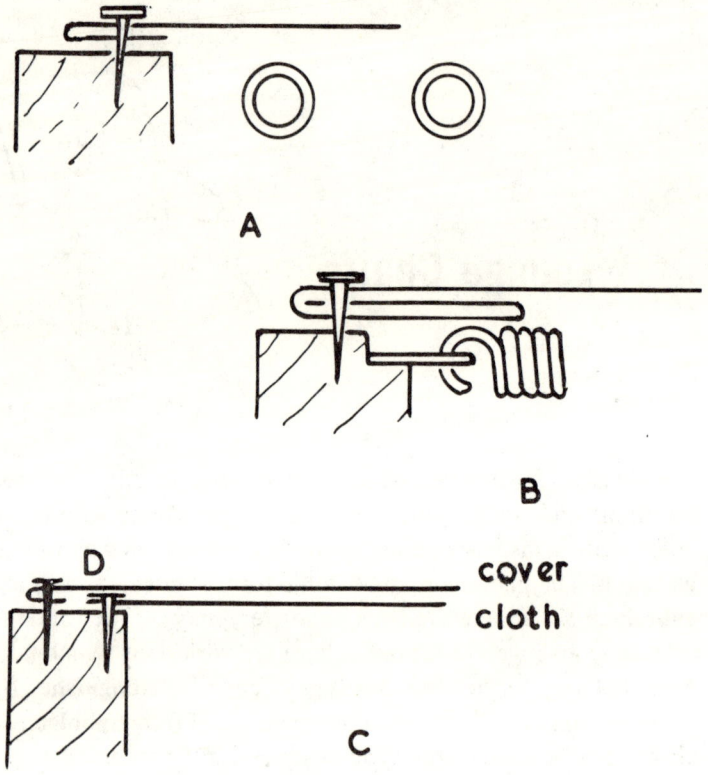

Fig. 8-1. Lounge chairs have loose cushions and little padding.

There is a similar problem of appearance at the back. If the chair is always used against a wall, the back may not be seen. But it is still usual to hide the springs. There may be a piece of plain canvas or cloth for this purpose. It looks best if it is a material matching that on the cushions. If it is a heavy material it may be put on without backing, but it may be better to have canvas, burlap, or other plain cloth first if there is not much strength in the outside cloth (Fig. 8-1C).

How this covering is fixed and arranged at the edges depends on the frame and the method of springing. It may be turned in and tacked to the back (Fig. 8-1D). Decorative nails or a piece of gimp could be put over the tacks. At the top the cloth may go over the rail and be taken far enough down the front to be hidden by the cushion. At the bottom back rail, the cloth can go under. If it is a suitable frame, the back cloth may be brought around the sides to the front so the wood is enclosed and the cloth edge is covered by the cushion.

This may be taken a step further: the front of the seat back may be covered as well, if the frame and springs permit. With zig-zag or tension springs across the back attached to rabbets or otherwise kept below the front line of the back rails, the covering may be brought around from the back. Another piece of cloth may be fixed over it (Fig. 8-2A) if the cushion will be wide enough to hide the joint. If the cushion is narrower it is better to take the front cloth around to the back and make the joint with decorative nails or gimp there (Fig. 8-2B).

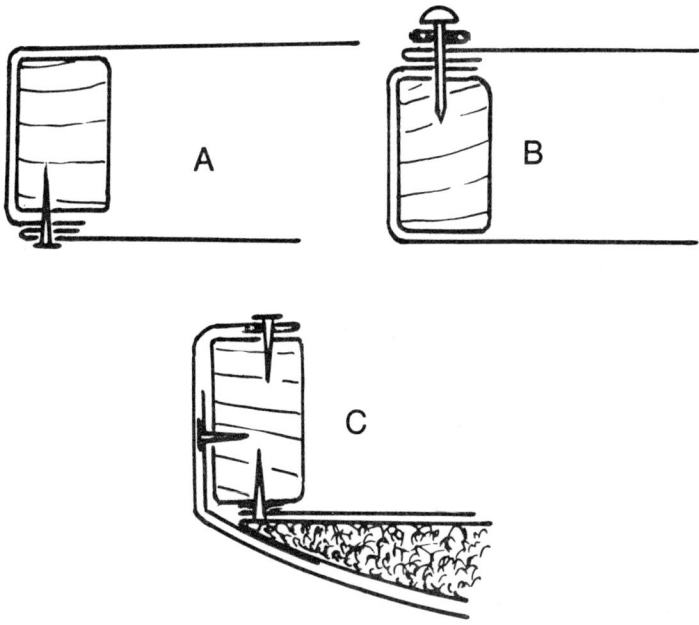

Fig. 8-2. The front of the seat may be covered as well.

Such a covering will press against the springs and their outline will show as a pattern on the surface after the chair has been in use some time. This may not matter, as the cushion will provide comfort, but it will look unsightly when the cushion is removed. It may also mark the cushion, which is often intended to be reversible. The back can be improved by upholstering thinly. Cover the springs with canvas or burlap. Over this put a layer of plastic foam about 1 inch thick or use cotton batting, or both, with the batting on the outside. Use an inner cover of light cloth and fix the covering material over this (Fig. 8-2C).

The cushions have to be planned in relation to the frame and any covering has to be applied to it. The seat cushion is nearly always a simple rectangular outline and the back cushion is nearly always a simple rectangular outline and the back cushion may also have straight edges, but in a chair where the arms are partly in front of the back uprights and are not wholly outside them, it may be better to step the cushion edge over the arm (Fig. 8-3). With foam or latex filling this shape is easily cut and the covering arranged to follow around.

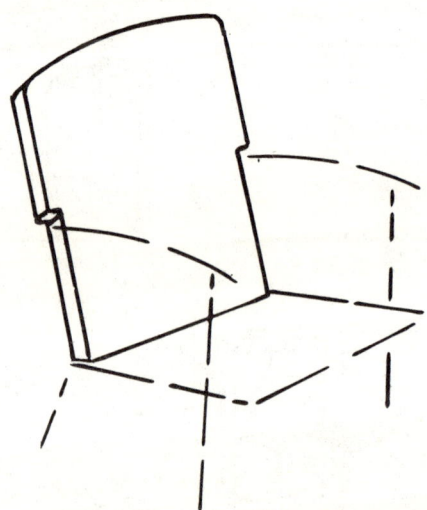

Fig. 8-3. It's sometimes best to step the cushion edge over the arm.

COVERING

Covering may have to be fitted around where the arms attach to the back or where the legs project (Fig. 8-4). Make sure the projecting or exposed wood has been given its polish, lacquer, or varnish far enough so no untreated wood appears. Cut the covering so there is enough to turn under. In most places it is

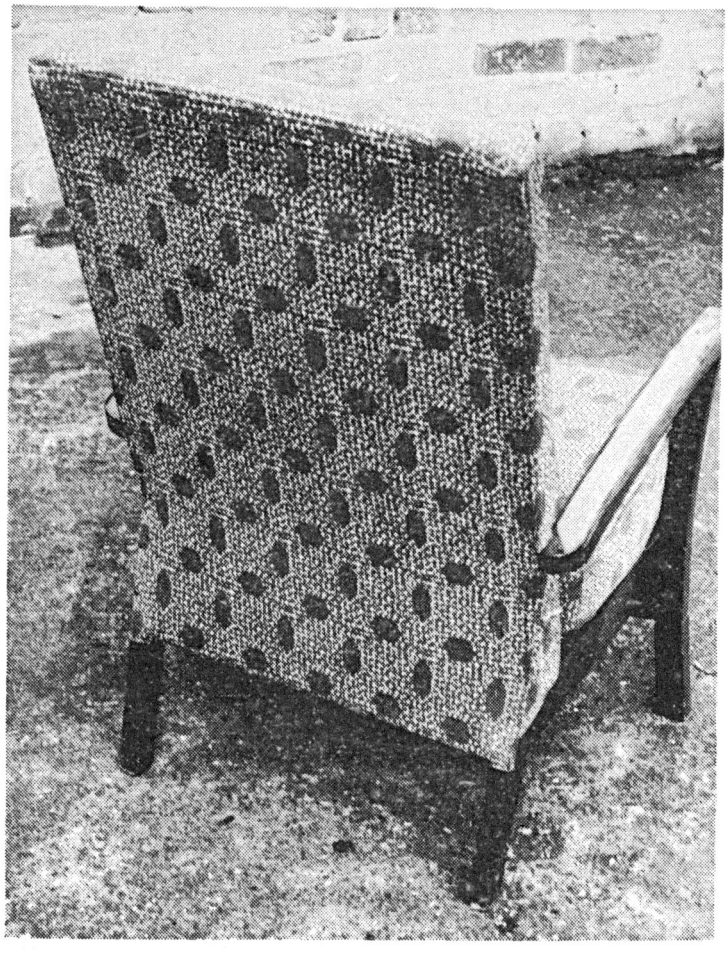

Fig. 8-4. The back springs are hidden by covering the back with the same material that is used for the cushions.

possible to arrange tacking on each side of the cutout so tension will be sufficient to hold a neat joint without tacks around its edges.

Another type of chair has the seat with the cushion replaced by a tight-covered upholstered seat. There may be a matching cushion above it or the seat alone may provide sufficient comfort. There could be traditional springing with hair or other stuffing, but it is more usual to use foam or latex padding over tension springs or rubber webbing.

In this case the rails should be at the same level and the covering is taken over them to fix outside (Fig. 8-5A). The stuffing is a piece of foam or latex thick enough for comfort, which means usually 4 inches at least. Edges are cut and rounded, being pulled down with strips attached (Fig. 8-5B) if a molded pad is unavailable. There may be thin foam fixed below if holes have to be covered and it may be necessary to edge some latex. This is the important part of the seat. There should be one or two layers of burlap or canvas over the springs. Bulk around the sides is reduced if this is tacked on the top of the frame (Fig. 8-5C). The stuffing pad goes over this and may have a layer of thin foam or cotton batting next, with inner and outer covers, which are carried down the outsides of the frames (Fig. 8-5D).

The edge may be merely turned under part way down the frame, and some decoration may be provided by nails or gimp (Fig. 8-5E). If the edge is taken to the bottom it can be wrapped under and tacked there (Fig. 8-5F), although the hard line of the edge can be broken by using a decorative edging with tassles (Fig. 8-6). If this is fixed with black gimp pins instead of tacks the fastenings are only visible from a close view (Fig. 8-7). How the covering is fixed to the back rail depends on design. It may be treated in the same way as the sides and front if it can be taken through below the back springing, or it may have to be tacked to the top of the back rail and this edge will be covered by the back upholstery or the loose cushion.

The front edge of any chair gets more use than the rest of the seat. Users often move forward to sit on the front edge. This means that the frame may be cut away and springs carried over to support a cushion with a good overlap (Fig. 8-8) or the cushion or seat swab itself may be strengthened along the front edge so it resists compression there and so the weight of a sitter does not push through to a hard line.

With traditional stuffing there would be fox edging, but if foam filling is used the edge may be built up with extra foam (Fig. 8-9A). With fixed seating the foam may be made oversize and pulled back to size so greater firmness is obtained there (Fig. 8-9B). A seat which comes up to a greater thickness near the front looks more luxurious and is more comfortable.

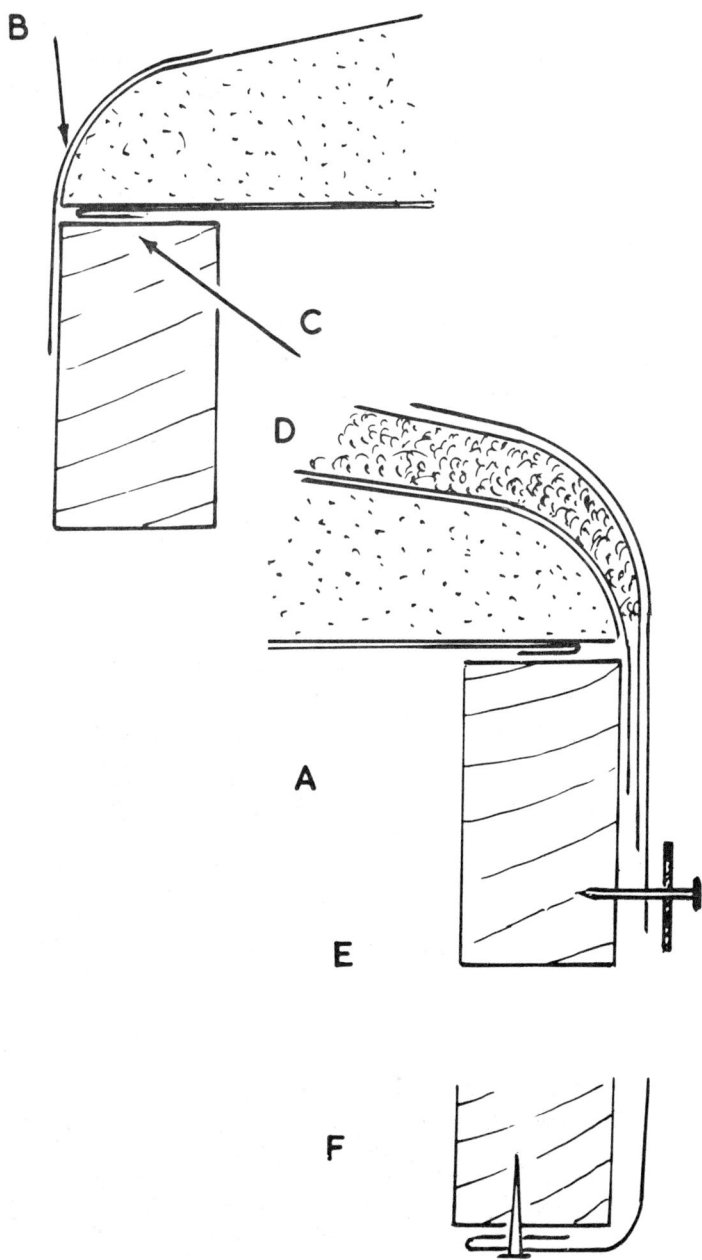

Fig. 8-5. A lounge chair may have its seat and back upholstered as well as using loose cushions.

Fig. 8-6. There are many decorative edgings. This chair has the hard line of an edge broken with a fringe.

Fig. 8-7. Gimp and other edgings can be fixed with adhesive and gimp pins, which are inconspicuous except on close inspection.

Fig. 8-8. The front of a seat has to be arranged so the weight of a user does not produce a hard edge. This chair has tension springs carried forward of a low front rail.

Another way of easing the hard line along the front edge is to round the edge with thin plywood bent over shaped pieces of wood, and let the stuffing be pulled over this (Fig. 8-9C).

FIXING CUSHIONS

Loose cushions may not always stay in place but they can be arranged with tapes or cords to fix them in. It is also possible to use snaps and other fasteners. These can be arranged on normal loose cushions with strips fixed to their edges, or it is possible to make a slip-over cushion that serves as a cover for the back. It rests against the back springs in the same way as a loose cushion, but a flap goes over the top and as far down as the rear seat rail where it is fixed with turnbutton fasteners.

Such a cushion can be made up with foam and the front seat can be piped (Fig. 8-10A). The rear seam may be plain. The front cover goes over in a continuous piece to cover the chair back (Fig. 8-10B). The filling may be a flat piece of foam or latex, although additional style and comfort can be provided by

157

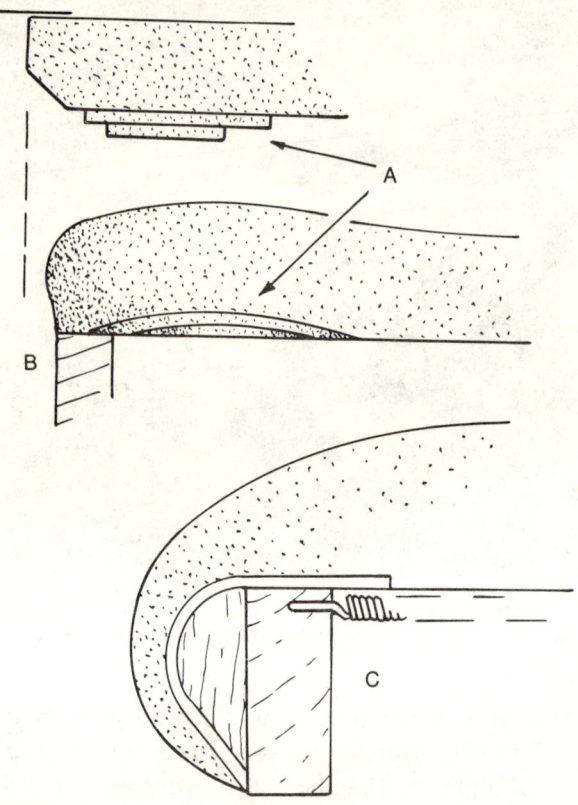

Fig. 8-9. There are several ways to ease the hard line along the front edge.

thickening to make a headrest. An increase in thickness at the base adds to comfort (Fig. 8-10C).

The cushion will have to be planned to suit the frame, but it will probably be best if the top comes a little higher than the frame so the wrapped-over part does not show at the front (Fig. 8-10D). The boxed edge cushion is seamed with the bottom open for inserting the padding (Fig. 8-10E). This edge is finally slip stitched.

There can be a strap included in the back seam at a point where it can be taken around the chair back (Fig. 8-10F). This may be a piece of the covering material sewn into a tube and turned inside out (Fig. 8-10G) if it is stiff enough, or a piece of webbing may be covered with thinner material. The strap ends join with fasteners, although the meeting point is covered by the back flap and it may be better to use a cord through grommets to give some adjustment (Fig. 8-10H).

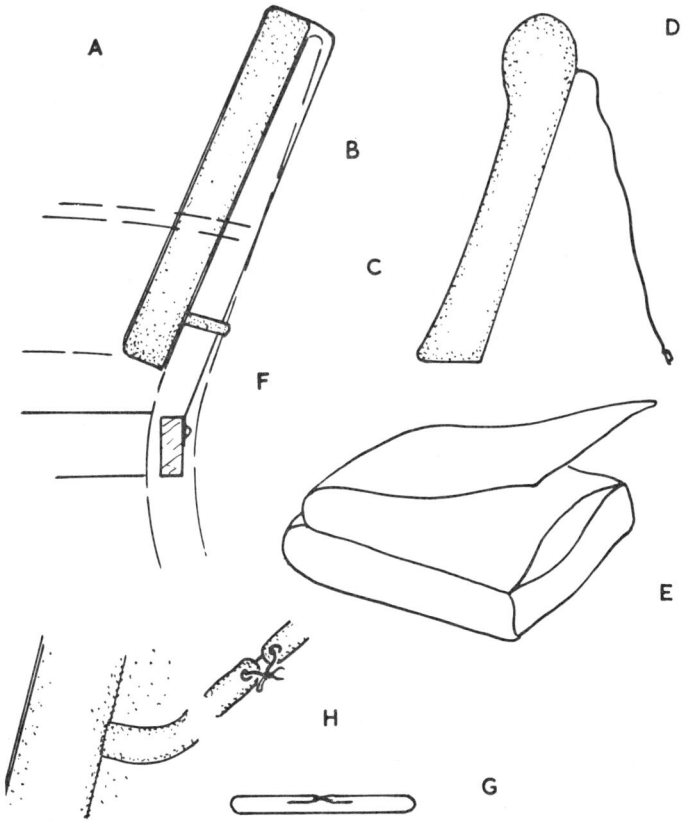

Fig. 8-10. Cushions can be fixed to prevent slipping. This one attaches to the chair back and its flap goes to the bottom rail.

The cushion should be given buttons on the front. Probably four will be enough. Their twines go through to flat buttons or pegs on the back (Fig. 8-11A).

The back flap has its edges turned in. It should be long enough to have a broad double turned-in edge at the bottom over the back rail (Fig. 8-11B), where it takes a row of turnbutton fasteners, with their bases held by wood screws to the rail. The turnbuttons can be made less obvious, if desired, by taking the flap under the back rail.

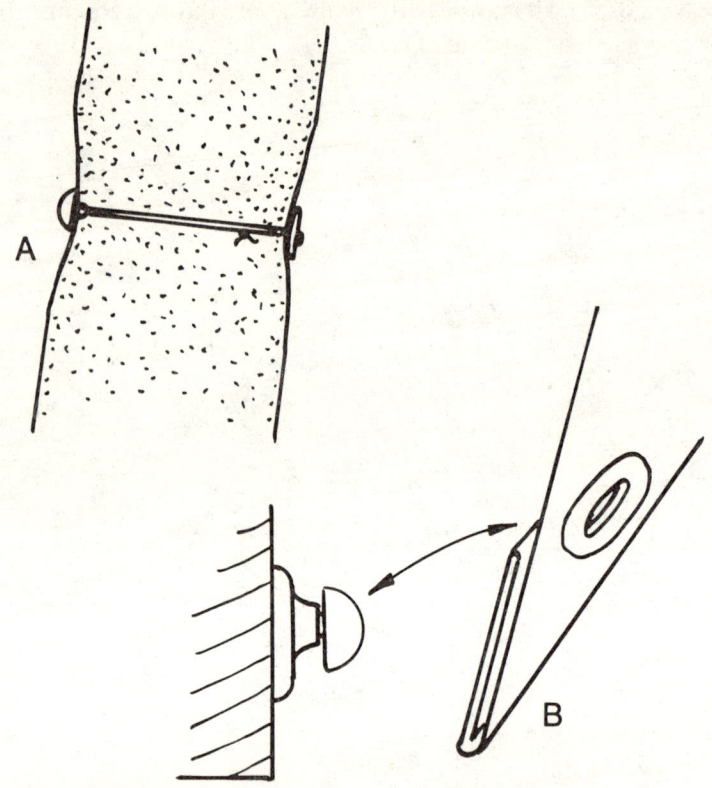

Fig. 8-11. Buttons and turnbutton fasteners may be used.

PADDED ARMS

It is common in this type of chair to have wood arms which contribute comfort by their shaping. They may be curved in both directions to conform to the expected positions of the user's arms. If they are nicely proportioned and well rounded this arrangement is adequate, but there are some chairs where a little padding is used on the top surface. This is not as much as might be used on a fully upholstered chair, but it gives softness where the sitter's arms will rest. The full length may be covered, or there may be padding at the forward ends only (Fig. 8-12A).

The narrow arrangement makes it easier to provide the padding in its own case and fix that, than to apply stuffing in position. There can be a cloth bag made up as a tube of sufficient size. It need not be specially shaped for the majority of arms. A piece of foam in one piece can be used, but it is easier to get a suitable degree of resilience by using foam pieces that are pushed in and arranged with a piece of wood. Then the end of the bag is sewn. Hair and other loose filling material can be used in the same way.

The bag is fixed down by wrapping over the cloth and the cover material (Fig. 8-12B), which may finish on the sides of the arm or be taken underneath. How the ends of the cover are dealt with depends on the shape of the wooden arm. The rear end may be tucked under the stuffing and held with adhesive or merely by the tension of the sides. If the front is rounded, the covering must be neatly pleated and turned under (Fig. 8-12C). The arm support must be cut around and the surplus cover material turned in.

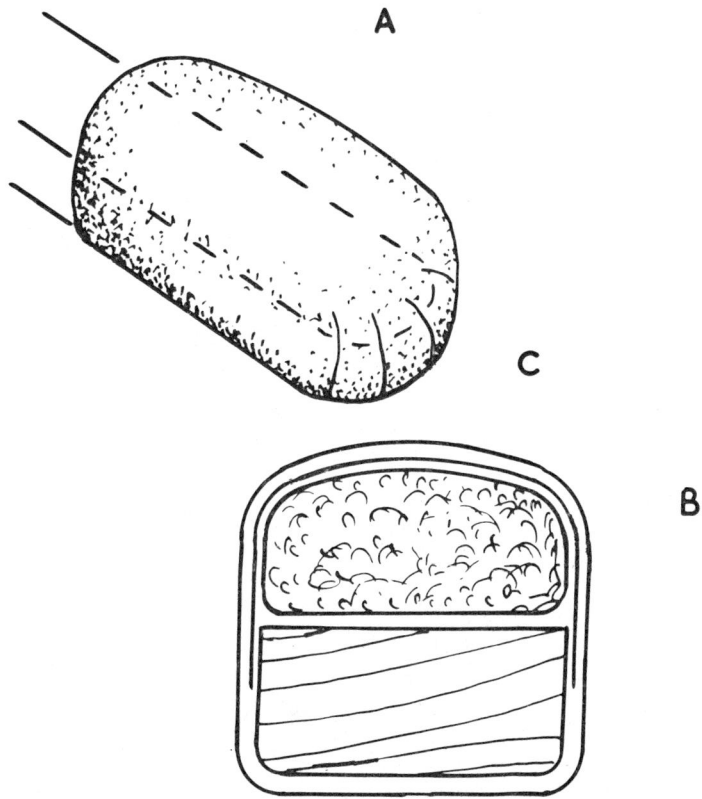

Fig. 8-12. The arm of a lounge chair can have a padded top.

SIDE PANELS

Sometimes the space between the side rails and the arms are filled with a panel, usually plywood (Fig. 8-13A). This could be left with the wood surfaces exposed and finished by staining and polishing with the rest of the woodwork. In that case it is not an upholstery problem, but appearance and comfort are improved if the panels are covered with the same material as the rest of the upholstery. This may lie flat on the wood or there may be some minimal padding included.

Covering is most neatly done before the panels are built into the chair. The plywood and its covering then fit into grooves (Fig. 8-13B). It is advisable to polish or varnish the parts

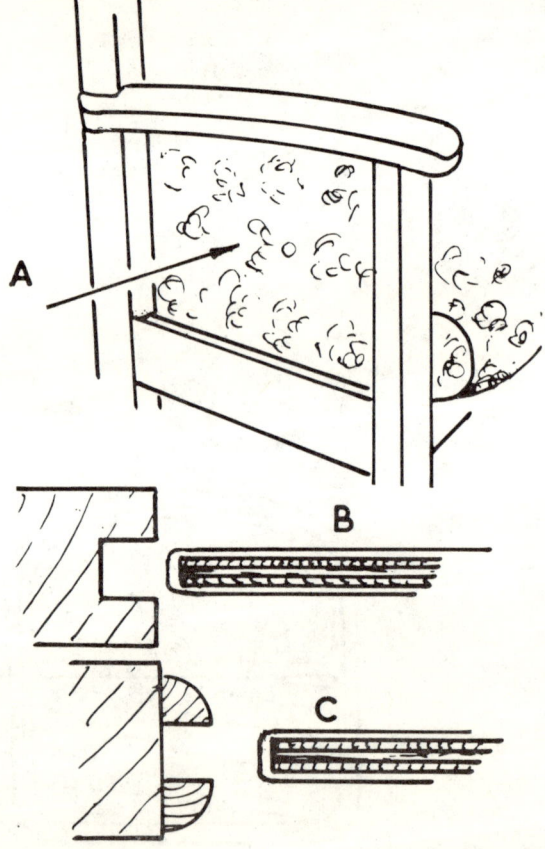

Fig. 8-13. If there is a side panel in a lounge chair it may be covered with the same material as the upholstery.

of the frame adjacent to the grooves before the panels are fitted, to avoid any risk of marking the cloth. Another way of fitting is to use quarter-round molding (Fig. 8-13C), which can be fixed to the frame with glue and panel pins or gimp pins.

Use an appropriate adhesive that is not too liquid. Care is needed to avoid the adhesive penetrating the cloth and making marks on the surface. If the covering material is light or an open weave, it may be advisable to first stick plain thin cloth to the plywood and attach the covering material to that.

If the covering material tends to stretch, care is needed not to distort any pattern by uneven pulling. So far as possible the cloth should be laid on the plywood without undue tension. However, it is necessary to avoid creases. With most cloths it is possible to lay the cloth on the wood and then press it down by rubbing with the hand from the center outwards. Let the cloth be too big and trim it to the plywood size after the adhesive has set. With vinyl or other non-porous material, lower it onto the adhesive-coated plywood from one side and follow through as it is put down by stroking with the other hand to force any air bubbles out (Fig. 8-14). As some of the adhesives that give the strongest bond are impact types that cannot be released, it is necessary to get the position and smoothness right the first time.

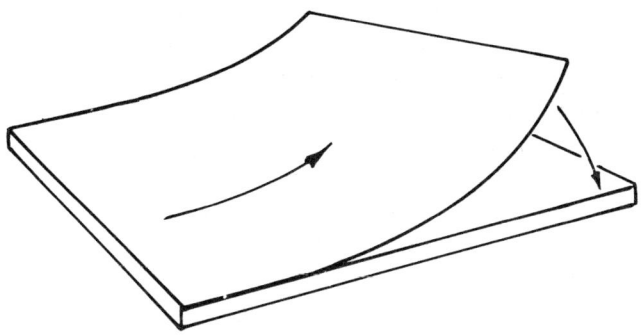

Fig. 8-14. Covering material must be applied carefully.

If the panel is already built into the frame, any cloth covering will have to be cut to size and cannot follow the plywood into a groove (Fig. 8-15A). It is advisable to make a paper or card template first. But with lighter cloths it is possible to press a

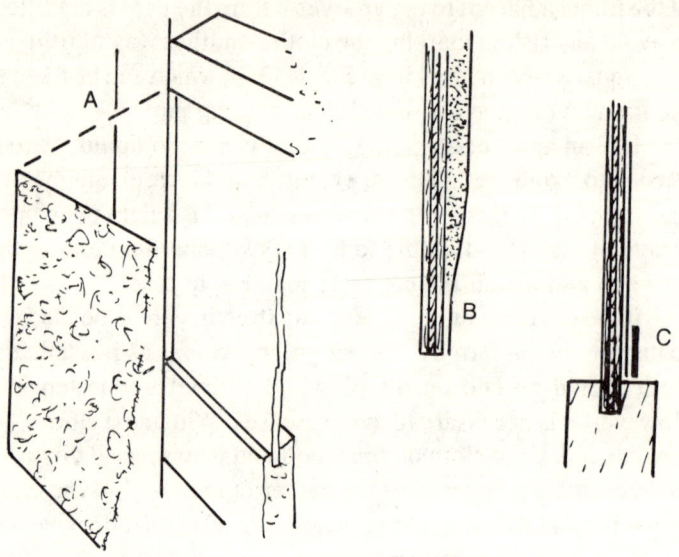

Fig. 8-15. Special steps must be taken if the panel is already built into the frame.

slightly oversize piece in on adhesive and trim around the edge with a sharp knife or razor blade.

If there is to be a little token padding this could be plastic foam 1/8 inch or a little more thick, held with a little adhesive. The covering can then be pulled down to the edges (Fig. 8-15B).

The covered panel can be edged around with gimp, although this is not usually done, but it may be appropriate if the cloth does not go into a groove and has not been accurately cut (Fig. 8-15C). If the plywood is thin it may not take gimp pins in the usual way, but gimp can be fixed with adhesive and thin pins can be taken right through and turned over.

Upholstered Arm and Wing Chairs

The chairs described in earlier chapters are mostly upholstered with cushions that lift out and have minimum padding at essential points only. Most lounge chairs have padded seats and backs, with either no padding on the arms or just a little token softening. At the other extreme are the fully upholstered chairs that give maximum luxury and comfort, but tend to be rather large. In between are chairs that often have seat and back padding similar to lounge chairs, but the arms have more padding and there may be wings to give added head comfort.

Where much of the upholstery of earlier chairs will lift out, in this type of chair some of it is fixed. For anyone starting to do upholstery, one of these chairs makes a good introduction to more ambitious work. There are a few techniques that should be understood.

If burlap or other cloth will show underneath a chair, it is usual to turn the edge under (Fig. 9-1A). The edge is folded at what is estimated to be the right place and tacks are put through the double thickness. This is satisfactory, but you have to get the size right before fitting. There are places inside where the burlap will not show. It is then more convenient to stretch it to the desired size and tension and put in a row of widely-spaced tacks. Then turn the edge over and tack again (Fig. 9-1B). There is no need to trim the final edge until after tacking. This method allows more even fitting; but having the cut edge outwards would not do for an exposed place.

It is sometimes desirable not to have tacks that show along the edge, and it is not always possible to cover a normally-tacked edge with gimp. There are two methods of tacking that can be used in this case, both called *blind* or *back tacking*. Strips of cardboard are needed. Pieces 1/2 inch or wider are suitable, depending on the type of cloth and the width of wood to take the tacking.

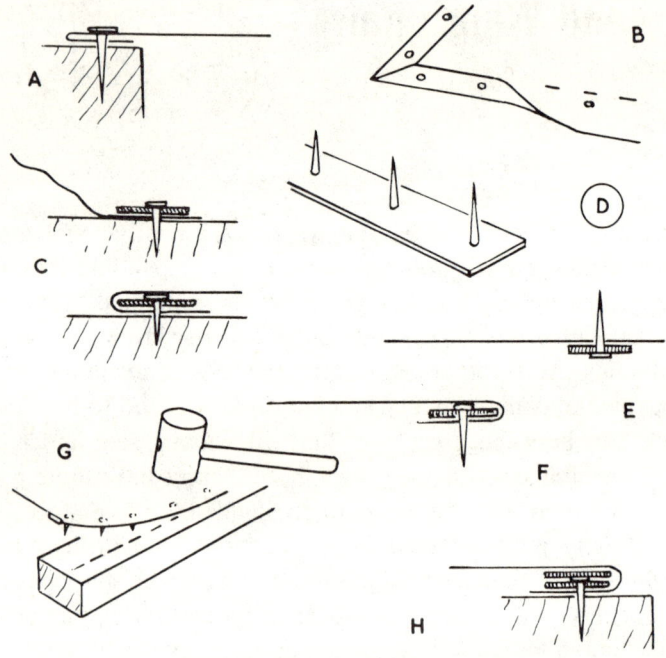

Fig. 9-1. There are several ways to hide tacks under fabric or wood.

In the simplest method the cover material is placed in position ready to fold back along the desired edge and fixed with a few widely-spaced temporary tacks. The cardboard strip is put with its edge where the cloth fold is to come, and tacked closely, so the cover can be pulled into place and there will be no fastenings visible along that edge (Fig. 9-1C).

It is possible to bend a straight strip of cardboard to follow a slightly curved edge, or card may be cut to a curve. For a curved edge it is necessary to experiment with the cloth and adjust the amount under the tack strip so the cover will be flat when pulled into place.

The other method can be used in similar situations. It provides a better spread of tension for material that may pull unevenly between simple tacking. It can be used with vinyl and other covers. Tacks are put through the cardboard strip first (Fig. 9-1D). The edge of the cover is pressed fully on to the tacks with a little surplus extending past its edge (Fig. 9-1E), then this is turned under with the folded edge along the intended line (Fig. 9-1F) and the tacks are driven with a rawhide or plastic mallet (Fig. 9-1G) that will not mark the cover, as might a hammer. Work along the strip with one hand guiding the strip as it is hit, then go back and pound again with the mallet to ensure the tacks all enter fully.

If there seems a risk that tack heads might mark or penetrate the particular material during driving, another piece of card can be put over the heads (Fig. 9-1H), or it may be sufficient to use a strip of masking tape or scotch tape. This would hold the tacks in the card during handling, in any case, if they tended to slip back.

A tack strip is sometimes useful inside upholstery, especially when the spread of pressure due to the cardboard will help cloth to fit more evenly around a shaped part, than it would if tacks were used without card. If stapling equipment is available, any of the blind or back tacking methods can be used with staples instead of tacks.

A similar idea can be used if a solid decorative panel has to be fixed. This may happen at the front of some arms, where a piece of plywood or stout cardboard is covered with fabric or may have its own front surface veneered or otherwise finished, yet fastenings through it would spoil the appearance. One or more tack strips are made and glued to the back of the panel (Fig. 9-2A), which can then be nailed into place by pounding the front with a rawhide mallet.

Blind tacking is convenient where there is piping or welt to come at an angle over wood. In some situations the meeting panels may be sewn with the piping included, then the assembly can be fitted over the wood. In this case it may be difficult to get the turned-in edges evenly arranged, so an unevenness will show through the cover. The alternative is to tack the seam. The piping is sewn to one cloth edge. This is brought up to the angle of the wood and the tail of the piping used to tack over the edge (Fig. 9-2B). The other panel is blind tacked so as to come close to the piping (Fig. 9-2C) to give a neat joint with no tacks visible.

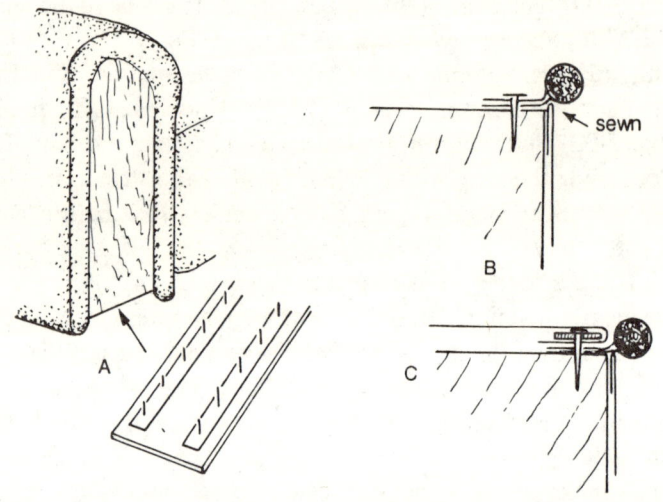

Fig. 9-2. Tack strips can be glued to the back of a panel. Seams can be tacked and piping used to hide tacks.

PADDED ARMS

It is the inside of the arms that needs padding for comfort, although in a fully-upholstered chair the outside will appear to be equally padded. It is possible to pad the sides and arms of a lounge chair while still exposing the wood frame to the outside (Fig. 9-3A).

In its simplest form the frame has a straight arm and the front leg is upright. If there is enough padding, the fact the straight lines are used will not detract from comfort. Such a design, with austere lines, looks well in a modern setting (Fig. 9-3B). The side panel can be filled with plywood, which has an outside finish to match the frame (Fig. 9-3C), so only the inside has an upholstered finish. Foam can be wrapped over the top and down the inside, but extra should be built up on top (Fig.

9-3D). This may carry a short distance down the inside and taper off. It may stop at the outside of the arm (Fig. 9-3E) or be wrapped under it, particularly if there is a cross member under the arm.

This will probably be sufficient padding, but cotton may be used over it, then muslin used to pull the padding to a smooth shape before the cover is put on (Fig. 9-3F). If the front of an arm extends over the top of the leg, the padding should be worked over it so as to give a neat curved front (Fig. 9-3G). How the covering is fixed depends on the desired finish. It could be tacked and the edges could be covered with gimp (Fig. 9-3H). Under the arms the cloth may be turned under and tacked inconspicuously (Fig. 9-3J). If there is to be no tack and gimp edge on the legs, the edges there can be blind tacked with a cardboard strip inside. Of course, this would have to be done before any other edge was fixed. At the bottom the edge will be hidden by the cushion so fixing is done to a strip above the one that supports the springs or rubber webbing (Fig. 9-3K).

If a softer side is wanted, plywood is omitted. Cover material is used and lined with burlap (Fig. 9-3L), then the arm is upholstered in the same way as with plywood. Another way of getting a cloth finish to the outside is to cover plywood or cardboard with covering material and fix this instead of the plain plywood panel. If a large chair has buttoned cushions, and if the pattern is to be carried through the sides, it is possible to include two or more buttons through each side. But it is more usual to make the arms without buttons. If buttons are fitted there will have to be similar ones at each side because both sides show. With the usual thickness of padding, the buttons would have to be pulled almost together with twine to get sufficient indentation at each setting.

Similar padding can be used with shaped arms. It may be advisable to make a paper template for the foam shapes, although if the shaping is not much, the foam can be fitted over the arm first and the part that comes inside can be trimmed to shape after folding over.

Completion of such a chair is similar to that for a lounge chair. The seat cushion should make a close fit between the padded sides. The rear cushion may be parallel between the

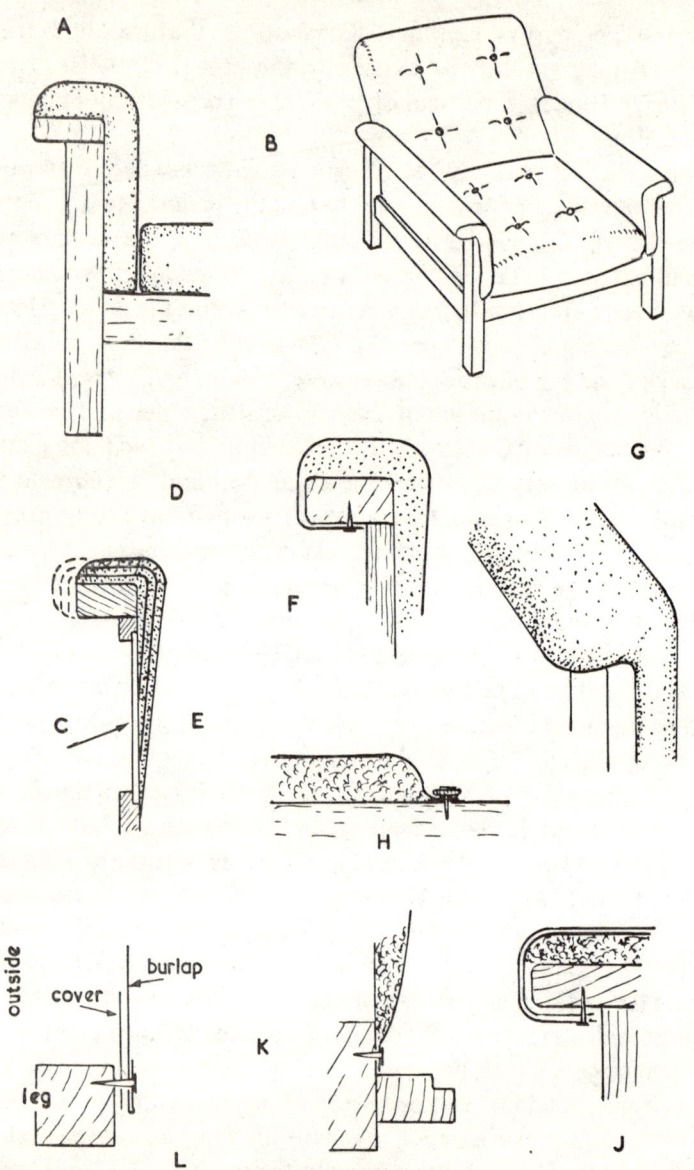

Fig. 9-3. In one form of upholstery, padding is provided on the areas located towards the body, but the wood is not covered on the outsides of the arms.

arms, but it will usually be better if it is stepped over them, so the lower part is a close fit and the upper part goes out to about the centers of the arms.

SADDLE ARMS

Another way of padding arms in a modern fashion is to arrange the upholstery to look as though it is a cushion wrapped over each arm, like a saddle (Fig. 9-4A).

The idea could be used with a frame having the arms built up from strips of wood joined together, but it lends itself particularly well to sides made of thick boards, usually plywood or particle board veneered attractively on one or both surfaces. Edges may be cut flat across and veneered or rounded and finished with a synthetic paint. With this sort of side to a chair, there will have to be some framing on the inside surfaces to take members that go across the chair.

With foam or latex filling a cushion may be made flat (Fig. 9-4B) and wrapped over, providing it is not too thick. However, this has the effect of thinning the filling where it is wrapped over, and it is along this edge that the most padding is required. If this method is used, the inner part of the cushion should go to below the seat cushion level and the outside may be semicircular.

Fix stud fasteners to hold the cushions in place (Fig. 9-4C). Closely fitting edges of the seat cushion will also help to hold the arm cushions. It is not usual to take them far enough back to fit against the back cushion, which will be full width, whether it is intended to be removable or it is a fixed upholstered back.

It is possible to upholster in position if a greater amount of padding is needed. There can be several thicknesses of foam wrapped over and fixed with muslin, using extra at the top and inside, with taper down the outside (Fig. 9-4D). The cover can be fixed by tacking, with gimp over the tacks (Fig. 9-4E). This may suit some designs, but it is not the finish for modern functional furniture. It may be possible to turn under the edges and fix them to the wood with adhesive.

For a luxurious thick saddle arm to combine with deep seat and back cushions, the cushion should be made to the saddle shape rather than being merely wrapped over.

The cushion should have boxed edges with piping around the outside seam, if that will match the other cushions of the chair. Make a cardboard or stiff paper template of an end of a cushion (Fig. 9-4F). The slot should be an easy fit over the wood arm. For square edges inside and out, both legs of the template will be the same, but for a semicircular outer shape, allow extra for the curve (Fig. 9-4G).

The inner part of the cushion may be plain cloth. Cut this to the intended shape against the wood (Fig. 9-4H). Allow about 1/2 inch all around for the seams.

Make the box edge from the template. For economy of material there will have to be joints at the bottom, inside and out. The thickness of the padding will determine the width needed, but for the type of cushion envisioned this will probably be about 3 inches. Add sufficient material for the seams.

The outside width will be the same as the inner part, but its length should be measured outside the thickness of padding (Fig. 9-4J). Some excess may be left on the part that will come inside the chair and this can be trimmed when that seam is made after the rest of the cushion has been assembled. Make up the cushion inside-out, taking in piping if necessary, but leave a part of what will come inside the chair to be sewn after the stuffing has been inserted (Fig. 9-4K).

Trim the foam padding and insert it, pressing it fully towards the outside curved end. Push it well into the casing so it does not thin around the bend. If it is slightly too long when the inner end is sewn closed, it will keep a good shape over the bend. There is no need for piping across the lower inner end as this will be hidden by the seat cushion.

If such a saddle cushion is big enough for a roomy chair, its surface area will be more than about one square foot and this is enough to warrant the use of buttons to prevent the outer cloth having a loose, uneven appearance over the filling. Two buttons outside should be enough (Fig. 9-4L). Ideally, the buttons should be covered with the same material as the cushion. If a button covering machine is unavailable, it may be possible to have them covered by someone with a machine. Otherwise, a plain button in a matching color can be used. Plain flat shirt buttons can be used inside.

Use a needle long enough to go through the cushion. If its eye is large enough to take two thicknesses of twine, put the button on the twine and pass both parts through at once (Fig. 9-4M), otherwise use single thread and take the needle through

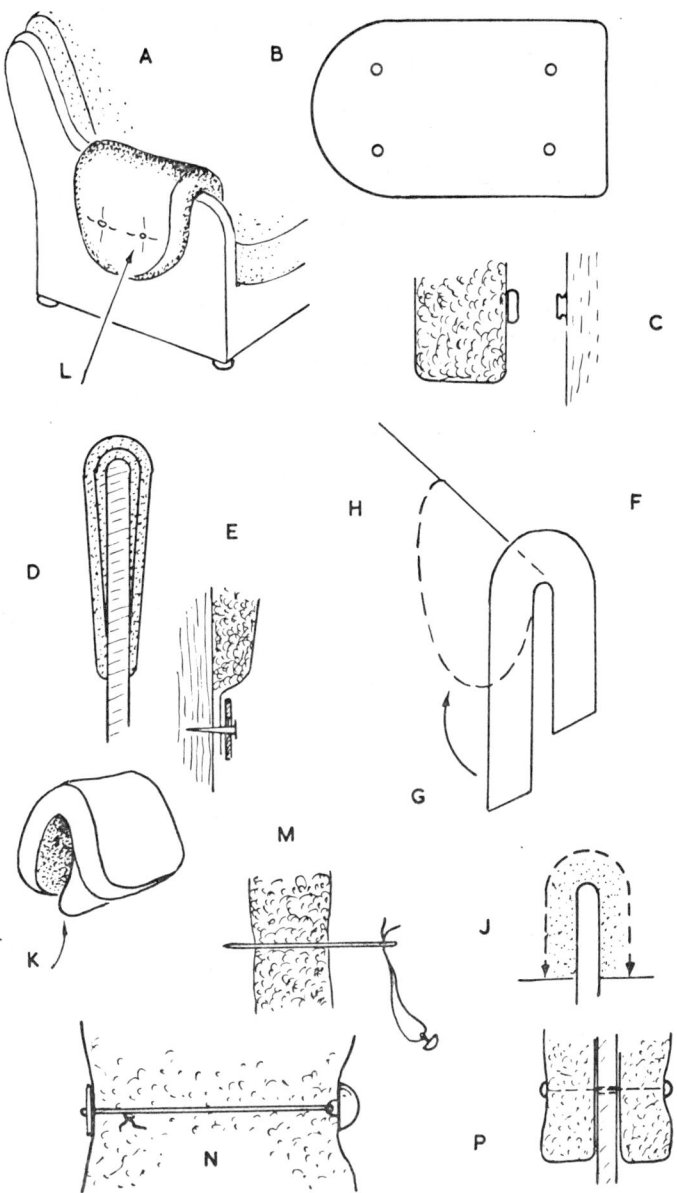

Fig. 9-4. One method of padding arms uses a cushion wrapped over like a saddle.

twice. Put on the inner button and joint the two parts of the twine with a slip knot. Adjust the twine to get the outer button just below the surface, then lock the knot. Compress the cush-

173

ion so the twine can be pulled to get the knot inside (Fig. 9-4N). The depth the button is pulled in should match the buttons on the other chair cushions. Fix press-stud fasteners under the arm cushions. Three under the outer flap should be enough, as the inner flap will be held by the seat cushion.

This type of arm padding can be used for any of the usual upholstery materials, but it looks particularly good in leather or vinyl, coupled with thick seat and back cushions to give a well-padded, comfortable chair of modern appearance.

Although the saddle cushions used as an example are semicircular outside and do not go back to the rear cushion, it is possible to use a similar idea for cushions that extend the full length of the arms and are parallel with the back as well as the seat cushions between the arms. A possible alternative method of fixing is to let the button twine go through holes in the plywood frame (Fig. 9-4P).

Foam is particularly suitable for padding arms. It may be possible to use felt, cotton, or any other of the prepared sheet materials, but it is unwise to use hair or any other loose filling material for any of the methods of arm upholstery described in this chapter. Loose filling is more appropriate for full upholstery, and even there has largely been superseded by foam and latex.

WINGS

Wings are characteristic of period and Early American chairs. They are less common on modern chairs, although their comfort is appreciated and some designs incorporate them. In some cases the wings are more ornamental than comfortable. They may then be made of plain wood or wood covered with fabric without padding. It is more usual to have wing frames that follow the outline, but are open in the center to give more scope for padding. In some early wings there is a double curvature so the flowing lines add to appearance and contribute something to comfort. Shaping in this way makes little difference to covering, except for the need to see that the covering material and stuffing are pulled into the hollows.

The frame may attach to the back only, but it is more likely to be joined to the arm as well (Fig. 9-5A) as this adds to strength as well as appearance. In normal use a wing should not have to withstand much strain, but the fact that it projects makes it subject to knocks. It is important that its design is strong and its joints secure.

How a wing frame is covered depends on its design, but it is convenient to regard it in two stages, with the inside getting covered before the outside. Wings are a prominent feature of a chair and it is important to give them a neat, attractive finish. It is usual for the inside upholstery to go around the front edge and for there to be piping or welt over the outer edge of the frame.

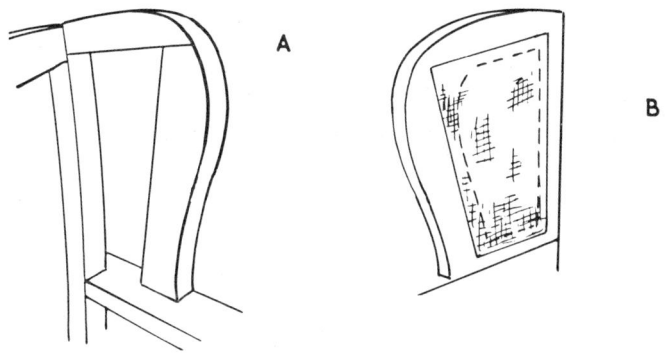

Fig. 9-5. Wings provide extra head rests and should be suitably padded.

If the frame is open, the first step in dealing with the inside is to cover the space with burlap, which may follow the shape or be cut with straight edges (Fig. 9-5B). This is turned over and tacked. A large wing may require one or more strips of webbing to provide additional support. A reasonably tight base is needed for the padding, but it should give under the weight of a head. If the wing is solid or has a plywood panel there is no need for burlap.

In a traditional wing the padding is made of curled hair, which is arranged to give a suitable shape and is held with twine through the burlap and with tacks around the edges (Fig. 9-6A). If the wing frame is solid there may be a layer of rubberized hair or other prepared stuffing, cut to the outline of the inner surface of the wing and held to it with adhesive or tacks. The loose hair can then be stitched to it. The hair stuffing comes to the edge of the frame, but not around it.

Cover the hair stuffing with cotton, using one or two layers. This should come against the back of the chair and be trimmed so it wraps over as far as the outer edge of the top and front of the wing frame. This is followed with muslin, which goes around the frame edge, to be tacked on the outside (Fig. 9-6B). What is done at the back depends on the design of the chair, but it can probably be taken around and tacked at the back. If not, it will have to be tacked close into the angle with the back cushion or padding. Adjust the muslin to bring the cotton and hair filling to an even shape and make sure that the pair of wings match. Use whatever number of tacks is needed on the outside to get a good shape. The tacks will be covered later.

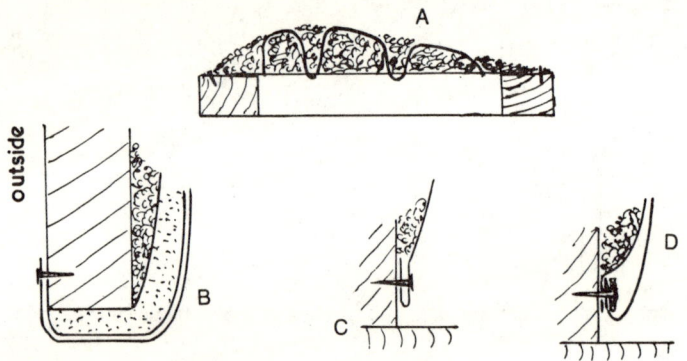

Fig. 9-6. Traditional wing padding is made of curled hair, covered with cotton and muslin, and tacked in various fashions.

Follow the muslin with the cover material, wrapped around and tacked in a similar way. When fitting the muslin and the cover, it is usually best to do the straighter edges first and tension the material from them. If the bottom of the wing comes against an arm, turn under the muslin and tack along this edge (Fig. 9-6C). If this edge will not be hidden by arm upholstery the cover material may start here with back tacking over the muslin (Fig. 9-6D). With some material, and with tight curves to the frame edge, it will be necessary to include some pleats. Arrange these evenly and see that opposite arms have the same pattern of pleats.

In a more modern treatment foam may be substituted for hair and may completely or partly take the place of cotton under the cover. With some covers there will be no need for muslin or other under-covering, but this relieves the cover of the need to pull any unevenness out of the stuffing. It holds the stuffing foam to shape and allows the cover to be given an even tension.

On the outside, the first step is to follow around the edge with piping, which can be made, as described earlier, from cover material. The edges of the piping are tacked to the outer surface of the frame, over the turned edge of the inner cover material (Fig. 9-7A). This goes from where the wing meets the arm around to where it meets the back. In some chairs the same piping can go across the top of the back to the other wing.

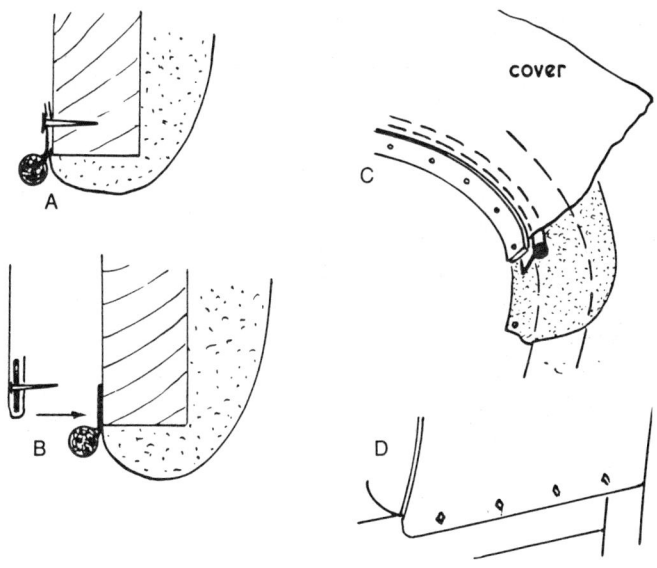

Fig. 9-7. The outside may also be covered.

If the wing frame is open, cover the space with burlap in the same way as on the inside.

The outside does not need padding. If the wing is solid there may be a piece of cover material flat on the wood, but usually there is a layer of cotton over an open frame.

To obtain a neat edge the cover is blind tacked close to the piping (Fig. 9-7B). Mark the shape of the wing on the cover and allow about 1 inch for blind tacking, as well as what is needed at

177

other edges. With the curved outline remember that it is the surface which has to come smooth so any creasing due to shaping will come under the tacking strip. You may have to cut into the edge to make it lie flat under the cardboard strip.

The cover is held in place with tacks widely spaced close to the piping. This is covered with cardboard strip about 1/2 inch wide (Fig. 9-7C). It may be possible to bend a strip around moderate curves by notching its edges, but it may be better to cut a piece to shape. Work around tacking the cardboard strip from the bottom upwards, keeping it close to the piping. It is the edge of cardboard that keeps the fold of the cover material close to the piping to make a neat finish.

Cut a piece of cotton to come close to the piping. Secure this to the frame with a few tacks or spots of adhesive. Pull the cover over the cotton. Get an even tension. What is done at the bottom, back, and the last few inches of the top depends on how the rest of the chair is to be treated. If further stages are not to be done immediately, use temporary tacks to hold the cover to the desired tension. If the chair back is to be covered, the wing cloth can be taken around and tacked far enough in to come under the rear cover. If there is to be no covering behind, the wing cover can be turned under and tacked to the frame. Along the arm there may be some arm or side covering that will hide a tacked wing edge, or it may be better to blind sew it to the arm cover. If there will be no adjoining cover the lower edge of the wing cover should be turned under and tacked or fixed with ornamental nails (Fig. 9-7D).

SECTION 2
ADVANCED UPHOLSTERY

Planning Materials Needs for Fully-Upholstered Furniture 10

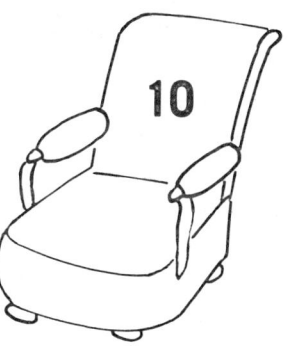

The various inner materials used in upholstery are much cheaper than the majority of cover materials. If more cotton, muslin, or other inside material is bought than is needed for a particular job, it should be suitable for another chair, stool, or sofa and will not be wasted. If an excess of cover material is obtained, the piece left over may prove a costly waste, however. Even worse, if the original order is not large enough and if more of the same material is not obtainable, the whole project could be a costly mistake. Consequently, careful planning is needed when it comes to covering material. The same planning will also serve as a guide to quantities of muslin and cotton needed.

Besides working out quantities according to the various shapes that have to be cut, it is necessary to allow for the pattern if it is prominent enough to need locating in particular places on the chair. Even if the pattern is made up of stripes it is necessary to decide which way they are to run on various parts, and cut the cloth accordingly. Some materials have a different appearance one way than another and this will influence cutting. With these problems it is often impossible to lay out the cloth as compactly as when plain cloth is used, so more will be required and there will be some waste.

So far as possible, joints in a single panel should be avoided. Vinyl and similar material should not be joined, but it is sometimes acceptable to joint woven cloth in inconspicuous places. It is also possible to use cheapter and plainer material where it will not show. The underside of a seat cushion is often treated in this way. Another way of economizing is to sew on *flys*. These are pieces of scrap or cheap material added to make up side in places where they will not show. A seat cover may be cut so the front and a short distance along each side is all in one piece, then there may be flys at the back and both sides, where they will be hidden in the finished chair (Fig. 10-1A).

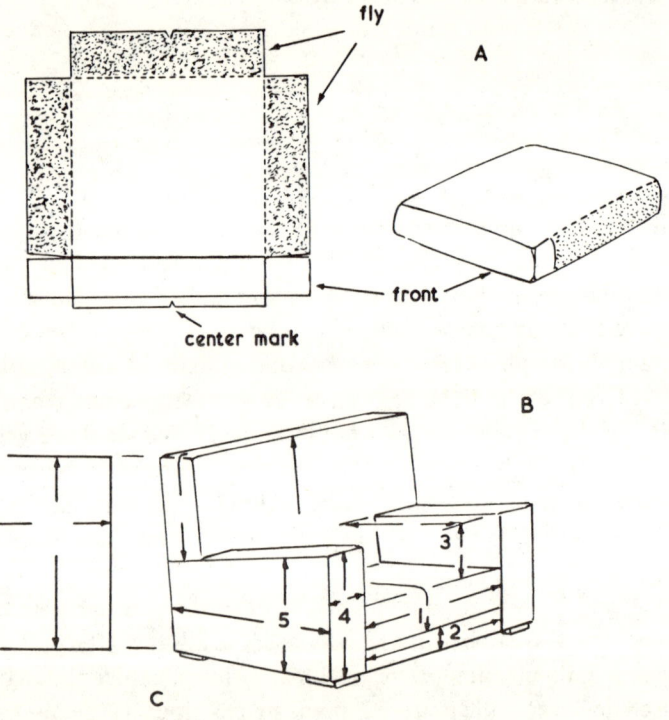

Fig. 10-1. Parts of a cushion that will not show may be made of other cloth as flys. Chair measuring should be done systematically.

The main joints in an upholstered chair are fairly obvious from the design. So far as possible cloth should be arranged to wrap over and follow on without joints, where this can be done, to allow the cloth to lay smoothly. However, it is sometimes possible to cut more economically by adding a joint. For instance, a boxed edge around a cushion might seem best in one length, but this could be quite long and it may be possible to cut the material better if there are two joints instead of one.

The way the cutting plan is arranged should take into account the largest pieces first. Then see how smaller pieces may be cut around them. If there is piping or welt to be made, that can be cut from offcuts after the main parts are laid out. Although piping should be cut diagonal to the weave, it need not be exactly 45 degrees if a waste piece will yield a greater length at a slightly different angle. The number of joints in a length of piping does not matter, although making piping is simpler if the lengths are long.

Many pieces of cloth have to be shaped. Although it may be convenient to treat them as rectangles using the greatest measurements, it is sometimes possible to cut curves to fit into each other and avoid waste. Paper templates may be made and moved around on the cloth, like a jigsaw puzzle, until the most satisfactory layout is found. Measuring is best done after the work has reached the muslin stage because at that point it is then possible to use a tape measure on the actual surface to be covered. If measurements have to be taken at an earlier stage, there will have to be a little extra allowed for variations that were not anticipated.

It is wise to establish a regular routine and keep to it when measuring. Always measure widths first and enter them first in any notes taken. If some of the measurements can be related to the width of material as supplied in the roll, this may assist in planning. Much material has been supplied in 54 inch widths, but with some imported material there are other standard widths. With the change to metric measure even other widths are possible. The quoted figure is not always exactly that of the cloth supplied, so measure what you have and work to what you find. Do not just rely on what is printed on the label.

MEASURING

Visualize the chair or sofa as a straight-lined assembly, (Fig. 10-1B), as some modern pieces may almost be. The measurements needed can be numbered. In each case there is a length and width (Fig. 10-1C). Wherever a simple seam appears, an allowance of about 3/8 inch will be enough for closely-woven fabric. Increase this allowance to 1/2 inch or more for loosely-woven or thick pile materials. If the cover has to go over an edge for tacking, allow 1 inch or whatever is necessary. It may be advisable to allow this much where piping is to come. For safety in shaping correctly, there should be more allowed on a curved edge or where the cloth has to be drawn to shape than when measuring a flat panel.

Use the end of the measuring tape close in to what will be the seam and take it to the other edge without tightening too much around a curve. In some cases, where cloth has to follow around a corner, this must be allowed for. At the front of a seat there must be enough material to go around the sides far enough to be hidden by the arm covering. Then more cloth may be sewn on in the form of flys.

Make a chart showing the number of the item required and what it is by name or number. Then record the size required, with the width first (Fig. 10-2A). Measure everything needed and list it all. Note what will be required for piping and any small parts, but list these at the end so they can be schemed into the final layout in a way that will use up spare pieces.

If there are cushions, get their sizes. A separate list may be made for other cloth that can be used for cushion bottoms, flys, and any other hidden places. The back may be made of a different material and recorded away from the main list.

With the straight-line shape used as an example there is little need for templates. The cloth may be marked out directly from measurements. Examine all the width measurements. Some of these may coincide with the width of the cloth, or come very near it. Try fitting these into place. It is useful to work on a scale drawing before actually marking the cloth, so different arrangements can be tried (Fig. 10-2B). Larger pieces may not allow much scope for variation in placing. They will have to be arranged in relation to each other so the best use of what comes beside them can be made for smaller parts.

Mark out the back of the material with chalk. Use a straight piece of wood as a guide for lines. A wooden yardstick is useful

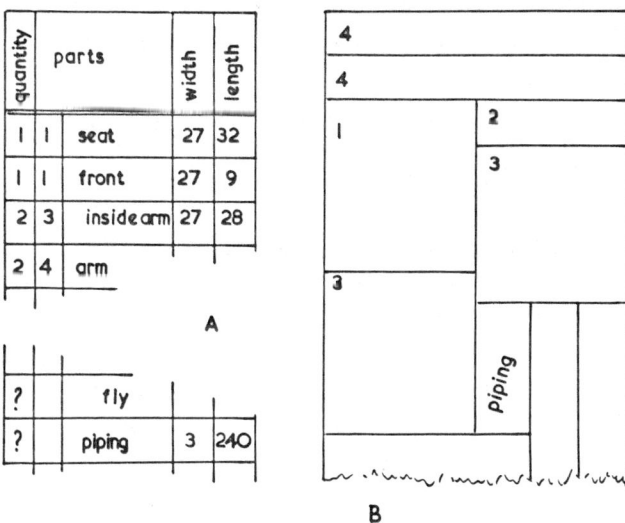

Fig. 10-2. Making a table of sizes allows fabric to be cut economically.

for this and for measuring, although an expanding steel rule is probably more convenient for most measuring. If the cloth has a pattern which cannot be turned around, mark the back the right way with something you will recognize, such as a 'T' for top. This is advisable with velvet or other piled material that has to be used one way to look right. Stick chalk that is rubbed to a chisel end (Fig. 10-3A) will draw a thin line.

Where there could be confusion between cut pieces, identify them with chalk marks. Cut them out with sharp scissors. Stack cut pieces in pairs face to face, so chalk from the back of one piece will not get on the face of another.

CURVED COVERS

Most chairs do not have severe straight lines. Some older ones had elaborate curves and cloth had to be cut very wastefully to cover them. Many modern chairs incorporate curves that are better marked out from templates than from measurements only. A typical club arm chair (Fig. 10-3B) has to be measured as shown, but it is helpful to make paper templates of the outside arm and the back facing (Fig. 10-3C). The outside arm pattern can then be marked for the inside arm as well. Allow for this going far enough down beside the seat. If there is to be a

185

seat cushion, much of the platform seat can be made of other material (Fig. 10-3D), as can be the underside and hidden parts of the cushion itself.

The arm panels have to be cut in relation to the weave of the material, but if the sloped edges are arranged to meet, they will use up less material than if square-cut pieces had been made to be shaped later (Fig. 10-3E).

Where a panel is symmetrical, as with seat and back parts, it is helpful to have the centers marked with darts or V cuts into the edge (Fig. 10-3F). Make them shallow enough to be hidden when a seam is sewn.

With traditional designs, such as a Victorian arm chair with rolled arms and wings (Fig. 10-3G), measurements have to follow curves. These curves may be compound, which means they may curve in both directions. The cloth therefore has to stretch and there will be pleats—both are requirements that do not allow for precise laying out. Some spare material will have to be allowed for.

The seat may have little shaping and its sizes may be obtained with reasonable precision. The width of the back may have to allow for varying curvature of the padding, so the edge line will not finish straight. It will usually be sufficiently straight to regard it as straight for the first cut (Fig. 10-3H). The back will probably have a flared outline, but will be flat, so a paper template can be made. Wings will require a paper template. Allow for the inner cover to wrap over the front and top edges, but the outer cover will stop at the edges. It is possible that its bottom edge will wrap under the arm, however. (Fig. 10-3J).

The amount of cloth needed for an arm is found by measuring back to front, with enough allowance at the back go right into the joint with the covered back. At the front of each arm the cloth usually has to wrap over with pleats, so enough material has to be allowed for this (Fig. 10-3K). However, a rectangle of the size obtained may cut wastefully. With some elaborately curved arms some part of the final shape may actually go outside this first rectangle. If you use soft paper that will wrap around reasonably closely, you will be able to find the shape of cloth to be cut, with reasonable accuracy. It may be better to use some scrap cloth to make a template, but avoid using anything with undue stretch.

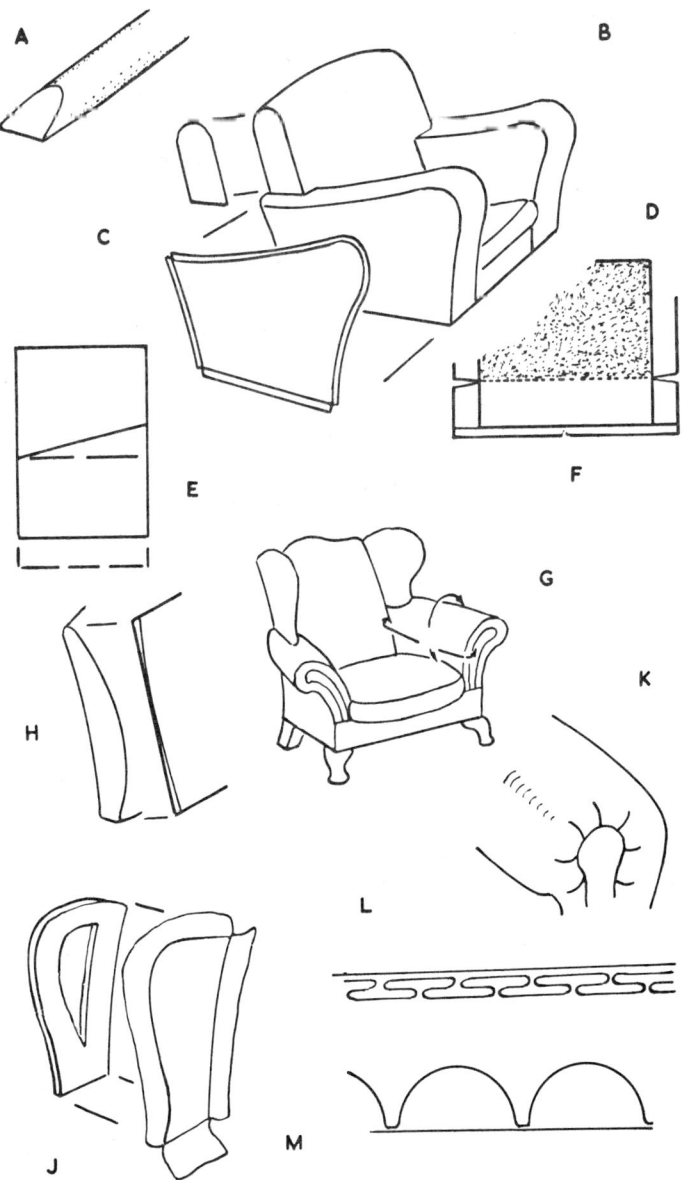

Fig. 10-3. Shaped surfaces require careful measuring and cutting, with allowances at edges for such things as flounces and channels.

If there is to be deep buttoning, some material allowance has to be made for this. The cloth has to go on looser in order to allow for pulling in at the buttons. If there is decoration by pleating or the use of *flounces* (Fig. 10-3L), you will have to allow enough material for this, too. In fact, this is a situation where sufficient spare material is advisable because the final make-up is unlikely to come exactly according to calculations.

Another place where measurements can only be regarded as approximate is in *channelling*. If the series of tubes to be stuffed are parallel, the overall width is found by measuring around the intended curves (Fig. 10-3M). Complications come when there is shaping so the lower part of a channelled chair back has a lesser distance around than the top, creating a conical effect. If there is curve in the height as well, the shape and size cannot be found very exactly by measurement. Some waste would have to be expected. If there are several chairs being made, though, the first chair will provide a guide to the way the cloth should be cut on other chairs.

Skill in planning for materials comes with experience. Time spent the best layout scheme for cutting the material is obviously well used. Although a beginner may be tempted to allow for too much material, this is obviously better than making too little allowance. If very little loosely-woven cloth is turned in at a seam, it may pull away.

Cowhides and morocco leather from goats are not often used because of the expense and the availability of vinyl and other materials that may have a leatherlike appearance. As real leather comes from animals, it suffers from uneven sizes and shapes and the fact that it may vary in thickness and have flaws due to injury to the animal. Leather has to planned for use very carefully and parts have to be cut to templates. At the same time, the best parts must come where they show and will get wear, while parts that are uneven in thickness or contain flaws may have to be used in less obvious places. Joints may have to be arranged where they will show least. The size of the original animal governs the size of a piece of leather, so large chairs will almost certainly contain some joints. In short, covering with leather should only be tackled after you have experience in marking out, cutting, and fitting other materials.

Fully Upholstered Chairs, Traditional and Modern

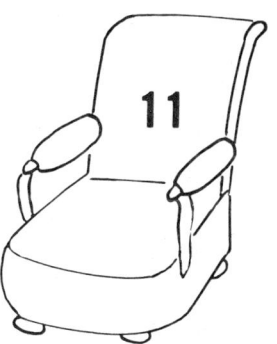

Designing a padded seat is a basically simple project, yet the variations seem almost limitless. Comfort comes from spreading the points of contact over as large an area of the body as possible. The greater the area there is in contact, the less weight there is on any particular part. This means that a shaped, rigid seat that conforms to the body pattern should be as comfortable as a smaller padded one. This only applies if the body does not move on the seat, though. As no one is likely to remain still for long, a shaped rigid seat ceases to be comfortable in any other position. This is where padding gains in efficiency; padding moves and will still conform to the body shape in the new position.

There are many seats that depend mainly on their shaping to give comfort. A flat bench supports the body on a few square inches of bone and soon becomes uncomfortable. The old shaped tractor seat, that conformed to the average-shaped person, was just as hard. But because a much greater area of seat was in contact with the body, the whole thing was much more comfortable, even when the tractor or implement was bouncing over rough ground. The same reasoning applies to a saddle for a horse, which has little resilience, yet provides comfort combined with control. In modern furniture some of the molded polystyrene and fiberglass seats rely on their shape for comfort and the amount of padding is negligible compared with more traditional frames.

The basic requirement of upholstery is to provide padding that will allow the body to press against it and give a good area of surface contact that will support without stiffness. If there is a firm backing, the padding must be thick enough to prevent the body pressure from going through to touch the hard back. Some resilience may be given by webbing and springs, but the upholstery above this provides the bearing for the body.

As gravity comes into the design, downward pressure is greater than that in other directions. This means that the padding of the actual seat should have to withstand greater loads than any other part of a chair, and should therefore be more generously upholstered. The arms also have loads to bear due to gravity, but they only have to provide comfort for the user's arms, and often intermittently, so arm upholstery need only be fairly firm and not very thick. However, well padded arms give a luxurious appearance, so you may want to make them thicker than is strictly necessary.

Although it may be argued that it is better for health and posture to have a rigid upright back to a chair, most people expect to lounge in a position that allows their body to become quite curved. This means that back padding needs to be thick enough and have enough resilience to allow the user's back to take the curve that he regards as comfortable.

There are chairs with ample upholstery that do not come much above waist height, but for comfort the chair back should be high enough to give support to the head. This has to be designed so the head part is correctly located, even when the body is relaxed deeply into a soft chair back.

Wings are less common on modern chairs, but they may be used as a decorative feature. If the head gets support even when it rolls sideways, this is obviously a gain in comfort. At one time the wings prevented drafts, but in a modern home they are unlikely to be called on for this purpose.

Size is also a consideration. If the seat is so deep from back to front that a person sitting on it is prevented by the angle under his knees from reaching the back—however comfortable that back may be—the chair is unsuccessful. Similarly, the feet must reach the floor, the chair arms must not be so far away that they cannot be used, and the back must not be contoured to suit a giant. There have been individually shaped chairs designed for particular persons, and such chairs may make an interesting project, but most furniture is designed to suit average people.

It is interesting to note that average people now are bigger than average people of only one hundred years ago. Much antique furniture will be found rather small for a modern user. Most people grow many inches taller than their ancestors. This is particularly noticeable if an old house is visited. Most door heights in such homes were intended for shorter people.

Besides size, there are angles and shapes to consider. Thick padding will allow for various postures that differ considerably from the angles of the frame underneath; but with more moderate padding, the shape of the frame plays a large part in determining the comfort of the finished chair. A dining chair has a seat parallel with the floor and a back that is not far off from being upright. The user's legs are near upright and the seat height is determined by leg length. As a chair becomes designed with a goal of greater relaxation, the seat gets lower and slopes back. With that there has to be some slope of the back. There is more slope if complete rest is intended than if the user may be expected to read. Some chairs have adjustments to their backs to permit various angles, but most have compromise angles and depend on the user adjusting to positions that the thick padding permits.

Most chairs are planned with the assumption that the user's feet will rest on the floor. If he wants to raise his legs, he will use a stool. Few older chairs made provision for attached leg rests; but modern recliners have adjustments to allow differing back angles and the raising of leg supports, so that anything between a near upright sitting position and a full-length, near-horizontal posture can be arranged.

Another way of arranging varying angles and a different approach to comfort was to mount the chair on rockers, maybe directly on curved bottoms that rolled on the floor, or by a spring arrangement over a base which did not move.

This feature points to another design requirement—stability. The base should normally be outside most other parts of the chair and certainly outside the parts occupied by the user, no matter how much he moves or how awkwardly he uses the chair. Most chairs have an ample area bounded by the leg positions, but this is a point that has to be watched with chairs that have reclining backs or can be adjusted to different extensions.

Nearly all chairs stand on four legs. In the usual modern house with flat floors, such a chair should stand firmly. If the number of legs is increased, slight variations of floor level become more apparent and a long sofa with six legs may have perfectly true bottoms to them, yet be found to need packing under one or more legs to prevent wobbles.

The leg arrangement that will stand without wobbling on any floor is a tripod. The old-fashioned milking stool had three legs to stand firm on the rough cowshed floor, and some chairs from pioneer days had three legs to suit earth floors.

FURNITURE PERIODS

It is not so very long ago in history that upholstery as we know it was found only on furniture of the comparatively wealthy few. Not much further back, even the wealthy and important people in many countries used extremely plain and hard furniture. Any padding was made of temporary cushioning with animal skins or anything else at hand. There were exceptions and some early civilizations did have padded furniture, but the types of furniture that may be regarded as earlier generations of our present upholstered furniture only go back a century or so.

In many early examples there does not seem to be much appreciation of the purpose of upholstery. There may not even have been much appreciation of the purpose of the particular piece of furniture, which was regarded more as an example of the craftsman's or designer's skill and ingenuity in producing an ornate specimen than in making something that was fit for its alleged purpose of support and comfort. In these cases, any upholstery used was of a token type. It was not permitted to interfere with a piece of carving or other decoration that may have detracted from comfort.

Periods that need to be noted are those of Louis XIV, XV, and XVI in France; William and Mary, Georgian, Queen Anne, and Victoria in England, plus the variations that took place at these times in America which usually is described as Colonial. Besides the furniture types identified by the monarchs of the time, there was the furniture of the great cabinetmakers, such as Chippendale and Hepplewhite. Besides the prolific output of some of their own workshops, many of these designers and cabinetmakers produced style books that were used by others as guides to make similar furniture. There is, as a result, a great amount of furniture described as Chippendale or another of the great furniture names. Such furniture may be of considerable value, so any re-upholstery undertaken on these pieces should be of a high standard and in the right materials, if the value of the piece is to be retained. If there is any doubt about the ability to do a successful job, the work should be passed to a specialist for attention.

Many of the designs of these earlier days are still being used for reproduction furniture. There is no attempt to pass the chairs off as antiques, but where an old design is obviously good it is sensible to work to it again. On such reproduction furniture the upholsterer may use modern materials. The chair is a new thing, even if it is based on an old design, so work on it should take advantage of progress in materials. This means that a reproduction chair could have joints held with a stronger glue and a covering of synthetic material which will wear much better than the older materials, as well as foam or latex filling that will be more comfortable and keep its shape for much longer. Of course, an old chair may be given modern upholstery, but only if it is of no great value to start with. If it has an antique value, renovation must be made with suitable materials. The use of modern materials on a genuine antique would reduce its value.

Much older domestic furniture may never rate much value as antique. Some of it will have passed through several generations and been repaired and recovered at various times. If it has reached a stage where common sense decrees that it should be discarded, taking it apart is a good education in traditional methods. The old techniques can be followed back as far as the frame. It may be that if the frame is sound, the chair can be rebuilt using traditional or modern materials and methods. Such a reproduction chair may be more valuable than one made on a modern frame, and it could be more comfortable.

If styles are followed through to the present day it will be seen that the coming of mass-production and factory methods in the early part of the twentieth century resulted in a lowering of design standards at first. Much of the furniture of this early period showed attempts to adapt the former hand methods to machine methods, or to regiment the hand worker into quick output, quantity-production with quality coming second. Most furniture of that time had little to commend it. Of course, there was some good early twentieth century furniture, but it is necessary to be selective if chairs of that time are to be taken as examples to copy or restore.

Later, the values of machine methods became appreciated and furniture was made to take advantage of the new techniques. Hand methods were retained where they could produce better results. In this way new styles evolved that were of a good standard, and they were able to take their place as good followers of earlier styles. In fact, they opened up new designs that were not copies of earlier models, but had character of their own.

A further step came with the introduction of plastics and synthetics towards the middle of the twentieth century. In many ways these materials revolutionized upholstery as well as many other crafts. There is, and always will be, a place for wood and natural fabrics, and they may always be appreciated as the highest quality materials, but there are many plastics and synthetic materials that have qualities that justify their use, and not just as substitutes for natural materials. A synthetic used where a natural material would be better is misused, and the object produced can only be regarded as one of inferior quality. But if the design takes advantage of the qualities of the new material, that practice constitutes good design. Much furniture of the latter half of the twentieth century is recognizable as a style different from what had gone before. Examples are the chairs based on frames of expanded polystyrene or fiberglass, which can be given shapes probably impossible with wood and conventional upholstery. Others are foam-filled chairs of comfortable, but unusual shape, on plastic or tubular metal frames.

Another development that has affected later twentieth century design has been the development of wood glues of exceptional strength and waterproof qualities never previously achieved. Besides making possible very strong wood joints, these glues have permitted laminations of considerable strength, so there are upholstered chairs with parts of laminated frames exposed. A shaped, laminated part can be much slimmer than one cut from solid wood to obtain the same strength, so a lighter chair is produced. With the grain following the laminations instead of crossing the shape in parts of curved work, greater curves are possible than would have been wise in solid construction. A decorative feature can be made of laminations in different woods, so there can be lines of different colors or grain markings. In fact, exposed laminated frames are a design feature of the period.

CHAIR DESIGNS

Of all modern designs, the club chair is probably the one that best adopts the basic design requirements for comfort, without concession to appearance or variations to feature special frames or decorative items. The seat is amply padded, sized, and located according to height. The back allows for most postures in comfort, and the arms give comfort to the sides of the body as well as to the user's arms. Any attractiveness in appearance is due mainly to the shape, which portrays fitness for purpose (Fig. 11-1), and the quality of cover material.

Fig. 11-1. The club chair, a commodious modern design, stresses abundant padding and forearm comfort.

Towards the other design extreme is an upholstered chair of the Victorian era. In those days it was expected that every piece of wood would be decorated in some way, possibly with veneer, but more likely by carving. Plain wood was considered unfinished. Today, we would be happy to enjoy the beauty of the grain, but the Victorians wanted to get into that wood with chisels and gouges to produce stylized leaves or other carved decorations. This reached the stage where upholstered furniture was expected to have enough exposed wood for the carver to exercise his art, even if this meant a reduction in the comfort provided by upholstery.

Such a chair might have a seat with ample cushioning, since that area provided little scope for carving, but the back might have just a padded panel for the middle of the back and another for the head. The fronts of the arms were considered places for carving (Fig. 11-2). The chair had some comfort, but it looked more like a royal throne. Its severe stance and lines seems to

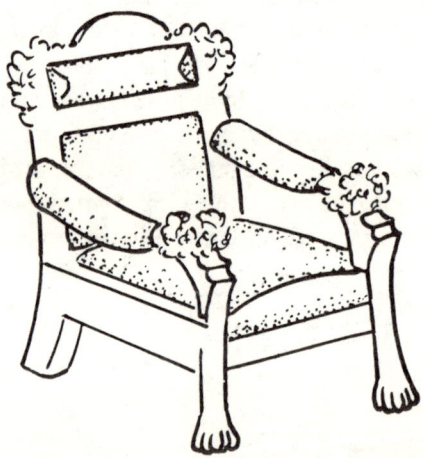

Fig. 11-2. The Victorian chair, though somewhat short on comfort, was marked by an austere elegance.

have suited the Victorian dress and attitude. One of these chairs may now have antique value so its upholstery could require attention; but if comfort is the goal, new work on it would probably not be worthwhile.

A little further back than Victorian days there was Georgian furniture that came before the preoccupation with carving.

Its upholstery had a greater coverage and the only exposed wood was the legs. These might have been turned in each case, or perhaps only the front legs were turned, leaving the back pair square. There was a severity about the lines compared with modern chairs, but the proportions were graceful (Fig. 11-3). When a modern chair is required without the bulk of a club chair, but with upholstery all round to give greater comfort than a simpler lounge chair, a modification of this Georgian design may be a good choice. The straight back can be changed to one with a frame adapted more to body shape, but the proportions can be kept the same to give a pleasing appearance.

Fig. 11-3. Pre-Victorian chairs are apt to look to use like modern chairs with the padded cushions removed.

Many modern chairs have their full upholstery complemented by seat cushions that can be lifted out. There may also be a back cushion that lifts out. In both cases the cushions are fitted and they form part of the chair. If loose cushions of plain shape are used additionally, that may mean that the basic upholstery is not as good as it should be. Much upholstered work of modern times comes in sets as a three-piece suite—two easy chairs and a two- or three-seat sofa or love seat—with similar upholstery throughout. This makes an attractive feature in a room. The problem is, though, any re-upholstery that has to be done to one damaged piece may have to be done to the other two pieces as well, in order to maintain a uniform appearance.

Many of these modern pieces are based on the club chair, but with some concessions to decoration. The outline of the back may have a curved shape. The arms may be covered in a way that gives a flared shape (Fig. 11-4). The cloth cover may be of a texture and appearance more suited to a home environment. Instead of using simple piping or welt there may be a loose or braided appearance. Buttons covered in the same material may make a pattern and be pulled quite deeply for special effect in some materials. They could also be used in places where they are not strictly needed to retain stuffing. There may be a fringe or flounce almost to floor level, so the legs are hidden.

Fig. 11-4. A modern piece based on the club chair emphasizes softness, warmth and domesticity. Note the use of ornamental buttons and fringe.

The wing chair and its accompanying sofa have followed through from Queen Anne days and are still popular in modern versions. In a modern chair the seat may project forward and have a loose cushion. The arms may have shaping or be fairly plain, while the back may also be plain. The wings may no longer have the double curvature found in the older chairs that started the fashion (Fig. 11-5). Modern chairs often do not stand far above floor level so legs are little more than blocks of wood, but if they have any length they are usually tapered and plain.

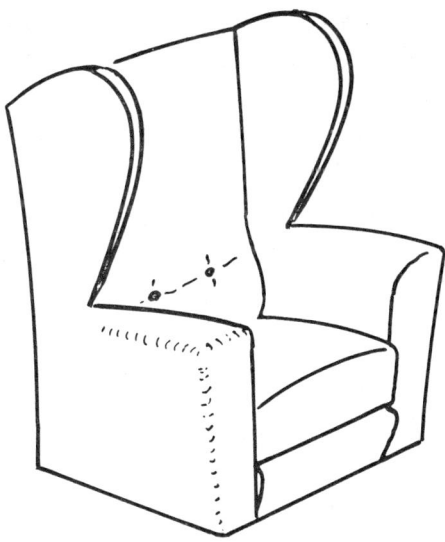

Fig. 11-5. The wing chair provides a certain amount of seclusion to the sitter. The projecting sides are fine for solitude but an impediment to peripheral conversations.

Compared with this new version, a reproduction of a period wing chair will be seen to have more curves to the upholstered parts. The legs could be turned or are more likely to be of the cabriole type, either carved with claw and ball feet or with a stylized leaf decoration. In some of these early chairs the arms did not come as far forward as the seat, to better accomodate the flowing and voluminous skirts of the period (Fig. 11-6). A fitted seat cushion was shaped around these shortened arms. The same cover material might be used all over, although there was a preference for plain material outside and a heavy quality material for the rest of the chair, with a more pronounced and vividly-colored pattern than would usually be favored by most people today.

Chairs based on wood frames have usually been of the type with back and arms joined at angles to the seat. This was largely because of practical considerations of construction. The early frame makers did not have the facilities to make elaborately

Fig. 11-6. This new version of the traditional wing chair incorporates shortness of legs and arms and consequently exaggerates the height of the back.

shaped frames for carved chairs. There were some curved wood frames, notably German, in which much skill and care had gone into joining wood parts so the resulting chair was without angles between the seat and its arms and back. Another way of getting a wrap-around effect as well as some compound curvature to the combined back and arms was to use an iron frame above seat level; but this needed special skill. The attachment of the various stages of upholstery had to be different and iron frames did not achieve much popularity.

Of course, not every traditional chair was intended to give support to the head. The back might be made in the same way as a higher chair, but if the back and arms were nearer the same level it was possible to follow the curve around to make what is called a *tub* chair (Fig. 11-7). This frame could be made by older methods, using several pieces lapped together for the curved rim, while in a modern version this is a place for lamination.

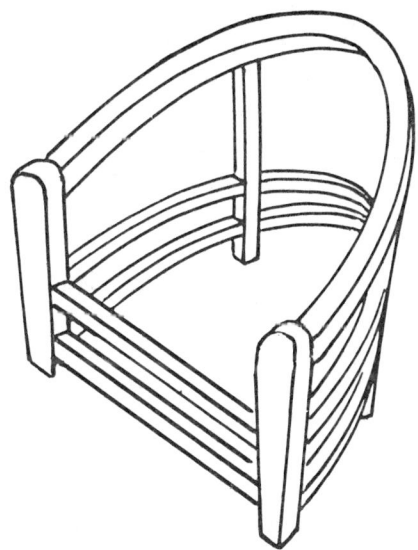

Fig. 11-7. The tub chair embodies a wrap-around frame but no provision for resting the head.

This type of frame was carried higher in Victorian furniture (Fig. 11-8). This design called for skill in working compound curves in wood and was wasteful of wood, however, because probably more than half the bulk of quite a large block had to be

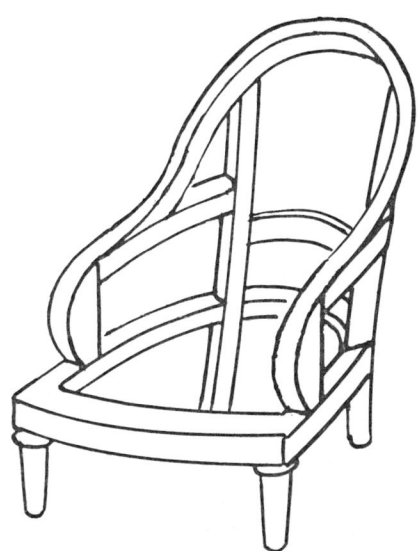

Fig. 11-8. The wrap-around frame becomes more difficult to construct when compound curves are part of the design.

cut to waste to make the parts sweeping from the arms to the high back. Even with modern laminations this shaping is wasteful and awkward. Today, this sort of frame is made with molded plastic seats, which go a stage further in shaping.

Hepplewhite, more than some of his contemporary designers, produced low-backed chairs and sofas that depended for their effect on proportions, with only a little shaping and comparatively plain exposed woodwork. Some other designers introduced more elaboration, which may have been regarded as good by the standards of those days, but a Hepplewhite piece may seem more acceptable by present-day standards.

A Chesterfield was a sofa in which the back and arms were given considerable rolled-over curvature while being kept at about the same height—not much above waist level. This is not a design for light floral fabrics, but was traditionally covered in hide and buttoned deeply (Fig. 11-9). With a good hide cover, such a piece of furniture might have an almost indefinite life, despite much use, so a club Chesterfield a century old is not unknown. Modern versions are more likely to be covered with vinyl.

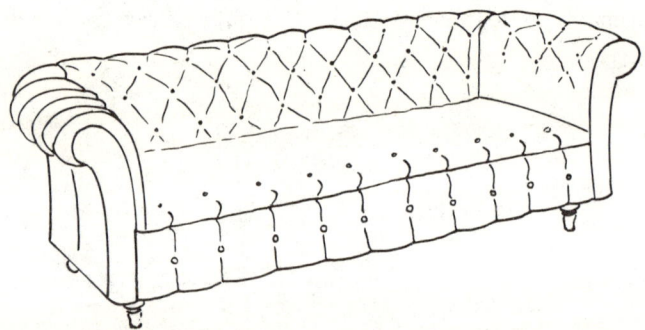

Fig. 11-9. The Chesterfield sofa was often fitted with a hide cover and deeply buttoned. Durability was one of its strong points.

The decoration given to older upholstery was mainly confined to placing of the buttons that were necessary, in any case, to anchor the twine that helped retain the loose stuffing. If buttons were not used, some other way had to be found to keep the stuffing in place. One way of doing this was to divide the upholstery into channels, so there were lines, usually vertically, on the back. This was not so suitable for seats, but it lent itself to tub chairs (Fig. 11-10). If there was much shaping, the channels had to be arranged with a flair, which was wasteful of material, but the result could be very effective.

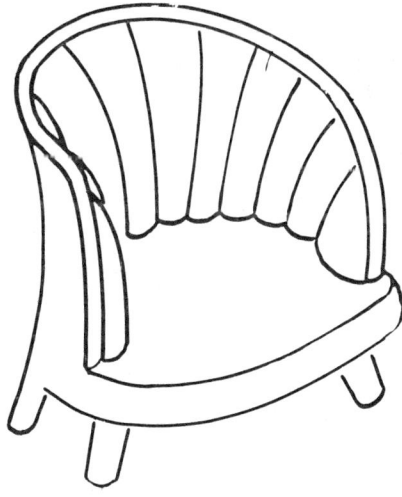

Fig. 11-10. One decorative method of securing the padding in the backrest is by channeling. When the channels are stuffed tightly and compressed closely to one another, they give firm support.

With foam and latex filling used instead of hair and other loose fillings there is less need for anything to retain the filling correctly in relation to the cover. It is still unwise to leave the filling too free to move, though, because it may take up a position that puts seams in the cover out of true and it may be difficult to reposition the pad without unpicking stitches. Buttons may still be used, or channelling may be wanted for the sake of appearance. In quantity-production furniture there are special pads with patterns of grooves into which the cover may be sewn or stuck to give a design on the surface. At the same time this prevents movement of the filling in relation to its cover.

Chairs intended for bedroom use were often classed as boudoir chairs. These were mostly for ladies' use and were of lighter construction and generally less bulky than chairs for use in living rooms. They were also covered with lighter and brighter fabrics, more in keeping with their situation. This tradition continues and there are boudoir chairs now made with modern materials. The design and the method of covering is similar to other chairs, but it is usual to provide flounces and pleats for a more feminine appearance (Fig. 11-11).

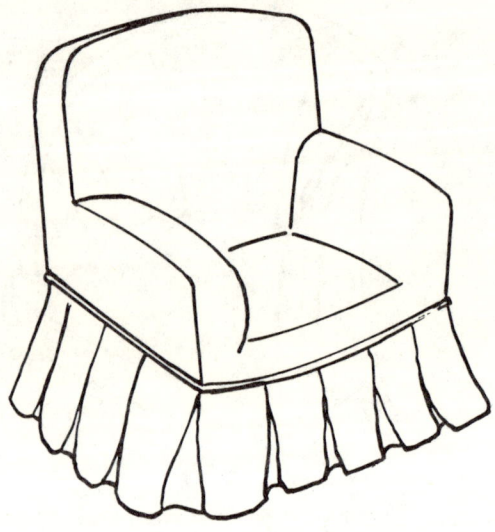

Fig. 11-11. Boudoir chairs are lightly constructed and smallish in size. With a bright, floral covering they are used in countless ladies' bedrooms.

Several variations on the basic chair theme have been used. Widening to suit two or three is an obvious change. Many Victorian sofas had only one end raised (Fig. 11-12), and a tapered, only lightly upholstered back, so a lady had room for her skirts while reclining.

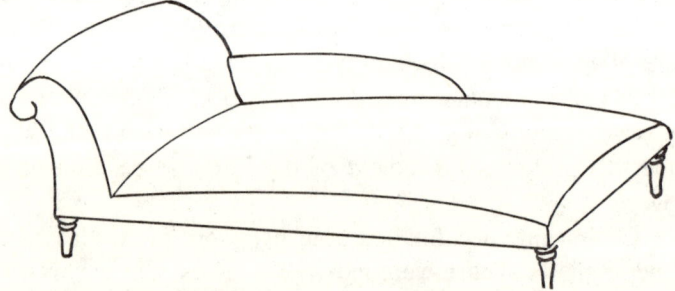

Fig. 11-12. Evolution in the function of a chair: from sitting to reclining. The seat is enlongated and the backrest repositioned to the side.

A chaise loungue (lounge) was a chair with an extended front for raising the legs (Fig. 11-13). In many cases the front

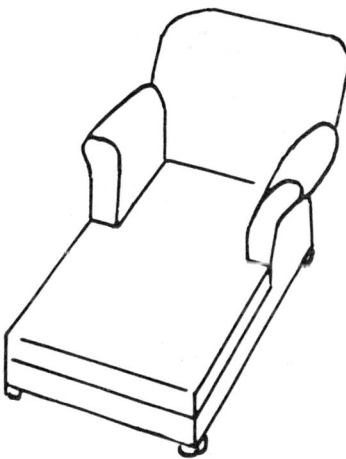

Fig. 11-13. The chaise lounge has two arm rests and a sloping back. It is a forerunner of our modern reclining chair.

could be removed to leave a normal seat. A modern version of this is seen in the reclining chair with a lifting leg rest.

The ottoman, in the form of a storage box with a padded top, has been found in sizes ranging from that of a footstool up to a bed (Fig. 11-14), and it is still a useful piece of furniture. The sofa-bed—a sofa that converts into a bed—is a fairly modern idea, which uses upholstery that is basically the same as the parts of a sofa.

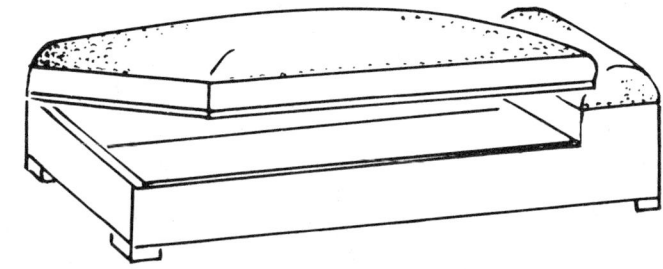

Fig. 11-14. The ottoman is a utilitarian combination of a seat footrest and chest. It has been built as wide as a bed or narrow as a pair of men's shoes.

There are novelty chairs from most ages. A three-legged chair may be designed to fit in the corner of a room. There are combined chairs on which two persons sit in opposite directions. Many of these novelties from Victorian days may still be found.

Modern chairs may be slung on laminated wood (Fig. 11-15) or tubular steel sides (Fig. 11-16). The actual supports for seat and back may be made of wood, and there may be upholstered arms on the sides, or saddle-type cushions.

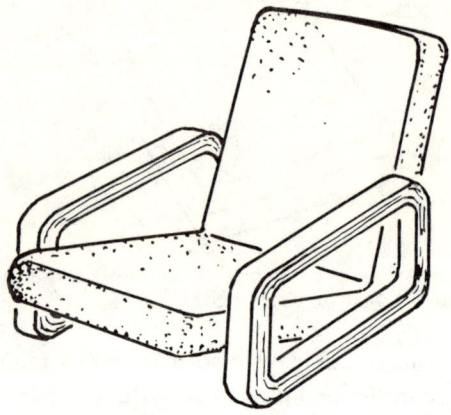

Fig. 11-15. The low-slung modern chairs often emphasize novelty of construction. This model uses laminated wood in an unbroken circuit for legs and armrest.

Sectional furniture has come about because of the need to rearrange furniture for watching television and then change back to other arrangements at other times. This type of furniture

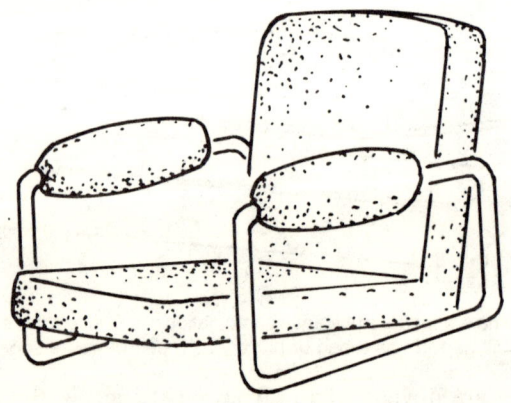

Fig. 11-16. Tubular metal sometimes replaces wood in the manufacture of contemporary novelty chairs.

features several identical chairs without fixed arms that can be used alone or brought together as a sofa. There are separate arms which may be fitted into sockets on the sides of any of the chairs. The seats and arms may build up into chairs of fairly normal appearance, although many of these sets have quite deep upholstery and cushion-style arms (Fig. 11-17), so the effect is that of a new pattern of furniture to suit modern living. Fabric patterned in ways not found on older furniture contributes to this effect.

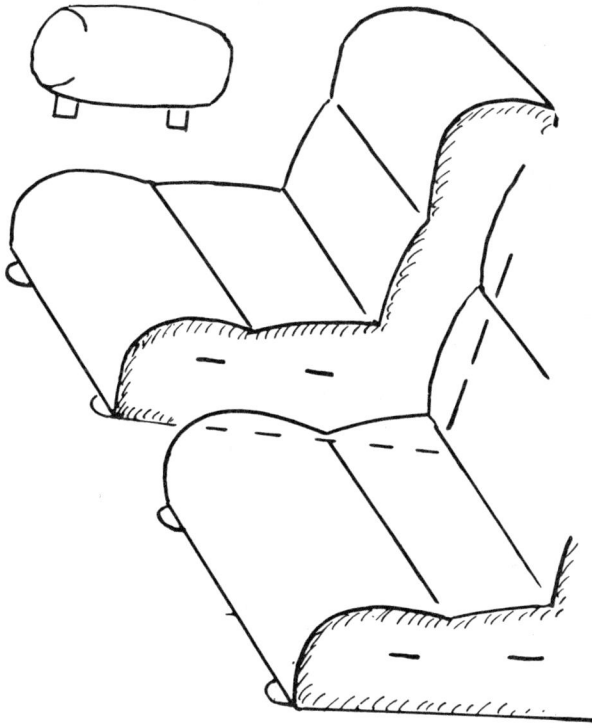

Fig. 11-17. The sectional sofa is the modern attempt to adapt a piece of furniture to a variety of uses.

Much use is made in modern furniture of bases on four arms with casters, to which the chair itself is fitted through an arrangement that allows both turning and rocking. This is usually used for office furniture, but there are versions for use in the home. Some deep comfortable chairs are based on molded

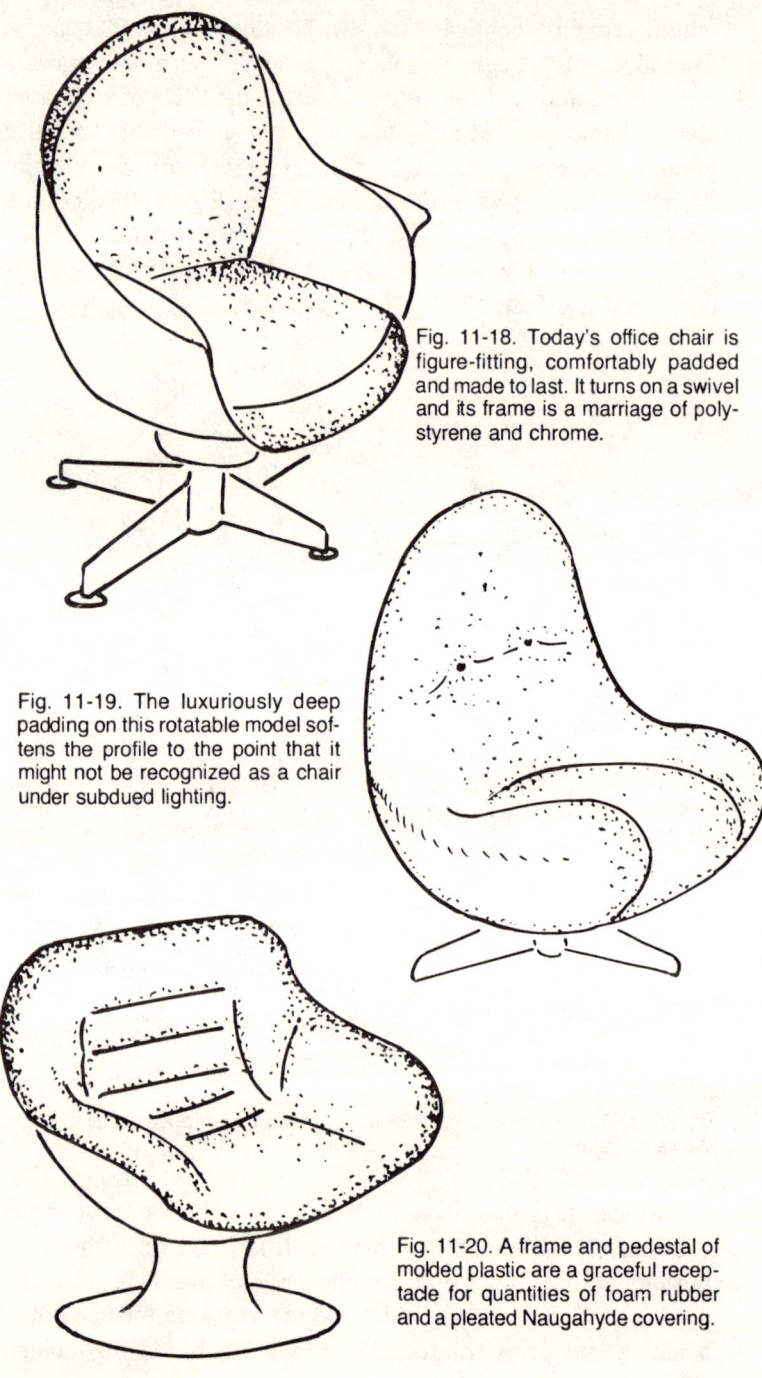

Fig. 11-18. Today's office chair is figure-fitting, comfortably padded and made to last. It turns on a swivel and its frame is a marriage of polystyrene and chrome.

Fig. 11-19. The luxuriously deep padding on this rotatable model softens the profile to the point that it might not be recognized as a chair under subdued lighting.

Fig. 11-20. A frame and pedestal of molded plastic are a graceful receptacle for quantities of foam rubber and a pleated Naugahyde covering.

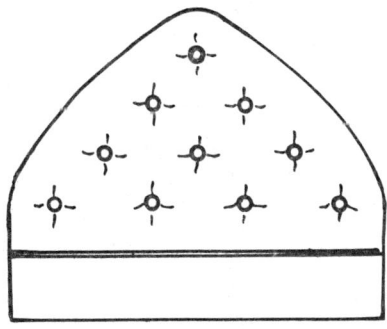

Fig. 11-21. Padded headboard decorated with buttons.

plastic frames and are more suitable for factory production than individual upholstery.

Chairs based on polystyrene and other molded frames are unlikely to be confused with other upholstered furniture. The shape is usually fairly closely figure-fitting. An office chair may be plain with little padding, but most furniture has some padding glued to the frame, then a stretch cover fitted over it. Over this go loose cushions, which are also profiled to fit (Fig. 11-18).

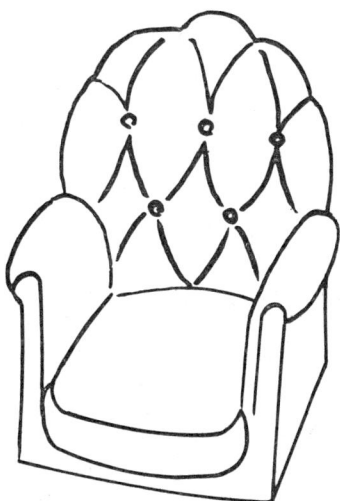

Fig. 11-22. A single design can be altered to create many variations of an easy chair. This and the remainder of the illustrations in the chapter should serve as inspiration to the home upholsterer.

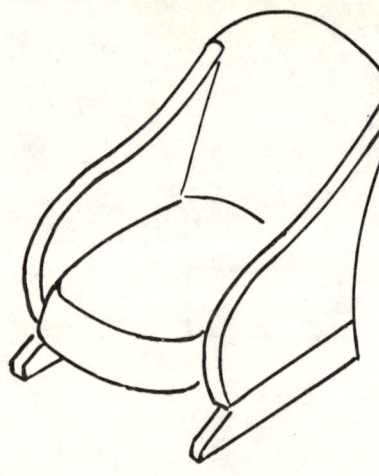

Fig. 11-23. Only the seat is deeply padded but the distinction of the appearance could make this chair a favorite item of a sitting room.

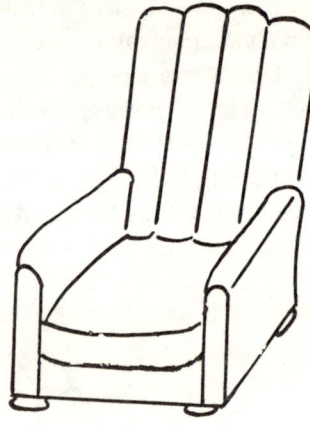

Fig. 11-24. Creating these attractive tubes isn't as difficult as it might seem. Closed off at the bottom, they can be loaded from the top before stitching.

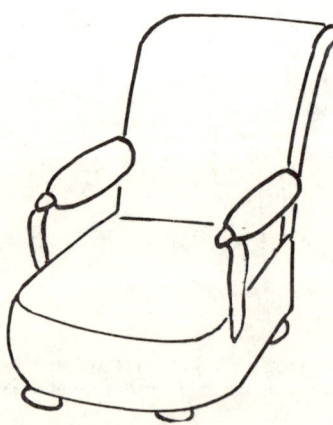

Fig. 11-25. This chair has been covered so that vestiges of its wooden construction are still evident. Only the armrest supports and the stubby feet still show through.

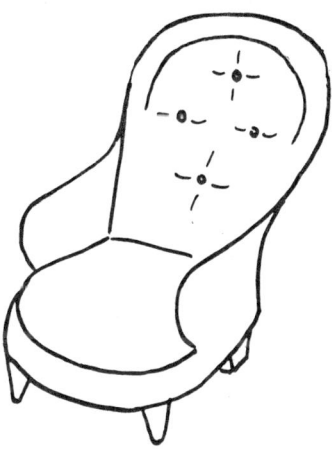

Fig. 11-26. Deeply-drawn cloth-covered buttons effectively retain the padding in the backrest and, at the same time, enhance the chair's beauty.

Other furniture of this type may have a greater thickness of padding and there may be buttons showing where twine is used (Fig. 11-19). Still other chairs may have molded supports and pleated padding (Fig. 11-20). Construction generally is more suited to factory methods than to invidiual craftsmen.

Beds have mostly only had mattresses made by upholstery methods, although some of the old four-posters were given padded heads and other parts to contribute to their comfort. In recent years, padded heads have taken the place of the more severe wood and metal ones. The usual form is a shaped board,

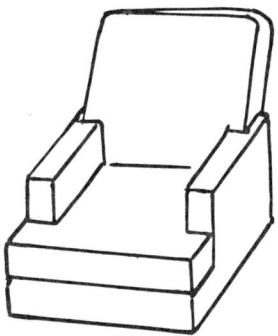

Fig. 11-27. Square edges are somewhat easier to form with foam rubber than with felt but may be worth the extra effort.

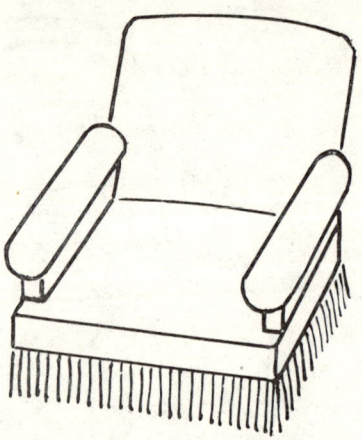

Fig. 11-28. Fringes always change the character of a chair. They're simple to apply as a fillip when everything else is completed.

padded and arranged with a pattern of buttons or other decoration (Fig. 11-21).

The examples used so far are only a few of the possible patterns of fully upholstered chairs and other items. Figures 11-22 through 11-29 show outlines of many other patterns that are possible.

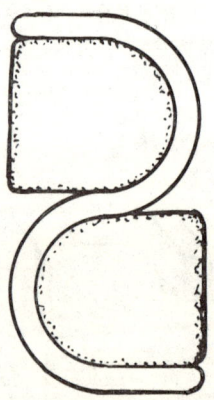

Fig. 11-29. A paradox: proximity and separation. This design never fails to evoke a comment from a visitor.

Fully Upholstered Chairs: Seats

The most important part of any chair is the seat. It has to be designed to suit various conditions. In normal use the occupant will put pressure on its center, but there are occasions when he will move forward and sit on the edge, while the seat may sometimes have to accomodate a person curled up. The greatest load tends to be placed forward of the center, with little direct load at the extreme back, although padding and springing there takes a share of the load from elsewhere.

With a sufficient thickness of modern foam or latex there would seem to be little need for any springing below this stuffing. Rigid bases are used for things like boat bunks, where the same cushioning is used for sitting and sleeping, but it is unusual for there to be a rigid base for the seat of a fully upholstered chair. Most chairs follow the conventional method of supporting the stuffing with springs on webbing, although tension springs may be found in some furniture. This applies whether the stuffing is made of curled hair or other loose filling, or is a pad which provides stuffing in one block.

The section through the seat is then fairly deep (see Chapter 2) with individual coil springs or units partly or completely built into a set. Enclosed springs may appear in Marshall units.

If tension springs are used the frame has to be prepared to suit the end attachments, although it is possible to use screws or tacks directly into the wood for spring anchorages. For most well-upholstered chairs it is usually preferable to use coil springs, but tension springs allow for shallower frames and they, or zig-zag springs, are more likely to be found in backs.

SPRINGS AND WEBBING

The layout of springs and the webbing that supports them has to be considered in relation to later treatment, as described later in this chapter, but in general the closer support is needed towards the front, where anyone sitting on the edge puts a more concentrated load. With Marshall units there is a close overall springing, but with individual springs, or rows mounted on steel webbing, the spacing is closed up towards the front (Fig. 12-1A). It is usually possible to use an even webbing spacing, so long as the springs get adequate support. It is not essential for webbing to cross under each spring, although this is convenient where it can be planned. Where the lines of springs close up towards the front, the circles of springs will be off-center (Fig. 12-1B).

Webbing is stretched and fixed, using one of the strainers described in Chapter 3, and in the manner described for a dining chair. The distance is greater, particularly for a sofa or love seat, although these may have additional crossbars, back to front, to give intermediate web tacking positions and avoid very long stretches of webbing (Fig. 12-1C). If there is any choice of webbing, a better quality is advisable for one of these chairs than for a dining chair.

Unless there are special requirements, the front springs are located close to the front of the frame, but it should be satisfactory to let the springs be about 2 inches from the other edges (Fig. 12-1D). The spaces between springs should not be more than the diameter of the springs, and usually even less (Fig. 12-1E). Mark the positions of the springs with chalk on the webbing, to avoid having to measure and locate as sewing proceeds. Use stout twine to sew the springs to the webbing in the marked positions. Work with a curved needle over the wire, going through the webbing close to the spring and knot on the outside each time. Let the needle go through so a pair of holes is slightly diagonal to the weave, then the twine will not pick up webbing threads in the same line. There should be little risk of stitches pulling along the weave of good webbing, but by going diagonal to it, any risk is removed (Fig. 12-1F).

Much of the truth of shape of the cover of the seat depends on the form the top pattern of the springs takes. Do not compress the springs any more than necessary, but tie with twine squarely and diagonally to get the upper surfaces of the springs to follow approximately the curves the seat top is intended to take. It may help in forming corners to let the twine go through the corner springs diagonally to tacks near the corners of the frame (Fig. 12-1G).

Although it is usual to use the same sort of springs all over a seat, it is possible by careful twine work to improve springing where it is needed along the front edge. Twine is taken from the front rail through the middle of each front spring, through the next spring to the top, along any other springs, and down across the back one (Fig. 12-1H). The effect is to pull up the lower turns of the front spring, so it stands higher at this stage. Although the top will be brought down in further tying, the twine first applied lifts and increases the tension in the body of the spring by using some of the thrust of adjoining springs. Another one, or sometimes two, lines of twine are taken over the springs from front to back to get the correct form to the line of spring tops (Fig. 12-1J). Make sure tacks are secure and long enough to grip. Although several lines of twine may originate from the same point, they need not all be attached to the same tack. A group of tacks in the same general area can be used. If one tack ever fails during the life of the upholstery, the others will still be taking a share of the load.

Of course, it is important that twine should not slip where it is attached to the springs and one of the knots suggested in Chapter 4 should be used every time.

Twine running from front to back is the most important link in forming the seat shape. It may be single or double twine, depending on the strength of twine, but as there are several strands over the same line of springs the effect is double or treble in any case. Do all of the front-to-back twine work first.

The twine from side to side may be single ply. Take each length from a tack in the rail, up through the outer spring, with a

215

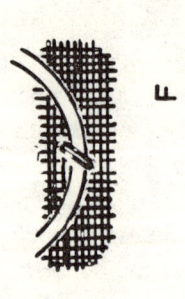
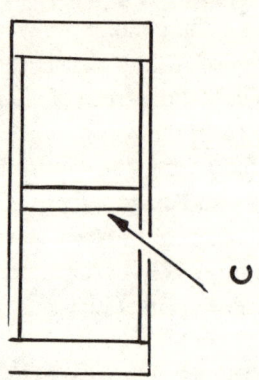
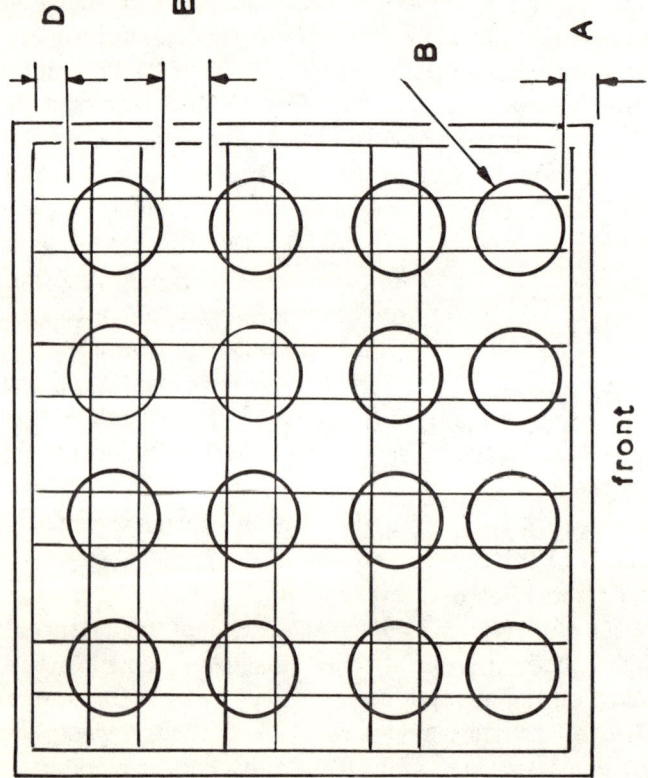

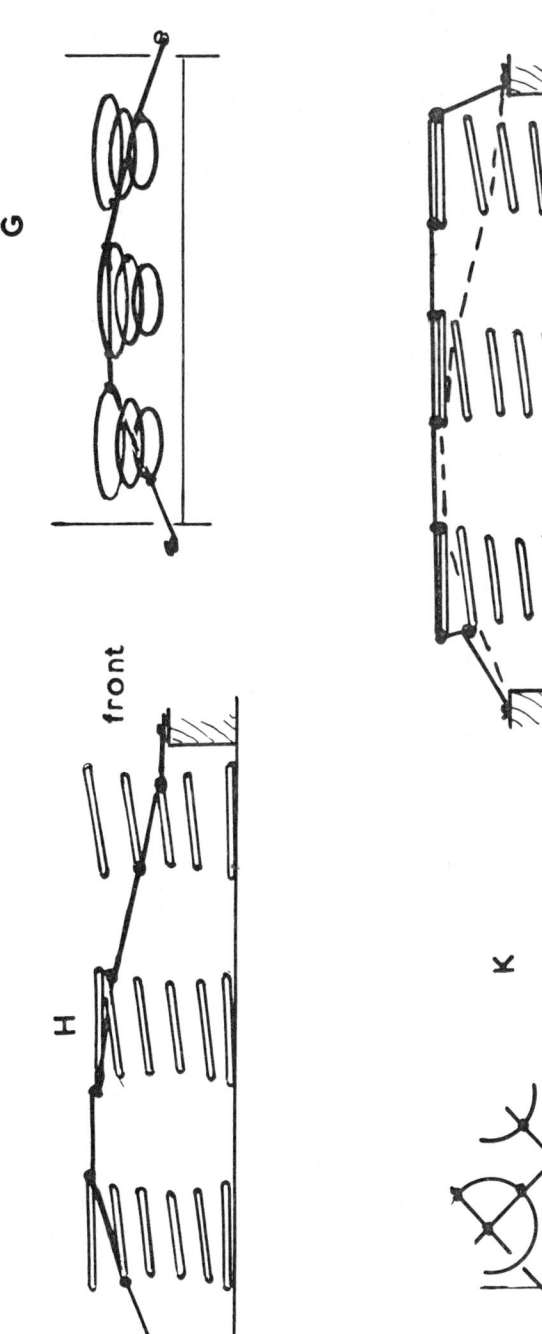

Fig. 12-1. Spring locations have to be planned and their tops tied to suit the upholstery.

knot on the third coil down, then across the top of other springs, and down in a matching way through the last spring to a tack. Diagonal ties are put on next. They cross each spring over its center in both directions, with knots tied in the same way as with the other ties. Bring each diagonal length of twine up through the outer springs (Fig. 12-1K) and across the tops of the others in the same way as the cross ties. With diagonals in both directions the result is called an *eight-way tie*.

An eight-way tie may be all that is needed, but some work is finished as a sixteen-way tie, by adding extra lengths of twine front to back and side to side over the existing twine, *between* the springs. At each crossing of an existing squarely-paced twine (not diagonals) there is a knot. For this additional tying to do its job in sharing the strain, tension between the knots has to be even, otherwise a tight length will be unduly loaded.

When all of the springs have been tied there will be quite a maze of twine ties, but the shape of the top should be even. If it is not, knots should be unpicked and adjusted. See that there is a reasonably even tension on all the ties. A slack piece between knots is not taking its share of the load and is overloading other lines. Perfection in tension may be difficult to achieve, but large differences should be avoided.

SPRINGS AND BURLAP

The complex tying of the tops of springs before proceeding further is done in the best work, but it is possible to reduce the amount of twine work if the tops of springs are sewn to the burlap or canvas which follows. There may have to be other work done, particularly to the front edge, before canvas is applied. But since the work is related to tying with twine, it is described here. The reader should remember to do whatever else is necessary at spring level before covering the frame and spring tops.

Burlap or canvas is tacked to the frame. Use temporary tacks, only partly driven, to get the material satisfactorily tensioned so the springs pressing up are brought to an even curvature. There may have to be several repositionings of the tacks before a satisfactory shape is obtained, so do not drive tightly until you are satisfied no tack will have to be withdrawn and driven in another place.

There may be a double thickness of burlap with cotton between (Fig. 12-2A). If so, it is only the bottom layer which is fixed at this stage, but enough must be left around the edges for turning over later. The springs thrusting upwards and the weight

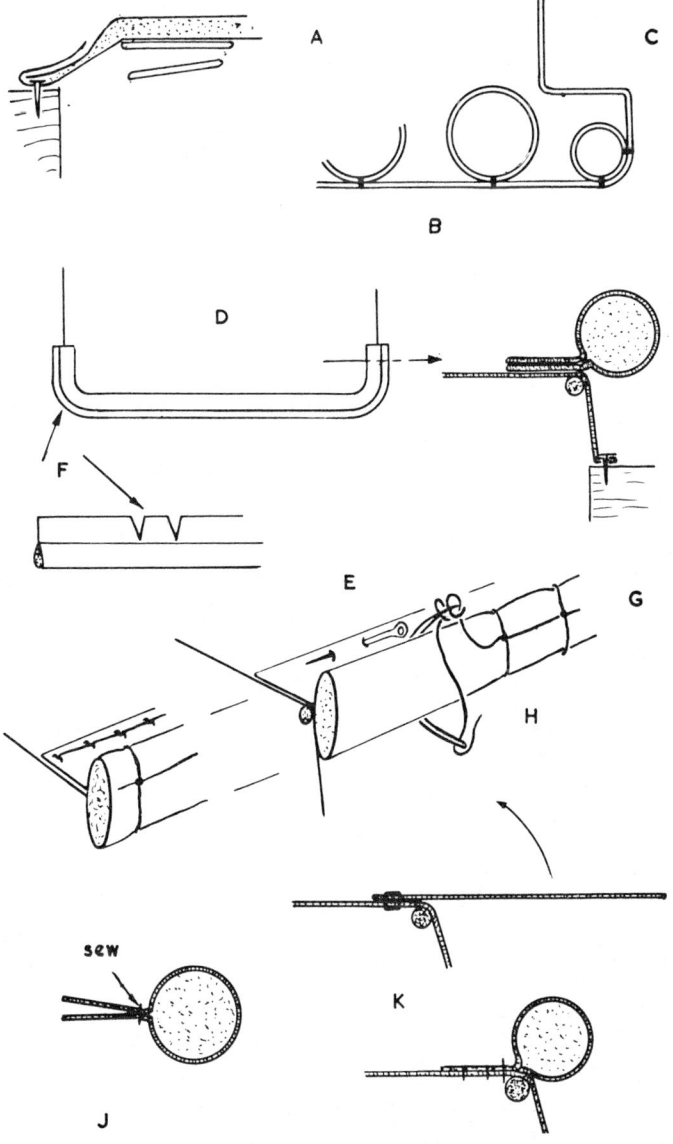

Fig. 12-2. Springs may be joined with wire. Edges are reinforced with rolls before stuffing is applied.

of a sitting person thrusting downwards can put considerable load on the tacks; so make sure there are enough tacks and all tightly driven. They cannot be reached once the cover is on.

There may be back-to-front and side-to-side ties put on, and the diagonal ties omitted, if the springs are to be sewn to burlap or canvas. These will fix the spring tops in position, so there is no difficulty in locating them under the burlap. In some chairs the springs may be only sewn to the burlap, without twine ties underneath. In this case, care is needed to get them correctly located. It may be necessary to view from below and above, then make chalk marks on the burlap.

Sew through the burlap or canvas in a way similar to that of sewing to webbing. Use a slip knot made with two half hitches to start sewing, then a single or double twist knot at four points on each spring. The twine does not have to be run in a continuous length. It can conveniently follow a zig-zag path. If there is to be cotton and another layer of burlap, this is taken in after sewing the springs. It is usual to wrap and sew the edge. Burlap may be fixed on the back and inside the arms at this stage.

FRONT EDGING

There are several ways of dealing with the front edge of a seat. In some cases it may be sufficient to carry the padding over the front edge. In some frames there is a shaped rail that allows for this, but in many frames there has to be additional upholstery work to strengthen and pad the front edge so a hard line is not felt when anyone sits on the edge.

To unite the front row of springs and provide a support for the front edge, the springs may be wired together. In some chairs the wiring is taken all around, but for many chairs the wire goes across the front and far enough back at the sides to come well within the boundary of the arms. Wire sizes vary and the spring supplier should be able to supply suitable wire and clips to go with it. A wired front edge is needed if the frame is narrow and without special shaping, so the springs stand a few inches above it (Fig. 12-2B). In a seat where the arms are set back, the wiring may take in a smaller spring to support the overlap at the corner (Fig. 12-2C).

Some upholsterers prefer to fix wires before tying the springs, but it is probably better to do all tying first. This allows the front springs to be adjusted with the twine through to get a better shape, and the wire is not in the way when arranging the run of twine and making knots near the edge. It is helpful in some seats to carry the wire all round. As this task requires little more work than to carry it only partly around, it should be done if there is any doubt about the seat cushion keeping its shape.

Clips can be attached to avoid knots, or the knots can be pushed aside. When bending the wire in position watch that the length is adjusted so the springs remain in their intended positions and are not distorted by incorrect locating of bends. If a Marshall spring unit has been used, wires can be fixed with clips through the cloth casings.

One way of softening the front edge is to apply roll edging, or fox edging. Fox edging is made like piping or welting, but much bigger. It is not impossible to make, but it is usual to buy it ready-made. It consists of a burlap flap attached to a padded tube. Its length should be sufficient to go around that part of the front of the seat that will project forward of the arms (Fig. 12-2D). Sometimes the fox edging is fixed to the frame before the burlap is put over the springs, but it is more usual to add it above the burlap.

Fix the fox edging at first with pins along the edge (Fig. 12-2E) using the burlap flap to hold so the roll comes over the wired edge. If the edging has to go around a corner, make one or more cuts in the flap so it will bend around smoothly (Fig. 12-2F). The roll part of the edging has to be sewn around the wire attached to the springs by tying it.

Use twine with a curved needle. Make the first stitch with a slip knot that is pulled tight (Fig. 12-2G), then make more stitches at wide intervals. A spacing of 1 1/2 inches should suit most chairs. The further stitches should lock in each place and not just be half hitches. One way of getting a sufficient lock is to twist the twine two or three times around the point of the needle, then pull tight (Fig. 12-2H). By the time the edging has been stitched all the way it should be held above and forward of the wire edge.

The next step is to sew down the flap which is being held with pins. The tightness of this flap on the burlap over the springs plays a part in preventing the roll from moving in use, so sew it securely. This can be done with stout thread or thin twine and a curved needle. Knot the first stitch, then make more stitches at about half the distance of the stitches over the roll; but form them in the same way, with a few turns around the point to provide a lock as each one is pulled tight.

If fox edging has to be made, use a piece of burlap or canvas about 6 inches wide. This can be filled with hair, which needs skill to spread evenly, or with rolled thin foam, then sewn close to the roll (Fig. 12-2J). Another way is to sew the burlap strip flat on the chair burlap so a sufficient amount overhangs. The filling is put in and the strip wrapped over and sewn by hand as filling progresses (Fig. 12-2K).

The front edge may be further softened after fox edging, or in place of it, by adding a square section of latex or foam ahead of the sprung framed seat. This makes a false front that projects ahead of the front rail (Fig. 12-3A). The foam block should be encased in muslin and attached to the rail to match with the sprung edge, to which it may be sewn. Later, the front will be included in the further padding with the main body of the seat.

There are other ways of dealing with front edge springing and not all upholsterers tie twine in the same way. Smaller springs may be brought out on to a front ledge, where those behind go down to webbing (Fig. 12-3B). Staples are convenient where springs have to be fixed to wood. They are the stout fencing type driven with a hammer (Fig. 12-3C) and not the light machine-driven ones that can be used instead of tacks through fabric. It is a help to restrain the front small springs with narrow webbing.

Another method of dealing with the front edge when the stuffing is to be made of hair or fiber uses a gutter and a roll made to serve a similar purpose to fox edging. The springs are prepared by tying, except the smaller springs of the front edge are not tied to the others; they are tied to each other. Burlap is brought over from where it is tacked at the back and pressed down to form a gutter behind the front row of springs (Fig. 12-3D). There can be a tack at each end of the gutter to stretch its bottom, then the sides of the seat can be temporarily tacked down. Use twine through the bottom of the gutter at wide intervals to loop down to tacks in the rail under the springs (Fig. 12-3E).

Pull the front part of the burlap over the front springs and the wired edge so it can be tacked with a turned-under edge to the lower rail and with a few tacks to the other rail (Fig. 12-3F). Tension the whole area evenly and put final tacks around the other edges. Sew the springs to the burlap, as already described.

A first or final layer of padding is made over the burlap. This is done with loose curled hair or other loose stuffing. Use muslin or another piece of burlap, first tacked along the back edge. Fill with stuffing, using a regulator to spread the hair evenly. If this is to be a first layer and there is to be more above it, a total thickness of 1 inch is about right. Fill the gutter tightly.

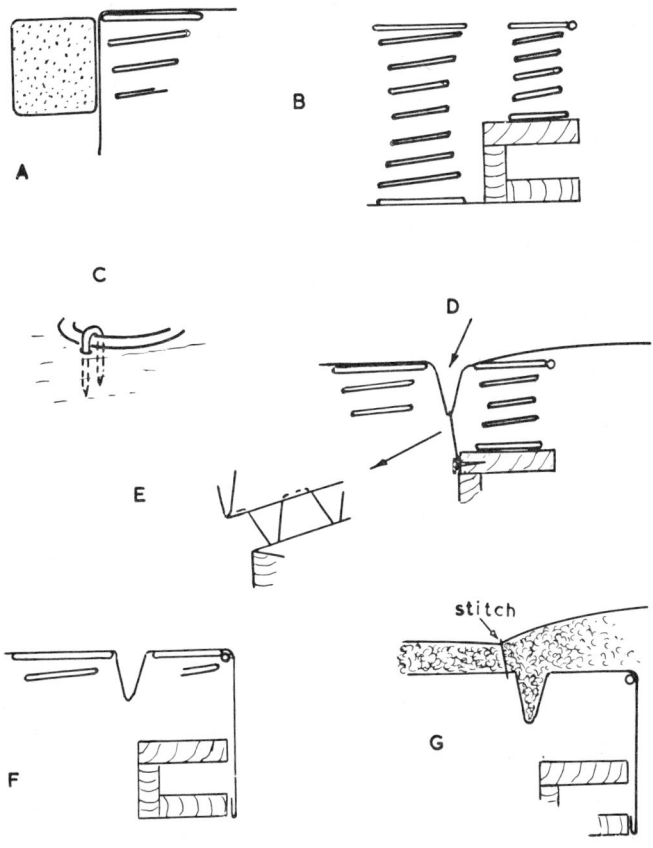

Fig. 12-3. A chair front may have extra small springs.

Sew through along the line behind the gutter with a long needle and large stitches to pull a straight hollow in the top surface (Fig. 12-3G). To get a neat secure line it may be necessary to make two or three lines of these stitches.

Pick over the stuffing forward of this line. Make sure the gutter is full. Bring the cloth over to a point below the line of wire. Add to and regulate the stuffing so there is enough to make a roll projecting forward.

Turn under the edge. Use a curved needle to make stitches (*sink* stitches) into the stuffing (Fig. 12-4A). Take the stitches in as far as possible and let them be as close as can be made conveniently with the needle. The effect is to draw the stuffing forward and make a roll that will not move back in use. As near as possible to that row of stitches, use a straight needle to go right through to the top and pull down a slight groove across the seat. This also acts as a barrier to stuffing working back from the edge (Fig. 12-4B). Finally sew along the turned under edge with half hitches that also go around the spring wire (Fig. 12-4C).

Many fully upholstered chairs have a fitted cushion that may be as thickly padded as the seat. This does much to soften the front edge as well as add to the general padding, but it is usual to still employ fox edging or other means of cushioning the front edge of the chair seat. Apart from any additional padding it provides, the edging helps to retain the cushion.

When the seat of a sofa or love seat is being sprung the springing arrangements and the front edge treatment are mostly the same as for a chair. Although the springs may be divided into sections by cross pieces underneath, this is for convenience in dealing with webbing and the springs are usually tied as one mass on top. Sometimes with a very long sofa that is to be fitted with cushions, the springs may be grouped under areas that will take the cushions, so each group supports a cushion as if it were a single seat. Twine ties keep the springs in these groups. There are no actual divisions in the support arrangements.

TENSION SPRINGS

Tension springs provide a simpler way of supporting a seat than does the arrangement of tied coil springs that has been traditionally used. In themselves the springs do not provide as

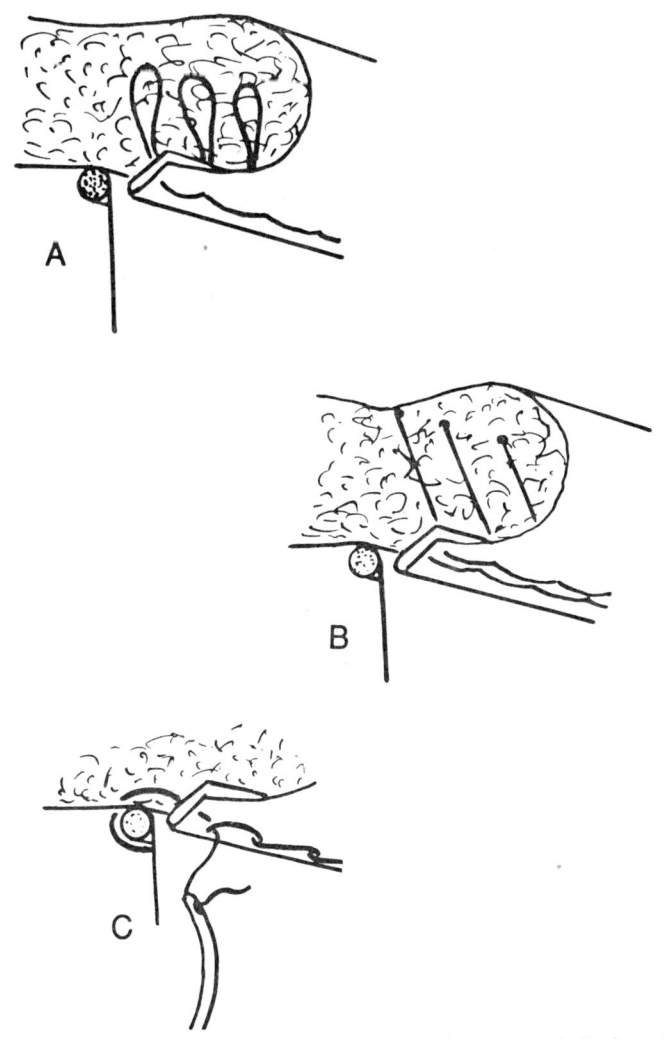

Fig. 12-4. When the stuffing is covered, special stitches are needed to keep the front edge in place.

comfortable a support, but with modern types of padding above them the result gives an almost equal degree of comfort. Tension springs are normally fitted in the shortest direction across a space. This means that in a chair they may go from side to side (Fig. 12-5A), but in a sofa they go from front to back (Fig. 12-5B). Any of the usual methods of mounting may be used, depending on how the frame has been prepared. In better work

225

there may be a strip of webbing or cardboard over the ends of the springs (Fig. 12-5C) and the springs may be encased in plastic sleeves. How close the springs are arranged will depend on their size and type as well as the area to be covered.

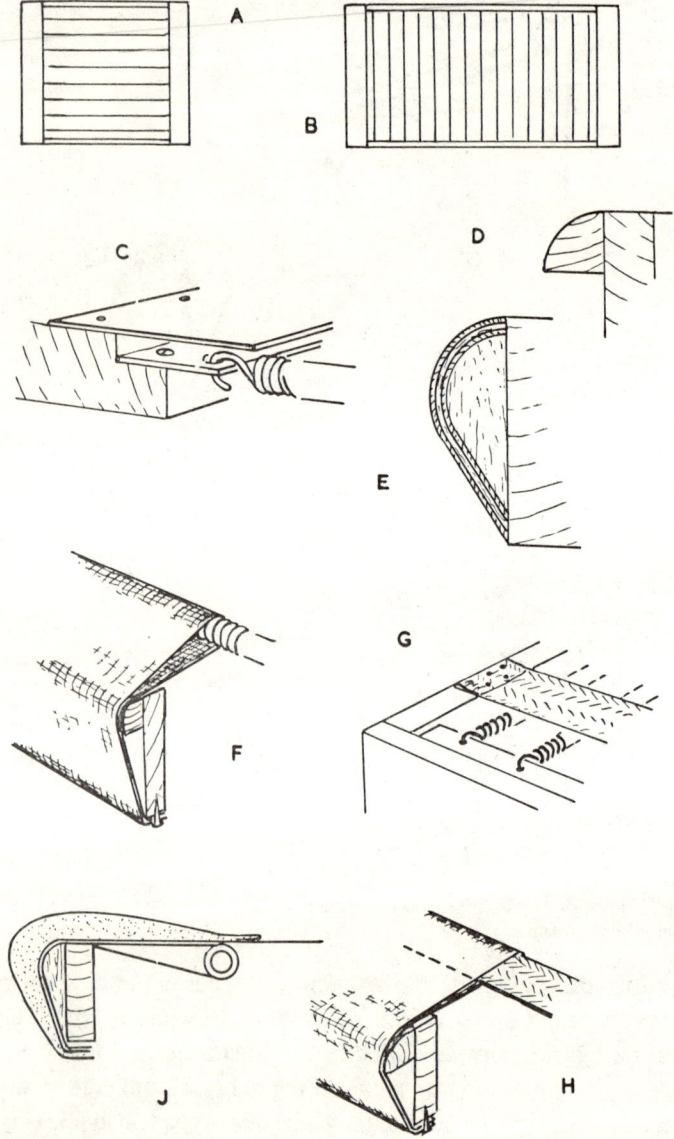

Fig. 12-5. Tension springs normally go the short way across a space. Front edges are then rounded and may be padded.

With tension springs, the type of front reinforcement described for coil spring supports cannot be used. Instead, it is usual to provide rounding on the front rail. It may be a quarter-round molding (Fig. 12-5D) or thin plywood around blocks (Fig. 12-5E). This eases the hard edge, even if it does nothing to soften it.

With chair springing a piece of burlap is looped around the front spring and taken double over the front, to be tacked below the rail (Fig. 12-5F).

With sofa springing this cannot be done. Instead, you must stretch a piece of webbing across above the springs and a few inches back from the front rail (Fig. 12-5G). Take the burlap around this and over the front (Fig. 12-5H), tacking below in the same way as the chair.

Another piece of burlap or canvas goes from the same front tacking position over the springs to be tacked at the back and sides. This has to be given sufficient tension for it to remain flat, but not enough to restrict the action of the springs when a weight is put on them.

How much padding is used over the whole seat depends on the amount of padding in the cushions. With good cushions there will be no need for any fixed padding. However, there should be some padding over the front. The front part of the outer cover should match the cloth on the arms and back. With the cushions in place not much of the seat cover will show, so only the front part need be made of patterned material. The rest of the panel need only be plain cloth.

This is convenient for holding the front padding. The plain platform material is made long enough to go around the front and continue to the back. The facing material is sewn to it at about the same line as the burlap goes around a spring or strip of webbing. The space is filled with padding, which may be cotton, felt, or foam. The padding may be increased in thickness around the front of the curve and tapered to nothing at the bottom (Fig. 12-5J). Stretch and tack the platform material in place, then position the padding and pull it over the facing material.

It is possible to use tension springs under fixed upholstery, but the upper part is then made more like a cushion which is fixed, using thick foam or latex, to provide padding. The inner and outer cover materials may go over the frame parts and be fixed by tacks and gimp or by decorative nails.

STUFFING AND COVERING

If a seat is to be stuffed traditionally with hair or other loose filling, the burlap over the springs is best covered with cotton and a further layer of burlap; although if canvas or something stronger and more closely woven than burlap is used, one layer may be enough. A risk with using a single layer of burlap is its failure after long use, enabling the springs to break through in places. Untreated burlap has little resistance to rot and in damp conditions the springs may rust. This rust, combined with the burlap's tendency to rot, may hasten failure. Of course, in normal use furniture does not suffer from dampness.

If curled hair or other loose filling is used, have a mass in the hand and pull it apart so it can be distributed over the seat in the places where it is needed. The very loose hair will build up to an apparent thickness considerably greater than it will finally become. At first, distribute the hair over the seat except for a few inches behind the fix edging.

Use a large curved needle and a length of twine to sew through the hair to the burlap with a pattern of large loose stitches (Fig. 12-6A). The pattern does not have to be geometrically exact, but it is convenient to work in large squares or diamonds. Pass the needle right through the burlap and up again close to where it went down, so the stitch can be locked with a knot at the crossing. Loops about 3 inches across should hold the normal amount of hair. What is needed is enough tension and closeness of stitches to prevent the hair from moving about, while allowing it to be loose and springy enough for a comfortable seat.

More hair has to be applied up to and over the fox or other edging so padding carries over the curve and tapers down the front. It will be necessary to tilt the chair as this is applied. Also, sewing will have to be progressive as hair is put in position, otherwise it will not stay in place. Rubberized hair can be used as part of the padding, but this is more appropriate for arms.

Hair needs something over it to give a smooth casing and prevent ends of hairs from working through woven fabric. It is usual to lay on cotton batting. This can be about 1 inch thick and is cut and arranged to completely cover the hair, including the area over the front rail (Fig. 12-6B). With this over a sufficient amount of hair padding, the front edge should have ample padding to provide a soft edge for anyone who sits over it instead of in the body of the chair. It will also give a good shape to the front of the seat, whether it is to be used alone or with a cushion over it.

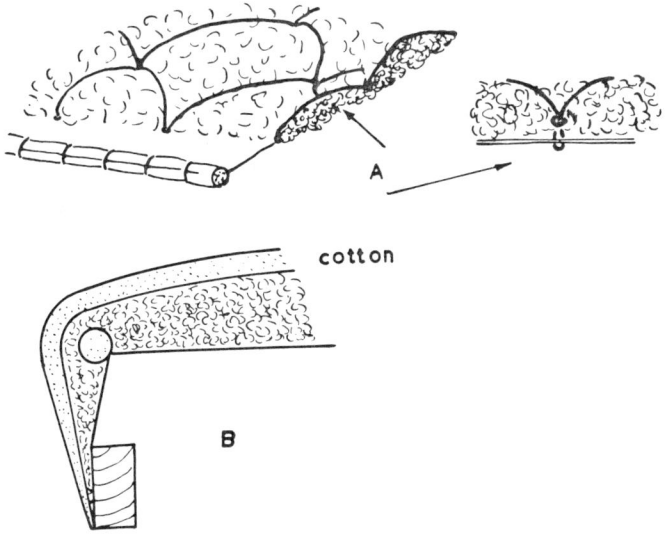

Fig. 12-6. Hair stuffing is retained with twine stitches.

The seat should usually be covered with muslin, although it is possible to proceed straight to the cover with some materials. Muslin pulls the padding to shape and relieves the outer cover of the need to do anything except fit what is underneath, avoiding any secondary considerations of easing out lumps or modifying shapes.

In the usual frame the muslin goes under the gut rails on the arms and the bottom rails under the back. There may have to be some cutting around legs and arms, but otherwise there is nothing to prevent a piece of muslin from being laid over and marked to size in position. Where there have to be cuts, allow the edge to turn under and do this at edges which will be tacked (Fig. 12-7A). At sides and front the muslin will go outside to be tacked, but do not take it so low that it will interfere with the fitting of outer cover material (Fig. 12-7B). It may go down the back rail on some chairs or it may have to be turned under on top of the frame (Fig. 12-7C).

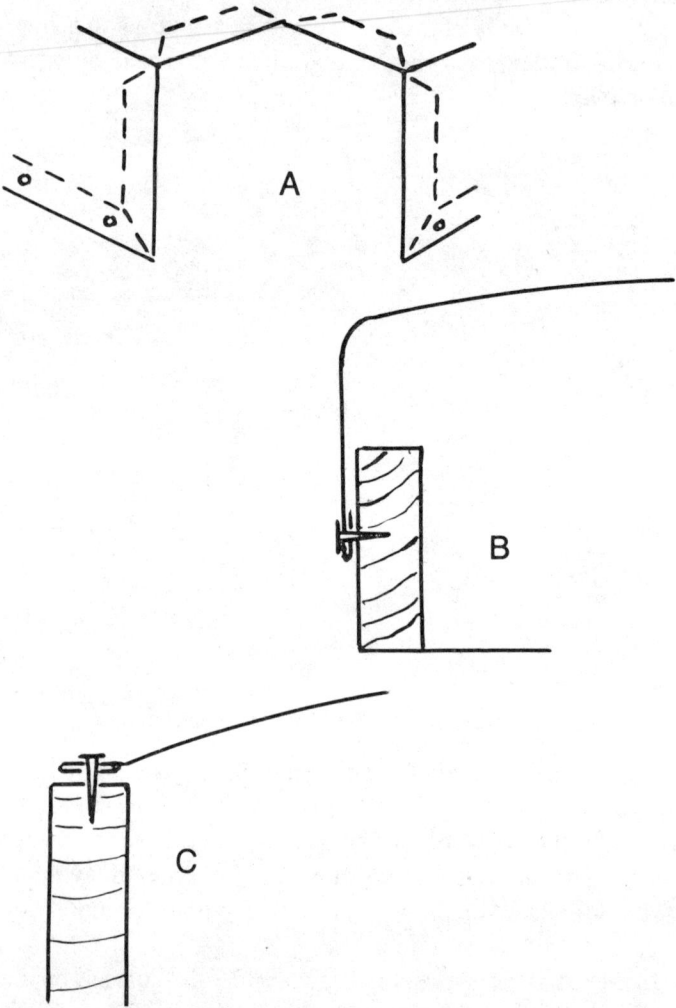

Fig. 12-7. Covering material is turned under the tacking.

Muslin needs careful stretching if it is to be smooth. Use temporary tacks partly driven to get an even tension without creases before finally tacking fairly closely around the edges. If there is difficulty in positioning the cotton, temporarily tack the muslin across the back and position the cotton as the muslin is pulled forward and across to the sides. To prevent movement in use, there may be a line of stitches across the seat a few inches back from the fox edging or other front roll. The stitches can be made with a small curved needle and thread. Pencil or chalk a guideline across the muslin. Start with a lock stitch around the wire at one side, then go across with stitches about 1/2 inch long taken deep enough to go through the cotton, and tight enough to hold it, but not so tight as to squeeze the cover out of shape. Finish with a lock stitch around the wire at the other side. Whether the cotton goes over the seat side depends on how the arms are to be covered.

Final covering of the seat will not usually be undertaken until the arms and back are also at the stage for covering, but the process is described here to complete the sequence on the seat. Anyone doing an upholstery job on a new chair, though, should leave this stage until after some of the work described in the following chapters has been done.

Seats are covered in many ways. The simplest method is similar to that for a plain cushion and the outer cover material is put on in a similar way to the muslin. If the front projects from the arms, the corners are neatly pleated (Fig. 12-8A). Edges are tacked or nailed and covered with gimp or there may be a flounce or other decorative treatment to the lower edge (Fig. 12-8B). That type of covering is more appropriate to traditional loose filling. If a boxed form is used, the traditional padding may be supported by front springs on a platform, as described, then the covering may have a boxed edge with piping if desired. Boxed edging is more appropriate with foam filling.

If foam or latex is to be used instead of loose stuffing the sequence of upholstery is very similar. If there is no stock piece of the right size, the filling material may be trimmed as described in Chapter 6, and the edges made up with strips fixed with adhesive. This pad is placed over the burlap on the springs instead of the sewn loose filling, then it is covered in the same way with cotton and muslin before the outer covering is added.

It is usual to use plain material as a platform for the main part of the top of the seat if a cushion is to be used over it. This may continue over the sides and back, which will be hidden, or

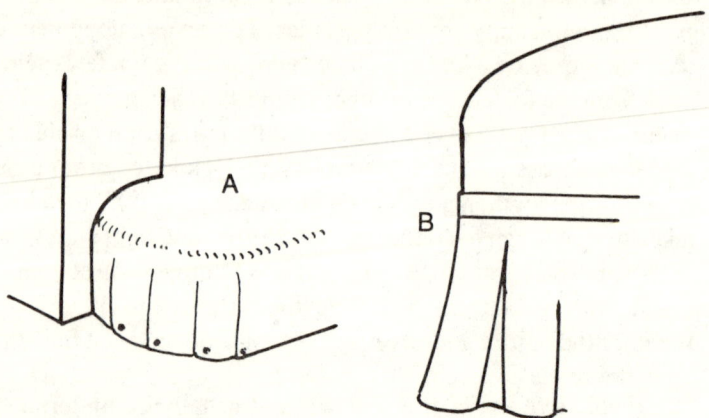

Fig. 12-8. Covering material is pleated around curves, or a chair may be finished with a flounce.

odd pieces of other fabric can be sewn on. If a platform of plain material is to be used, sew this to a strip of the outer cover material, arranging the sizes of the pieces and the position of the seam so the joint will be far enough back to be hidden between the arms by the cushion. If other material is to be used for flys, get the size of the seat piece, with a paper template if necessary, and sew on the flys. Make sure the seams will be folded on to the edges and not show on top (Fig. 12-9A). It is helpful to mark the center back and front for correct positioning.

If the cushion seat is to project forward and have a piped edge, cut the front of the top to shape, with about 1/2 inch allowance for sewing to the piping (Fig. 12-9B). Prepare a strip of cloth to go around the front. This must have an allowance for sewing to the piping and enough hanging down to cover the chair front and tack below, if that is the method of covering used (Fig. 12-9C)—or enough to reach low enough for any other sort of finish. Sew the piped edge inside-out. Do not sew it to the flys. Turn the cover the right way and try it in position. Get the correct positions of the seams between the box-edged front and the flys, then pin in readiness for sewing the seams (Fig. 12-9D).

When the cover has been made to fit, use center marks as a guide positioning and stretch it in place. Use temporary, partly driven tacks to get it correct. It should be tight enough to slightly compress the foam. When a satisfactory fit has been obtained,

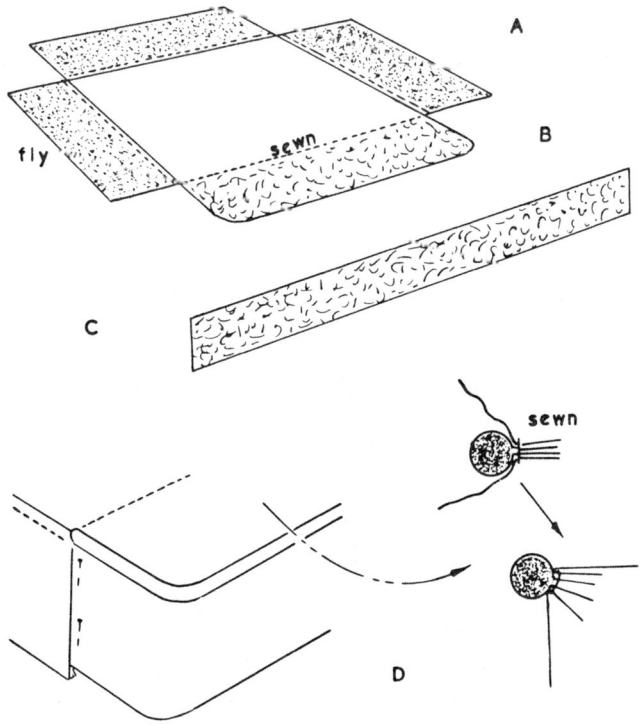

Fig. 12-9. The platform of a chair has its boxed front finished with cover material, but flys are added elsewhere.

final tack in the same way as the muslin, but allow for the way the back and arm material may have to cover it, and the method of finishing the front if the cloth does not go under the frame.

In many chairs there will be buttoning. The edges of the covering may be finished in several ways, and there are applied decorations that can be used. Details of finishing methods are given in Chapter 15.

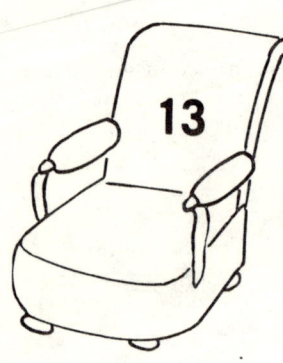

13

Fully Upholstered Chairs: Arms

The seat may be the most important part of a chair—without it, it would cease to be a chair—and the back plays an important part in providing comfort, but the parts that are most obvious and that contribute most to appearance are the two arms. They also add to comfort. A chair without arms is not as comfortable for full relaxation as one with arms. At one time arms, and their wings, played a part in protecting the sitter from drafts, but that need is unlikely in a modern home.

Hard arms have their uses and they are found in the simpler lounge chairs, but it is more comfortable to have some padding for the forearm and hand to rest on. Height in relation to the seat is important. If this is wrong, the chair arm cannot be used to rest the arms or to use for an elbow when supporting the head with a hand. In normal use the weight is not much and is spread, but there should be enough padding to allow weight to go on the small area of an elbow, without pressing through to anything hard below.

Padding on the top of the arm is most important, but this is usually carried around the edges, both to allow for indirect loads and for the sake of appearance. The outside of an arm is usually faced with the covering material, but this does not usually have padding to back it. Inside the arm there may be no padding in some chairs, but it is more usual for padding to be provided there, and this is often arranged as a continuation from the top.

In some older furniture it was usual for arms to have a curved top section, combined with a curve in the length, possibly even with a flared shape. This caused a compound curvature, which had to be provided by the frame. Curved sections are still used and may be very comfortable and good looking, but many modern pieces of furniture have flat-topped arms to the frames and this is carried through to the covering, with only slight curving at the edges. These arms provide plenty of comfort due to the use of modern padding materials, although they would not retain their effectiveness if used with loose stuffing materials.

As will be seen, arms may be stuffed with loose hair and other materials, but, more than in other parts of upholstery, the use of sheet foam, rubberized hair, and other stuffing in sheet form makes for ease in doing the work and upholstery that should provide more lasting comfort.

As will be seen, arms may be stuffed with loose hair and other materials, but, more than in other parts of upholstery, the use of sheet foam, rubberized hair, and other stuffing in sheet form makes for ease in doing the work and upholstery that should provide more lasting comfort.

In some designs there are exposed parts of the frame, usually at the front of the arm, although sometimes these appear where the arm meets the back. These parts have to be given a finish and it is usual to do at least part of the finishing before adding covering. In some cases the frame is covered, but there is a wood facing or panel added to the front of each arm.

The various stages in upholstering all parts of a chair have to be integrated and it is unusual to complete covering arms or another part before starting on the upholstery of adjoining surfaces. For convenience in describing the work on arms, however, they are dealt with completely in this chapter. The information should be used with that in the previous and following chapters, though.

If a frame is intended to have padded arms, it will have a top surface to each arm that will form a base for the intended covering. It is often possible to adapt a frame by reshaping its arms, or adding pieces to it to alter the shape. But it can usually be assumed that the original frame was made with the arms at the correct height in relation to the seat, and there should not be too much alteration in this distance if modifications are made.

Another important part of the frame for dealing with the arms is a *gut rail* (Fig. 13-1A). This is located just above where the cushioning of the seat will come, so the upholstery of the arm can be arranged close to it, but materials from the seat can pass under it. This is related to a similar rail at the back, where back covering has to be dealt with close to the seat. It is unlikely that the gut rail will need alteration, but the seat and inside arm should be visualized in relation to each other.

The arm frame should be checked before commencing covering. If it is an older rounded type, it will probably have been smoothed in the shaping process, but some modern square-armed frames may be rather rough and angular. Abrupt angles should be rounded. Although the padding and covering will soften angles, a sharp angle may press into padding and eventually spoil the surface cover lines or make a hard spot that can be felt from outside. Round any sharp angles and take off corners as much as construction will allow, but do not go so far in the process as might result in a weak joint.

An arm frame will usually have an opening towards the inside, bounded by the top, the gut rail, the back, and the front leg. This opening has to be covered to form a base for padding. Normally this is done with burlap and a backing of webbing.

In a modern chair with a flat top the size of the opening is such that two upright bands of webbing should be enough. Space them evenly (Fig. 13-1B). This may be the same 2 inch webbing that is used under springs, or there is an advantage in having a wider grade if available. For a large opening or a narrow webbing there can be more bands used vertically and there could also be an interwoven horizontal band, but this is not usually necessary.

Cover this area with burlap. How far it extends past the edge of the opening depends on the area of wood, but in most chair frames it will come close to the top surface and to the front edge. It should go on to the gut rail enough to grip it (Fig. 13-1C), but should not extend below if this is close to what will be the seat level; space for working there might be restricted.

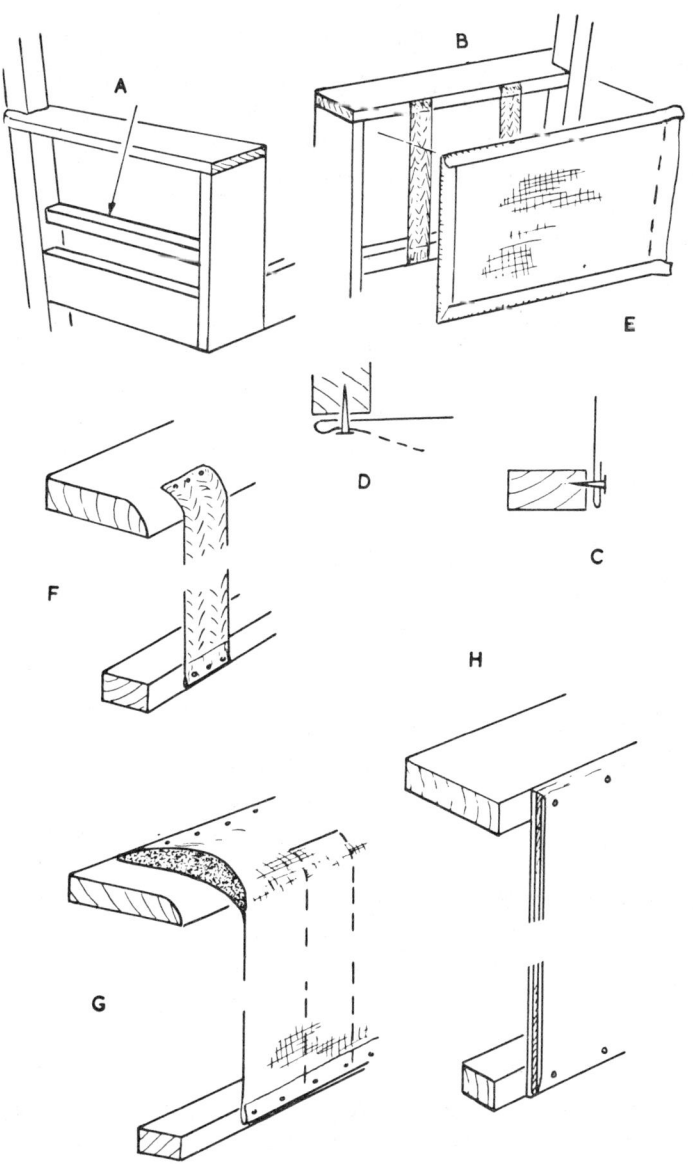

Fig. 13-1. The inside arm is lined with burlap or plywood.

Spread the burlap evenly with a few temporary tacks, then turn in the edges and tack through the double thickness. Trim neatly, although this will be covered under padding and the state of the edge is not very important (Fig. 13-1D). In some chairs the

237

rear edge of the burlap has to be joined into the back. For this purpose, leave some extra and do not complete tacking there until it is joined to the back (Fig. 13-1E).

On some types of arm the top may be mainly flat, but there is a curve where the top and inside blend into each other. Where this occurs there is still a need for webbing inside, but the top of each piece can go over the top of the arm (Fig. 13-1F), if this is more convenient. The burlap may be taken over the edge of the arm so it is tacked to the gut rail and across to the outside edge of the top of the arm, while taking in the first layer of cotton or rubberized hair next to the wood (Fig. 13-1G).

The treatment of the inside of the arms of an antique chair is very similar. The amount of webbing and the overlap of the burlap will have to be arranged to suit circumstances, but most of these frames need an inside backing to the padding that will follow. However, there are some chairs where the burlap from the inside may go all round the top of a rounded arm, to provide an unbroken support for the padding which follows, so as to get a smooth line. If an old frame is stripped for recovering, check how the previous upholstery was arranged. Early upholsterers had different ideas. The practices were not necessarily better than more recent methods, but in restoration work it may be preferable to follow the original method—even if it will be hidden and the outside will look the same whatever base technique is used.

In some chairs there are wings attached to the arms. Their method of covering has already been dealt with (see Chapter 9), but their inside surfaces should be burlapped at the same time as the insides of the arms. Also, subsequent covering should be done together so the final coverings will blend into each other inconspicuously.

In some chairs the inside padding is given a more rigid backing with a piece of thin plywood or other board (Fig. 13-1H). Chipboard or other manufactured rigid board that will not break easily can be used, but avoid cardboard or other weak board that may crack in use and become very difficult to get at to replace. Fix with nails, not tacks, which might loosen due to their tapered form.

COVERING ARMS

Any of the padding materials may be used on arms, whether square or rounded. If loose hair is used it is placed on the inside of each arm in a very similar way to that used for a seat. It is helpful to tilt the chair on its side so gravity helps the curled hair fall into place (Fig. 13-2A).

Hair is opened out and dropped on to the burlap of the inside arm of a square-sectioned example, and sewn with large loops to the burlap, either diamond fashion or with the stitches parallel to front and bottom (Fig. 13-2B). Making each loop about 3 inches should be satisfactory. Judge the amount of hair to give a finished thickness of about 1 inch for most chairs. If the edge is straight, it may help in getting a good finish to tack on cardboard strips (Fig. 13-2C).

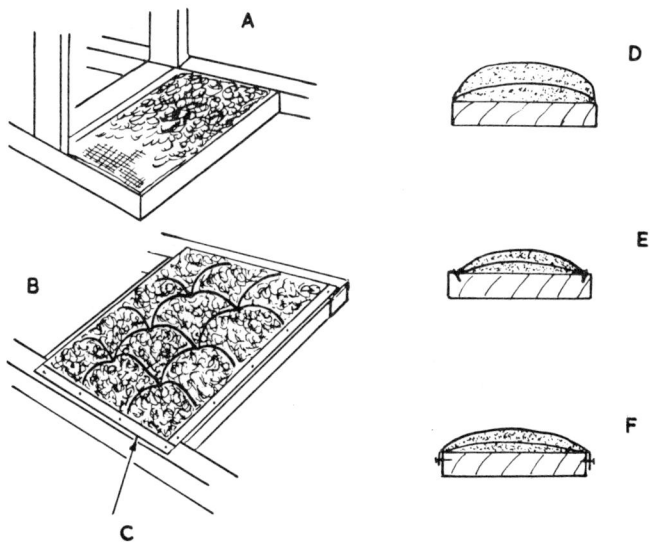

Fig. 13-2. The arm may have hair stuffing.

Loose hair is not so convenient for the top of a square arm, although it can be used. Burlap might be stretched and tacked over the wood, then stitches made into it to hold the loose hair. It is simpler to use rubberized hair or hair bought already attached to burlap, but this can be further padded with loose hair underneath (Fig. 13-2D). Fix the rubberized hair with tacks around the edges. The tacks may be on top (Fig. 13-2E) or the material taken over the edges (Fig. 13-2F).

If foam is used, pieces about 1 inch thick may be put on, and built up to give extra padding where required. Pieces should be cut to wrap over the top and down the inside, with enough at the front to round over the edge (Fig. 13-3A). Extra padding may be put under the top part and should be carried down the inside if that has a plywood or other rigid lining (Fig. 13-3B). At the outside the amount carried over will have to suit the intended design, but there will usually be enough to soften the angle. Use enough tacks or staples to hold the foam in place.

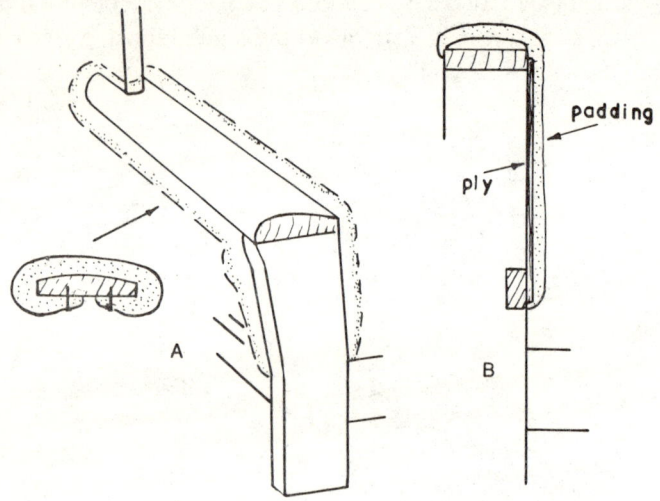

Fig. 13-3. Padding may be carried over the top of the arm.

Whether there is hair, foam, or other padding, the next step in covering a square-topped arm is to completely cover with cotton about 1 inch thick, except for the front if there is to be a wood facing. Let the cotton go in one piece from the gut rail inside, over the top, and down to the gut rail outside. Let the cotton inside go under the gut rail for its width and tack it there. Let the width of this piece of cotton be enough to fit closely to the back and project a short distance forward of the front so it wraps over (Fig. 13-4A), or allow enough to go under whatever wood facing is to be attached. If the front is to be covered with the same cloth or vinyl as the rest of the chair, use another piece of cotton, cut to fit inside the other cotton (Fig. 13-4B). Fix the cotton with enough tacks to stop it from moving when covered. The tacks need not be very close.

The arm should be covered with muslin before the finish cover is put on. This is best done by sewing parts rather than tacking them; then there will be no unevenness where the tacks pull the cotton in. Cut muslin pieces to the inside and outside sizes of the arm panels, with another piece long enough to go along the top and down the front. Make an allowance for seams (Fig. 13-4C) and sew these parts together inside out. Use sizes that will give a tight fit, by making the measurements nearer those of the frame than the outside of the uncompressed cotton.

This has to be fitted over the arm without disturbing the lay of the cotton. It helps to put a piece of cloth over the arm and lower the muslin onto it by folding down from the inside-out position (Fig. 13-4D).

Stretch the muslin evenly. Inside, let it go under the gut rail so it is between the inside arm and the seat. Tack it under the gut rail. There will be more tacks at the back, and it may be necessary to trim the muslin at the front to fit around the leg below the level of the top of a front rail. It will usually be necessary to get inside the muslin at the bottom outside in subsequent work, so only drive a few tacks partly there. This way, those tacks can be lifted if necessary and final tacking can be done later.

Many square arms are covered with the outside cloth in a way similar to that described for muslin. Allow enough for fixing to the back inside and enough to wrap around and be covered by a back piece outside. The front and the outside arm should go low enough to be fixed at the level needed to suit the design, which will be below the edge of the muslin. In many frames the muslin is tacked outside to the gut rail, but the covering cloth goes to the seat rail.

In some square-armed chairs, the cover material is sewn like the muslin cover, but with piping or welt in the seams (Fig. 13-5A). This needs careful measuring so the piping looks right when the cover is fixed. In particular, it is important that the two lines of seams are parallel. Carefully manipulating the material as it is stretched and tacked will ensure a neat fit. Use a few temporary tacks until a satisfactory appearance is obtained before final tacking. It will probably be necessary to leave final

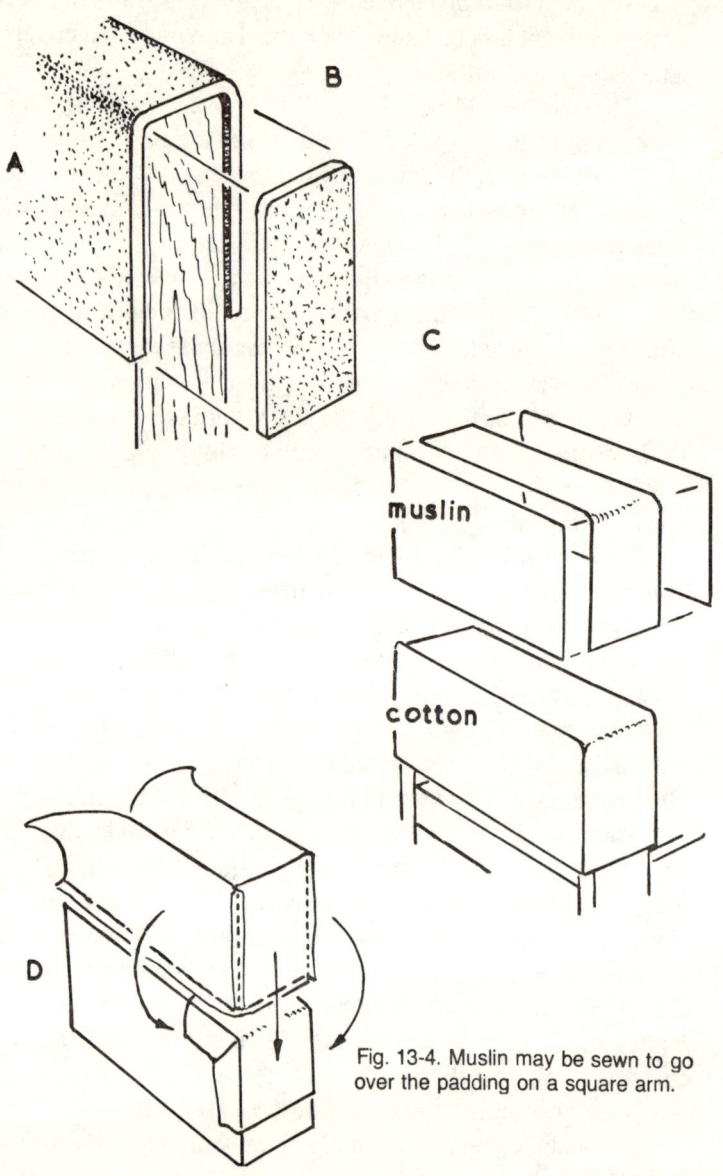

Fig. 13-4. Muslin may be sewn to go over the padding on a square arm.

tacking where the arm meets the back until the covering of the back reaches the same stage. Similarly, the lower edge will have to follow on the lower edge of the seat front and the finishing along this line should be done to both parts at the same time.

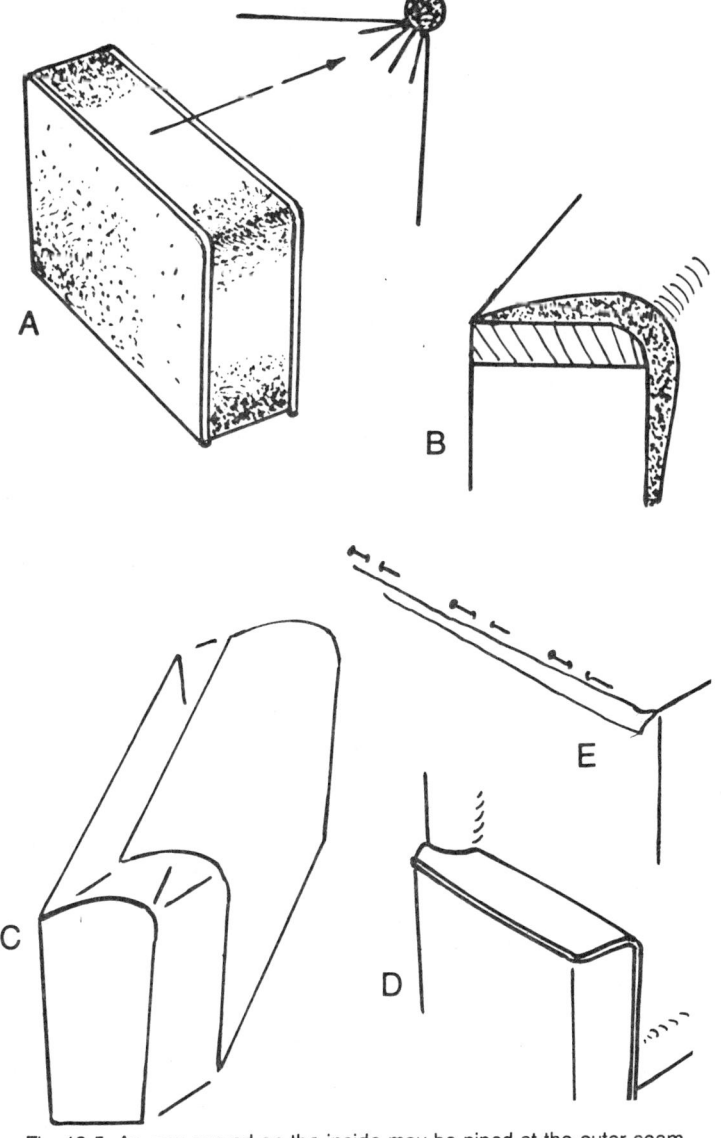

Fig. 13-5. An arm curved on the inside may be piped at the outer seam.

If an arm has a rounded inner edge (Fig. 13-5B), further covering of the already padded burlap consists of using a piece of foam or rubberized hair about 1 inch thick over the burlap and about the same size and shape, although there should be enough to spare at the edges to compress it a little. It may be possible to use a few tacks. To avoid compressing with tacks where a hollow might show through, the padding may be located with a little adhesive around the edges.

This can be followed with a fitted muslin cover. The outside can wrap around the front and be sewn to a piece that covers the inside and top (Fig. 13-5C). As with the square-topped arm, cut this so it pulls tight. This type of arm may have cotton for the depth of the arm outside, or there may be only enough to roll over the top edge enough to round it. In both cases the muslin can be taken right down the outside.

Strain evenly with temporary tacks, then tack in a similar way to the muslin on a square-armed chair, leaving some of the final tacking until adjoining parts are covered, if necessary.

The outer cover for this sort of chair is made with the seam in a similar place to that of the muslin, so there may be a piped line along the outside edge of the top, curving to come down the inside line of the front of the arm (Fig. 13-5D). If there are curves or flares in the arms, it will be advisable to make paper patterns, although a good shape can be obtained by putting on the cover material inside-out and pinning along the line of the seam (Fig. 13-5E). In some chairs with this type of arm, a different pattern is used inside and out and the change of pattern comes along the line of the seam, to make an attractive feature of the design.

If an arm is rounded, it will have a burlap inner surface similar to a square-topped arm, but the curve over the top needs an even padding all over. In traditional upholstery the hair is sewn to the burlap, but that hair located over the curved top is only kept in place by the cotton wrapped over it (Fig. 13-6A). It may help in locating the hair to coat the top of the frame with adhesive, or there may be burlap stretched and tacked tightly over it, and some stitches taken through that.

With loose hair it helps to retain it and give a good front edge to make a welt that is between ordinary piping and fox edging in size. This is made of burlap with a cord up to 1/2 inch thick enclosed and tacked around the arm front so it projects forward slightly (Fig. 13-6B). Take this from near the lower upholstered position outside, around the front and down to the seat rail inside. Tack frequently enough to hold it, probably every two inches.

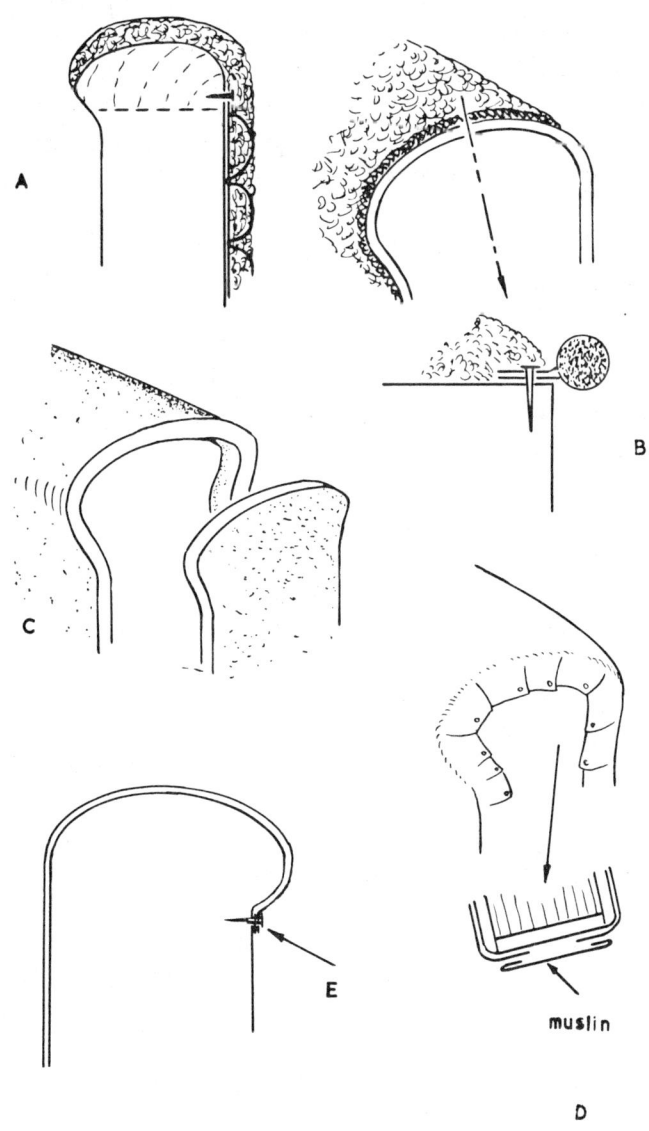

Fig. 13-6. With a traditional rounded arm, hair and cotton go over the top.

Fit cotton in a similar way to that described for a square-topped arm. If the front is to be padded, let the main cotton project forward and enclose another piece in it (Fig. 13-6C). If there is to be a wooden front added, turn in enough for that to cover and omit the front padding.

It would be difficult to make a sewn cover for most rounded arms so muslin over cotton is best drawn over the front and tacked (Fig. 13-6D). Both cotton and muslin may need careful trimming to completely cover a shaped arm and fill the area right to the back. Small pieces of cotton may be used as fillers at the back, but you should get the front right with a single piece. Allow ample muslin for pleating at the front, and trim off surplus after tacking.

The outer covering cloth is fitted in a way very similar to that for the muslin. How far the piece from the top goes down the outside depends on the design. If the top rolls over and there may be curve in the arm when viewed from above, it is better to let the cloth cover the inside and go over the top to the inner angle (Fig. 13-6E), otherwise there would be creases that could not be avoided if the same cloth was taken down the outside. The cloth is tacked inside the angle and another piece used outside.

A modern chair with rounded arms may be padded with foam, but otherwise it is treated in a way similar to that of a traditional chair using hair padding. With some outer covering material there may be no need to use muslin, but even if it is not essential, it helps to get the padding into an even shape before the cover is applied.

OUTSIDE ARMS

If the top overhangs the outside of an arm, as it does in many rounded arms (Fig. 13-7A) and in some modern styles, the outer covering material is best made of a separate piece of cloth. This may have to be done, even if there is no overhang, when there is a wing attached to the arm.

If the front of the arm is covered and not intended to have a wooden piece added, cotton, muslin, and covering material may be fitted there first, with the covering material taken around the edge of the front frame (Fig. 13-7B). If there is to be an added wooden front, it may be better to take the side padding and cover around the front (Fig. 13-7C).

The material over the top should be tacked along the angle under the overhanging edge (Fig. 13-7D). If the face is open, there should be burlap tacked on (Fig. 13-7E) and this may be backed with webbing in the same way as the inside was. Over this goes a piece of cotton or a piece of thin foam, although in some cheaper work this may be omitted.

Blind tack the outside fabric close under the rolled top. Crease the cloth that is to turn under, then tack through a strip of cardboard (Fig. 13-7F). Pull the cloth down and temporarily tack through its lower corners so it lies in place without creases. How the bottom edge is to be dealt with depends on the design. It may be best to take the edge of the cloth under the bottom rail, where it is folded back and tacked. It may have to finish on the outside, where it is turned under and tacked in a straight line. If there is to be a flounce or other addition, the cloth may be temporarily tacked at this stage, and finally fixed when the additional work is done.

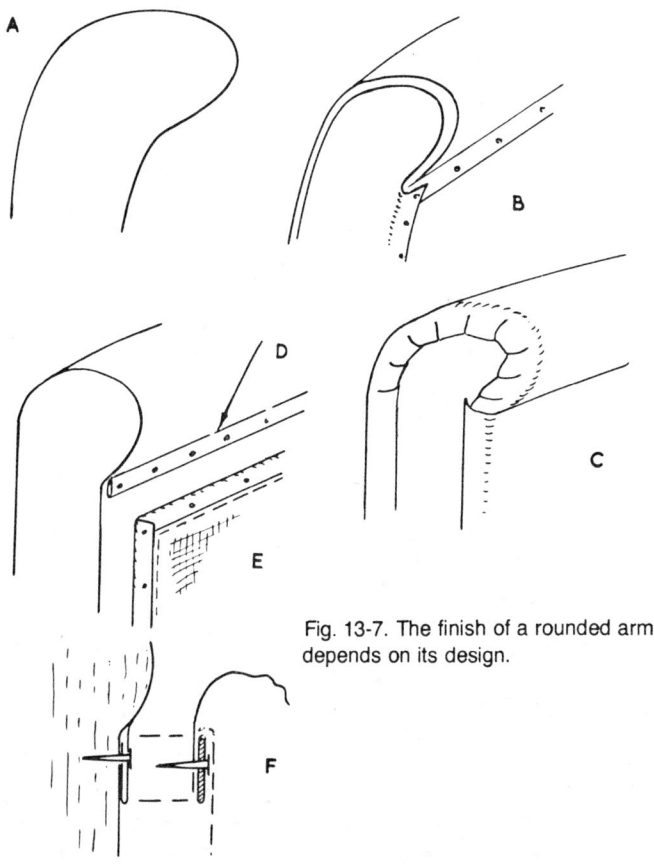

Fig. 13-7. The finish of a rounded arm depends on its design.

247

At the back the cloth outside the arm will usually wrap around the back and eventually be covered by a back piece. If the muslin has been carried around the front, the cover material also goes around and is tacked. In some chairs with rounded arms there is piping around the front. This would be included in the front joint of the inside and top, with enough left hanging to be included in the outside arm joint (Fig. 13-8A). In that case the front of the outside fabric is carefully turned under and tacked through the piping (Fig. 13-8B). Although blind tacking would have been better here, this cannot be done along two edges of any panel. In some chairs it may be better to use blind tacking here and use ordinary tacking under the overhang at the top.

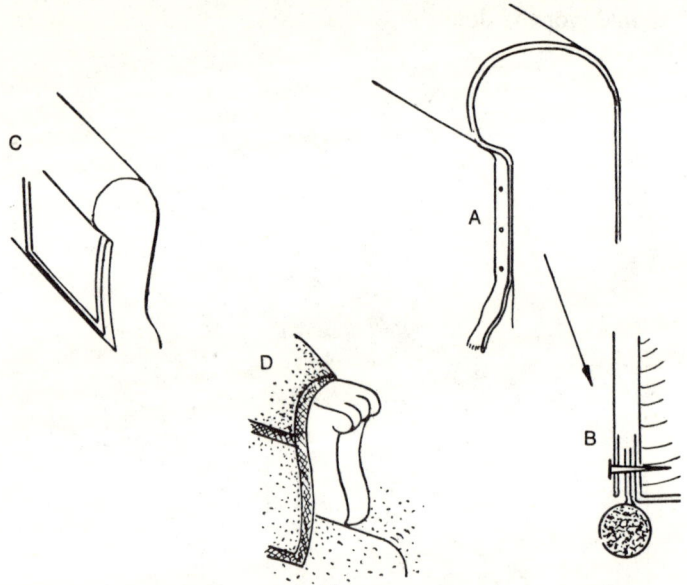

Fig. 13-8. Seams are arranged inconspicuously, with gimp and piping used to hide joints.

Where there are exposed tack heads, it is customary to cover them with gimp. Traditionally this was held only with gimp pins, but in new work it helps to use a modern adhesive, either in place of or in addition to the pins. However, be careful that no adhesive goes where it should not be, as most of these adhesives are impossible to remove completely. Put adhesive on the back of the gimp with a narrow piece of wood.

Tacks or pins through gimp should be staggered to hold down the edges. Some upholsterers tack narrow cardboard strip and glue the gimp to that, but this is difficult to do neatly so the cardboard is completely hidden. Even if back tacking is used or the tacks are hidden where the cloth turns over an edge, there may be a complete border of gimp for the sake of appearance or the maintaining of a pattern. (Fig. 13-8C).

Much of the older style of antique furniture with exposed wood at the front of the arm and other parts of the frame exposed, needed the covering material carefully turned under and the edges covered with gimp (Fig. 13-8D). Care is needed to see that the final edge follows the intended pattern, which may not necessarily be parallel with the edge of the opening. It is more likely that the edge has to be parallel with an outer line of the exposed wood.

FRONT ARM PANELS

False front panels may be used, particularly with rolled-over tops and flat fronts to the frames. The attached front piece makes a neat finish in a prominent place which might otherwise be difficult to deal with efficiently and to give a satisfactory appearance.

If the padded edge is turned in all round, the panel needs to show an even border, so it should be carefully marked out (Fig. 13-9A). A preliminary shape made from cardboard or other scrap material may be used as a template. Sometimes stout cardboard is used as the actual panel, but it is better to use something that will retain its stiffness. Thin plywood is the best choice.

The plywood may be merely covered directly with material similar to that of the rest of the chair. For this finish it is advisable to round the edges of the plywood. The cloth is wrapped over and held to the back with adhesive (Fig. 13-9B). If it is a cloth with any pattern, nails with small or no heads can be used and they will not show on the surface (Fig. 13-9C). It may be possible to drive nails and cut their heads off so enough is left projecting to enter the back of the panel when the nail is driven further with a rawhide or rubber mallet (Fig. 13-9D).

If the covering is plain fabric or vinyl, nail heads might be too obvious. The alternative is to use one or two tack strips on the back (Fig. 13-9E). Fix the strips with glue and let the glue set before proceeding, then use a rawhide mallet to drive the whole assembly into position.

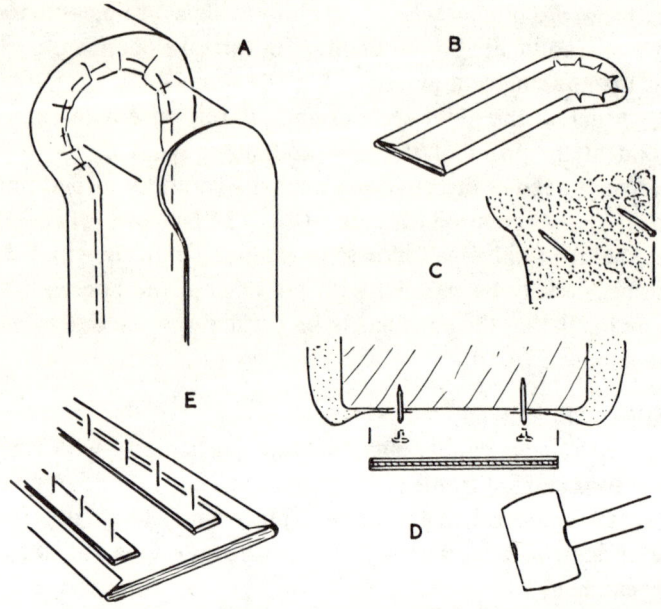

Fig. 13-9. The front of an arm can have a piece of wood fixed in several ways which disguise the method of fixing.

With soft and open weave material it is possible to nail through from the front so the nails do not show. The weave is eased open with the point of a regulator so the nail can be inserted. It is driven and the head brought close to the plywood surface with a punch, then the point of the regulator used to bring the weave back into place over the head again.

The appearance of vinyl and some fabric panels may be improved by including piping around the edge of the panel. Let the piping be loose around the edge so it is pressed up to the surface when the panel is fitted (Fig. 13-10A). Fix the piping with adhesive and short tacks into the back of the panel.

A panel may be given some padding. This can be made of cotton, cut to the same size as the panel, and pulled to a curved section with the covering (Fig. 13-10B). Piping with similar material makes a neat division between the panel and the surrounding padded edges (Fig. 13-10C). This may be fixed with tack strips, although with a loose fabric it is possible to open the weave and drive a nail, using a punch through the cotton (Fig. 13-10D) and then to close the weave again after driving.

It is possible to fill the space in the front of an arm with fabric only, or fabric backed by cotton or foam, but this has to be done carefully to get an even border. When a plywood or other rigid shape is used, an even shape is automatic. Covering with fabric only also means that it is almost impossible to hide the fastenings, so tacks around the edges could be covered with gimp (Fig. 13-10E), although vinyl of the imitation leather type looks attractive with decorative nails (Fig. 13-10F).

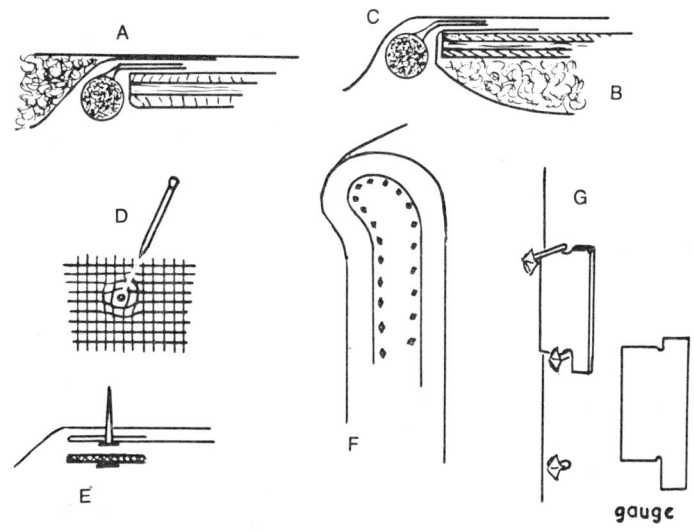

Fig. 13-10. Sometimes piping is used, along with cotton padding, or fabric is used alone, with gimp or nails.

When nails are used for decoration it is important that they are evenly spaced. In some leather or imitation leather upholstery, large decorative heads are arranged so they touch, or almost touch. Other nails may look better if they are spaced further apart, but then it is important that the spacing between the nails and their distance from the edge of the fabric panel be even. Any discrepancies may be very apparent in this conspicuous position. A card template can be used to check both distances. Drive a nail until its head is still a short distance above the surface, put the gauge against it and start and next nail (Fig. 13-10G). Remove the gauge and drive the second nail to the same position and use the gauge to locate and start the third nail. Continue like this all round. Stand back and check the pattern of nails. If it is satisfactory, drive the nails tight. If any need moving, it is still possible to lift them without damage.

Fully Upholstered Chairs: Backs

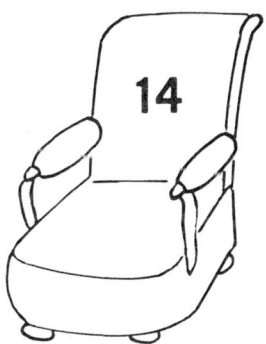

When anyone is sitting, the seat takes the main load and contributes most to comfort—or discomfort if it is badly designed. Arms may be a convenience, but it is possible to use a chair without arms for a long time without noticeable discomfort. However, anyone sitting expects to find some back support if the chair is to be used for long. A stool or other seat without a back is only suitable for brief use. Similarly, a plain wood back or a simple rail does not provide acceptable comfort for long. Even a dining chair with its usual padding does not remain comfortable if it is used as a means of rest for a long period.

The back of an upholstered chair has to be built at a good angle to the seat to provide comfort. This is decided mainly by the frame, but there can be slight variations provided by the way upholstery is applied. Padding has to suit the body. If there is little padding, the back may be contoured to suit the body. This is done in molded polystyrene and other similar frames, but it is unusual today to provide any contouring in a wooden frame. Some old chairs that did not have the benefit of modern padding materials were given shape to their wooden parts, and there were some examples of very clever woodworking craftsmanship that backed the less effective padding of Victorian and other times. One of these frames makes an interesting recovering project, but most work will be with straight-backed frames.

There are several ways of providing padding to a chair back. Although it might seem reasonable to use a rigid back, such as a piece of plywood, and cover it with thick padding, this is not done, and there is always some flexible support behind whatever padding is used.

There could just be a pattern or webbing immediately behind the padding. Rubber webbing might be substituted for ordinary webbing to give more flexibility. Zig-zag springs are used more for backs than for other parts of a chair, and in some fully upholstered chairs there may be tension springs. Although all of these methods of springing are used in the backs of fully upholstered chairs, they are more appropriate to the more lightly upholstered lounge chairs already described.

It is more usual in a fully upholstered chair that is well-padded in the seat and arms to use coil springs in the back, particularly if this is the method of springing the seat.

LIGHT SPRINGING

If a frame is intended for webbing as the only support behind cushioning, it will have the forward faces of the frame level and there will usually be an extension over the full width above the arms (Fig. 14-1). Webbing will usually be spaced evenly but there could be slightly closer spacing behind the body than behind the head. It is usually sufficient for the gaps between the pieces of webbing to be rather more than the width of the webbing in both directions. This applies whether the webbing is ordinary or rubber.

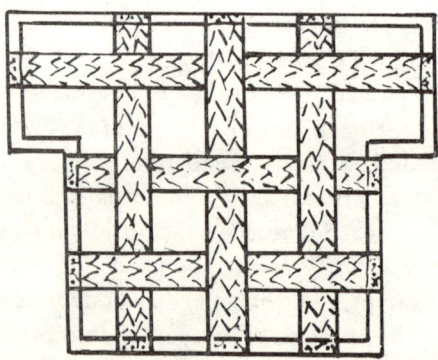

Fig. 14-1. The nature of the chair back dictates the design of the springing.

Zig-zag springs are stiffer than tension springs, and they may be used the long way of a space if that is more convenient. In a chair back they probably give a more natural support if they are upright. Spacing about 6 inch centers should be satisfactory in most chairs (Fig. 14-2).

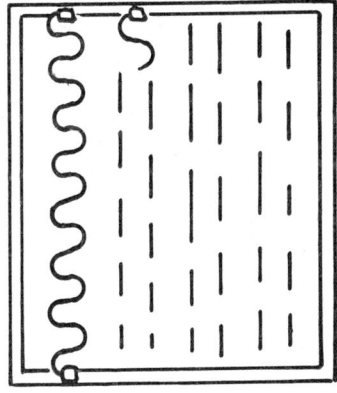

Fig. 14-2. Six-inch spacing of the springs should be sufficient.

If the support is to use tension springs, they will usually be placed across a chair back, because that is the shortest direction of the panel (Fig. 14-3), but in a loveseat or sofa, the width is too great and they have to be upright.

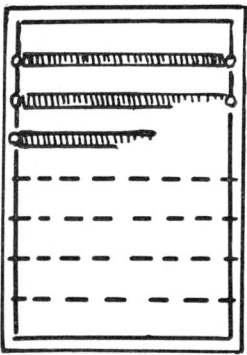

Fig. 14-3. In most chair backs tension springs are positioned crosswise.

With any of these methods of springing the padding applied directly may be quite light and little more than a covering for the sake of appearance. The main padding is then provided by a cushion, which may be fitted and shaped, but it is removable and an independent thing, even if it is not often removed.

COIL SPRINGING

Coil springs in a chair back are used in a way similar to that of the springs in a seat, but they are often smaller and lighter. The back frame is not usually as thick as the base for the seat, so the springs are shallower. Webbing is fixed on the rear surface in a pattern to suit the springs, but not usually as closely as under a seat. In some frames the bottom rail is not as thick as the outer frame parts and is set in so its front edge is level. This means the webbing has to curve in and to allow for this it is helpful to have a close double line of webbing to support the bend (Fig. 14-4). By taking the webbing forward in this way, the lower line of springs will then be made to force forward more than those higher up, giving a greater curve to the covering where it is needed.

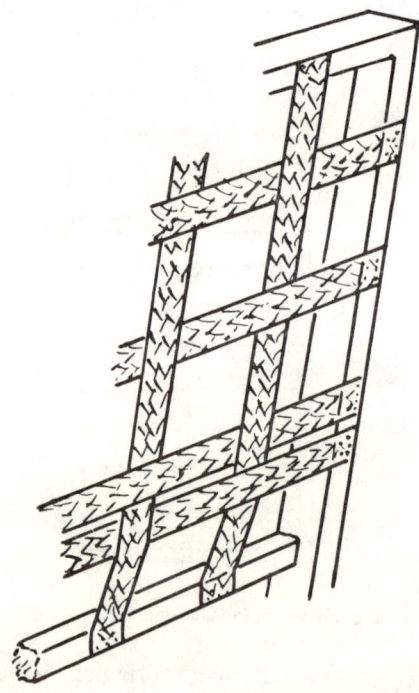

Fig. 14-4. Webbing is positioned according to where the coil springs are to be located.

Coil springs are usually located over the webbing crossings, but where the back overlaps the arms the springs may go on single parts of webbing (Fig. 14-5). It is also possible to have close-fitting Marshall springs in their cloth cases. Small springs of this type, with wire edging to retain their positions, can make a very comfortable back.

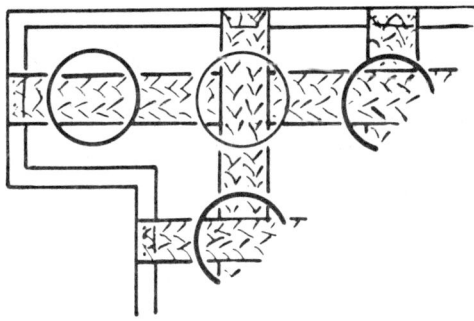

Fig. 14-5. Where possible, coil springs are located atop webbing crossings.

In production work there are spring assemblies used for chair backs, where the springs are on steel webbing, and there is a wire mesh front to spread the thrust against the front padding (Fig. 14-6).

Fig. 14-6. A wire mesh diffuses the support of the springs to all points.

Spring spacing depends on the style of finish on the back. If there is to be a wire around the springs and the edge of the upholstery is to be finished squarely, the outer edges of the springs should be close enough to the outside of the frame to allow the padding and covering to take the intended shape, which means within about 2 inches of the outside of the frame in most chairs. If the edge is to be rounded or it has to blend into wings or sides, the springs can be located further from the edge.

Have the chair so the back is horizontal and locate the springs on the webbing. Mark with chalk or other means. Sew with twine and a curved needle, in the same way as described for the seat. Use lock knots and make sure the springs are secure as any failure means partial dismantling to correct the error.

The free parts of the springs have to be tied in a way similar to those of the seat. The strain is not usually as great, so it is possible to use single instead of double twine and to reduce the number of crossings, unless it is known that the chair will get heavy use. If this latter is the case, treatment in the same way as a seat may be advisable.

Ties are taken squarely across the frame in both directions and then diagonally. If there is to be a wire edge, the twine is taken up through the outer springs and the top edge may be pulled down to help shaping. The twine starts on the top edge, goes down to a tack, then up through that spring, into the next, and over any more, to drop through to a tack on the bottom rail (Fig. 14-7). As with seats, the wire edge is fitted after all twine is fixed.

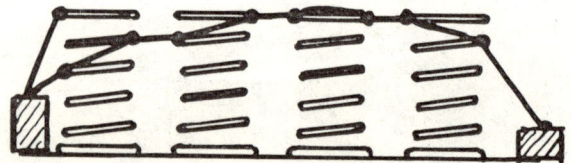

Fig. 14-7. Twine is tied to each coil spring and affixed to tacks driven in the frame.

If the back is to finish rounded, the twine may go over the springs across the chair, then the upright ones can go through to pull down the top springs and return over all the springs to the bottom (Fig. 14-8). Although Marshall spring units are already linked, it is advisable to use twine over them as well.

The back has to be related to the seat. Make sure that when the seat has been fully upholstered there is space for the back to be completed and the stuffing and covering taken underneath for fixing. It is the position of the bottom row of springs that affects this.

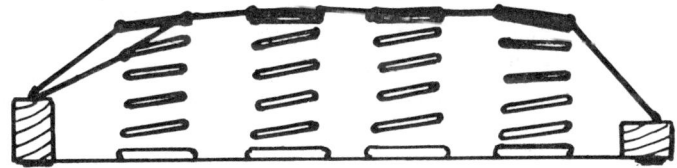

Fig. 14-8. Springs are tied in a different way if the back is to be rounded.

Individual upholsterers have their own methods of weaving the twine through back springs. To a certain extent the main purpose of the twine is to prevent the springs from moving as they are covered and to reduce movement when the chair is in use. Twine going across may go through the springs instead of over them, leaving the twine that goes up and down to help with shaping.

FIRST PADDING OF BACK

The method of upholstering the back should be related to the method used for the seat and arms. If there are wings, they will be worked in the same way as the back and their covering will be done in stages at the same time as the back.

The springs are covered with burlap. For some chairs the burlap may be a single thickness with the edges turned in or out and tacked to the frame. Use temporary tacks and move the burlap as necessary to get an even tension over the springs before finally tacking around the edges. Sew the springs to the burlap in the same way as described for the seat.

The back may have double burlap with cotton or hair between the layers. Apart from any value in padding the back, this can help in giving the final back a good shape. It can serve in a way similar to fox edging on a seat.

Fix the first layer of burlap with tacks, but leave several spare inches around the edges (Fig. 14-9A). Cut another piece of burlap to fit inside the first. If cotton is to be used, use a piece almost as large as the first piece of burlap. Put it in position with the second piece of burlap ready to fix. Roll over the edge of the cotton and sew through to secure this in place (Fig. 14-9B). Do this all round the exposed sides and across the top. Where the padding comes within the arms and across the bottom there is no need for the roll and the edge can be fixed by sewing through or by tacking through all thicknesses (Fig. 14-9C). With some frames it may be more convenient to take the burlap under the bottom rail (Fig. 14-9D).

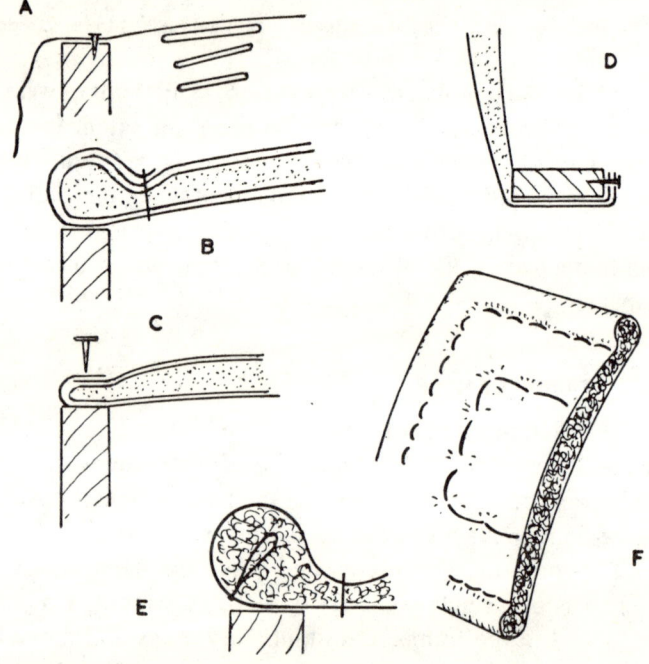

Fig. 14-9. First padding of the back.

If loose hair is used instead of cotton or other sheet material, hold the back horizontally and drop picked out hair on to the burlap to give a finished thickness of about 1 inch, then build up enough to make a roll at the exposed edges and sew around in the same way as with cotton. With loose hair it is advisable to use sink stitches at intervals all round into the rolled edge (Fig. 14-9E).

With a large back and loose hair something has to be done to prevent the hair from moving and settling at the bottom. There may be more thickness at the bottom than higher up for the sake of comfort, but no more should be allowed to drop. Large, loose, running-through stitches can be made in a pattern over the back. In a small chair one square may be enough, but use more if necessary (Fig. 14-9F).

If the back is to be padded with plastic foam or latex rubber, it will probably be satisfactory to only use one layer of burlap against the springs, but there could be a layer of about 1 inch plastic foam between layers of burlap in the same way as described for cotton. This spreads the thrust of the springs and should result in a more even final shape to the covered back. It will also add to its comfort.

SECOND PADDING OF BACK

Padding with hair is done in a way similar to that for the seat, except that the chair is tilted so the back is horizontal. Pick the hair carefully and spread it evenly over the back to a good thickness. Sew with large loops to the burlap (Fig. 14-10A). If there are wings do these at the same time. With wired springs and a square edge the stitches will have to retain the hair as it wraps over (Fig. 14-10B). Get a good shape and an even density of hair, although it may be slightly greater at the bottom than near the top.

In some chairs the top edge is also required to be padded. If hair is being used, this can be taken over the top (Fig. 14-10C). As loose hair would be difficult to keep in place, it may be better to use rubberized hair, at least for part of the thickness.

Rubberized hair can be used over the main area for part of the thickness if preferred. It would not be sufficient padding alone, but it could be laid first and more loose hair put over it to make up a good thickness, preferably with retaining stitches pulled through in the same way as for an entire padding of loose hair.

In much modern upholstery the padding is made of foam or latex and this does not need as much attention to get a good fit as does hair. It may be possible to use several layers of thin foam to make up the thickness and get the required shape, bringing it around the edges of the springs to the frame (Fig. 14-10D) or carrying it around to provide padding on a broad top or side (Fig. 14-10E).

In some chairs it may be better to use the foam or latex in one thick pad. Whether it is in one or more thicknesses, it will have to be cut to fit inside the arms. It may be possible to extend a front pad with pieces held to it with adhesive to overlap frame edges. This may also be advisable if trimming latex exposes hollows that should be covered.

If a very large piece of foam is used, it may be advisable to put a few loose stitches through it to retain its position, especially if the final covering is not to include buttoning. Adhesive can also be used to hold foam or latex in place.

When hair is used as a padding, it should be covered with cotton and this is best arranged in a single piece. Within the arms and seat let it come close to these other surfaces. At the sides above the arms and along the top, let it overlap enough to retain the hair and provide additional padding (Fig. 14-10F). There will probably be no need to fix the cotton, but if necessary use a few tacks or pins until the cotton is covered.

If the top and exposed edges of the back frame are narrow and rounded, take the inside padding far enough over the edge so it will eventually join with the outside of the back and the appearance from the front shows a clean pattern, with any joints beyond normal view from the front. The covering of a back with a flat edge will go over in the same way, but padding of that has to be considered in two steps, while the narrower edge can be dealt with in one operation.

The cotton should be covered with muslin. This should also be used over foam or latex. Without it there is a risk of friction on the cover causing the plastic to wear and crumble, particularly around the edges or anywhere that twine or fastenings pass through. Muslin acts as a guard against this.

Trim the muslin approximately to shape. Arrange it centrally. Tack it temporarily to the bottom rail. Pull it over the padding and tack it temporarily to the top rail. Stand the chair upright. Cut the muslin so it can be tucked between the back and the inside of each arm and be long enough to project at the back.

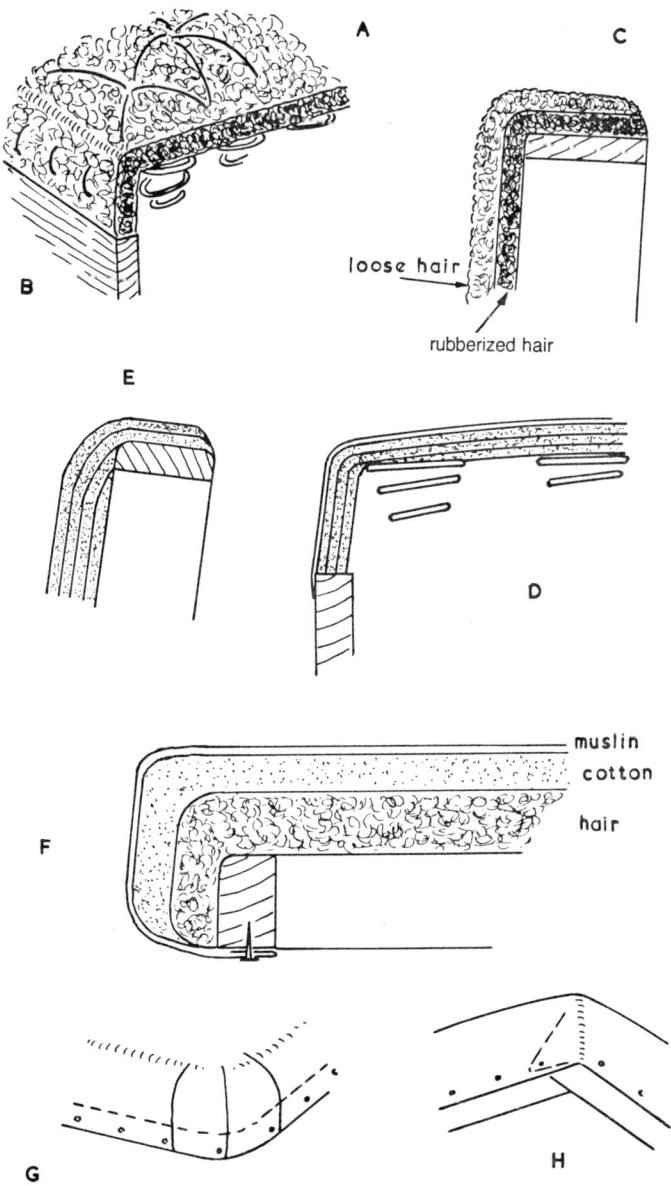

Fig. 14-10. The upholstery of backs is similar to that of seats, and may continue over the top and sides.

Temporarily tack it to the back. Adjust the lay of the muslin. Move the temporary tacks as necessary until a good fit is obtained. Tuck muslin under the bottom back rail above the seat.

When the fit is satisfactory, do final tacking all round. With a square-edged outline, the muslin may go to the back and be turned under along the edge, where it is tacked. If there is a rounded corner, pleat the muslin evenly (Fig. 14-10G). If the corner is more nearly square, use one large pleat (Fig. 14-10H). This is better than making cuts at the corners.

The cover material has to go over the same area as the muslin, with a little extra to overlap on to the back, where the edges will be covered. If there is any prominent pattern it will have to be carefully centered. A paper template is advisable. If the back is square-edged, it will have to be given boxed edges. It may be possible to make up parts that will be out of sight by using other material as flys.

The seam may be plain or have piping. In some designs there are special edgings which are sewn in like piping, but the edge shows a fringe, decorative cord, or other ornamental seam. This would have to be carried through to other parts of the chair as well. The border, which forms the boxing, needs to be wide enough to wrap over the back. With the boxing and any piping sewn on, there can be flys, and the assembled cover should be ready to slip over the back muslin (Fig. 14-11A). If flys of other material are used, leave collars of the cover material for a short distance beyond the seams or piping, so there is no risk of a wrong material showing in the joints inside the arms.

Take the bottom fly under the back and adjust its tension so the cover makes a good fit. If there is a piped top edge, this is very obvious, so it is important that it is symmetrical and not pulled unevenly over the padding. In some chairs the bottom fly is tacked to the bottom back rail. In others it may be taken down and tacked to the back seat rail (Fig. 14-11B). Pull the side flys through and tack them in the same way as the muslin.

Pull the border over the back and temporarily tack until it is seen to be even, then tack all round, far enough in to be covered by the back cloth (Fig. 14-11C). If the back is rounded in section the front cover material may be wrapped over and fixed with tacks in the same way (Fig. 14-11D).

An alternative way of dealing with that type of back is to sew the back and front together. Then they can be slipped over, but they cannot be sewn below arm level. The flys are pulled through from the front. When the top of the cover has been adjusted to fit symmetrically, the flys are tacked and the back is taken down as far as the bottom of the chair rail (Fig. 14-11E).

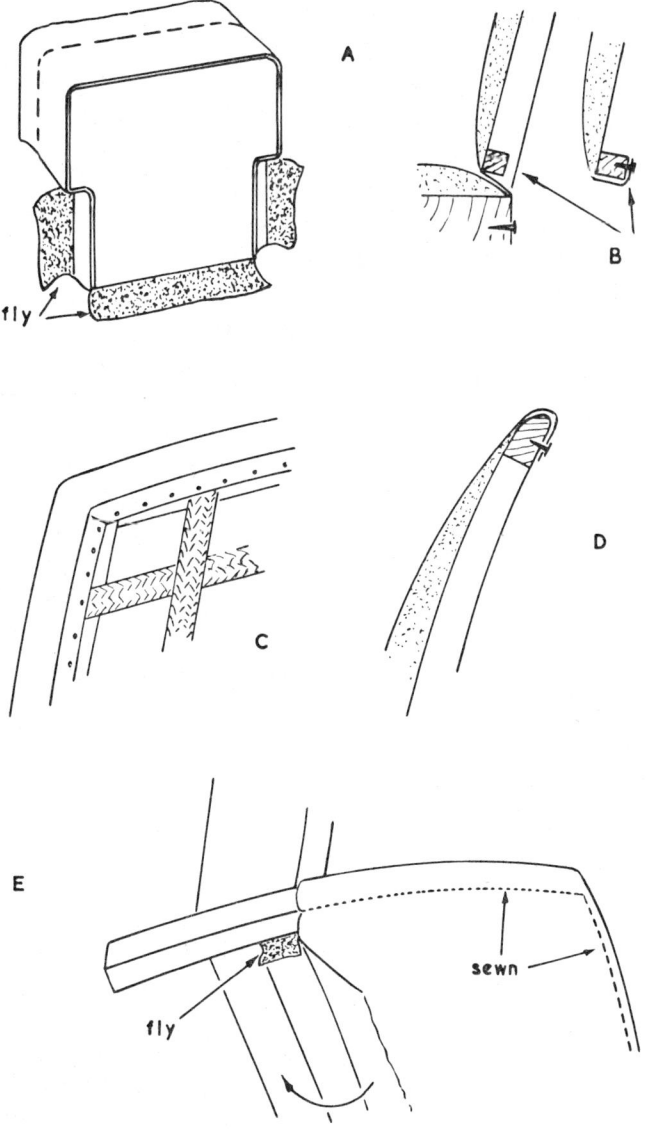

Fig. 14-11. The back cover fits around the padding and blends into the arms and seat; then the fabric is sewn on the back.

OUTSIDE BACK

If a chair is used against a wall the appearance of the outside back may not matter much, but if it is brought to the center of the room, the back may be very prominent, so it needs to be neat and match the rest of the chair. The back material should be the same as the rest of the chair.

For a simple back there may be burlap put on first to close the open part of the back, then cover material placed over it with its edges turned in and tacked an even distance from the edge (Fig. 14-12A). Another way is to use piping around the edge over the wrapped-over cover material from the front. This is tacked to the wood (Fig. 14-12B). If there are straight sides, start at the bottom of one side with a tack and stretch well towards the top, to get the piping straight. Burlap is used, but its edge is kept inside the piping. Use the cover material up to the piping (Fig. 14-12C). It could be tacked. With some patterned material, black gimp pins or other small nails will be hidden by the design (Fig. 14-12D). For the neatest finish, slip stitch the turned-in edge to the cloth of the piping all round (Fig. 14-12E). The lower edge can be taken under the bottom rail and tacked.

The back may include some cotton between the burlap and the outer cover to give a softer feel there (Fig. 14-12F). If the top of the back is straight across it is possible to avoid slip or blind stitching across there by using blind tacking instead. Piping or welt is put all round, but at the top edge the cover material is put under a cardboard strip, which is tacked close to the top piping (Fig. 14-12G).

Stretch down and temporarily tack under the bottom rail. Get a good tension at the center and work outwards from there. Tension across the width in the same way, working from the centers of each side upwards and downwards. If the pattern is suitable for hiding nails, nail the turned-under edges close to the piping or, preferably, slip stitch them to the piping (Fig. 14-12H).

If the back is curved, as it usually is in older furniture, the covering method is similar, but greater care and skill are needed to get good results. Blind tacking through a cardboard tacking strip can be used as far as possible around the curve at the top. It is usually possible to start at the center and bend the cardboard

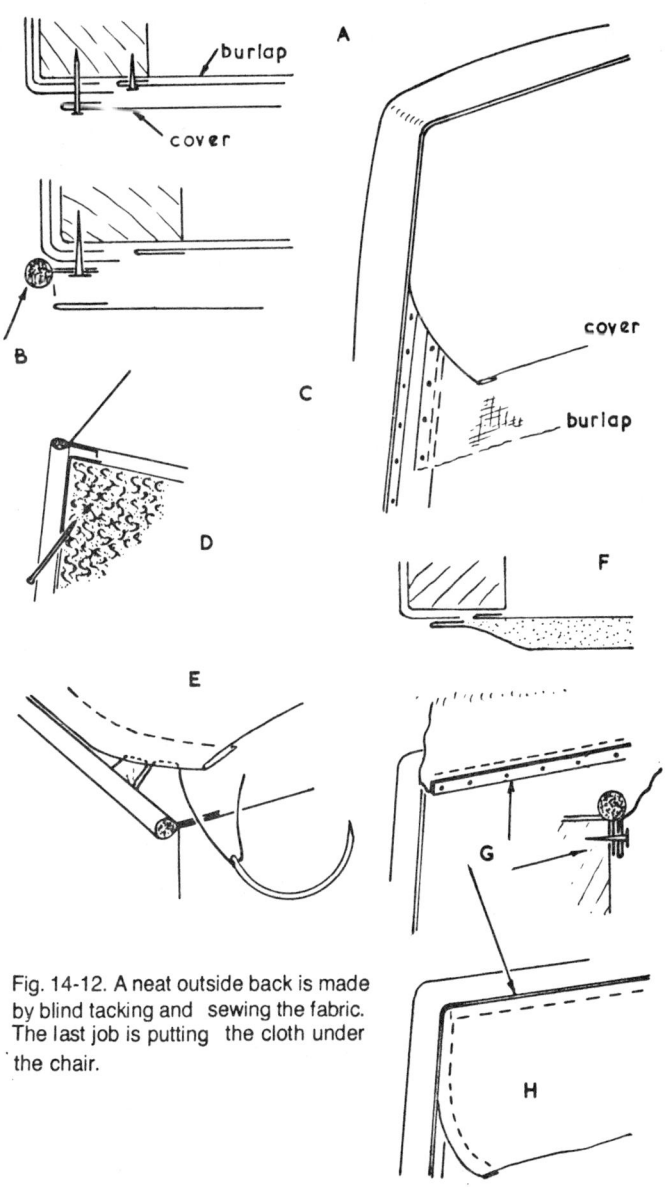

Fig. 14-12. A neat outside back is made by blind tacking and sewing the fabric. The last job is putting the cloth under the chair.

as you progress outward until the amount of curve prevents you from stretching the cloth out of the way any further. From that point, stretch the material down to temporarily tack below the bottom rail, then work outwards from the end of the blind tacking with slip or blind stitches taken through the piping, if used, to the cloth wrapped over from the front. Follow the contour of the back. Pins or temporary tacks will help to position the fabric and get it evenly tensioned. See that the back is not pulled out of shape by uneven stitching. Blind sewing may be tedious over a long seam, but it makes the best finish.

UNDERNEATH A CHAIR

The underside of a fully upholstered chair will rarely be seen, so its appearance may not be important. However, it is a fairly large volume of exposed springs and webbing, closed at the top with the burlap under the padding. Dust may gather around the springs, either rising from the floor or dropping from the burlap or stuffing. This could later fall on a clean floor. It is more hygienic to avoid an accumulation of dust, so it is better to cover the underside of the frame with something to prevent dust from passing through. Sometimes this cover has been made of ordinary burlap, but there are other materials, treated to make them dustproof, which are more suitable. A flat bottom merely has the material turned in and tacked, or it can be fitted around legs (Fig. 14-13).

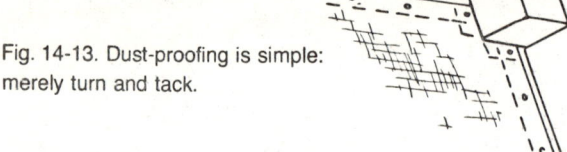

Fig. 14-13. Dust-proofing is simple: merely turn and tack.

A fully upholstered chair of traditional form is quite heavy, so it is usual to provide it with casters or some other form of glider so it can be moved without lifting. The corners of a flat bottom may have wood blocks to take casters. Legs may be drilled to take the type with a long stem. In many modern designs the blocks or leg projections to take the casters are the only exposed woodwork. These should be stained and varnished or otherwise finished almost to completion before the covering material is fitted, to avoid the risk of marking with wood finish. A final coat of polish may be left until upholstery is completed, in case the wood gets marked during handling.

It is interesting and useful to provide a finished piece with some record for future reference by you or some other upholsterer. This record may be a card fixed inside the bottom frame before the dust cover is tacked underneath. It can give your name and the date of the work, or any other information that might be of use, such as the type of material used and any reference numbers or other data that might be of use when a repair has to be made. What you are making now is the antique of a century hence. Some future collector may be glad to have the information you provide!

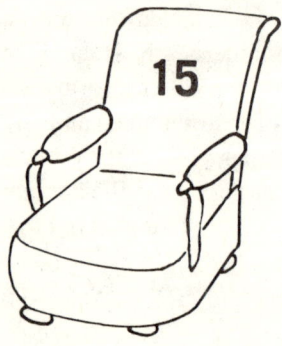

15

Fully Upholstered Chairs: Finishing

The instructions in the preceding chapters deal with the basic upholstery work to pad and cover a chair almost completely, but there are some finishing touches that are also needed. Some of these have been mentioned where they are incidental to other processes, but more detailed information is given in this chapter.

When the arms, seat, and back have been sprung, stuffed, and covered, the chair, sofa, or couch is fit to use and may look quite attractive; but the difference between a hasty or unskilled piece of upholstery is often in the care given to the work which rounds off the process. In some cases these finishing techniques are needed for strength. Sometimes they are purely decorative. In many cases they combine both functions.

BUTTONING

In early upholstery, which used a variety of loose filling materials, it was necessary to sew through to prevent the filling from moving about. Despite some internal stitching before the cover was added, gravity would eventually cause the stuffing to settle to the lowest point, or it would be pushed aside in use. This would cause the point where the greatest weight was applied, and therefore the greatest padding needes, to actually have less padding.

This process of sewing through has been used with buttons on the front for a very long time in upholstery history. In fact, buttoning has become accepted as a normal part of most upholstered furniture, whether stitching through in a particular case is necessary or not with modern stuffing materials. Even with the stuffing in the form of a single pad there is a risk of the cover moving in relation to the pad, so a few sewn-through buttons are worth having.

Some information on buttoning has been given in the instructions on covering stools. The technique is basically similar for other pieces, but in most fully-upholstered furniture there is a soft back as well as front. The buttons used in these cases are usually a domed type (Fig. 15-1A). It is possible to buy buttons already covered and it may be possible to obtain some that have patterns to suit the finishing fabric. Buttons do not have to be the same as the fabric and it helps in some designs to have them contrast, but in many chairs the buttons are covered with the exact same material as the chair.

Covering buttons by hand is difficult and not always very satisfactory. In commercial production a button-covering machine is used. It may be small and operated by hand with a lever. A disc of material is stamped out, then a mold put in the machine between dies; it pressure wraps the material around the mold and forms the button. For hand covering, a disc may be cut with a round hollow punch or scissors. It is put around a plain button and fixed with adhesive. For vinyl or leather there may be stock buttons that will match, but if the cover material has to be put on a button, it is helpful to heat it, so it becomes more pliable and will take the compound curvature without creasing.

If the stitches go through to webbing or burlap there is usually no need for anything on the back. If the anchorage for the stitch is only open-weave burlap or you have doubts about security, put a plain button (Fig. 15-1B) on the back. An alternative to this plain button is a small strip of wood with a hole through (Fig. 15-1C).

The buttons are a design feature. If they are accurately placed they improve appearance, but if they are out of line or off center, they are so obvious that the fault will be very apparent.

On a square or near-square item like a seat, there will be a symmetrical pattern (Fig. 15-1D), but on backs there are several ways that the buttons can be arranged (Fig. 15-1E).

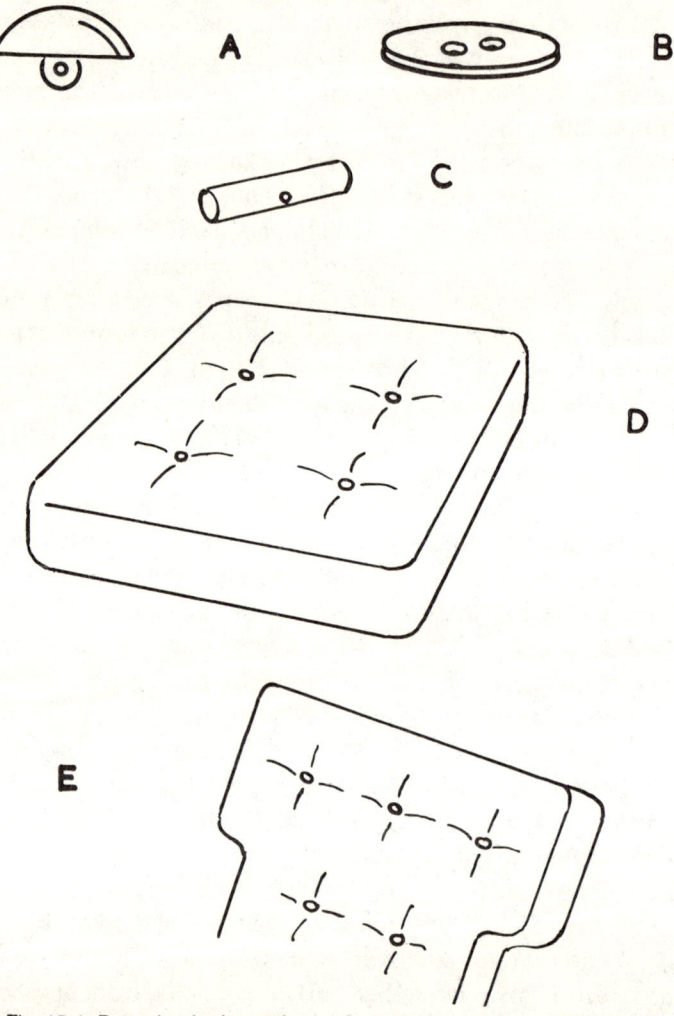

Fig. 15-1. Buttoning is decorative and prevents movement of the stuffing.

For normal buttoning there are no special needs to keep in mind while fixing the muslin and covering fabric. Buttoning is not done until after final fixing has been done around the edges of the panel to be buttoned. Measure and mark out the button positions with light chalk marks. Use pins at the button positions if that will help in locating them. If the other side is normally hidden there is no need for special marking out there. It does not matter if the stitches do not go through at right-angles to the surface, but they should not be far out, or a diagonal pull may be apparent in the lay of the button. Diverting the stitch to miss a spring will not matter, however.

Use a straight needle long enough to go through, and fairly stout twine. If the eye of the needle will take double twine, the button can be threaded on and both parts of the twine taken through in one pass (Fig. 15-2A). Otherwise it will be necessary to go through and back. Both parts come out at the same point at the front.

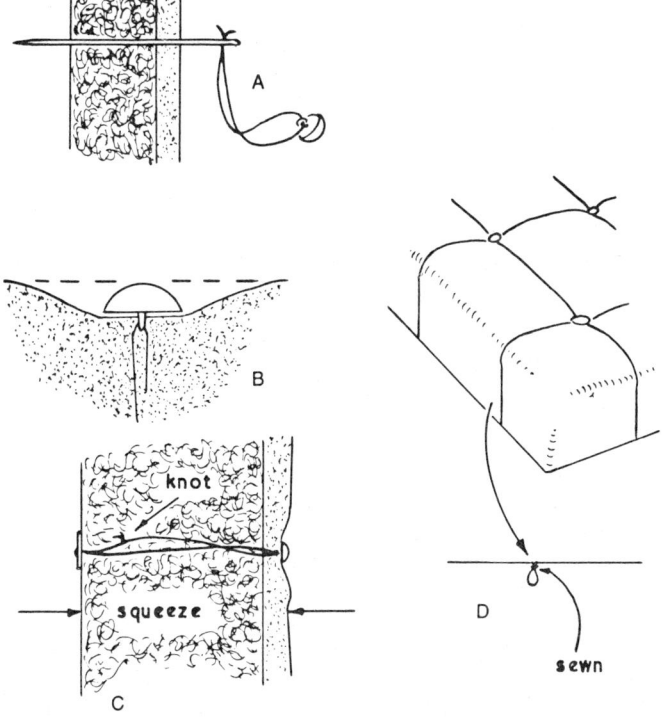

Fig. 15-2. Buttoning techniques.

Tie the twine with a slip knot that can be locked later after it is adjusted, but do not pull the first one tight until all buttons have been positioned. In normal buttoning the button is drawn in until its top is just below the normal line of the surface (Fig.

15-2B). Adjust all buttons in a panel by moving the slip knots and see that the indentations match so there is a uniform appearance. When this is satisfactory, lock the knot and cut off surplus twine, but not so close to the knot that it might work loose. If there is a button or piece of wood with a hole in it, work and adjust through this in the same way. If the thread runs directly through webbing or burlap, a small wad of cotton put under the loop of twine will reduce any risk of pulling through.

If the chair has a seat cushion that can be lifted out, it is usually made so it will turn over and be used with either side up. If this is buttoned there will have to be similar buttons on both sides. In this case both panels should be marked out with chalk and the button positions carefully located. The long needle going through will have to be manipulated until the point comes out in the right place on the second side. When all twine has been adjusted and the knots locked under one button, the cushion is compressed and the knot worked out of the way into the body of the cushion (Fig. 15-2C).

The buttoning can be emphasized by lines across the fabric. In some vinyl and other plastic, commercially produced upholstery the effect is obtained by molding in lines. In woven fabric the lines can be made before the cover is fitted, by sewing across so a tiny loop of fabric is taken up. This has to be allowed for and the fabric positioned correctly when it is fitted, but this is no more difficult than centering a prominent pattern (Fig. 15-2D).

There was a fashion for very deep buttoning some time ago, and some antique furniture may be seen with the buttons pulled in very much more than in most upholstery. This is also a feature of some modern furniture. It may make its own pattern or it may be combined with lines across, either squarely or, more often, in a diamond pattern. The action of deep buttoning, in any case, tends to crease lines from one button to another.

Deep buttoning has to be planned before the chair is covered. There is too much fabric to be pulled in for covering to be done tightly before buttoning. Deep buttoning that is obviously strained does not look right. Deep buttoning was evolved in the days of hair and other loose stuffings. Although it can be used with foam and latex, the effect of pulling in the cover material may not always be effective, as the creases may not pull in as markedly or neatly.

For deep buttoning, the seat or back is covered to the stage where cotton is put over the stuffing and covered with muslin, but the muslin should only be held with a few tacks temporarily. Leave some surplus muslin around the edges. Do an experimental marking out on the muslin and try pulling through with temporary stitches to the back. Tacks will have to be released to allow the muslin to pull in. When a satisfactory pattern has been obtained, do final tacking around the sides. How much material will be taken up by the deep buttoning stitches depends on the size and pattern, but expect about 2 inches of fullness to be needed on a seat about 18 inches square and 5 inches thick.

The finishing fabric should also be amply large. It may be marked with chalk in a pattern to match the muslin. It can be placed over the muslin, then as each temporary stitch is released, another, with the button slipped on, can be made in the same place (Fig. 15-3A). With care it is possible to get the deep-buttoned pattern in this way before any fixings are made around the edges (Fig. 15-3B). When all of the buttons are fixed, tension the twine so all buttons pull in the same amount. It may be necessary to ease some out and adjust creases to make a neat pattern before finally drawing in and locking the knots. If there have been any temporary tacks around the sides, release them and position the fabric evenly. Tack around the sides in the usual way.

In this type of buttoning it is usual to place the knot under the button. There is considerable pull on the twine, so do whatever is necessary to prevent it from pulling through at the back. Cut the twine ends off close enough to be hidden by the button and use the point of a regulator to get the knot under the button (Fig. 15-3C).

Most plastic covering materials are affected by temperature. If vinyl or similar material is to be used for deep buttoning, it needs to be soft to take up the deeply indented shape. Heat is needed to soften it. If the weather is hot, or the work is being done in a hot shop, that may be sufficient, but otherwise some local heat will help. This can be any sort of electric heater, directed towards the part being worked, although it is desirable to maintain a uniform heat over the surface that is to be deep

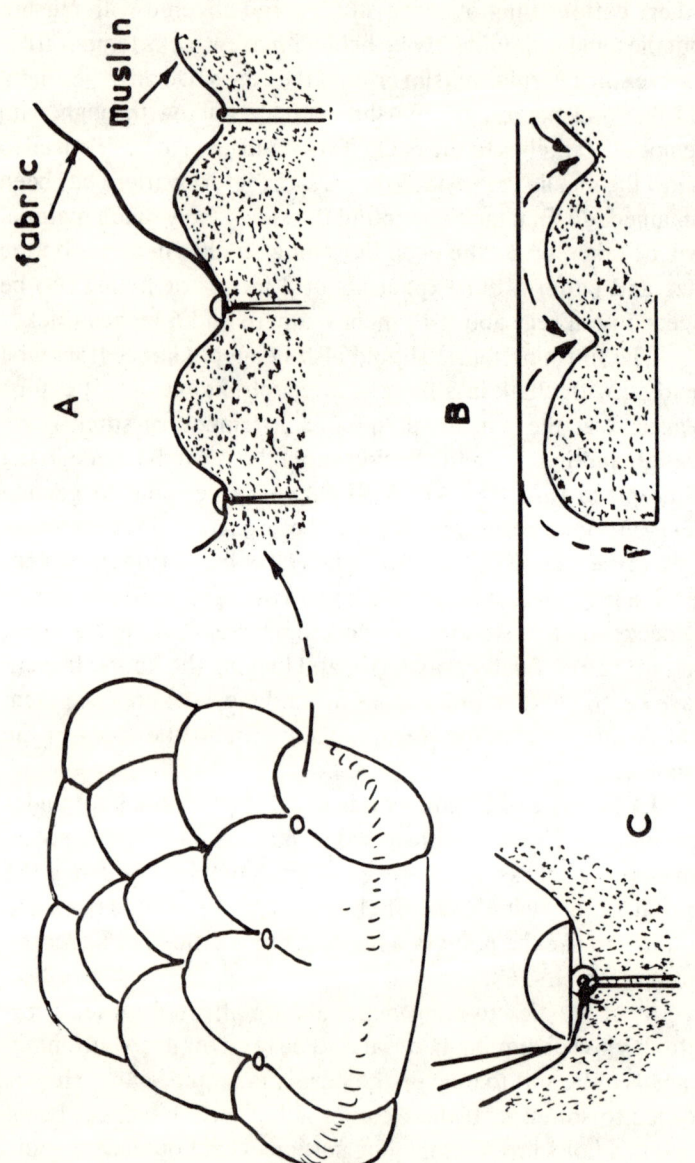

Fig. 15-3. Deep buttoning requires allowance in the fabric before fixing the edges.

buttoned. Experiment to find the amount of heat that can be used. It is usually possible to heat the surface so it is uncomfortable to touch, without damaging the material. The material will then take the intended shape and keep it when cooled.

DECORATIVE NAILS

An ordinary nail head may not be regarded as a thing of beauty, but if arranged in a pattern even plain nails can look attractive. This can be seen in some colonial and pioneer furniture, where available materials had to be used and nails that could not be hidden were arranged to look neat. For example, a simple diagonal arrangement along a joint is effective (Fig. 15-4A).

With leather or plastic imitation leather, nails can often make an adequate decoration without the addition of any other decorative feature. A club chair or similar piece of furniture in vinyl or leather gets its effect from its proportions and decorative nails at seams and joints.

Nail heads are from 1/4 inch to 1/2 inch across and the length of the nail portion is usually 1/2 inch, which is enough for most purposes (Fig. 15-4B).

Head patterns are basically round, but they may come in various patterns of intertwined lines, formal flowers, or haphazard hammering (Fig. 15-4C). The heads may be given an antique or oxidized finish, which will not be in much contrast to natural leather color, or they may be plated so they show up against a leather background.

It is important that the heads are not damaged when the nails are driven. It is advisable to push a spike into the wood to make an easy entry for each nail. Some nails may not be damaged by hitting with a hammer, but it would be better to use a rawhide or plastic mallet. However, the size of the end of this mallet makes precision hitting difficult and it may be better to use a punch.

The ideal punch would have a hollow in the end to match the nail head, but a reasonable substitute is a piece of soft wood, with its end grain against the nail (Fig. 15-4D). It may not last long, but it is easily replaced.

Decorative nails may be driven directly through a seam or a turned-under edge. This may be all that is required where the lower edge of the outside arm or front covering comes over wood that is partly exposed (Fig. 15-4E), but in some places a strip of vinyl can be laid like gimp where the nails are to come. This can be done where pieces meet and overlap. There may be

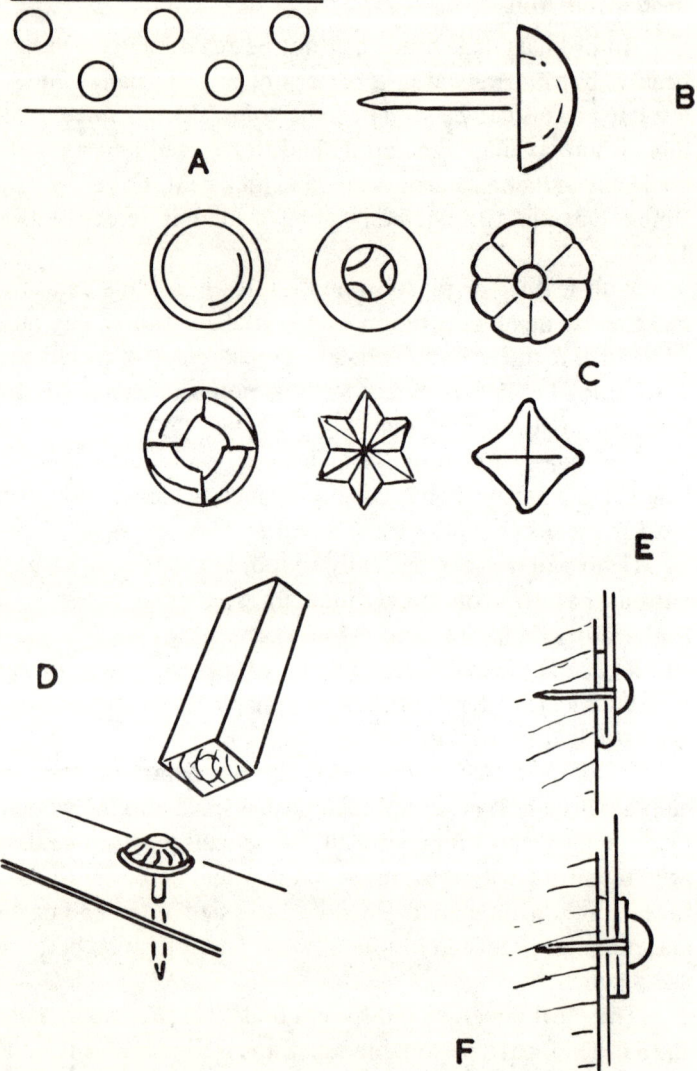

Fig. 15-4. Decorative nails are used mostly with leather and vinyl.

adhesive and tacks to take the initial load, but a strip over will hide the joint and make a background for the nail heads (Fig. 15-4F).

If an edge of vinyl or similar material is to be nailed and it is difficult to get the intended shape without creases, work from the middle of the edge outwards. Get the required tension near the center and progress each side of that nail. If necessary, apply heat with an electric heater or lamp and adjust the material as required as you progress. Do not use any more heat than needed to get the material soft enough to pull to shape.

GIMP, RUCHINGS, AND WELT

Gimp has already been mentioned in chapters dealing with places where gimp is needed for construction. A very large range of gimps are made in sufficient colors to match any finishing fabric. The widths and patterns vary, but the most useful is a little more than 1/2 inch across. There is scrollwork on the surface. This scrollwork, or another uneven surface, allows black gimp pins to be driven. Their heads will be very inconspicuous after being driven level. With modern adhesives it is now possible to safely stick gimp over joints and to limit pins or nails to the few needed to keep the gimp in place while the adhesive sets.

Ruchings are like gimp, but they are more elaborate, with tassels, looped cords, and other decorative work that has bulk to stand out from the surface. They are intended to make a more prominent decoration than gimp and a chair design has to be planned to treat them as a feature (Fig. 15-5A). The ruching has to be related to the covering material and be complementary to it. If the fabric is comparatively plain it may be the ruching that is important.

Another form of ruching is arranged like welt or piping with a piece to be sewn into a seam (Fig. 15-5B). This allows the same decorative feature to be carried around a soft edge and where the fabric fixes to wood.

Welt or piping has been described earlier. Plastic piping can be obtained for use with vinyl. It is possible to make piping from offcuts of the covering fabric, preferably cut on the bias, diagonal to the weave. For decorative purposes it is possible to make welt of other materials, to give a design feature something like the use of ruching, where attention is drawn to the different welt framing panels of covering material.

A similar effect can be obtained by making the welt with cord larger than the usual piping cord, so although the welt is the same material as the covering, it shows up more. Some furniture uses double piping (Fig. 15-5C), which may not always be very tight, so its varying line around and edge gives an unusual design feature. This makes a good division between upholstery fabric and an exposed polished wood frame.

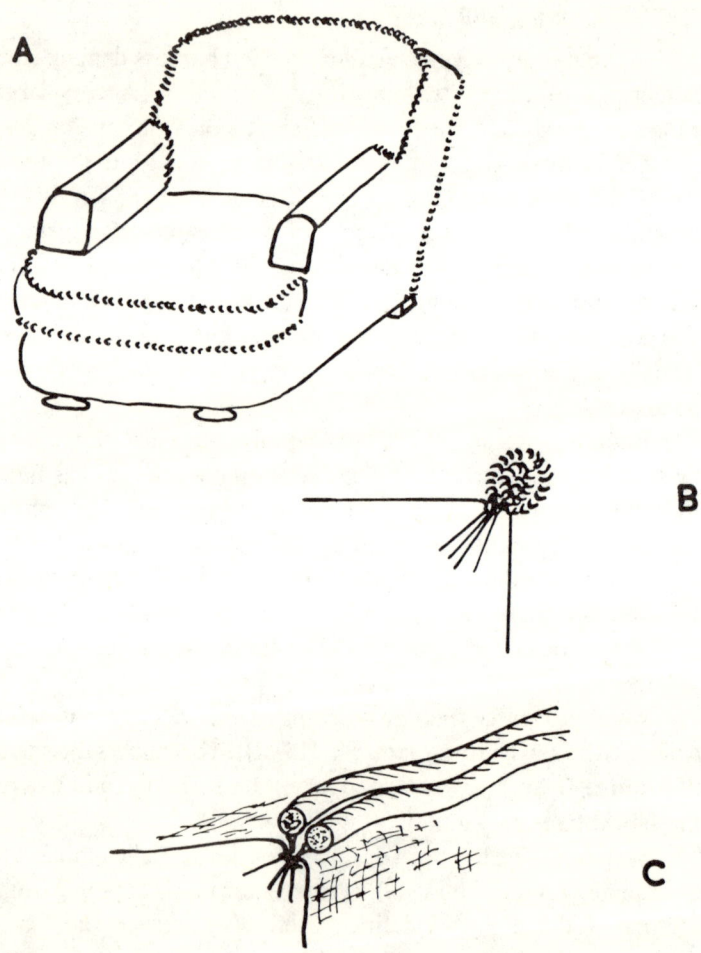

Fig. 15-5. Special decoration can be made by alternatives to single piping.

BOTTOM BAND

In some fully upholstered chairs the seat fabric covers all there is of the front frame, but in some chairs there is a band across the chair below the seat. This bottom band (Fig. 15-6A) is not usually very wide, but the few inches of width has to be decorated in some way. The band may be covered by a flounce, as described later in this chapter. It could be covered with fabric surrounded by gimp or ruching to match the rest of the chair, or it could be provided with some padding, which is usually preferable.

In many chairs the bottom band comes between the arms and its covering stops there. It is unusual for it to go across the arms at the same level, but in a chair where the seat projects forward of the arms, the bottom band will also do so (Fig. 15-6B). The only difference in covering is the need to take the upholstery around the angles at each end.

To cover the bottom band with upholstery, the method is very similar to that used for fixing a padded back to a chair. Fix piping along the top edge of the wooden band (Fig. 15-6C). Tack at the ends and stretch—around the corners if it is a projecting seat—then use sufficient tacks along the length to keep the piping in place.

Have a piece of cover material large enough to allow for back tacking at the top and turning in at the ends. Fix the top edge with a cardboard strip so it is close to the piping (Fig. 15-6D). Tack firmly with the covering fabric turned up out of the way.

The stuffing can be a single or double thickness of cotton or foam. It helps the appearance if the greatest thickness of the curved front is towards the top. This can be arranged if a double-width piece is allowed to overlap (Fig. 15-6E), and is then folded back (Fig. 15-6F). If a single layer is considered sufficient, this is laid in place and the covering fabric pulled over it. The fabric goes below the bottom edge of the band and is tacked there (Fig. 15-6G). Before tacking below for the full length, turn under at the ends to make a neat fold against the edges of the arms. If the arm is covered with fabric the neatest finish is to blind sew the ends to it. Otherwise it may be necessary to tack. Blind tacking might be used, with the type of tack

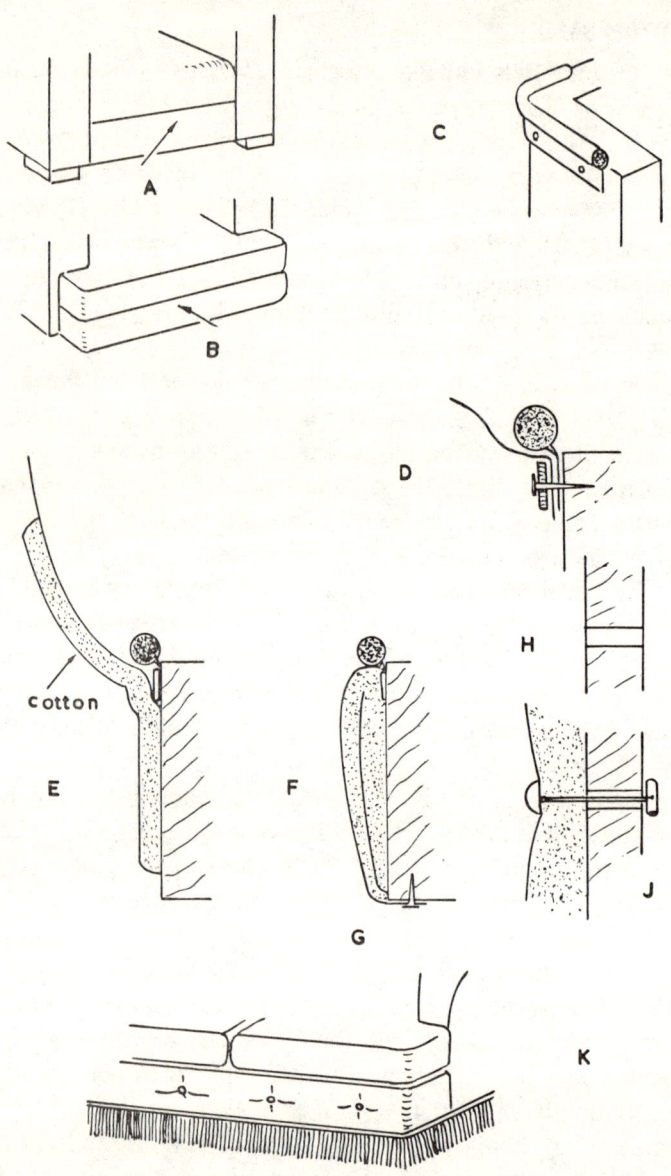

Fig. 15-6. A bottom band is an extra feature of some chairs.

strip that has the tacks through the cardboard before putting inside the fold, but this is awkward. Tacks on the surface may be covered with gimp.

If other parts of the upholstery have edges decorated with ruching, this could be carried around the bottom band, and there would be no need for blind tacking.

A broad bottom band might be decorated with buttons, if they will fit in with the general design. The bottom band is usually a fairly substantial piece of wood as it forms part of the structure of the frame. If buttons are to be used, the wood should be drilled for the thread before covering is begun. Holes about 1/4 inch diameter will make it easy for the probing needle point to find the way through from the front (Fig. 15-6H). Use a strip of wood or a button at the back (Fig. 15-6J).

A buttoned bottom band with ruched edges may be given a finish by having a fringe around the bottom. This is obtained already made on a band to be fixed like gimp to the lower edge of the upholstery (Fig. 15-6K) and should be arranged so it just clears the floor and hides the legs.

FLOUNCE OR SKIRT

Some chairs are given a skirt that goes all round and fills the gap between the bottom of the upholstery and the floor. In fact, the skirt or flounce finishes 1/2 inch or more above floor level, depending on types and depth of carpet. There should be enough clearance to prevent it from catching or dragging on the floor.

The skirt may be pleated at the corners only on a chair, although there may be pleats under the joints between cushions on a sofa. Another flounce may have pleats at regular intervals, up to the point where pleats and the spaces between them are the same. There are other methods of making flounces, too, and anyone with dressmaking or interior decorating experience may gather the skirt material in various ways to get special effects.

If there are pleats only at the corners (Fig. 15-7A), the length of material needed is much less than with close, or box, pleating (Fig. 15-7B). To match the rest of the upholstery the strips to make the skirt should be cut across the material. If cut lengthwise, even with unpatterned material, the difference would be apparent. A pleat that folds back 4 inches uses up about 16 inches of material. Allow for this when measuring around a chair. Joints to make up length should be arranged in the back of a pleat, if possible, so they will be hidden. Allow for the final joint to come in this way, probably at one of the back legs.

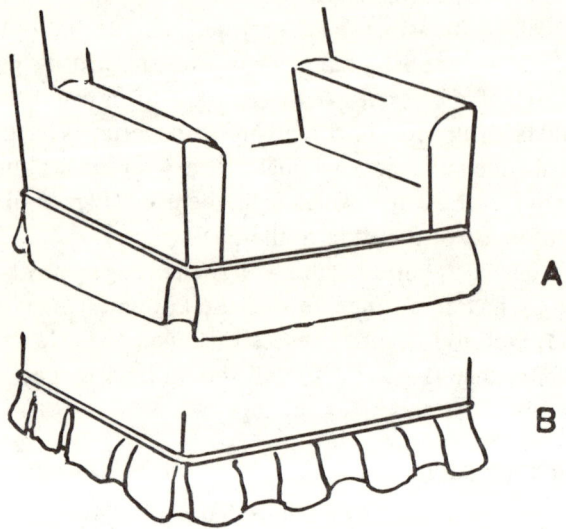

Fig. 15-7. Flounces are pleated in several ways.

The fabric might be merely seamed at the bottom (Fig. 15-8A), or it could be doubled (Fig. 15-8B). This is better lined with muslin (Fig. 15-8C). It will then hang better. What is done at the top depends on the design of the chair. The edge of the flounce could come under a length of gimp where it joins the chair upholstery (Fig. 15-8D), or it would hang out better if there was blind tacking against a length of piping (Fig. 15-8E). The method of fixing determines the width of material to be cut. A small amount of surplus can be hidden when the edge is fixed.

Sew strips to make up a sufficient length to go around the chair. If the skirt is to be lined, cut and join up muslin, keeping it about 1 inch narrower than the skirt fabric. Sew a line of stitches along what will be the inside of the skirt to keep the cloth and muslin in the correct relation to each other. Fold the skirt along its center and sew the edges together (Fig. 15-9A). Press the fold, either by ironing or with a commercial press.

Locate the places where the pleats are to be (the corners of a chair plus the front of a sofa). Fold back the two sides of each

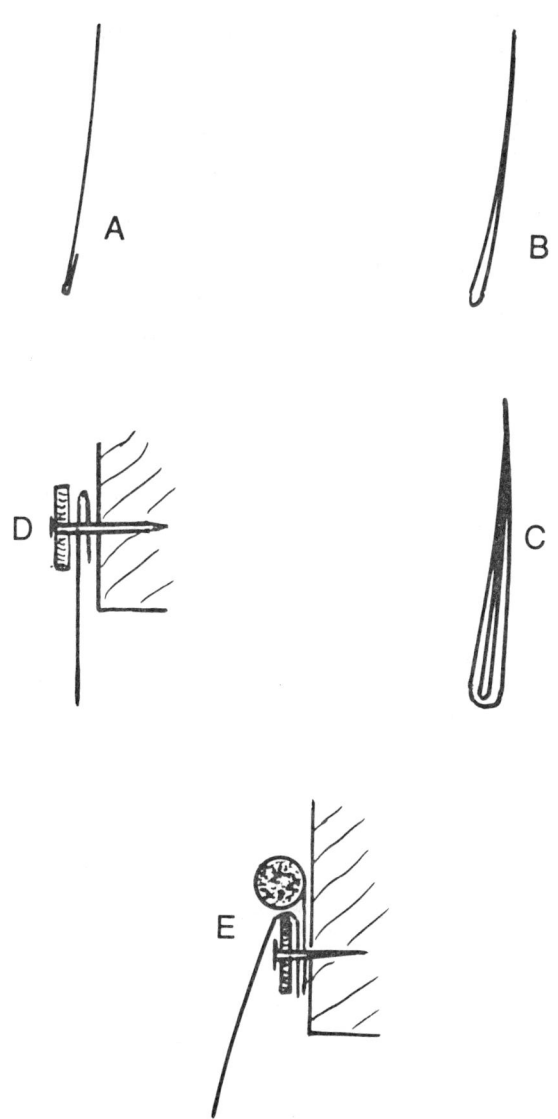

Fig. 15-8. Flounces must be planned to give an even result and are usually fixed below piping.

pleat equally and pin the folds (Fig. 15-9B). Leave enough to make the joint inside a pleat at the previous corner.

Have the skirt material on the actual chair and get the pleat positions by putting them over the corners—not by measuring.

When all pleats have been folded and pinned, sew across the top of each pleat to hold it in shape, then remove the pins. The joint between the two ends of the skirt can be sewn, but that corner can be left with its pleat unsewn, then slight adjustment can be made there if the distance around after fixing does not prove exactly the same as first estimated.

If the top edge is to have piping and blind tacking, sew on a length of piping that will allow the flounce to hang to the intended depth when it folds over (Fig. 15-9C). Check the length of piping around the chair and let the meeting ends come at the back.

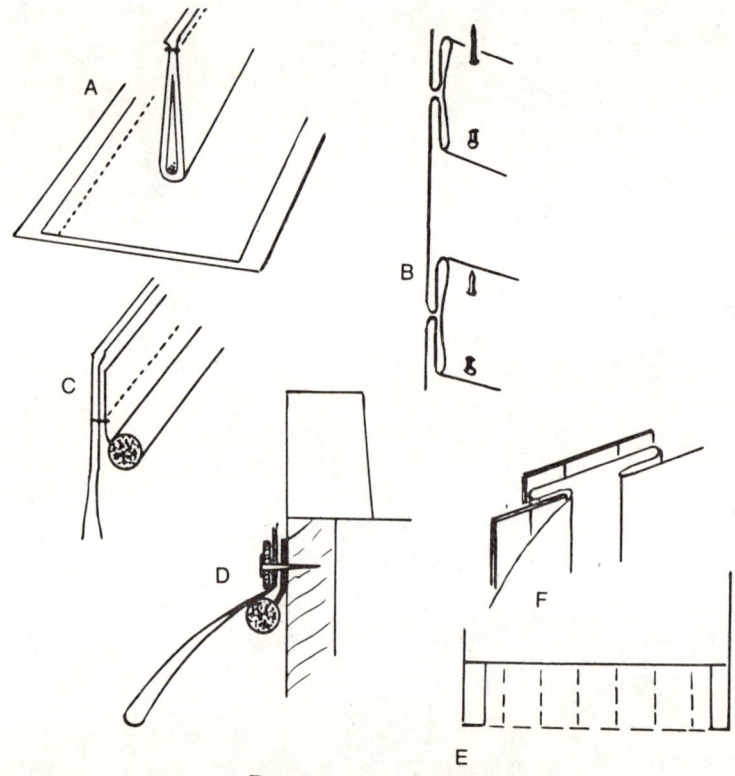

Fig. 15-9. Making flounces.

Mark where the piping is to come around the chair, if it is not clear from an edge of the existing upholstery. Have the chair upside down so the flounce will hang clear while the tacking strip is located. Check that the pleats are correctly positioned. Use a few temporary tacks to hold the flounce in place.

With the flounce hanging out of the way and the piping hidden by it, tack on cardboard strips (Fig. 15-9D) close to the piping all round. Use whatever number of strips are needed, but do not bend around corners—make joints there instead. Turn the chair the right way and the flounce should hang down correctly.

If the pleats are to be close to give a box-pleated effect, the pleats are made in the same way but it is necessary to adjust their sizes so they are evenly spaced across the front of the chair and along the sides if possible. Get the length across the front and divide this into a suitable number to allow pleats and spaces that match (Fig. 15-9E). Make up a length of lined flounce similar to that for corner pleats, but the amount will be much more. Arrange for the joint to come at the back of the chair at the back of one of the pleats.

It is important that the pleats be even in size. This can be checked by measuring each one, but it is simpler to use templates of cardboard or thin plywood. Let them be about as deep as the flounce. One is the total width between centers of pleats and the other is half that. In use, the wide one is placed over the cloth, then a narrow one pushed into the cloth over it until the edges are level. That process automatically gets the size of a fold (Fig. 15-9F).

From this point the method of fixing the flounce is the same as for a corner-pleated one. Both corner and box pleats should usually be pressed before they are fitted. Some fabrics may look better if they are allowed to curve as they spread towards the floor, but the majority are better if the folds at each pleat are pressed. Some of the sharpness may eventually disappear from the folds, but they will have settled into an attractive form.

CURVED PARTS

Much modern furniture has straight edges and moderate curves, but some antique and reproduction furniture has the upholstery material taken over shaped edges. Some parts have considerable curves in both directions, with the frames taking the padded surfaces into compound curves. If covering is tackled wrongly there may be creases that cannot be removed or a panel of cloth may be distorted so the weave is pulled out of shape or a pattern is askew.

Most woven cloth may be stretched. Sometimes the stretch is more one way than the other. It may be more across the width of the cloth in the roll, or it could be lengthwise. This should be checked before using the cloth. If there is no stretch, or it is so slight that it has little effect, it will be impossible to cover a pronounced double curve without having to use pleats or creases. Vinyl and similar plastic material on a fabric backing may have little stretch when cold, but if warmed the plastic will soften and allow the fabric to stretch. Leather varies in its ability to stretch. Moistening leather will make it more flexible, but this property is not much use for upholstery because dampness has to be avoided. Wetting is used to allow shaping of leather in saddlery and other leather crafts, however.

When a panel with a compound curve has to be covered, it is usually best to pull the fabric across its center in the direction that has greater stretch first (Fig. 15-10A). Fix with temporary tacks. Next pull across the center in the other direction (Fig. 15-10B). If one direction takes more compound curvature than the other, work in that direction first with further shaping, progressing from the center tacks outwards (Fig. 15-10C). Do some straining in that direction and change to the other direction alternately until the whole panel is temporarily tacked.

It is probable in the first straining that the pull will be uneven. This may show in the pattern. There will have to be some adjustment of tacks to get this right. If creases occur around the edges and adjusting tacks will not remove them, leaving the work for a day may cure the trouble because the stresses in woven material tend to even out naturally. Do final tacking progressively, without removing temporary tacks until just before each is about to be replaced by a new tack. A persistent crease can sometimes be worked out by pulling and tacking its center while relaxing the strain slightly at nearby tacks.

If the fabric has to be taken over a shaped edge the problem is comparable to a compound curve, but not as great. In this case get a reasonable strain in the straighter direction (Fig. 15-10D). This will allow the cloth to be pulled in the other direction with the minimum risk of creasing (Fig. 15-10E) as it is turned over the edge.

Any edge which is high when viewed usually looks best if it is rounded. It is more comfortable to handle in any case. If an edge is low when viewed, it looks better if the angle is sharp. This applies to the lower edges around a chair. The cloth is usually taken below the wooden frame and tacked underneath. If the frame has suffered knocks or the wood was not straight in any case, any flaws will show through the cloth fold. If the edge is unsatisfactory, it may be possible to plane it true before covering, but work on the wood is inadvisable after upholstery has been commenced. A simple way of getting a good edge is to tack or staple a piece of cardboard along the edge, with a very slight overhang to disguise the flaws in the wood (Fig. 15-10F). This could be a narrow strip intended for back tacking, or a wider piece that can be taken under any padding, so tacks there could not show through the covering cloth, as might happen with some driven close to the edge if their heads were not sunk flush with the cardboard.

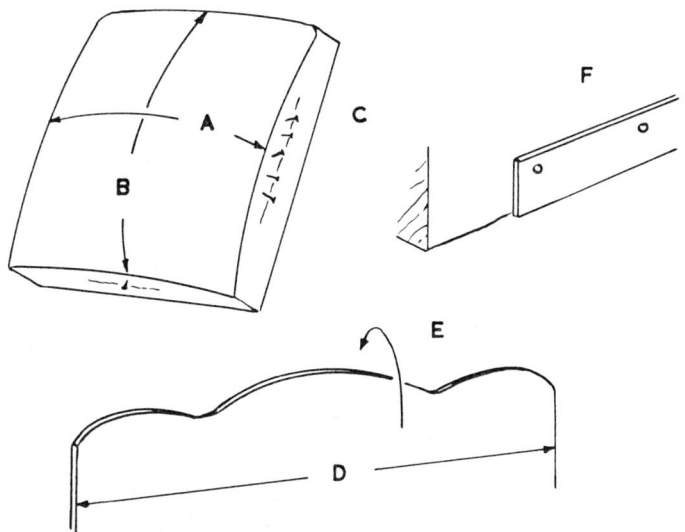

Fig. 15-10. Compound curves need special tensioning to avoid creases.

GLIDES AND ROCKERS

It is unusual for a chair or other piece of furniture to merely stand on the ends of its legs, particularly if it is to be moved about. With modern floor coverings the wood ends might mark carpets or other floor matting, linoleum, or plastic tiles. Older furniture nearly always had casters (Fig. 15-11A). They are still used, but there are now alternatives to the simple wheel that turns to trail in the direction the chair is to be moved.

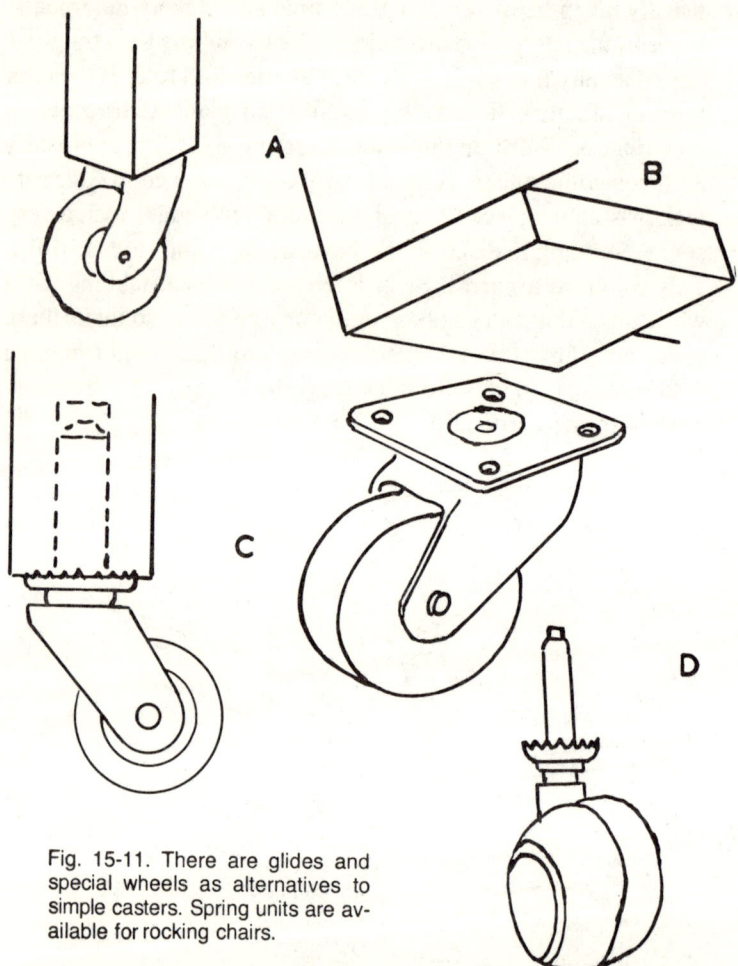

Fig. 15-11. There are glides and special wheels as alternatives to simple casters. Spring units are available for rocking chairs.

The basic caster usually has a hard rubber wheel and a plate to screw under the chair. This suits a broad base in the form of a block under the chair (Fig. 15-11B). Fixing is done with ordinary wood screws. The smaller casters have plain bearings, but there are ball races in the larger and better casters.

For legs that do not present a sufficient area to take a plate there are casters with stems to fit into holes. The stem is a tube that should be a tight fit in the hole. A toothed ring grips the end grain (Fig. 15-11C). The stem is about 3/8 inch in diameter, so it can be used in quite slender legs.

Today, ordinary wheel casters are more likely to be found on industrial and office equipment. For household use there are better looking ball casters (Bassick) that present a broader surface to the floor (Fig. 15-11D), and are less likely to damage carpets. The wheels are 2 inches or 2 1/2 inches and there may be a stem to go in a leg hole or a plate 1 1/2 inches square to screw on.

Instead of a revolving wheel there may be a domed sliding surface to make a glide. Only the larger ones are suitable for large, fully upholstered chairs. They may have a screw adjustment, which is useful if a chair has legs of uneven length. Some also have ball and socket joints so the glide follows any unevenness on the floor. This may be an advantage on other things with adjustable legs or folding arrangements, but does not matter much on a chair. The fixing is a plate with spikes to grip end grain and tubular part to fit a hole (Fig. 15-12A). The actual glide is about 1 1/4 inches in diameter. One type is made of steel and is more suitable for hard floors. For carpets there are nylon faces that are less liable to mark and will not leave rust marks.

One simple glide is made of pressed steel and is plated. It has spiked edges so it can be driven into end grain with a mallet (Fig. 15-12B).

Some simple glides are made like nails with large plated heads. The largest is 7/8 inch across, so this type (Fig. 15-12C) is more suitable for lighter furniture. A variation on this includes rubber cushioning (Fig. 15-12D). The base is made of plated steel, but the rubber allows some flexing as a chair is moved. The largest size is about 1 1/16 inches in diameter, which may be adequate for a chair of moderate size.

A rocking chair may rock directly on the floor, in which case there is nothing to concern the upholsterer. For a platform rocking chair, thought, the movement of the upper part on the base is controlled by powerful springs. For the standard springs the upper part should be made to 16 inch radius and the meeting surfaces should be smoothed so they roll quietly and without jarring.

Two sizes of springs are normally available for large chairs. The larger size, with springs about 2 inches in height and diameter, suits the largest type of club chair. The other has springs about 1 3/4 inches each way and suits any smaller rocking chair. There may have to be some cutting of the wood to clear the springs, but otherwise the assembly screws on the sides (Fig. 15-12E).

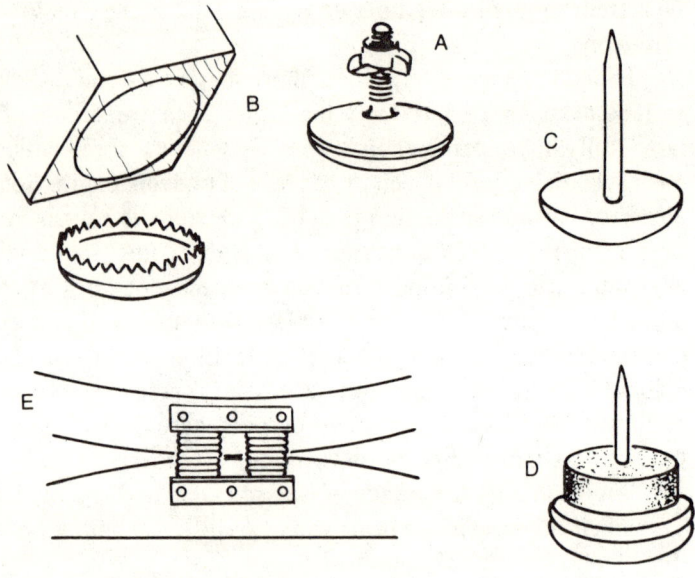

Fig. 15-12. Several types of foot glides and the springing mechanism of a modern rocking chair are illustrated.

For swivel chairs there are devices consisting of two plates with a large diameter ball race between. A typical one has a ball race about 5 inches across and each plate has lugs to take four screws each way at 8 inch centers. The whole thing is 5/8 inch thick. So long as there is a sufficient area of substantial wood to fix to, installation is only a matter of centering and screwing in place. The size quoted will suit all but the largest swivel chairs. Of course, swivel and rocking may be combined in one chair.

Chairs: Special Fully Upholstered Styles and Effects

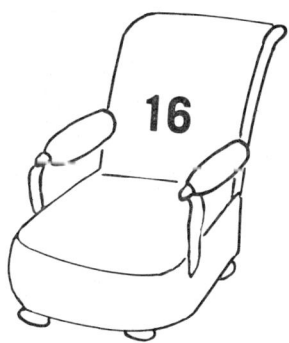

The upholstery methods and techniques described so far can be adapted to most types of furniture, but over the years there have been fashions that did not conform exactly to other methods and it was necessary to use new techniques, rather than modifications of old ones. These changes are still going on. Polystyrene and other plastic frames have to be covered with methods and materials that an earlier upholsterer would not understand.

BOWED BACKS

The back of a chair may blend into its wings without an angle, so the back is bowed in one curve when viewed from above (Fig. 16-1A). This type of back has been made with traditional wood frames, but it is particularly adaptable to molded plastic frames. Compared with conventional chairs, the difference in upholstery is the need to deal with a hollow curve. Drawing fabric over an outside convex curve is no problem, but if the surface is concave, something has to be done to draw and keep the fabric into the hollow.

A typical chair with a wood frame (Fig. 16-1B) has little curve crosswise for the greater part of the depth of the back, but most of the hollowing is nearer the top where the wings flare out. Springs may be used and burlap put over them in the usual way, but there may have to be some temporary tacking around the edges of the greatest hollowing to allow for adjustment as further stages of covering are performed.

Covering over this may be made of foam padding and cotton, or foam may be adequate alone. Cover with muslin. Pull the muslin in to the hollow with a few large stitches taken right through. Do this pulling in before the muslin is tacked around the edges. Mark on the muslin a pattern of button positions.

Put the fabric in place without fixing around the edges, except for a few temporary tacks to prevent the cloth from falling off. Locate the button positions from the marks on the muslin and fix buttons with twine taken through. Do not lock the knots yet. Get all the buttons in position and try stretching the fabric to see that it settles down smoothly and with the buttons symmetrically placed.

There may be shaped parts of the frame to which buttons should have their twine anchored so as to get the intended shape. Otherwise twine goes through to the burlap in the usual way. When the button pattern is seen to be correct, lock the button twine knots and finally stretch and fix the fabric around the edges.

Molded frames or shells make much use of adhesives in covering. Some of these shells rely mainly on their contours for comfort and any padding is provided by one or more loose pillows or cushions. Polystyrene always feels warm.

Added padding is usually foam about 1 inch thick, stuck on with adhesive. Use correct adhesives as some will dissolve polystyrene. So far as possible, avoid joints near edges as it is easier to make a wider piece conform to the curve and stick securely if it wraps over on to a reasonably flat surface to meet another piece (Fig. 16-1C).

Covering is often made from knitted fabric which will stretch and conform to the shape. This may be a loose cover that can be removed and replaced with another if a different pattern is desired. If it is to be fixed, it will have to be sewn or held back by buttons in the hollows. It may be necessary to go right through the mold, but it is also possible to sew to strips of webbing or other cloth stuck to the mold (Fig. 16-1D). A convenient alternative to using sewn strips is to use Velcro strips, which are cloth with an interlocking hooked surface. Strips fixed to the covering engage with strips stuck to the mold. They hold under normal use, but a pull will disengage them. They can also be used instead of zippers for cushion closures.

It is usual to put thinner foam on the outside as well as the normal thickness on the inside of a molded chair. Most of these seats are mounted so they swivel or rock on a leg assembly. The attachment arrangement is usually a plywood platform supplied already bonded to the seat. This should be left exposed by the padding, both for the need to fix the legs and for a convenient surface for tacking cloth.

If a loose cover is to be made, work on the actual chair, using the fabric inside out and pinning around the seams. This will have to be arranged so it will slip over when finished, but the stretch in the material allows moderate curves to be passed. Where stretch cannot be relied on to pass over a shape, there can be zippers, or it may be possible to arrange the cover to pull tight with a tape or cord through a sewn edge (Fig. 16-1E) below the seat. When the cover has been fitted with pins, cut marking Vs in the edges and sew the seams. In some designs there may have to be a zipper a short distance up the back to pull the cloth into shape before using a drawstring through a hem at the bottom.

For a close-fitted cover the fabric is marked out in a similar way to a loose cover and it may be helpful to sew some parts together before fitting. If there are to be cushions, it may be possible to stick down plain fabric for much of the area that will be hidden and bring the outside fabric around to be stuck to it far enough in to be hidden by the cushions (Fig. 16-1F).

If the fabric is to be used without cushions to hide it, the seat and back covering are more important than the outside. It may be possible to let the inner covering go over the edges and meet the outside fabric where it will be inconspicuous under the turn of the arms or back. It is stuck or sewn, either on the surface or through to webbing underneath (Fig. 16-1G).

Within the hollow a covering that will not have cushions may be pulled down at the back of the seat by stitches into a line of webbing (Fig. 16-1H). In some molded seats there is a piece of plywood molded into the plastic and there may be a line of staples driven through into this to serve the same purpose.

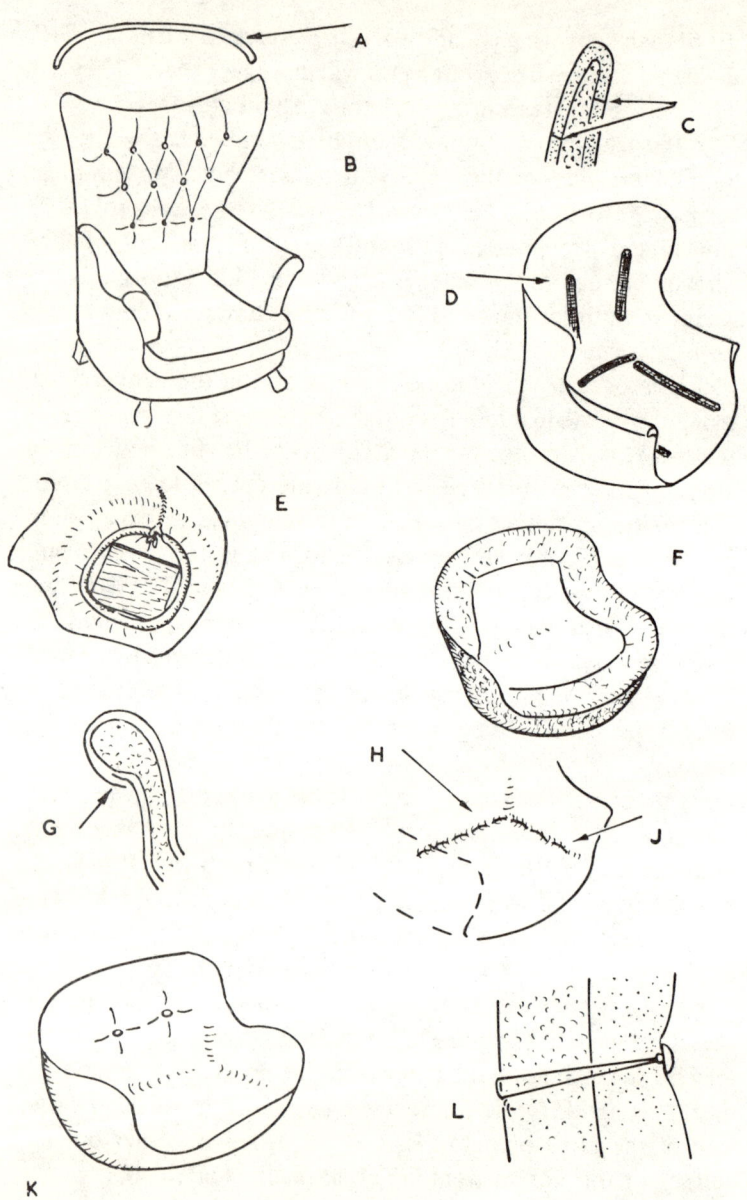

Fig. 16-1. Special shapes of wood and plastic frames need buttons or strips to hold fabric to the hollow curves.

There may be a similar line to mark the hollows between the seat and the arms (Fig. 16-1J). The hollow of the back can usually be taken care of by two buttons (Fig. 16-1K). Their twine may be taken through to webbing on the surface, but polystyrene is soft enough for a needle to be pushed through and it is possible to take twine right through, but the two parts of twine should be spaced apart, so the knot has something to pull against without a button on the outside. This can also be done with thin wire, and the twisted ends will bury in polystyrene (Fig. 16-1L). Of course, this must be done before the covering material is put on the outside. It is also possible to put in wire ties before covering a chair, so buttons can be tied to these loops with twine.

An alternative to fully upholstering the inside of a molded chair is to use fitted cushions which are fixed in place. These are made in the normal way, but are provided with buttons, which are not fitted until the cushions are put in place. The twine is then taken right through the molded seat to secure the cushion. If the knot is under the button, the loop of twine is unlikely to be very obvious at the back. The cushions can be removed by cutting the twine. In a deep chair there may be a large seat cushion overhanging the front, then another cushion resting on it and one above that shaped to suit the head.

PILLOW BACK CHAIRS

Pillows as the main padding have been used long before the coming of molded frames. Many upholstered chairs have matching cushions and these are regarded as part of the chair, although they may be removable. In some chairs and sofas the cushions rest against supports with little or no padding. In others the back is fully upholstered and the chair could be used without its cushions, although the depth from front to back may then be quite a lot. There is a traditional pattern known as a pillow back (Fig. 16-2A) in which the main back padding is a cushion, but the chair itself is upholstered in a way that complements the cushion. This type of chair is not intended to be used without a cushion.

The pillow is made in the usual way (Fig. 16-2B). A modern one would be filled with foam or latex, but traditional ones had hair covered with cotton, or some were filled with feathers, down, or other very soft loose stuffing. Anything of this sort tends to settle, even when there are plenty of pieces of twine

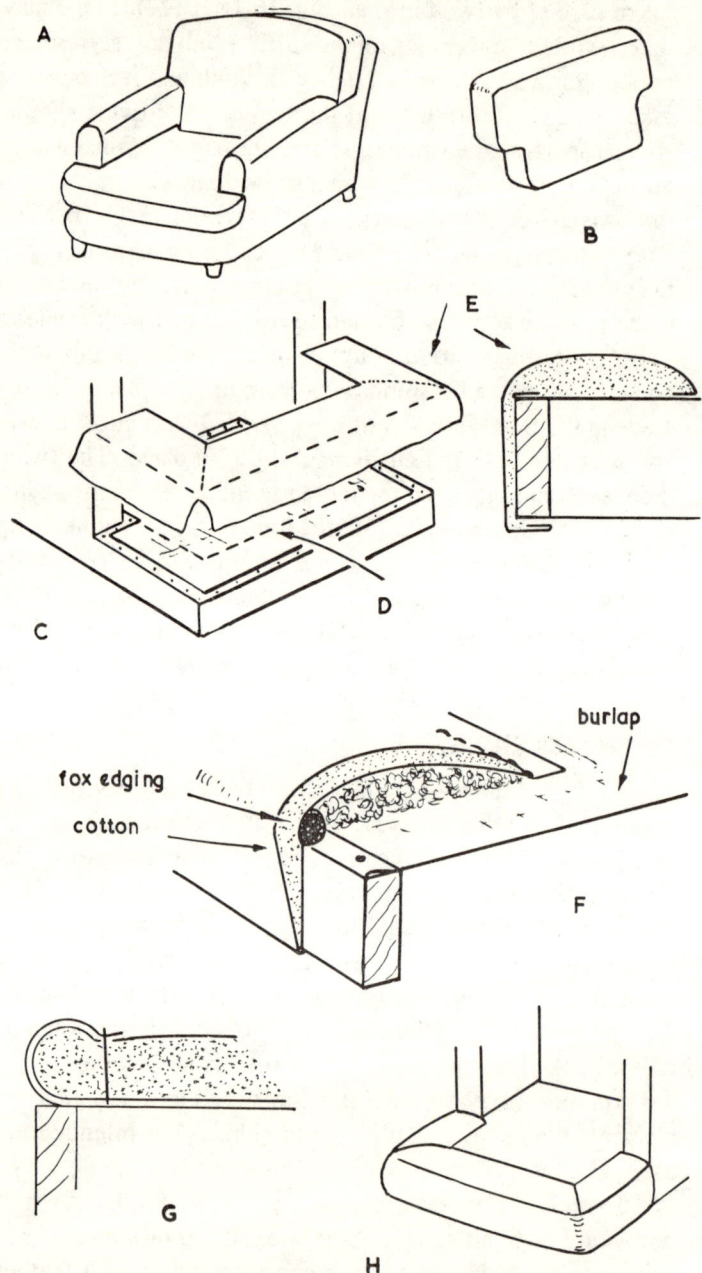

Fig. 16-2. In a pillow-back chair, the chair back is given a borderded upholstery to support the pillow.

passing through to buttons. It is possible to sew muslin or other material into compartments to keep the stuffing in place. The divisions may follow the lines of the button pattern. Without this it is necessary to remove and shake a cushion occasionally to spread the stuffing. If feathers or down are used, they should be enclosed in a down-proof cambric, otherwise they will work through to the surface of any other fabric.

The size of the cushion depends on the design, but normally it fits closely to the seat and between the arms, then may match or slightly overlap the chair back. It is usually possible to make up a boxed cover and leave the lower part and a short distance up each side to be hand-sewn after the cushion has been filled. The cushion may be made reversible, so either side may face outwards.

The actual chair back may be made in a number of ways. In a traditional form it has springs covered with burlap and a layer of cotton, or just a single layer of burlap. This is all over the front of the frame in the same way as for other upholstery (Fig. 16-2C). In a modern version it might be acceptable to close the back with plywood and fill the area with foam covered with burlap. In any case it is the layer of burlap which forms the base for the upholstery that is peculiar to the pillow back design.

Padding is only provided around the edges. This serves to let the pillow drop into a comfortable hollow, which also keeps it in place. The upper part of the back gives extra comfort to the head.

For traditional covering, the burlap is marked out to follow around at about the width of the arms, or about 5 inches if the arms are narrow (Fig. 16-2D). Make a muslin cover large enough to sew around the marked line, go over a stuffing between that and the frame and around the frame to the back. Sew the corner miters (Fig. 16-2E). Hand sew the muslin to the burlap. Large stitches with a curved needle are suitable. At the outer edge of the frame apply fox edging. Between this and the muslin seam cover the burlap with stitched hair in the usual way (Fig. 16-2F). Bring the muslin over cotton on the hair. Miter the corners of the cotton, but make sure the edges butt tightly and there are no gaps where the cotton comes against the arms. The cotton may go over the frame to soften its edge, or both cotton and muslin may stop short to expose wood, if it is a frame intended for polished wood to show.

For a modern treatment foam could be substituted for hair and fox edging. The burlap could be left full enough at the edges to go over wrapped foam to give a fuller edge than would be obtained otherwise (Fig. 16-2G).

When the final covering is put on the chair, it is taken over the muslin from the back. The central area may be covered with the same material or it could be plain fabric, turned under around the edges and sewn through the cover to the burlap, inside the line of stuffing (Fig. 16-2H).

CHANNEL OR FLUTED BACKS

Instead of overall pads, possibly divided by buttons, it is possible to arrange the upholstery so padding comes in a series of tubes, usually arranged upright. These flutes or channels go best with a curved back, when the back and arms blend into each other. Such a design allows the channels to taper and fan out towards the top (Fig. 16-3A).

The initial support is the same as for other upholstery. There may be springs in the back. Rubber webbing may be used in some chairs. As the covering is not a large pad, avoid an angular system of springs and do not edge with wire as might be done behind a squarely-shaped pad, even if the channel back is a fairly flat surface between arms. Cover the springs with burlap. Tack cotton or foam over that.

Initial support is the same as for other upholstery. There may be springs in the back. Rubber webbing may be used in some chairs. As the covering is not a large pad, avoid an angular system of springs and do not edge with wire as might be done behind a squarely-shaped pad, even if the channel back is a fairly flat surface between arms. Cover the springs with burlap. Tack cotton or foam over that.

The channels are made between two layers of muslin. There is a piece that goes around the chair without shaping in section and another piece that goes around in a series of channels. This piece is considerably longer than the first. Fix the first piece of muslin around the chair. Let it go all over the frame with enough overlap for eventual fixing, but only use partly-driven temporary tacks at this stage. Mark the shape that is to be covered with channels. Locate and mark the mid-points along the top and bottom edges. Remove the muslin and draw a center line between these points. It is important that the channels will make a symmetrical pattern when they are fitted. The center line will help, as final fitting will be done outwards from the center. Mark the centers of the top and bottom rails as well as guides for locating the muslin.

Lay the muslin flat. If cotton has been used over the burlap it will probably be advisable to cover that permanently with muslin and use another piece over it for the channel backs. It may not be necessary to use muslin for the front channel piece and then cover with finishing fabric. With some materials the finishing fabric can go directly over the channel filling.

Measure across the flat piece of muslin. Divide this into the number of channels required. They should all be the same width, except the outside ones may be slightly wider. This may help in getting the other divisions even (Fig. 16-3B). How wide the channels are depends on the design and what figure will divide evenly. The larger the channels are, the thicker the padding will be, but a few large channels may not look as good as a larger number of narrower ones. The size has to be related to the piece of furniture and may be anything between 3 inches and 9 inches, with 5 inches as a reasonable average size. If the chair back has considerable flair it may be necessary to taper the channels, but moderate taper can be taken care of in fitting parallel channels or it is possible to slightly taper the fillings while keeping the cases parallel.

The outer piece has to be made large enough to allow for bowing out at each channel (Fig. 16-3C). An experiment will show how much extra to allow to get the right amount, but it will probably be something like 2 inches at each place. Allow a little more at the outside channels. The total width will probably be wider than the available material will cut. Arrange seams to come along the bottoms of the flutes. Mark where the seams will come on the back of the fabric.

Sew with strong thread along each seam, but leave the outside channels open (Fig. 16-3D). On most chairs the outside channels will have to conform to the size and shape of the arms or edge and will have to be filled and trimmed in position.

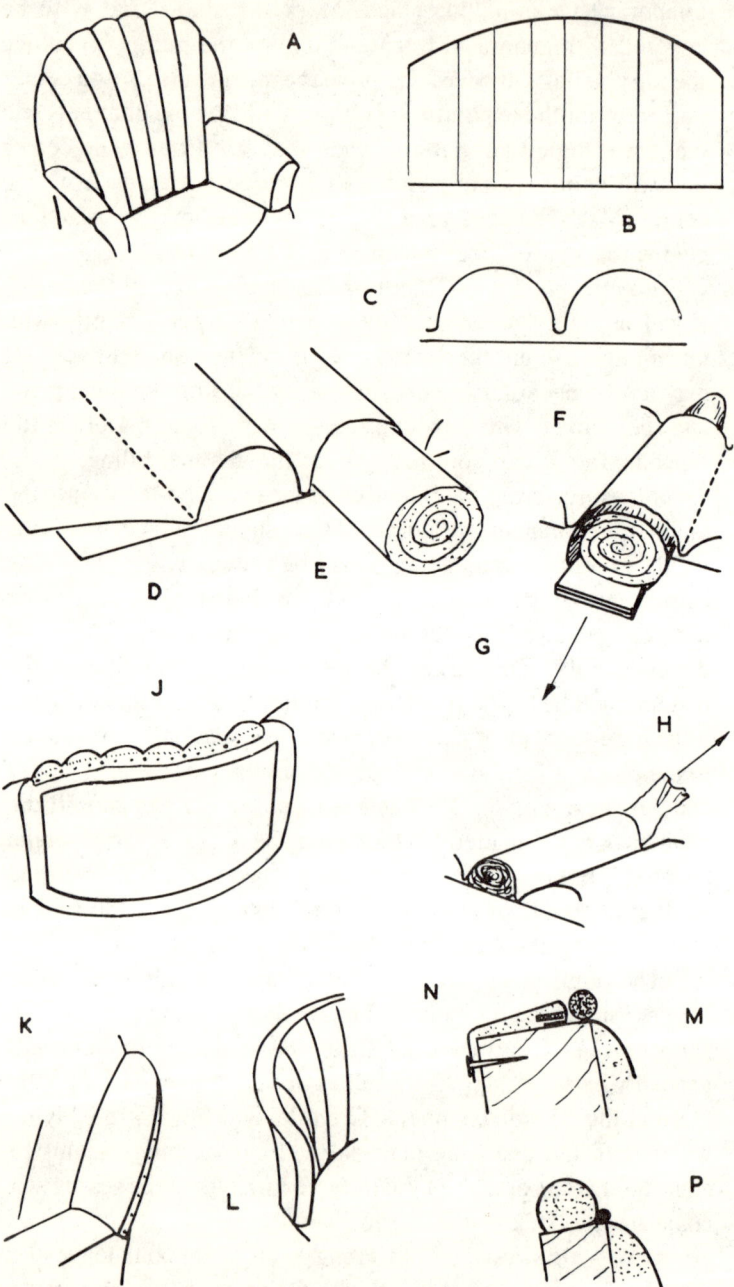

Fig. 16-3. A channel-back chair has the upholstery put in fabric channels before it is shaped and fitted into the chair.

Plastic foam is the easiest filling to use. Squeeze a very tight roll and introduce it to a channel. Keep it tight and push it in as far as it will go (Fig. 16-3E). This will probably be about halfway. Put your arm into the other end of the channel and pull it through. It may help to trim the foam slightly tapered and face this towards the bottom of the chair back. Besides making it easier to thrust the foam into the channel it reduces the bulk at the bottom end slightly, where some reduction may be an advantage when fitting to the chair.

Traditionally the filling was made of cotton, rolled in the same way as foam, but because of the tendency for cotton to come apart, a more careful method of stuffing had to be used. A thin piece of plywood is used as a guide and the roll of cotton is held to it with a piece of cloth. The whole assembly is thrust into a channel until the cotton is right through (Fig. 16-3F). While the cotton and cloth are held, the plywood is withdrawn (Fig. 16-3G). With this out, and before the cotton expands, the cotton is held and the cloth pulled through (Fig. 16-3H). The filling should be a few inches longer than the channel it goes in, because it will be compressed to make a tight fit when the assembly is fitted to the chair. Make sure the filling material does not bunch up or otherwise become uneven, because this would affect appearance.

With all the channels filled, except the outside ones, put the channelled fabric in the chair. Move it around so the center matches the marked center on the chair. The bottom of the back will be slightly narrower than the top on most chairs. As the work is arranged, this will have to be allowed for. Tuck the bottoms of the channels temporarily under the bottom rail. Spread the tops evenly. Stand back and view from a distance to see if the spacing is correct. Mark the positions of the tops of the flutes, to help with final fixing.

At the bottom rail, pull the channels through. So far as possible let at least some of the filling go between the rail and the seat upholstery. It will probably be tight, but get as much as possible tightly packed there. Some may have to be eased back into the channels, but be careful of causing lumps to show through the fabric. Use a few temporary tacks to hold the fabric, preferably located at the ends of the flutes between channels.

At the top, start by pulling up a center flute, and temporarily tack to the top rail. Do this at the other flutes and watch that the spacing is even. If there is much filling extending above a flute, cut away some, but leave enough to press down into the flute to make a rounded end. At each channel pull over the center, then midway between that and the flute tack each side. Regulate the amount of pull to get a rounded top to the channel (Fig. 16-3J). Adjust any tacks to get an even effect, then permanently tack into the back of the frame.

This leaves the outer channels to fill. Prepare rolls to bring these out to the same sizes as the adjoining channels. In an arm chair, these rolls will come above the arms and the fabric can be taken around the sides of the frame for tacking, and turned under against the arms (Fig. 16-3K).

For many chairs that completes the channel back, which will show the characteristic rounded top. At the back, the space over any springs may be covered with burlap. This could be followed by cotton or foam and the covering fabric, turned in all round over the tacked front material.

Another possible finish to the edge of the back is created by bringing the channels to a flat edge, which is covered (Fig. 16-3L). All of the filling is kept below the edge, so the line of the frame is followed (Fig. 16-3M). Piping goes above this and facing material is back tacked against that (Fig. 16-3N). It is taken over the back edge of the frame, where it is covered by the back fabric. Ruching, or other decorative edge, could be used instead of piping. An alternative to back tacking flat on the frame is to make a roll of cotton or foam, and draw the fabric back over that (Fig. 16-3P).

TUFTING

At one time, going far back into history, a treatment that looked something like deep buttoning was used. In buttoning the fabric is laid over the padding and pulled back, so it is stretched to conform to the intended shape and the stuffing is also compressed where the button and twine come. Tufting is related to channelling in that it forms the outer fabric into pockets, which are filled separately. A diamond pattern is usual and a row of diamonds is partly sewn, then the filling material inserted and those diamonds completed. This leaves another row of partial diamonds to be treated in the same way. Great care is needed to achieve a uniform pattern and this work is rarely done today. With modern materials buttoning can produce a similar effect.

Bar fronts and bed heads are sometimes given what is described as a tufted finish, but it is really only buttoning. The only resemblance to tufting is in the manner thick foam is sometimes partially cut to fit between the lines of a button pattern (see Chapter 17).

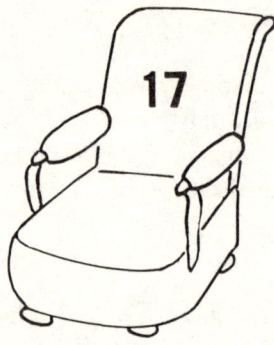

17

Beds, Divans, Ottomans, Head Panels, and Boxes

There are many things, not always intended to be sat on, that have to be upholstered. In some cases upholstery is an alternative to another form of decoration and is applied mainly to give a luxurious appearance, while in other cases there is value in the padding applied as an aid to comfort or a means of minimizing the risk of damage to the article or to a person coming into contact with it. In most cases the application of upholstery is a simpler process than dealing with a chair. Anyone who can upholster a chair should have no difficulty in adapting the methods to the particular form of an unusual project.

BUNK SEATS

Yachts and trailer homes have seats that convert to bunks for sleeping. Many of these have loose cushions, made as described earlier, but some are fixed and often have to be shaped to suit the curves of the yacht or recreation vehicle. They may also have to adapt when changed from seat to bed, so there are joints in the upholstery as well as in the wood supports.

The standard type of cushion to rest on a plywood top is usually made with foam or latex filling. It may have a piped edge or be merely wrapped over with seams at the bottom. It can be sewn inside-out, then turned the right way on the pad and the open end closed by hand sewing, or with a zipper (Fig. 17-1A).

For a long narrow cushion, such as may form a back to a bunk seat, there can be a zipper for most of the length of the center of the back. The foam pad may be inserted or adjusted through the back. Such a back cushion may be fixed to the seat cushion, so it drops down to make up a bed width (Fig. 17-1B). One piece of fabric may be used for the tops of both cushions and the underneath pieces brought up to make a seam along the fold line. Alternatively, both cushions may be seamed where they meet, with the edges of the fabric outwards so they can be sewn together.

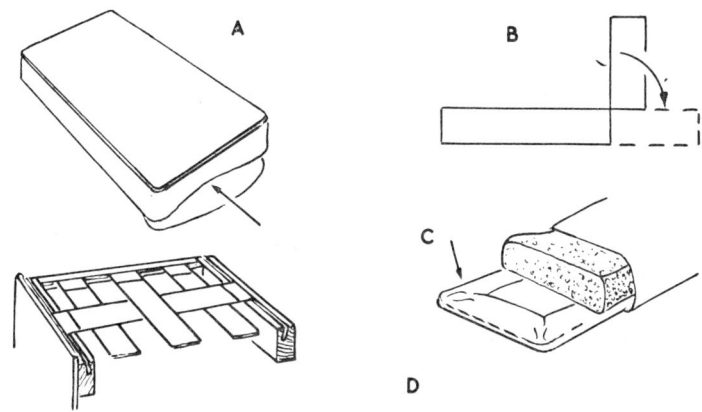

Fig. 17-1. Bunk cushions are foam-filled and may be supported on rubber webbing.

In some of these conversions it is necessary for a cushion to rest on rails or to be otherwise only partly supported when the assembly is made into a bed. In that case there should be some stiffening of the cushion itself if the use of a loose piece of plywood is to be avoided. Plywood can be enclosed in the cushion, but to reduce the risk of damaging the fabric, all corners and edges should be well rounded and it would help to enclose the plywood in a piece of muslin or other cloth before putting it in the cushion (Fig. 17-1C). Except for this, the cushion is made up in the usual way.

In most bunks there is no resilience in the support, which is usually made of plywood. With at least 4 inches of foam in the cushion, there is a reasonable degree of sleeping comfort. This can be improved by using rubber webbing instead of plywood, preferably with metal clips into grooves at the ends (Fig. 17-1D), so replacement is easy; but this means that the method has to be planned from the start, because the wood has to be grooved before assembly. If it is existing woodwork, the rubber webbing may be tacked in place. In a boat it is better to use copper or other non-ferrous tacks or nails, because of the risk of rust in a damp situation. For the same reason it is inadvisable to use normal upholstery springs, which would soon rust. Apart from any damage this would do to the springs themselves, adjoining cloth, thread, or twine would be stained and weakened by rust.

For the same reason—damage by dampness—it is advisable to use synthetic fabrics on a boat. These fabrics do not rot and their moisture absorption from a damp atmosphere is negligible. Cotton, wool, and other natural materials will absorb moisture and eventually rot.

Bunks in a recreation vehicle, where damp is unlikely to be present, could have full springing and be treated in the same way as a bed or settee/ottoman, as described later. In the type of accommodation large enough for a bed to be separate from the daytime living area, and conversion from seat to bed is not required, the bed can be as comfortably upholstered as a bed at home.

BOXES AND OTTOMANS

A box with an upholstered top can be anything from a small box for use as a foot stool, with storage space for slippers and shoes, to one large enough to be used as a bed or a sofa for lounging, with large enough storage space for blankets and sheets. The box part may be finished by staining and varnishing or polishing the wood, and only the top is upholstered. The box may also be covered with cloth or vinyl and the inside can be lined with a material to suit the intended contents—something robust for shoes, or something more delicate for bedding or clothing.

The traditional way of dealing with the top uses a frame over which there may be burlap only for a stool, but for a rather bigger box there could be a few lines of webbing (Fig. 17-2A). An ottoman large enough for sleeping needs more springing.

This will be discussed later. Over the burlap goes fiber or hair with large stitches arranged in the usual way. If any have to go to points over the frame, they can be secured with tacks (Fig. 17-2B). The hair is covered with muslin, temporarily tacked at first. Put in some sink stitches all round to keep hair pulled towards the edges (Fig. 17-2C). Follow this with roll stitches right through (Fig. 17-2D). They can be about 2 inches long and taken all round (Fig. 17-2E). The final tacking may be to the top of the wood or around the outside if it is a deeper frame.

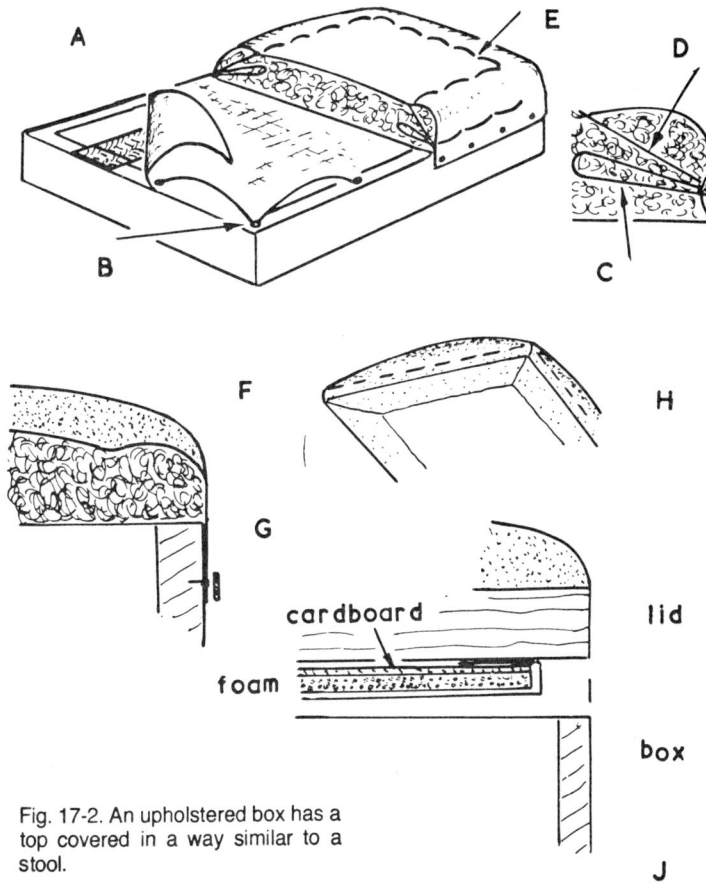

Fig. 17-2. An upholstered box has a top covered in a way similar to a stool.

Over this goes cotton or foam (Fig. 17-2F), which is pulled to shape by the cover fabric. This may be tacked around the outside if the top frame is deep and the lower part is to be exposed wood. Gimp goes over the tacks (Fig. 17-2G). For a shallower lid the cover fabric goes underneath, where it can be fixed with adhesive or tacks (Fig. 17-2H). Take it far enough in to come well inside the line of the top edge of the box.

The underside of the lid can be covered with lining material, stretched and turned under for tacking. A neater lining is made by cutting a piece of cardboard to fit within the bounds of the box. Cover this with lining fabric turned over it and held with adhesive. A piece of thin foam may be included as well (Fig. 17-2J). It may be possible to glue this assembly to the lid or it may be better to use nails, which could have ornamental heads, if the material is leather-like vinyl in a shoe box.

If foam or latex is used it may take the place of the hair and there will be no need for any stitching, but keep the foam slightly oversized so it compresses. If it is undersized, there may be gaps showing at the edges of the finished top. There may be no need for cotton over the foam, although this gives a more luxurious feel and appearance to the upholstery.

The wooden part of the top may be solid, either thin plywood on a solid wood frame, or one piece of thicker plywood or chipboard. In that case the foam or latex can be in sufficient thickness to not need other springing or padding. Round the edges as described earlier. Take the covering fabric underneath and cover the underside of the top in the way described for traditional upholstery.

It is a help in fitting a neat lining to have the bottom off the box, as tacks can come underneath and be hidden by the bottom when it is fitted.

The inside of the box can have thin foam stuck on if padding is required. Cover the longer dimension inside first. Let the lining cloth go over the top edge, where it is tacked. Strain downwards and tack underneath (Fig. 17-3A). Make sure the cloth is a full width—if some turns around the corner slightly it will be covered by the end lining and ensure avoidance of gaps. When the ends are lined, do this in the same way, but turn under and rub down folds for the corners, so there is a sharp crease when the cloth is fitted. When the ends are tacked, pull hard down the corners (Fig. 17-3B). Make sure all tacks are driven tight so none will show through the fabric over the top or interfere with a close fit of the bottom. Cover the bottom with fabric inside, using adhesive or small tacks around the edges, then nail or screw the bottom on.

The neatest way to deal with covering the outside is to back tack inside the top edge (Fig. 17-3C). Use a sufficient length of cloth to go under the bottom for tacking. Have a sufficient width to more than cover a side and fold it to a miter as it goes over the corner (Fig. 17-3D). Each corner may be sewn with soft fabric to bring the panels of cloth close together. With vinyl it would be difficult to sew the outside corners neatly. A strip of the same material about 1 inch wide may be folded to an L shape and used over the corners, where it is fixed with decorative nails.

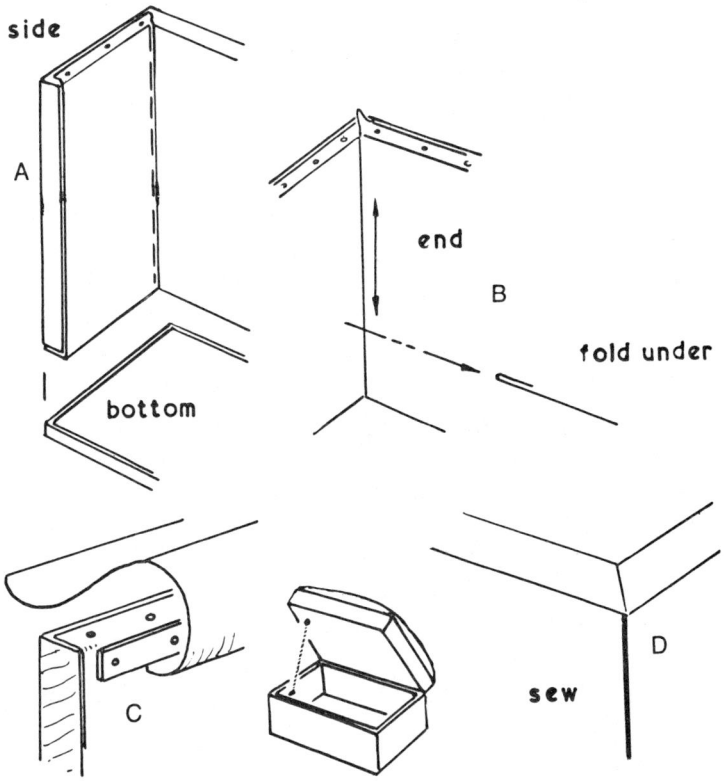

Fig. 17-3. The box is covered inside and out.

A box lid is hinged. It may have a chain to prevent it from opening too wide, and there may be a fastener. Whether these things will go over the upholstery or directly against the wood depends on their design, but the method of fitting should be discovered before completing upholstery, and it may be advisable to have a trial assembly, then take the things off until upholstery is completed.

The name 'ottoman' may be applied to quite a small boxed stool, but it usually refers to something rather larger, which can be used as a backless seat for two or more people or it may be large enough to serve as a bed for a child or adult. One form may be made to match chairs and sofas to form part of the matching furniture in a room. In that case it may be made a suitable height to be brought up to a chair and convert it to a chaise lounge. The way the chairs are upholstered will be a guide to how the ottoman should be treated.

A smaller ottoman can be treated in the same way as a boxed stool. An ottoman does not necessarily have a box below, but it is likely to have a fairly deep frame and there may be legs or feet.

If the ottoman has to match other furniture it should be upholstered in the same way. Where a chair only has a front edge to be finished, an ottoman must have finished edge all round the top.

If the top is to be traditionally upholstered there will be webbing and springs, but as the seat may be used in any direction, have the springs reasonably close and not too far from any of the edges. There may be wiring around the springs, if that was the method on matching chairs.

Cover with burlap, followed by hair, although the first layer may be made of rubberized hair. Use cotton and muslin in the same way as for a chair. Stitching around the edge as described for a boxed stool is advisable. What to do with the covering fabric depends on any matching furniture. It may be taken to the bottom of the frame and tacked under its edges. If the matching chairs have a bottom band, the top fabric may go far enough down the outside to be covered by it, then tacked on the outside.

A bottom band on a box should match that on any chair, in its width and distance from the floor. Make it in the same way, back tacking along the top and including cotton if that is in the chair bottom band. If there are any lines of gimp on the chairs, fix matching lines on the ottoman.

The usual method of springing a seat with a pattern of webbing below means there is some flexibility on the underside. As weight is put on the seat, the compressing springs thrust the webbing downwards to an extent which gets greater as the furniture gets older. If there is a box below, this could damage the contents; so it is usual in a box ottoman, particularly if it is a large size, to support the springs with wood strips (Fig. 17-4A) or a solid piece of plywood or chipboard. If the padding is to be made of foam and no springs are to be used, the top becomes similar to a bunk and the plywood is fixed on top (Fig. 17-4B). If thin plywood is used there should be some stiffening pieces at intervals under a large top.

For traditional upholstery the springs are located on the wood crossbars instead of on webbing (Fig. 17-4C), but otherwise covering is very similar to that of a chair or a smaller stool. On a large ottoman with hair stuffing, it is important that the hair should not move and it should keep its bulk to the edge. There may be fox edging all round (Fig. 17-4D). It is also possible to have the burlap overwide and make *thumb rolls* with it. Use hair or rolled cotton and tack this with the burlap around the edge (Fig. 17-4E) to serve the same purpose as fox edging. For the usual covering, a roll as thick as your thumb is about right, but keep it the same size all round.

The stuffing of hair is stitched and covered with cotton and muslin. The cotton may be taken over the edge and the cover fabric pulled over it to make a rounded edge (Fig. 17-4F). For a square edge, which may be preferable if the ottoman is to be used for sleeping, the top can be made with a boxed edge and piping along the seam. In that case the cotton should not go over the edge (Fig. 17-4G).

The underside of the lid may have the usual burlap, which is covered with lining material, backed by cardboard or thin plywood and foam, in the way described for a smaller box. The box itself is lined in the same way, preferably with the bottom fitted after the lining has been added. A large box ottoman will be too heavy to lift about. It may be on feet or blocks. Casters will be used, or there may be glides for a smaller ottoman. If the blocks and casters can be left until after the cloth has been fitted and turned under, the need to cut around them will be avoided,

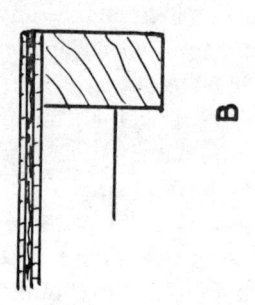

B

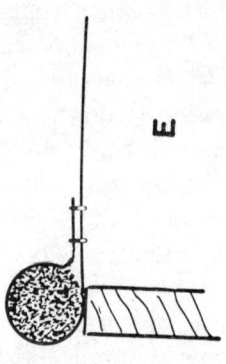

E

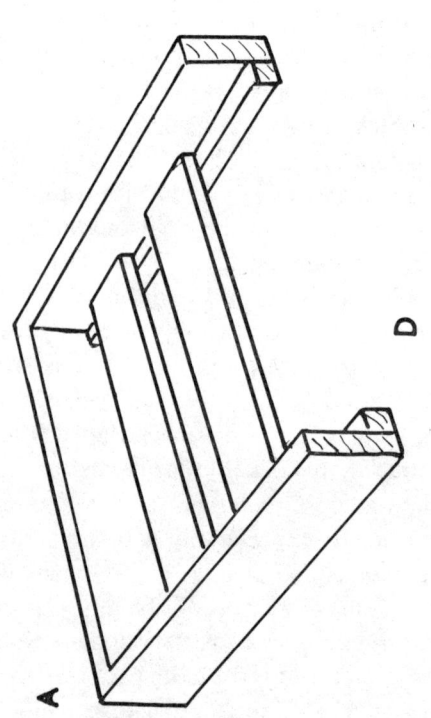

A

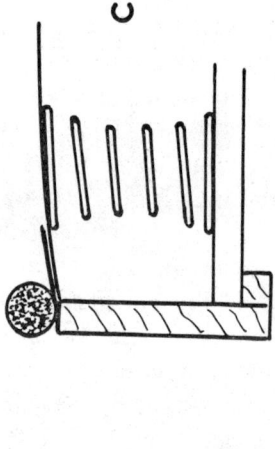

C

D

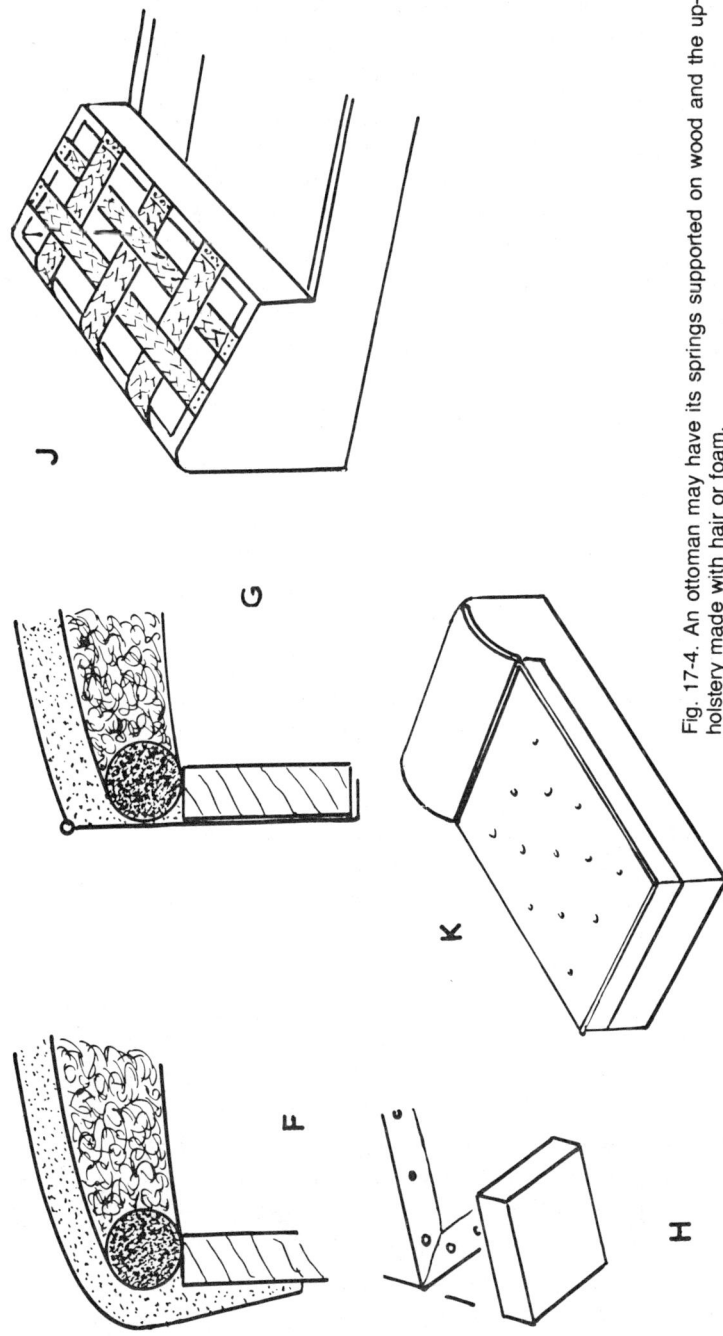

Fig. 17-4. An ottoman may have its springs supported on wood and the upholstery made with hair or foam.

and it will be easier to get a neat fit (Fig. 17-4H). A layer of burlap or cambric underneath the box makes a good finish, but when the piece of furniture may never be turned over, it is not very important.

Hinges for a large ottoman need to be fairly substantial and they may have to be fitted as an experiment early in upholstering, then removed for final fitting later. There can be a chain as a lid stay, but a piece of webbing will also serve, and will be kinder to bedding or clothing inside when the lid is closed. The lid will stay down under its own weight and there will probably be no need for a fastener. However, it is useful to have some sort of handle to grip and a piece of covering material can be sewn inside-out to make a tube. Pull it back the right way and sew it as a loop to the edge of the lid.

If the ottoman is used for sleeping, loose pillows may be used. If it is used for reclining during the day, there can be a built-in raised part at one end to support a cushion (Fig. 17-4J). This is part of the box, with its lower edge about level with the closed lid and a suitable slope. The upper surface is covered with plain or rubber webbing, which may be covered with burlap and the usual hair, cotton, muslin, and covering fabric, or there may be a latex or foam pad. In any case, finish the edges to match the lid covering, with a boxed and piped edge, if that was used (Fig. 17-4K). The lower edge should blend into the line of the covered lid, but do not have the joint too close, or the lid will chafe and damage the fabric.

As with other upholstery a large area on the top of an ottoman is best finished by buttoning. Foam may not rise and make a rounded top. Hair stuffing might become too rounded. This needs buttons and foam will benefit in appearance by using them. There need not be many. Spacing about 12 inches apart should be enough for holding the padding in shape, but more can be used if that suits the pattern wanted. If there is a plywood top under foam it will have to be drilled for twine. Have two holes at each place, so the twine goes down one and up the other. Make the holes large enough to pass the needle easily, as its point will have to find them through the foam. For upholstery on burlap the twine goes through to that, where a wad of cotton or a plain button prevents the twine from pulling back.

BEDS AND DIVANS

The ordinary bed with a box spring mattress over springs made as manufactured units does not offer much scope for the individual upholsterer. He may be able to do some repairs, but these are not usually made completely as a new project except in a factory.

There are sofas that convert to beds. Their parts are arranged to fold down, so the back joins the seat to make a bed width. Except for the folding arrangements, the upholstery of the parts is similar to that of chairs or an ottoman.

A divan bed is somewhere between a sofa and a bed. It may be used as it is, or there may be a thin mattress put over it. Such a divan bed is a good partner to a padded headboard. This is discussed later in this chapter.

The frame may be made of softwood if it is to be covered with cloth or it might be made of hardwood for varnishing or polishing. A deep frame looks better than a shallow one, but strips inside for the springs may be raised (Fig. 17-5A); otherwise unnecessarily deep springs would have to be fitted. The back edge will have square corners to fit against a backboard. The front corners may be rounded with blocks of wood built in (Fig. 17-5B). There may be bracing inside, but this is arranged out of the way of upholstery.

If the framing is softwood, heavy staples are better than tacks for holding twine and are needed in any case to fix down the springs. Use twine squarely across the tops of the springs and other lines of twine may be taken diagonally as well, in the same way as a chair. The twine should set the tops of the springs to a reasonable curve above the level of the frame (Fig. 17-5C).

This is covered with burlap tacked around the top of the frame. If hair is to be used there may be fox edging around the edge, or the burlap can be used to make a thumb roll (Fig. 17-5D). Cover the top with hair and use sink and roll stitches to take care of edges, where the roll edge is not very large. The edge should be finished by boxing, with piping if wanted, so the padding finishes close up to the edges without any great increase in thickness at the center. When cotton is put on, let this also finish at the edge and not turn over. If foam is used instead of cotton, or in place of hair and cotton, it may be a little too large, but make sure it is compressed as the cover is fitted.

Mark out the fabric for the top and cut the strip to make up the boxed edge. This will probably have to be made up from several pieces cut across the width of the cloth. Arrange a piece across the foot of the bed and let it go around the sides an equal amount, with whatever other pieces are needed to make up, and a final joint along the back rail. Pin the parts of the cover inside out over the divan, then sew the seams.

With a cloth-covered frame the boxing is deep enough to go under the frame. If part of the wood is to be exposed, mark where the fabric is to come and turn it under along that line. Whichever method is used, tack temporarily at first and adjust the temporary tacks until the seam or piping follows around evenly. When that is satisfactorily arranged, do the final tacking.

The top will require twine through, whether there is hair or foam stuffing. Buttons can be used, but on a bed tufting is an alternative.

Tufts are short piece of wool, cotton, or synthetic material of about the thickness of knitting wool. Sew through from the top and back through a different part of the burlap to the same point. Tie a slip knot on top and cut off to leave a few inches of twine for handling. Do the same at every tuft position. Put a bundle of tufting material under the twine (Fig. 17-5E) and pull the slip knot until the tuft sinks into the surface. See that this is done to the same depth at each place, then lock the slip knots. Cut off surplus twine. It may be possible to work the knot into the thickness of the upholstery, but will not show if left in the body of the tuft.

Divan frames usually suit standard size mattresses, so a commercially-made mattress can be used with a cover hanging over during the day.

If a mattress is to be made, it is possible to use a box spring unit, but this is unnecessarily complicated when there is already springing in the divan. It would be better to use a piece of foam about 3 inches thick and big enough to cover the bed. Treat it as a large cushion. Use the same covering fabric as was used on the divan and make it the same on both sides so it can be turned over.

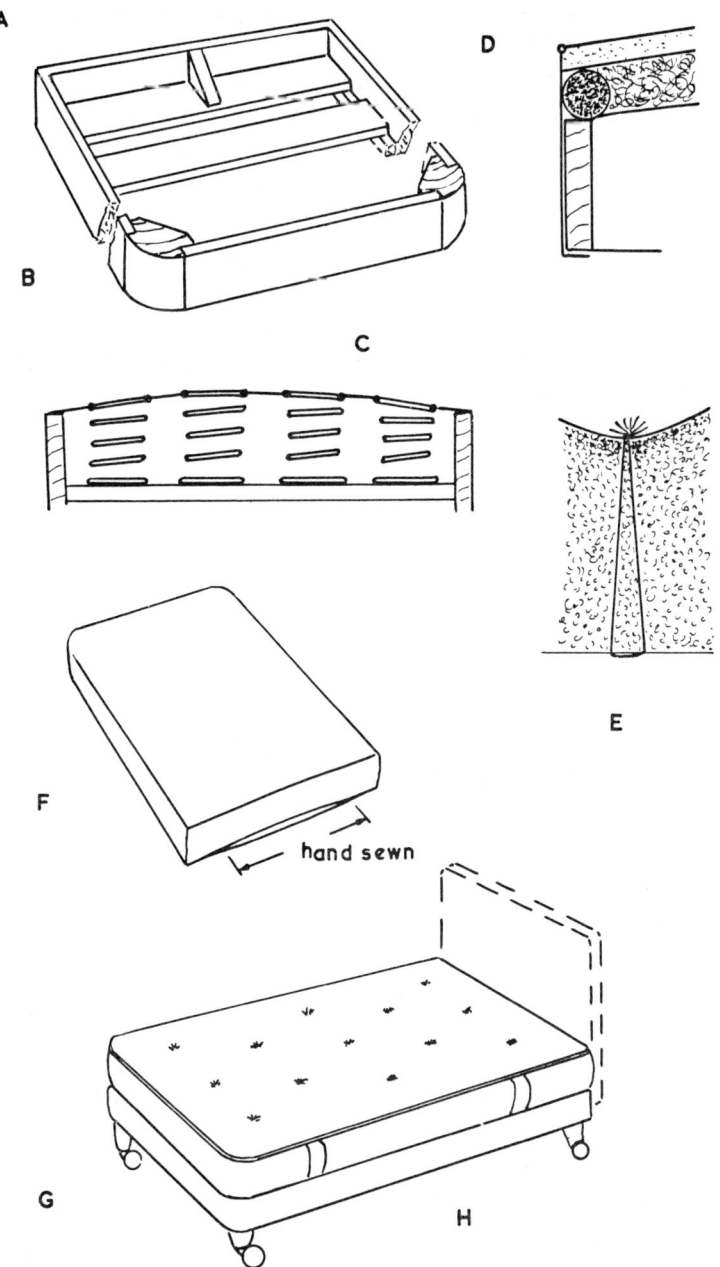

Fig. 17-5. A divan is framed like an ottoman, is fitted with a mattress, and may have tufts instead of buttons.

Carefully get the shape of the top, allowing for the seams, but also keeping the cover slightly smaller than the foam. Make sure edges are straight, even if the foam shows an uneven edge. Draw the edges along a straight piece of wood while the cloth is on a sheet of plywood or a flat floor. Discrepancies due to inaccurate marking out may be too obvious in the finished mattress. Similarly, make sure the seams in the edge boxing pieces are parallel and the same distance apart all round.

Most foam is sufficiently flexible to be curved enough to push through an opening narrower than its size, so make up the cover completely stitched around except for a part of one seam at the back edge (Fig. 17-5F). When the foam has been inserted and adjusted the remainder of the seam can be sewn by hand. However, it may be advisable to delay doing this until after tufting.

Tufting should be done in a similar pattern to that on the divan, with tufts on both sides. Pull in to get a reasonable depth on both sides, but not so much as to cause unevenness in the surface that can be felt by anyone on the bed.

A divan bed usually has short legs. The type of legs to be used should be decided before upholstery has progressed far. Many legs can be fixed with plates screwed under the bed. Make sure there are blocks built into the frame with sufficient area to take the plates. A divan is too heavy to lift and the legs should be fitted with casters (Fig. 17-5G). It may be a help in turning the mattress to sew in loops as handles on each side (Fig. 17-5H).

HEAD PANELS

Padded bed heads, padded panels on walls, padded fronts to counters or bars, have all been used for some time, but the use of foam in many thicknesses for upholstery, coupled with adhesives and synthetic materials have made these things easier to make and more satisfactory in use. Natural materials used in this way have been difficult to clean once they became soiled. Most synthetic materials are easier to clean in position, so they are more acceptable.

It is important that the bed head or other panel be stiff enough not to warp after treatment, because this would spoil the effect and very little could be done about it. A fairly stout piece of plywood or particle board should hold its shape without special stiffening, except for a very large area. If thinner plywood, Masonite, or other material of comparable thinness is used, it needs to be framed with solid wood, which need not be very thick, but to prevent distortion there should be another piece on the back (Fig. 17-6A). Framing with plywood or other thin material on one side only may develop a twist or become hollow after a few weeks. Of course, if the panel is part of an assembly, such as a bar, with other framing and parts attached, there is no risk of distortion.

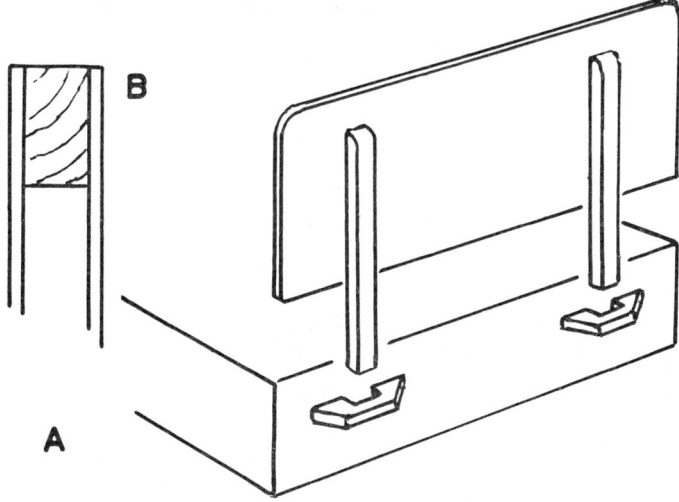

Fig. 17-6. A head board for a divan or single bed may have bordered padding.

A bed head panel may be fixed to the wall and a divan or other bed brought to it, but it is more usual for the panel to be attached to the divan, although it is possible for it to lift off. There are several methods of attachment, but in a simple one, two uprights behind the panel drop into sockets behind the bed (Fig. 17-6B). The uprights provide stiffness for the panel as well. Their exposed edges should be rounded in any case, but if they are liable to mark a wall they could be given a little token upholstery in the form of some foam or cotton enclosed in any available material and tacked on (Fig. 17-7).

For some types of head board the edges of the wood should be well rounded, but even when the design requires square edges, the sharpness should be taken off and corners rounded slightly with a few strokes of a plane, or light sanding.

Much of the purpose of a head panel is decoration, as anyone sitting in bed is likely to have a pillow to provide soft-

Fig. 17-7. Head panel uprights can be padded to prevent damage to walls.

ness. However, the headboard should be designed to suit a normal person sitting, with support for the back and enough height for the head. If it is a double bed, the panel should be arranged accordingly—a single bed may have a panel going to something like a point at the center, but a broader top would be more appropriate for two people.

One type for a single or a double bed is square-cornered, or nearly so, and the main padding comes around the edges, rather like the back of a pillow-back chair. It has the advantage of retaining pillows used to support anyone sitting.

A border is marked around the back board (Fig. 17-8). A piece of foam is cut to fit this and stuck on. The foam may be 1 inch or not more than 2 inches thick. It would be possible to use cotton. At the lower edge continue down or frame around

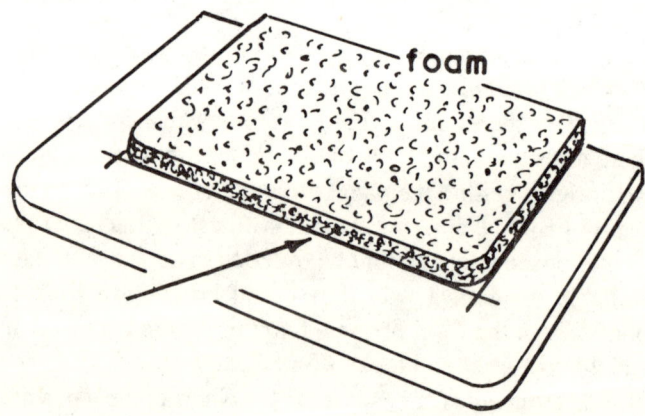

Fig. 17-8. A thin layer of foam provides cushioning for the head panel.

behind the upholstery of the bed, but make sure the padding will not interfere with the fitting arrangements. Cover this padding with muslin or other cloth and tack all round the border line (Fig. 17-9). Use cover fabric over muslin, tacked in the same way. Some fabrics can be used directly over foam without muslin.

Fig. 17-9. The foam is covered with muslin or fabric and tacked at the borders.

Tack piping over the tacked center panel (Fig. 17-10) so the piped edge makes a straight line. Stretch between tacks at the ends of lines to tension and straighten the piping before driving intermediate tacks. The piping marks the dividing line around the panel and should be parallel with the edges.

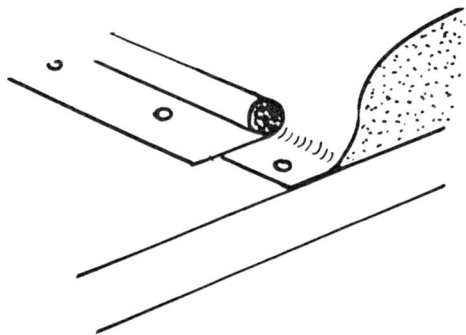

Fig. 17-10. Piping is tacked over the center panel.

Back tack a strip of card and a length of covering material over the edge of the piping, making the covering material wide enough to wrap over more foam and go around to the back of the panel (Fig. 17-11). There have to be miters at the top corners. The only length that is critical is across the top. The sides can have some spare length at the bottom. Put the top piece temporarily in position and get its length and the cut of the miter. Allow something for seaming. Cut the miters on the sides and sew the three parts together. Back tack all round.

323

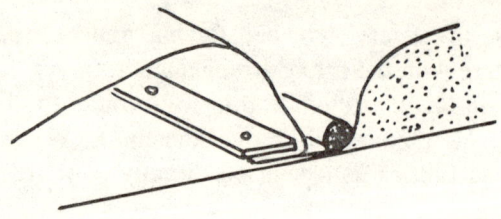

Fig. 17-11. Back tack a strip of card and a length of the cover over piping's edge.

Cut foam to fit around the border. It may stop at the edge of the panel or be wrapped over. Miter the corners closely. Pull the cover material over evenly with temporary tacks at first. When appearance is seen to be right, finally tack at the back all round. For the neatest finish on the back, remove the uprights and cover the back with similar material that overlaps the wrapped edges, then replace the uprights (Fig. 17-12).

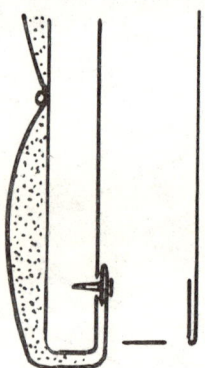

Fig. 17-12. The uprights can be upholstered in the same manner as the panel.

Head boards are often buttoned (Fig. 17-13). In a traditional form the board is covered with burlap and the padding is hair, with the usual sewing and a covering of cotton under muslin and the covering material. This would not be justified in modern work, as the padding is better in the form of foam. Deep buttoning, or something comparable to the older tufting (as distinct from mattress tufting), can be used by cutting foam.

If the foam is cut partly through along the line between buttons (Fig. 17-14) and the buttons drawn down, some of the

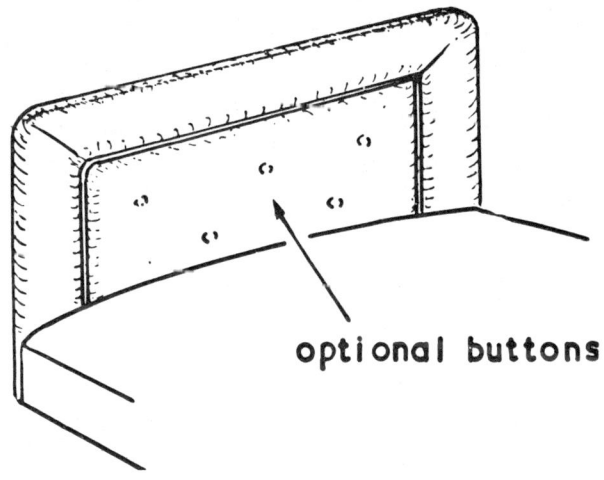

Fig. 17-13. Buttons enhance the panel's appearance.

foam will be forced to each side to give a more rounded effect (Fig. 17-15).

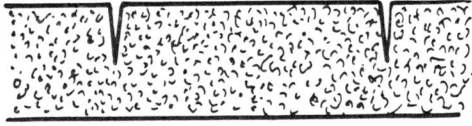

Fig. 17-14. To create tufting in the foam, first slice partly through the thickness.

The board may have a shaped outline, but the arrangement of buttons should be worked out to give a pleasing pattern. If the creases between buttons will come in a diamond pattern, this is usually more effective than a square pattern. In the overall

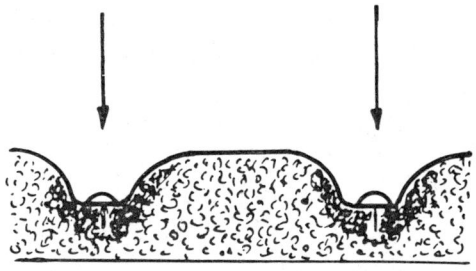

Fig. 17-15. Buttons give a soft contour to the slices.

design, diamonds emphasize height, while a square pattern makes the board seem broader (Figs. 7-16 and 7-17).

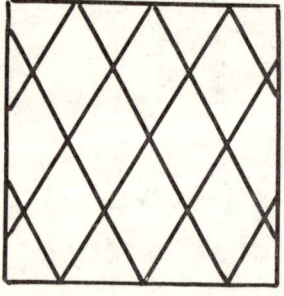

Fig. 17-16. Placing the buttons in a diamond pattern emphasizes height of a panel.

Stick the foam to the board. Mark the positions of the buttons. A spike or nail may be put temporarily in each position.

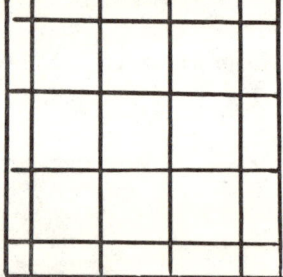

Fig. 17-17. A square pattern of buttons seems to broaden the panel.

Use a straightedge across these points as a guide to a knife to cut partly through (Fig. 17-18). Drill through the back in each

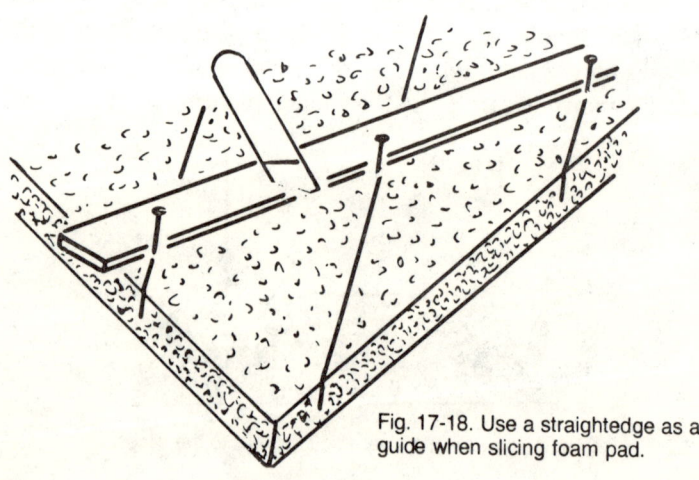

Fig. 17-18. Use a straightedge as a guide when slicing foam pad.

button position and pass a nail through so it can be pushed up to mark the covering fabric, which is temporarily tacked in place all round (Fig. 17-19).

Start near the middle of the pattern and push a nail through; then fix a button in that position with a slip knot. Work from the middle outwards, locating and fixing buttons. When they have all been fixed, begin tightening progressively so the buttons draw down the same amount (Fig. 17-20). Lock the knots and

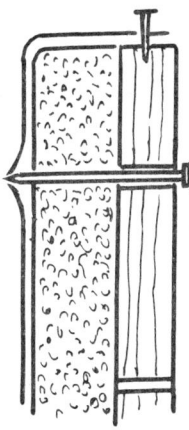

Fig. 17-19. Push nails through drilled holes in back to mark button positions on fabric.

cut off surplus twine. There may have to be some adjusting of tension around the edges to get a good appearance. When this is right, drive the final tacks around the edge and finish the back as described for the other head board.

Fig. 17-20. Work from the center of panel outwards when placing buttons.

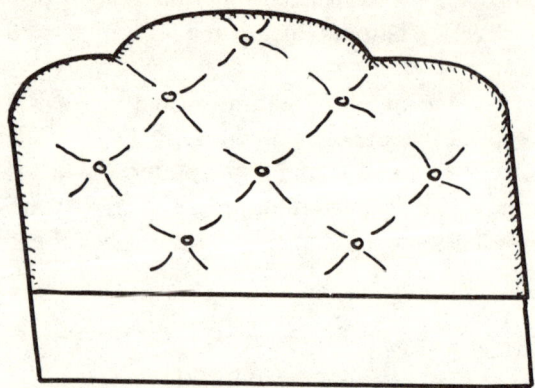

Fig. 17-21. A border and a buttoned center is a decorative combination for a head border.

The center panel of the first head board can be buttoned if desired, and the same idea can be used for a shaped board, with a border and buttoned center (Fig. 17-21). Care is needed in mitering the border.

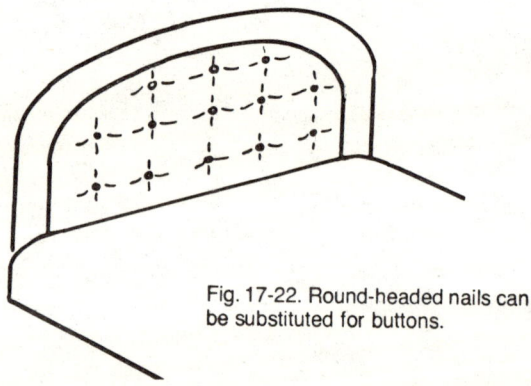

Fig. 17-22. Round-headed nails can be substituted for buttons.

A simpler type of buttoning, suitable for other panels, such as bar panels, uses round-headed nails instead of buttons to pull the padding in (Fig. 17-22).

Repairing Minor Damage

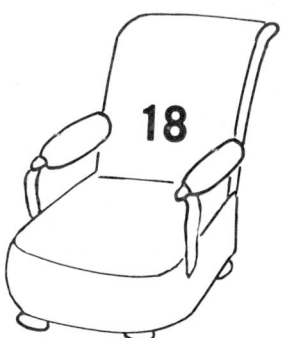

The saying, 'A stitch in time saves nine,' comes for the days of square-rigged sailing ships, when a seam in a sail had to be attended to as soon as it began parting or it might rip much further. It might have also applied to upholstery, although the results of neglect are not quite as serious. However, prompt repair to minor damage will often prevent it from developing into more serious trouble. Slight damage quickly dealt with can often be repaired so the result is inconspicuous, but if it has been left, the effects of chafe and wear may make it impossible to conceal what has been done.

Minor damage may be regarded as the sort of thing that can be repaired without dismantling at all, or by only a slight opening of the upholstery. In most cases the existing materials will be used, or new material only brought in to supplement or repair the things already there. Replacement of any extensive part of the upholstery necessitates stripping and recovering, following the instructions in the next chapter and the methods outlined in the rest of the book.

Of course, an early repair to minor damage necessitates having the ability and equipment available, so an elementary knowledge of the techniques involved is worth having, even if more ambitious work is not anticipated.

TORN FABRIC

A common piece of minor damage is a cut or tear in the outer or finishing fabric. If this is woven material the first break is usually clean—if it has been a direct cut—although it may be ragged if the break has been made by something that hit with a glancing blow. The threads will soon loosen and come away from the torn edges in both cases, so an early repair makes it easier to bring the edges together again with the best chance of the repair not showing. If there are loose threads that cannot be put back in place, cut them off, but avoid removing any more than necessary as missing threads make it more difficult to close the gap neatly without affecting the appearance of any pattern.

In some cases it is necessary to sew the edges; but in a very obvious place, such as the top of an arm, it is better to use a patch underneath secured by adhesive. Select an adhesive intended for the material. There are rubber-based adhesives that are suitable for many natural materials, but different adhesives are needed for synthetics. If an adhesive not primarily intended for upholstery is used, be careful that it is not so thin that there is a risk of it penetrating the cloth and showing on the surface.

The patch need not be of the same material as that that it is to repair, but it should be of a reasonably close weave and obviously suitable for the same adhesive as will suit the outside fabric. Try not to enlarge the hole. Make the patch bigger all round (Fig. 18-1A). As it has to be pushed through the hole, its size will have to be related to the available gap. It may help to cut off the corners of the patch. Fold it in order to get it through the hole. A blunt table knife is a suitable tool to push through and make the patch lie flat and in the correct place (Fig. 18-1B). It is important that the patch is flat and without creases.

Read the adhesive instructions. If it is a type which allows the surfaces to be brought together immediately, hold up one side of the damage and use the knife blade or a thin piece of wood to push adhesive under one side, with as good a spread as is possible. Press down and do the same to the other side. This type of adhesive usually allows movement. Manipulate the meeting edges so they are worked close together, then hold them while the adhesive sets to the point where it will not slip. If the adhesive has to be allowed to become tacky before bringing the surfaces together, push adhesive under one side and make sure the underside of the cloth as well as the patch becomes coated. Then hold up the cloth at that side while the surfaces become tacky, and bring them together with the outer surface brought as near as can be judged to its original position. Prepare the other side in the same way, then bring the edges together as the cloth is lowered onto the patch. Of course, care is needed to avoid getting adhesive on the surface that will show. How any surplus adhesive is dealt with depends on its type, but if it is still liquid, it can usually be removed with a clean cloth. Make sure a part of the cloth that has previously been soiled is not used again.

With extensive damage, such as a long cut, it may be impossible to pull the edges together sufficiently for a patch and adhesive only to keep them in place. They will then have to be sewn, preferably over a patch. Sewing to the patch transfers the strain to it. In some places it may not be possible to get a patch underneath, and it will be necessary to use stitches that draw and lock the edges together.

A small curved needle and thread to match the material can be used to sew along each side of the cut (Fig. 18-1C). If the lines of stitches are kept back from the edges, but the edges are brought into register with each other as the stitches are made, sewing can be followed by adhesive applied in the same way as a simpler repair so the edges are kept neatly together. Stitches should be kept small, but the curve of the needle and the flexibility and tightness of the fabric will affect stitch size. Let the stitches go a short distance further than the damage, so there can be no distortion of the cloth that might affect appearance, particularly if there is a prominent pattern.

If the cut is in a less obvious place and a patch cannot be put underneath, it may be satisfactory to pull the edges together with a simple zig-zag stitch (Fig. 18-1D). Because the thread goes diagonal to the weave it may be too obvious for a prominent repair. It may be better in such a case to use half-hitches. The edges are pulled with stitches directly across and the thread goes along the cut between stitches (Fig. 18-1E). As each stitch is made, the needle goes behind it and enough tension is put on for the crossing to bring the line from the previous stitch along the seam (Fig. 18-1F).

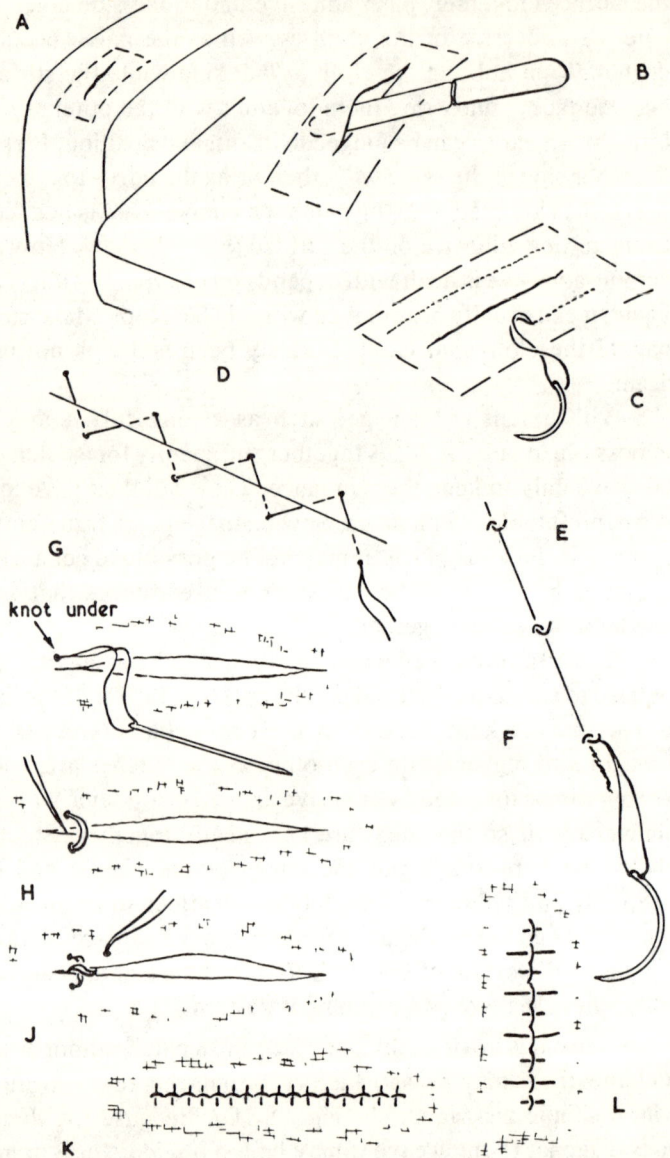

Fig. 18-1. Fabric repairs usually involve sewing and the method used depends on circumstances.

A herringbone stitch is the least obvious stitch, but in a place where considerable tension is needed to bring the edges together, it may be necessary to use it. This has the advantage of holding the tension as each stitch is made, but it is more obvious when finished and is better suited to a hidden part, like the inside of an arm or the underside of the chair.

To make a herringbone stitch, use a single or double thread and either a straight or curved needle. Knot the end of the thread and pass the needle up through the far side at the left of the damage (Fig. 18-1G)—assuming right-handed working. Come across and down through the near side, with the needle point emerging to the left of the stitch through the gap (Fig. 18-1H). Draw this tight and go over the stitch and up through the far side again (Fig. 18-1J). This completes a stitch. The action is repeated by going down through the near side, up on the left of the stitch, over it and on to the next one, and so on (Fig. 18-1K). How close the stitches are made depends on the material and the amount of tension needed. The closest stitches may be about six to an inch, but four to an inch may be adequate. With heavy material larger stitches may be all that are needed. Although it is neatest to keep all the stitches the same length, it may be better on loosely-woven cloth to let them be of different lengths so the tension is taken on different threads of the cloth. Alternating long and short stitches also allows the stitches to be closer (Fig. 18-1L), which may be an advantage if much strain has to be taken.

Vinyl and other sheet plastic material can be repaired in the same way as woven cloth, by using a patch underneath with adhesive and stitches if needed. Many of the general adhesives will not adhere to plastics and an adhesive for one plastic may not adhere to another. If the plastic being treated is not known, it will be advisable to try the effect on a scrap piece, possibly cut from a turned-under edge.

Because of its texture and appearance, a repair done in this way may not finish very neatly. Although the repair may be strong, it may not look very good. Vinyl on a fabric backing does not usually tear very far, so the problem may only be an L-shaped break with legs less than 1/2 inch long. There are ways of dealing with this type of damage that require special materials, but which produce an invisible repair when properly done.

In one system there is a two-part filler which can be colored with pigments to match the vinyl being repaired. This goes into the damage and is smoothed to match. It is cured with an electric heater supplied with the kit. Grain effects can be introduced and it is possible to fill the damage so the finished surface shows no sign of having been repaired.

To get a good match on any damaged vinyl by that method means having a large selection of color pigments to draw on. Another system uses a liquid that will dissolve vinyl. A scrap piece cut from the material being repaired is dissolved, and this produces repair solution of the same color without the need for the large number of pigments.

It is possible to make a texture impression—a sort of mold of a patterned surface—and use this over the inserted repair solution. Then when heat is applied the repair sets with a surface pattern matching the surrounding material.

Vinyl becomes dull and may lose its color with use and age, but this can be corrected so the finish is almost as good as new. There are cleaning materials and others for reviving colors. If these are used on undamaged furniture or in association with a repair, it is possible to rejuvenate vinyl upholstery so the appearance is enhanced.

A rip close to a piped edge is a special repair as the usual patch underneath or stitched edges cannot be arranged. The stitching may have to be arranged to suit the type of damage, but for a tear in any material close to the piping, the best way to hide the stitches that pull the damage close may be to turn in the edge and pull it towards the piping with stitches that go below it (Fig. 18-2A). The torn edge nearest the piping is kept under and the other edge will probably have to be turned under to give the

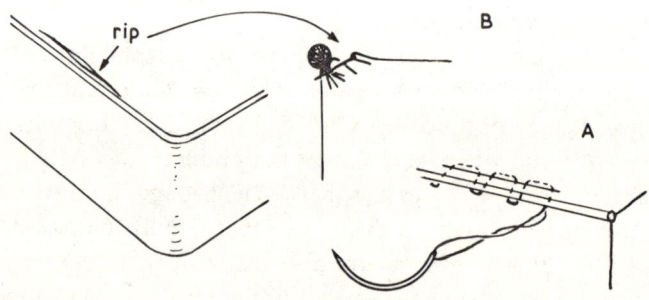

Fig. 18-2. A rip near piping can be sewn through below the piping.

uneven support. This means that it is often advisable to replace the whole pattern of webbing, which is not usually a very big undertaking on an average chair.

When the whole pattern of webbing is to be replaced, all of the old webbing is removed with the twine that held springs to it, but notice the pattern followed by the twine if the same system of sewing is to be followed again. Any of the methods described for new work may be used, however.

To get a good tension the strips of webbing should be fitted one way without compressing the springs, but letting them overlap (Fig. 18-3B). When the webbing is fitted the other way, compress the springs and tension the webbing so it does not sag under pressure from the springs (Fig. 18-3C). Finally, replace the burlap or other covering. It may be advisable to reposition tacks as they may not hold very well if all are driven into old holes.

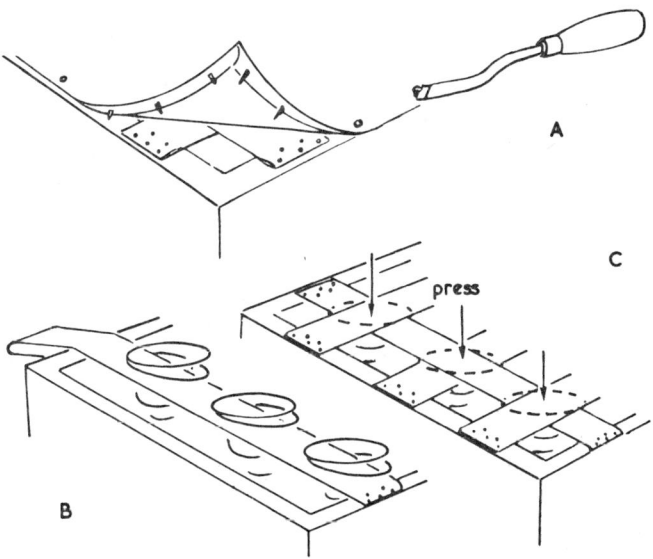

Fig. 18-3. If webbing has to be replaced it should be tensioned and the springs positioned later.

RENEWING BURLAP

In a fully upholstered dining chair, and in some other chairs, the springs thrust upwards against one or more pieces of burlap, which come below the padding or stuffing inside the edge enough strength to prevent stitches from pulling out (Fig. 18-2B). Stitches are taken through the turned-under edge being repaired and kept close under the piping at the sides, where they will be hidden.

WEBBING

When a seat is upholstered it starts from the webbing upwards. In use, the varying loads on the seat cause downward thrusts through the stuffing and other components of the seat to the springs, which, in turn, finally thrust on the webbing. The webbing has nowhere to pass the load. Although the load has been reduced through the springs, the thrust on the webbing may cause it to fail after long use.

An uneven appearance on the top of a seat may be evidence that the webbing has partially failed. A complete break in a piece of webbing will be obvious below the seat. There may even be a spring hanging loosely below. If the underside of the seat is covered with burlap or other material, the pattern of webbing will show through and any damage can be seen.

The under covering material may have its edges turned in and tacked. Lift the tacks carefully and remove the covering material with its folded edges undisturbed if it is fit to use again (Fig. 18-3A).

It may only be necessary to replace one or two pieces of webbing. If so, notice how the old pieces are interlaced and cut the twine to springs, preferably in a way that does not affect the tying to springs on undisturbed webbing. Fix an occasional strip of webbing in the way described for new work, using a similar arrangement of tacks at the ends as in adjoining pieces. As the webbing is strained across, compress the springs so the strip can be given a tension comparable to what it would have had when fitted to a new frame before springs were added.

Even if only one piece of webbing has reached the stage where immediate replacement is necessary, the rest of the pattern of webbing may be at a stage where it could not be expected to last much longer. In that case it would be foolish to replace just the one piece and be faced with replacement of the other webbing in the near future. Old webbing may have stretched, so the introduction of only one or two new pieces may produce covering of the chair top (Fig. 18-4A). This may suffer from the effect of the metal spring tops wearing through, so the spring thrusts against the stuffing, making the seat uncomfortable and probably showing unevenly on top. In some chairs there may be two layers of burlap with cotton batting between (Fig. 18-4B).

In both cases it is necessary to remove the top to replace damaged burlap. If the top is in good condition it should be removed with minimum of disturbance so it can be refitted without difficulty. How this is done depends on its construction, but a start is made by removing nails or tacks around the edge (Fig. 18-4C) so the gimp or other decorative strip can be removed to expose the tacks holding the covering material. These tacks are withdrawn and the cover lifted off.

If the filling is made of foam or rubber it can be lifted out, but if the chair has hair or other stuffing material held to the burlap with large twine loops, the twine should be cut and the hair removed with as little disturbance as possible, so it can be replaced as far as possible as a unit. Remove the old burlap and note how it was fitted.

If the springs had their tops held by a pattern of twine unconnected with the burlap, the twine should be checked for its condition and security. It need not be disturbed if it doesn't need repair. If the springs are sewn to the burlap, note the arrangement so it can be repeated with the replacement material.

If there is a single piece of burlap, cut it to the size of the old piece and turn in its edges in the same way. Stretch it evenly and avoid the old tack holes when fixing it.

If there is a double thickness of burlap with cotton between, the traditional method of fitting makes the lower piece about 2 inches bigger all round. It is tacked in place, then the cotton and the other piece put over it (Fig. 18-4D). The under piece is wrapped over and stitches made through the three thicknesses. The twine is half hitched or knotted (Fig. 18-4E), then taken in a long stitch (about 1 1/2 inches is suitable) to the next point (Fig. 18-4F). Do this all round. There is no need for other stitching or fastenings.

Replace the top. If hair is used for the stuffing, reposition it and make retaining twine loops, as described for new work. If

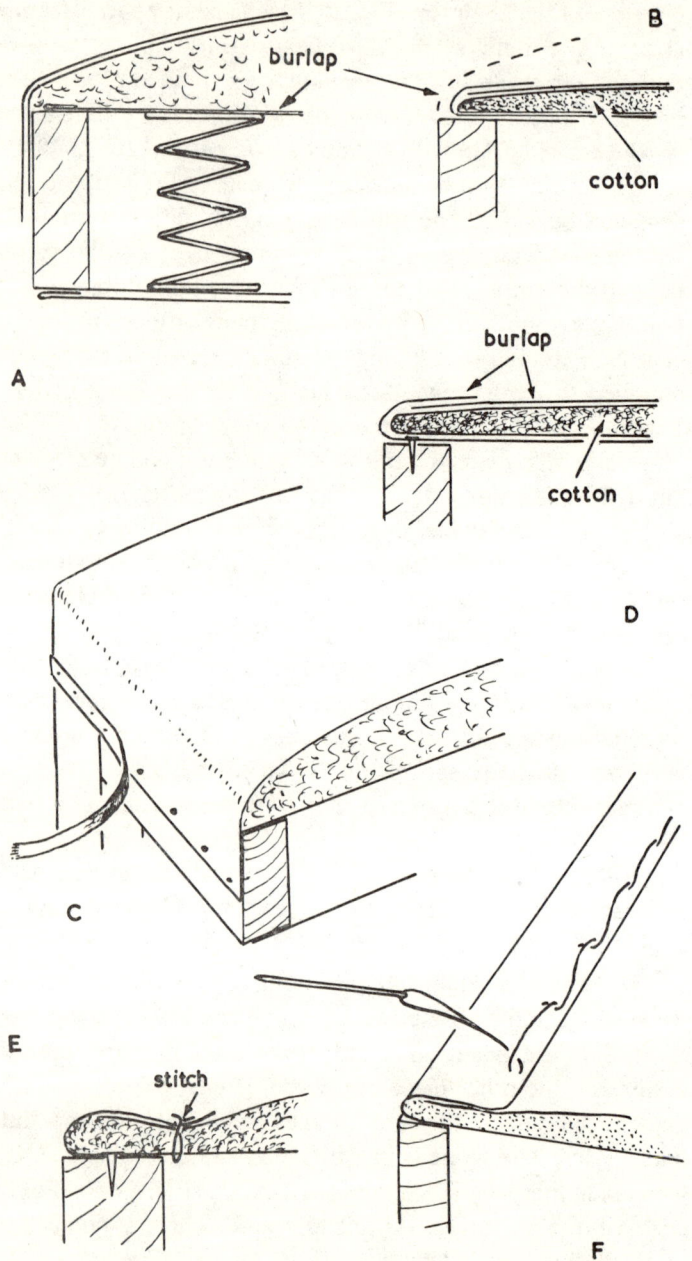

Fig. 18-4. The burlap above the springs can be improved by putting cotton between it and another layer.

there is cotton batting over this, it may be advisable to fit a new piece if the old part has become compressed. If the filling is made of a latex or foam pad, check its condition. If it is a symmetrical shape, it may be possible to turn it so a new edge is to the front where the greatest compression and wear may be expected.

On some traditional chairs there may be extra burlap along the front edge and maybe at the sides. This will be discovered when the top is removed, and it is usually tacked to the frame and wrapped over the filling to which it is sewn at intervals. If this is found, new burlap will probably have to be used when the top is replaced.

Fit the top and its gimp, using the old markings and tack holes as a guide, but drive at least some of the tacks in new positions for greatest strength.

BUTTONS

Buttons may be purely decorative, particularly if the filling is made of foam or other material in block form. But if hair or other loose filling is used, the button supports twine that plays a part in preventing the filling from moving about. To a lesser extent buttons may do something to prevent movement of a foam pad which is not a tight fit in its covering.

If the twine breaks it should be renewed without delay, both to restore appearance and to go through the filling before that has had a chance to move in relation to the cover. Even if the button is matching and has been lost, it may be advisable to put a temporary thread and button in place to hold the filling until a matching button can be obtained or a plain button can be covered with material cut from a waste part of the covering.

If parts of the twine remain through the pad, withdraw it from the back. Note if there is a button or peg at the back. Check sound buttoning elsewhere and use the same method on the repair if possible, although if the back part of the assembly is hidden, it will not matter if a different, more convenient method is used.

Fitting new twine and buttons is the same method as that used when making new furniture, but it may be necessary to reinforce at front or back if the fabric has become worn or torn.

A patch small enough to be hidden by the button can be fixed with adhesive at the front. It may not be necessary to keep it as small at the back (Fig. 18-5A). Use a long needle and thread the front button on the twine. Check at another position to see if the twine has been used single or double.

Pass the needle through and take in the back button or peg. Make a slip knot so the twine tension can be adjusted (Fig. 18-5B). Compress the cushion and regulate the knot so that when pressure is released, the amount the button pulls in at the front matches the other buttons. Compress again so the slip knot can be locked and surplus twine cut off (Fig. 18-5C). Pull the twine so the knot goes into the body of the cushion (Fig. 18-5D).

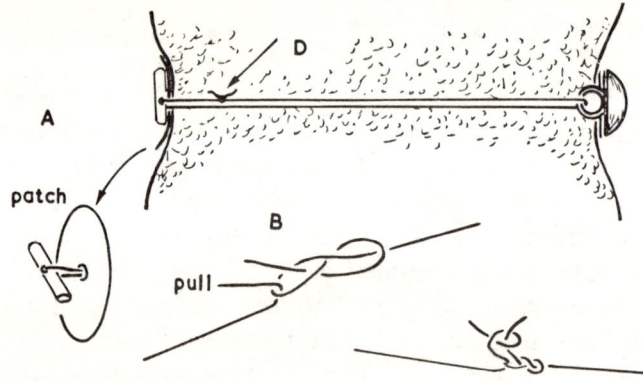

Fig. 18-5. When buttons are replaced use a slip knot until the tension is correct, then lock it into the body of the stuffing.

LOOSE FASTENINGS

The problem of loose fastenings in frame structures is dealt with in Chapter 27, but fastenings holding the fabric and other upholstery materials may also loosen. In many cases it is a simple matter of driving the nail or tack in a slightly different place. If this would affect appearance and the head should be in the same spot, it may be possible to push a sliver of wood into the hole and drive again (Fig. 18-6A). Another way is to drive the tack or nail diagonally so it penetrates new fibers, then the final hammer blow knocks the head flat (Fig. 18-6B). A series of nails driven diagonally in alternate directions (Fig. 18-6C) have a combined strength better than if they were driven straight.

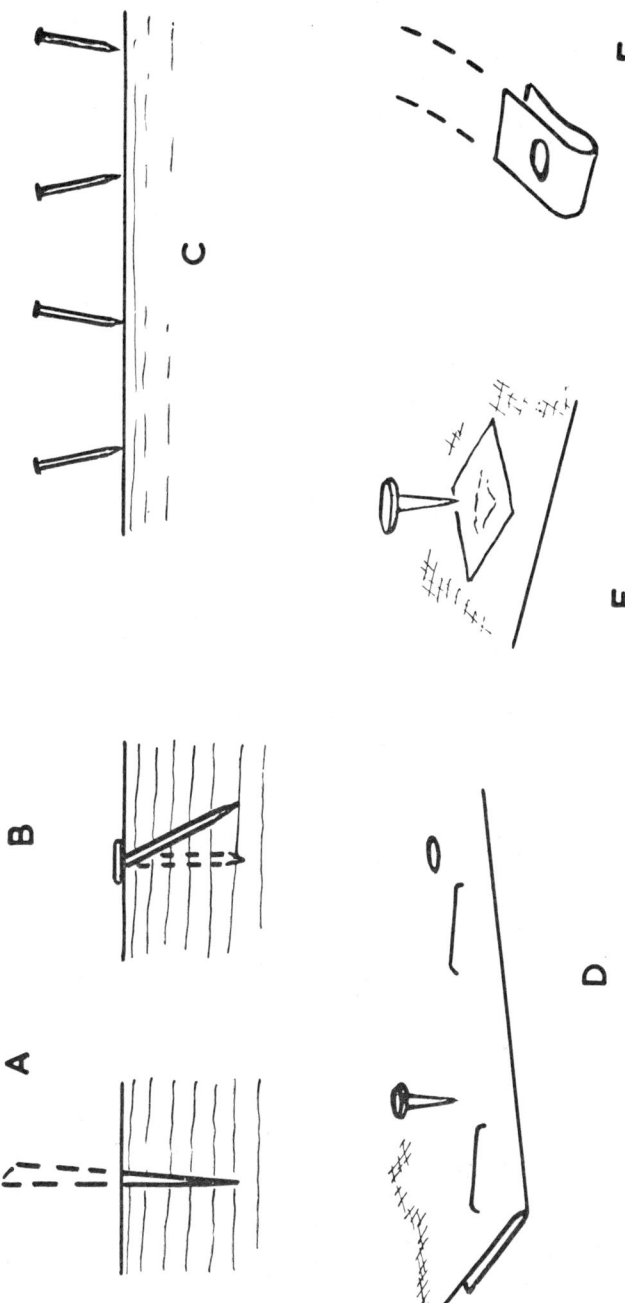

Fig. 18-6. Nails get a better grip if sloping. Tape under a head will reinforce over a tear.

If staples have been used and they have loosened, they will probably not hold well enough if merely tightened by hammering, although this can be tried. If stapling equipment is available more staples can be driven alongside the loose ones. If this cannot be done, it may be possible to carefully lift staples and drive them again in slightly different places with a hammer. Alternatively, drive tacks alongside the loose staples (Fig. 18-6D).

It is sometimes possible to find slightly thicker or longer tacks to substitute for the loose ones, but make sure the wood underneath is stout enough to take them. If the hole in the fabric has worn large or torn, it may be advisable to fix a patch with adhesive before driving a new tack (Fig. 18-6E), although for small damage in a place that is hidden, a piece of tape folded over may spread the pressure under a tack head (Fig. 18-6F).

If fabric held with adhesive has come away it is not always satisfactory to merely apply more adhesive. Adhesive grips by penetrating the pores and interstices of the materials being joined. If adhesive has already been used, this will have sealed the surfaces. The newly-applied adhesive may bond to the old, but in many cases it will not grip the old dry adhesive surface. The old hard surface should be broken up by scraping with a knife blade, rubbing with abrasive paper or sometimes by just flexing the material.

Adhesives are used now much more extensively than in earlier years, so it may be possible to use them in repairs to old furniture to either reinforce old fastenings which are replaced for the sake of appearance, or in place of other fastenings. Gimp and other decorative material added to the surface covering may be much more secure with adhesive in addition to occasional tacks or pins.

BROKEN SPRINGS

It is not usually advisable to attempt to repair broken springs. It is much better to replace them. There is such a variety available that a replacement for any spring should be obtainable. For a temporary repair it may be possible to stretch a broken part of a compression spring and use it until another can be fitted. It may be possible to pad a broken end to make up the length so it provides support for a short period, but take care to see that there is no risk of the rough end penetrating the filling or covering.

A tension spring that breaks somewhere within its coils cannot be repaired satisfactorily and must be discarded. The adjoining springs may take the load adequately until a new spring can be fitted. If something has to be used for support, a piece of cord or rope may be passed through the spring. If it can be brought out between the coils and tied, the end coils will still provide some springing (Fig. 18-7A). A new spring should be substituted as soon as possible.

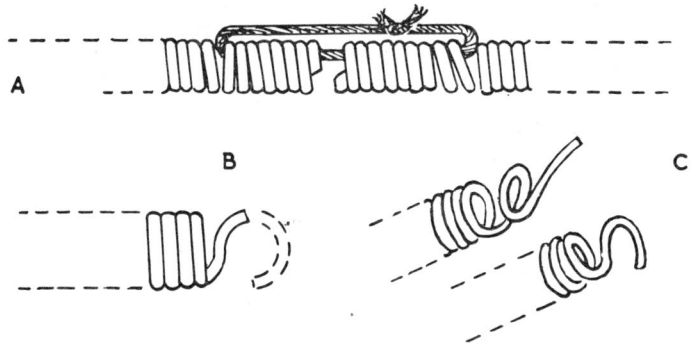

Fig. 18-7. Broken tension springs may be tied temporarily, or the ends may be refashioned.

A tension spring is more likely to break at one end (Fig. 18-7B). In some springs the temper of the steel at the ends is not as high as in the body of the springs. This means that the ends are softer than the rest of the spring, which is hard and comparatively brittle. If the end is soft enough it may be possible to reshape the broken part with two pairs of pliers or a pair of pliers and a vise to make a new hook (Fig. 18-7C). It may not be as precise a shape as the original hooked end, but it will grip the metal plate or other fixing.

If the end of the spring is too hard to be bent into a new hook shape, do not persist in trying or the brittle steel may snap again. If a replacement spring is not available, it is possible to draw the temper from the end so it can be bent. Use a blowlamp flame, or even the flame of a gas cooker. Great heat is not needed. It is best if part of the steel is rubbed bright with emery cloth or other abrasive. Heat gently and watch the bright surface. It will start to turn to several colors. Heat just a little more than is necessary to obtain these oxide colors on the surface, but do not go on to red heat, or too much of the end of the spring will be softened. Let the steel cool slowly. If you try to hasten it by dipping in water, that will harden the steel again. The annealed end should bend easily to a new hook shape and need not be given any further heat treatment—it will be strong enough in its annealed state.

Like tension springs, rubber webbing is better replaced than repaired. Any repair is best regarded as a temporary expedient while a replacement is obtained. If one piece of rubber webbing breaks, other pieces in that assembly should be examined as they may also be badly worn or have deteriorated rubber. If the rubber is stretched well and minute cracks become visible, this is a sign that the rubber is becoming *perished* or *denatured* and the material is nearing the end of its life. General replacement is advisable if the piece of furniture is to be brought back into good condition.

If the break is at an end, it may be possible to carefully open the end fitting, then cut the webbing and refix to the new end, providing there is enough stretch in the webbing to adjust to the new length. Also, the tightened piece should not be so much tighter than adjoining pieces that the set of the cushion which is supported will be affected. If the end is tacked it may be possible to cut off the minimum to give a sound end and arrange the tacking a little further in than before to allow for the shorter webbing and to give it a tension comparable with the other full-length pieces.

If rubber webbing breaks within its length instead of at the ends it may be possible to repair it by overlapping and sewing the ends (Fig. 18-8A), providing this does not shorten it too much to reach the frame and still give a tension that is not excessively greater than the nearby undamaged webbing. Let the parts overlap and sew with two needles. Have double thread or twine and make stitches from opposite sides (Fig. 18-8B). Twine may be used, but a stout thread, such as that used for carpets, is preferable.

If such an overlap would shorten the webbing too much, the ends can butt against each other and have another piece sewn below (Fig. 18-8C). This is satisfactory with another piece of similar rubber webbing, but it is possible to use ordinary webbing or other stout cloth. In that case it is better to have it above and below (Fig. 18-8D).

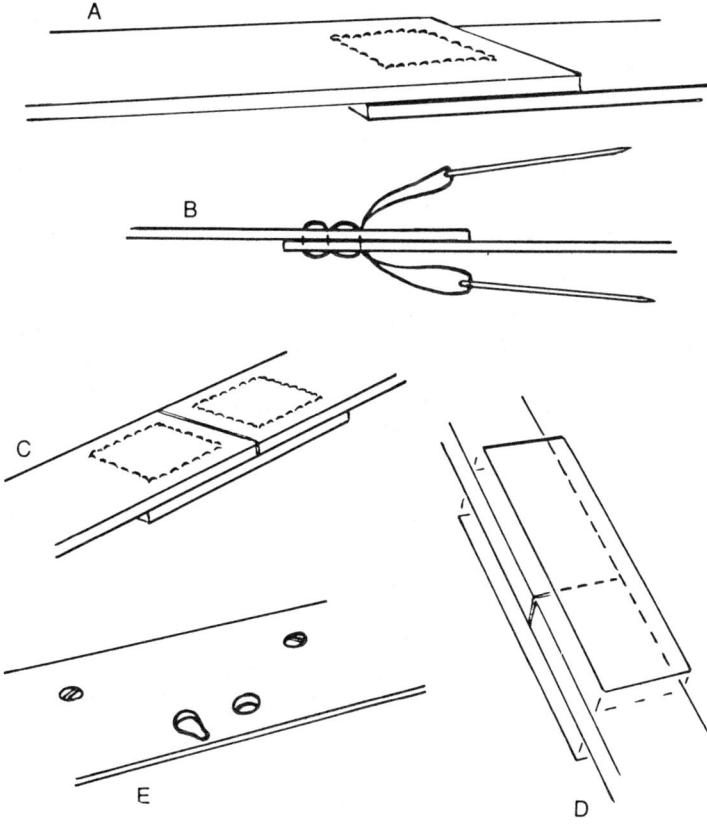

Fig. 18-8. Rubber webbing breaks can be sewn.

If springs or rubber webbing breaks, it is probably because it is at the position of greatest strain. When replacing a repaired length it may be better to rearrange the whole pattern so this piece gets less load, by placing it towards the back of a seat or near the bottom of a back.

Springs across a seat usually hook into a drilled plate. The spring is tempered steel and the plate is much softer mild steel, so after long use the steel may wear the hole out of shape—so much so that there may be little of the plate left for the spring to pull against (Fig. 18-8E). The simplest repair is to drill a new hole a short distance to one side of the old one. Altering the line of the pull of the spring by that short amount will not make any difference to the support given to the cushion.

It is unlikely that zig-zag springs will break. If one does, there is no satisfactory method of repair and it should be replaced. Temporary support might be given by using a length of rubber webbing, if the chair has to be used, but this is only a short-term expedient.

REPAIRING FOAM

Some types of foam filling tend to crumble, particularly at edges that get most wear, such as the front edge of a seat cushion. If it is a cushion that can be turned and used in several ways the risk of this happening can be reduced or delayed by periodic turning. If an edge has crumbled it may be possible to join on a new piece of foam instead of replacing the filling completely.

If the cushion is fitted with a zipper it is easy to withdraw the foam. If the zipper is not full-width, reach in and fold over the foam for withdrawal. If the cushion is sewn all round, find the hand-sewn seam and unpick the stitches. In a fitted cushion this will probably be the lower rear seam. With a fitted cushion that turns or a loose cushion, the seam that has been sewn from outside will have to be located and unpicked. Like the zipper this may not extend full-width.

Withdraw the foam and examine it. Cut off the damaged part parallel with the edge (Fig. 18-9A). A carving knife or any knife with a long, thin, sharp blade will do. Have a new piece of foam with a similar section to the old material, but cut it wider than is necessary to make up the original size. This will ensure that the cover will press tightly on the foam so as to compress it and hold the joint together.

Coat the surfaces with adhesive and press them together on a flat surface. It may help in getting an even pressure to press with flat pieces of wood (Fig. 18-9B). Adhesive alone may be sufficient, but if it is considered advisable, thin cloth may be stuck with adhesive over the joint (Fig. 18-9C). Self-adhesive

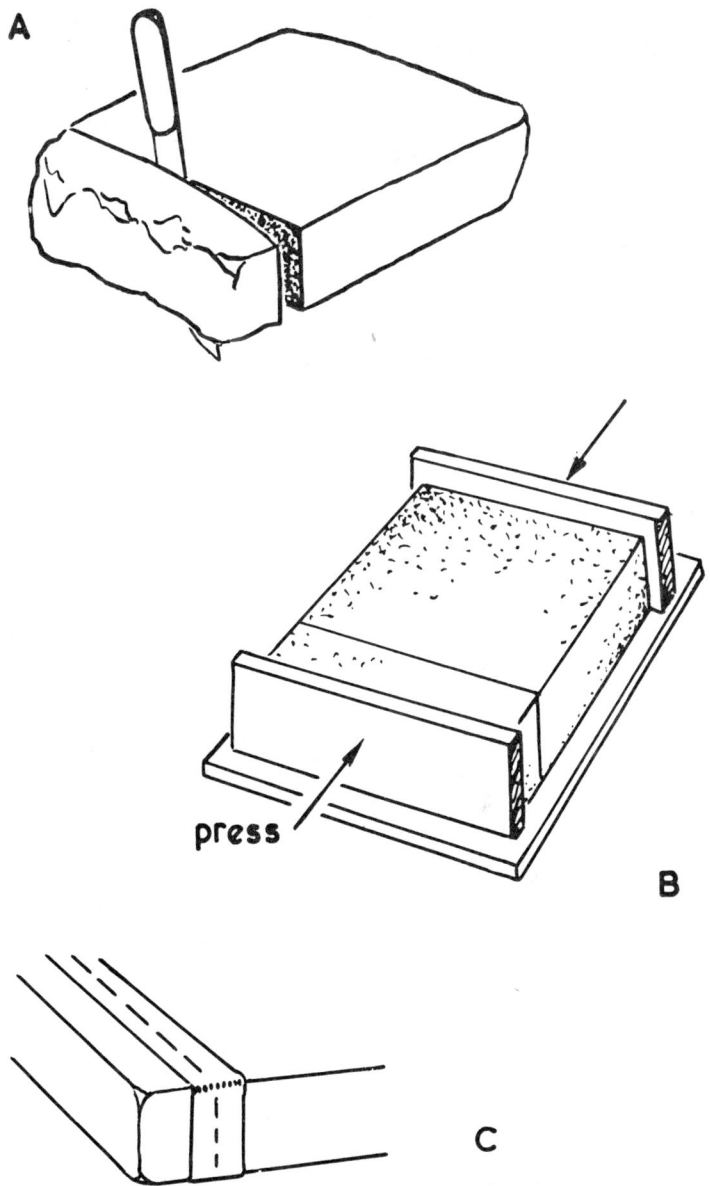

Fig. 18-9. A crumbled foam edge can be cut off and a new piece stuck on.

plastic strip might be used for the same purpose. The new edge that will be taking the same wear that caused the old edge to fail may be reinforced by thin cloth stuck on. Allow all stuck joints ample time for the adhesive to set before putting the foam back in the cover.

Fold the foam to fit it in the cover. Reach in and position it. Adjust it so the repair is under compression from the cover when that is closed. Close the zipper or resew the seam to complete the repair.

DINING CHAIR BACK

Many modern dining chairs are only upholstered on their seats and have wood backs without padding. Many older dining chairs, however, had a small padded panel to provide a little softening to a fairly straight back. Modern chairs achieve comfort by having more shape to conform to the body.

The small panel has a hole right through the frame and a cloth cover back and front (Fig. 18-10). The cloth at the back is flat, but that at the front may be slightly domed. The space

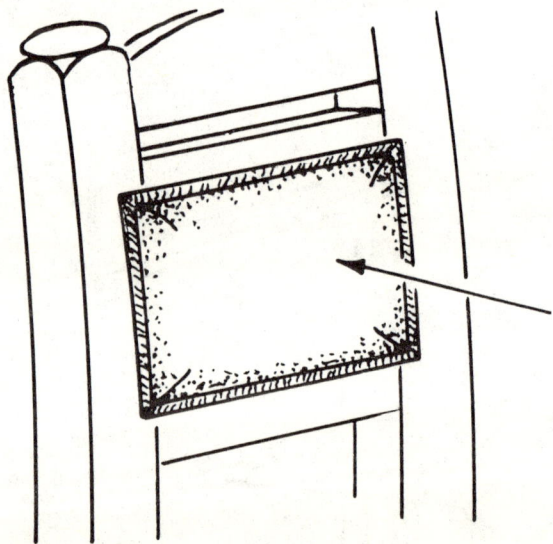

Fig. 18-10. The upholstery of a dining chair back may have to be built out with extra padding.

between is filled with a stuffing, which may have been any of the traditional types of filling (Fig. 18-11). A repair may be needed because the stuffing has compressed and become hard or slack, or because the covering has become worn.

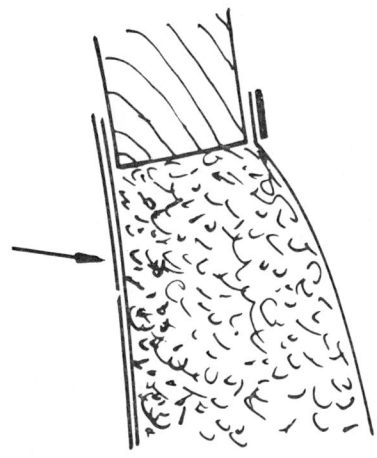

Fig. 18-11. The back panel of a dining chair is lightly padded.

If the old covering is to be retained and does not need repair, it is simplest to leave the front untouched and remove the back panel. Usually this has gimp to be lifted to expose tacks through the covering, which may be lined with burlap (Fig. 18-12). Pick out the stuffing, which may be made of hair, felt, or cotton. Almost certainly this will have to be discarded, but if it is in reasonable condition although compressed so it no longer fills the space, it may be possible to face it with cotton batting, thin foam sheeting, or other material against the front to make up

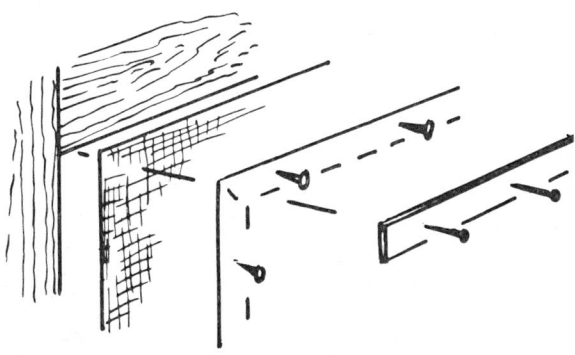

Fig. 18-12. If the old cover is to be retained, padding can be renewed by working from behind.

enough padding (Fig. 18-13). The alternative is to fill the space with loose pieces of foam or build up with sheet foam to give the front a good shape (Fig. 18-14). The back material is replaced and kept flat to complete that repair.

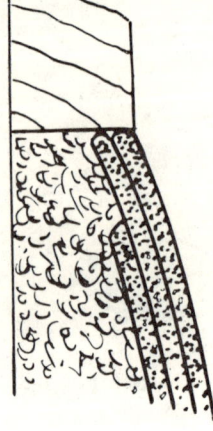

Fig. 18-13. Compressed padding can be rejuvenated by the addition of layers of cotton batting or thin foam.

If new covering material is to be used, the back panel is flat and the front may have to be given one or more pleats at the corners to allow for shaping. The back is fixed first, then the filling inserted and the front covering stretched over it. It is important that the two panels have true edges which are straight

Fig. 18-14. Back panel can be contoured entirely with sheet foam arranged in this manner.

and parallel with the square parts of the frame. Because of the proximity of parallel wood edges, any errors in shaping the panels will be very obvious.

It is advisable to pencil the outlines of the cloth panels on the wood. Although the cloth may be marked apparently accurately, the pencil markings rather than the cloth shape should be the final guide when fixing. The back panel is flat and easily fixed with straight edges. Start at the center of the bottom and tack outwards with enough tension to keep the edge straight without distorting any pattern (Fig. 18-15). Put a temporary tack in the center of the top and try the layout of the cloth. Tack across the top from the center outwards, regulating the turned-

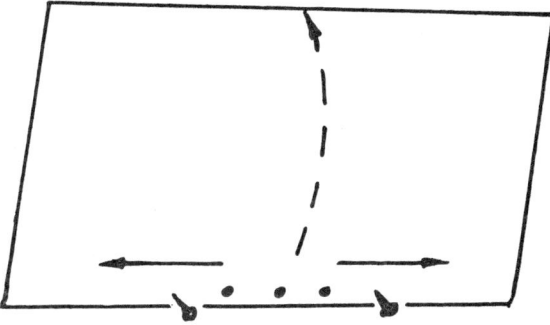

Fig. 18-15. Tack the cloth cover at bottom first, from center outwards. Tack the top in same fashion.

in edge to conform to the pencil lines. Do the same at the sides, working from their centers up and down. Do not tack right to the corners in any direction at first, but leave enough material there to carefully fold in. With most material it is possible to fold the uncut cloth in without causing too much thickness there (Fig. 18-16). With thicker material a cut into the corner helps (Fig. 18-17), while with very thick material the corner can be cut across (Fig. 18-18). Cuts at the corners should not come right to the turned-in outline, but a small amount of uncut cloth should be turned under. If a cut is taken right to the fold it may show as a raw edge at the corner.

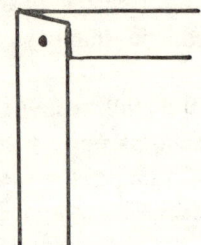

Fig. 18-16. Thin layers of material can be folded at corners without undue bulk.

The front is covered in a similar way, but there has to be an allowance for shaping over the padding. Turn in the lower edge and tack from the center outwards, but leave the corners. Pull up and over the padding to the center of the top. Turn in there to

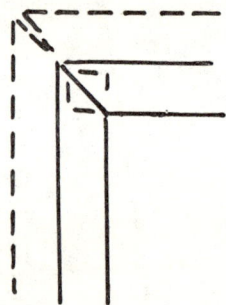

Fig. 18-17. Thicker layers of material will need a diagonal cut to make them fold easier at corners.

the pencil line and work outwards towards the corners. Treat the sides in the same way. At the corners pull and turn in the edges with one or two evenly-spaced pleats to allow for the curve over the padding (Fig. 18-19).

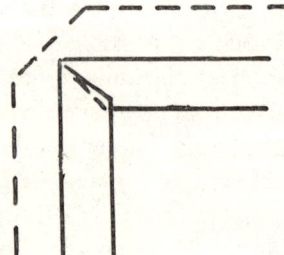

Fig. 18-18. Thickest layers won't fold well at corners unless ome of the material is scissored off.

This type of padding is usually bordered with gimp, but the back should match the seat, and the method of edging should be the same as that of the seat.

LOOSE COVERS

Sometimes a piece of upholstery is still sound, but because of wear and age its appearance is poor. The alternative to

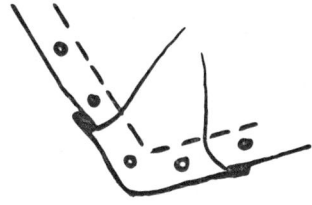

Fig. 18-19. Material on front of panel may have to be pleated at corners for smoothest appearance.

recovering is to hide the unattractive, but strong, existing covering under another layer of cloth. In some cases this might be fixed in the same way as normal covering, so the old covering can be regarded as a lining. The procedure then is very much the same as when fixing new covering material, except that in a fully upholstered chair there may be difficulty in making the same joints between back, seat, and arms that would be used in a new work.

Another way is to use removable covers. For cushions these are simple. They are made up with zippers so the cushion can be thrust in. If the cushion has boxed edges, the cover should be made the same way, although it is not usual to include piping in a light loose cover. With piping inside, another line of piping would cause an excessive and uneven bulge.

For other parts it is advisable to make paper patterns or templates and scheme the covering so it can have joints, usually at the back, where tapes or fasteners can be used. It is then possible to take off the cover for cleaning. Such a cover need not conform exactly to the chair outline, although it should be a good fit around the actual seating and reclining area. At sides and front there can be pleated, or otherwise decorated, drapes below and around the legs. Of course, any separate cushions should be covered separately, and a cushion fitted into the loose covering of the chair will help to keep it in place.

For a partly upholstered lounge chair, a loose back cover can drop over as a sewn-up pocket as far down as the arms and be fitted with tapes or fasteners below there. A loose seat cover may be cut around the legs at each corner with enough then to go under the seat and be held down by straps across with fasteners, or by using grommets and cord lacing underneath.

19 Stripping and Recovering

Wood, particularly if it is a hardwood and properly seasoned, as it would be for a good chair frame, is a more durable material than most fabrics. This means that a chair frame is likely to outlast the upholstery which has been put on it. If the external appearance of an upholstered chair shows that it is no longer fit to use, its frame may still be as good as new or in a condition where a little work would put it back into good order. It may then be used as the base for a new chair—not necessarily exactly the same as before.

Whether stripping and recovering is justified depends on a number of factors, including economic ones. For a professional upholsterer, time means money and he may not feel it is worth the trouble to strip a chair and recover it and then offer it for sale. If the work is done to order and the customer is willing to pay for the time involved, the work then becomes economically feasible. An amateur faced with the same chair may find the work of stripping and recovering interesting and satisfying. He may learn something new as he investigates the upholstery he removes and the finished chair will be something he will be proud of. When he does the work as a hobby and does not have to equate his time with money, material costs may be low in relation to the value of the finished chair. In any case, he or she may not regard the value in money terms, but in the satisfaction of a job well done.

Where a factory is engaged in production upholstery, the methods are geared to manufacturing a large number of identical pieces of furniture and there is no place for individual items. All work is done on new frames. There is no place for single chairs, even with new frames. There is certainly no place for frames extracted from discarded and worn out chairs.

The individual upholsterer, whether professional or amateur, will find that much of his work is concerned with recovering. Even when the work is not custom upholstery for particular order, it is worthwhile to accumulate old frames, which can be extracted from other people's discarded chairs during periods when there is no more pressing work. The frames can then be used to recover to suit individual requirements. Even frames which are found to be too damaged to justify recovering may yield useful wood for repairing other frames.

The state of the frame in an apparent wreck can be tested by resting the chair on one corner and pressing from the opposite side. Movement in the frame can be felt through the old upholstery. There may be creaks and groans that indicate loose joints or broken wood. Try this in several directions—resting on each corner in turn and maybe inverted on the corners of the back. Signs of movement do not necessarily condemn the frame, but they show that some work on it will be necessary. Experience will show what to expect when the frame is revealed and you may decide that the chair is not worth bothering with after all.

A chair does not always have to be stripped down to the bare frame. You may discover that some of the lower stages of upholstery are in good enough condition to remain, so stripping need only be taken that far. This may happen with a chair that has not been misused, but subject to fair wear and tear that has left the outer fabric so shabby it is no longer acceptable. Even then there may be more work to do than just putting on new outer fabric. Stuffing may have settled, springs may have become displaced, and other things may need attention inside. Attention to these matters can be paid without doing more than lifting parts or building up, as described later in the chapter. Minor repairs were described in Chapter 18.

A very old chair may have antique value. When reupholstering, you should keep this in mind. It may be advisable not to strip any further than is necessary to replace material obviously worn out and beyond refurbishing rather than renewing. Materials and methods used should be the same as those in the original chair. It would be wrong to use synthetic fabrics or foam filling, even if these might be considered an improvement on the old materials. It may be advisable to salvage old stuffing materials, if the hair or fiber used is unlikely to be obtainable for replacement. Old and compressed stuffings can often be teased out to make them fit to use again.

The value of an antique may be destroyed if it is repaired and recovered in a modern way. It may then be a better chair, but it can no longer be regarded as antique. If such a chair is accepted from a customer who specifies work of this sort, it is important that he understands the change in status of the piece of furniture.

REMOVING UPHOLSTERY

There are at least two schools of thought about removing material from a frame. Many workers argue that it is useless to keep old materials, either for re-use or as patterns for new material. They would prefer to start with their own measurements. Others favor taking old material off carefully so it will give the shape for its replacement. This method should be approached rather guardedly. Old fabric will have stretched in use, and may be uneven, so the shape you remove is not necessarily the same as the original shape.

A fabric part carefully removed will provide a clue to the shape of a new piece of fabric, but the new piece should be marked from measurements. The old piece will then be used for comparison and show if mistakes have been made or there is a wide divergence in shape.

If time is valuable and you know that the chair will have to be stripped down to the bare frame, it can be tackled with a knife and everything removed as speedily as possible. If it is uncertain how much will have to be removed, or there is interest in finding out how the original upholstery was done, it is better to take off layers in the opposite sequence to which they were applied. This is also the method to use if you are uncertain how far stripping will have to be taken.

The ripping chisel is the main tool. This may be used in the hand as a lever or hit with a hammer or mallet. More than one chisel may be advisable. A normal one with a claw end (Fig. 19-1) will go into most places, but where a tack has been driven

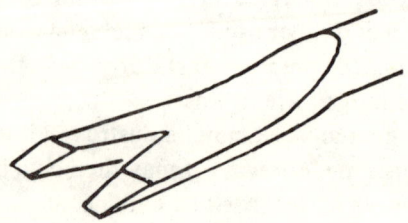

Fig. 19-1. A claw end ripping chisel.

deeply a thin straight end is of more use (Fig. 19-2). This can be made from a screwdriver ground down almost to a knife edge. The chisel can be pushed cornerwise under the head of a buried tack, and twisted sideways to start the tack coming out (Fig.

Fig. 19-2. A straight blade ripping chisel.

19-3). This ripping chisel is also useful for staples, which will have been power-driven and may be deeply embedded. A corner of the end can be worked under the staple and twisted to

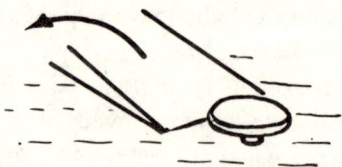

Fig. 19-3. A screwdriver with the blade ground thin makes a good prying tool.

lift its center, or one leg may come out (Fig. 19-4). Final extraction may then be done with pliers.

Fig. 19-4. Use one corner of the chisel to pry out a staple.

It is not always necessary to lift every tack. If a long tacked edge is released for a short distance at one end, the rest of the tacks can often be released by a sharp pull on the loosened part (Fig. 19-5).

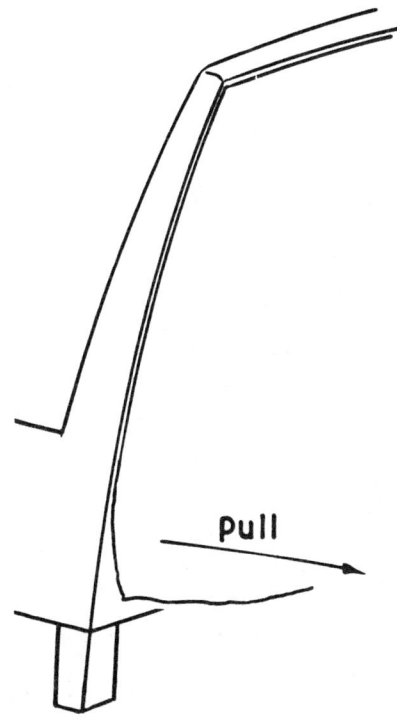

Fig. 19-5. After prying out the tacks near the corner, try to remove the remainder by grasping the material and tugging.

Pliers and pincers are needed. Besides their obvious use in pulling metal, pliers may also provide a means of levering and pulling cloth. Broad-ended upholstery pliers are particularly good for this, but ordinary engineer's pliers can be used for stripping, where the fact that their narrow noses may damage the material will not matter. Pincers are mainly used for pulling nails. With a stubborn nail or tack, it may be possible to drive the ripping chisel with the grain both sides of the head, then tilt the edge of the pincers into the grooves to get a grip (Fig. 19-6). If pincers have to be used on a varnished surface, protect the

Fig. 19-6. With deep-set tacks you may have to gouge out the wood to enable the pincers to clasp the tack head.

surface with a piece of cardboard or thin plywood, so rolling to get the nail out does not make an impression on the surface (Fig. 19-7).

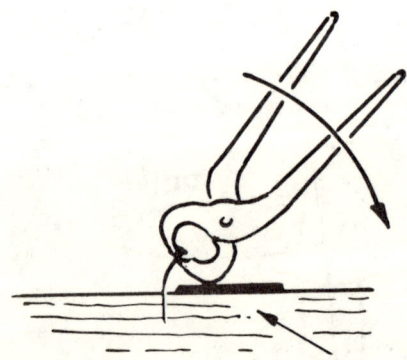

Fig. 19-7. Protect the finish of wood by placing a piece of cardboard under the pincers.

If a nail breaks or its head pulls off, or one leg of a staple snaps and is left, pliers may grip and lift it. If this method is unsuccessful, punch the metal below the surface (Fig. 19-8). It is advisable to do this as the break occurs, otherwise it may be overlooked and the rough end will tear fabric or scratch the hand. It would also damage a plane if that has to be used to level the wood.

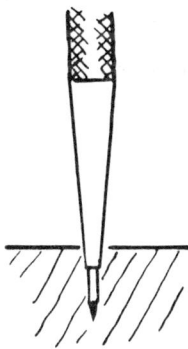

Fig. 19-8. Broken nails that can't be extracted easily may be driven below the surface with a punch.

If the sequence of covering detailed in earlier chapters has been followed, a piece of burlap or cambric is normally the last thing to go on a chair, underneath the frame. Invert the chair and remove this first. Driving the chisel under a few tack heads will allow the material to be gripped and pulled off. This will be your opportunity to examine the webbing and springs (Fig. 19-9). The webbing will almost certainly have suffered, but the springs may have further uses.

The next part that was fitted was probably the outside back. Tacks will be found at the bottom and they can be levered out, but it is possible there is some sewing higher at the sides and the top edge may be back-tacked. Cut stitches with a knife point (Fig. 19-10). Scissors may be used, but a sharp knife is more convenient. Lever off the back-tacked cardboard strip at the top. Note how this was fitted. Also note any blind sewing. For a beginner, seeing how a professional made the cover and left joints and seams so they were inconspicuous will probably be a

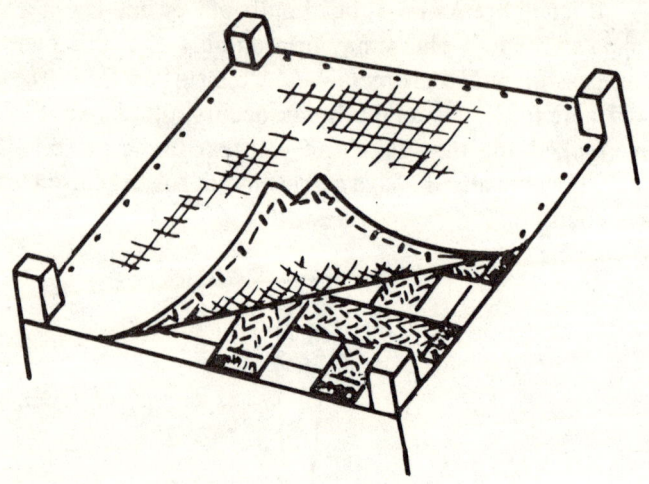

Fig. 19-9. Webbing and springs can be examined by turning over the chair and unfastening a corner of burlap (or cambric) which covers the bottom.

better education than reading about the techniques. Observation will amplify other instruction, in any case.

The outside arms usually come next. Their method of attachment will vary according to the design and the inside arm fabric may overlap, depending on the type of arms. In most cases the bottom edge will be tacked under the frame. Start

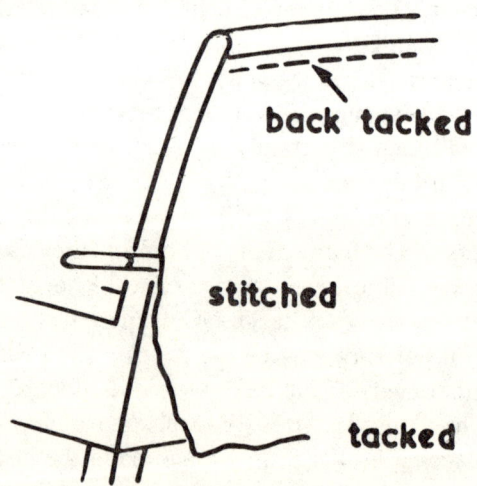

Fig. 19-10. Use a knife point to cut stitching at top and sides.

362

loosening from there and work upwards, noting how the fabric has been fixed. Also note what padding is provided on the outside and over the tops of the arms, if it is expected that the chair will be covered in the same way again.

If there are front panels to the arms, they may come off next. If there are not visible fastenings through them, they are probably fixed with nail strips on the back and can be pried off by levering with the ripping chisel around the edges (Fig. 19-11). The covering on the bottom band under the seat front can also be lifted. Note how this was made. The fabric may go under the frame and be back-tacked along the top edge. Look for stitching at the ends.

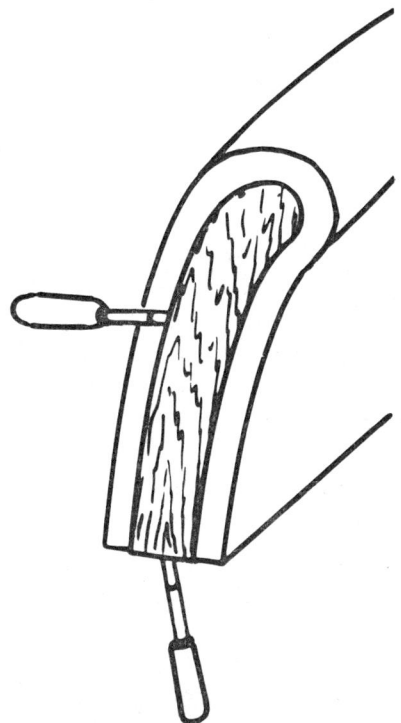

Fig. 19-11. The front panels of arm rests are often secured by concealed tack strips. Prying under the panels loosens the strips.

Check how the fabric over seat, back, and inside arms has been arranged. Loosen tacks and remove these pieces in the reverse order that they were fitted. It may be found that it is only the cover material of the back or seat that needs replacing, so the springs, the padding over them, and the muslin cover may be left; but if there is any doubt, it is better to completely strip. An early failure, due to using old parts under new, would show false economy.

If any of the old upholstery is to remain, it ought to be thoroughly cleaned. There will almost certainly be a considerable amount of dust to be removed with a vacuum cleaner.

Springs may be used again if they are still sound, but the shape the seat or back takes will show if any of the springs have lost any of their tension or are otherwise deformed. If springs are defective it is wiser to fit a new set completely than to mix old and new springs, unless it can be seen that the load will still be taken evenly.

Tension and zig-zag springs will show if they are still satisfactory, but like coil springs, it is unwise to mix old and new springs. Pressing rubber webbing will show if it is still serviceable.

Webbing and burlap are the materials that deteriorate most, so they should be discarded and replaced, even if some other material is re-used. Nails and tacks can be discarded, unless there are unusual types that cannot be replaced. Trying to use tacks again can be very difficult, as the slightest flaw will make a tack enter on the skew or the point will curl over instead of enter. It is better to use all new tacks. They are cheap.

If the chair is stripped down to the frame and this needs any attention, refer to Chapter 27. If the frame is apparently sound, make sure there is no roughness and feel for projecting broken nails or other metal that should be removed or punched down. Check for rot, which is unlikely to be present unless you have a discarded chair that has been exposed to the weather for some time. Look for signs of borers (worms). Any small holes should be suspect. A few holes may not matter, but the wood should be treated with a chemical that kills borers. If nothing is known about the old chair, treatment of the wood by a preservative and possibly a chemical to counteract borers may be a worthwhile precaution to take before recovering.

If a frame shows signs of having been covered more than once before, by the number of tack holes that can be found in addition to those you have drawn tacks from, check if you can reasonably expect to get a grip with the majority of tacks you will be driving in the new upholstery. Tacks entering old holes may not grip well enough. If you have doubts, add extra tack rails (see Chapter 27).

PARTIAL RECOVERING

If a chair has no obvious breakages, but the outer covering needs replacing, either because it is worn or it has to be made to match other furniture, stripping of the outer fabric should be done carefully so as not to disturb anything underneath any more than possible. This means using the ripping chisel carefully for the first lifting along any seam, until the locations of tacks through muslin or other hidden parts are discovered (Fig. 19-12). Follow through the sequence that the original fabric was fitted. When the outside arms and outside back have been removed, it should be possible to see how the fabric over the seat, inside arms, and back was fitted.

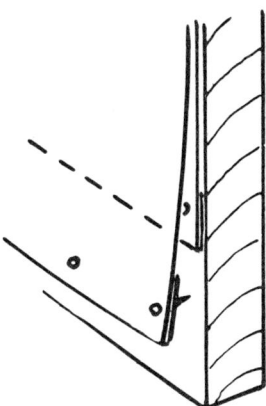

Fig. 19-12. Pry off the tacks gingerly to avoid damaging the muslin beneath the outer covering.

If it is a chair in which foam or latex has been used for padding, there may be no muslin or other material between the covering fabric and the padding. So far as possible, avoid disturbing the padding. However, examine it—particularly at the front of the seat, where it may be crumbling. It should either be replaced completely or a new piece should be stuck on (see Chapter 18).

If the stuffing is made of hair or other loose material, it will probably have settled under the points of greatest load—at the center of the seat and above the middle of the back (Fig. 19-13). If the muslin is partially removed it may be possible to pick over the filling to get it back into shape, but more likely some more

Fig. 19-13. Depressions in the stuffing occur at points of greatest load.

will be added to make up the bulk and give a good shape when the muslin is brought back into place (Fig. 19-14). The best result will probably be obtained by working the new material under the old.

A similar problem comes on the arms. Padding there is not usually as thick or as resilient as on the seat, and may be rubberized hair or other padding, which does not allow much expanding or opening up. It would only settle back again after a short time. It may be advisable to use new padding, but the compressed padding can often be brought back to a good shape by padding under it with more of the same material, some hair,

Fig. 19-14. Although fluffing up the old stuffing will help the situation, it will usually be necessary to add new material.

or pieces of foam (Fig. 19-15). The top can be made more comfortable and even by using a thin layer of foam before putting on the finishing fabric (Fig. 19-16).

Before making the new outer cover, examine all the parts that will be hidden again. If there is buttoning, new twine will be

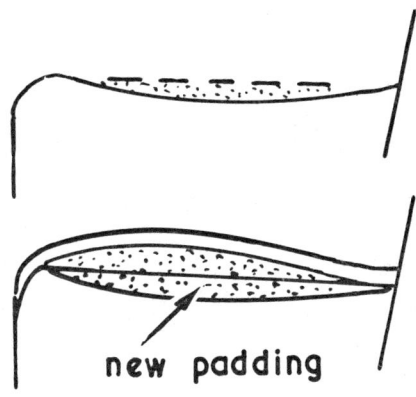

Fig. 19-15. To add stuffing, place the new material under the old.

used. It should go through at the same places in the front, but it may be stronger to go through a slightly different point on the burlap at the back, where burlap fibers have not been strained (Fig. 19-17). In any case make sure all remnants of old twine and cotton have been removed. Check twine ties on springs. See that tacks or staples are firm. Extra twine or reinforcing tacks are easy to fit at this stage, but a failure here at a later stage could be troublesome. If there are coil or zig-zag springs in the back,

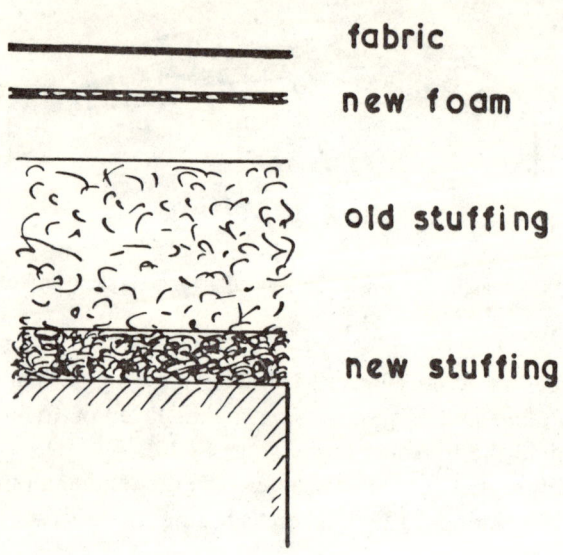

Fig. 19-16. A thin layer of foam placed atop the old and new stuffing contributes substantially to comfort.

check their security. Zig-zag springs may have short, interconnecting coil springs and there may be ties to the frame. Check that none of these are displaced. It is possible for them to be moved while stripping the outer covering.

Thin sheet foam is a useful material for giving a little more padding to any surface. Its compression is enough for it to be pulled in at the edges where necessary. The only place where its extra thickness may not go is between the bottom of the back

Fig. 19-17. The twine securing the buttons should be passed through new openings in the old burlap.

and the seat. It can be used over muslin (if that has not been removed). If it has to be held in place while the covering is fitted, there can be some spots of adhesive around the edges.

The covering fabric is fitted in the ways described for new work, but the old fabric can be used as a guide. Use measurements and try the new material on the chair, rather than just draw around the old material. If there is piping it may have to be made up from offcuts of the new material. Then covers for arms will have to be sewn inside-out to fit as they are reversed. Allow ample material at the edges of the fabric parts for adjustment.

Any new buttons should take up the old positions. Mark the positions with chalk, using the holes through the muslin as guides. In some chairs it may be simplest to put the back or seat fabric temporarily in position with a few tacks around the sides, while the buttons are located and fixed, then the edges are pulled to shape and permanently fixed (Fig. 19-18).

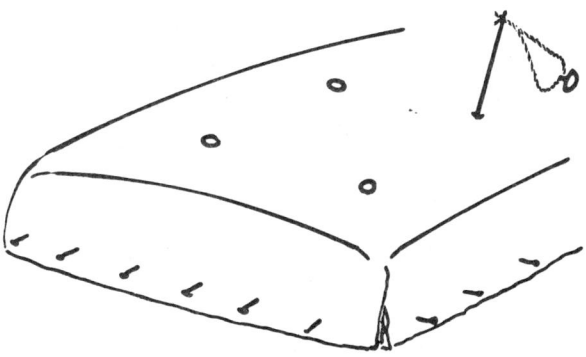

Fig. 19-18. Fabric may be tacked temporarily along the sides while the buttons are being mounted through the front.

If the seat has a cushion over it, it may have a platform made from plain material. Unless it is necessary to repeat another method for the sake of keeping an antique construction, a new cushion is best made with a foam or latex interior. If the existing cushion has foam or latex in it, check that this is in good condition. Look for crumbled edges. Both materials tend to settle slightly with age, so they no longer fill their casing.

It may be necessary to make up a crumbled edge with new material (see Chapter 18) or if the cushion has compressed, there may be a layer of thinner foam added to increase the thickness and make a better fit in the cover. Even if there was not a muslin case inside the cover material in the original cushion, it will be worthwhile making a case to go around a repaired foam filling. If a new cover has to be made, follow instructions described earlier.

ADAPTED RECOVERING

An old chair may not have the shape and lines that are desired today. Drastic alterations would have to be made to the frame by modifying parts and rebuilding as necessary. Guidance on this work is given in Section 2. However, some alterations are possible by using padding. In particular, arm design has changed. The curves of Victorian chair arms have given place to straighter lines, with more thickness of padding. A hollow arm can be brought up to a straight line by building up with felt, rubberized hair, or other pad material (Fig. 19-19A). Adhesive can be used to retain it.

Several layers of foam can be stuck over the arm to increase its bulk from the rather narrow ones favored in earlier chairs (Fig. 19-19B). Some older chairs had the front of the arm frame finished with carving, which stood out from the padding. This can be cut off so as not to weaken the joint, then the front padded with more layers of foam (Fig. 19-19C). If this is too resilient, the first layers might be made of felt or other more dense material, but use foam on the outside. Use adhesive to hold the layers in place. Encase all this in muslin (Fig. 19-19D) before fitting the outer covering fabric.

Some older chairs had rather sparse padding in the seat. If the old stuffing is to be retained it may be possible to add a shaped latex pad that tapers to the edges to give more padding where it is needed (Fig. 19-19E) without adding to the thickness where there may be no room for it in the joints to back and arms. It would probably be better to abandon the old stuffing and replace it completely with foam or latex, but make sure there is enough thickness to give a satisfactory shape to the finally covered seat top.

Older chairs often had the upholstery brought only a short distance over the side and front seat rails (Fig. 19-20A). They can be modernized by taking the cloth down to tack under the

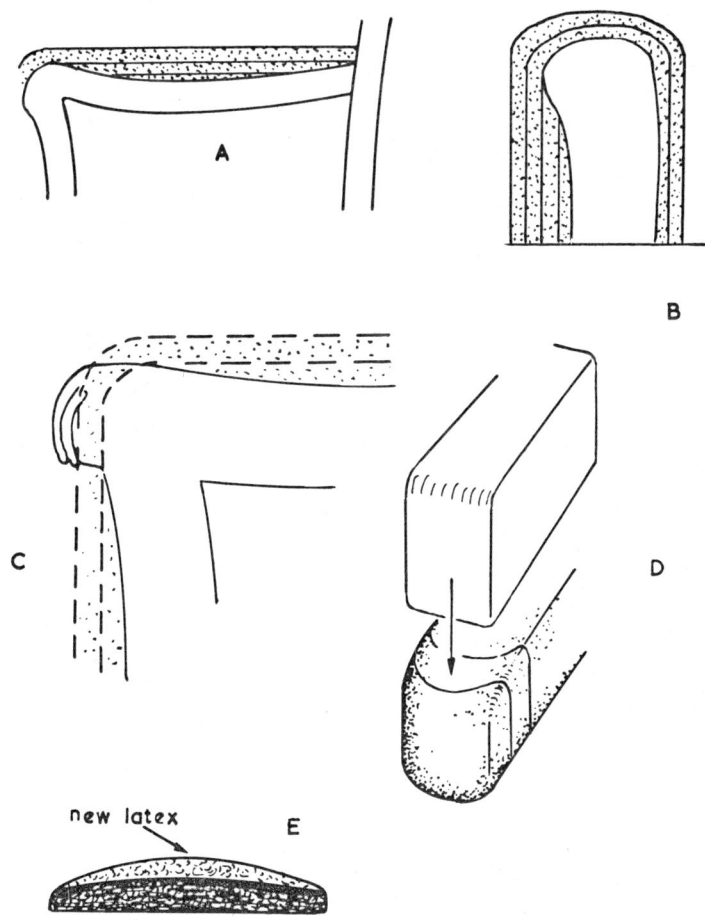

Fig. 19-19. Old frames can be modernized by building up with foam.

rails. If the rails are shaped on the underside, plywood can be used to give a new line (Fig. 19-20B). This might also lend itself to the addition of a bottom band (Fig. 19-21A), if there was not one on the original design.

There is not much that can be done to alter the back of a chair without structural alterations to the frame, but a variation in the padding will give a different effect. There can be a padded headrest across the top (Fig. 19-21B). If there are wings, it may be possible to fill the angles with padding, so the back and wings are covered in a single sweep (Fig. 19-21C).

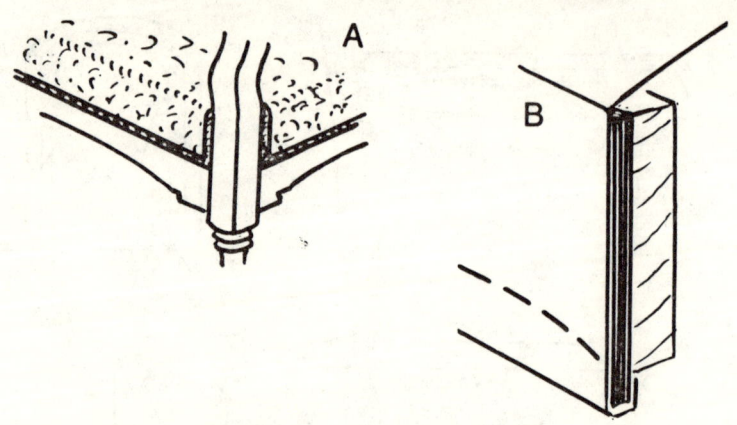

Fig. 19-20. Altering the covering scheme is also possible.

A change in height will alter the appearance of a chair. Obviously, the seat height has to be correct, but cutting off the legs can be counterbalanced by having a greater depth of cushioning. Carrying the cloth around the seat to the bottoms of the rails will make the seat look deeper. Cutting off the often rather slender legs of an old chair and replacing them with solid blocks and casters will give a different appearance to a chair (Fig. 19-21D).

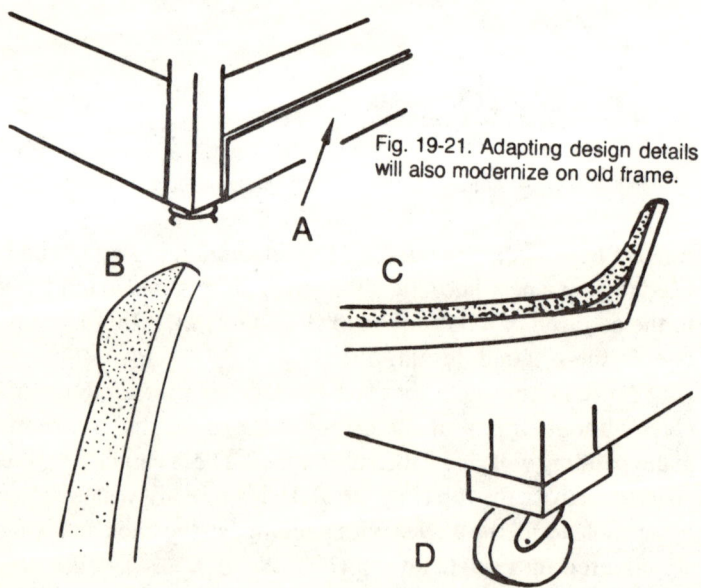

Fig. 19-21. Adapting design details will also modernize on old frame.

Even without much basic alteration to the shape, a change in the style of covering material will alter appearances. A lighter color will make a chair seem more roomy. A darker color may emphasize depth and comfort. It will seem warmer than a light color. A pleasant colorful pattern, even on a chair of older style, will modernize appearance compared with a plain sombre color. Breaking up the design by using two patterns of cloth will also give a modern effect. Outsides of arms and back may be a different material from that used on the seat and insides of arms and back. If it is a chair with cushions, it may be sufficient to have the fitted cushions a different pattern fabric from that of the chair.

FULL RECOVERING

If a chair is stripped to the frame and recovering is to start from that stage, the work is as described in preceding chapters. Take particular account of the way the existing upholstery has been done while stripping. The older materials may be different and it would be better to use modern materials, but the old methods will serve as a guide to the way that particular frame may be covered.

The old material will serve as a guide to quantities and might be used as templates to find the best way to cut the new material economically from the roll. If the frame is from a really old chair it is unlikely to be of a size to suit standard latex or foam pads. Pads will have to be cut and made up as described earlier. The old layout of springs probably cannot be improved on, so the original arrangement of webbing and springs can be followed, although it is advisable to stagger the locations slightly so tacks are driven into new parts of the wood and the old holes are avoided. This also applies to tacking muslin and covering fabric. The amount of overlap on the frame can be made slightly different from previously, so the line of tacks will be in undamaged wood. When fitting the outside arms and the outside back, the width of overlaps can be altered slightly, so the tacks follow a new line—1/8 inch from the old line will be enough.

When a frame has been stripped and is recovered, it is advisable to dispose of all the old materials, particularly if it was a derelict chair of unknown origin. Old and dusty natural materials may harbor pests and the fabric should be burned. Be careful of old tacks and other metal fastenings. Drop them into a container and not on the floor of the shop. If any are dropped, sweep them up before they damage shoes or enter feet. If any of the wood has to be refinished before recovering, do varnishing and polishing well away from the dusty area where stripping was done.

Rush and Cord Seats

20

There is a type of seat that is neither a hard wooden one nor a fully upholstered one. This type is a soft strip material worked in a pattern within the frame. There is some flexibility in the support under a sitting person which provides a measure of comfort. This type of seating is found in varying forms in many parts of the world and may be anything from a very crude interlacing of rough ropes to intricate patterns in cane or synthetic cords. Certain types have become associated with particular items of furniture and there are traditional rush and cane seated chairs that are established as antiques. Besides these patterns there are many more that have been devised and some of them take advantage of new materials.

Although seating in this way may not be strictly upholstery in its more narrowly accepted sense, the techniques are related and it is unlikely that a specialist craftsman will be available, so an upholsterer may be called on to deal with these other types of seat, too. In any case, they are attractive and make good alternatives to normal upholstery for some types of furniture.

MATERIALS

Many types of rushes and grasses have been used for seating. Rural craftsmen used whatever was available. Almost any sedges, rushes, and grasses can be twisted into ropes and used for seating, but some lose their strength with age. Despite this, European craftsmen followed basically similar patterns with different natural materials, and pioneer settlers in America followed a similar tradition using whatever material came to hand.

Rushes grow along river banks and in marshes. Some only grow in salt marshes. The earlier use of rushes was for scattering on the floor to provide a primitive form of carpeting. Rushes used for seating grow long and may be up to 10 feet high. The cut rushes are dried to retain their green/brown color.

An alternative to rush is seagrass. Rushes have to be moistened and twisted as the work progresses. Seagrass is a sedge plant that is processed and made into a form of rope, which is supplied in long lengths ready to use. The natural color is very similar to rushes and coarse seagrass can be used for similar patterns to rush, with very similar finished appearance. Rush is only used in its natural color, but seagrass may be dyed. The rope form is usually two-stranded, and it is possible to get seagrass with the strands in different colors or with one strand plain and the other dyed.

Ropes and cords of various sorts can be used. These can be normal lines intended for other purposes or special lines for seating, which are dyed and comparatively free from stretch. A line that is too elastic may finish as a slack seat after a little use. Natural hemp or cotton cord may be suitable. Intricate designs can be worked with macrame cord. Very thin line may take a long time to work into a seat pattern, which might not be as satisfactory in use as a stouter line.

Cane is used for a different type of seat, although there are some patterns that finish with surface patterns similar to those worked with cord. Cane or rattan palm is a wild climbing plant that grows in the jungle of tropical forests. It grows to considerable lengths and trails along the ground as well as climbing trees. It may be up to 1 1/2 inches thick. Processed cane is cut down to various narrow widths up to about 1/8 inch. Its natural color is yellow/brown, but it can be obtained enameled in several colors. Cane is supplied in lengths which may be 6 foot to 9 foot.

TOOLS

The only tool needed for much rush seating is a sharp knife, but a piece of square-edged wood can be used for pushing and ramming. This is also used with other seating materials and a craftsman may call it a *commander* or *rapping iron*, although it is merely an oddment of wood. Some workers prefer scissors for general cutting, but there is much trimming of small pieces of projecting rush which is better done with a knife.

For seagrass or any form of cord or rope it is helpful to have a few shuttles (Fig. 20-1A). Exact sizes are not important, but 9 inches long and 2 inches wide from wood about 3/8 inch thick should be suitable for most jobs. Round the exposed ends. A very narrow shuttle may allow for tucking further towards the end of a pattern than a wide one, but it will not hold as much, and by the time that stage is reached it is only little more trouble to work with a loose end of line.

For some patterns it is useful to have a wooden needle (Fig. 20-1B). It should be longer than the distance across the chair or stool and as thin as the strength of the wood permits—1/2 inch wide and 3/16 inch thick is reasonable. The two holes should be just large enough to pass the seagrass or cord. A pointed round rod (Fig. 20-1C) about the same length as the needle is used for forcing spaces between woven strands and may be laid across a stool to regulate tension in some patterns.

For cane work there are several tools of the awl type. A parallel type with a flat end (Fig. 20-2A) is used for pushing old cane out of holes in repair work. A pointed awl (Fig. 20-2B) may be called a doubler, and is used as a peg to hold cane in a hole. There may be a wooden version (Fig. 20-2C) used for the same purpose.

For both cane and seagrass there is sometimes a need for a large needle with a bent end (Fig. 20-3A). It may be a curved upholstery needle, but it should have an eye large enough to take seagrass or cane. The alternative to a needle is a tool for pulling through. It can be a shell bodkin (Fig. 20-3B), with an awl handle that pulls through a little at a time, or in some seat patterns it is better to have a long wire weaver (Fig. 20-3C) to pull a strand across a full width.

At the start and finish of some patterns the end has to be tacked to a rail, so a hammer is needed and the tack can be the usual upholstery type. Pliers will withdraw tacks and pull through strands in very tight work.

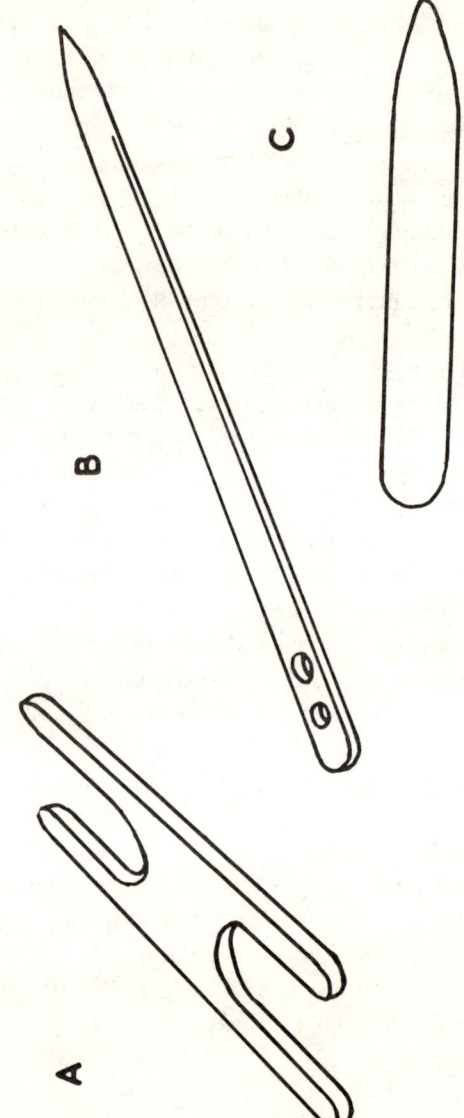

Fig. 20-1. A few special tools are needed to wind the covering material for rush seats and to manipulate the strands of cane seating.

RUSH PATTERN

Rushes are rarely used for anything except a traditional pattern which has strands, at right angles to the rails, which meet in miters from the corners. The pattern underneath is the same, but there are lengthwise strands hidden inside and the result is a strong, comfortable seat. This is known as rush pattern, even if seagrass or other material is used (Fig. 20-4).

Rushes should be used damp, not wet. To prepare them, soak them briefly in cold water, then spread them out and cover with a damp cloth. Leave them for about twelve hours. The water will penetrate and make the rushes pliable. If rushes are used dry they will crack. Some rushes may absorb water quicker, so experiment will show how long to leave them; but do not try to hurry the process by using the rushes wet.

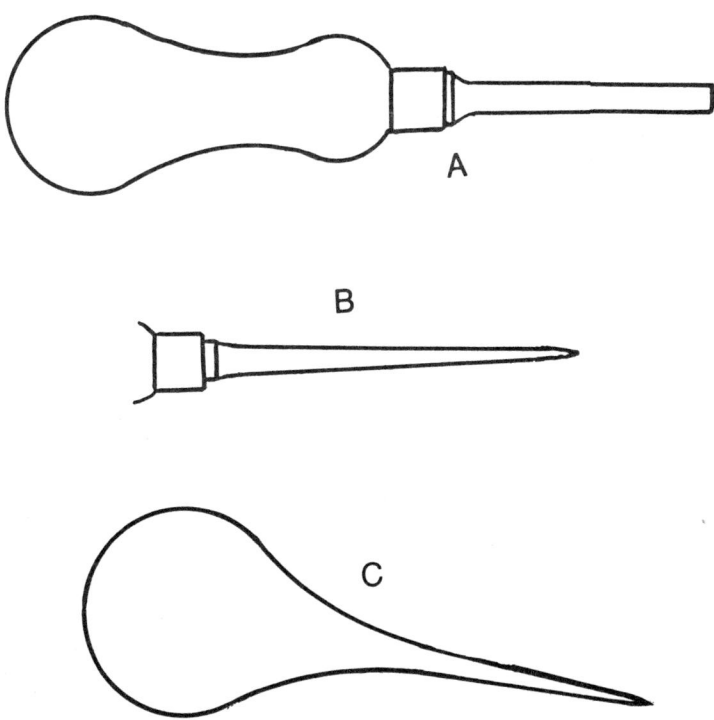

Fig. 20-2. Several awl-type tools may be needed for cane work.

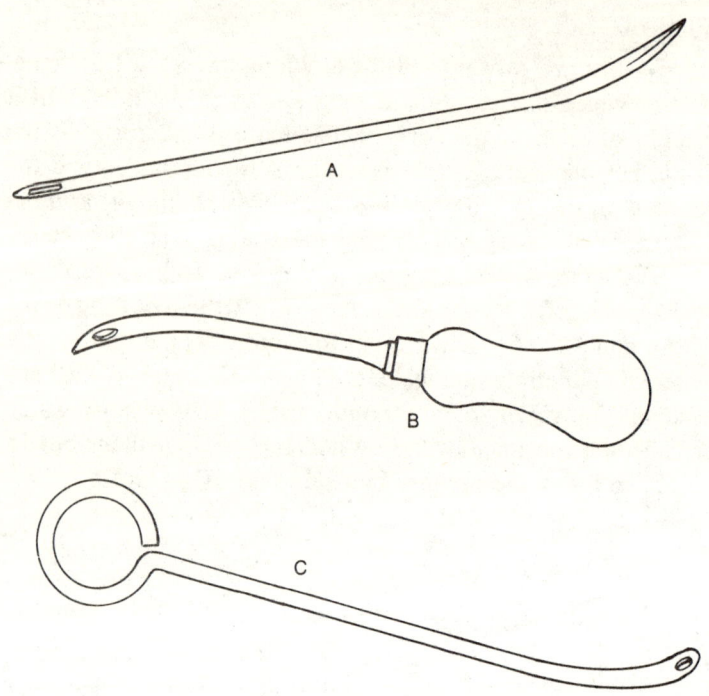

Fig. 20-3. Large bent-ended needle, shell bodkin, and long wire weaver are used for cane and seagrass work.

Rushes have to be twisted as they are worked. How many are used together depends on their thickness and the desired total thickness. It may be sufficient to twist only one rush, or maybe two. The aim is to get a rope-like appearance on the top surface. Regular twisting is not as important underneath. As the end of a rush is being approached, twist in a new piece. It will probably be sufficient to twist the end of the new rush closely around the old and tuck it under. So far as possible keep these joints underneath or in the lines going between corners, which will be hidden when the seat has been finished.

With seagrass or rope, the method is the same as with rushes, except the material is ready for use in a long length and does not have to be soaked or twisted. Wind several shuttles full, so the work can proceed quickly. Seagrass is supplied in hanks. The securing knots should be untied and the hank hung around a chair back to avoid tangles as line is drawn off to wind on a shuttle.

The actual technique of seating is quite simple, although the method of construction looks like a mystery in a finished seat. Care is needed to get a neat formation, but the covering of a square seat is a repetition of a simple action. For seagrass, cord, or rope, knot the end and fix it with a tack inside a rail (Fig. 20-5A). Rush may lock itself sufficiently at a corner without a knot. It does not matter which way the work is done around the stool or chair, but most workers favor a clockwise direction.

At a corner, go over a rail, under it, then over the other rail (Fig. 20-5B), so as to enclose the leg. This is a complete action, which has to be repeated until the top is full. Pull the work tight at each stage—get every wrap tight as it is made. Do not try to pull several turns tightly together. From the first corner, cross to the next, bringing the line from under the first corner to the top of the next, and do the actions again (Fig. 20-5C).

Go all round the frame in this way. As the first corner is reached, let the line follow round inside the first turns (Fig. 20-5D). Continue in this way, keeping a good tension on the line. After a few complete circuits the top pattern will build up at each corner. Watch that turns do not ride up on each other and keep the working end crossings all at the same level so a neat miter is formed.

Fig. 20-4. The top of a stool covered in the traditional rush-pattern method using seagrass. Color has been introduced by working a few strands in the corners.

Another thing to watch is the squareness of the pattern at each corner (Fig. 20-5E). Use a piece of wood to push the turns along a rail if necessary. If the fault is the other way, use a wooden needle or rod to pull the crossings towards the leg. The line to the other corner gives a clue to squareness. The pattern should be parallel with it. Checking should be a continuous process. Watch for squareness as turns are made. This is better than having to stop for correction after several turns.

Joints in rushes occur as necessary and do not usually involve knots, but seagrass and cord have to be knotted when a new length is brought in. If a knot is placed in the line as it goes between corners, it will eventually be hidden. Towards the end of making a seat there may have to be one or two knots on the underside, but if their ends are left long and tucked inside they will be inconspicuous.

A reef knot (Fig. 20-5F) is sometimes used, but with slippery line, such as seagrass and synthetic cord, it is better to use a sheet bend (Fig. 20-5G). Bend one end back and work the other through it (Fig. 20-5H). With very slippery material, the working end can go around a second time (Fig. 20-5J).

On a square frame and using line of even size, all four sides will be filled at the same time. The end of line is then taken over a rail and tacked to it underneath. It is cut off a few inches from the tack and buried in the seat.

If the top is rectangular, the ends will be filled first. The rest of the pattern is made by working over and under opposite rails and through the middle space until the seat is filled (Fig. 20-5K) before tacking and cutting off.

Many chairs are wider at the front than the back. The normal method of working around the frame would result in the back rail becoming filled before the other sides. One method of allowing for this with rush is to mark the front rail centrally to the same distance as the length of the back rail (Fig. 20-5L). Pieces of rush are used to work from near a back leg, around both front legs and to near the other back leg. This is done until the front rail is filled to leave a space matching the back rail. The ends are tied temporarily to the side rails (Fig. 20-5M). From this stage the top is worked all round in the usual way. When a few complete rounds have been made they will hold the first work and the temporary ties can be removed.

That method is only satisfactory with rush. Another method is suitable for other materials and rush. Work around the frame in a normal manner, but occasionally go twice around each of the front legs (Fig. 20-5N). Do this until the remaining space along the front rail is the same as that remaining at the back. How often it is necessary to go twice around front legs depends on how much has to be made up, but every second or third circuit will do. Double turns too often may become apparent in the final appearance.

As the pattern is worked, on any shape top, spaces will be seen inside towards the corners. With seagrass or any other prepared cord there is no need to do anything about this, but with rush the pockets each side of the miters should be stuffed with scrap pieces of rush. Without this there is a risk of the seat loosening and developing a sag after a little use. If the top is being recovered, some of the old rushes can be used for stuffing, or waste from the new rushes can be used. Push the stuffing in with a piece of wood. Do this progressively as the pattern is built up. In a rectangular top, final pieces can be worked in by forcing strands apart on the underside.

As can be seen, the rush pattern does not permit any variation. For most purposes, the standard pattern is acceptable and it is usual in traditional furniture to prefer this. If seagrass is used, it is possible to make the whole top in a color or it can be mostly natural or one color with more colors worked into the corners. It is possible to work in colors at any point in the design, but the more attractive designs have color at the corners and the rest of the top plain. It can be done with several colors working outwards from the legs, or bands of a color can be broken by natural strands. The bands may taper off in width. Knots can be hidden in the inside strands. Obviously, the same amount should be done at each corner (see Fig. 20-4).

It is unusual to cover the edges of seagrass or cord tops, but some traditional rush chairs had strips of wood nailed around the outside. They protect the rush from chafe and help keep it in place. The nails through the wood stop twisted rushes from loosening. If strips are used, they can be quite thin and should be given well rounded edges.

CHECKER PATTERN

Seagrass and the various cords can be worked in an over-

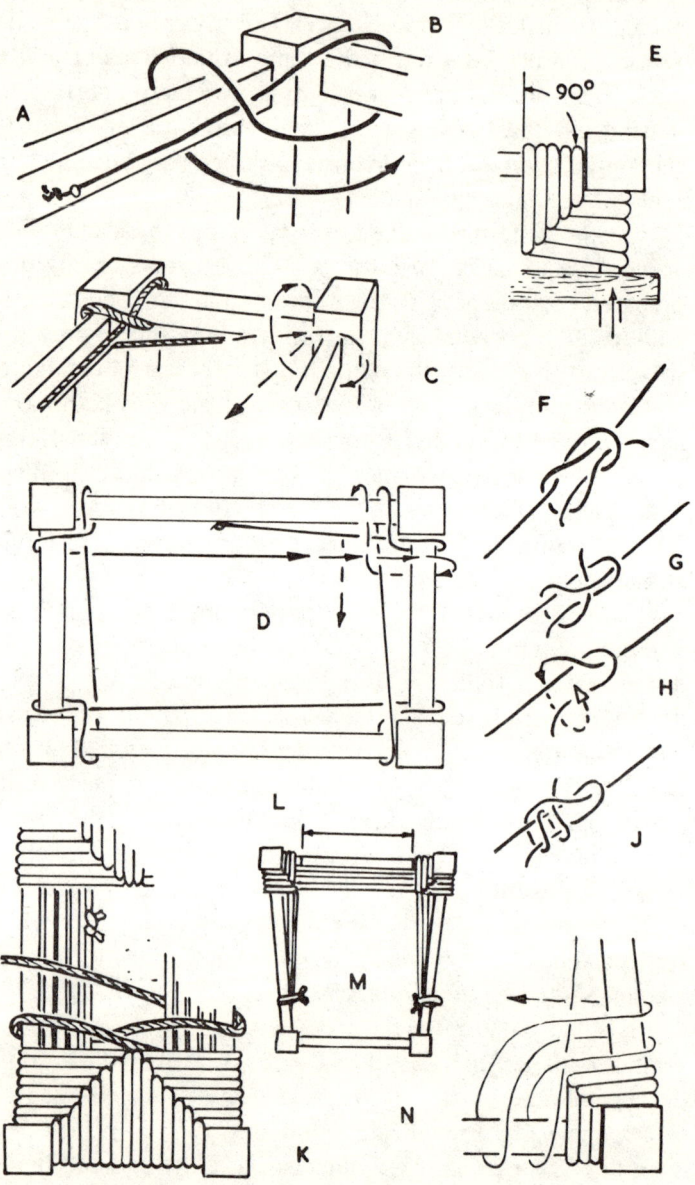

Fig. 20-5. This is the traditional method of working a rush pattern around the top of a stool or chair. Joints are made between the corners. The pattern changes to allow for tapered tops or long stools.

and-under pattern, which allows for several variations, particularly if colors are used. The quickest work has a fairly open pattern, but a more effective pattern has the crossing bands separated by narrow spaces. When the spaces are quite narrow there has to be some careful judging of first tensions if the final top is to finish with an adequate tension and not be slack at the finish or so tight that the pattern cannot be completed. Some experience with a less demanding pattern is advisable first, so you can learn the amount of tension desirable.

A basic pattern has four strands across and two wraps around the rail (Fig. 20-6A). If the square of a leg does not project far inside the lines of the rails, there may have to be wraps next to the leg (Fig. 20-6B), but if the legs are a reasonable size the top will look better with strands going across immediately next to the legs (Fig. 20-6C). Wraps in the first instance are needed to give working clearance when going the second way.

For the first stage (*warp*), the seagrass or cord can be on a shuttle. It is a help in getting the tension right to put a rod across the frame. Knot the end of the seagrass and tack it close up to a rail inside a leg. To get an even pattern it helps to mark the centers of the two rails that are to be covered. Put on the turns over the rod, getting a comfortable hand tightness. When one set of cross strands (in this case four) have been put on, make the wraps around the farther rail first, then return underneath to make the wraps around the starting rail. The line goes diagonally underneath (Fig. 20-6D). If the nearside wraps had been put on first, it would have gone diagonally on top and spoiled the pattern.

Continue in this way. When the center marks are reached, check that the turns will be symmetrical. You have to finish with the same number of turns or wraps as you used at the start. It may be necessary to compress the turns along the rails by pushing with a piece of wood. In any case, there should be no bare rail showing between turns. When you have gone about three-quarters of the way along the rails, check again that there will be room to finish the pattern properly, and either spread or compress the turns to suit. If there have to be joins, make the knots on the underside, preferably about halfway across the

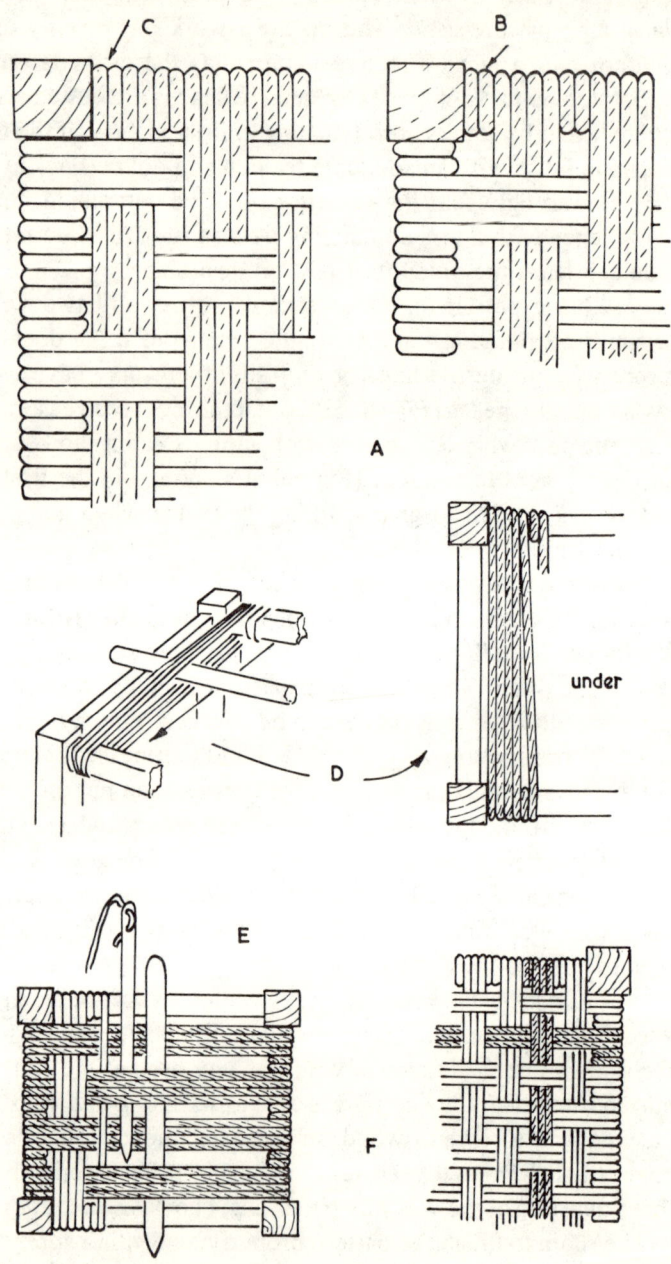

Fig. 20-6. An attractive pattern can be made by a simple weaving of strands over and under, either in the same or different colors.

frame. Finish by tacking to a leg under a rail in the same way as at the start.

In the other direction (*weft*) the line cannot be used on a shuttle, but a suitable length has its ends taken through the holes in a wooden needle. A long length avoids knots, but much time has to be spent pulling through, so a compromise length has to be accepted. Knots are arranged underneath and may be hidden by the strands the other way. Start with a tacked knot. The needle can be picked over and under alternate groups of the first strands, but it is quicker to use another needle or the pointed rod to open the strands and let the needle through (Fig. 20-6E and F). It is possible to arrange something like the same pattern underneath as on top, but because of the diagonal lines between wraps, there will be changes. An alternative is to work a large pattern on the underside, possibly three groups in each direction (Fig. 20-7). Keep a good tension, so the four crossings on the top are close, then do the wraps at the far side before coming back to do two on the nearside. Withdraw the second needle or rod and use it to pick up the alternate sets of strands.

Tucking can continue in this way a few times, but then the first strands will have tightened too much to allow the rod or second needle as well as the working needle. Continue by picking your way across with the working needle only. Almost certainly the new lines will not be straight. If nothing is done about it, they tend to bow out into the body of the pattern. Use a needle as a straightedge while the point of another is used to pull the strands back into line. Do this frequently as the pattern progresses and keep the turns on the rails pulled close so no wood shows through. Watch the spacing of the second sets of strands so the end of the pattern that way will finish even.

As the pattern proceeds and the last part is reached, **there may be no space and possibly too much tension for the wooden needle to be used.** Change to the bent steel needle. The last few crossings will have to be taken by going over and under one group of the first sets at a time. Be careful to get sufficient tension on these last crossings. It may be helpful to press the turns on the rails back as tight as possible to provide clearance, and let them spring back after all the crossings have been made.

Finally, use a straightedge across the pattern both ways

and use the point of a wooden needle to get all lines straight and even.

While such a checker top looks good all in one color, the first variation is to use natural one way and a color the other way. Another interesting variation uses color as one or two sets of bands to form a border (Fig. 20-6F).

Another variation uses two colors both ways. This has to be done with two shuttles at first and two wooden needles for the second way. The pattern has to be arranged so the colors alternate along a rail. In this case there are five lines in each crossing group and single wraps around the rails. As double lines are used all the time, it is helpful to work with a partner on opposite sides of the frame.

OTHER PATTERNS

The over and under method of weaving of the checker pattern can be developed to give a diagonal or twill weave, while altering the diagonal weave at intervals can turn it into a chevron or zig-zag pattern. The first part (warp) is put on with single crossing strands separated by single wraps. The weft is put on

Fig. 20-7. The underside of a checker pattern does not follow the same arrangement as the top, but can be in large squares.

with a wooden needle and the pattern looks best if this is done without wraps. The warp must not be too tight as there is a considerable amount of interweaving to be done.

The basic pattern on the top has the weft going over and under groups of three warp strands (Fig. 20-8A). By staggering these crossings the diagonal effect is obtained. On the underside the strands can make a large checker pattern of three or four crossings each way. Knots come underneath and can mostly be hidden in the pattern. As each crossing on top is individual, there is no need to use a second needle to open the strands, unless it is preferred to do it this way to get the crossings correct before passing through the needle drawing the strand. The design looks best with a contrasting color the second way.

Start at one corner with the weft and go over the first three warp strands. Continue all the way going under and over groups of three to the far side. Let that side come as it will. Pull tight and straight, then return underneath. Next time go over two strands at first, then work in threes all the way across. Pull tight and return underneath. Next time go over one only at the start and then threes all the way (Fig. 20-8B).

Next start by going under three and in threes across, under two and across then the sixth time under one at the start (Fig. 20-8C). The seventh, eighth, and ninth crossings are a repeat of the first three. To make a diagonal or twill weave continue in the same sequence. To make a chevron pattern (Fig. 20-9) treat the ninth row as the middle of a pattern and work the sequence the other way, with the tenth row the same as the eighth, the eleventh row the same as the seventh, and so on, until the 17th row is the same as the first (Fig. 20-8D).

Check the tightness and straightness of all the rows. Almost certainly they can be pressed along the rails to get a neater effect with no wood showing through, then the point of a needle is used to pull the lines straight. The last row (the 17th) is also the first row of the next complete pattern, so continue from there to make another complete sequence of crossings and do this as often as necessary to fill the frame. With this pattern there is no need for a complete pattern at the end. Draw the weft strands tightly back along the rails and get in as many crossings as possible. Use a bent steel needle for the last few crossings.

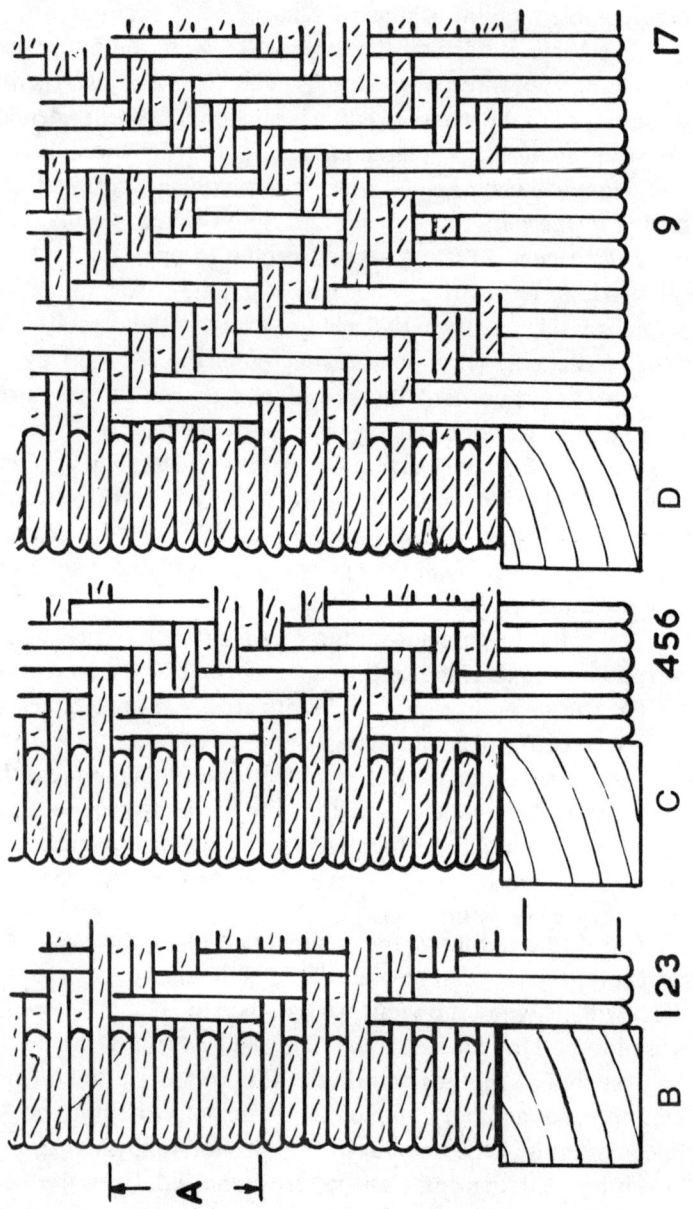

Fig. 20-8. Using single strands and tucking in steps produces either a diagonal or a chevron pattern.

390

Once the method of weaving is understood it is possible to use different numbers to get other diagonal weaves, such as diamonds and squares, as well as chevrons of different proportions.

If very fine cord is used, such as macrame twine, similar tops can be worked in chevron and checker patterns, but it is usual to have several strands laid side by side taking up the width of the larger material. Except for this the technique is the same. The fine line makes a very neat and attractive top, particularly when suitable colors are mixed.

Nearly all seat patterns have the line crossing above and below the rails. This gives a measure of flexibility and a neat appearance underneath, which may not be important in a stool or chair that is rarely lifted. There is a method of making a seat in a single thickness, which is suitable for twine and fine cord on stools or other small items. It is less suitable for stouter line or larger seats.

The warp must have enough slack to allow tucking the

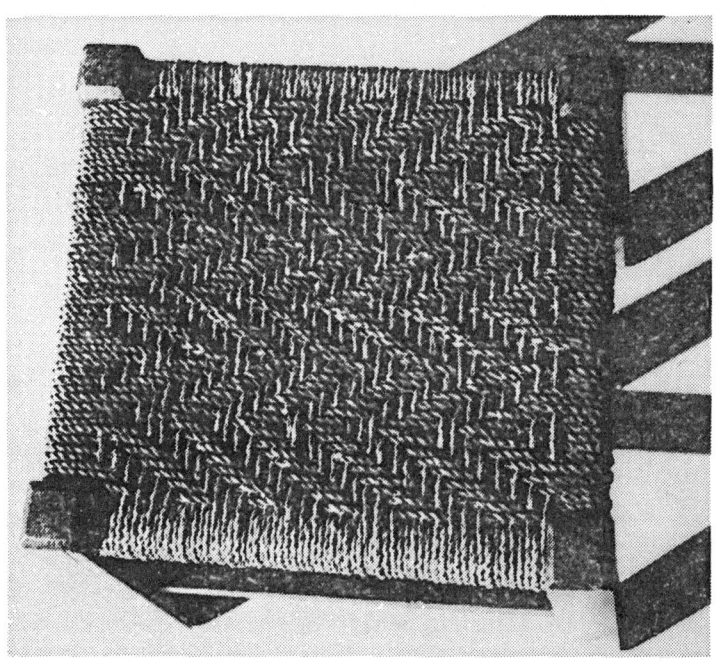

Fig. 20-9. A stool top worked in a chevron pattern as shown in Fig. 20-8.

other way and an even tension of the right degree can be made over a rod laid across the frame. Start at one leg, either by tacking or by tying to a lower rail. Wrap around the rail and cross to the other side, where the line goes around the rail and up on the leg side (Fig. 20-10A). Go over the crossing strand, under the rail, and back to the first side (Fig. 20-10B). Go around the rail and up so as to take in the previous strand and itself (Fig. 20-10C). Go back to the other side and do the same there. Continue back and forth this way until the width is made up. Remove the rod and start working the other way.

Use a needle on the line and work the chosen pattern. A simple checker with four or six sets of strands in a different color is effective. At the rails, deal with the line in the same way as in the first direction, except it will not be possible to get all the lines close without wraps on the rails. After each half hitch on a rail, take the line around again before going across (Fig. 20-10D). Use the point of a needle to get all the lines straight across.

This type of seat tends to move down to the midpoint of the rails, so it is more effective with round rails than with square-edged ones.

CANE SEATING

There are several ways of seating chairs with cane, but the best known method makes an open pattern using holes drilled in the frame. Doing the work is time-consuming and there are substitutes in the form of plastic or cane sheet of woven appearance that can be fixed as a panel, but any of these things are substitutes that would not be acceptable on good work. There is plastic strip available that looks like cane and can be used as an alternative, but it would be unsuitable on antique or reproduction furniture.

The size of cane has to be related to the size of hole in the frame. In use, the cane goes down one hole, underneath, and up the next, without twisting (Fig. 20-11A). The glossy side should be uppermost on all exposed surfaces. Cane can be fixed in a hole with a wooden peg, driven, and broken off. For a joint the old and new ends may be pegged together in a hole. An alternative is to push the new end down the hole beside the old end and half hitch it (Fig. 20-11B). Ends can be cut off later.

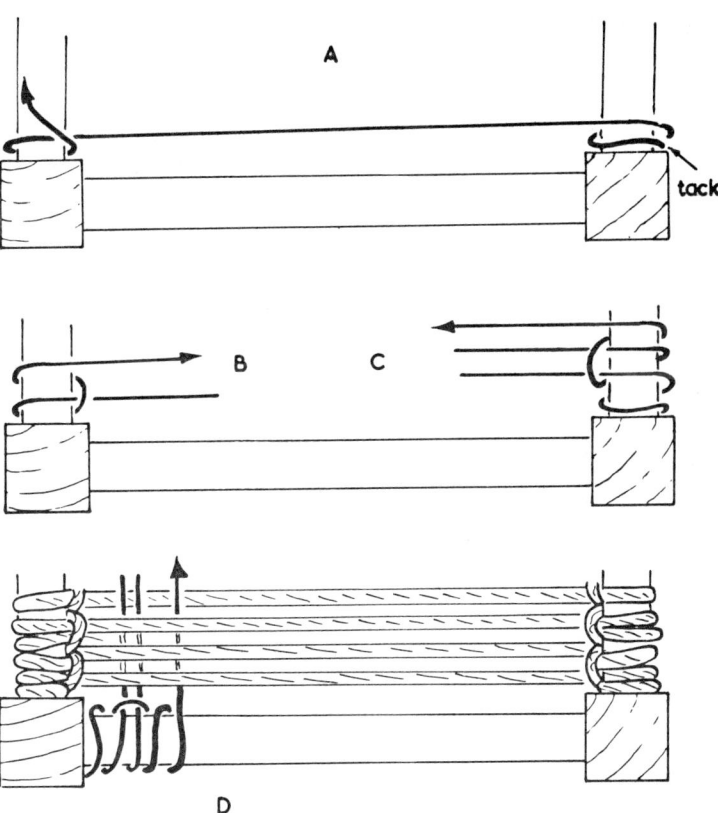

Fig. 20-10. It is possible to work a stool top in a single thickness by knotting at each rail.

The usual patterns have strands directly across the top of the frame at right angles to each other, then more strands are woven diagonally. There are variations, mostly due to the number of strands and how the overlaps are arranged. Two basic patterns likely to be met are *single-setting*, with only one cane between opposite holes in the first weaving, and *double-setting*, where there are two canes between opposite holes. The basic instructions that follow are for double-setting. The single-setting pattern is similar, but less complicated.

Use a single strand. Let it go through a hole near a corner with about 3 inches below and secure it with a peg. Go across the frame to the opposite hole, down this, and up the next. Continue across all but the corner holes in that direction. Put on

393

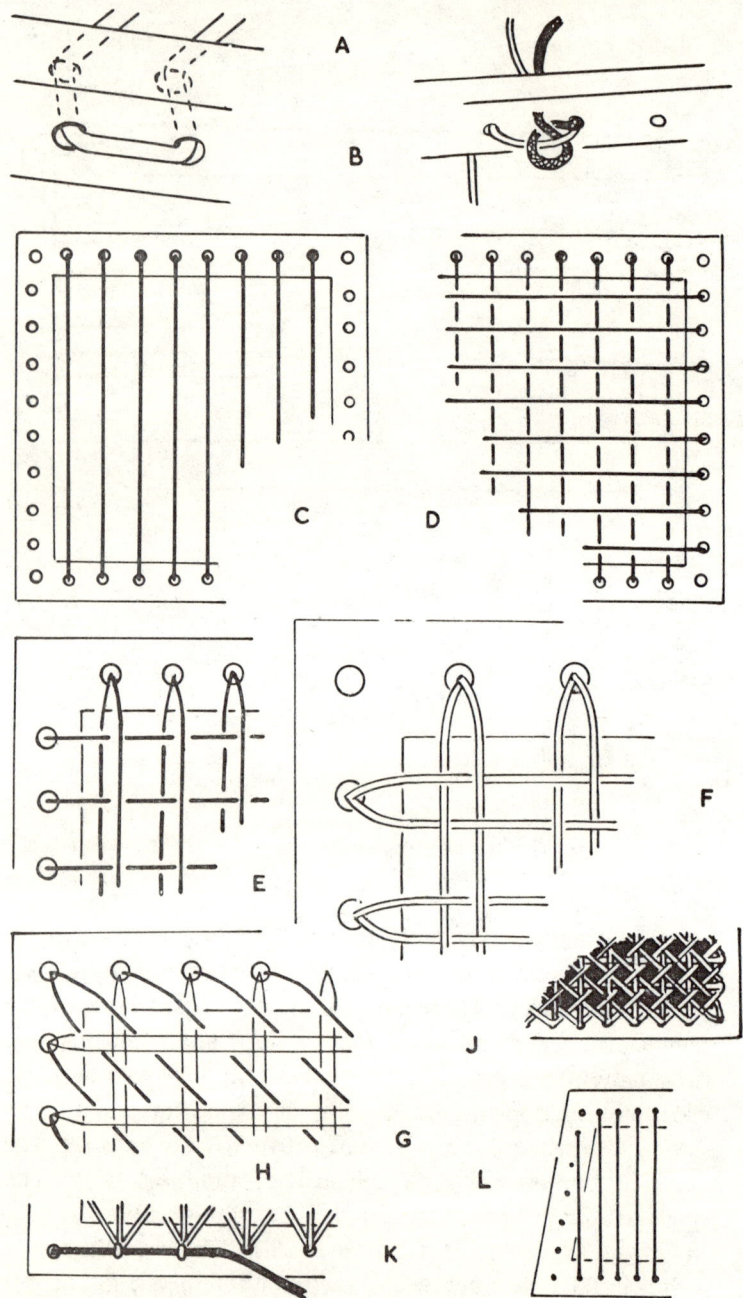

Fig. 20-11. A cane seat is made by working the strips of cane through holes in the frame and weaving them into each other in a variety of patterns.

a good tension each time and use a temporary peg to hold the tension at each hole while the cane is being worked to the next stage. This puts lines of cane across one way (Fig. 20-11C). Do the same the other way, with the strands on top of the first (Fig. 20-11D). Go back to the first direction, use the same holes, but take the new canes *over* the second ones (Fig. 20-11E).

It is at this point that weaving takes place. The second strands in the second direction are taken over and under, to make a pattern at each crossing (Fig. 20-11F). This can be done by hand, but it is quicker to use a bodkin, inserted back through about four strands. Then insert the cane in its hole and pull it through, repeating as often as necessary across the seat.

For a single-setting pattern, only one strand of stouter cane is used instead of the pairs of canes each way. From this point onward, weaving is very similar. As all canes are passed through holes, tension should be put on and held by pegs until further work will hold the load and the peg can be removed.

With double-setting, push the crossing patterns close together so there is no doubt which are the spaces to be used for diagnoal weaving. Pairs of strands in double-setting are treated as single strands when doing diagonal weaves.

Start at a corner hole and go across to the opposite corner, over and under all the way (Fig. 20-11G). Do this again between the same holes, but start under if the previous tucking started over, or vice versa (Fig. 20-11H). Do this parallel to those canes across between the other holes until they are all connected.

Change to the other direction and do the same thing that way, starting with two strands corner to corner and continuing until all holes are linked (Fig. 20-11J). The pattern will be getting very tight and a bodkin will be needed near the corner, if not also in the body of the seat.

Although this completes the pattern, the holes in the frame are exposed and this would have an untidy appearance if left. The final step is covering the holes with a strip of cane, which may be wider than that used for weaving the pattern. It is held with thinner cane through the holes. The *beading* cane is a single length along one side, then another piece is used on the next side. It is not bent around a corner.

Point the end of the beading cane and push this end down a

corner hole. Bend it and lay it over the holes along one side. Bring the thin cane up a hole, over the beading, and down the same hole, to go underneath to the next hole, where the action is repeated (Fig. 20-11K). Do this all the way along the side, with a good tension, then point the end of the beading cane and thrust it down the next corner hole.

Repeat on the other sides. Where any ends have to be secured, pegs can be used and concealed by the beading. Ends of diagonals may be secured by twisting around any convenient loops underneath. Stray ends should be cut off flush.

Complications come when seats are not square or true rectangles. It is usual to make the woven pattern squared, rather than try to conform to the frame shape. Traditional chairs are often wider at the front than the back. The original arrangement will almost certainly have allowed for a square pattern. Start by caning between center holes at back and front. Work outwards. When all of the rear holes, except the corners, have been used up, keep the canes parallel, but go to convenient side holes (Fig. 20-11L).

A round seat can be visualized as a circular frame imposed on exactly the same body pattern as on a square seat, but holes around the curved perimeter have to be taken up where they are convenient to make the pattern. This means that not every hole is used every time, but tucking through holes is arranged as needed to keep pattern lines parallel.

With a circular or elliptical seat, count the holes and divide by four so as to obtain four points which can be regarded as centers of four sides of the pattern. Work from the center outwards and keep the canes parallel. Further around the curve it may be necessary to miss some holes to retain parallel lines.

Arrange the diagonals so they will cross the first setting strands at 45°. With a circular seat this means starting at the holes halfway between those used to start the setting canes, but with any other sort of curve, positions will have to be judged that will give the correct angles.

The foregoing instructions cover what is probably the best known pattern, but if an existing seat is examined, many variations can be seen. Setting strands may not be woven, or they may be woven as pairs instead of individually at each crossing.

The seat may have had the diagonals put on first and the parallel canes put on singly or in pairs in a variety of patterns through them. Different sizes of cane may be mixed to give a different appearance. In all cases the basic technique and tool work is the same as described, but the different patterns have to be followed.

Section 3
FRAMES

Frame Types

The frame of a chair or other seat is the skeleton that provides strength to the body which, in turn, may almost completely hide it with upholstery. The structure has to be reliable as it is usually inaccessible after it has been covered. It has to have adequate strength, not only to withstand direct loads, but to resist the strains imposed by occupants who rock it on two legs or put on loads due to moving or tilting.

Where parts of the frame are exposed it needs to have a cabinetmaking quality finish, although in the hidden parts it need not have the same surface finish. The important parts are the joints. It is often impossible to strengthen by using diagonal bracing across parts of a frame, or by using panels to stiffen a structure, because of the upholstery requirements, so there are often wracking strains on joints of comparatively small area, and these need to be good. Any devices designed to reinforce them may be worth having.

A great many woods have been used for frames. It is largely a matter of local availability, but softwoods are not usually chosen. They may have sufficient strength to carry loads, but they do not make such secure joints as hardwoods. The bent frames are made of close-grained hardwoods. Quebec birch has wood characteristics that are regarded as ideal. Whatever wood is chosen, it should have been properly seasoned. Even then it may be advisable to store the wood for a few weeks in conditions similar to those where it will finally stand.

Wood absorbs and gives out moisture. This causes it to expand and contract, but not in amounts that will matter. What might be more serious is the tendency to warp with varying amounts of moisture content. A chair frame might twist after being put into use, and little could be done to it. Seasoned wood contains some moisture. If the frame will be regularly used in a hot, centrally heated room, more of this moisture may be lost than was originally intended in seasoning, with a resultant risk of warping. If the wood is stored in a similar atmosphere before being made into a frame, however, this risk will be reduced.

Wood is not the only material used for frames. In the past there have been iron frames and some Victorian iron frame chairs produced a degree of comfort that has probably not been equalled. Bottom and legs may have been made of wood, but the back and arms were made of iron, using substantial round rod for the outline and flat slats for shape and support (Fig. 21-1).

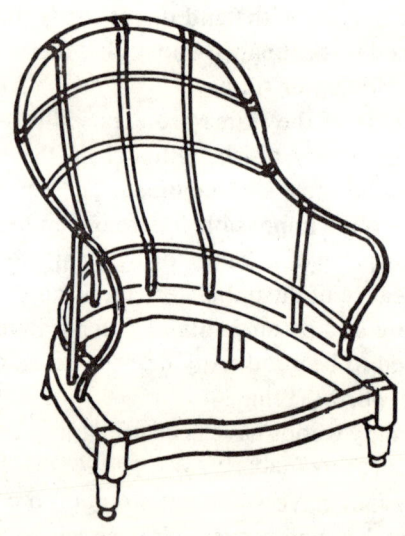

Fig. 21-1. The frame of this chair is a combination of wood and metal. Legs and bottom are of wood while the arms and back are fabricated from bands and rods or iron.

Today other metals besides iron are used for frames, although the amateur and individual who makes single pieces of furniture probably still favors wood. While it is not impossible to produce a frame of almost any shape in wood, the time and skill needed may render some shapes almost impossible to make. A shape similar to the iron frame would involve many wood joints and the cutting of much wasted wood to get the desired curves; but there are examples of Victorian and later chair frames with much shaped wood (Figs. 21-2 and 21-3).

Fig. 21-2. Much time and skill are required to produce the elaborate wooden curves of this chair.

It is possible to modify shapes so the wood framing has less pronounced curves, yet the upholstered covering is given more curving in the right places by the arrangement of padding. Fortunately modern design and styling favors straighter lines. A frame for a contemporary chair may include more straight lines, with the minimum of curving, but appearance is enhanced by tapering outlines instead of curves (Fig. 21-4).

With latex and foam upholstery it is now much more usual to have quite thick padding compared with some traditional work which was stuffed with hair and similar materials. This

Fig. 21-3. To produce these graceful curves, as much wood was cut away as used.

means that a chair pattern closely conforming to the shape of the occupant is less important, although obviously the shape and proportions of the user have to be considered. With thicker comfortable padding the frame is farther from the user than in

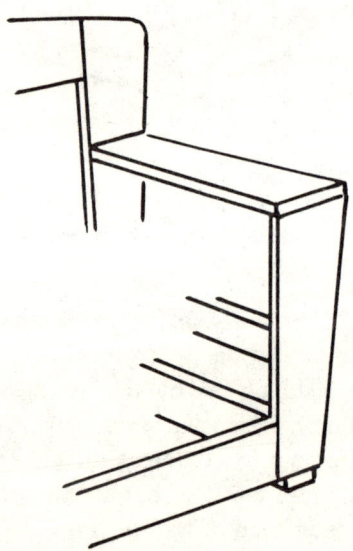

Fig. 21-4. Modern frames favor straighter lines. Curvature is achieved by modifications to the padding.

earlier padded seats and this allows the frame to be a simpler shape. Some quite satisfactory shapes are made of entirely or almost entirely straight pieces of wood (Fig. 21-5) or with slight

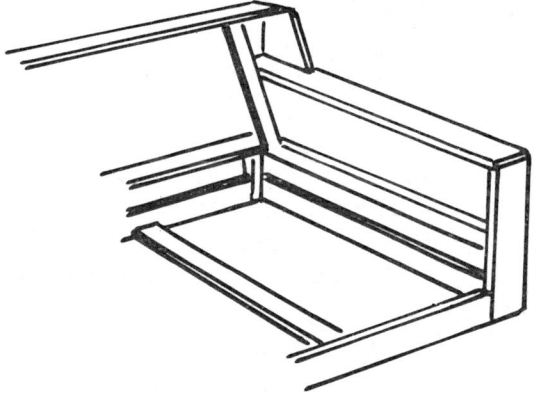

Fig. 21-5. Chairs of the present era are generously padded with latex and foam, precluding the necessity for the craftsman to build frames closely conforming to the shape of the human body.

concessions to shaping by curving outlines of arms or back (Fig. 2-16).

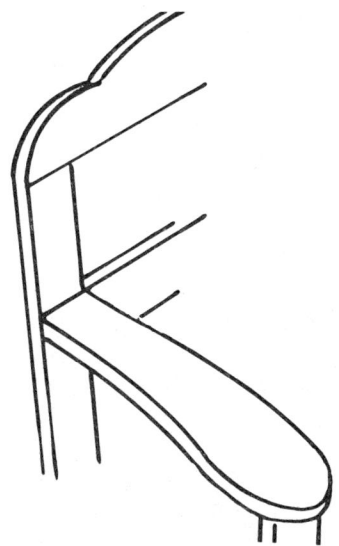

Fig. 21-6. Except for the slight curve of the armrest, this chair is constructed entirely of straight lines.

A frame for a dining or lightly upholstered lounge chair, where most of the woodwork is exposed, requires more skill to make because the wood is much more a feature of the finished piece of furniture. Such a chair requires more woodworking skill to produce an acceptable shape and finish. Parts that are straight when covered by enough upholstery may need delicate curving when exposed, so they are more difficult to make. A dining chair of good appearance and comfort is probably more difficult to make successfully than any other sort of frame, so chair-making of this type may be better left to an expert unless the reader has enough skill and sufficient tools and facilities. A further problem is that these chairs are usually in a set of four or six, and making a matching set is always more difficult than making one chair.

There are some fireside or lounge chairs with many curves to the exposed wood, but because comfort is provided by cushions, it is possible to make this type with mostly straight lines (Fig. 21-7). The skill required then, in addition to that needed for a frame that is to be covered, is related to the ability to produce a good finish on the wood surfaces.

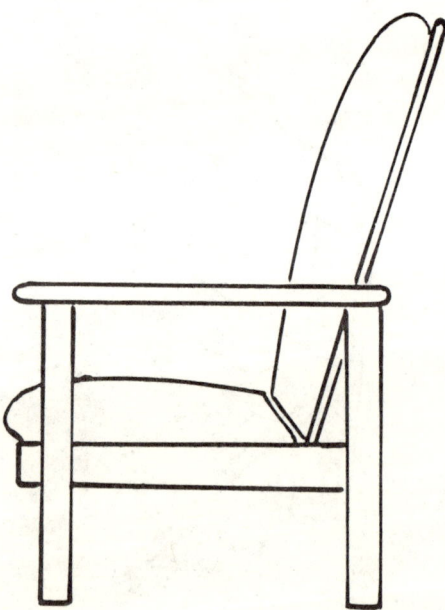

Fig. 21-7. The comfort of this fireside chair derives from the plump cushions.

Frames for sofas and other multiple seats are made in basically the same way as chair seats. Quite often a sofa is used with matching chairs, so the ends are often the same and the only frame differences are in the length of the seat. Structurally, the sofa frame needs enough strength for the extra width and weight, which will still be supported only at the ends. There will have to be some bracing to prevent distorting of the longer crosswise members and possibly some stiffeners under to provide additional support for the seat (Fig. 21-8A).

Simpler frames are needed for stools and there need be little shaping to the components (Fig. 21-8B) although legs and rails may be turned. A stool, because it is lighter and more easily moved, may be subject to more wracking strain than a chair. Its joints need to be good to resist these loads caused by tilting on two legs. For a fully upholstered top the rails should be as deep as the design allows (Fig. 21-8C) to make way for broad—and therefore strong—joints. If it is a stool with a lift-out upholstered top, construction becomes more like a dining chair, with the quality of the woodwork being a more important feature. However, lines are usually straight and there is no problem of a curved back, so a reasonably competent woodworker should be able to make one.

For beds and ottomans or other reclining upholstery work the basic frame is more like a shallow box, usually with cross members to support springs (Fig. 21-8D). As the framework is then fairly substantial, although straight, this is one type of frame where softwood may be acceptable because it is sufficiently strong and generally lighter than hardwood. The basic box frame may be further built up with a sloping end for a pillow or supports for a head board.

An entirely different type of frame is being used increasingly, mostly in factory production. This is molded in plastic and is usually designed to give the finished shape of the seat in one piece, merely requiring covering with the outside cloth. There is no padding or other work, except there may be loose cushions. There are variations on fiberglass and resin, as well as several close-celled foams such as polyurethane, polythene, and polystyrene. The shape may be complete or there may be one or more holes to facilitate fixing the cover. There may be a

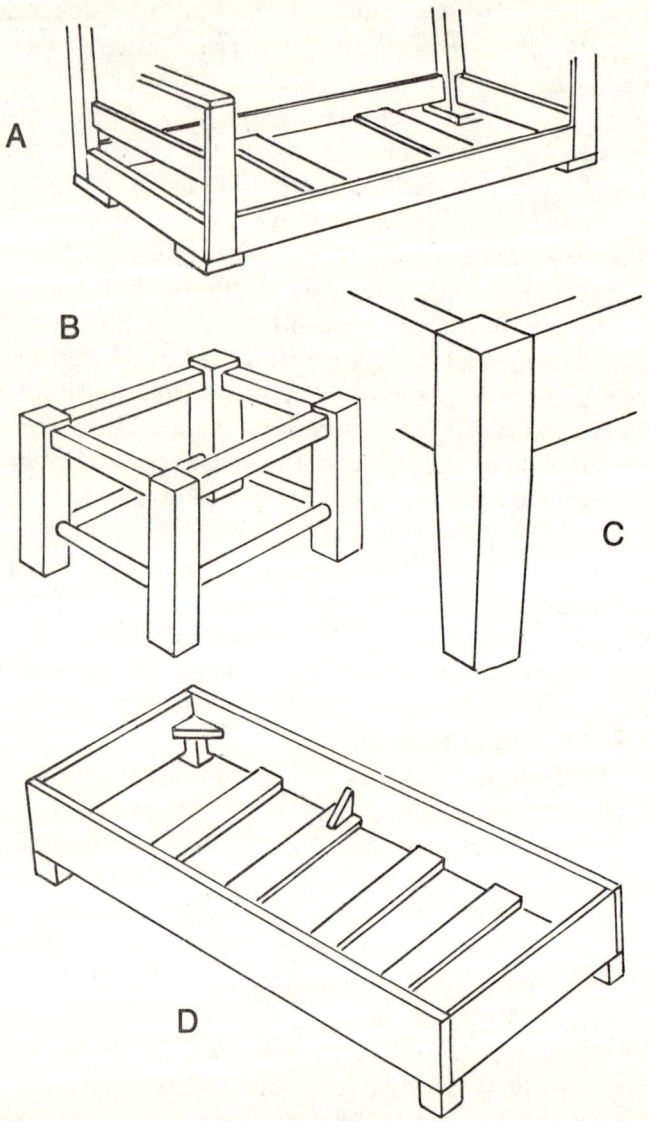

Fig. 21-8. The simplest frames are made of boxed or rectangular stool shapes.

wood base molded in or it may have to be attached, or there may be some other arrangement for mounting the molding on a support.

Although that type of plastic molded shape seems particularly appropriate for office furniture there are examples where different covering materials and suitable cushions make the basic pattern into attractive home furnishings.

Although such modern chair shapes seem particularly appropriate to mounting on pedestals where they can rotate and possibly tilt, they can be given more conventional wooden legs and supporting frames. There are many tubular plated metal supports and mechanisms available. They are suitable for some wood frames chairs as well as those with plastic frames.

At one time the only way to provide adjustment for a reclining chair back or other movement was by using struts in notches, made up with the wood framework. This can still be done and may be the most appropriate way of providing a suitable action in some circumstances, but there are many mechanisms available through upholstery suppliers to allow tilting and rocking as well as adjustments where chairs adapt to reclining backs or lifting leg supports. There are supports that let the chair swivel and adjust in height. These are mostly central pedestals on spread legs which may be of a rather utilitarian appearance for office use, or more attractive for use in the home.

If a seat is to be permitted any movement, this should be considered at the frame stage so allowances can be made and none of the subsequent upholstery arranged in a way that might interfere with or become damaged by the movement. It may also be necessary to fit bolts or other attachments to take the mechanism to some part of the frame that will not be accessible for insertion after covering. Reinforcement may have to be considered. If all of the load has to be taken by a comparatively small part of the framework bolted to a metal fitting and all the use and misuse of the chair anticipated, it may be wiser to reinforce with more wood or a metal plate to reduce the risk of breaking or of bolts pulling into the wood when strained. There should be large washers under bolt heads and nuts in any case.

22 Frame Construction Details

The types of frames made by an individual depend on his skill and equipment. A simple frame like a stool or the base for an ottoman might be made with just a few hand tools and only a modest woodworking skill. Other frames need more skill if the equipment is sparse than if a well equipped shop is available. Some work may be long and tedious with hand tools, although having power tools available may make completion of the same task more accurate as well as quicker. Not everything can be done with power tools and any craftsman worthy of the name should be able to carry out many hand tool techniques properly.

Wood is very much stronger along the grain than across it. If a piece of wood has the grain lines approximately parallel to its sides (Fig. 22-1A) it will exhibit its maximum strength when subjected to a bending load. If the grain lines run off the sides there is a risk of cracking under a bending load (Fig. 22-1B). In planning a frame design it is advisable to avoid *short grain*. For instance, if a curve is cut too far around in one piece of wood, the grain which is about parallel with the circumference at one point becomes cross-grain and weak at another point (Fig. 22-1C). If such a piece has to be cut it is better to dowel two pieces together so their grain is stronger (Fig. 22-1D).

If you examine a frame you will see that although there may be curves, the majority of joints are at right angles to the straight lines of the components before they are shaped (Fig. 22-1E). Meeting surfaces are flat and straight (Fig. 22-1F). It is unusual to bring a rail or other part against a curved surface. A flat is formed so the joint is made to it, even if it means cutting into a turned part.

If there is a double curvature in a part, such as a chair arm, this is cut in two stages. The solid wood has to be big enough in cross section to contain the shape and this may mean cutting quite a lot of wood to waste to make what is finally a light and slender arm that is curved. Avoid excessive curvature, both for economy of material and for avoiding the risk of weak short grain.

Draw the shape on one surface (Fig. 22-1G). Cut this. If a band saw is available, the cut can be made at a known right angle to the surface, and this is the best way of achieving success. If hand sawing has to be used, mark the shape on the opposite surface as well. This is best done by using a card template, which is advisable as a guide in any case if a pair of arms are being made. For hand sawing it helps to make a number of cuts into the waste part so parts of the waste will come away as the saw moves around the curve. If there is no suitable saw for following a curve, the waste can be removed by using a series of saw cuts in the waste parts towards the final line. Then you can chop the waste away with a broad chisel.

If the waste is cut away in a single piece with a band saw, use this as a guide for the shape the other way (Fig. 22-1H). Mark the shape on this and hold it over the arm while cutting the outline with a band saw. If the waste has been cut into pieces, mark the second shape directly on the arm and cut it out.

Before going further, mark and cut the ends including the laying out of any joints. Then if the arms have to be shaped, work on them with a spokeshave, rasp, or chisel to get the desired section. There need not be an exactly rounded section if the arm is to be upholstered, but be careful of discrepancies that are very great, because they may affect the padding enough to show or make smooth covering difficult. If it is an exposed arm, there will have to be much work down through successively finer abrasive papers to get a good surface after shaping with tools.

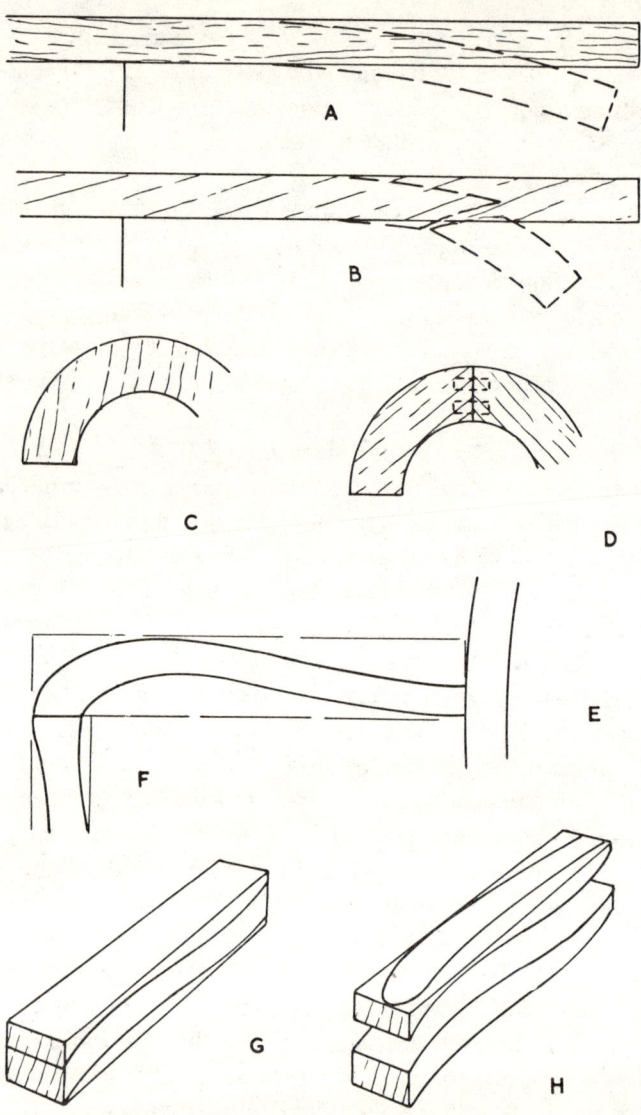

Fig. 22-1. The effect of grain must be considered when planning and making a wooden frame. Wood is much stronger in the direction of the grain than across it, so care has to be taken to avoid parts with grain running across.

Although many chairs have tapering shapes that incorporate curves, it is important that they stand upright and are symmetrical. Shapes that should be the same or two opposite hands may be tested by putting one on top of the other. They can also be tested for twisting in this way. It is possible to put together a set of parts that appear to be accurate, yet they have a built-in twist. This can be checked by sighting across. If two opposite sides of a frame should be parallel edgewise, look across one towards the other and see if lines that should agree really do. If you can stand back a short distance and look toward a background of contrasting color, any discrepancy will be more easily seen.

There are many right angles and the best tool for checking is a try square, preferably 12 inches long (Fig. 22-2A). Angles often have to be compared and the tool for doing this is an adjustable bevel (Fig. 22-2B). When wood has to be cut across the grain accurately it is better to mark the line with a knife than to use a pencil. Although a straight steel rule and a longer expanding rule will be needed, much measuring is done best by comparison. If several pieces of wood have to be the same length or have joints at the same distance, mark them all together. Precision in relation to each other is more important than precision in relation to the markings on a rule. If all parts are 1/4 inch different from what you intended, they will match and it is unlikely that the error will matter, but if each is measured with a rule individually and there is an error in one or more parts, the trouble is more serious.

It is also helpful to have a large set square, which could be a triangle cut from the corner of a plywood sheet, maybe 3 feet on its long side (Fig. 22-2C). This can stand on the floor to check if a leg is vertical, or be used to check that a corner assembly is square when viewed from above. Another way to check symmetry is to measure diagonals. This can be done with a tapered shape as well as one with square corners. Although a rule might be used, a strip of wood with pencil marks (Fig. 22-2D) gives less risk of error.

DOWELLED JOINTS

A dowel is a round wood rod. Most frames today are joined with dowels. This is probably because dowelling is more suitable for machine work than the mortise and tenon or other traditional joints. Dowelling does not have so many advantages

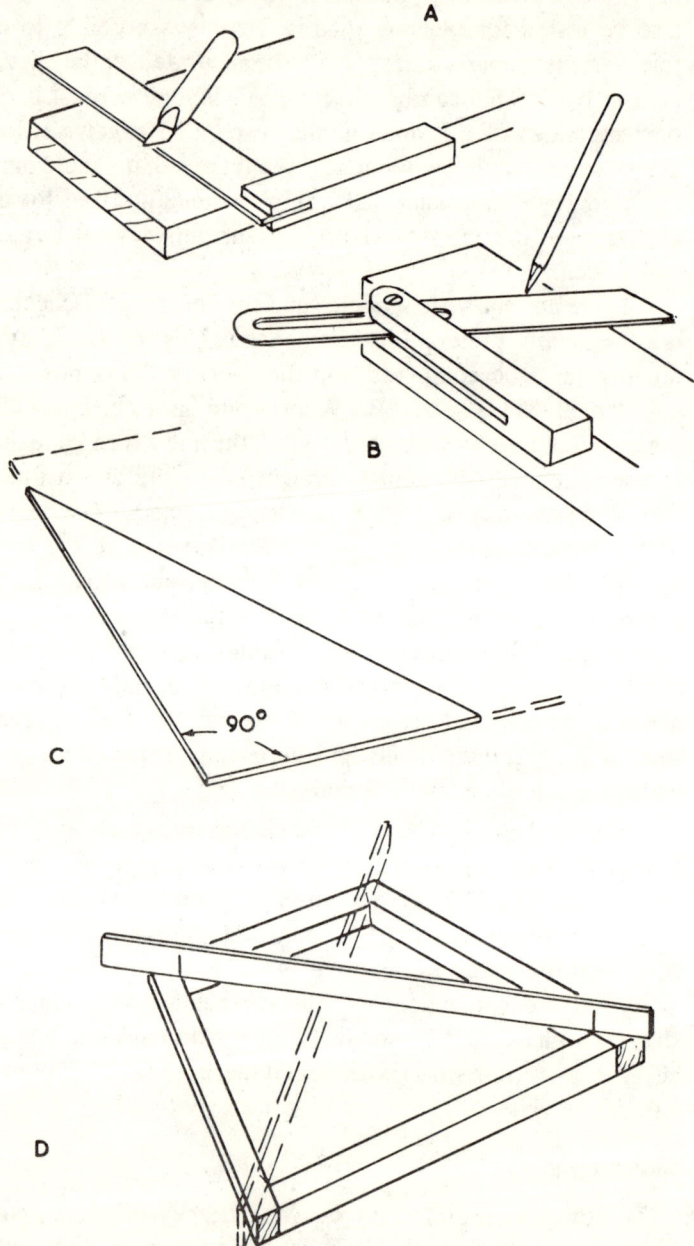

Fig. 22-2. It is important that chairs and other furniture are made symmetrical and to stand upright. Squares and adjustable bevels are used for marking out and diagonal checks made to ensure symmetry.

if the work has to be done with hand tools, but it is still probably the type of joint to choose in most circumstances. In early work dowels were made individually by driving a roughly shaped piece of wood through a hole in a steel plate. Today, dowels are usually bought ready-made in long lengths and cut as needed. There are, however, some dowels obtainable already cut to length with the ends bevelled. The dowel goes into a hole in each piece being joined and is glued there. It is helpful to bevel the ends slightly. A dowel going into a hole is like a piston in a cylinder, compressing the glue. Because of this it is usual to let the dowel be slightly short and arrange a groove to let air and surplus glue escape (Fig. 22-3A). The groove may be sawn, although in some prepared dowels it is spiral and pressed into the wood.

There are stock diameter dowels and it is usual to choose a size between 1/3 and 1/2 the width of the narrowest piece of wood to be joined. How far a dowel should go into the wood is mainly a matter of experience and has to be related to the actual parts. If there is ample wood, a 1/2 inch dowel might go in 2 inches, but at a corner into a leg the dowels can only go as far as they will meet (Fig. 22-3B) if they are at the same level.

Of course, no joint is made with a single dowel, except something like a small square-sectioned rail, and even that may have two slim dowels arranged diagonally. Two or more dowels are strong and they prevent the parts from moving in relation to each other.

The success of a dowelled joint depends on accurate marking out, and the exact location of the drill center when making a hole. Also, the hole must be drilled at right angles to the surface. The use of a bench drilling machine ensures the holes will be truly at right angles, but for hand drilling there are guides and jigs available that can be adjusted so the holes in the meeting parts will match and the drill enters at the correct angle. Although it is possible to drill for dowelled joints by freehand methods with a brace or a hand electric drill the use of a guide is advisable and essential for quick accurate work if there are many joints to be made.

If a dowelled joint is to be made without the aid of a guide, mark out both parts together (Fig. 22-3C). Gauge from edges

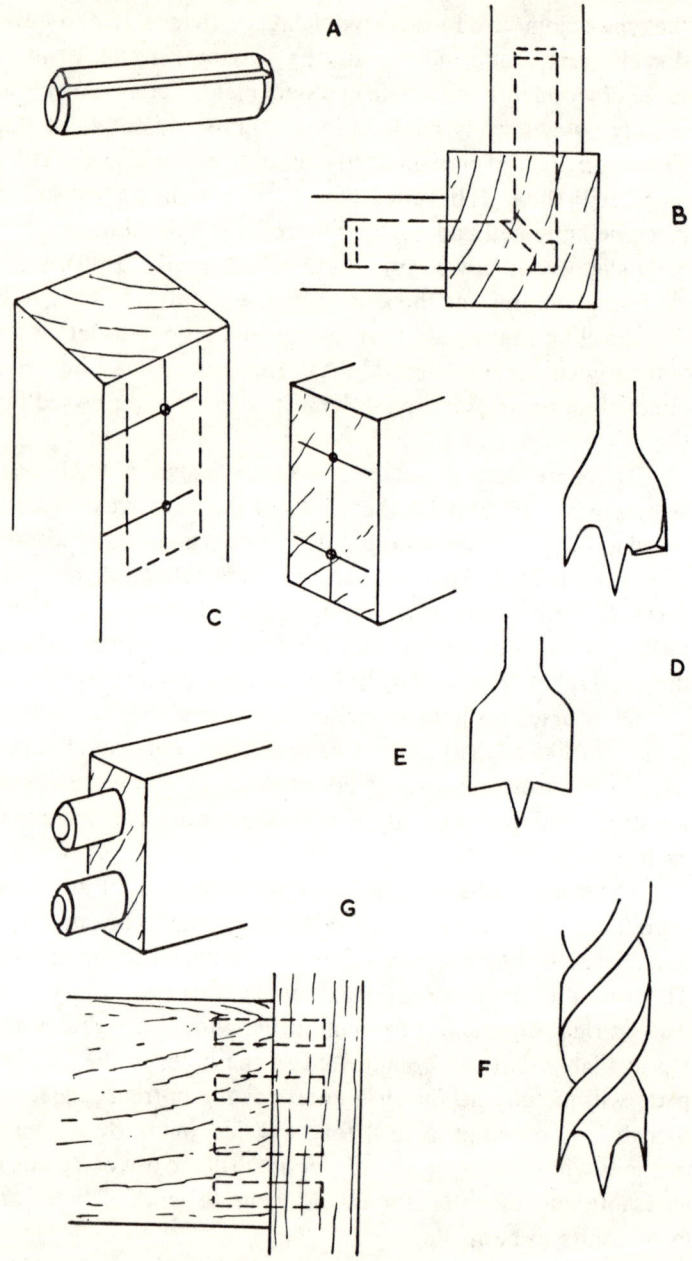

Fig. 22-3. The most popular method of joining frames today is by dowels which have to be carefully matched.

and mark the hole centers by pressing in an awl. Use a wood boring bit even for small holes, if possible, as it makes a cleaner hole than a twist drill. The spade type of bit for a hand brace (Fig. 22-3D) or electric drill (Fig. 22-3E) may be satisfactory, but in a deep hole it may wander and the type with twisted flutes behind the cutting edges (Fig. 22-3F) is better able to keep straight.

The strength of a dowelled joint lies in the glued dowels, not in the meeting wood surfaces, where glue against end grain is not very strong—so have enough dowels. Examples are 2 inch by 1 inch section rails with two 5/8 inch dowels and a 5 inch by 3/4 inch rail with four 1/2 inch dowels (Fig. 22-3G). If possible, have a depth stop on the drill so the hole is made slightly deeper than the dowel is to penetrate.

CLAMPS

Dowelled and other joints have to be pulled together and usually held tight while the glue sets. It may be possible to hammer parts together. Use a mallet or have a piece of wood to spread the hammer blow and prevent damage. If the joint is tight it may hold in close contact without clamps, but these are usually needed. Although it is possible to improvise clamps for some purposes, proper C and bar clamps (Fig. 22-4) are worth

Fig. 22-4. C clamps are useful for small thicknesses, but a bar clamp is needed for places where a greater capacity has to be spanned. Note the scrap wood to prevent damage by the clamp heads on the chair frame.

having. C clamps in several sizes hold smaller parts within their capacity, but bar clamps pull frame assemblies together.

Without a bar clamp it is possible to use wedges and blocks of wood on a stiff board (Fig. 22-5A) to apply pressure. It is also sometimes useful to apply a Spanish windlass by twisting several turns of rope (Fig. 22-5B). It is often possible to correct lack of symmetry when clamping. If an assembly resists coming square when diagonals are checked, putting a clamp slightly diagonally will pull the frame to shape as well as secure the joint (Fig. 22-5C).

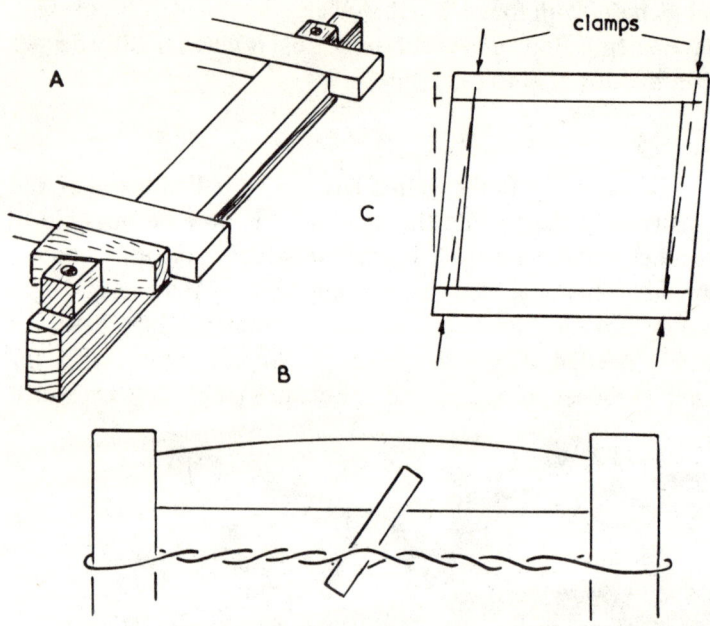

Fig. 22-5. Frames can be pulled together with wedges or twisted cord and it is possible to correct shape by using clamps slightly diagonally.

MORTISE AND TENON JOINTS

Although dowels are commonly used and are satisfactory, many of the joints traditionally used were mortise and tenons. These still have many uses and may be preferred by some workers instead of dowels. They are appropriate for reproduction furniture and should be used when repairing antique chairs. When the part of a frame is concealed by upholstery, it may not matter what joint is used, but an experienced observer can usually detect whether dowels or tenons have been used at the corners of an exposed chair arm or other wood joint. A tenon may offer a better glue area and provide a better integrating of the two wood parts, to give the greatest strength possible in a joint that may get considerable loading.

In the basic mortise and tenon joint between two pieces of the same thickness, the tenon (the projecting part) is one-third the thickness of the wood (Fig. 22-6A). The tenon may go right through the other piece, but in most furniture construction it is *stopped* or *stub*.

To make this joint with hand tools, mark both pieces at the same time. It is helpful to have a mortise gauge (one with two adjustable points) to scratch the thickness of tenon and mortise. Use a knife to mark lines that will be sawn. If the tenon is to go right through it can be left a little long. In that case mark the mortise on both sides of the wood (Fig. 22-6B).

Use a back saw with fine teeth to cut the shoulders of the tenon while the wood is held in a vise or pushed against a bench hook (Fig. 22-6C). Cut down the sides of the tenon with the saw *kerf* kept on the waste sides of the lines and first cutting diagonally, watching the lines on end and side of the wood (Fig. 22-6D). Do the same with the wood tilted the other way and finally cut straight through (Fig. 22-6E).

At one time mortises were chopped completely with a mallet and chisel, but it is easier and has less risk of splitting if you drill a number of overlapping holes first (Fig. 22-6F). These can be slightly less in diameter than the width of the mortise and they are made without marking out, but there are jigs available to control the spacing of the holes and guide the drill with such a close overlap of holes that there is very little to remove with a chisel.

Use a chisel of the same width as the mortise to chop out the waste. Do not cut right up to the end lines until the last cuts, otherwise the edge will be rounded when levering out the chips. If the mortise goes right through, do the chiselling from opposite sides. In any case have the wood on a solid bench top while hitting the chisel with a mallet, otherwise there is a risk of the grain breaking out on the underside, if the wood is in a vise or otherwise unsupported below.

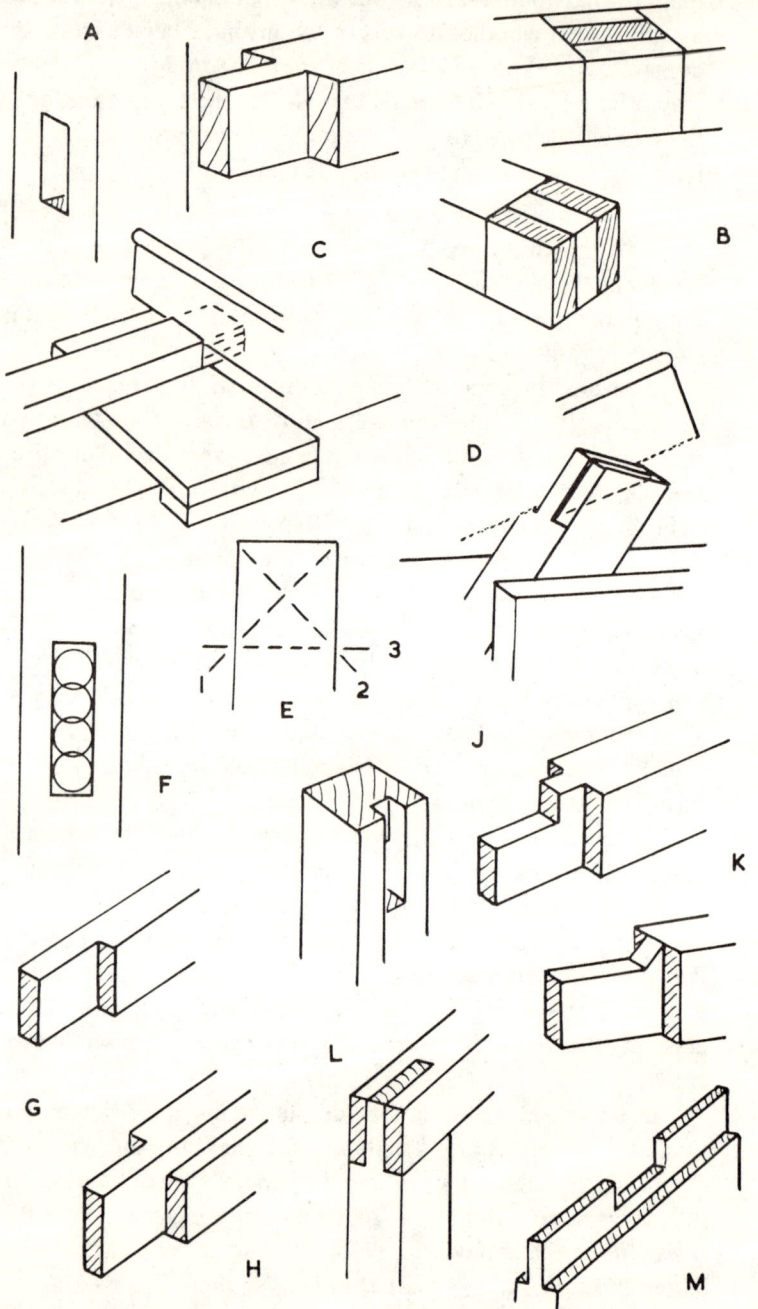

Fig. 22-6. There are several varieties of mortise and tenon joint used in frames, particularly those of a traditional type.

If the mortised piece is wider than the other, as it often is in furniture, the joint will be stronger if the tenon is thicker than one-third the thickness of the narrower piece. It need not always be central. If located completely to one side it is called a *bare-faced* tenon (Fig. 22-6G). For a molded or rounded edge or a rail to take a drop-in seat, the tenon position and width may have to be regulated to suit, but it should never be less than one-third the thickness of the wood (Fig. 22-6H).

If the tenoned piece comes near the end of the other piece, the joint has to be haunched. If the end will not show the tenon is cut short (Fig. 22-6J) to fit a groove; but where it is exposed, as with some chair rails into legs, the cutback part is angled (Fig. 22-6K). In some hidden parts of a frame it may be satisfactory to make a corner with an open mortise and tenon joint, sometimes called a *bridle* joint (Fig. 22-6L). Where a broad rail is tenoned it is usual to cut back the middle, so not so much mortise has to be cut away (Fig. 22-6M), with possible weakening of that part.

DADO AND LAP JOINTS

If a broad board meets another like a shelf it is not very satisfactory to merely fix it with a few screws. It is better to make a dado joint (Fig. 22-7A). The dado should not be more than about one-quarter of the thickness of the wood and there may be a reinforcing block glued below (Fig. 22-7B). This helps the joint resist the wracking strains it may receive in a chair frame. Use the actual wood as a guide to the width of the dado and cut the lines with a knife. Gauge the depth and saw down the sides of the dado. It is a help in keeping the saw kerf on the waste side of the line to chisel across angled towards the knife cut (Fig. 22-7C) as a guide for the saw.

The waste wood between the saw cuts may be removed by chiselling or with a router. Check that the bottom of the dado is flat across the width of the board, otherwise the board may be distorted when the joint is pulled tight.

If a dado joint is hidden by upholstery it can be cut right across, but if an edge is exposed it looks better if it is *stopped* on the visible edge (Fig. 22-7D). The piece that fits in the dado has a notch cut, but for a neat appearance work to a knife line on the front edge.

It is necessary to remove a short section at the stopped end (Fig. 22-7E) so that a saw can be used in the stopped dado. This can be done with a chisel, chopping across the grain before levering out the waste wood. Do not cut back to the lines until most of the waste has gone. It may be advisable to leave a little waste wood (Fig. 22-7F) until the rest of the dado has been cut, otherwise the saw may damage that end. Saw the sides of the dado with short strokes of the saw, with its end kept within the chopped out part. After the waste has been removed, trim the stopped end of the groove.

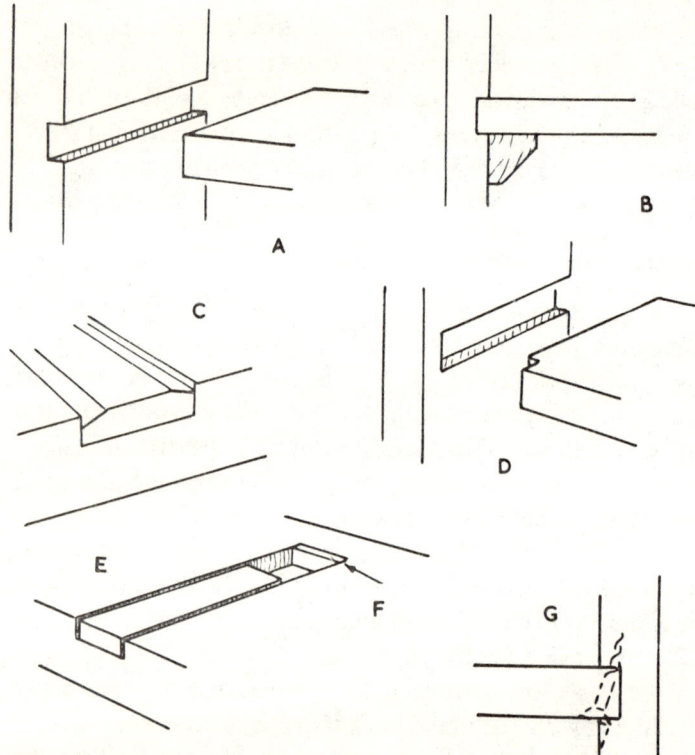

Fig. 22-7. When flat parts meet, a dado joint is appropriate.

Besides putting glue in a dado joint, there should be some screws. If they will not show they can be driven from outside, but if the outside is visible, and for a possibly stronger joint in any case, screws may be driven diagonally from below (Fig. 22-7G).

If two pieces cross at the same level they are joined with a lap (or halving) joint. In its simplest form half is cut from each piece (Fig. 22-8A). The cuts are made in the same way as those for a dado, using the actual wood to mark widths and gauging the depth from the top surface on both pieces. The same joint is used where there is a T-pattern meeting (Fig. 22-8B), as may occur where wood is used instead of webbing to support springs.

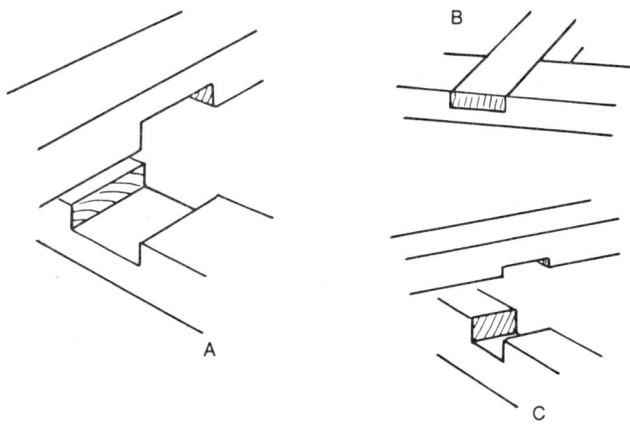

Fig. 22-8. Where flat parts cross, a lap joint is the one to use.

A lap joint is less satisfactory at a corner, but it may have to be used instead of dowels or mortise and tenon joints if the pieces are fairly thin and meet edgewise.

Cutting away half the thickness for a lap joint obviously weakens a piece of wood, but in a good joint the two parts are mutually supporting. If there is a difference in thickness the joint is stronger if less is cut from the thinner piece (Fig. 22-8C).

DOVETAIL JOINTS

There are some complicated and difficult traditional dovetail joints. The principle is a good one, as the design of the joint resists pulling apart in one direction without reliance on glue or fastenings.

A single through dovetail (Fig. 22-9A) makes a good corner joint, while several dovetails may be used on a wider corner. The slope of the side of a dovetail is usually about 1 in 8 (Fig.

22-9B). Mark the dovetails and saw on the waste sides of the lines (Fig. 22-9C). Remove the waste by chiselling, working from opposite sides to avoid breaking out the grain. Mark the end of the other piece from the first, with a finely sharpened pencil. Square down the lines to the marked depth (Fig. 22-9D). Saw to this depth on the waste sides of the lines. Some waste wood can be removed by diagonal cuts (Fig. 22-9E), then the joint is finally trimmed with a chisel.

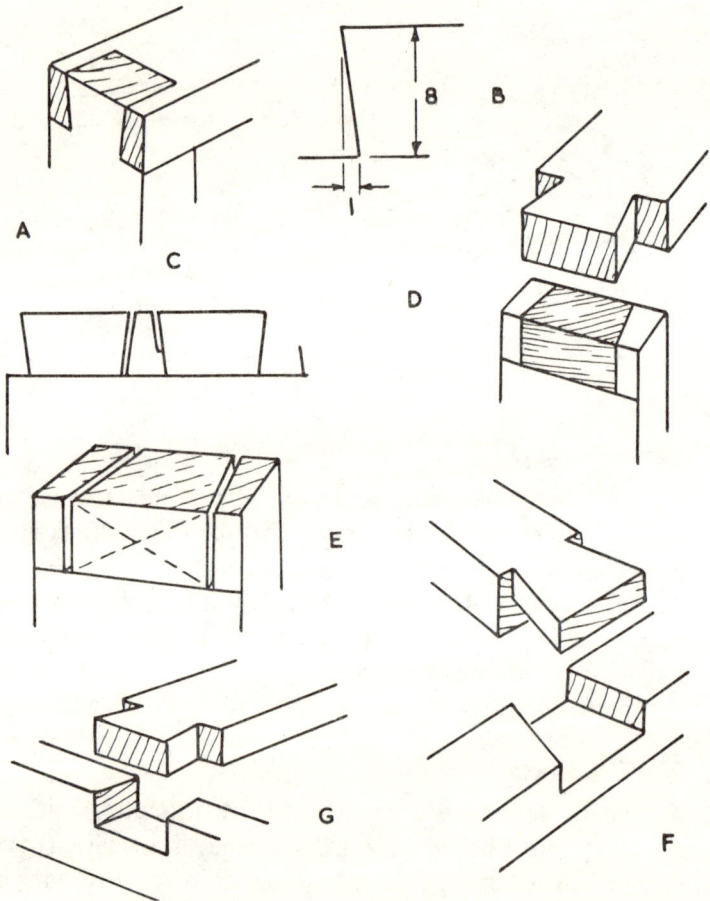

Fig. 22-9. A dovetail locks parts together better than most other joints.

There are guides for using a special tool, which may be driven by an electric drill, to make multiple dovetails mechanically. This may be used in making frame joints if it is available, but wide multiple dovetail joints are not often needed in chair or sofa frames.

Dovetail lapped joints are useful for holding together parts which may tend to open in use. The battens across an ottoman may be fixed in this way. The basic joint is a variation of the lap, with both parts the same thickness and half cut from each, but using a dovetail form (Fig. 22-9F). If one part is thicker, the dovetail piece need not be cut away to half thickness or not at all if the difference is great (Fig. 22-9G).

SCREWED JOINTS

Common wood screws make good joints between many parts in a frame. Besides pulling parts together they contribute strength across grain. Be sure to drill holes of the right size in order to avoid the risk of splitting the wood. Although a screw may be expected to enter some softwoods without drilling, with hardwoods there must be drilled holes. With the harder and more closely grained woods, the holes have to be bigger than when the wood fibers are more flexible, so exact sizes cannot always be specified.

A screw normally pulls two parts together by pressure under the head reacting to the grip of the threaded part. Consequently, the hole in the top part should be a sliding fit on the neck of the screw (Fig. 22-10A). Tightness there is the reverse of what is wanted. The hole in the lower part should be about the same diameter as the root of the threads (Fig. 22-10B), with a little tolerance according to the hardness of the wood. In very hard wood this hole should go the full depth of the screw, but in softer wood the point can be left to penetrate a short distance without the aid of a hole (Fig. 22-10C).

A screw head may pull into softwood, but for hardwoods the mouth of the hole should be countersunk. A countersink bit works best if turned slowly, so even if other drilling is done with a power drill there is an advantage in countersinking with a hand-turned brace.

If a screw has to be used on an exposed surface, it is sometimes possible to use a decorative head, but more often it is better to hide the screw. One way of doing this is by counterboring (Fig. 22-10D). A hole to clear the head is drilled shallowly.

This can be filled with stopping after driving the screw. It could be plugged with a piece of dowel, but that will show end grain. It is better to use a plug cutter, which is a sort of hollow drill used in a power drill. It makes round plugs with the grain across. If the same wood as that being plugged is used, the counterbored hole may finish almost invisible.

Sometimes pocket screwing can be used to avoid having a screw on a visible surface. A hole is drilled diagonally from inside, then a pocket is cut out with chisel or gouge so the head is partly buried (Fig. 22-10E).

Screws hold best across the grain. If they have to be driven into end grain they should be long and plentiful. One way of strengthening such a joint is to fit a dowel through the wood so the screw goes into it and benefits from that much cross grain (Fig. 22-10F).

In the hidden parts of a frame joints can be strengthened with blocks glued and screwed into angles (Fig. 22-10G). Screws may be square to one piece and joined to it before fitting to the second piece, then more screws can be used to pull the joint together, assisting or taking the place of clamps. If the joint is already made, screws can be driven diagonally to pull the block into the angle.

The blocks can be used more in the form of angle brackets. Grain should be across the bracket and short grain avoided near the end of an arm, particularly if the bracket is curved (Fig. 22-10H). Curving may be necessary to allow a reasonable length and direction of screw. In some corners the bracket will have to be shaped around a leg or other part.

It may be possible to strengthen hidden parts with metal brackets of the type intended for shelves or other purposes. In some cases a wooden bracket may be needed less for strengthening a joint than for preventing a frame from distorting. A large diagonal brace would do this, but in many cases it would interfere with springing or some other function. Instead there can be diagonal pieces across corners, fixed at their ends, but not fitted into the corners (Fig. 22-10J).

There are a few bolts used in making frames, but in general they should be avoided except for parts which may have to be dismantled. Nuts and bolts used on wood should have large

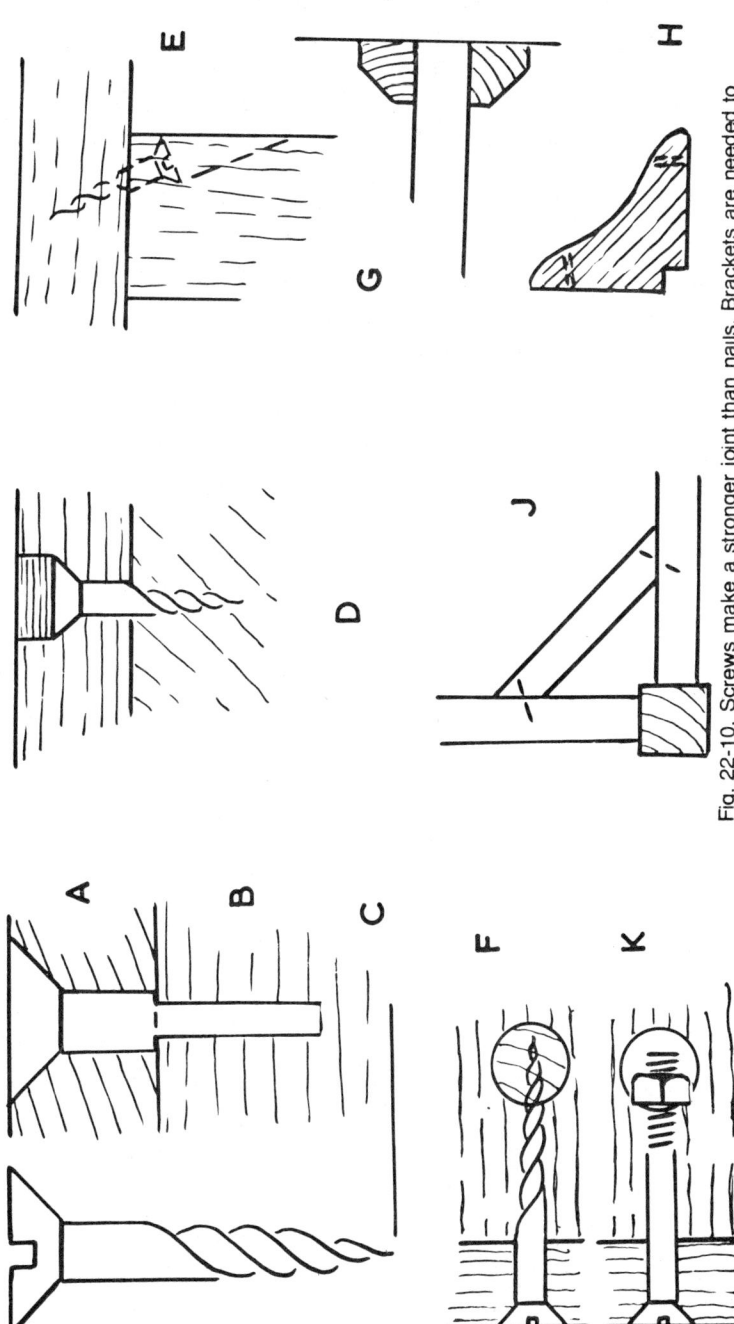

Fig. 22-10. Screws make a stronger joint than nails. Brackets are needed to stiffen some corners.

washers to take pressure. These should be of larger diameter than the engineering size washers often supplied with the bolts. A metal-threaded screw and nut may be used for a similar purpose to a wood screw and dowel for a difficult end grain fastening, where the nut is let in instead of using a dowel and the metal-thread screw pulls into it (Fig. 22-10K).

Whatever joints or fastenings are used, they should be considered in relation to the whole frame. A very strong reinforcement at one point may not compensate for a weak joint at another point. A large number of reinforcements of about the same strength will mutually share strains and support each other. Consider any added reinforcement in relation to the upholstery. Avoid screw heads which stand above the surface or ragged edges of wood that may catch in the filling material. If a bracket is added, make sure it will not foul webbing or other upholstery material yet to be added. Even if it is clear during construction, use of the chair may force parts together. It is good practice to round exposed edges inside in any case, even if there seems little risk of fouling.

23

Stools and Simple Frames

The frame for a stool usually has the advantage of being symmetrical and having parallel sides. This makes for ease of marking out and cutting joints. There may be no great difficulty in scheming the angles for a seat flared in the width or curved at the back, but having parts the same width and parallel reduces complications, particularly for a beginner. One possible disadvantage, however, is the need for accuracy—a slight error in squareness or size may be more obvious to the casual observer than a similar error in a flared or curved frame.

A basic frame (Fig. 23-1A) has four square legs with rails at the top and another set lower down. There are many variations possible, but such a frame, possibly for rush or seagrass seating or covering with a plywood panel for a padded top, will serve as an example of the sequence of work needed to get a satisfactory result. Obviously, the wood should be straight and square. It will almost certainly be bought machine-planed. Check its straightness by sighting along and using a straightedge. Check the squareness with a try square. Correct any errors, if necessary, by hand planing. In any case, exposed surfaces should be planed with a finely set hand plane to remove any machine plane marks.

There may be a single dowel in each rail, but a small stool with light section rails will be made up stronger with mortise and tenon joints. All parts that should be the same length should be marked out together. Put all four legs together and mark across with a try square and knife for cut parts, or pencil for other parts. If the wood is too long, leave cutting to length until after joints have been cut. Use the actual rails as a guide to widths of joints (Fig. 23-1B).

Mark all around where the ends will be cut and mark the joints onto a second surface. Mark the four rails in one direction together and cut off the ends (Fig. 23-1C). Mark the other four in the same way. Gauge the widths of the tenons and keep the gauge points the same width to mark the mortises. Drill out some of the waste in the mortises. Normally, the mortises are allowed to meet, so the maximum length of tenon can be used (Fig. 23-1D). Cut the tenons and miter the meeting ends. If rails have to be level with the tops of the legs under a flat top, haunch the tenon.

Although a beginner may want to try joints together, it is better to have confidence in your workmanship and depend on accurate cutting, so the only assembly is the final one. This should result in a stronger joint than one that has been given several trial assemblies.

Saw the ends of the legs carefully on the waste side of the cut lines. Plane or sand the ends carefully if they are not to be covered, as they will be prominent in the finished stool. There are several ways of decorating them, but a neat finish is created with a bevel all round (Fig. 23-1E).

ASSEMBLY SEQUENCE

Assembly of a three-dimensional frame has to be done systematically to avoid twist and inaccuracies of shape, despite having made matching parts the same size. Assemble one side with glue and bar clamps (Fig. 23-1F). Check squareness and sight across two rails to see that there is no twist. A nail can be driven into the inside of a joint (Fig. 23-1G). This will permit the clamps to be removed. Put the assembly on a flat surface. Make up the opposite side in the same way, but before the glue has started to set, put the second frame on the first, with jointing surfaces meeting. See that the two assemblies match and are flat. If there is a tendency to distort, put a board and weight over the frame until the glue has set (Fig. 23-1H).

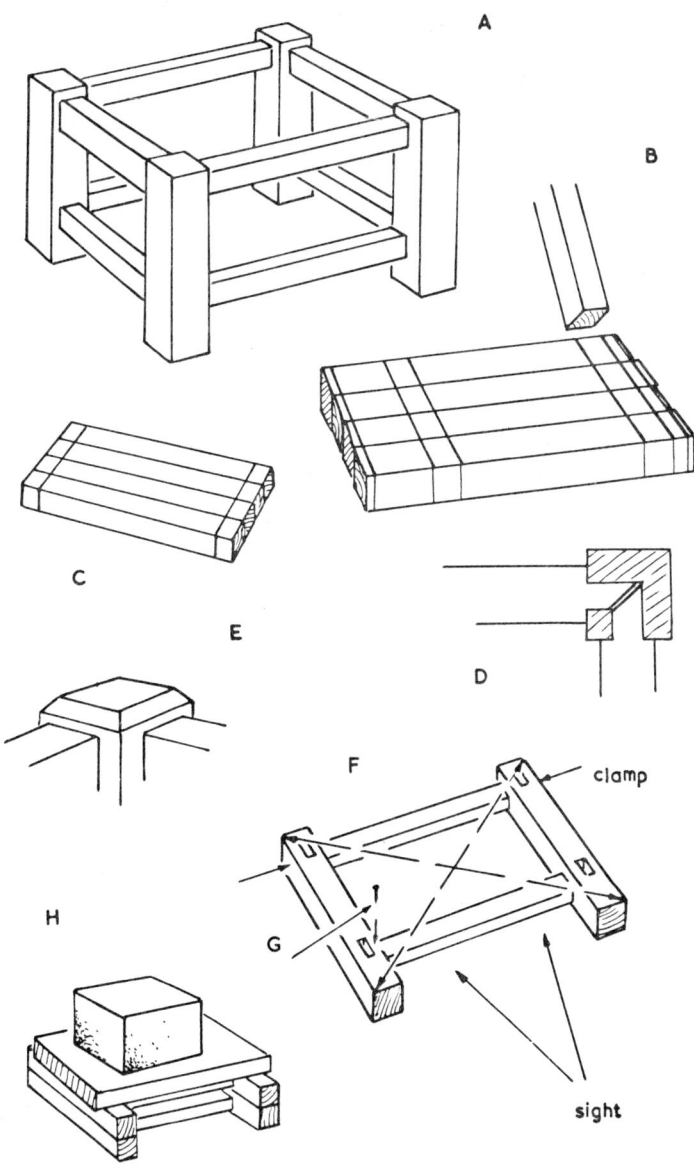

Fig. 23-1. A basic stool frame is the shape of a simple rectangle, but care is needed to make sure parts match and the assembly is square.

Add the rails the other way. Use clamps. Nails may be driven inside again. Check and correct squareness of each side before the glue starts setting. Finally check for squareness and distortion when viewed from above. See that the pattern of the lower rails is not twisted in relation to the top rails, when viewed from above.

Leave the stool frame standing on a level surface until the glue has set. If there is any tendency to twist or distort, put a board on top, with a weight to hold the stool down.

Resistance to wracking strains comes from the depth of the joints, so a rail that is deeper than it is wide may be stronger than a square one of a similar cross-sectional area. Longer, and therefore stronger, tenons on lower rails can be arranged if the joints are staggered (Fig. 23-2A).

Round rails can be used. Their joints are simple to make because only matching holes are needed (Fig. 23-2B), but a rail that is thick enough for the top of a rush seat may need holes so large that the tops of the legs may be weakened. It is more usual to use square tenoned rails at the top and round rails at the bottom. Although prepared dowel rods are convenient, it may be difficult to match wood with the legs so the finish is satisfactory.

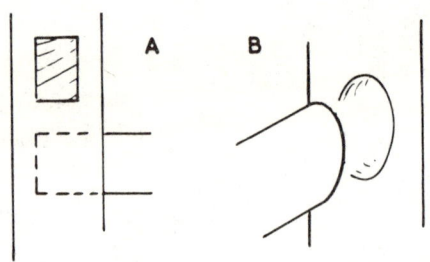

Fig. 23-2. Parts of a stool may be joined with mortise and tenons or dowels.

A single level of rails will be enough for a foot stool, but for a tall stool there should be double rails (Figs. 23-3A and 23-4). Traditional rush seats had rails deeper at the middle and these give a pleasant appearance to a modern version (Fig. 23-3B).

If a lathe is available, legs and rails may be turned (Fig. 23-5), but is is advisable to leave the wood square where joints come, to allow the strongest construction (Fig. 23-3C). A joint into a substantial round leg may be satisfactory, but there is a

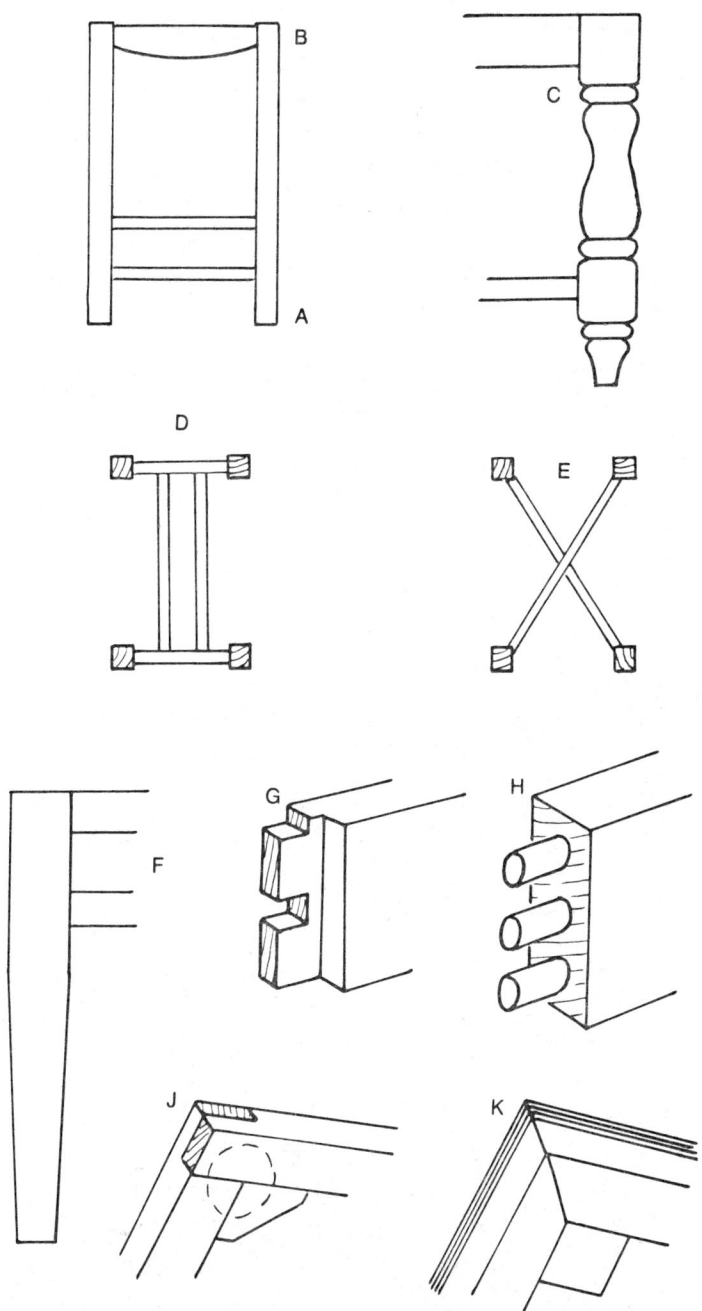

Fig. 23-3. Rails may be arranged in several ways and a solid top can be built up.

loss of glue area compared with a square leg. Rail joints to slender round legs should be avoided.

It is simplest and strongest to let the lower rails go from leg to leg, but other arrangements are possible, such as one or two rails joined into crossing ones (Fig. 23-3D). Allowing rails to cross creates a weaker construction (Fig. 23-3E), so if this pattern is used the size of wood should be adequate.

There is no need for lower rails if the top assembly can provide stiffness in the joints. Normally lower rails could be

Fig. 23-4. A tall stool frame needs double rails to give sufficient stiffness.

taken around fairly close to the top (Fig. 23-3F). If the top is to be upholstered, either on a board or more fully over the rails, the top rails can be quite wide and they will provide stiffness in the joints, whether tenon (Fig. 23-3G) or dowels (Fig. 23-3H). There can be additional support provided by brackets in the corners.

By the nature of its use, a stool may be subject to distorting loads, so legs should usually be braced by rails lower down. A stool that depends only on the top joints should have legs which are sufficiently stiff and not too long.

There are prepared legs of many sorts, such as tapered wood with metal ends, plastic rods with metal trim, or completely metal legs, which are supplied ready to screw under a table or stool top. All that is necessary is a pad of sufficient thickness to take screws. For a stool there should be enough thickness to allow a good looking depth of top. It may be a frame for webbing with corner reinforcements large enough to take the let tops (Fig. 23-3J), then webbing supports the upholstery, or it may be reinforced plywood for latex or foam upholstery (Fig. 23-3K).

OTTOMANS

An ottoman or divan bed may be based on a frame which is really just a box. If it is to rely on a good thickness of latex or foam for cushioning, it may be a sort of inverted box, with a piece of plywood or particle board over a frame that can have a few crossbars for stiffness (Fig. 23-6A). Ideally, corners would be dovetailed, but it is more usual to glue and screw, possibly with a reinforcing block inside (Fig. 23-6B).

If springs are to be used, there may be battens across to support them (Fig. 23-6C). They can go through, preferably with dovetail ends, or be supported on strips inside (Fig. 23-6D). If there are to be corner legs, they can double as reinforcements for the corner joints (Fig. 23-6E).

If the frame is to be a base for a divan bed, it may have to be given rounded corners at one end. These are best made by shaping solid pieces, into which the sides are notched (Fig. 23-6F).

The deeper one of these frames is, the less risk there is of it twisting. If it is more shallow it may twist, possibly only after

Fig. 23-5. If turned legs are used the strongest structure comes from leaving the joint positions square.

being put into use. To guard against this, do all assembly on a truly flat surface and make sure the frame is held flat on this while glue sets. Build in brackets. They may come horizontally in the corners as reinforcements there, but the ones that have greatest resistance to twisting are between battens and the sides (Fig. 23-6G).

For a box ottoman one of these frames, no deeper than is necessary to contain the springs or support foam without twisting, can be hinged over a box (Fig. 23-6H). This may be a fairly small storage box which doubles as a seat, or a full-length divan large enough to be used as an occasional bed. In this sort of construction a finished thickness of 7/8 inch should be regarded as the minimum if distortion is to be avoided. A frame depth of about 4 inches will take adequate springing. If there is a plywood top for foam it could be shallower, but for a bed size it should not be reduced much.

SEAT TOPS

For a lift-out seat, the simplest base is a sheet of plywood or manufactured board. It should not be too thin or it may warp,

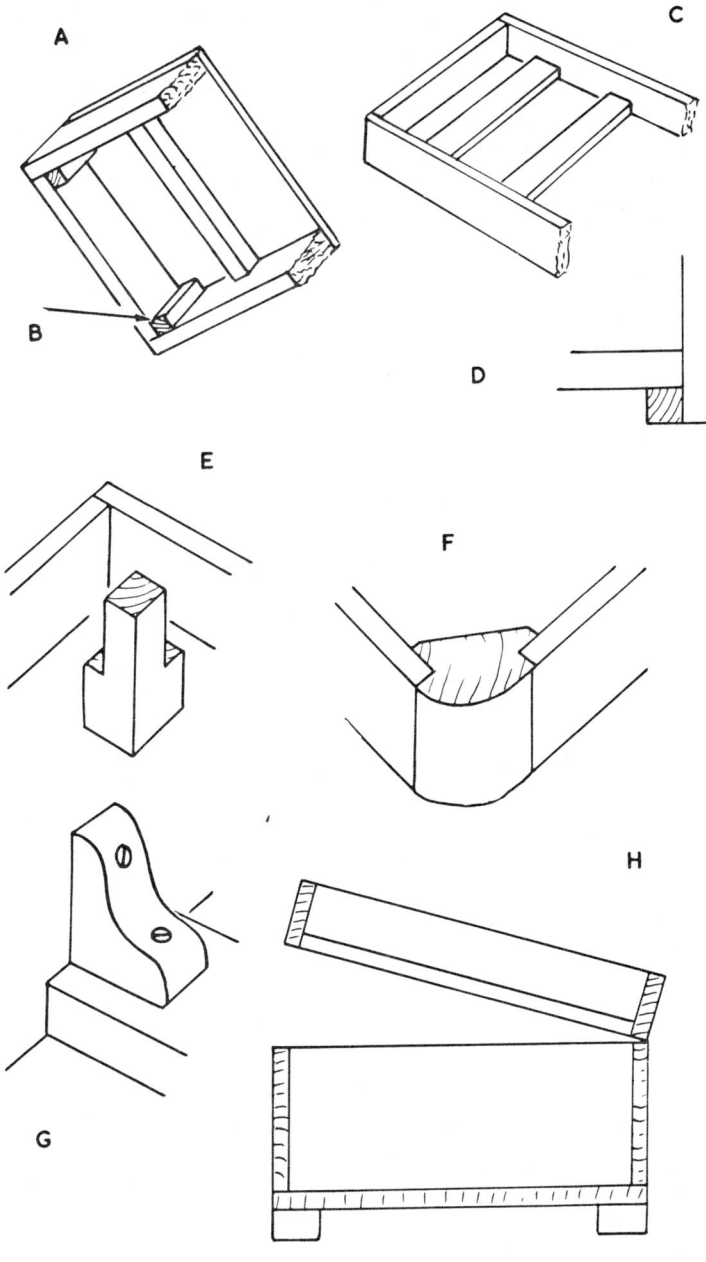

Fig. 23-6. For beds and ottomans a simple box-shaped frame is all that is needed.

even if it is strong enough. One-half inch is the thinnest advisable. The size depends on the place it is to go and the total thickness of cloth to go around it. Round the edges and slightly round the corners. The aim should be to arrive at a size that will just drop in after covering, and be reasonably easy to remove yet tight enough to stay in position during normal handling of the chair. Drill a few holes to allow air in and out of the upholstery (Fig. 23-7A).

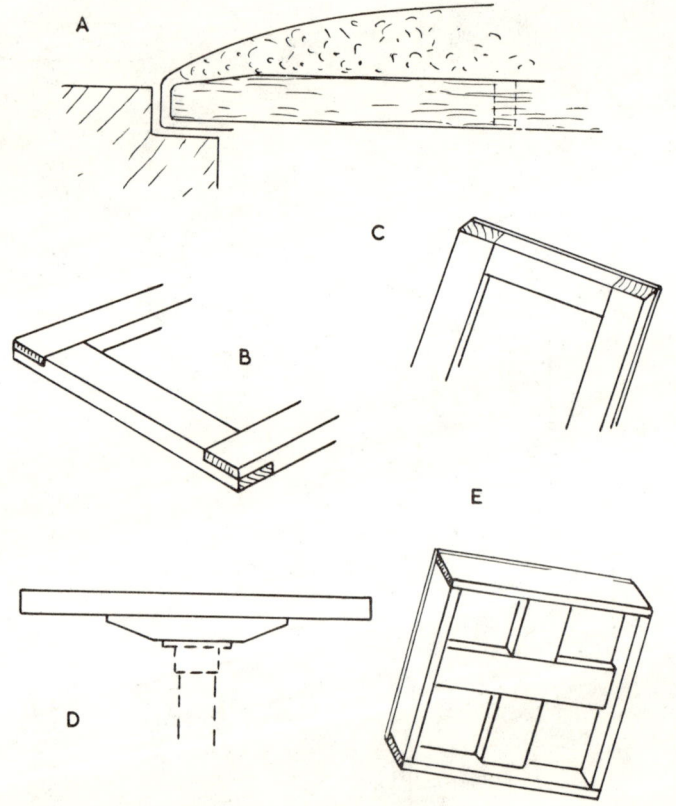

Fig. 23-7. A seat top may be solid, with holes to let air in and out, or built up.

If the seat is to have webbing to support upholstery, the frame cannot usually be very deep so corner joints will probably have to be laps (Fig. 23-7B). Screws can reinforce glue. Round the inner edges so as not to chafe the webbing. The outer size needs the same careful fitting to the chair as described for a plywood seat.

If the seat is fairly large there may have to be a combination of plywood and framing to get stiffness without excessive weight. The plywood can then be thin because the battens around will provide stiffness (Fig. 23-7C). For a revolving stool or chair, the support comes at the center. The whole seat may be a piece of plywood that is thick enough, but it is good design to strengthen the center with a pad, tapered at the edges (Fig. 23-7D). Another way of making the seat stiff enough and give it a great depth around the edges for a more chunky look when upholstered is to frame plywood with cross members for the central attachment (Fig. 23-7E).

24

Open Frames

Lounge and fireside chairs are often only lightly upholstered and the padding may be entirely in the form of removable cushions. If properly shaped and proportioned, such a chair can be very comfortable. It is usually more compact than a fully upholstered chair. As all, or nearly all, of the frame is exposed, it should be made of a hardwood that will take a good finish, and the workmanship needs to be of such a quality that the uncovered wood has a good appearance.

In much covered framing, parts are often fairly wide. In an open frame the sections of wood tend to be rather slimmer as large sections would be ugly. This means that joints are of smaller area, so they need to be close fitting and well made. A light chair tends to get rougher usage than a heavy one, so an open framed lounge chair may have to resist tilting or handling in a way that puts twisting strains on joints.

In a basic side frame there is an arm, of perhaps 2 1/2 inches by 1 1/2 inches section, with front and rear uprights a little over 1 1/2 inches square. Stiffness is obtained by making the seat rail fairly wide—possibly 4 inches by 1 1/4 inches in section (Fig. 24-1A).

There could be mortise and tenon joints at all meetings, but if dowels are used there should be two where legs meet the arm (Fig. 24-1B). They are easy to mark accurately if they are in line with each other, but there might be more strength if they are set diagonally (Fig. 24-1C). One aid for marking dowel positions from one piece on to another is a turned pointed plug that fits into a hole and will accurately locate a center on another piece when they are pressed together (Fig. 24-1D).

There should be at least three dowels between the seat rail and the legs and they should be taken as deeply into both parts as the wood will allow without risk of splitting or breaking through (Fig. 24-1E). The two sides should be made as a matched pair, with one assembled over the other.

Strength in the width is provided mainly by back and front seat rails, usually of similar section to the side seat rails and dowelled to the legs or to the side rails (Fig. 24-1F). Whether there are lower rails and how they are designed depends on the height and construction of the seat. A low seat with seat rails of good depth and stout legs does not need lower rails. They would not look right in any case. Sides should be checked for squareness during assembly and the glue should be allowed to set with the sides under weights to prevent twist. Squareness should be checked when cross rails are fitted. If legs do not stand upright any error will be very obvious to casual viewers. Check also that the assembly is symmetrical in the plan view. This type of chair usually has parallel sides, but it could be wider at the front than the back.

A simple back consists of a flat frame to take webbing or zig-zag springing (Fig. 24-1G). The corners are lapped and screwed. This has to be supported at an angle. Users have different ideas about the angle of a seat back, which is why many of these chairs have adjustable backs. A compromise angle may have to be found by experiment, but a slope of 15 degrees from the vertical is about right. The lower part of the frame goes behind a rear seat rail that may be set forward of the legs (Fig. 24-1H) and rests against a top rail that may be joined to extended arms or let into the rear uprights (Fig. 24-1J). The strain on a back may sometimes be considerable, so joints should be strong and the greatest resistance to leverage is obtained by having the upper support as far above the lower attachment as the design will allow.

Such a chair, with straight lines and little in the way of embellishment, may be acceptable and can look quite attractive

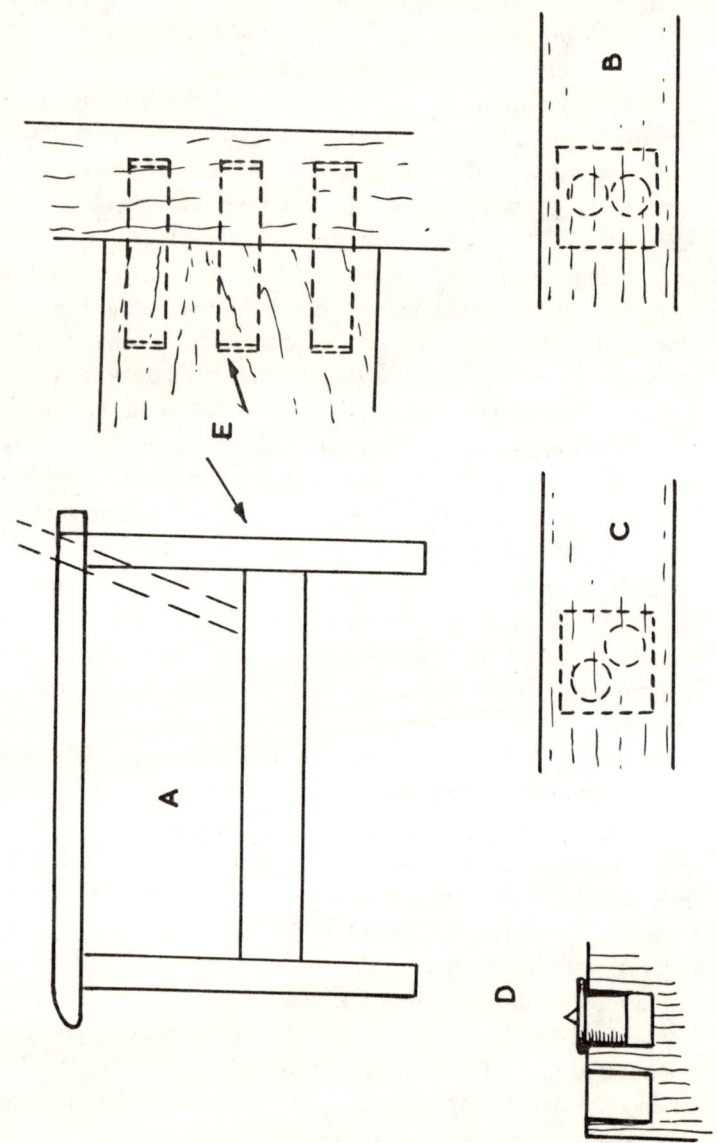

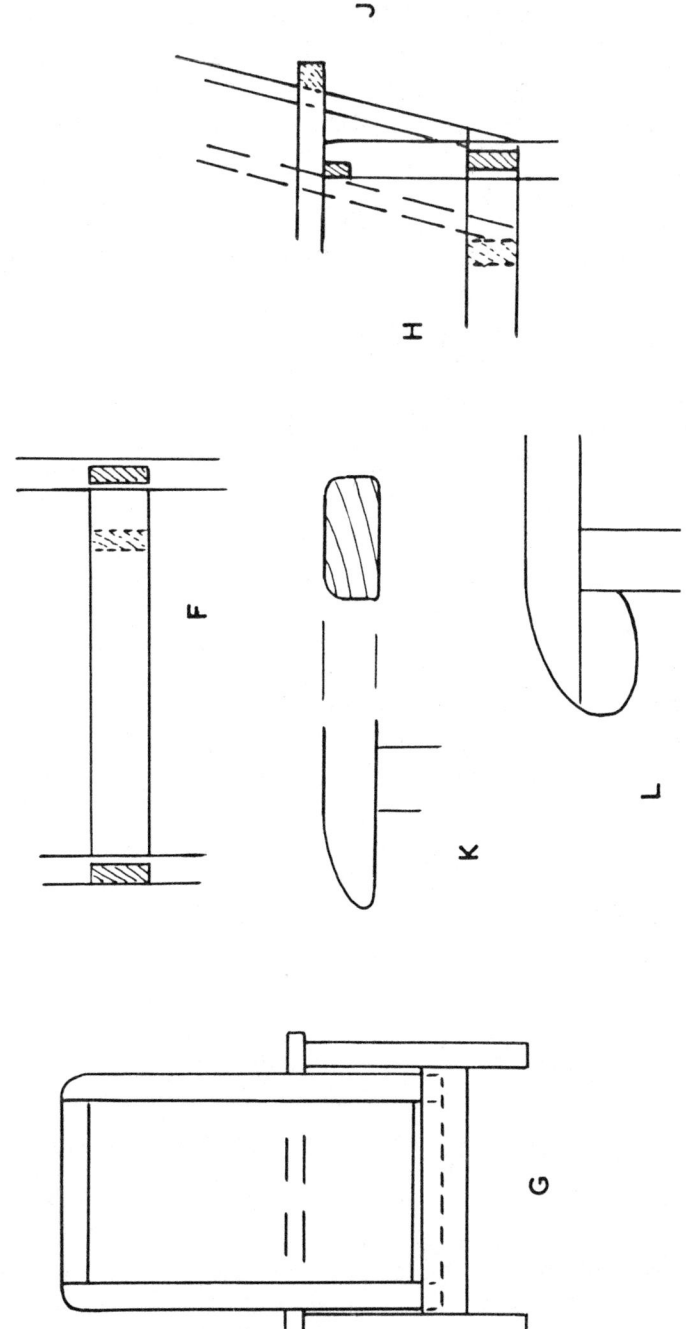

Fig. 24-1. A simple lounge chair can have straight lines and rely on cushioning to provide comfort.

in the right setting, particularly if the two cushions have patterned coverings to match surroundings. If thick foam or latex cushions are used, it may be satisfactory to merely have plywood panels over seat and back, but a more comfortable chair will result if the back has webbing or zig-zag springs and the seat has tension springs or rubber webbing. The type of springing has to be considered and allowed for in construction. The wood may have to be grooved or rabbetted before assembly to suit the method of attachment.

Even in a severely plain chair there have to be concessions to comfort. The arms should be well rounded on top and at the forward ends (Fig. 24-1K), which could also be thickened (Fig. 24-1L). Other edges should be rounded to varying degrees. There should be no sharp edges on which stockings might be snagged and parts that may be handled should be rounded more.

There are many possible variations on the basic design, but sizes should be considered. A dining chair with a top that does not compress much may have its seat about 16 inches from the floor. A lounge chair needs to be lower, but since there may be 4 inches or more of cushioning that will compress when sat on, the height of the rigid part of the seat is not so easy to settle. Something like 12 inches at the front is reasonable, although some people may not want to sink too low because of the difficulty in rising. There should be plenty of seat area, permitting some movement on the cushions, and 20 inches square between legs may be enough. In some of these chairs the back may not be intended to give head support, but where this is required the back will have to be about 30 inches above the seat frame (Fig. 24-2A).

The seat cushion may finish in line with the front legs, but there can be a supporting frame resting on the crosswise seat rails and projecting forward a little (Fig. 24-2B). These seats are often horizontal, but it is more natural to have the back a little lower than the front—1 1/2 inches in 20 inches should be enough (Fig. 24-2C).

Legs and arms can be shaped in many ways. A leg can keep its full width at joints and be curved away (Fig. 24-2D). The arm may be its full depth at joints and be made thinner elsewhere. It may be shaped in plan view as well (Fig. 24-2E); then the whole

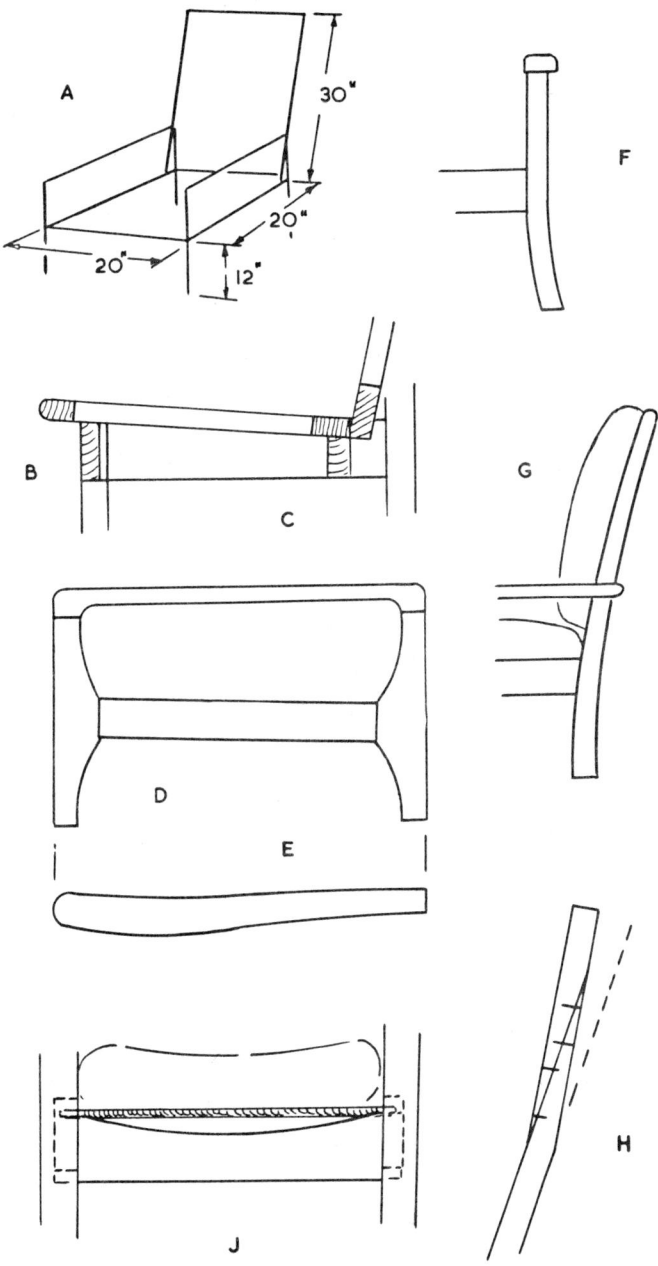

Fig. 24-2. A lounge chair should be properly proportioned and the straight line shape can be modified with curves.

section may be well rounded away from the joints, where the parts blend into each other.

If a band saw or other saw for curves is available, the legs may be cut to curves. The front legs can flare outwards (Fig. 24-2F). The rear legs can be cut so they continue upwards to form the back (Fig. 24-2G). So far as possible choose wood with grain that will follow the shape. Avoid cutting into so many lines of grain that only weak cross grain is left.

The back does not have to be flat. Head support slightly forward of that at shoulder level may be allowed by the upholstery, although it is possible to either cut the back frame sides to curves or splice the straight sides (Fig. 24-2H). The difference in angle need not be much. The splices are then quite long and the glue may be supplemented with screws. A variation would be to make the top slightly narrower by sloping in the spliced pieces.

A rigid support under the front of the seat may press through and be felt as a hard edge. Springs or webbing will give under the user's weight and the inflexible edge felt, despite the thickness of cushioning. If springs or webbing are front to back nothing can be done about it, but if tension springs or rubber webbing is used across, the top edge of the front rail can be curved to provide clearance (Fig. 24-2J). This puts more load on the front springs, which should be as close to the rail as possible. There may have to be two which are close together.

ARMLESS CHAIRS

A low chair without arms is convenient for many uses besides just lounging. It allows a mother to deal with a baby in comfort and anyone working at a task like using a typewriter on the knees or sewing a sail has freedom of movement coupled with comfort. The problem for the framemaker is getting a strong enough joint between back and seat without the aid that would be given by arms. Fortunately modern glues have considerable strength in correctly formed joints, but where the wood is of very light section there may have to be some metal bracket for reinforcement.

A typical chair has lift-out cushions, which may be located and retained by studs, and the cushions may fit between the sides, rather than on them (Fig. 24-3A). Tension springs can be

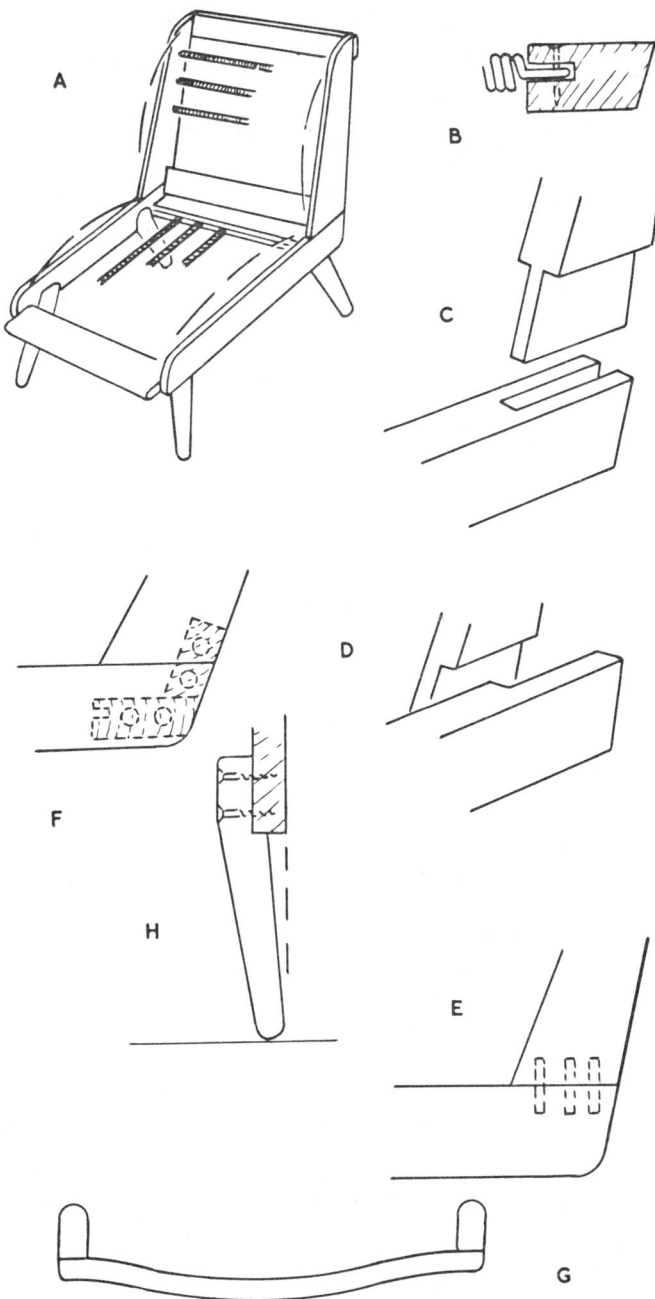

Fig. 24-3. The joint between back and side rails is very important.

arranged front to back under the seat and across the back. Grooves in front and back seat rails will take the spring ends (Fig. 24-3B). Springs across the back may be fixed in the same way, or the spring ends can go into individual holes and screws be driven from the back.

The important part of the construction is the joint between the back and side rails. If the parts are thick enough, there may be a bridle joint (Fig. 24-3C). A glued and screwed lap joint (Fig. 24-3D) is possible, or three dowels (Fig. 24-3E) should be strong enough if the joint is carefully fitted. Cross members are dowelled into the side assemblies (Fig. 24-3F). As the cushions fit

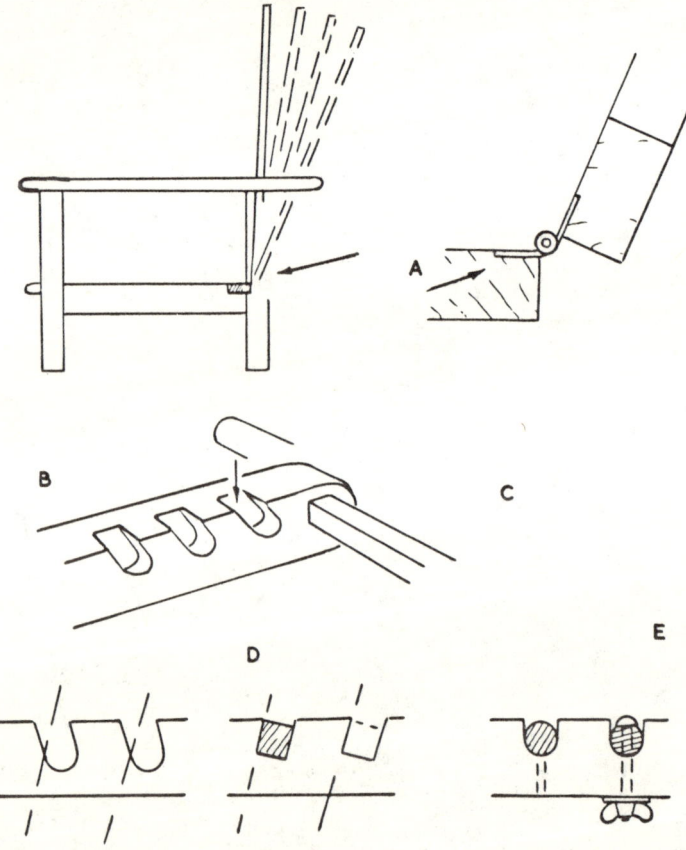

Fig. 24-4. An adjustable back on a lounge chair needs a strut to drop into slots behind the seat.

between the sides the top cross member should be kept to the back and may even be packed out from the sides. If it can be curved, that will make for more comfort (Fig. 24-3G).

Legs may be tapered flat or they may be turned ones, fitted by notching to go inside the seat frame where they are fixed with glue and screws (Fig. 24-3H). As with an arm chair, all exposed wood should be well rounded. The top of the sides of the back and the fronts of the seat sides may be given some decorative shaping, but otherwise the wood parts are plain and thoroughly sanded before staining and varnishing or polishing.

ADJUSTMENTS

A lounge chair may be given an adjustable back or there may be an adjustable leg support. The back frame can be hinged to the rear seat rail (Fig. 24-4A). There are metal fittings for providing adjustment, but there can be a rail behind the back that drops into sockets in extended arms (Fig. 24-4B). As a safety precaution there may be a permanent rail, so the back cannot drop completely (Fig. 24-4C). The notches should be angled or arranged so there is little risk of the adjusting rail lifting out accidentally (Fig. 24-4D). If adjustment will be rare, you can use nuts and bolts (Fig. 24-4E).

A leg support may be a flap that is hinged to the front seat rail, usually with a padded top. Its width is limited by the height it can hang down when out of use. It may be given a strut that folds back underneath.

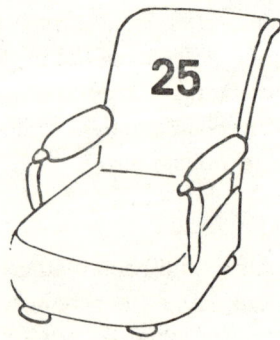

25

Enclosed Frames

For a fully upholstered chair or other piece of furniture not much of the frame is visible in the finished work. This means that the quality of finish on the hidden parts is not important, although smoothness and rounding of certain edges may be advisable where parts of the filling are met, or the outline of the wood may affect the smoothness or shape of the outer covering. It may be possible to use wood that has flaws affecting appearance so it would be unsuitable for an exterior part.

Another consideration is strength. After covering has been finished it may be very difficult to get at the frame again to make a repair. This means that the wood used must be sound and free from flaws that affect strength. It should have been properly seasoned because wood drying out after being built into a chair may warp with enough power to affect the shape of the chair. Joints also have to be strong enough to withstand the anticipated loads. This really means giving the joints more than what is considered just enough strength. You don't want to risk failure in use, because getting at a broken joint may mean dismantling the covering possibly to the stage of wrecking it.

In old frames most of the joints were variations on the mortise and tenon. This is still a good method of jointing. Most newer frames have dowelled joints, however. These are easier to make in most locations because they lend themselves to power drilling and the use of prepared dowel rods. The strength of dowels lies in their fit and in the glue area presented by their surfaces, particularly where the side grain of the dowel meets the side grain of the hole. End grain does not hold as well, although it contributes something to the total strength. These points should be remembered when planning a joint to have enough strength.

Larger diameter dowels have better glue areas than smaller ones and the more dowels that can be included in a joint without cutting away so much wood that it is weakened, the stronger should be the joint. There are many types of glue and almost any woodworking glue can be used, but one of the two-part synthetic resins will produce the strongest joints. It will also have the greatest resistance to moisture. This aspect may not have much bearing on its choice in most circumstances, although if a damp atmosphere may be expected, as in yacht furnishings, it is a valuable property to have.

It may be possible to reinforce a hidden joint in a way that would not be acceptable for an open visible frame. Pieces meeting edgewise may be dowelled and a strip may be glued and screwed below to provide more strength (Fig. 25-1A) if the reinforcing piece would not project or affect the appearance of the covering. Brackets can be used. They may be metal angle braces (Fig. 25-1B) or shaped blocks of wood (Fig. 25-1C). Metal brackets project less, but wood brackets can be glued as well as screwed. Where two flat parts meet, the thickness may not be enough to make a very strong joint unaided, but a block can be glued and screwed inside the angle (Fig. 25-1D). It can be kept short and its ends rounded if there is a risk that it might affect the shape of filling and covering.

In some furniture it is only the short legs or feet that are visible wood parts. If they are part of the overall structure, they will provide strength and this is a good method of construction; but the frame has to be made so these parts will have the required shape and finish, yet be part of a longer piece of wood that is enclosed and therefore need not be completed to the same quality.

More often in modern furniture the feet project only a small amount and are separate parts. In this case there is an opportun-

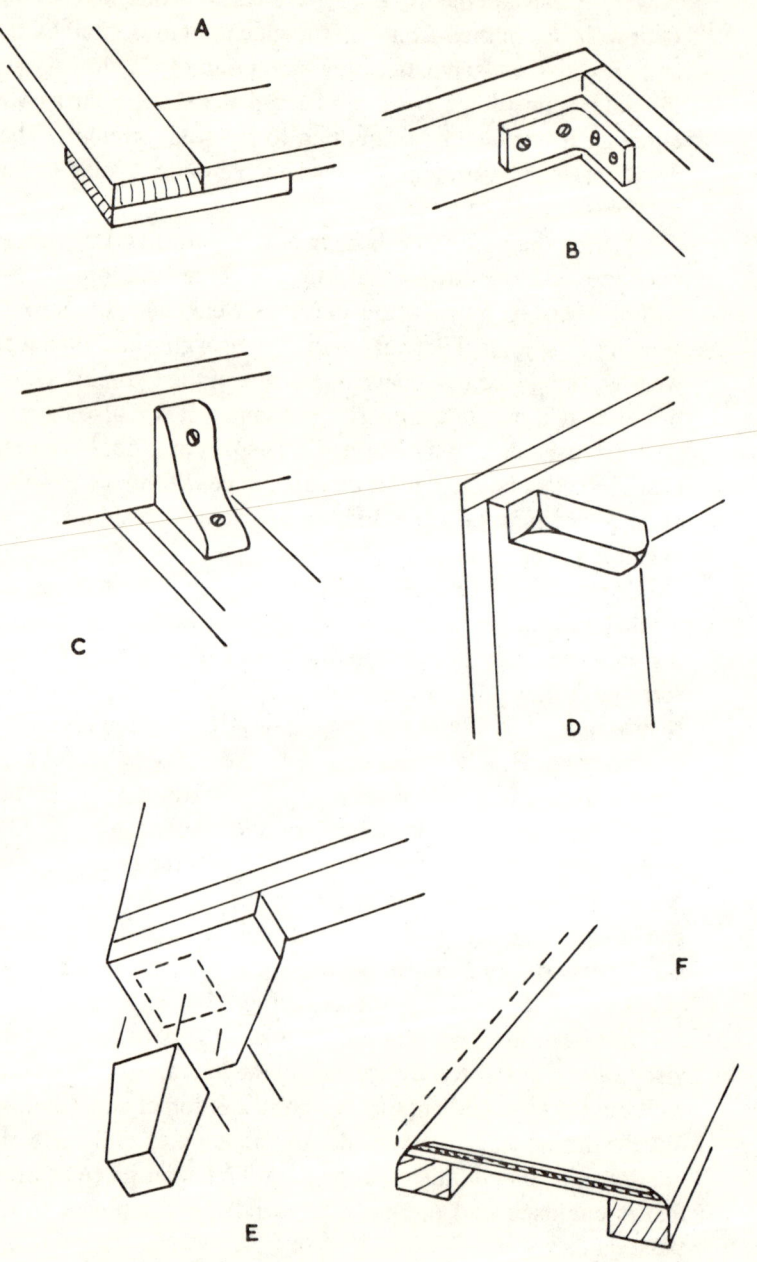

Fig. 25-1. A frame that will be hidden can be reinforced in many ways without affecting its appearance.

ity to brace the frame with a pad that supports the feet. The pad can extend a short distance each way and be cut diagonally across the corner (Fig. 25-1E). The turned or block foot fixes below. If necessary, the outer edges of the pad may be rounded so the edge line of the frame is not affected.

CURVED PARTS

At one time many frames had several curved parts. A frame with single or double curvature can certainly conform better to the shape of the user, but modern frames use more straight lines and rely on the thickness of the upholstery to adapt to body shape and provide comfort. In the days when wood was cheaper and waste could be tolerated a double-curved piece was cut from solid wood, with the finished piece being perhaps less in bulk than the parts cut away and scrapped.

In some frames there are still curves to be included. This is seen in arms and backs. In commercial production the shape may be made with a band saw of sufficient capacity, but the individual worker is unlikely to have a band saw with the required capacity of upwards of 4 inches, and a different method is needed.

With strong, modern glues it is possible to build up and laminate wood parts in ways that are cheaper and often stronger than cutting from solid wood. Plywood can sometimes be used to provide strength and lightness. A chair arm that requires considerable curve at the edges may be made with plywood on battens (Fig. 25-1F), either with glue only or supplemented by a few nails. Keep these clear of the parts that will be curved and make sure there is solid wood where tacks will be driven later.

For moderate curves in the length of a piece of wood, parts may be glued to give enough thickness at the shaped parts (Fig. 25-2A). Edges underneath may have to be cut back so there are no undesirable projections. This method lends itself to joints to other parts as it provides flat meeting surfaces. When the curve has been made in the built-up direction, there can be shaping in the other direction if the design requires it, but be careful that there is enough remaining overlap of the glued joints after the second shaping. Although modern glues make a very strong bond, it is advisable to allow them a good area of contact.

Another way of producing a shaped part is by laminating. This can be several thicknesses of thin wood or even pieces of plywood. They have to be bent around a form or mold and clamped to it while the glue sets. The method also ensures two or more parts matching. Even with one chair there will probably be two matching curved parts and with several, uniformity of shape is important.

The former is made from fairly stout wood that will resist bending. Except for the surface where the laminations will come, it can be quite rough, but it should be of a thickness that will allow C clamps to span it. It can be built up (Fig. 25-2B). Work the surface to the curve required and check that it is flat across. Make it a little longer than the finished parts will be so they can be assembled and trimmed to length after curving.

If solid wood is used, it should be thin enough to bend fairly easily. For moderate curves most woods 1/2 inch thick will do. Let the finished part have at least three laminations. Coat the parts with glue and clamp to the former. Have wood pads under the clamps. For a wide piece have a clamp each side, at each position (Fig. 25-2C). Paper may be put between the first layer and the former to prevent any glue that oozes out from sticking these parts together. Leave the clamps on until the glue has set hard. With some two-part synthetic glues, first setting may be in a few hours, but greatest strength builds up over a day or more. If there is no urgency, leave the clamps on for this time.

This method is particularly suitable for chair arms or shaped back uprights. It can also be used for a curved chair back. A laminated part is then much stronger than a piece cut from the solid or built up by pieces dowelled together. For this sort of shape, which has a section approximately square (Fig. 25-2D), it is convenient to make the mold on a base that projects and guides the strips as they are bent (Fig. 25-2E). Clamps may be used, or it is possible to use wedges to supplement or take the place of clamps (Fig. 25-2F). As with other laminations, make the former and the strips longer than the final length around the curve, to allow for trimming after making.

Another semi-laminating method sometimes has uses if a part has to be straight for most of its length but there is a curve at the end, as with an arm that sweeps up to blend into the back. One way of dealing with this is to splice on a curved part cut

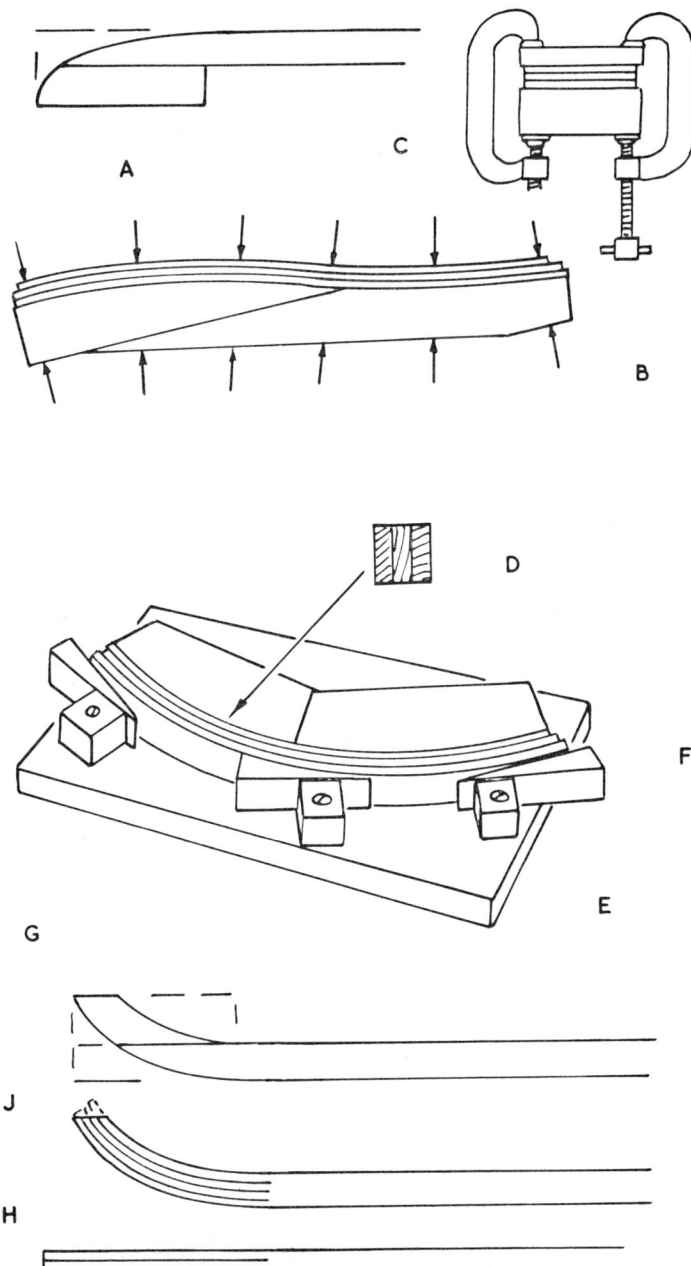

Fig. 25-2. A shaped part can be built up or made by laminating strips around a former. It can also be given a curve after making several saw cuts in its end.

from solid wood (Fig. 25-2G), but another way is to make several saw cuts lengthwise (Fig. 25-2H), then put glue in the cuts and pull the wood around a former (Fig. 25-2J). Clamp the straight part as well as the curve, so it does not distort; otherwise the bending strains tend to put a slight curve in the uncut part as well.

FRAME DESIGN

A frame has to provide a basic shape, but it also has to be planned to provide strength and rigidity. The two requirements have to be related in a good design. Four narrow pieces of wood making up a frame will have very little joint area at the corners, even if they would give the required shape. A diagonal brace across them might give stiffness, or a plywood panel included would steady them, but in many designs this would not suit the method of upholstery, so strength has to come in other ways.

In a typical modern frame the front and top of an arm are wide, but not very thick. Their breadth provides resistance to sideways loads, but there is not much resistance to downward or tilting loads (Fig. 25-3A). If a side rail can be made fairly deep and maybe a gut rail provided as well (Fig. 25-3B), the ample depth of joints gives the needed stiffness to resist tilting and downward loads. Similar considerations come into the layout of lengthwise members. There is usually a deep front rail (Fig. 25-3C) that gives some bracing effect due to the broad joints. There may be a similar back rail, and a bottom rail to the gut rails also contributes strenght as well as shape (Fig. 25-3D). So far there is little resistance to the whole assembly pushing out of shape in the direction viewes from above. There can be rails underneath (Fig. 25-3E) and corner brackets where they can be arranged without interfering with covering (Fig. 25-3F).

There are other ways of making up frames, but the considerations quoted should be kept in mind when planning a special chair or other enclosed frame. Usually the finished shape has to be visualized, then the skeleton that suits the body planned so it will support and strengthen as well as give shape.

The first departure from straight lines usually comes in the arms, which may have tapered fronts and rounded as well as tapered tops (Fig. 25-4A). The front may be brought forward

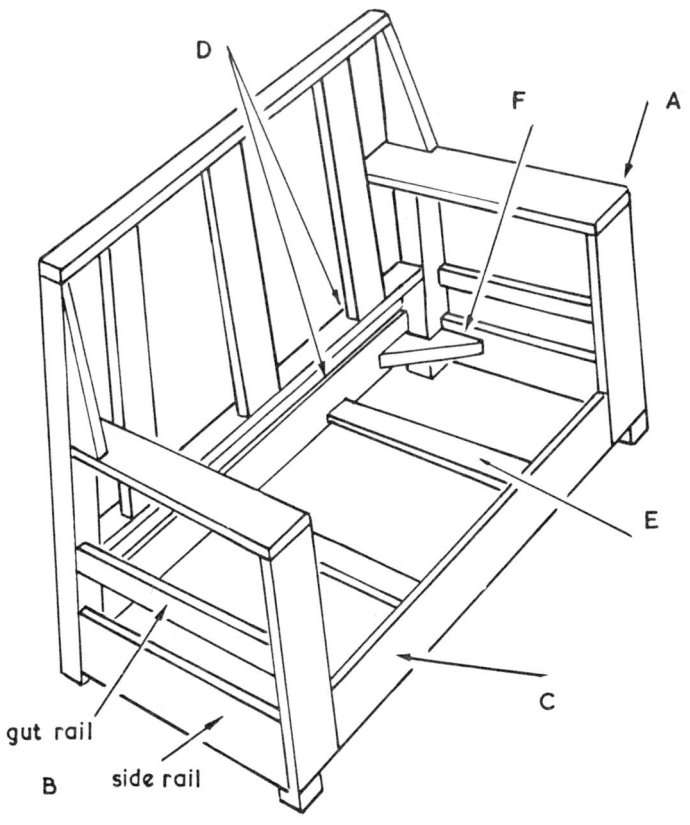

Fig. 25-3. Not all frames are straight, as in this example, but the method of assembly is very similar.

and two rails may take the place of the simpler front rail (Fig. 25-4B). Gut rails can be doubled and there are two rails at the back to suit the method of covering (Fig. 25-4C). In this case the back is straight, but there could be shaping to the top. Wood brackets are included for stiffness.

Wings add complications, but can contribute stiffness (Fig. 25-5A). They are dowelled to the arms and the rear uprights, with another joint between their two parts. This gives the shape usual in modern furniture, but in traditional and reproduction pieces there may be a double curvature as well. With straight wings a curve to the top back rail is appropriate (Fig. 25-5B). In such a chair on short legs there may not be a very good oppor-

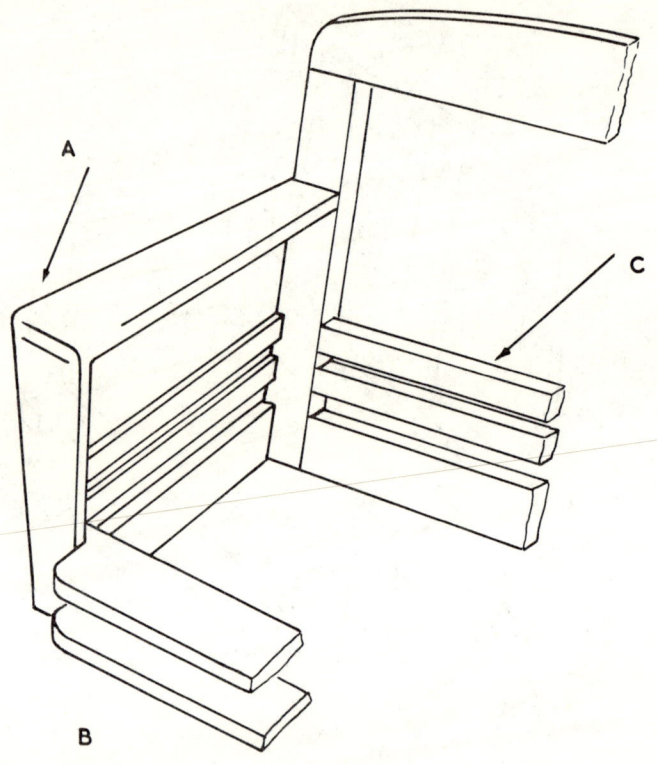

Fig. 25-4. A chair frame can be given shape with tapered arms and a curved back, as well as an extended front.

tunity to brace back to front with deep rails. In this case strength in that direction is provided by a solid filling towards the back at each side (Fig. 25-5C). This does not interfere with the covering nor lie in a position where it could be felt by the user. There is a deep front rail, but another way of carrying the seat forward is achieved by using plywood sprung over shaped blocks (Fig. 25-5D).

If a traditional frame is examined it will be seen to have many more curves. Front legs were mostly more decorative and these did not usually continue up to form the arm fronts (Fig. 25-6A). This meant that the main frame was often comparable to a stool and the rest of the frame was built up on that. Arm fronts were curved in several ways (Fig. 25-6B and C), but were never

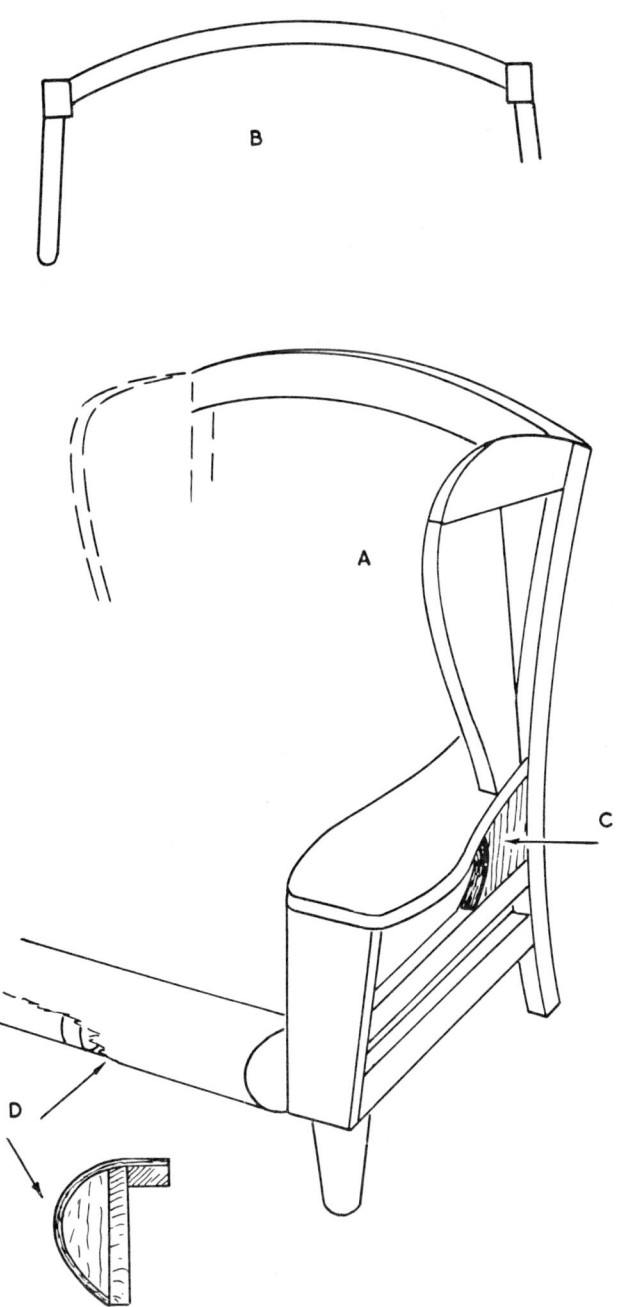

Fig. 25-5. Wings add comfort and quality to a chair. The front edges can be rolled instead of extending flat.

straight. Back legs always curved (Fig. 25-6D), but might be plainer than the front legs. There may be some straight parts in a frame, but in this type of seat almost every wood part has some curve. If reproduction furniture is to be authentic there has to be shaping and this means mainly bandsawing from solid wood, with subsequent waste.

Sizes and details of construction depend on many factors. Seat height is related to its size. With a large seat the user leans back more and is more comfortable in a lower seat than if the size of the seat had made a more upright posture desirable. Where the dining chair has a small area and a seat height between 15 inches and 17 inches, chairs intended for relaxation get lower at the front as the depth from front to back gets greater, down to 13 inches or so. This is to the height of the compressed upholstery and is only an estimate for average circumstances, but the rigid frame front will be several inches lower than this. To a lesser extent the arm height has to be related to the seating posture in the same way. If there is much padding on the arms, the amount of compression has to be estimated. The arms are usually about 12 inches above the seat level. Heights of backs vary from quite low, with minimum body support in some modern chairs, to about 30 inches above the seat level if good head support is to be given. Anyone unused to chair designing should take a few measurements from a chair intended for the same purpose, although not necessarily of the same design as that intended.

Open framed lounge chairs do not differ much in their requirements, so the same basic parts occur, even if there are many differences in overall design. For a fully upholstered chair the frame details may have a general similarity, but it is necessary to consider how the upholstery is to be done as this will affect the layout of wood parts. If it is necessary to drive a row of tacks anywhere at the upholstery stage, it is obviously important that there should be wood in the right place to take them. If arms are to have springs, the frame must allow for this so the finished covering takes the right form and comes to the right height. The covering material for seat, arms, and back has to be fixed to frame parts in the correct relation to each other, so wood has to be correctly located. If the filling is to be mainly

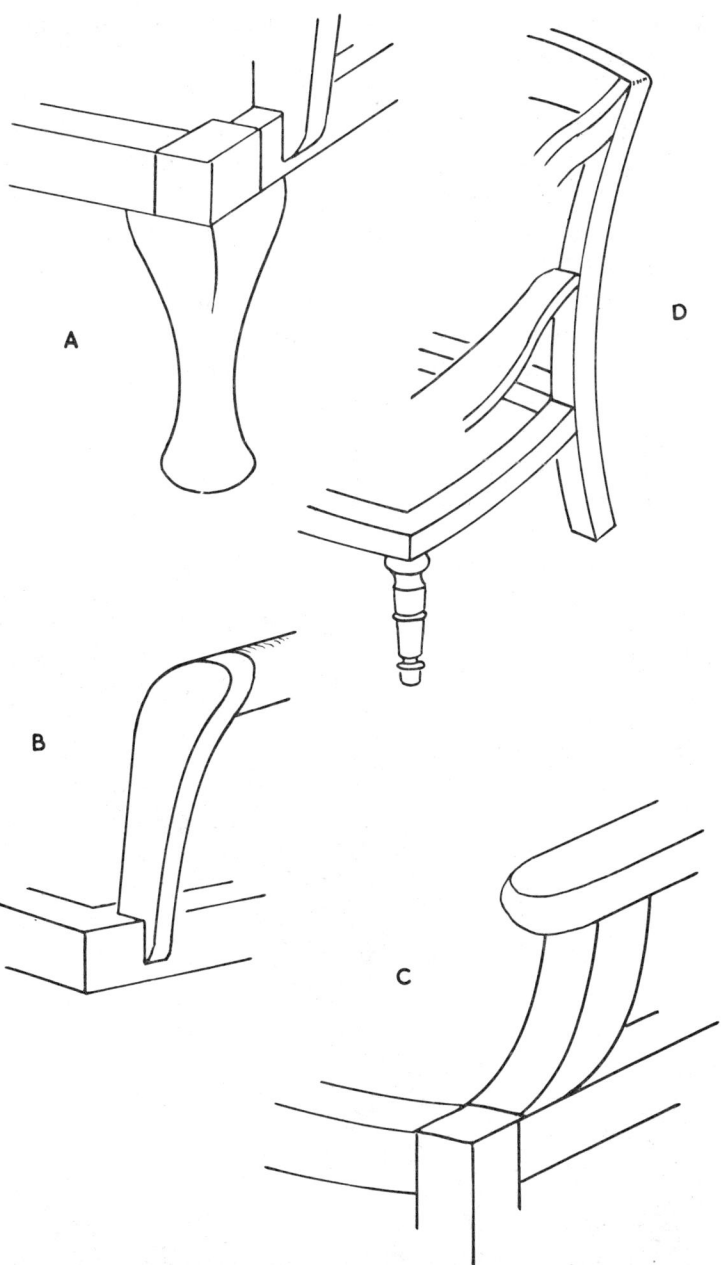

Fig. 25-6. Many traditional chair frames had the legs fixed to the seat and the other parts built up on that. Many styles of curving parts and arm fronts were used.

made of foam or latex, the layout of some frame parts will be different from, and more simply arranged than if, springs and traditional fillings and coverings are to be used.

The type of support or springing needs to be settled fairly early in designing a frame as it is simple enough to groove or rabbet parts when they are merely lengths of wood on the bench, but difficult or impossible to do if the need is only realized after the part has been joined to other parts.

Polystyrene, fiberglass, and similar seats that come as a complete molded shape need very little preparation for covering and there is really nothing that can be done if the standard shape does not satisfy you. This is not a type of material that permits modification, certainly not by cutting away, as the surface then exposed may crumble or be otherwise unsuitable (Fig. 25-7).

Some of these molded seats need a solid wood or plywood base to fit to the supporting pedestal and this is the only prepara-

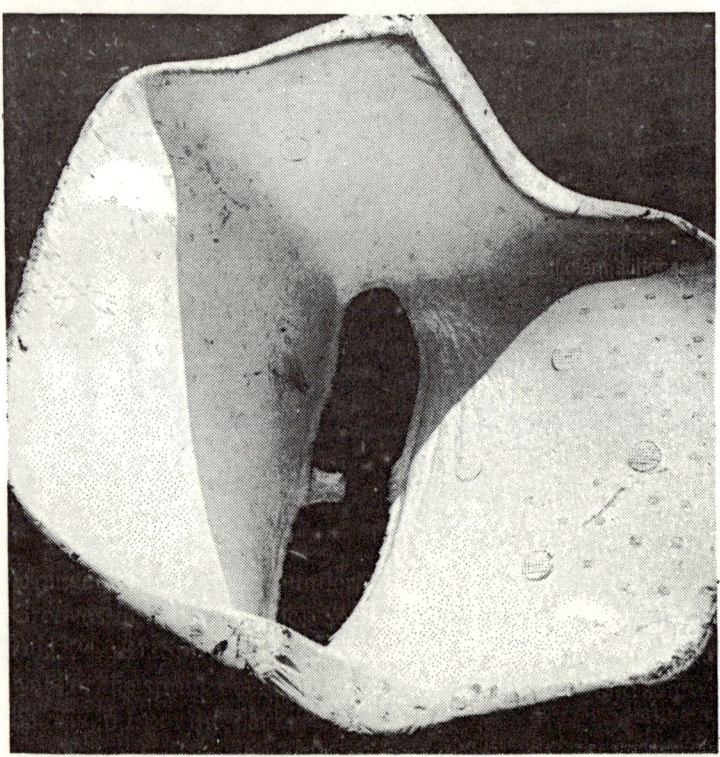

Fig. 25-7. A molded foam seat is complete to the final shape and does not permit modifications.

tion to be done before covering. How it is fitted depends on the design. There may be built-in bolts or sockets to take screws. If a glue has to be used, make sure it is compatible with the type of plastic used in molding the seat. With some types of expanded foam there is a risk of some adhesives dissolving the material. Check the instructions with the seat and adhesive.

As the frame has to be related to the method of covering and the type of filling and padding used, the design of a closed frame must be considered in relation to the upholstery which is to follow, so the information in this chapter should be read in conjunction with that in Chapters 11 to 16.

Making a frame from first principles is an interesting project, but there are many considerations, both in design and construction, that may not come right the first time. A beginner may therefore find it rewarding to first use old frames that can be repaired or altered. New frames can be made later based on the experience gained. Information on this approach is given in Chapter 27.

26

Wood Finishing

Most upholstered furniture has a part of the woodwork exposed. In some chairs with removable cushions or lift-out seats almost all of the wood of the frame is visible at some time. In a very fully upholstered chair there may be little more than some small projecting feet. Although the finish of the wood, on a piece where the upholstered part does not make up much of the whole, may be considered the responsibility of another craftsman, an upholsterer still needs to know about wood finishing. He may wish to see a whole project through from the making of a frame to the finishing of it, as well as the upholstering of it. He may need to renovate damaged exposed wood or he may have to complete the finishing of exposed wood parts after upholstering.

What makes the predominant feature has to be considered. If the chair is almost completely upholstered, the short lengths of legs or feet will not attract much attention. The general design of the upholstered parts and the pattern of the fabric are what attract the eyes. Providing that the finish on the wood is not in glaring contrast, its quality is not so important. Obviously, a finish should be as good as possible, but a few inches at floor level need not be up to the standard of a large expanse of wood at a higher level. If the chair has little upholstery—maybe a lift-out seat and a small cushioned back—the wood plays a much larger part in the visual effect. It may have to match other wood furniture. In any case, its coloring and polish are the prime motifs and much more attention may have to be given to preparing and finishing the wood.

The most important step in a wood finish is the preparation of the surface before applying the finishing material. It is possible to build up what amounts to a new surface to work on if it is to be covered with opaque paint, but most furniture has a transparent or translucent finish and the wood grain shows through, so the best finish is obtained when the wood surface is as near perfect as it can be made.

Most wood used in furniture frames is close-grained hardwood. Hardwoods will take a better surface than the open-grained softwoods, although the hardwoods may need more physical effort.

Sawn wood leaves a coarse surface, which is smoothed by planing. If the wood is machine-planed slowly over a sharp blade, the finish may be quite good; but if the blade is blunt or the wood is pushed quickly over it, the surface may have a pattern of marks across the grain. Ideally, machine planing is followed by hand planing, but in a frame already assembled this may not be possible. Very thorough sanding is then needed. The marks may not be obvious until a gloss finish has been applied, so looking at the surface with a cross light or trying a finish on a hidden part may be advisable where there is doubt.

If wood is hand planed, the tool should be finely set and sharp. Most grain has a tendency to tear up when planed one way, so if the first stroke does not produce a smooth surface, plane the other way. With difficult grain it is a help to use the plane diagonally, so the cutting edge travels at an angle with a slicing action. Be careful of the risk of end grain breaking out. If end grain is exposed in a joint, plane from the edge, not towards it (Fig. 26-1).

Much of the beauty of wood lies in its irregular grain, so a piece may be selected to show the twisted pattern on the surface. With some woods, this may not plane smooth in any direction. The tool to use then is a scraper. There are hooked scrapers with replaceable blades, which are pulled over the surface, but the expert cabinetmaker favors a flat steel scraper.

Fig. 26-1. End grain should be planed in a direction that will not break out.

This is a piece of saw steel with its edge turned over. A new edge or a badly worn one may be filed true and rubbed on an oilstone (Fig. 26-2). Use a piece of hard steel, such as a chisel or gouge,

Fig. 26-2. Difficult grain is better finished with a scraper used as shown.

to rub along the edge hard and at a slight angle (Fig. 26-3A). This turns over a fine cutting edge. When this is pushed at an angle over the wood (Fig. 26-3B) it takes off much finer shavings than a plane, with no risk of tearing up a confused grain. It is usual to hold the scraper with both hands, using the thumbs to force it to a slight curve as it is pushed forward (Fig. 26-4). Although much preparation of furniture wood can be done by sanding, a scraper is a useful tool to have.

Plywood is made by gluing veneers at right angles to each other. These veneers are cut like shavings from a rotating log and then flattened. This means that in some woods the grain can be very open when made into plywood. The surface has usually been power sanded during manufacture, but in some cases there are many tiny fibers that may stand up and spoil a finish. More sanding may merely bend them, and scraping is a better treatment.

SANDING

The process usually called *sanding* is a carry-over from the distant past when sand was used. Modern abrasive paper and cloth may be coated with glass, garnet, or other natural grit, or by a manufactured grit. Some abrasive paper is intended for materials other than wood. Avoid this type. Otherwise it is the grade that may be more important than the actual substance used.

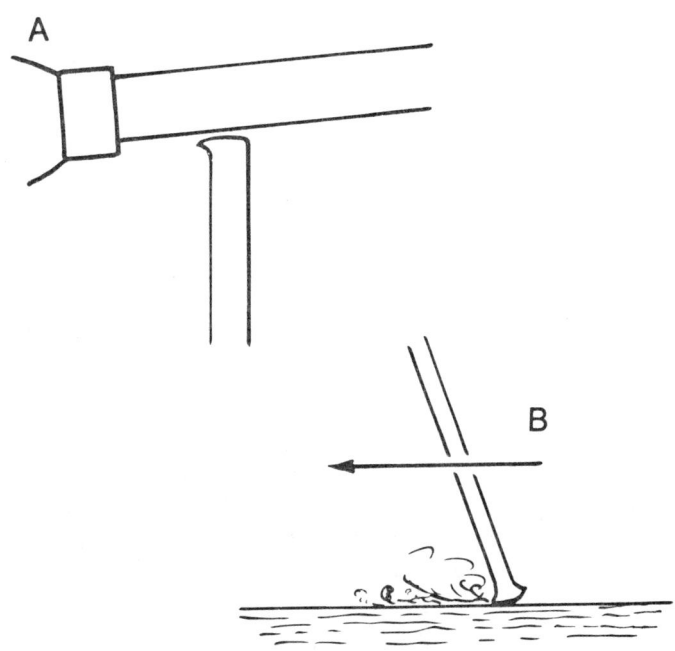

Fig. 26-3. Hard steel is used to rub along the edge.

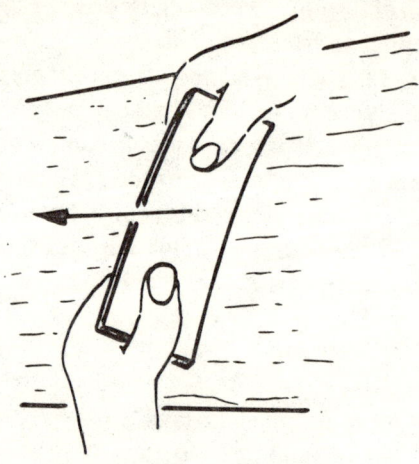

Fig. 26-4. Using the scraper.

There are several ways of grading abrasives. The best is by the number of grits per square inch with 50 as very coarse for wood and 320 as fine. Fineness may continue to 600 or more for some other materials. A traditional method of grading has 2 as the coarsest (36 grit) down by halves to 0 (80 grit), then finer by 2/0, 3/0 and so on, with 7/0 (240 grit) as the finest likely to be needed on wood.

Unless the surface is very rough the first sanding can be done with grade 0 or 80 grit and the wood surface finished with grade 5/0 (180 grit). If a varnish or polish has to be rubbed down there may be a need for grade 7/0 (240 grit). Some suppliers talk of *cabinet* papers for those intended for bare wood, and *finishing* papers for those intended to be used on an applied finish.

Power sanding can use a coarser grit than the equivalent hand sanding to get a similar effect. This is due to the high speed. Except in making a new frame, it is advisable to only use hand sanding when preparing exposed surfaces of furniture. Power sanding can very quickly take off too much, and some types, such as disk sanders, leave disfiguring marks. On a surface, sanding should be in the same direction as the grain, so the very fine scratches are inconspicuous.

Sheet abrasive paper and cloth are usually in a size that can conveniently be torn or cut into four for use. A folded piece can be used on a shaped part, but freehand sanding of flat surfaces is not advised. It is better to wrap the paper around a block (Fig. 26-5). There are cork and rubber-faced wood blocks for this purpose, but a piece of wood can be used. Let it be of a small enough surface area to come within the paper and deep enough to provide a comfortable grip. Much abrasive paper has the grit bonded with a waterproof adhesive, but if a non-waterproof glue is used, the paper can be given a longer life if it is warmed before use. This drives off any moisture in the glue.

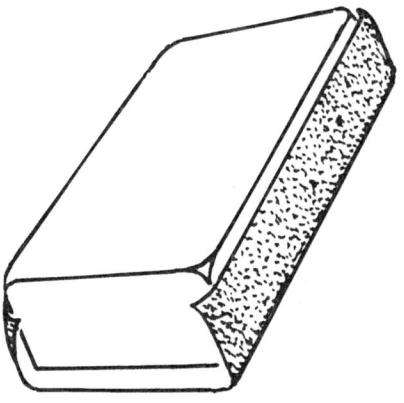

Fig. 26-5. Hand or power sanding is also acceptable.

Abrasive in powder form may be used to rub down between coats of a finish, using a cloth or felt pad. Pumice or a household scouring powder can be used. Steel wool is also used as an abrasive. Do not use the type sold for domestic scouring; there are finishing grades from 000 through 0 to 3 (coarsest). Do not use anything coarser than 1 on wood, followed by the finer grades for finishing. Steel wool has possibilities in intricate shapes that might be difficult with sheet abrasive paper. Some woods, particularly oak, can be discolored by the use of steel wool. In any case, make sure the particles are removed by wiping with a damp cloth.

In a normal preparation sequence, machine plane marks are removed, either by hand planing, scraping, or coarse sanding. This is followed by sanding with a medium grade abrasive and then a fine one. With some woods, fibers tend to bend instead of rub off. Dampening a surface and allowing it to dry will raise these fibers so they will sand away. Wiping a surface with a cotton glove or with the hand in a nylon stocking will show any roughness.

Finishing a wood surface up to the stage where it is ready for stain or polish leaves it very vulnerable to damage or dirt. It may be advisable to only partly follow through the sequence before doing other work on the furniture, and only finally finishing the surface just before staining, varnishing, or polishing. If a finally sanded surface has to be left some time, it may be advisable to give it a coat of shellac. This will seal the grain and prevent it from absorbing dirt. Light sanding will remove the shellac and allow further treatment.

WOOD BLEMISHES

Because wood is a natural product, it may contain flaws. When old furniture is reupholstered, the wood may have sustained damage. Some treatment has to be left until after staining, but other work is better done to the bare wood.

A dent from a knock or misdirected hammer blow has not removed wood, but has compressed cells. A few drops of water on the hollow may make it expand to its original level and remain there after drying. Heat, in the form of a really hot spoon or other metal article, can be applied to the water to make it steam. This may penetrate better than cold water. In any case there will have to be a final sanding.

There are several compounds for filling cracks, open joints, and knot holes or covering sunken nails or screws. Some will absorb stain, so can be used on the bare wood before staining, but others are colored and intended to be used after staining. For a painted finish the color of the stopping does not matter, of course.

Stick shellac or plastic stopping (sometimes called *beaumontage*) can be melted and pressed in with a hot knife. This is colored and useful for covering nails and similar small holes after staining. Plastic water putty is a powder which is mixed with water into a paste and has to be pressed in and cleaned off fairly quickly. It will take stain or it can have added color. Plastic wood has more of the character of wood when set and can be chiselled or otherwise worked to a limited extent when hard.

Stoppings do not provide any strength. If the strength of glue is needed as well as the ability to fill a gap, it is unsatisfactory to use glue thickly. In these circumstances most glues will *craze*, so they dry with a mass of cracks and no strength. Instead, the glue should be mixed to a thick paste with sawdust, preferably from the same wood as the frame. The sawdust prevents crazing and the joint should be almost as strong as close gluing.

At one time glazier's putty (linseed oil and whiting) and dental plaster (plaster of Paris) were used for stoppings, but the other stoppings are better.

STAINING

The color of wood may be changed by staining and then applying a polish or other finish, or by incorporating the stain into the finish. It is considered more craftsmanlike to apply the stain first. If it is in the applied finish it does not penetrate the wood as well and may not enter the grain at all. In subsequent wear this will result in parts of the wood color showing through in a shade different from the unworn parts. Color in varnish does not look as clear and may have a muddy appearance depending on the degree of darkening.

Wood does not have to be stained and many woods are most attractive if their color is not altered. Staining should usually emphasize the existing color, although there are occasions when different woods have to be matched, or the furniture may be brought to the same shade as something else in the same room. Mahogany usually has its redness emphasized. Oak and walnut may be made more brown.

Stain has the color dissolved in a liquid so it penetrates the grain and is left there when the solvent evaporates. Although it is possible to make up stains, prepared stains are usually more appropriate and economical for the small amount of wood associated with upholstery.

There are penetrating oil stains, which are brushed on fairly liberally and allowed to soak in. The intensity of staining is partly dependent on the soaking time. Surplus can be wiped off with a cloth when the color is judged right. In general, you should work from the least important part to the more important part. End grain and sapwood absorb quickest and may have to be wiped before other parts.

Water stains are powders to mix with water. They are brushed on and not usually wiped afterwards. It is not quite as easy to get an even effect as with oil stains, but several thin, light coats will build up a more even effect than one heavy, dark one.

Spirit stains are powders to dissolve in alcohol. There is not such a large range of wood colors, but there are other colors, such as blues and yellows, that may be used for special effects. These stains penetrate well and dry quickly. This may be helpful for small parts, but it is almost impossible to get an even appearance over a large area. Brushing has to be done rapidly and the brush must not be allowed to dwell on a spot. Spirit stains should be used for small, narrow things, although they can be used for touching up damaged finishes.

FILLING

It is necessary to fill the cells of some open-grained wood, such as oak; otherwise an applied finish will soak into the hollows even after repeated coats. Fillers are broadly divided into *paste fillers* for the more open-grained woods and *liquid fillers* for close-grained woods.

Plaster of Paris and whiting have been used as fillers, but the powder ingredient of most newer fillers is finely ground crystal quartz, called Silex. This is bound into a paste with coloring matter. Some fillers may be used before staining and they will absorb stain with the wood.

Paste filler is rubbed on to the wood in all directions so it becomes trapped in the grain cells. Go over this with a piece of burlap or other coarse cloth to force the filler into the grain and even the coating. Change to a soft cloth and work along the grain to remove excess filler. For moldings or carvings use a stiff shoe brush or similar tool to remove excess filler.

If oil stain has been used, give the wood a thin coat of shellac before filling, but apply direct over other stains. Let the filler be slightly darker than the stained wood, as it tends to dry lighter.

Liquid filler on close-grained wood is more of a sealer than a filler. Paste filler can be diluted with benzene or turpentine. It is then brushed on and wiped with coarse and soft cloths, as for open-grained wood. It is also possible to use shellac, varnish, or lacquer. Shellac should be brushed on thinly and allowed to dry, then another thin coat applied. This is lightly sanded after it has dried. Common shellac is orange colored and may be used over dark stain. There is also a bleached white shellac, which is better over natural or lightly stained woods.

Varnish should only be used as a filler on close-grained wood if it is to be followed by more varnish of the same sort. Lacquer can be sprayed on as a filler and lightly sanded after drying, as a preparation for a final lacquer finish. It should not be used under other finishes.

With some close-grained woods there is no need for a filling stage and finishing steps can be applied directly. Most of these are not common furniture woods. Woods that may not need filling or may need only liquid filler are beech, birch, gum, maple, and sycamore. Mahogany, rosewood, sapele, and walnut are woods that need medium filling. Some open-grained woods that need paste filling are ash, chestnut, elm, oak, and teak.

VARNISH AND SHELLAC

The most convenient way of applying a finish to a frame where not much wood is exposed outside the upholstery is by brush. In particular, short legs and feet do not warrant a sprayed or rubbed finish. Varnishes made from natural lacs and resins have been used for a very long time, but in recent years these materials have been replaced by synthetic ones that are superior in many ways.

Varnish gives a pleasant gloss. If properly applied, there should be no obvious brush marks. Varnish is tough and durable, with a good resistance to solvents and knocks by heavy objects.

Older varnishes needed dry conditions within certain temperature ranges; they were affected by humidity. While modern varnishes still benefit from dry, clean conditions and are better applied in moderate temperatures, they are more tolerant.

If a varnish is described as a *boat varnish* it is almost certainly synthetic as are most of those described as *quick drying* or *four-hour*. There are two-part synthetic varnishes, which have to be mixed before use. They are not used on furniture, but are meant for exterior and wet conditions. Ordinary synthetic varnishes are dust-free in an hour or so and touch-hard in a few hours, but they continue to harden over at least a day.

Varnish is sluggish below about 65°F. Varnish may be stood in hot water to make it more fluid. Avoid the fumes of burning oil, gas, or solid fuel when using varnish. If portable heating has to be used, let it be electric. Apply varnish with a good brush and with a minimum of strokes. Do not work out the varnish by brushing in many directions, but get it on evenly without going over the same part again, if possible. Too much brushing over one part causes the varnish to lift or not dry evenly. Brush along the grain where possible.

If bare wood is varnished directly, it helps to thin the first coat slightly with the thinners recommended by the makers. Sand the first coat, as it may have raised wood fibers. There will probably have to be three or more coats to get a good finish. Follow the maker's instructions about intervals between coats. Some specify a maximum as well as a minimum time between coats.

Shellac is imported as flakes which dissolve readily in denatured alcohol. It can be bought already dissolved in various strengths, which are described as *cuts*. A "5 pound cut" means 5 pound of shellac in 1 gallon of alcohol. Weaker dilutions are available, a thinning can be done by adding alcohol. Common shellac is orange and suitable for all dark finishes, but there is a white or bleached shallac, with only a slight tinge, that is better for light colored woods. White shellac does not keep as well when stored.

Shellac can be used as a sealer under paint as well as under a shellac finish. If there are resinous knots in softwoods, they can be sealed with shellac under paint, even if it is not used elsewhere.

If shellac is brushed on, many coats are needed, but as the drying time is short, several coats can be applied in a day. Five or six coats of 3 pound cut shellac will give a better finish than fewer coats of a stronger cut. Sand lightly between coats. Avoid humid conditions. Work quickly and spread each coat. Shellac becomes dustfree in a few minutes.

Both shellac and varnish can be smoothed with fine steel wool and followed with wax polish. Clean varnish brushes with the solvent recommended by the makers. If a varnish brush has to be kept overnight between coats, suspend it in varnish. Shellac will dry rapidly in a brush, so clean it with alcohol and store it suspended in alcohol, but seal the container to limit evaporation.

French polishing is a method of applying shellac that builds up a polished surface of great beauty. French polish is shellac of about 2 1/2 pound cut, but it should be free from the resin which is in some shellac varnish. A *rubber* is used—this is a pad of cotton batting wrapped in a piece of fluffless cotton cloth. The polish is applied to the pad and the cloth wrapped around it so liquid oozes through.

There are three stages: bodying-in, building-up, and spiriting-out. Bodying-in puts a base of shellac on the wood. Use enough shellac and rub across and with the grain, then use circular movements, but do not stop on the surface. Lift off or go over an edge to stop. Cover the whole surface. Let it dry and do it again.

Leave this to harden for about a day. Lightly go over the surface with steel wool. Apply more polish. If the rubber tends to stick, moisten the surface with a drop of linseed oil on the finger. Build up by more polishing, but do not charge the rubber with as much polish. An occasional drop of oil will be needed to prevent dragging. Work over the surface with circular motions and do not stop on the surface. Work at a reasonable speed, but there is no need to press very hard or go very fast.

After at least five hours, use a fresh rubber to spirit-out with a little alcohol only. Polish lightly. This gives a burnishing action that should bring up the final gloss.

French polishing is really intended for large areas. For moldings, carvings, and fretted parts the polish has to be applied with a brush. For most woodwork associated with upholstery, a brushed finish is likely to be more appropriate than French polishing.

LACQUERING

A spray gun has uses in furniture manufacture and may be convenient for dealing with the exposed parts of frames that are to be upholstered, but for a single piece of furniture the comparatively narrow parts do not provide a very big target, and much of the spray is liable to be wasted. For most of this work a brushed finish may be preferable.

Modern lacquer is a complex chemical composition intended for spraying. Most of it is unsuitable for any other method of application. It is a clear gloss finish, although there are versions for shading and coloring. Lacquer will attack other finishes so it should not be used over an existing finish of another type or even sprayed alongside it.

Lacquer is inflammable so care is needed. Anyone unused to the process should practice on scrap materials because it is very easy to get sags and streaks, orange peel effect, and blooming. Thinners are needed to clean the gun. The amount of work involved in preparing and cleaning afterwards is only justified when a considerable amount of spraying may be expected to be done at one session.

OIL AND WAX POLISHING

Very old furniture has acquired its patina and finish through use and age. Originally it may have been rubbed with an oil, but it has been the rubbing of clothing and flesh that has given the finish.

Many oils have been used for polishing. Getting a polish with oil is a slow process spread over years, so oil polishing is not to be considered today. Wax also has a long history. There are many waxes, the best-known being beeswax. The hardest wax is carnauba from a Brazilian palm tree. It is brittle alone, but can be mixed with other waxes. Paraffin wax is soft. Like ceresine, it can be mixed with other waxes.

Wax polish is made by mixing waxes with turpentine, either to make a liquid or a paste. Using wax to build up a polish on bare wood is a lengthy process. It is possible to seal the wood with something else and build up a wax polish on that. Wax is rubbed on with a cloth and it slowly builds up its own surface film.

Most applications of wax today are in prepared polishes that are used to revive other finishes. Shellac, varnish, or lacquer may all be followed by wax polish. Furniture polishes and creams in prepared form contain wax and are good for periodically polishing furniture that was originally treated with another finish.

PAINTING

Like varnishes, paints have undergone changes from natural to synthetic constituents. Paint may be regarded as varnish with coloring pigments added. At one time there was a great variety of paints for particular purposes and for building up the different stages of a paint finish. If paint is to be used on furniture it is advisable to use all of the products of one maker and follow his advice on what to use at different stages.

Traditionally the first coat was a primer, which was a thin paint of a color that was not related to the final one. Its purpose was to enter the pores of the wood to gain a bond and provide a base for further coats. This was followed by one or more undercoats of a color compatible with the final coat and with a matte surface. Over this went the top coat, which usually had a gloss finish.

Modern paint systems are variations on that, but in many it is possible to use a smaller variety of paints. Shellac can be used instead of primer in some cases. The top coat may be used to put on several layers, without using an undercoat. Read the maker's recommendations.

The notes on varnishing apply to synthetic paints. Do not work the surface with a brush any more than is necessary to get an even spread. To avoid brush marks, make final strokes back towards an earlier coating of wet paint and lift the brush as it goes over it.

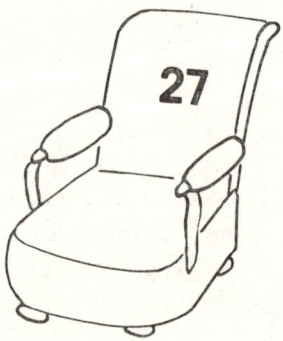

27

Repairing and Restyling Frames

Some furniture gets considerable abuse, which it usually withstands for quite a long life. Eventually, however, it may reach a stage where the old covering has to be stripped and the frame may be found to be damaged as well. Unless a frame is in a very bad state, it is worthwhile repairing it—especially if recovering is considered worthwhile.

An exception may be if rot is present. Rot starts in damp conditions, so furniture that has always been used indoors should not be rotten. If you hope to revive a discarded chair that has been left outside for some time, though, examine the wood for rot. Rotten wood has lost most of the normal wood characteristics. It will be dead and powdery to the touch. It may have already crumbled. Rot is caused by the spores of a fungus. It is not only the part obviously affected that has to be discarded—the spores are almost certainly present in wood that appears to be unaffected. Treatment consists of cutting away for some distance each side of the worst part, and the specified distance is so much that in the average piece of furniture the whole frame has to be discarded. The spores travel in the air and may attach themselves to other wood; so if rot is discovered, the affected furniture should be moved away quickly and burned.

There are preservatives that can be applied to wood to prevent rot, and furniture intended for use in damp situations should be treated by them. They are preventatives and cannot be used as a cure once rot has attacked.

Another problem in an old frame may be the presence of borers, often described as worms. There are several borers. Their presence is indicated by small holes on the surface, but inside the wood there may be many passages eaten away behind each surface hole. If left unchecked the wood may be eaten away so much that it is weakened to the point of breaking. It may be necessary to cut away and replace a badly affected part. If the attack is only slight it is possible to treat the wood with a substance that kills any borers present and prevents further attack. Follow the maker's directions. The treatment can be used on wood that has not been attacked as a guard against future attacks. Borers tend to favor certain woods and even particular parts of those woods, so an attack may be quite localized and it will submit to treatment.

LOOSENESS

A common fault with an old frame is looseness of fastenings or joints. If a screw has loosened, it may be possible to replace it with a longer or thicker one, but this may still leave many wood fibers broken or compressed so they contribute nothing to the grip of the screw. It may be better to plug the hole and drill this for the screw (Fig. 27-1A). The plug can be a piece of wood, or it can be one of the plugs used for screwing to plaster or brick walls. It may be possible to plug a screw hole with a mixture of glue and sawdust, then drive the screw into that before it has set.

Glues have changed. An old frame almost certainly has its joints made with a natural glue, manufactured from fish bones, horse hooves, and similar materials. Such glue had a good strength when dry, but in damp conditions—not necessarily very damp—much of the strength was lost. Strength may have been recovered when the glue dried, but if by then a joint had moved, the damage was done.

These glues are almost obsolete. Modern glues are synthetic and they come in a great variety of trade names. Nearly all have a good resistance to moisture and a strength greater than that of the old glues. Be careful that any glue chosen for repairs to frames is described as a wood glue. If it is also described as suitable for paper and fabric, it is not a glue intended to have strength sufficient for furniture. Probably the strongest glue generally available is epoxy. This comes in two parts, which have to be mixed just before use. Besides bonding wood to wood, epoxy will join most materials, including metals, to themselves or to other materials. An epoxy joint in wood is among the strongest possible. The strongest epoxy glue is slow getting, and this should be used if a glued joint can be left a day or more. There are also quick acting epoxys, which are not as strong.

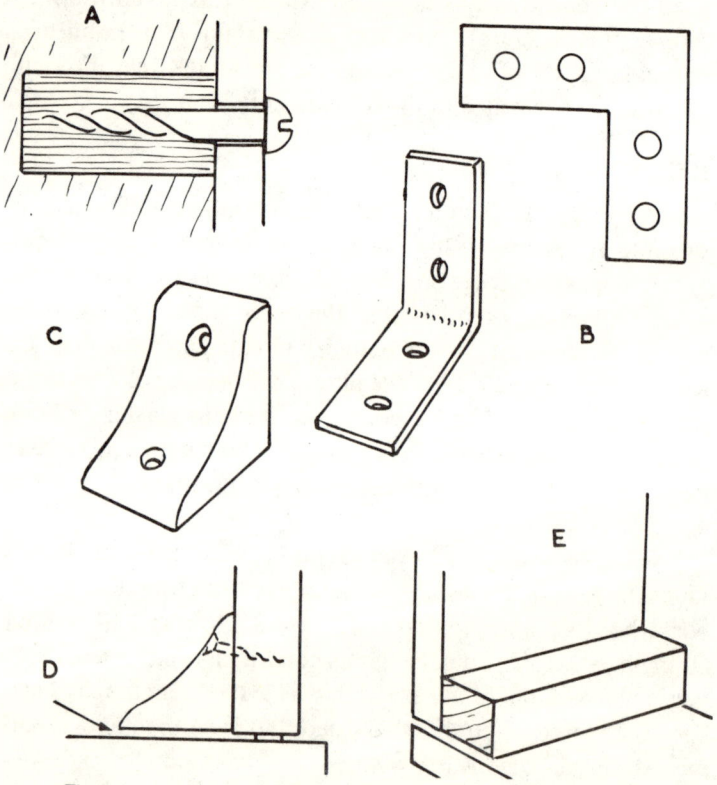

Fig. 27-1. Weaknesses in framing can be corrected with brackets.

There are other two-part wood glues and these are generally stronger than one-part wood glues, although these may still be stronger than traditional glues. A problem with modern glues is that they are not gap-filling, which means that if the parts of a joint are not in close contact the glue *crazes* as it hardens and produces little strength. A way to avoid this trouble in repair work, where wood parts cannot be brought as tight as might be desired, is to mix sawdust with the glue to a thick consistency. If this fills a gaping joint, the glue bonds to the sawdust as well as to the surfaces and dries without crazing.

Unfortunately, many glues are not compatible with each other. This means that if an old joint with traces of natural glue in it is to be reglued with a modern glue, it is necessary to remove as much as possible of the old glue before applying the new glue.

For glue to get a grip it is helpful to scratch the surfaces to expose new wood fibers. A fine saw, such as a back saw, drawn sideways in several directions over the wood will make a pattern of scratches that will give the glue new fibers to grip.

Traditional glued joints had to be tightly clamped until set. With most modern glues it is only necessary to hold the parts in contact. In many repairs, the assembly is such that clamps could not be applied, but it may be possible to bind the parts temporarily together with string, masking tape, or something similar.

If the glue has failed in a joint which can be taken apart, there is little difficulty in scraping away old glue and remaking the joint with new glue. If the joint is loose and cannot be taken apart, new glue should not be put on old glue, even if it is possible to introduce it. It may help to squeeze some new glue in, but there will have to be some reinforcing as well.

There are standard repair plates and brackets that can be bought in many sizes (Fig. 27-1B). They can be used to strengthen a weak joint. It may also be possible to make wood repair brackets, similar to those described for the making of some new frames (Fig. 27-1C). If a joint is open and has to be pulled together as well as strengthened, it is possible to fix a wood bracket with glue and screws to one part, but leave a gap in the direction of tightening (Fig. 27-1D). When the glue has set in this first direction, glue is introduced into the new joint as much as possible and the bracket is glued and screwed in the other direction, so the action of screwing pulls the joint together.

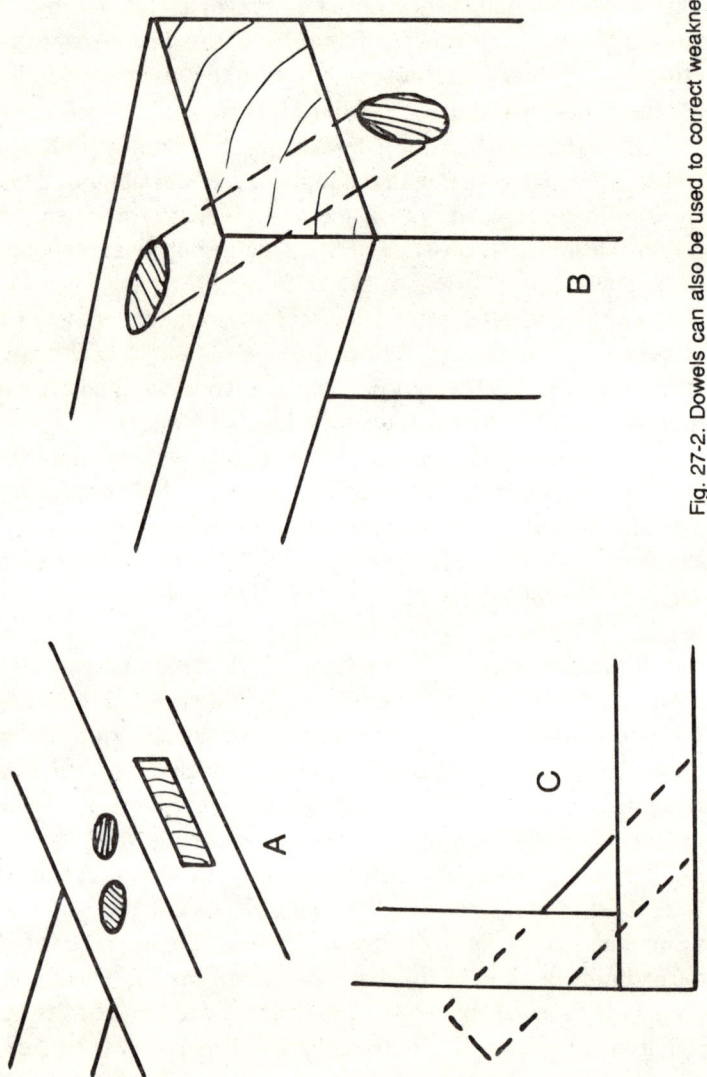

Fig. 27-2. Dowels can also be used to correct weaknesses.

482

A similar idea may be used in a weakened angle between broad boards. A block is fixed first to one part, with a gap in the direction that tightening is needed (Fig. 27-1E) and this pulls the joint tight.

Dowels can be used to strengthen weakened joints that cannot be taken apart. A dowel with a modern glue will strengthen a joint even when fixed in an improbable direction. A loose mortise and tenon joint may be pressed together, then several dowels put through holes across the tenon (Fig. 27-2A). In a joint between thick parts a repair dowel may go across at an angle (Fig. 27-2B). If the parts are thin and projections inside would not interfere with covering, the dowels may be exposed in the inside angle (Fig. 27-2C).

The reason many parts of a frame have loosened is that they are made up of unbraced, four-sided panels. Any assembly of four sides is very vulnerable if pushed at a corner (Fig. 27-3A). A three-sided figure cannot be pushed out of shape (Fig. 27-3B). The four-sided figure can be given the strength of triangles by putting in a diagonal (Fig. 27-3C). It may not be possible to triangulate many parts of a frame because the braces would interfere with upholstery, but the principle should be remembered when making repairs to frames that have failed for this reason.

The effect of a diagonal is partly obtained by a smaller brace or bracket (Fig. 27-3D), which may be a solid block or a strip of wood. This method of bracing may be possible at one or more corners of a four-sided frame. Even at only one corner, some of the stiffening effect is transferred to the other corners as well.

Plywood is useful for bracketing if it can be fixed on the face of a weakened angle. It may come underneath the corner of a frame (Fig. 27-3E), where its effect increases with size, so it should be as big as reasonably possible. Fixing any type of brace with glue as well as screws or nails gives the greatest strength.

SCARFING

If a part of a wood frame has split or cracked, the treatment depends on the type of damage. If there is a split along the grain and it can be opened enough to introduce glue, it may be a sufficient repair if you glue and hold the parts together until set.

A crack across the grain cannot be treated in this way. Glue does not hold well to end grain and could not be trusted alone to make a repair. There should be some reinforcing splints around

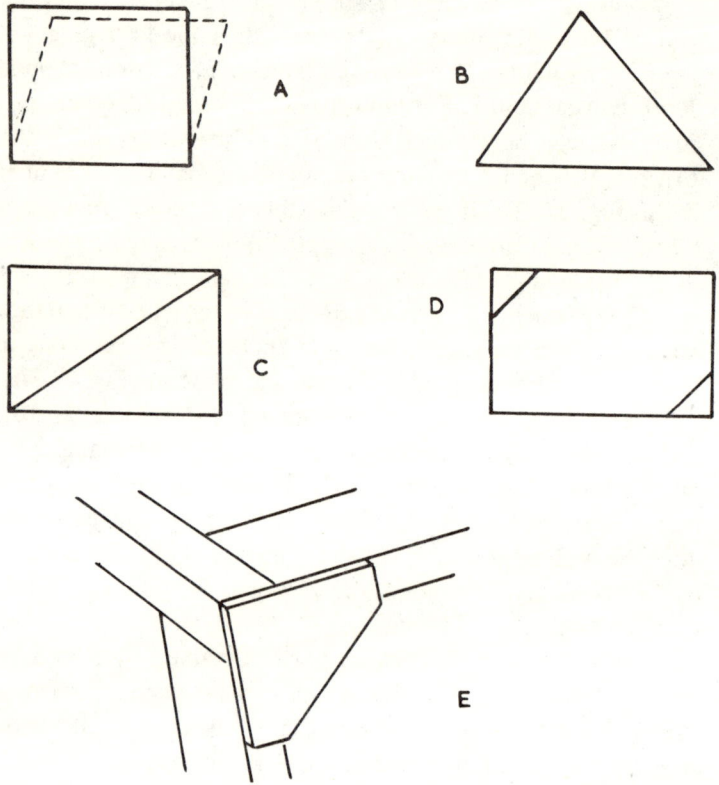

Fig. 27-3. A triangle cannot be pushed out of shape so diagonals or corner braces will give a triangular effect to a square frame or corner.

the joint (Fig. 27-4A). It may be possible to do this only on the sides least likely to affect covering later, particularly if the parts are tapered. If wood strips would interfere with covering, it may be possible to make metal plates to screw on (Fig. 27-4B).

Another way to deal with splits and cracks is to use fiberglass. This can be obtained in the form of woven cloth or tape. With suitably activated resin it is bandaged tightly around the damage and left for the resin to set. One or two layers can be wrapped without increasing the size enough to affect the upholstery that will follow.

If a part is badly damaged it may be better to join on a new piece of wood. The damaged part may be cut square across and the new piece butted against it, then splints put along the sides of the joint as described for dealing with a crack. Quite often this increase in cross section is unacceptable. A better joint is a *scarf*, which joins pieces that have been angled.

Glue makes the strongest joint when the surfaces meeting have the grain parallel with the surfaces. It is possible to join pieces if they are cut so there are parallel surfaces with slightly angled ends (Fig. 27-4C). It is simpler to merely cut the ends straight across to long angles. The grain is not then exactly parallel, but it is approaching parallel sufficiently to provide a good glue bond. The angle should be one in seven or flatter (Fig. 27-4D). If the wood is 1 inch thick the scarf should be at least 7 inches long. Such a joint may be clamped with overlapping strips of wood and clamps beyond the joint as well as over it. Paper under the clamping strips prevents them from becoming stuck with surplus glue (Fig. 27-4E).

If a shaped part has to be repaired by scarfing on a new piece, it is often better to let the new part be slightly too big; then it is shaped to match the old part after the glue has set. Precision in the joint is not then so important as when the new part is fully shaped first.

FRAME FINISH

When the covering is removed from an old frame it is often difficult to withdraw all fastenings. Tacks and staples should be removed if possible. The wood can sometimes be punched down each side of a broken nail or staple so pincers or pliers can grip the end. If this is impossible, punch the offending metal below the surface. In a very old frame, nails may be found to be used for joints that would now be screwed. It is advisable in refurbishing an old frame to replace nails with screws, if the nails can be removed without too much damage to surrounding wood.

If a frame has already been stripped and recovered before, some wood may already have a great many tack holes and it might be difficult to get a good grip with the next lot of tacks. In this case it may be possible to fix a new tack rail along a

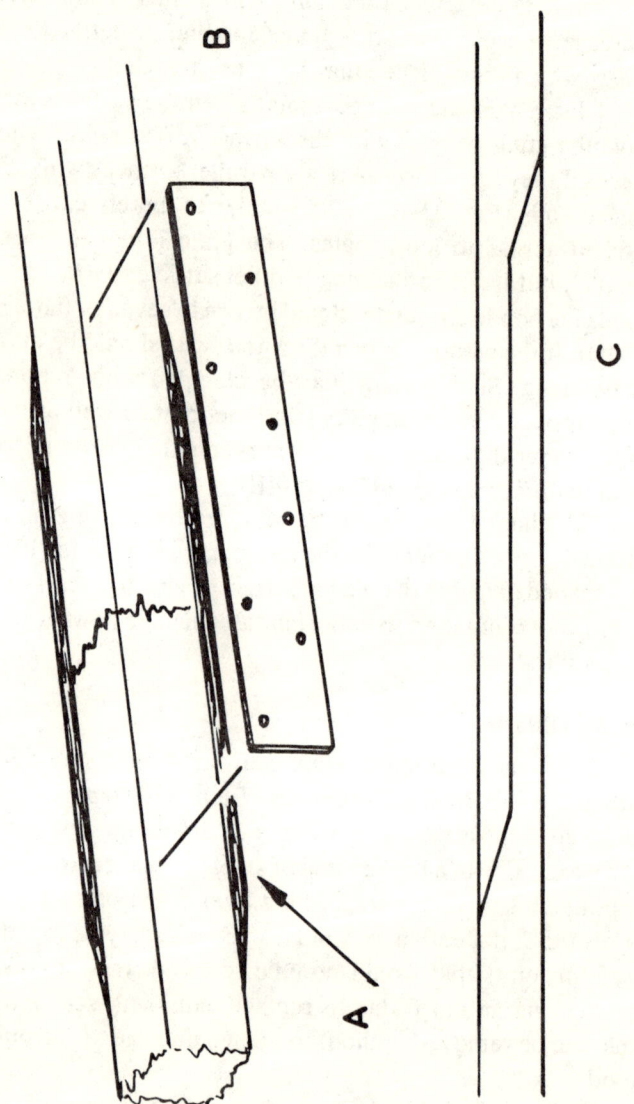

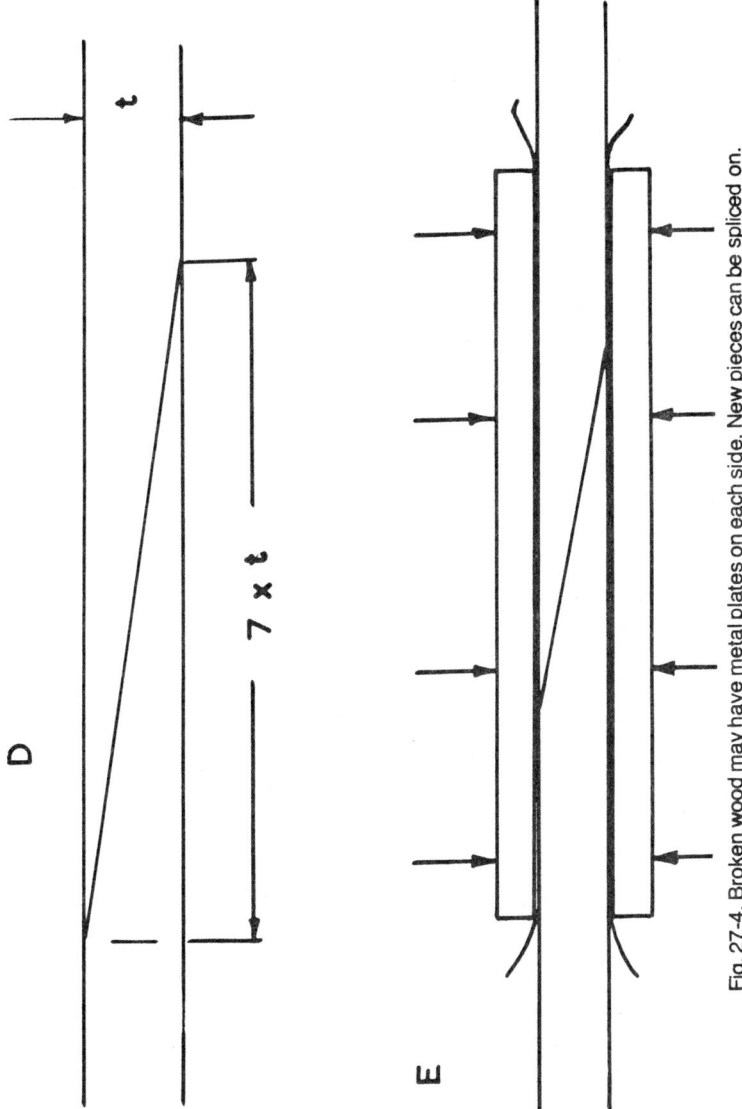

Fig. 27.-4. Broken wood may have metal plates on each side. New pieces can be spliced on.

damaged edge. This depends on where the part is. If the covering material comes over a rail and is tacked underneath there can be a new tack rail inside (Fig. 27-5).

If the much-tacked wood is in a place where a new tack rail could not be used, it may be possible to plug old holes with slivers of wood. Then the edge can be wiped along with a

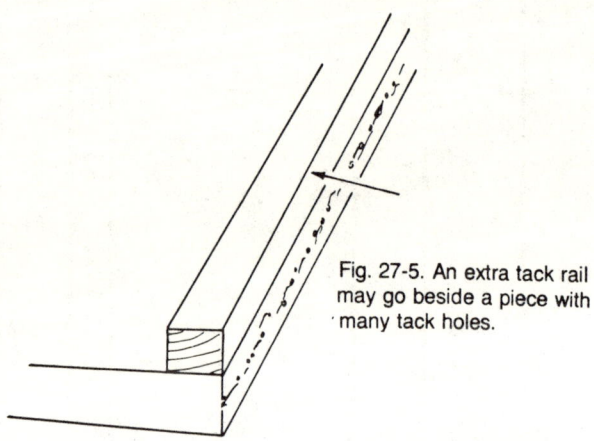

Fig. 27-5. An extra tack rail may go beside a piece with many tack holes.

mixture of glue or stopping and sawdust, pressed down with a chisel or putty knife, and the whole edge can be sanded smooth before recovering. If the length of the previous tacks is known, it may be possible to use longer ones next time.

Removing the covering from a frame usually does some damage to it, if only tearing up the grain where tacks are levered out. Although a high finish may not be needed on hidden parts of the frame, roughness could affect the positioning and lay of the stuffing and various layers of covering. A rasp, or similar tool, may be needed to smooth very rough parts. Splinters or pieces chipped by removing tacks may be better broken off than laid back in place, where they may lift later. Coarse abrasive paper can be used all over the frame, and particularly along rough or sharp angles. Even if this work may not be seen until the frame is stripped again, such a finish encourages good work in the finished chair.

RESTYLING

Taking an existing frame and altering it is a project to approach with caution. In many frames the parts are interdependent. Suppose the frame for an arm chair is being considered for conversion to a chair without arms. Can the arms be merely cut off? If the frame is examined it may be found that the back may still be strong enough without the arms, and the front legs may be unaffected, but it is more likely that the front legs and arm fronts are the same piece and the arm tops obviously provide strength for the back so both unsupported parts might move (Fig. 27-6A). It may be possible to brace the front legs in some way after their tops have been cut off, but it would not be a very craftsmanlike job. The back may be more of a problem as the joint between back and seat frame is not strong enough after the support of the arms has gone. Any brackets for strength there may be so large that they affect the covering appearance.

Cutting down is usually a safer choice. Lowering a chair is only a matter of cutting off the legs the desired amount, but this has to be done very carefully if the chair is still to stand level. If reduction is to be the same all around, use a marking gauge to get exactly the same distance from each end. If the tilt of the seat is to be altered make sure the cuts on the two back legs match and that both front legs are cut the same amount.

Reducing the height of a back is usually a simple task. Care is needed to take out equal amounts and have close-fitting meeting surfaces. If the back is parallel, the sides can be cut and the new surfaces joined with dowels (Fig. 27-6B) without disturbing the top. This can be effective with a frame that will be covered, but for a lounge chair with exposed wood sides, the top has to be repositioned further down. Old dowels have to be carefully drilled out and new ones used in the lower position (Fig. 27-6C).

A sofa frame can be reduced in width to any point down to a single-seat chair, if it is a straightforward design. If there are shaped parts in the back, reduction will have to be related to matching parts of the back design, if a change is possible at all. For a straight frame the center can be cut from the crosswise members, which are then joined again. The simplest joints have covers on the inside or underneath, where they will not affect fabric covering (Fig. 27-6D). Normally, the wood removed should be at the center; then the new assembly will be symmetrical. In some designs this is not important and it may be possible to cut out a part off-center to avoid displacing some part of the cross bracing. Reduction has to be related to the springs available. If made-up springs are being used, the new frame size should be made to suit a stock assembly.

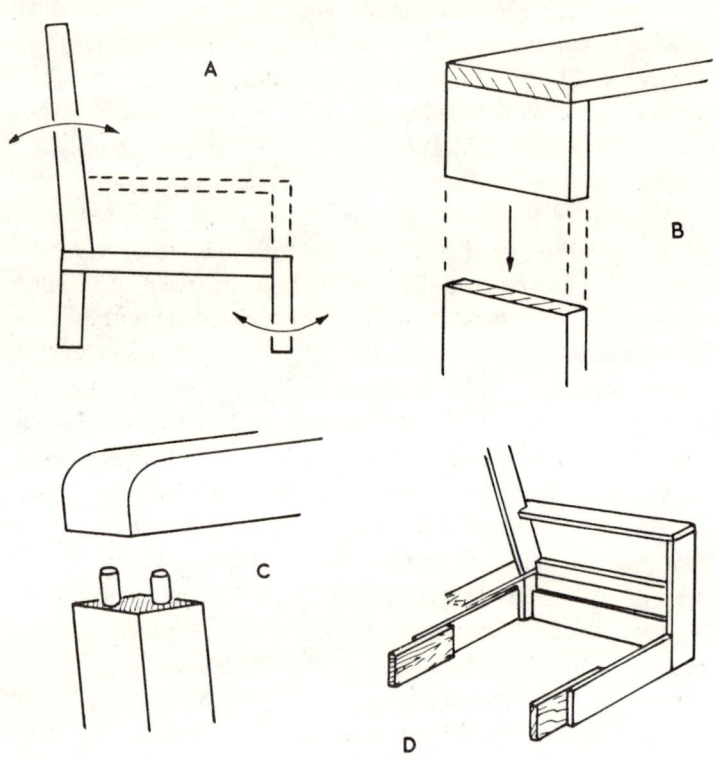

Fig. 27-6. An old frame can be altered by removing arms, lowering its sides, or cutting it in width.

FINISHING

The steps in finishing the exposed parts of a frame are described in Chapter 26, but in dealing with an old frame it may be necessary to strip an old finish and start again or patch up the old finish and revive its appearance.

If the only exposed parts are legs projecting below a fully upholstered chair, the old finish is best removed mechanically by scraping and sanding. If there is a larger expanse of old paint or varnish to be removed it may be better to use a chemical stripper, but read the instructions and follow them carefully. The frame to be treated should be absolutely bare of upholstery. The work should preferably be done outside, in a place where it is possible to hose away the residue with plenty of water. With most strippers the chemical is applied and the blistering finish scraped off; then the surface has to be neutralized with another chemical or with water. After drying a new finish can be applied.

If the old finish does not need stripping it may be revived in several ways. Much old furniture is very dirty, particularly around floor level. A start should be made with a scrubbing brush and a strong detergent. Make sure all of this is washed off with clean water. If the result is an even, acceptable color but all gloss has gone, it may be sufficient to brush on a modern synthetic varnish, possibly two coats. If this gloss is considered too brilliant and a more mellow finish is wanted, the shine can be reduced by rubbing with a fine abrasive paper if it is reasonably flat wood, or with pumice or other abrasive powder if the part is carved or turned. This is followed by rubbing with a furniture wax or cream.

If the old finish has been chipped or damaged, yet it is not to be stripped, rough edges of damaged varnish or lacquer should be rubbed and tapered with a piece of abrasive paper over the thumb. Spirit stain may be wiped over the damage to even the color. Much depends on the treatment previously received, but spirit stain will penetrate some other finishes and its color can be adjusted by wiping. This sets quickly and can be followed by wax polish.

It may be possible to get a satisfactory darker color by using a varnish stain over a damaged earlier finish. The surface is sanded level, without rubbing through to the bare wood. Varnish stain has the coloring matter in the varnish, so the stain stays on the surface. When treating bare wood it is always better to stain the wood before varnishing, but the stain would not penetrate the old finish and varnish stain may cover blemishes in the old finish by darkening the whole surface.

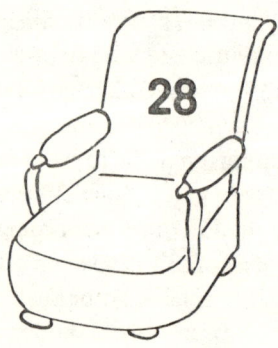

28
Safety

Upholstery, as practiced by the individual worker, is almost completely a hand craft. For quantity production of furniture in a factory there may be elaborate machinery, for which many safety precautions are necessary. An upholsterer working on single pieces of furniture may have an electric sewing machine and there may be an electric drill, but all other tools are comparatively simple, hand ones. If the work is more ambitious, there may be a cushion stuffer or a button covering machine, but these things are only developments of the hand technique.

Safety under these circumstances is largely applied common sense. Electrical equipment should be properly grounded, insulation should be adequate and undamaged, and the machines should be handled in a proper manner. An electric drill should not be used toward any part of the body. It is better to have the work held in a vise than to hold it in place with one hand. If both hands are on the drill they cannot be damaged by the rotating bit. A sewing machine is not very hazardous because certain things that have to be done to make it perform properly also have a second purpose of making the process safe.

If much work is done on frames there may be an electric grinder for sharpening tools. Grit from the rapidly rotating stones is hazardous and goggles should be worn. A container of water should be placed alongside your work so tools can be dipped to prevent overheating. Overheating draws the temper of the steel and may cause the steel to burn the hands so the shock releases the grip and the tool may fly away dangerously.

Scissors do not have knifelike cutting edges and are unlikely to do damage if left around, but the points may scratch flesh if the tool is casually left in an unexpected spot.

Knives, chisels, and other edge tools should be handled with care and put down in places that are reserved for them whenever possible, so there is no risk of inadvertently touching a sharp blade when feeling for something else in a place where the edge tool is not expected. This may not always be possible, but you should put down a knife on a clear surface where it is easily seen, not among waste material and a collection of other tools. Apart from personal safety, a fine edge on a knife is quickly blunted if it is mixed with other steel tools.

A hand should not be placed ahead of an edge tool. If it is necessary to steady the wood being cut, the hand should be behind the cut. Far better, whenever possible, you should hold the wood by a clamp or vise. Two hands on a chisel give better control, as well as safety. Besides doing better work, a sharp tool is often safer than a blunt one that needs excessive effort to use. The blunt tool may jerk and jump while being forced to work.

Some furniture is quite heavy. Be careful when lifting it. Your legs should take the load, not your back. Lift with a straight back. Bend your knees, not your back. Be careful that when furniture is placed in position for working, it is safe and unlikely to move and fall. Use edged trestles under legs. Support furniture evenly. If it has to be moved or inverted at working height, get help—lifting a high load higher to turn it may put more strain on your back than when lifting from the ground in the proper way.

Springs and needles are made of tempered steel. Steel cannot be made hard without giving it a degree of brittleness. Be careful when stretching or manipulating springs in case they break. In particular, keep your face out of line of the stretch. A long needle may break if it is levered and such an unexpected break may cause the end to enter your hand.

Needles have to be sharp to do their job. An occasional prick from a needle may be regarded as an occupational hazard of upholstery, but even a minor prick should not have happened. It happened due to carelessness. There should be a box or other recognized storage place for needles. Apart from safety, this storage avoids losing needles and prevents them from being blunted by other tools. If an apron is worn there may be a pad of soft material high on the bib or maybe the pocket of other protective clothing, so a needle temporarily out of use can be stuck there. Such a high position is away from the area where hands are normally placed and used, so there is little risk of pricking. Single-ended needles can be pushed into a bottle cork. Double-ended needles are better in a container.

The oldtime practice of having a mouthful of tacks ready to use is certainly not hygienic, even if there seems to be no record of anyone swallowing tacks. It is better to have the tacks nearby in a container. A turned wood bowl is more convenient than an angular box because the tacks can be drawn up the side as needed, and the last few will not be difficult to get at. Hitting the tack and not your thumb is mainly a matter of practice. If any form of stapler is used instead of hammer and tacks, remember it throws a staple with considerable force if you use it in the air to check its action. Be careful that it is not directed at anyone or anything that could be damaged.

It is probably too much to expect that in a busy shop there will be no tacks and other waste on the floor. The floor should be frequently swept, however, and it is good practice to have a container for waste nearby so discarded items can be dropped in it. It needs to have a closed bottom, so small things, like tacks, cannot pass through spaces. Even in the best kept shop it is wise to proceed as if there are tacks on the floor. Wear shoes with thick soles. Avoid kneeling or otherwise touching the floor except with your shoes. If you have to get low to work on furniture, check the floor first.

Frames may have ragged edges, so handle them as if expecting splinters. This may apply to a new frame, because there is no need to smooth wood that will be covered, or an old frame, which may have become rough when old covering and tacks were removed.

Be careful of loose clothing. This is very important with machinery, but there can be a risk when doing hand work, too.

A hanging tie or a flapping jacket may catch in something unexpectedly and distract you from the work at hand; it may cause you to handle a tool badly or otherwise put yourself in a hazardous situation.

Upholstery is the sort of craft that can be carried out in comfortable conditions. Light should be adequate so there is no strain in seeing what you are doing. So far as possible, all around lighting is better than too much from one side. Temperature does not have much effect on the natural materials of upholstery, but some synthetic materials get very stiff at low temperatures. Some varieties of vinyl may be almost rigid near freezing point, but at normal room temperatures they are more flexible than leather. Raising their temperature to a point almost too hot to comfortably hold makes them very pliable. In general, have the shop at a comfortable working temperature. You are less accident-prone then than if you are concerned with how cold or hot you feel.

Ventilation is important for comfort and some upholstery produces dust that should not be allowed to accumulate. If you are finishing wood parts, some of the things used require exceptional ventilation or they will be hazardous to health. Some of the materials are also acid or caustic and dangerous to the skin. Read and follow the instructions provided with bleaches, paint strippers, and other chemicals for treating wood. Used properly they may be expected to do their task. Besides care in using these things, be careful how you dispose of them or the products of their action. Some paint stripper, for instance, produces a waste product that may cause spontaneous combustion if this "gunk" is compressed together in a waste bucket. Read directions and precautions, and believe them.

Allow yourself room to work. You should be able to get all around the piece of furniture being upholstered. Additionally, there may have to be a work place for rolling out and cutting cloth. A sheet of plywood temporarily supported on chairs, benches, and stools that happen to be around does not encourage good work and may cause an accident. Occasional upholstery work may have to be done in a shop normally used for other crafts. Be careful of other equipment that might cause damage, or may be set in motion due to the contortions you make in trying to work in a confined space.

A well-ordered shop, with plenty of space, good natural and artificial lighting, with tools neatly stored, materials racked or in drawers, with the floor swept and no dust anywhere, may be something of a dream, but it is a fact that a tidy efficient shop encourages good work and is much less likely to cause accidents than an untidy muddled shop, however much the latter may be considered to have character and be traditional.

Glossary

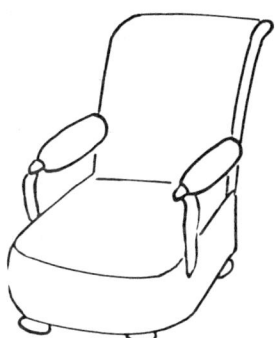

Back tacking—Tacks positioned through a cardboard strip so the fabric may be turned back to hide them. Also called blind tacking.

Baker clips—Clips for fixing edge wires to springs.

Batting, cotton—Padding material.

Bayonet-pointed needle—Needle with flattened faces behind point.

Bias—Diagonal to weave.

Blind sewing—Alternative name for slip sewing.

Blind tacking—Alternative name for back tacking.

Borer—Beetle grub that attacks wood, leaving holes on surface. Also called wood worm.

Bottom band—Lower part across front of seat. Also called bottom border.

Boxing—An edge strip sewn to a face piece of cloth to provide a square edge to a cushion or other padding, possibly with piping in the seam.

Box ottoman—Padded seat arranged as lid of a storage box.

Box pleating—Pleats close together.

Burlap—Coarse weave jute cloth. Also called hessian or sacking.

Buttons—Round or shaped disks used on twine through upholstery for appearance and for retaining stuffing.

Buttoning, deep—Buttons on twine pulled deeply into the padding to create a pattern.
Cable spring—Alternative name for tension spring.
Cabriole hammer—Hammer with small diameter face to its head, for getting into confined places.
Calico—Cotton cloth.
Cambric—Plain woven cotton treated to prevent down from pushing through. Cloth coated to make it dust-proof and used below springs underneath a chair.
Carcase—The body of a box or other container.
Cavity latex rubber—Cushion material with cavities on underside.
Chaise lounge or longue—Long low chair with leg supports.
Channel back chair—Chair with padding arranged in upright tubes.
Chipboard—Board made of wood particles in plastic. Also called particleboard.
Chisel, ripping—Tool for removing tacks.
Clips, baker—Clips for fixing edge wires to springs.
Clove hitch—Knot made by jamming two half hitches.
Coil spring—Compression spring used to support padding.
Cording foot—Used on sewing machine to get close to piping.
Cord, piping—Cord made of cotton, paper or plastic for making piping.
Cotton—Natural material, woven in many ways and used loosely compounded for padding.
Cotton batting—Padding material.
Couch—Alternative name for sofa.
Crumb, polyether—Small pieces of plastic used for filling.
Cushion—Loose pad that does not fix down.
Cushion, scatter—Individual cushion not intended for a particular place. Also called throw cushion or pillow.
Cushion stuffer—Machine used as an aid in filling cushions.
Dacron—Polyester synthetic fiber, used to make cloth.
Deep buttoning—Buttons on twine pulled deeply into the padding to create a pattern.
Divan—Sofa for use as bed or bed upholstered in the same way as a seat.
Double coil spring—Compression spring, narrow at center.

Dowel—Wood peg used to make joints in frames.
Down—Feathers from the breast of a duck.
Drop-in unit—Coils mounted on bar to fit in frame.
Edge wire—Wire fixed around group of springs to stabilize them.
Edging, fox—Roll of stuffing material used at edge of seat.
Edging, roll—Alternative name for fox edging.
Eider down—The best feather filling, from the breast of the eider duck.
Facing—Flat surface, usually wood, covered with fabric.
Felt—Loose strands made into a pad.
Felt, linter's—Waste cotton linters made into felt, similar to cotton batting.
Fiber—Older stuffing material made from leaves and fibrous plants.
Fiber rush—Manufactured alternative to natural rush.
Fiberglass—Glass-reinforced plastic used for frames.
Fireside chair—Alternative name for lounge chair.
Flexibead—Half-round flexible molding to cover with fabric or leather as a border.
Flock—Re-used wool from rags, used for stuffing.
Flounce—Hanging border below edge of chair.
Fly—Piece of cloth sewn to another, usually as an extension, where it will not show.
Foam—General name for plastic and rubber filling.
Fox edging—Roll of stuffing material used at the edge of seat.
Frame—Wood or metal structure forming support for upholstery. May also be a molded plastic shape for covering.
French polish—Shellac finish for wood.
Gimp—Prepared decorative strip to cover tacked edge.
Gimp pins—Thin nails, usually black.
Gut rail—Mid rail along chair side.
Gutter—Groove pulled in cover by stitching parallel with edge.
Hair—Stuffing material, usually mixed from the hair of hogs, cattle, and horses.
Hair-circular needle—Curved needle with regular semi-circular shape.
Hair, rubberized—Sheet material with hair bonded with rubber.
Hessian—Alternative name for burlap.

Hide—Leather from cow.
Insiding—Dealing with the inner surfaces.
Kapok—Vegetable stuffing material that is buoyant and used for upholstery on boats, but superseded by closed-cell plastic foam.
Knot, lock—Twine knot that can be adjusted and locked.
Lacing—Pulling together with cord. Tying springs with twine.
Lacquer—Synthetic spray finish for wood.
Laid twine—Twine made to resist stretching.
Latex—Foam rubber.
Latex, cavity—Cushion material with cavities on underside.
Latex, pin-core—Rubber pad with many holes.
Leathercloth—Plastic surfaced imitation leather.
Lining—Inside covering of a box or similar object. Inner cloth behind outer fabric.
Linter's felt—Waste cotton linters made into felt similar to cotton batting.
Lock knot—Twine knot that can be adjusted and locked.
Lounge chair—Lightly upholstered chair with padded seat and back, but usually plain wood arms.
Love seat—Seat for two.
Mallet—Wood, hide, or plastic hitting tool.
Marshall units—Group of coil springs in cloth sleeves.
Mattress needle—Long, straight, double-ended needle.
Morocco—Leather from goat skin.
Mortise and tenon joint—Traditional frame joint—tenon fits into mortise.
Muslin—Open weave cotton cloth used to cover stuffing.
Naugahyde—Trade name for a vinyl material.
Needle, bayonet pointed—Needle with flattened faces behind point.
Needle, half-circular—Curved needle with regular semi-circular shape.
Needle, mattress—Long, straight, double-ended needle.
Needle, spear pointed—Alternative name for bayonet-pointed needle.
Needle, spring—Curved needle, straighter at eye end.
Needle, tufting—Alternative name for mattress needle.
No-sag spring—Trade name for a type of zig-zag spring.

Nylon—Plastic material that may be woven.
Ottoman—Padded seat without back or sides.
Ottoman, box—Hinged padded seat with storage box under.
Outsiding—Dealing with outside surfaces.
Overstuffing—Upholstering.
Padding—Covering on stuffing before applying outside fabric. The softening material used in upholstery.
Particleboard—Board made of wood particles in plastic. Also called chipboard.
Period style—Design from earlier days.
Picking—Adjusting stuffing.
Pillow-back chair—Chair with the main upholstery of the back in the form of a cushion.
Pincers, web—Pincers with broad jaws.
Pin-core latex—Rubber pad with many holes.
Pin, gimp—Thin nail, usually black.
Piping—Cord in cloth sewn into seam. Also called welt.
Piping cord—Cord made of cotton, paper, or plastic for making piping.
Platform—Center area of top of seat.
Pleat—Fold and crease fabric over curved edge.
Plywood—Boards made with many wood veneers laid at right angles to each other.
Polish, French—Shellac finish for wood.
Polyether—Plastic used for foam filling.
Polyether crumbs—Small pieces of plastic used for filling.
Polystyrene—Plastic used for molding frames.
Polyurethane—Plastic used for molding frames.
P.V.C.—Polyvinyl chloride—the full chemical name of vinyl.
Rag tacker—Slang name for upholsterer.
Rail, gut—Mid rail along chair side.
Rawhide mallet—Mallet made with rolled leather head.
Rayon—Synthetic fabric made from cellulose.
Regulator—Pointed tool for adjusting stuffing.
Ripping chisel—Tool for removing tacks.
Roll edging—Alternative name for fox edging.
Roll stitches—Large stitches through covered stuffing parallel with edge to create roll and retain stuffing.
Roll, thumb—Alternative name for fox edging.

Rubberized hair—Sheet material made of hair bonded with rubber.
Rubber webbing—Rubber and fabric stretch webbing.
Runner—Cover strip, such as over ends of tension springs.
Rush—Marsh plant, dried and used for seating.
Sacking—Alternative name for burlap.
Saddle—Cushion over arm.
Scatter cushion—Individual cushion not intended for a particular place.
Scrim—Open-weave cloth to cover stuffing.
Seagrass—Rope made of grass and used for seating.
Seam—Sewn joint between pieces of cloth.
Setee—Alternative name for sofa.
Sewing, blind—Alternative name for slip sewing.
Sewing, slip—Stitching edges so finished seam does not show stitches.
Shirring—Closely gathered cloth to make a decorative border.
Single coil spring—Compression spring, narrow at bottom.
Sink stitch—Stitch looping from edge of cover into loose stuffing to hold it near edge.
Sinuous-coil spring—Alternative name for zig-zag spring.
Skewer—Pin with eye end for temporarily holding cloth.
Slip sewing—Stitching edges so finished seam does not show stitches.
Sofa—Seat, usually for three people.
Spear-pointed needle—Alternative name for bayonet-pointed needle.
Spring, cable—Alternative name for tension spring.
Spring, coil—Compression spring used to support padding.
Spring, double coil—Compression spring, narrow at center.
Spring needle—Curved needle, straighter at eye end.
Spring, No-sag—Trade name for zig-zag spring.
Spring, single coil—Compression spring, narrow at bottom.
Spring, sinuous-coil—Alternative name for zig-zag spring.
Spring, stabilizer—Small coil spring to fit between zig-zag springs.
Spring, tension—Long coil spring used under cushions.
Spring, zig-zag—Serpentine-shaped spring to support cushion.
Stabilizer spring—Small coil spring to fit between zig-zag springs.

Staple—Two-legged fastener alternative to tack and driven with special tool. Two-ended nail used for fixing coil springs to wood.

Stay tack—Temporary tack.

Steel webbing unit—Several springs on steel strip.

Stitch, roll—Large stitch through covered stuffing parallel with edge to create roll and retain stuffing near edge.

Stitch, sink—Stitch looping from edge of cover into loose stuffing to hold it near edge.

Stretcher, webbing—Tool for tensioning webbing.

Stripping—Removing old upholstery from a frame.

Studs—Decorative nails.

Stuffing—The filling material in upholstery.

Stuffing, top—Second layer of stuffing, often foam or cotton, outside the main stuffing.

Suite—Set of matching furniture.

Tack—Tapered nail.

Tack, stay—Temporary tack.

Tacking, blind—Alternative name for back tacking.

Tacking rail—Extra strip of wood in frame to take tacks.

Tension spring—Long coil spring used under cushions.

Throw pillow—Individual cushion, not intended for a particular place. Also called scatter cushion or pillow.

Thumb roll—Alternative name for fox edging.

Top stuffing—Second layer of stuffing, often foam or cotton, outside the main stuffing.

Trestle—Support to bring work to a convenient height.

Tufting—A traditional method of filling pockets of fabric with stuffing, with buttons at the crossings of seams, to give an effect similar to deep buttoning. Using tufts of wool or other material held by twine through padding, in the same way as buttoning.

Tufting needle—Alternative name for mattress needle.

Twine—Thin string or stout thread.

Twine, laid—Twine made to resist stretching.

Velvet—Short cut warp pile cloth, traditionally silk.

Vinyl—Plastic material that can have a leather-like appearance.

Wadding—Alternative name for cotton batting.

Walling—Strip of fabric around edge of cushion to give square edge. Also called boxing.

Warp—Lengthwise strands in woven cloth.

Webbing—Strap-like strip made from flax, cotton, hemp, or jute.

Webbing, rubber—Rubber and fabric stretch webbing.

Webbing stretcher—Tool for tensioning webbing.

Web pincers—Pincers with broad jaws.

Weft—Crosswise strands in woven cloth.

Welt—Alternative name for piping.

Wing—Side head rest.

Wood worm—Alternative name for borer.

Wool—Hair from sheep and similar animals.

Y knot—Lock knot for twine to spring.

Zig-zag spring—Serpentine-shaped spring to support cushion.

Index

Index

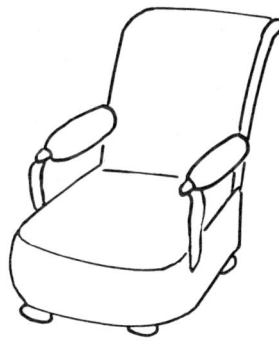

A

Adhesives	28
Arms	235
covering	139
outside	246
Arm chairs	
padded arms	164
saddle arms	171
wings	174
Arm panels, front	149
Awl	71

B

Back	
channel	300
chairs	153
coil springing	256
fluted	300
front padding	259
outside	266
pillow	293
second padding	261
springing	254
Band, bottom	281
Beds	317
Bottom band	281
Bowed backs	293
Box seat	104
Boxes	308

Bunk seats 306
Burlap 218
    repairing 336
Buttoned stool seat 119
Buttoning 270
Buttons, repairing 339

C

Cabinetmakers 17
Cabriole hammer 43
Cane seating 393
Chairs
    arm 165
    armless 446
    backs 253
    bowed backs 293
    buttoning 270
    channel back 300
    curved parts 287
    cushions 143
    designs 195
    finishing 270
    flounce 283
    fluted backs 300
    lounge 149
    pillow back 197
    plywood 108
    office 125
    skirt 283
    underneath 268
    wing 165
Chalk 59
Chisel 66
    ripping 48
Clamps 68, 417
Coil springs 81, 256
Cord seats 375
Corners, curved 185
Covering 37, 228
    arms 239, 234
    inner 36
    repairing 353
Curved corners 185
Cushions 129
    chair 143
    covering scatter 133
    filled 129
    fixing on lounge chairs 157
    molded 131
    wall-edged 140
    wall-edged bunk 134
Cutting 44

D

Dado joints 421
Decorative nails 277
Designs, chair 195
Divans 317
Dovetail joints 423
Dowelled joints 413

E

Early upholstery materials 18
Edging, front 220
Egyptian furniture 14
Enclosed frames 450

F

Fastenings, repairing 340
Filling 472
Finishing
    a frame 485
    chairs 270
    wood 464
Flax 25
Flounce 283
Foam, repair 346
Frame
    construction details 410
    design 456
    types 401
Frames 401
    armless chair 446
    curved parts 453
    enclosed 450
    finish 485
    looseness 479
    open 440
    ottomans 435
    restyling 488
    scarfing 483
    seat tops 436
    stool 429
Front
    arm panels 249
    edging 220
Furniture
    Egyptian 14
    middle ages 15
    periods 192
    Roman 13
    sectional 207

G

Gimp 279
    pins 26
Guild, upholstery 17

H

Hair, stuffing 18
Hammer
    cabriole 43
    magnetic 44
Head panels 320
Hemp 25
Holding 58

I

Inner coverings 36

J

Joints
    dado 421
    dovetail 423
    dowelled 413
    lap 421
    mortise and tenon 418
    screwed 425
Jute 25

K

Knife
    general-purpose 44
    sharpening 15

L

Lacquering 476
Lap joints 421
Loose
    rigid seats 92
    soft seats 98
Looseness, frame 479
Lounge chairs 149
    covering 152
    fixing cushions 157
    padded arms 160
    side panels 162

M

Magnetic hammer 44
Marking chalk 58
Materials 24
    natural 22
Mattress needles 52

Measuring 58, 183
Middle ages, furniture 15
Modern upholstery 22
Mortise and tenon joints 418

N

Nails 26
    decorative 277
Needles 49
    mattress 52
    spring 52

O

Office chair 125
Oil polishing 476
Oilstone 45
Open frames 440
Ottomans 308, 435
Outside
    arms 146
    back 266

P

Painting 477
Piped stool seat 114
Piping 113
Planes 66
Plywood chair 108
Polishing
    oil 476
    wax 476
Punches 68

R

Recovering 355
    adapted 370
    full 373
    partial 365
Regulator 52
Removing upholstery 357
Repairing foam 346
Repairs 329
    burlap 336
    buttons 339
    coverings 353
    dining chair back 348
    fastenings 340
    springs 342
    torn fabric 330
    webbing 335
Restyling frames 488

Ripping 48
    chisel 48
Rockers 289
Roman furniture 13
Round seat 122
Rubber webbing 77
Ruchings 279
Rush pattern 377
    checker 380
Rush seats 375

S

Safety 492
Sanding 467
Scissors 44
Screwed joints 425
Seat
    piped stool 114
    tops 436
Seating 112
    simple 91
Seats
    box 104
    bunk 306
    buttoned stool 119
    cane 393
    cord 375
    loose rigid 92
    loose soft 98
    round 122
    rush 375
    stool 104
Sectional furniture 207
Shellac 473
Simple seating 91
Skewers, steel 52
Shirt 283
Spring
    needles 52
    repairs 342
Springing 73, 254
    coil 256
Springs 30, 215, 218
    coil 78
    tension 78, 224
Staining 471
Staples 28
Steel skewers 52
Stool frame, assembly 429
Stool seats 104
    buttoned 119
    piped 115

Strainers, web 54
Stripping 355
Stuffing 18, 33, 228

T

Tacks 26
Tension springs **78, 224**
Thread 29
Tools 42
    special 70
    woodworking 61
Tufting 304
Twine 29

U

Upholstered arm chairs 165
Upholstery
    development 13
    guild 17
    materials, early 18
    modern 22
    removing 357
    stuffing, hair 18

V

Varnish 473
Victorian furniture 17

W

Wax polishing 476
Web
    pincers 53
    strainers 54
Webbing 25, 73, 215
    flax 25
    jute 25
    repairing 335
    rubber 77
Welt 279
Wing chairs 165
Wood
    blemishes 470
    finishing 464
Woodworking tools 61